CITY OF CHAMPIONS

CITY OF CHAMPIONS

Hank Gola

TATRA PRESS LLC

Printed in the United States of America by Tatra Press LLC
Library of Congress Cataloging-in-Publication Data has been applied for.

ISBN: 9781732222700
First Edition: November, 2018
Tatra Press LLC
Distributed by: Midpoint Trade Books, Baker & Taylor and Ingram
Edited by Tom Biersdorfer
Cover designed by Mimi Bark
Interior designed by Isabella Piestrzynska, Umbrella Graphics
Printed and bound in the USA by Sheridan, Chelsea, Michigan

Media, special sales and permissions: Chris Sulavik (Tatra Press) at tatrapress@gmail.com or 646-644-6236
Foreign translation rights: Whitney Lee (The Fielding Agency) at wlee@fieldingagency.com or 323-461-4791

Tatra Press
4 Park Trail
Croton-on-Hudson, New York 10525
www.tatrapress.com

To Mom

An honorary Boilermaker since 1950

&

To the memory of Walter Young

My friend

&

To Boilermakers and Stingarees Everywhere

ALMA MATER SONGS

MIAMI HIGH SCHOOL

Where the royal palms stand proudly
Underneath the summer sky
Where the tropic sun shines golden
Stands our proud Miami High
Fair blue skies and golden sunshine
Lift our colors gold and blue
As we lift our voices singing
Hail! Miami High, to you!

Loyal hearts, Miami High School,
Hail your name in joy and pride
Alma Mater, our devotion
Praises you as honored guide
Years will crowd through time but always
Shall they add to your fair frame
And out hearts, Miami High School
Ever sing to your dear name

GARFIELD HIGH SCHOOL

Our voices swell with true emotion
Our hearts e'er leap with joyous zeal
We sing our song of strong devotion
In praises of our dear Garfield

Oh Garfield High School alma mater
E'er faithful true and tried art thou
To Garfield High School alma mater
We consecrate our hearts right now

Even though we all shall have to leave thee
And wander far from sight of you
Our hearts will ever, ever praise thee
Our love for Garfield still rings true

Oh Garfield High School alma mater
E'er faithful true and tried art thou
To Garfield High School alma mater
We consecrate our hearts right now

TABLE OF CONTENTS

ACKNOWLEDGMENTS

Whatever we do in life begins with family, and mine was instrumental in supporting what became a virtual obsession over almost four years—the research and writing of "City of Champions." Without the intrepid transcribing and later proof reading of my wife, Lillian (the valedictorian of the Garfield High School Class of '72, by the way), I would have never made my deadlines. She was always there to assuage my doubts or prop me up. My son Henry and my daughter Julianne were the first to encourage me to write a book while Julie's critical mind provided invaluable suggestions for both the words and appearance. My incredible mother, Ann, is, at age 95, an inspiration who promoted the book to anyone who would listen. My sister Sandy, too, was an asset when it came to design suggestions and spreading the word. Thoughts of my twin granddaughters, Rose and Ruby, helped get me through the day while my grandson Elliot always provided relief on our babysitting days by asking, "Why is Dampa working again?" My love also goes out to my daughter-in-law Alice Ann and son-in-law Jason and to all my extended family. And, of course, where would I have been without my writing companion, my faithful pug, Freddie?

I also received tremendous cooperation from everyone I contacted. Those interviews were among the most enjoyable parts of the process. Sadly, several interview subjects have since passed away since we spoke: notably, my beloved high school history teacher, Florence Adler, Lou Mallia, Anna Kurilec Laboda, former Garfield High principal Ciro Barcelona, former Garfield great Ken Huebner, Anne Whritenour, and, of course, Walter Young. Walter's son David, Angelo Miranda Jr., Molly Brady, Jack Boyle's granddaughter, Steve Jenkins, and Larry Mike Osceola Jr. provided many of the pictures that help the book come alive. Dave Sistaro, Violet Kolbek, Florence Klecha, Barbara Burek, Blake Reilly and Sal Costa provided archive materials. Betty Knoepfel sent me many of Art Argauer's personal mementos. Louise Greer provided the same for her father, Jesse Yarborough.

Chris Stevens, the head football coach at Xavier High School in New York City, broke down game films for me and lent insight into the single wing formation he still uses. Theresa Payne contributed rigorous digital research on a number of topics. Steve Adamek, Ralph

Vacchiano, Bill Westhoven and Ian O'Connor reviewed early chapters and encouraged me to continue.

My eternal gratitude goes to Chris Sulavik of Tatra Press for his faith and belief in this project. We had a chance meeting at a golf media day, where I explained the difficulties I was having getting the book published. After reading the few chapters I'd written, Chris recognized the book's potential and took a chance on it. His devotion as an editor and sounding board was constant. Additional thanks to Tom Biersdorfer, my old *New York Daily News* colleague, for contributing his editing skills and to cover designer Mimi Bark and interior designer Isabella Piestrzynska for making it look so good. A special Dziękuję! goes to Isabella for correcting my Polish. Thanks, as well, go to Eric Kampmann and Annette Hughes of Midpoint Trade Books for their remarkable enthusiasm.

Special thanks to Howard Lanza and Chris Shupenko of the Garfield Historical Society, Fred Darwick of the Miami High Alumni Association and Passaic City Historian Mark Auerbach, who helped guide my research, as did Ashley Trujillo and Kristen Lachterman at HistoryMiami, John Shipley at the Miami-Dade Public Library, Peter Lavagna at the Carlstadt Historical Society and Tom Anker and Beth Zak-Cohen at the Charles F. Cummings New Jersey Information Center at the Newark Public Library. Miami historian Paul George provided a wonderfully informative tour of book sites and lent me his perspective whenever needed. Garfield High School athletic director Mike Alfonso and former football coach Steve Mucha generously loaned me the old game films, including a fantastic color version of the 1939 Passaic game.

I'd also like to recognize the staffs at these other libraries and history centers, where I no doubt operated every microfilm reader or scanner ever manufactured: Garfield Public Library, Clifton Public Library, Passaic Public Library, Morristown Public Library, Morris County Library, Johnson Public Library (Hackensack), Paterson Free Public Library, New York Public Library, Hoboken Public Library, Jersey City Free Public Library, Vineland Public Library, Bloomfield Public Library, Atlantic City Free Public Library, Chester County Library, Toledo Lucas County Public Library, Alachua County Library, Jacksonville Public Library, Knox County Public Library, McKeesport History Center, Nutley Public Library, East Orange Public Library, Elizabeth Public Library, Oak Park Public Library and the Live Oak Public Library.

Finally, I'd like to thank Ian O'Connor for offering me my best piece of advice. "Write the book you want to write," he told me. I did.

PROLOGUE

Anyone driving into Garfield, New Jersey will be greeted by a sign proclaiming it as the "City of Champions." It might seem like an idle boast for a time-worn town, yet it has been that way for over eight decades. And, if the city is a bit dog-eared, its pride is justifiable.

In the tumultuous year of 1939, Americans across the country sat awestruck as the big screens of their movie palaces transported a Kansas farm girl to Munchkinland. *The Wizard of Oz* was a metaphor for life at the close of the decade when Americans teetered between cold reality and bright hope, not quite out of the Depression and not quite into World War II. That same year, a group of gutsy football players from Garfield High School embarked on their journey over the rainbow to a place beyond their imagination—glamorous Miami, Florida, where they had the opportunity to play for the "mythical" national championship.

How I came to that mostly forgotten place in time is easy. I am a Boilermaker. Garfield is my hometown. Early on in life—somewhere between diapers and dungarees—I sat down with my father to receive the talk that was bestowed upon almost all Garfield boys of my generation. No, not *that* talk. With the air of any other Christmas story, Dad told me of the night of December 25, 1939. It was a lesson in the essence of being from Garfield, encapsulated in a single, wondrous name.

Benny Babula.

As time dwindled down on the Orange Bowl clock, the great Babula booted the winning field goal. I could see it in my mind as my father spoke. I didn't yet know the meaning of the word Homeric, but that is how Babula appeared to me, with a laurel wreath of purple and gold worn on his head. He was Garfield's hero, my hero, the embodiment of the underdog mentality that insisted Garfield kids could compete against—and beat—the big boys. It was a reason to puff out your chest, no matter how old one got, how far away one settled.

I never settled that far from Garfield in any respect. My mom, an honorary Boilermaker by way of Bayonne, New Jersey, still lives in the house where I grew up, a short 20-minute ride back to the 60s. The blue-collar town of my youth has changed, but not entirely. Many of the landmarks remain. The mind supplies the old images of those that do not. It's easy to think back on one in particular—being a kid when Babula was running a meat distribution business. Hiding at a distance, we would marvel at him. Dressed in this long white coat, blood-stained near the bottom, he'd casually sling a side of beef over his shoulder and carry it out of his truck into to Fila's Market on Lanza Avenue.

We'd elbow and prod each other. "That's him. Benny Babula." No other words were necessary.

My father would have graduated with Benny and the boys had he, like so many Depression kids, not dropped out of school to go to work. My Polish-born grandparents owned a butcher shop in Garfield but my grandfather allowed his customers to "pay on the books" and seldom collected in full. In the end, he was driven out of business and he and my grandmother joined the other workers at the Forstmann woolen mill.

My love of sports was indelibly sealed at Dad's telling of Garfield High's great victory. Before I started rooting for any pro team, and even before I was a fan of LaSalle All-American and NBA star Tom Gola, I was, foremost, a fan of the Garfield Boilermakers. The worst Thanksgiving of my young life was in 1962 after Dad called the paper to get the results of the game against traditional rival Clifton. Unbeaten Garfield had lost. Once I got a little older, I started riding the student buses to away games. Garfield was still a state power. The best Thanksgiving of my young life was in 1965 sitting next to Dad in the crowded stadium and watching Garfield finally break the Clifton hex.

In high school, Coach John Hollis, an assistant on the '39 staff, reinforced the Babula legend. On rainy days, he'd pull out the projector during gym class and show the old game films.

Eventually, I got to wear the purple and gold myself, though not in football. I was too scrawny for that. I played baseball, modestly, at best, but proudly. Benched after I criticized my coach's tactics in the school paper—"Jokers sit"—I knew my future was not on the field. I'm convinced, though, that those Babula stories also had something to do my eventual vocation. At least this Garfield kid made it to the major leagues of

The author's grandparents, Walenty and Katarzyna Gola, proudly pose on the stoop of their butcher shop on Banta Avenue in Garfield, circa 1939.

Courtesy of Gola family collection.

sports sections in the New York papers.

This all came full circle one day in 2014 as I was driving home from Foxboro on I-95 after covering an early season Patriots game for the *Daily News*. I don't know why the thought occurred to me, but I calculated that it was precisely 75 years since Garfield's magical moment in Miami. The paper granted my request to commemorate the anniversary by writing an End Zone, the big feature story at the back of the Sunday section. It turned out that my 2,800 words fell far short of telling the whole story. And, the more I learned about that mythic game and all that had preceded it, I became convinced there was a book there. I could flesh it out with the Miami side—the Stingarees had their tales too—and try to depict what life was like in those years between Depression and War. Indeed, it was more than a story of an American game. It was a story of America.

The reader should know that this is a slightly different animal than most sports books. Nearly four years of research through reels of microfilm, digital searches, game films, game paraphernalia and numerous interviews opened up avenues of inquiry I could not have imagined when I began telling the story of how, some eight decades ago, a small New Jersey high school football team made it on the national stage.

What I discovered was how this story was inextricably linked to—and supported by—other stories. In the end, this team and this sport and this era capture an America at a dramatic point in its history. So, orbiting this game were numerous characters beyond the gridiron— the cities, the families, the river-town factories, the Florida swamps, the neighborhood tavern, the sportswriters. As I researched news and learned of personal histories, it became clear how much the world touched—and shaped—the Boilermakers and the Stingarees.

For example, I surely did not expect that the sinking of the *Athenia* at the start of World War II would be a part of the narrative. Yet, it is. A Garfield immigrant from Slovakia almost lost his family en route to New Jersey. This experience and others defined lives and attitudes toward citizenship and duty, as well as America's attitude toward the European war and the concerns the immigrant parents of Garfield's players might have held.

Similarly, southern segregation wasn't a planned topic until I discovered its relevance to the history of Miami High School football and as a window into southern sensibilities and attitudes in general. The game's larger social aspects, then, begged exploring and, in the end, revealed surprises. It was an exciting process to uncover stories and facts buried long ago but worth telling again and, I hope, that tell more completely the story of these two legendary teams.

Of all my sources, one touched me most of all. I'd met Walter Young at Garfield's Homecoming Game that year when he and Leonard Macaluso, two of the three surviving members of the '39 team, were honored at halftime. He was an incredibly vibrant man who had built a rich life, rising to the top of his profession as the founder of a scale manufacturing company while raising six children. He was at the time the oldest active CEO in his field and was still driving twice a week from his home in New Jersey to his office in Connecticut. But more than that, he was a man of faith and principle who was still guided by what his parents—and coach—had instilled in him.

Mitch Albom had his *Tuesdays with Morrie*. I had my Fridays with Walter. He would fill my voice recorder with his memories, and I would supplement those with my research. He told me I knew more about the game than he did, and we both found that pretty funny.

Walter was one of the finest men I'd ever met. He was the same age as my father, and it was as if I were talking again to Dad, who died in 1986. Walter gave me a real sense of the character of those players and why they, as ordinary kids, were able to accomplish the extraordinary.

Walter only occasionally mentioned the pain in his back, but in February of 2016, he called to tell me the results of some tests. He was diagnosed with stage-four colon cancer, news that he faced with utmost courage and dignity, news that made my heart sink to my stomach.

"Oh Walter, I'm so sorry," I said.

"Don't be sorry, Hank," he said. "What am I bargaining for, to live to be 100?"

Selfishly I thought, "why not?"

As he made plans for his final months, Walter gave me three prized possessions from high school, his two letterman sweaters and his 1939 championship jacket, which looked as if it had hardly been worn. It is now one of my prized possessions. The last time I visited Walter, he told me he had one regret, that he hadn't really done enough on Earth. To me, it was ridiculous, of course, and I couldn't help thinking about how his old coach, Art Argauer, would have been so proud of the man he became. A devout follower of the New Apostolic Church and a member of its clergy, Walter was tearfully yet joyfully celebrated at his funeral in October 2016. The small, plain, church was filled with family, friends and admirers listening to the minister eulogizing Walter's "abundant life." It truly was. He'd outlived most of his teammates, and they could not have chosen a better representative to carry on for them.

Before he died, I rushed to finish the first chapter of this book and send it to his son, Dave. He read the words to his father on his hospice bed. Though Walter seemed to flicker in and out, Dave was sure he heard them. They were the last he ever spoke to his father. Walter died the next morning.

While I had already been fairly convinced of the merits of bringing to life Walter's (and all the others') pasts, his passing sealed it for me. I had to write this book and tell the story of Walter and his team, no matter how many people tried to convince me it would be of little popular interest.

I have one regret—that I didn't start 15 years sooner, when so many more players from both teams were still around. The people from Garfield who lived through that year's euphoria, such as my Dad and Walter, have been leaving us—and at a sad clip. Yet, the game's mark is indelible in those who remain. Consider John Kurilec, for example, of whom I write in Chapter 2, and who could not be interviewed for the book. He'd suffered two strokes and his communication skills were badly compromised. His son said he mostly answers, "I don't know," to questions. Yet when his son asked him if he remembers the Garfield football team winning the national championship, he looked at him and said plainly: "1939."

Still, there was one other moment that made the story come alive for me. Around Christmas 2015, I visited Leonard Macaluso, hoping to coax a few memories out of him. He was living in the V.A. Hospital in Paramus, New Jersey, which, sadly, had all the appearances of a place where old soldiers went to die. As the case of many of his fellow World War II vets, much of Leonard's life had faded away. Dementia had blurred and tangled up his memories but not his instincts. While he struggled with details, confusing games and years, his demeanor sharpened when I asked him about the techniques of line play. Suddenly, he practically sprung out of his wheelchair, leading with his forearm, aiming for my solar plexus, just as he had all those years ago. He said he played football because he loved to hit people. I was seeing firsthand what it was like to play against the mighty Boilermakers of coach Art Argauer.

I hope I can make readers of this story feel as if they lived the game and the time. I want to strap them in a leather helmet or seat them amid the excitement of the stands on that sweltering Miami night. I want them to experience 1939. I only hope I prove as worthy of the task as the Garfield players were of theirs.

I asked Walter near the end, when he got to where he was going, to tell Benny and all his teammates what I was writing.

I owe this to all of them . . . and, especially, to Dad.

ONE

THE BLOCK

For 75 years, Walter Young had something on his mind that he just couldn't let go.

He was, by that time, a very accomplished man in every respect. Yet Young always had a burning desire to do his best and a constant fear that he hadn't. So it was that one unresolved detail weighed inconveniently on his conscience; a specter of guilt that revisited every time he looked back on a long-ago Christmas night in 1939. The outcome was perfect that night, at least for Young and his Garfield High School teammates. The New Jersey team had already beaten the odds by just getting to the "Health Bowl," but to have defeated powerful Miami High for the "mythical" national championship was beyond their dreams.

Now, after all those years, Young finally had the chance to salve that pesky and recurring pang of guilt. His nerves tingled so that he might as well have been sprawled on the playing surface of Miami's Orange Bowl, when he was a raw-boned 17-year-old football player with wide eyes. "Mythical" was a good word, because, all these years later, it still seemed surreal to the man peering into the glare of the laptop—and into unveiled truth itself.

Social media, of all things, offered Young his redemptive moment. And he could hardly believe it.

Before him on his kitchen table sat a computer streaming a YouTube video. Smoky images of that game appeared in black and white, although he could easily imagine them in color— the green grass, the yellow uniforms, the blond hair of "Li'l Davey" Eldredge barely peeking out from under his tight-fitting dark blue, leather helmet, all lit up by the stadium's soft arc lights and the blinding pops of news photographers' flashbulbs. Eldredge was the star of Miami's Stingarees. Young had cut him down with the key block on a Garfield Boilermaker touchdown, leaving the two boys together on the gridiron surface, each upset for different reasons—one terribly angry, the other thoroughly frantic.

The deceptive play, with the simple, stark name of "Naked Reverse," had worked to perfection—thanks to Young's final role in it. As Garfield's left end lifted his head over Eldredge, Young could see his teammate, John Grembowitz, alone in the end zone—although he wouldn't allow himself to admire the scene. He hurriedly scanned the field for something else: a penalty flag. There was none.

The thousands in Miami's home crowd, unaccustomed to anything but celebrating plays, had gone silent, their usually clanging cowbells hanging by their knees. It only made the little voice inside Young's head all the louder. Where he should have felt relief, there was dread.

"One little block," Young explained, recalling the play in detail. "My job was to pick up Gremby as he came around left end. And he was wide open. Davey Eldredge was the kid way back, the final safety. He had the speed to catch John, and I was supposed to block him. I did. But I misjudged. He was so much faster than I was, so that instead of blocking him in a safe way, I clipped on the side. I said to myself, 'Oh my God, I fouled him.' I looked around and . . . no flag . . . and Gremby was over."

With that, Young turned his attention to the video of the old game. His coach, Art Argauer, was an early proponent of game film. Shot from the sideline, it was cut up to show each snap. In the game's aftermath, it was a hit in Garfield's Ritz Theatre and at various banquets. Eventually the reel was transferred to video and then to disc before a copy left behind in somebody's attic made its way onto YouTube, a journey through time and technology before intersecting with Young's life again.

Young admitted he hadn't thought much about the game for long stretches. His life was too busy to dwell on it. A self-made man who'd built his own scale company, he was, at 92, the oldest active CEO in his industry, someone who still drove the often traffic-tangled route from his home in New Jersey to his office in Connecticut twice a week.

Above all, Young was a man of faith. He had officially retired from the pulpit of the New Apostolic Church, but he remained deeply involved in its ministries and bound by its teachings. He was Priest Young to the congregation.

It was a life well lived. He'd followed his older brothers into college, and he followed his patriotism into the Army Air Corps, where he served as a meteorologist in World War II, in both Africa and Europe. He married and had a family. After his first wife, Edith, died too young, he married Alida, a fellow church member who had lost her husband. There were grandkids and great grandkids. And with his day-to-day life filled with such matters, the game never seemed all that important.

Oh, he remained tremendously proud of his team and friends with one teammate in particular. Now and then, there would be an anniversary celebration or reunion and there was the night he was inducted into Garfield's Hall of Fame. Now and then, Young would admire the game program with his teammates' autographs or the certificate he'd been presented at the 1940 New York World's Fair, which proclaimed him a national champion for Garfield's 16-13 win. But given his strict Germanic upbringing, there was little room for sentimentality or nostalgia.

His hometown, however, felt otherwise. To working-class Garfield, the 1939 team was the embodiment of its grit, its pride and its underdog mentality—why the city called itself "City of Champions." In Garfield, the story of the 1939 game was legend, passed down from father to son. If there were a test for Garfield citizenship, one of its questions would surely be: "Who kicked the winning field goal in 1939?" If you couldn't answer, "Benny Babula," you might as well move across the river to Clifton.

Babula was gone for almost twelve years now. Young was among just a few survivors from either squad. The game's 75th Anniversary had arrived, and Young was invited to Garfield's

Homecoming Game to be honored at the coin toss along with former teammate Leonard Macaluso. He walked proudly to the middle of the field, still erect and athletic-looking. And, as he glanced at the sign above the scoreboard reading "Art Argauer Field" he began to fully absorb the mark his team left on the community. In an interview that night, Young admitted he had never appreciated it all until recently, and he confessed to his long-held torment about the block.

"But Walter, you do know that the game film is on line? That we can actually watch the play?"

So, here he was at his kitchen table as familiar images—unfolding frame by frame—filled the screen. The power of Babula's runs. The precision of the blocking of Garfield's single wing. The speed of Miami's short punt formation.

Young took it all in.

As the video reached the third quarter, he knew what was coming. He rose out of his seat a bit and put his well-worn, big hands on the table as his face flushed with the amazement and excitement of a teenager.

"This is it? Yeah, by God it is! I don't think I've ever seen it the way I'm looking at it right now . . . Can you stop it? . . . Now Gremby's got the ball."

Frozen on the left side of the screen, a shadowy figure, Garfield's left end, can be seen.

Young.

Looking more closely, a solitary Miami player looms in the secondary.

Eldredge.

As the film progresses, they meet. Head on. Eldredge goes down.

Legally.

"I'll be damned," he said.

The man who made the block asked to rewind the play over and over. The block was legal every time. He was damned no longer. His conscience had been cleared. Those old butterflies, cocooned so long, were emancipated. It was as if the game had finally ended.

But even the proof of a legitimate victory left Young in amazement. "I still don't know how we did it. Some day, I'm sure it's all going to be exposed as some sort of elaborate hoax, that it never really happened," he said with a chuckle.

Garfield's path to a national championship was more than circuitous. It was filled with roadblocks and detours. Serendipity and happenstance powered the street lamps. Fate was the road map, the destination finally reached under the spell of a full moon.

The Boilermakers would exploit every opportunity and manage every fine line. It shouldn't have happened.

But, just as Walter Young's block, it did.

"Can you play it again?"

TWO

THE BUBBLE

The final weeks of the summer of 1939 waned into autumn. In the industrial city of Garfield, New Jersey, kids hung on to every breath of warm air just as leaves cling to trees, savoring every minute of the outdoors as the school term began. It was a good time, a "swell" time to be alive and young.

The Depression loosened its grip as the decade neared its end and, with its many factories in operation, Garfield carried on as well as could be expected. People were making a living, and that was fine.

What's more, a special anticipation was palpable throughout the sports-crazy town. Down at rocky Belmont Oval, along the railroad tracks and across from the pump house, coach Art Argauer was gathering his championship Garfield High School football team for another season. Usually, Argauer would have started poor-mouthing his chances to those guffawing buddies in the local press. But this year, there was no reason not to be cocky about the tools at his disposal.

Garfield was pivoting off an undefeated state championship season. A few holes needed plugging but as Argauer scanned the practice field, whistle in hand, the sweaty scene would have been the envy of any high school coach in the country, not just in New Jersey.

Stretching out his powerful legs with a tug on his high-top cleats was Benny Babula, son of a Polish immigrant who had managed to prosper through tough times with his meat distribution business. Babula, a classic triple-threat, single-wing tailback with movie star looks, was already creating a stir among the big-time college recruiters from Notre Dame to Tennessee.

Next to Babula was his best friend on the team and partner on the '38 All-State teams. Rugged-faced, sandy-haired John Grembowitz was part of a hybrid brood of seven. His mom and stepdad ran a tavern around the corner from St. Stanislaus Kostka Church, whose pastor, Msgr. John Wetula, was hardly averse to stopping in for quick belt . . . or two. Grembowitz's stepbrother, Ed Klecha, had starred for Argauer a couple of seasons earlier. Now, with his combination of toughness, explosiveness and smarts, Grembowitz was the perfect man to lead Babula on power sweeps.

There was plenty of complementary talent as well, almost all culled from the pool of Eastern European and Italian boys that seemed to pass through Argauer's machine-like system each year. The boys were playful and frisky as they went through calisthenics, knowing Argauer would soon have them pushing in earnest. Summer was good—they had bathed in their hero status along with the sun—but they were eager to get back into action, emboldened by their last season's spoils. Well-drilled, deep and confident, Garfield was primed to repeat as state champion although every opponent would make its date with the Boilermakers the biggest game of the season.

For certain, all of Garfield was stepping a little livelier, from the street peddlers to the factory workers to the cops and city councilmen.

So, it was no wonder that when the morning newspaper hit the stoop, Garfielders turned first to the sports pages and past the troubling news from Europe. There, another conflict fomented from the very ground that many had abandoned before the last war ravaged their former homelands.

Now, just as the team's September workouts set the stage for the momentous year to come, September's front pages foreshadowed the dark conflict that would eventually shake all lives in Garfield. And it was in those early days of September when the first ominous winds of the that hurricane touched the city, reaching the Grand Street front steps of one Vasil "William" Kurilec, a 31-year-old Rusyn immigrant separated from his family by a treacherous ocean and a budding war.

Kurilec was anxious for word from his wife, Maria, traveling out of Grizny-Svidnik, Slovakia, with their 10-year-old son, Jan, and 5-year-old daughter Anna. For the decade since arriving in America, Vasil had been living with his sister and brother-in-law, scraping together savings from a job as a cable machine operator in the Okonite plant in Passaic, New Jersey, sending as many American dollars as he could back home.

He'd made only two trips back to Grizny-Svidnik, where his two children were born. He had never seen Anna.

The people in Svidnik were dirt poor, literally. The floors of their homes were without flooring, the roofs thatched. Still, situated in a valley of the Carpathian Mountains near the Dukla Pass and the confluence of the Ondava and Ladomírka rivers, it was a lovely place, particularly when the dogwoods and sour cherry trees bloomed.

Quaint, beautifully crafted wooden churches dotted the landscape. The inhabitants of Svidnik were Greek Catholic Carpatho-Rusyns, the "people from nowhere." They had settled for hundreds of years on both what is now the Polish and Slovakian sides of the Carpathians and on into Ukraine. Although governments came and went, and the borders were redrawn over the centuries, their loyalties lay with their cultural, ethnic and religious heritage— Rusnaks in Slovakia, Lemkos in Poland.

Vasil Kurilec originally planned to return and acquire land with savings from his stint in the U.S. Considering his modest beginnings, his ambitions were relatively grand. He would go to Vienna and, with his American earnings, buy a tractor. He would become the only farmer in Svidnik to own one. He and his family would prosper off the land. But the war drums changed the script. Now it was imperative he get his family out—and quickly. Everything moved suddenly and furiously.

Kurilec cleared the first hurdle when final papers for his U.S. citizenship came through in December. That meant he needed to deposit the sum of $500 (roughly $8,600 today) required by U.S. authorities to admit his family. Had he not been a citizen, it would have cost an additional $3,000.[1]

In January 1939, he began the process negotiations for his family's immigration. However, by March, Hitler's armies stormed into Czechoslovakia, and the situation quickly darkened. Slovakia became a Nazi puppet state whose troops would even participate in the invasion of Poland.

Vasil's brother, a policeman in Svidnik, was pressed into guard service by the Wehrmacht and sent to the Sudetenland. When he saw the arms buildup, he wrote to Vasil and made a thick black mark on the back of the envelope, the signal that a family member had died. He wanted Vasil to be sure to open it. "Get them out NOW," he wrote.

Diplomatic offices were shut down for two months but, finally, Kurilec was able to deposit the $500 and wire the money for the trip. He learned his family had left Grizny-Svidnik on August 13. While they were en route to the former Czech border, the German government sent an edict that no residents of the just-dissolved Czechoslovakia nation could pass but, because Vasil was a U.S. citizen, his wife and children were considered Americans and allowed to cross.

Their ill-fated adventure continued. Originally, they were able to book passage on the *Queen Mary* but, at the top of the gangplank, a stern-faced official blocked their access. It seems that Joseph P. Kennedy, the U.S. Ambassador to the U.K., had bumped several among the "huddled masses" to enable his American friends to flee Europe while the fleeing was good.

Turned away, the Kurilecs spent the rest of that day outside an hotel, not knowing English, until a relief agency took care of them. Days passed. The authorities were ready to send the children to Scotland, along with misplaced British kids. At the last minute, they were told they would be sailing on the British passenger ship, the *S.S. Athenia*. The date was September 2, a day after Adolf Hitler's blitzkrieg tore into Poland.

As the British headlines screamed WAR, the Kurilecs and 543 other passengers shuffled across the *Athenia*'s gangplank at the murky docks in Liverpool, joining those who had boarded in Glasgow and Belfast, all on their way to Montreal. When the *Athenia* headed up the River Mersey toward sea, it carried 1,418 people, including crew. The Kurilecs were among 150 European refugees, mostly women and children, and they were in imminent danger.

The ship's captain, James Cook, had just been advised by the British Admiralty to use anti-submarine measures. He was to follow a zig-zag course north of the usual trade routes and sail with the ship blacked out, even down to any lit cigarettes or pipes. Those orders became paramount around 11 a.m. when the captain received a not-unexpected message. England was officially at war. The news was relayed over the ship's public address system to the passengers.

That is how the *Athenia* appeared in front of the itchy trigger finger of Oberleutnant Fritz-Julius Lemp and his U-Boat, some 200 miles west of the Hebrides just before twilight on September 3. Lemp's *U-30* had been one of 14 submarines to slink away from Hamburg in mid-August as Germany prepared for war. Now the 26-year-old commander received a coded message from Kriegsmarine headquarters: "Do not wait to be attacked. Make war on merchant shipping in accordance with operational orders."[2]

It was direct but not simple. Urgency ought to have been tempered by discretion—not exactly a common military protocol under Hitler. But the Fuhrer was still hopeful of pulling off another diplomatic heist with France and, mindful of how the *Lusitania* sinking drew the United States into World War I, he was wary of American casualties. He'd play it coy for the time being. U-Boats were under orders to follow the Prize Regulations of 1936, which stipulated the merchant ships first be boarded, searched and evacuated. Only warships could be sunk without warning.

As twilight approached on the third, Lemp peered through his periscope at a vessel that was obviously taking evasive measures—zig-zagging, blacked out and moving beyond normal travel routes of passenger ships. Caught between the Adrenaline-filled urge to attack and the innate desire to obey orders, Lemp's instincts and judgment were tested. He suspected a passenger ship fitted with naval guns. If that were so, it was fair game, and, for Lemp, an early prize of war on the war's first day.

Lemp did not hesitate. He turned the sub so the moon was at its back and gave the order from 1,500 meters away. "Feuer!" The first torpedo shot out of its tube and slammed squarely into the *Athenia*'s hull with its 600 pounds of explosives. The second missed, preventing even greater loss of life. But the *S.S. Athenia* was doomed.[3]

At that moment, Vasil Kurilec was halfway through his shift at Okonite, unaware that his son was playing with a friend on the *Athenia*'s top deck. Jan's mother was looking after an older boy, Jan Olear, also bound from Slovakia to his father in New Jersey, but traveling alone. Ever since the *Athenia* left port, they were doing what boys do—tearing up and down the stairs and ramps, exploring every corner, inventing games.

Down below, Jan's mother slept with Anna, trying to nurse her through her seasickness. She was in the bottom bunk in a small cabin they shared with another family on the overcrowded ship. There were six bunks in all in this cramped arrangement.

Yet, Anna wasn't sleeping. Music and laughter lofted from above and Anna, longing to be on the upper deck, was captivated by it.

"All of a sudden there was a large noise," she remembered in a 1989 interview. "As a child, you don't know it's an explosion."

Jan knew. From across the ship he and his friend saw and heard the terrific blast, described by one passenger as an earthquake on the ocean. They saw the thick towers of dark, suffocating smoke and a plume of water shooting high into the air as the torpedo gouged a hole in the *Athenia*'s port side. According to the official report, which Ambassador Kennedy relayed back to Washington, the explosion "destroyed the bulkhead between fire room and engine room, shattering the oil tank and destroying access of stairs from the third class and tourist dining saloons to the upper decks."[4]

Passengers with the misfortune of being on the nearby deck, cabins or staterooms died instantly—or drowned. Deaths also occurred on the stairwell and in the dining area, where, as the second seating was about to take dinner, instead witnessed lights going black and the ceiling crumpling to the waterline.

The once-peaceful deck, with many enjoying the sun setting into the water's horizon, descended in chaos. Terrified screams erupted. Passengers ran in all directions, from what, exactly, they did not know—just away from danger. Several near the boys shouted desperately: "The ship is sinking! The ship is sinking!"

Young Kurilec didn't witness the horrors detailed by several survivors—blackened bodies, a 12-year-old girl still in a deck chair, her body torn to ribbons, or those engulfed by flame.

But he and his friend acted more calmly than many of the adults. Knowing the ins and outs of the ship from their adventures, they scurried down below deck to shepherd Maria and Anna Kurilec to safety, fighting through and slipping past people as if all their previous games had prepared them for this very real mission.

At last, they burst into the cabin.

"Mama! Mama! Wake up Mama!" Jan shouted in his native Rusyn, rousing her from sleep. "Everybody's drowning! The ship is going down!"[5]

Amid the confusion, the quick-thinking boy helped his mother and sister into life preservers before strapping one on to his own body.

"He told us to get along to our life station on deck," Anna remembered, years later. "My mother's reaction, being from a landlocked country, was that we would die right there at sea."

In his haste, Jan hurried up the stairs, assuming his mother and sister were right behind him. They weren't, and there were too many people between them to rejoin. Mayhem ensued. People pushed and shoved without knowing what to do, where to go. The refugees did not understand commands in English, making it even more difficult to swiftly board the ship's 26 lifeboats. In many cases, the crew simply chucked passengers in—children first.

Anna was wide-eyed at the desperation surrounding her. Maria was terrified. The most imposing bodies of water she'd ever encountered were the calm Rivers Ondava and Ladomírka near Grizny-Svidnik. Now she was being directed to abandon a sinking ship in the icy, turbulent North Atlantic. As she peered over the rail, she saw a lifeboat's occupants being jerked around and jostled as they were lowered by ropes toward the sea.

But she never forgot this stark, incongruous *tableau vivant:* a woman bedecked in a fur and jewelry, with crewmen removing her life preserver. She had just died in her wheelchair.

By then, someone had grabbed Jan and dragged him away to the nearest lifeboat station. The 10-year-old boy was on his own. By luck, Maria wasn't separated from her daughter. A Czech sailor had ushered them up to the deck and got them into the same lifeboat. He told Maria to keep her child tight—between her legs—so she wouldn't be thrown loose when the boat was tossed about in the churning water. Her boat was on the floor of the ship, waiting to be lowered, as Anna and her clutched daughter waited their turn. All Anna could see was the water coming in over the side of the boat.

Maria's thoughts were of Jan. Frantically, she searched for him among the bobbing lifeboats below and spotted him in one. Maria held her daughter tightly and prayed—prayed for them, prayed for Jan—as she crossed herself three times in the manner of Greek Catholics.

"She always said she never prayed before or after the way she prayed that night," Anna said.

Jan was safe, albeit starting a harrowing adventure of his own. As his boat was clumsily lowered, he feared it would never make it to the water, that he'd be spilled into the ocean. As the gears of the davit creaked, the two crewmen responsible for operating the block-and-tackle system struggled to lower the lifeboat on its manila rope falls. The process, which relied on gravity, became a real-life version of a tilt-a-whirl, one end lurching, then the other, dipping the occupants toward the cresting waves so that they had to cling on to stay secure. At last it slammed on the water's surface and bobbed among so many others—for the moment safe. As for the future, no one knew.

Jan noticed the *Athenia* was listing and orders came to get away from the ship to avert the lifeboats being sucked down if the big ship were to sink suddenly and speedily. Farther and farther away they rowed, powered by cumbersome oars in the arms of ordinary passengers until, as darkness encroached, Jan lost sight of the other small boats. Finally, sensing a degree of security, Jan moved from the bottom of the boat, where water had collected, to a seat. But if he was dry, he was also cold, having been soaked and only wearing summer clothing.

At one point, a launch pulled up to Jan's lifeboat and let off two sailors to help man the oars. Some in his lifeboat started to sing, feigning, or at least encouraging cheerfulness and strong will as emotional ballast to trauma. They floated for hours, bailing water, with the lights of three ships visible in the distance but too far off to save them.

One of those ships was luxury yacht *Southern Cross*, owned by retired Swedish utilities tycoon Axel Wenner-Gren, who purchased it from Howard Hughes. At 338 feet, it was one of the largest luxury yachts in the world. It had left Norway bound for its winter berth in Nassau, Bahamas, where Wenner-Gren made a home on Hogg Island.

Shortly after 9 p.m. on September 3, radiomen on the *Southern Cross* picked up the SOS signal from the *Athenia*. They were on a course north of the Shetland Islands, about 63 miles from the sinking steamer. When they came upon the drifting survivors at roughly 2:30 a.m., scudding clouds obstructed the moonlight. The crew cast floodlights onto a horrifying scene with the desperate survivors screaming while buffeted by 15-foot swales.

It was later described by Marguerite Wenner-Gren, wife of the yacht's owner. "It was a terrible sight," she said. "Everywhere were people in *Athenia* lifeboats, some up to their necks in water, others lying on top of each other and packed in like sardines. Others were floating around in life belts and they were pretty rotten too."[6]

The yacht circled the survivors so it could do its rescue work from the outside in to prevent people from drifting further away. Six crewmen took an empty *Athenia* lifeboat and began to pull people in and row them to safety.

"The rest of us on board hauled in the victims," Mrs. Wenner-Gren explained. "Some of the women's hands were raw to the bone from trying to row those heavy old boats. Others we pulled aboard by ropes or by hand."[7]

Among those were Maria and Anna, extremely fortunate to escape any further calamity. Safely on board, they watched while the *Southern Cross* crew yelled through megaphones to others to stay away from the stern of the boat. Even so, the swells hurled at least two overloaded lifeboats against the stern, capsizing them. The occupants scrambled to crawl onto the upturned bottom. One man stood on the keel, dragging drowning people from the water, but not everyone made it.

A Russian Jewish couple, hoping to flee the madness in Europe, saw their two sons disappear and drown. According to Mrs. Wenner-Gren, the lucky ones were hauled onto the decks of the *Southern Cross*, covered with oil from head to foot.

One young woman sat for a moment, exhausted. Then she realized her baby wasn't with her. "My baby!" she screamed and leapt back into the water, committing suicide.[8]

The *Southern Cross* rescued 376 persons with another 440 saved by the Norwegian freighter *Knute Nelson*. At 10:30 the next morning, the America-bound survivors were transferred to the *City of Flint*, a freighter bound for Canada and then New York. As grateful as they were that God had answered their prayers, Maria and Anna still had no idea whether Jan was safe. They couldn't have known that his rescue happened at daybreak when a British destroyer came upon his lifeboat.

They put Jan into a boatswain's chair with its plank of wood for a seat, and hauled him up.

"I skinned my knuckles pretty badly going up, hitting against the side of the boat. I didn't know enough," he said. "But finally I was up on deck." He was taken to Belfast, then to Glasgow, where, to his surprise, he was reunited with Jan Olear. Signs of war were everywhere. Anti-aircraft balloons were up just outside the hotel. Inside, the *Athenia* survivors were instructed on how to use a gas mask. Eventually, they were moved to the village of Dollar and housed in Campbell Castle, where they awaited transport to the U.S.

Safe aboard the *City of Flint*, Maria Kurilec had been fruitlessly sending daily cablegrams asking about her son. All the while, Vasil was without any information. The last communication was from his wife on August 30. He didn't learn they were on the *Athenia* until September 13. That's when he received a telegram that his wife and daughter were safe in Halifax, where the *City of Flint* first landed, bound for Hoboken the next day. He telegraphed back, asking about his son. He learned he was on a list of the missing. There was just no way to know.

Although Mrs. Kurilec had seen Jan in another lifeboat, she knew there was no guarantee he was alive. As an example, the death toll expanded when, while rescuing passengers in the 10-foot seas, the *Knute Nelson* ram-rodded its propellers into one of those lifeboats. Fearing Jan drowned, it was a tearful reunion for William, Maria and Anna on the Hoboken water-front. *The Herald-News* of Passaic headline summed it up: "City of Flint brings unhappy climax to William Kurilec's 10-year dream."[9]

Edward Davis, a *Jersey Journal* photographer who was on the pier as Kurilec—described as a "pathetic figure" in the *Associated Press* accounts—awaited a reunion with his wife and daughter. Davis was asked by his paper to put his impressions into words. He captured the emotion of the scene, even if he embellished some details:

> *Contrasting strangely with the beautiful sunlit morning which saw its arrival in the North River; the* City of Flint *brought into Hoboken Saturday morning the final load of misery and suffering—an aftermath of the torpedoing of the* SS Athenia.
>
> *Not even a news photographer inured to tales and sights of suffering through experiences in covering picture stories for the* Jersey Journal *could help being deeply moved by the story told by William Kurilec, husband of Mrs. Maria Kurilec, who lost one son on the* Athenia *when it sunk.*
>
> *The father stood on the pier talking to me when the* City of Flint *came into view. With tears rolling down his cheeks he waved to the boat which was bringing his wife and the six-year-old daughter he had never seen. When the gangplank was lowered, he was one of the first on board and the sight of him embracing his wife and daughter is one I think will always be stamped on my mind. His son, John, 10, was swept from his mother's arms when the* Athenia *gave a lurch and was swept into the Atlantic. Officers of the boat had quite a time holding the mother from going after her son but finally prevailed upon her to save herself and her daughter.*[10]

After speaking to reporters, the Kurilecs left the dock driven by Vasil's cousin, Michael Kudla, a steamship agent who had been assisting him. Just before they reached Garfield, Kudla stopped at his office on Monroe Street in Passaic. He soon burst back out, running to the car, breathlessly reporting the news. The Kurilecs could hardly believe what he told them. Their son was safe. A telegram from the Cunard Line came across that Jan had been located among the survivors in Scotland. A month later, the *SS Cameronia* brought him home. He spent a couple of idle days roaming about at Ellis Island, detained because he didn't have his papers. He remembered picking up American papers left behind on the long rows of benches and looking at the pictures because he couldn't read English. Finally, New Jersey Congressmen George M. Seger and J. Parnell Thomas cleared the red tape and the family was reunited in Garfield.

"Now, all our prayers have been answered," Vasil said, but it wasn't until his mother saw him walk through the front door that she said: "He's home."[11]

Jan Olear, the boy who played with Kurilec aboard the *Athenia*, lived the next four years in Clifton, New Jersey, before joining the Army in 1943. A year later, four years after he survived the sinking of the *Athenia*, Private Olear was killed at the Battle of Anzio in Italy with the 179th Regiment, 45th "Thunderbird" Division. The boy from Svidnik is buried in the American Cemetery in Naples.

Jan Kurilec graduated Garfield High School in 1949. His name was Americanized to "John" by then. His nickname, according to his yearbook picture, was "Yanko." He was, "good-natured—winning the favor of all," a member of the High Y and Purple and Gold club.

He was also lucky. The attack on the *Athenia* claimed the lives of 93 passengers and 19 members of the crew. The last to die was a 10-year-girl who succumbed to her injuries aboard the *City of Flint*.

It could have been worse. Unlike the *Lusitania*, the *Athenia* didn't sink immediately and that enabled the crew to fully evacuate the ship. Somewhat miraculously, a third torpedo from *U-30* also missed its mark. The *Athenia* captain and some of the passengers swore they saw Lemp bring the *U-30* to the surface and shell the ship with its cannon but that was later disproven. Rather, what they likely saw was the third torpedo exploding near the ship. Whatever the case, the survivors were fortunate. After Lemp was able to confirm he fired on a passenger ship, he ignored the Prize Rules by leaving the scene and not assisting in rescue efforts. Indeed, Germany didn't acknowledge it sank the *Athenia* until Admiral Karl Donitz testified at the Nuremburg trials in 1946.[12]

Lemp never made radio contact with Berlin, which learned of the sinking from the BBC. Lemp reported it three weeks later, after having sunk three additional ships. But all references to the *Athenia* were stricken from the U-Boat's log. Lemp's role in the war turned out to loom large. Awarded the Knight's Cross, he didn't survive the war. Commanding the *U-100*, he was forced to surface by depth charges and made an unsuccessful attempt to scuttle the sub as it was cornered by British warships. He died trying to return to it. When the Brits got on board, they were able to recover an Enigma machine, the key to breaking the German code. So, it could be said that Lemp helped start the war, and later helped finish it.

At first, the Germans claimed the *Athenia* hit a mine, then they submitted that Winston Churchill, Britain's newly appointed first lord of the Admiralty, had ordered the sinking as part of a scheme to drag the United States into the war.

The detestable Nazi propaganda minister, Joseph Goebells, put those charges into hyper-rhetoric in a speech broadcast throughout the world on October 23. "But the United States did not fall for your plan . . . the United States has not lost its senses," he screeched.[13]

It mattered which story Americans believed. Even if the Nazis had taken credit for the sinking, it would have unlikely eventuated in a *Lusitania*-like catalyst to arms. Perhaps it played a role in helping President Franklin Roosevelt sell his cash-and-carry program to Congress. But, at that moment, there was simply no stomach for another war.

In the immediate wake of the sinking, *The Herald-News* could not have been more forceful in its isolationist editorial of September 5, even to the point of accepting some inevitable American deaths at Axis hands.

> *We Americans are resolved to keep out of it!*
> *We must keep out of it!*
> *Already, in the sinking of the Cunard liner* Athenia *by a German U-Boat we see how factors that brought us into war in 1917 are at work now in 1939 to bring us into this second tragic conflict. There were Americans on that ship; there will be Americans on other ships that will be sunk before this war is over and some of those Americans will die.*
> *We must not let such factors stir our passions to the extent of our Country's becoming involved in this war as a belligerent.*
> *Our sympathy must not, and does not, shake our unalterable conviction, decision and will, that America must stay out of this war. Our first duty is to ourselves. That duty is to "keep America out of war and war out of America."*
> *Let all feeling of selfishness and partisanship be put aside! We must be prepared to do right, whatever comes, and no matter how much we may suffer in the doing.*[14]

Those sentiments were everywhere.

The *Athenia* survivors barely disembarked from the ships that brought them safely to the New York docks before they saw women carrying placards that screamed, "Keep our boys out of war!"

Inimitable 1930s commentator Boake Carter, in his nationally syndicated column, warned of letting the *Athenia* incident spark the wrong emotions.

> *We may therefore hold total disgust for such warfare and those who resort to it but keep cool enough to realize that we can destroy America if we permit our emotions to run riot to such extent that we begin agitating to get into this war.*[15]

It was telling that Edward Davis, the *Jersey Journal* photographer, closed his brief description of Kurilec at the Hoboken pier with relief, not outrage.

> *Leaving the scene, I realized more than ever before that this country has no business over there in Europe and I was more happy than ever before to feel the good earth of Hoboken beneath my feet.*[16]

Even in the Polish and Slovak communities of Garfield, there was no call for intervention, not even with Nazi boots trampling their homelands. Polish immigrants contributed to relief efforts but kept their sympathies at bay. Their feeling was that they left Europe before the war supposedly fought to end all wars. They were not about to send their sons back to Europe to fight the next one.

It was as though, from the onset of World War II, America was in a temporary bubble, happily insulated as it whistled past the European graveyard while it reveled in distinctly American culture—not as a distraction but as an expression of freedom.

It would take the Japanese attack on Pearl Harbor to burst that bubble and shift America's preoccupation en masse, like the coordinated pivot of a single wing formation, turning its focus to one spot in the line.

In 1939, as Europe and the Far East boiled over, America's attention focused on the premieres of screen classics such as *The Wizard of Oz* and *Gone with the Wind*. Something called a television was wowing crowds at the New York World's Fair. America reveled in the Yankees' fourth straight World Series championship after Lou Gehrig's retirement and in Joe Louis, fresh off his KO of Germany's Max Schmeling, training for his next fight in Pompton Lakes, New Jersey.

Americans made *The Grapes of Wrath* the best-selling novel of 1939 and marveled at the new Mercury sedan. They slow-danced to Glenn Miller's *Moonlight Serenade* and tuned in to Edgar Bergen and Charlie McCarthy on CBS Radio's Chase and Sanborn Hour.

And, all across America in big cities and small towns, they turned out for high school football in the fall.

Roughly 1,000 miles to the South of Garfield, another team was drilling for the 1939 season. Coach Jesse Yarborough was making his Miami Stingarees sweat in the subtropical heat. Miami had established itself as somewhat of a dynasty in Southern football but was coming off an 8-2-1 season, disappointing by Stingaree standards.

Yarborough bemoaned his lack of veterans to his boys in the press, but those scribes weren't buying the "Colonel's" complaints. They knew all about a deep program that routinely filled holes left by graduation. As Yarborough scanned the well-groomed practice field behind the big high school, there was the blonde Davey Eldredge effortlessly turning on the speed, pulling away from some outmatched scrubs. His brother Knox had starred for Yarborough a few years earlier. Intent on showing him up, Davey had the confidence of a game breaker. Then there was Jay Kendrick, looking even bigger than the season before when he dominated anyone the opposition put in front of him.

Nope. Yarborough may have had the typical coach's nerves, but odds were his team would be able to avenge a 1938 loss to Jacksonville Lee in its opening game.

No one on that practice field—or on Garfield's—was thinking about war. And the papers in both places were determined to keep it that way.

No Miamians were aboard the *Athenia* when it sank but the city made its connection in another way. On September 22, three weeks after the sinking (and four days after Vasil Kurilec was reunited with his wife and daughter), the *Southern Cross* slipped down the channel toward her moorings on Pier 1 at the Miami city yacht basin.

An oily imprint of a hand was still visible on the starboard side of the yacht, left there by someone who perhaps had been lost, grasping in desperation. The yacht would receive a fresh coat of gleaming white paint while in port. There, as the newsmen hovered in the bright sunshine, far removed from the frantic scene in the Atlantic, Mrs. Wenner-Gren and her sister, Mrs. Gene Gauntier, retold the story of the rescue. "It was the worst experience of my life," Wenner-Gren said in despair. "I never want to see anything like it again."[17]

It wasn't the first brush Miami had with the war. In June, the *S.S. St. Louis*, full of Jewish refugees who had been refused safe haven by the Cuban government, anchored off the Miami coast. The occupants could see the bright lights of the city, but they would not turn out to be beacons of safety as President Franklin D. Roosevelt, too, turned his back on them. A Coast Guard patrol boat stood guard as the *St. Louis* turned back toward Europe to prevent any possibility of refugees jumping off and swimming ashore. One crewman told the *Miami Daily News*, "It doesn't seem possible that so many people could crowd aboard one ship."[18]

In the end, of the 1,008 refugees on board, 254 were lost in the Holocaust.

While Miamians seemed sympathetic to war's victims, they were, like most Americans, not about to get involved. A few days after the *Athenia* had been sunk, an editorial in the *Miami News*, headlined "On Keeping Sane," urged readers to distract themselves from war news.

> *A drop of water falling hour after hour on the same spot of a man's body will make that man a raving maniac. Well the keepers of the torture chambers of the world have known that. Focus the mind too long on one thought, one sense of injury, one fear, and mental balance is lost. This brings us to this war.*
>
> *Because the war in Europe, with its many repercussions here, is so far and away the most pressing and important of events, we are tempted to think and talk and hear of it exclusively.*
>
> *Each day now each side will be telling the world how many men it has killed, how much property destroyed, how much ground it has gained. The tale of horror, heard too oft, will warp our reason, distort our judgment, weaken our mind and nerves. It is a mistake to subject oneself to torture as this. If it did any good to seek this punishment, then take it we should. It does only harm. More important to America than the war in Europe is the keeping of our own minds clear, our judgments sound. Failing this, we could easily be where Europe is.*
>
> *No normal person will wish to ignore the hideous scene abroad. Every normal person will seek the diversion requisite to keeping himself in balance, sane. The baseball season still offers its salubrious help. The struggles of football will soon relieve the tensions of more serious wars. The movies will continue to relax such as they do relax, and we hope with no excessive accompaniment of reproductions and reminders of the war.*
>
> *Books offer their continuing lure away from the heart-breaking events. We even promise, though it is a promise hard to keep, to reserve some portion of these columns for subjects removed from and more permanent than the wholesale slaughter precipitated by ephemeral maniacs.*
>
> *Be calm, even if not happy, despite the war. That is no sin. It is simple sanity.*[19]

Miami High's students were just as ambivalent toward American involvement. As the student body excitedly prepared for another Stingaree football season, the editors of the *Miami High Times* left no doubt where they wanted their interests to remain:

As football season begins in America, another great sporting event is taking place in Europe and while the European method of playing differs radically from American standards of sportsmanship, essentially both countries are concerned with the same problem, the gaining of territory from the opposition.

Wrangling for two years over the exact date of the combat, both Germany and England have disagreed at last, and are at it hammer and tongs. So tremendous have been their enterprises, it has taken over a score of announcers and the facilities of three great networks to translate their activities.

The European contest has been interesting to Americans due to the lack of other diversions. However, the time has come for America to stop worrying whether or not Hitler will undermine the allies and to concentrate on whether or not Edison will defeat the Stingarees. In other words, the sooner American citizens get their thoughts out of the backyards of Europe into the yards of the football field, the better off they will be.[20]

Similarly, on the opening day of the 1939 high school football season in New Jersey, readers of *The Herald-News* editorial page found a syndicated cartoon by Alan Klein that thumbed its nose at the ominous events overseas. A burly gridder, with No. '39 on his jersey, jaunted along, his chest puffed out and a girl on each arm. Frazzled and left behind were two military officers in oversized uniforms. Klein titled it, "Today's Hero."

In December, a couple of months after they arrived safely in America, the Kurilec kids began assimilating to their new permanent home in Garfield. They could not have been further removed from the Carpathians, yet they had found safety in this unfamiliar spot in the world. They were just beginning to learn English but, as most everyone in Garfield, they were also caught up in excitement in the town.

The high school football team was leaving for their big game in Miami, and it seemed the entire city was turning out to see them off. Their cousin, Anna Korotky, was a Boilermaker cheerleader, and they were at the high school with the whole family when the buses pulled out. Anna cheered along with her big cousin even if she didn't know whether a football was blown up or stuffed with feathers.

"How wonderful is this place?" she asked herself.

They were already Americans. And like all of America, they were giving war the stiff-arm.

THREE

THE CITIES

Miami and Garfield. Glamour and grit. Sand and clay. Soft Southern drawls and thick European accents. Coconut palms and linden trees. One a destination, the other a dead end. Leave it to high school football to provide a stage on which small, hustling Garfield and big, bustling Miami could stand head-to-head as equals.

By the time the cities collided in 1939, Miami and Garfield could not have been further apart. Each originally sprouted in the decades following the Civil War: Miami from the tangled wilderness of South Florida, Garfield from the sweeping New Jersey farmland along the Passaic River. Each would then experience explosive growth spurts that ultimately defined them.

Miami was a frontier, yet a different sort for America—as one of the tropics, built outwardly from the shores of Biscayne Bay and the Miami River. Land was wild and abundant. Urban planning was simple. When a high school was needed, for instance, a few acres of pine and mangrove would simply be cleared out a few miles from the city center. The city seemed boundless and sprawled with ease. Even the Everglades could not contain it.

Things were markedly different up in Jersey. Garfield had no area to expand. Its borders—both municipal and psychological—were fixed. Instead, growth meant greater urban and social density. Then, as now, Garfield appears on the map as a tilted anvil strangely apt for the industrialized city it was. It is defined by two rivers, the energy-giving Passaic and the Saddle, which was barely more than a creek.

Conceived as a tidy collection area for the city of Passaic's overflow, Garfield eventually absorbed the immigrant flood of the late 19th and early 20th centuries. Bucolic it wasn't, despite its founder's intentions. There were open areas to be sure, but they hardly conveyed a feeling of spaciousness. They were more empty lots that served as impromptu sandlot ball fields or shortcuts skipping through factories and small businesses.

Each city owed its existence to the Industrial Revolution. Miami's future was set by the arrival of the railroad, bringing both new inhabitants and a constant parade of visitors. Tourism, real estate and, later, commercial aviation were its economic engines. Garfield was strictly blue collar, with its nest of factories lubricated by the elbow grease of the immigrant labor force that had begun to pour through Ellis Island at the turn of the century. By escaping, for the most part, the lot of old-world (and often backwards) agrarianism in Europe, men rolled up their sleeves to perform dangerous jobs in exchange for some semblance of economic mobility and promise in America.

Each city, too, had its visionary. Garfield had Gilbert Ditmas Bogart. Florida had Julia DeForest Tuttle.

Southeast Florida was scorched by heat and teaming with bugs when the Seminole Wars of the 1800s discouraged and drove out settlement. It was truly one of America's last frontiers, an uninhabitable terrain still covered with mangrove and pine when, in 1891, Tuttle purchased the land around the old Fort Dallas outpost and made it her home. Tuttle envisioned a great gateway city and center of trade with South America. But, outside of the Brickell family, which had been in the area since 1870 investing in real estate, few paid attention to her . . . that is until the fortuitous "Great Freeze" of 1895.

Henry M. Flagler had helped make John D. Rockefeller millions as the brains behind Standard Oil with a 25 percent share of the monopoly. But Flagler's visits to Florida, first as therapy for his dying wife, Mary, then on vacations with his second wife, Ida, stirred his imagination and he left Standard Oil to embark on a dream of turning the Sunshine State into a tourist mecca.

Flagler's first Florida enterprise was the 540-room Ponce de Leon Hotel in St. Augustine, completed in 1888. Now, to connect what he described as the "American Riviera" to the rest of the East Coast, Flagler needed a railroad. As the Florida Railroad snaked its way southward, so did modern civilization, development and prosperity. In 1894, Flagler's rails finally reached Palm Beach.

Tuttle, 72 miles to the south, knew Flagler and was also aware of his ambitious goal of bridging the turquoise blue water to Key West. She could be patient and wait for the railroad's inevitable arrival but, suddenly, the bad fortune of others became her windfall.

Four days after Christmas, 1894, temperatures plummeted from Jacksonville on down as an Arctic front swept across the state. Temperatures in Orlando reached 19 degrees. Snow fell outside Tampa. A man froze to death in Lake City. Citrus fruit was frozen solid, with an estimated 2.5 million boxes of oranges still on the trees. Losses were put at $2 million by farmers, $500,000 by truckers. That's $55 million and $14 million, respectively, in 2018 dollars.[1]

Some of the older orange trees were able to survive, with new growth appearing with over a month of warm weather into February. But that warm spell also made citrus more vulnerable. When a second, even more devastating, freeze hit on February 7, it claimed what remained, killing not just the fruit, but entire trees, at least north of Miami, to the roots.

Outside her home, Tuttle kept a small orange grove that had survived in temperatures above freezing. As proof she (as the story supposedly goes) boxed up some fragrant orange blossoms and shipped them to Flagler, then huddled up in northern Florida. The thought of tourists basking in more hospitable weather than his was enough incentive for him to start laying track from Palm Beach to Miami, with 100 acres of land provided by Tuttle.

Flagler dispatched one of his railway superintendents, John Sewell, to begin clearing out the piney woods. He arrived with a small workforce of 12 black laborers, along with his brother Everest St. George Sewell, to be better known as "E.G." They worked fast. The first train chugged into Miami, belching smoke, clanging its bell, in April of 1896. From an area which contained only nine inhabitants, Flagler created a city. He dredged a channel, built streets, instituted the first water and power systems, and financed the town's first newspaper. Miami was incorporated in July after Flagler scoffed at suggestions it be named after him. From these quickly-built foundations, the city grew. Flagler's master plan worked. The magnificent Royal Palm Hotel completed the venture and lured Gilded Age elite. It wasn't long before the parents of the 1939 Miami High School football team had made their way to this new beacon of opportunity.

Garfield's actual beginning came in 1873 when Civil War veteran Gilbert Bogart purchased the farm of John Barkley and most of the 87 acres that would comprise the future city. He planned to offer affordable lots for the construction of one- and two-family homes, each with front and back yards, and all within walking distance of Passaic's factories. Bad timing. The Panic of 1873 forced him into bankruptcy and it took eight years for him to regain the funds to buy back the land.

When Bogart first laid out his lots, he called his creation "East Passaic" but, on its rebirth in 1881, he took a grander view.

"Tell everyone (to) speak no more of East Passaic," he proclaimed, naming it instead after "the man who will lead this great country to prosperity," just elected President James A. Garfield.[2]

Within months of his inauguration, the new president was shot down by an assassin and died a slow, protracted death from infection. His was, however, an apt metaphor for the new town. Born poor, Garfield had risen through the Republican Party by wit and hard work to gain the 1880 nomination as the unlikeliest of candidates and the biggest of underdogs. As a staunch opponent of machine politics and the champion of the disenfranchised, particularly ex-slaves, the president was a fitting representation of his namesake city and its gutsy football team.

Rather than pay the high tariffs imposed by a protectionist U.S. Congress in the late 19th century, German manufacturers, in particular, opened factories in the United States. In looking for sites for their plants, they could see that the Dundee Canal along the Passaic River and the Dundee Dam, across it, provided the perfect location with ample supplies of power and water for manufacturing and easy access to New York City via rail. The entire area, including Bogart's suburb, boomed.

Botany Worsted Mills opened in Passaic in 1889 and the industrialization spread across the river into Garfield, followed by a new workforce from abroad. At first, many of these men—the great majority from Eastern Europe and Italy—arrived as migrant workers of sorts, sending money back to their families and planning to return in a year or two. Others came to America with their wives and children, leaving their parents behind, never to see them again. This migration, as with so many to the New World over the centuries, brought in its wake a trail of countless broken family ties and lost family records.

Eventually, many transient workers did send for their remaining family members to make America their permanent home. However difficult it was, for most it was a rung up compared to what they were leaving. Garfield thus evolved from its colonial Dutch roots, from sleepy patriot farms to busy factories. As time progressed, names prefixed with "Van" and "Den" become less common than those ending in "ski" and "o." Broken English became Garfield's "unofficial" language. Two sections emerged, soon to be dubbed Guinea Heights and Polack Valley.

Bushy's Sweet Shop, a typical Garfield storefront amid the shops on Passaic Street. Courtesy Howard Lanza.

Garfield, as such, was highly political but hardly politically correct. The nicknames reflected generations-old sources of self-identity and pride among two European groups that had lived amongst each other so well for so long but who didn't mind needling each other. In fact, even in the 1970s, the beloved John Hollis, an assistant coach on the '39 team, would pull out a big rope on the last day of gym class at GHS. "Guineas on this side, Polacks over here," he'd bark in a gravelly voice. The few leftovers would be split up and they'd have at it. Those days, that's how it was in that town. It was, clearly, a "Garfield thing."

The rope dividing Garfield ran along the railroad tracks. Along the eastern edge, the land rose to a plateau at the top from those tracks. Streets could be laid out in terraces, not unlike the villages of Italy or Sicily but without the lush vegetation. The Italian immigrants were attracted to those hills, a comfortable milieu in a strange world. What was once called Bogart Heights earned an earthier but more descriptive new nickname. The "Valley," meanwhile, spread downward to the rivers. Polish, Slovak, Rusyn and German immigrants formed pockets and established churches as the centers of their communities.

Our Lady of Mount Virgin Church was erected in the Renaissance Revival style on the highest point of the Heights, its facade reminiscent of St. John Lateran in Rome and the other churches back home. The altars, which would survive a devastating fire in 1940, were of Bronzetto marble.

Oddly, its two leading priests at the time weren't Italian, but Irish. Father Joseph Dooling was the pastor, and Father Charles Casserly his young assistant, active with the parish youth as a trusted counselor and popular with the adults as the originator of the church bingo games. Born in Jersey City, Casserly was part of a family that sent several sons and grandsons into the priesthood, although his nephew Charley eventually became the general manager of the Washington Redskins.

Mount Virgin, like the other three Catholic churches in Garfield, ran its own elementary school staffed by nuns at such a nominal cost that all the church schools were filled. Mount Virgin was also no different than the other Catholic churches in its appeal to the

An aerial view of a typical Garfield neighborhood. Note the two-family homes amid empty lots.
Courtesy Estate of Angelo Miranda.

congregation for funds. Each week, it included a list of the previous Sunday's donations in the church bulletin. Joe Barbato remembered, as a boy, how his mother sent him off to church with a quarter for the collection basket before the offertory.

"They would take up the second collection and there was one time when the priest made the comment he was going to be taking up the collection and Blessed Mother was going to be behind him and if she heard any tinkling of coins, she would blush," Barbato said.

The church and its surrounding shops provided the center of culture where old traditions were kept alive. Makeshift bocce courts dotted the neighborhood. Families planted vegetable gardens filled with tomatoes. Some raised grape vines for homemade wine, and fig trees, wrapping them throughout the harsh winters. Many Italian immigrant women were talented seamstresses. In 1939, the Heights contained 23 small dress and suit-making shops to employ them. They did piece work, paid just over one dollar per garment. A skilled seamstress could turn out seven dresses in an hour.

The main employers for Garfield's 29,739 inhabitants (11,103 were foreign-born, 17,000 were the offspring of foreign-born parents) were its factories. In 1940, the Garfield Chamber of Commerce published a promotional brochure entitled, "Garfield, City of Industrial Peace." Inside, it listed 64 separate industries scattered across the city's 2.16 square miles. Those included Heyden Chemical, Hammersly Manufacturing Corporation (where waxed paper was first developed), Presto Lock, Hartmann Embroidery Works, Castle Ice Cream Company and many others, including the woolen mills.[3] The biggest of those was also Garfield's biggest employer, Forstmann Woolens, with its sprawling plant in the middle of the Fourth Ward and the heart of Polack Valley.

All the factory whistles kept time in Garfield. Their sharp screams would mark the routine of daily life, announcing the beginning and end of shifts, lunch and dinner, from across the town and across the Passaic River as well. The first blast came at 7 a.m., then 11, noon, 3, 4, 5, 7 and 11. Workers would file in and out and walk—few families owned automobiles— to and from home. The streets of the Valley were lined by block after block of neatly kept two-story houses. One family lived below, one above. Front yards were squat, but tidy, and most families, despite their modest homes, were proud, adorning their yards with flowers and blooming fruit trees. Back yards were larger, but not bigger than a baseball diamond, and could accommodate vegetable gardens or a baseball catch. Life was simple with few requirements. One was the ready availability of a shot and a beer—a Boilermaker, what else? As prohibition ended, corner taverns popped up everywhere, numbering as many as 55. They were social hubs, fielding sports teams, sponsoring day trips. A few featured basement bowling alleys, others dancing halls. In Garfield, a man was identified by where he drank and where he prayed. The churches were as packed on Sunday morning as the many "gin mills" were on Saturday night.

St. Stanislaus Kostka Church stood two blocks away from the Forstmann plant. Monsignor Jan Wetula, one of the football team's biggest boosters, was its pastor, and its annual picnic was one of the most popular events in town. As was the case in the city's other churches, St. Stan's was a pillar that provided the moral foundation for its parishioners' uncertain future in America. Faith was the one possession that immigrants could be bring along on those crowded vessels that steamed into New York Harbor, a constant comfort as the last link to home. Masses were said in native tongues. At St. Stan's, Polish hymns were sung, not always on key, by devout women. Decades later, these women, now "Stare Babas," were still singing with creakier, but no less reverential, voices.

Another Catholic church, Our Lady of Sorrows, sat not far from St. Stan's. It served a smaller Italian population in the Jewell Street neighborhood, a planned community of sorts. Antonio Lanza worked as a night watchman guarding the building supplies when the Forstmann plant went up in the first decade of the century. He was a Sicilian immigrant and the company needed workers. It asked him if he could lure some of his compatriots down from the Heights to settle near the plant. Lanza agreed under one condition: that the street in front of the factory be named after him. Lanza Avenue still runs from River Drive to Midland Avenue. Garfield was always a deal-making town.

The Slovaks who settled in Garfield were Lutheran. Most settled in the Second Ward atop Belmont Hill, where they established Holy Trinity Church. The Slovaks always provided top athletes to the high school. In 1926, the 1,000 members of the congregation raised $100,000 to build a new brick Gothic structure. Its 195-foot steeple towered above all else in the city and can still be seen plainly from across the river. The Rusyn population lived in the blocks near Heyden Chemical, where they built Three Saints Russian Orthodox Church, with its distinctive cupola and three-barred cross. Several parishioners were on the Boilermakers' 1939 roster.

The fourth Catholic parish, Most Holy Name, run by the Franciscans, had no real ethnic identification. But, as the others, it contributed to the city's culture by sponsoring the Holy

Name Cadets, a drum and bugle corps that would bring home 11 national championships, beginning in 1940. When the Cadets turned toward them, audiences got goosebumps, feeling as though they were being hit by a wall of sound.

Other Protestant denominations were represented as well, including Calvary Baptist, which served the small black population. All the congregations made Sunday a ritual. Church was usually followed by dinner in the afternoon—roast beef, if the family could afford it.

For the most part, people didn't have to leave town. Businesses selling everything from automobiles, hardware, shoes and clothing to vegetables and meats were within walking distance. Whatever wasn't that close was still within a short bus ride away in Passaic. In addition, peddlers came around with their wares: knife sharpeners, umbrella repairers, even those hawking laundry supplies rode trucks up and down the streets beckoning customers. Fruit peddlers bellowed, "Watermelon!" while the fish mongers' cry of "Pesc-e, Pesc-e" echoed throughout the Heights. Fresh milk, naturally, was delivered to the front door. In the winter months, the cream on top would freeze and kids ate it like an ice cream pop. When the iceman made his deliveries in the summer (most houses didn't have refrigerators yet), kids chased after the truck and refreshed themselves with the ice chips as they flew off the back of the truck. On wash day, mothers boiled the clothes clean in big galvanized vats and hung them out to dry in the breeze. They came off smelling as fresh as earth. Outdoors was busy. The scarcity of automobiles meant people had to hoof it. There was interaction. Everyone knew each other's business.

Florence Adler, who later was a long-time history teacher at the high school, remembered growing up on Wessington Avenue in the heart of town, not far from Palisade Avenue and Passaic Street, both of which were lined with small stores, none of them self-service. The person behind the counter would somehow extricate whatever sundry items that were possibly needed.

"I didn't even know that there was a Depression, except that my father wasn't working a full week. He worked at Samuel Hird, sorting the wool. He'd work three days and get two off, work just the morning, something like that," she explained. "But my parents made do. They planted vegetables. I still remember the corn because we would pick it in the morning when it was still juicy. People tried to raise as much food as they could and if you had friends living in apartments who didn't have gardens, you would help them out because the job situation was the same way for them."

The Adlers also raised chickens and ducks, as did many of their neighbors. There was even a store on Belmont Avenue that did a fantastic business selling feed.

"There's nothing like a well-fed chicken," she said, practically smacking her lips. "It would take about two years to raise a duck. My mother would mix corn with water and some butter; she would put the duck under her arm and open its mouth and force feed it. I watched what was going on but I never tried doing it."

Women sewed clothes for their children instead of buying them. The dry goods store on Passaic Street, owned by the Berensons, one of the few Jewish families in town, supplied the materials. Every now and then, Forstmann opened its doors to sell its woolen goods to the public. Adler fondly remembered the coat her mother made for her from the fabric she bought there.

For entertainment, the Montauk and Central theatres in Passaic had the first-run movies while the Ritz in Garfield showed them late. Most kids entertained themselves.

Girls played hopscotch and glided on strap-on roller skates if they could find smooth streets. Boys played pick-up games in the empty lots without parental oversight. They fished in the Passaic River, and the more daring leapt from the waterfalls at the Dundee Dam, at the peril of a broken nose. Ice skating was available in the winter at the pond near the "pump house" and at one near then what was called the "brickyard". That pond had an interesting story that went back to Gilbert Bogart.

Bogart was ultra-competitive, and he had a rivalry with a friendly antagonist, Richard Morrell, a brick maker from Passaic. He determined to go him one better after hearing that the clay in one section of Garfield might be perfect for making higher grade terracotta bricks. He obtained the services of a geologist and, because he didn't want to be recognized, disguised himself as a hobo to visit the site. Sure enough, the geologist told Bogart that it was good clay well-suited for making quality terracotta tiles, so Bogart began to buy up the Banta family property that contained it. He built a small factory with a track for the carts to haul out the clay and a storage building in which to keep it. Unfortunately, as they started to dig the clay, they discovered that the geologist's findings weren't accurate. It wasn't of high quality.

"But that was not the disaster," explained Garfield historian Howard Lanza. "The disaster came when they hit the underground springs. It flooded, forming the brickyard pond."

According to Lanza, those springs were the cause of several drownings. It wasn't the depth. It was its ice-cold temperature that brought on leg cramps. Many a parent warned their kids not to go swimming at the brickyard.

The dynamic between parents and children helped keep society together in Garfield. The mother tongues were still spoken in most immigrant homes. Benny Babula's mother, for instance, spoke just a few words of English. In many cases, a child didn't speak English until Kindergarten. Yet, it was very important to these parents that they assimilate into American society by being good citizens and good workers and learning the "American way." Once these kids left the house and interacted with each other, they did so as American kids, playing American games, telling American jokes. But they also maintained their "home" identities, even calling themselves "Polish," or "Italian," for instance. While they grew into the American social fabric, their strongest ties remained tethered to their parents and their cultures, to be handed down to the next generation as well.

Al Kachadurian didn't grow up in Garfield. He played against Garfield for Paterson Eastside High School. But, his experience as the son of Armenian immigrants in Paterson was very similar to the sons and daughters of immigrants in Garfield.

"The kids were poor, they played hard, they went home, they studied," he said. "We were proud to get good grades for our parents. We would go home with our report cards, show them to our parents and they were proud of us. We knew how they struggled to get to this country. They didn't come over easily. You would never do anything that would reflect poorly on your parents. Everything you did was to honor them."

Above all, Garfield was a sports town. The Garfield Indians, the Jewells and Jinx were a few of the several athletic clubs in town. The YMCA on Outwater Lane near the Samuel Hird woolen plant was popular with both sexes. It featured a pool and tennis courts and entered a basketball team in the state's YMCA league. There were factory leagues in softball and basketball. St. Stan's sponsored a basketball team while teams like the Blue Bishops took on all comers. There were several semi-pro football teams, including the colorful Hippo Rubes. Bowling leagues flourished.

Boxing was extremely popular. There were weekly fight cards, both indoor and outdoor, at Belmont Park, often featuring top names. The city itself turned out plenty of good boxers.

Joey Barcelona went by the name Joey Harrison after Harrison Avenue. He had started his amateur career as the "Masked Marvel," taking on all comers and never defeated. A smooth technician known for his good footwork, he ended his professional career at the age of 23 in 1933 after 126 fights, never having lost by KO or TKO, and was later inducted into the New Jersey Boxing Hall of Fame. He'd serve two terms as a Garfield city councilman and five years on the Board of Education.[4] His son, Ciro, quarterbacked Garfield in the late 40s and coached Garfield in the early 60s.

Charlie Blood and Joey Harrison engage in an outdoor sparring session in the Heights. Courtesy Howard Lanza.

Charlie "Blood" Benanti, another Hall of Famer, earned his nickname by spilling a lot of it as a street fighter in his school days. Just 5-4, 127 pounds, he turned pro at the age of 16 to help support the family, earning $10 for four rounds, and won the New Jersey Lightweight Championship in 1928 and retired in 1931 with a record of 65-5.

"I gave up fighting after a Garfield boy, Joey Biss, stood up for eight rounds of pounding. I was mad because I couldn't knock him out . . . and the depression had cut my purses from $300 and $400 to $50 and $75. Not worth it," he'd later explain.[5]

Benanti took over a tavern on Frederick Street from his father-in-law in 1938 and named it "Charlie Blood's." His son's family still runs it today.

Joey Biss was one of two fighting brothers. Mickey was the other, and they claimed both Garfield and Passaic as their homes. Mickey was known locally as the bad boy of boxing, or "The Killer," often getting into it with the fight patrons, relishing their boos while winking to the boys in the press row. Before Biss' 1932 grudge rematch with Frankie Turrano at the Paterson Armory, Art McMahon of *The Herald-News* eerily wrote that "there is murder in the eyes of the Garfield comeback expert if his friends can be believed."[6] That night, Biss pummeled his opponent so badly that, in the fifth round of the scheduled eight rounder, he asked referee Danny Sullivan to stop the fight. He didn't. In the seventh, Biss landed a right hook to Turrano's stomach and what McMahon described as a "whistling" left hook to his neck as Turrano slumped to the canvas with a sickening thud.

Turrano could not be revived by the ringside doctor and was taken to Paterson General Hospital, where he died the next day. Biss was held on manslaughter charges but was exonerated. The fight should have been stopped. Turrano's mother, Amelia, rejected offers to stage a benefit fight for her son with an emotional statement to the papers:

> *There will be no benefit bout for the family of Frankie Turrano. They do not want blood money. It was bad enough to lose their own beloved son and brother without being the cause of letting some other mother go through the heartaches they are going through.*
>
> *If the law would only put a stop to fighting it would be doing something really worthwhile. Frankie Turrano's mother appeals to all the other young boys to get out of the boxing game while they have the chance.[7]*

Tippy Larkin was the best of the Garfield boxers, another reason for the city's "City of Champions" slogan. Born Anthony Pilliteri in the Heights, he was known as the "Garfield Gunner" with a career that coincided with Garfield High's great run in football and brought him to Madison Square Garden and to national fame. His devastating right hand earned him 58 knockouts in a career that began in 1935 and lasted 17 years with a record of 133-14-1. In 1946, he won the light welterweight world title by decision in a classic bout with Chicago's Willie Joyce.

No sport in Garfield, however, compared to the excitement of high school football. It even had its own smell in a city that could generally have been recognized by one's nose. The factories produced their own telltale odors, like the faint vinegar smell from the soaking tanks in the woolen mills and a pungent, intoxicating fragrance from the Heyden Chemical plant. There was also the enticing scent of homemade bread baking in ovens and kielbasa hanging in the butcher shops in the Polish sections and, from the Italian kitchens, the aroma of Sunday gravy, plump with Jersey tomatoes from the garden, tinged with garlic and herbs simmering on the stove all day.

But there was one smell that enchanted all of Garfield—that of leaves burning in the crisp fall air, heralding the arrival of another high school football season. The Boilermakers played their games on Saturday afternoons when the streets were left so deserted it was said a thief could break into any bank in Garfield. With no home field of their own, the Boilermakers played their games a few miles across the river at Passaic Schools Stadium, where its concrete grandstand peered up at the railroad tracks on the opposite ridge as passenger trains rumbled by during play.

It was a festive atmosphere. Red Simko had been a student at Garfield in the late 1920s. He was a slight man with a short-cropped head of copper and he was Garfield's unofficial head cheerleader. Red tossed lollipops into the stands before games as the Garfield High marching band played the fight song to the tune of *On Wisconsin!*: "Garfield High School, Garfield High School, Plunge on through that line."

Florence Sluja was in high school at the time. She pasted every newspaper article she saw on the team in a scrapbook that she still keeps.

"I went to all the games with my friends," she said. "We took the bus to the Jefferson Street terminal in Passaic and walked to the stadium up Main Street. For the away games, they

The home grandstand at Passaic School Stadium was filled for Garfield's 1939 battle with Clifton. Here Ray Butts hauls in a pass from Benny Babula. Courtesy Estate of Angelo Miranda.

always had a bus going for the students. I remember the Asbury Park game in 1939. We were sitting with a few duds in front of us. We got them up and cheering, though."

The big day often continued into the night. The full-page ad on the back inside cover of the 1939 game program suggested that fans "head straight for" Frank Dailey's brand new Meadowbrook in Cedar Grove. There was dancing starting at 4 o'clock to music by the Meadowbrook Boys, with cocktails priced at 35 cents and dinner at one dollar with no minimum. Afternoon patrons could hang until 7:30, when the feature band took the stage: Jimmy Dorsey and his orchestra with Helen O'Connell and Bob Eberle, vocalists.

Miami, too, loved sports, everything from prize fights to ice skating and especially the dog and pony tracks—all in a big way. By 1939, Miami stood as one of the great young, modern cities of the country, brashly erected as a result of the Florida land boom of the 1920s, which took it from dusty dirt roads and frontier-like wooden buildings to hot concrete sidewalks and soaring skyscrapers.

Post-World War I prosperity created upwardly mobile Americans, who, suddenly flush with money and time, began to pour into Florida in general and in Miami in particular. Get-rich-quick schemes filled many an imagination and with the Everglades being drained and cleared, real estate appeared to be the ticket. Advertising lured them in. In the middle of winter, developer Carl Fisher, a promotional genius, lit up Times Square with a billboard that boasted, "It's June in Miami." Filled with real estate ads, the *Miami Herald* was the heaviest newspaper in the country. Credit was cheap—a 10 percent "binder" did the trick—with quick, enormous profits to be made on resale.

Hoyt Frazure was a "binder boy."

"You bought a property (in the) morning by paying five per cent down with an agreement to close the deal in 30 days and in the afternoon you peddled the property for a higher price," he explained years later. "At the height of the boom I was earning $160 a week selling ads and even more selling land. My biggest single deal was the sale of an eight-unit apartment house . . . for $57,500. I received 60 per cent of a $2,750 commission."[8]

Visitors were besieged with offers as soon as they reached the train station. One described his carriage being "swarmed round . . . like a hive of angry bees; most of them shouting all purple in the face with heat and excitement."[9] Nights on Flagler Street resembled those in the New Orleans French quarter with titles to land thrown around like beads. Developers hired bands to create interest as realtors moved through the crowd hawking their parcels. Miami's population doubled between 1920 and 1923, and in 1925, as building permits topped $60 million, the city expanded from 13 to 43 square miles as various communities such as Lemon City, Coconut Grove and Allapattah approved annexation. Inevitably, as land prices and the cost of living got out of control, the bubble burst at the end of that same year but not before $90 million was spent to develop Miami's bay front skyline. In 1925 alone, 16 new hotels and office buildings were added.[10]

Cranes filled the air all at once as the McAllister, Columbus, Everglades and Alcazar Hotels rose from the sandy ground. For its new headquarters, the *Miami News* erected the iconic News Tower with its design based on Seville's 12th century Giralda bell tower. Fronting the new buildings, city planners recreated the grand boulevards of Europe with palm-lined Biscayne Boulevard and laid out Bayfront Park at the water's edge. Lush with colorful tropical trees, shrubs and flower beds, the park also included a band shell. Nearby, in 1933, an assassin attempted to take the life of President-elect Franklin D. Roosevelt and instead mortally wounded Chicago mayor Anton Cermak. Construction also began on the towering—if over-sized—Dade County Courthouse, which, when finally completed in 1928, was the nation's tallest building south of Cincinnati.

The great hurricane that ravaged Miami in September 1926 dealt the city a crippling blow, forcing Miami into the Depression faster than the rest of the country. But even the Depression couldn't completely put an end to its allure as a getaway spot for those travelers who could spare the dime. And they came from everywhere to mingle.

Damon Runyon captured that convergence of American culture in December of 1929, when he wrote of the coming exodus south from frigid climes and looked forward to revisiting his favorite Biscayne Boulevard Hotel in time to watch the ponies start running at Hialeah, the traditional start of the tourist season. Miami was the nation's gathering place.

The old McAllister, however, preserves a smiling countenance, despite Mine Host Muller's bleak attitude toward the reservation-less and you can sit on the wide veranda in a wicker rocking chair when the Florida moon comes on and watch the milling mob on the sidewalk below in ease and comfort.

You see the same faces that you see on Broadway, or in Saratoga during the racing season. You hear the argot of the big town mingled with the patois of the high grass, for there on the sidewalk in front of the McAllister—"the paddock"—the dudes from the effete east rub cheek by jowl with the crackers from Florida and Georgia and with the small towners from the Midwest.[11]

A grand view of Biscayne Boulevard as seen from Flagler Street, along hotel row. Note the islands of palm trees separating traffic.

The view across Bayfront Park toward Biscayne Boulevard. The park was alive with tropical ferns, brightly colored flowers . . . and pigeons.

With its economy untethered to manufacturing but driven by tourism and a budding commercial aviation industry, Miami would also emerge from the Depression earlier than most of the nation. This was evidenced by the numerous art deco hotels that popped up in Miami Beach in the late 30s. In 1940, Miami Beach had only 28,000 year-round residents, and yet it ranked among the country's top 10 cities in the number of building permits it had approved.

And, as if to announce and symbolize Miami's recovery, the 17-story DuPont Building, with its Rockefeller Center influences, started rising in 1937 after the demolition of the old Halcyon Hotel on Flagler and Northeast Second Avenue. Built solidly and squarely out of Wisconsin black granite and Alabama limestone—it could withstand 225-mile per hour winds—its street-level shops led to an escalator lifting customers to the magnificent mezzanine lobby of the Florida National Bank, bedecked with marble floors, a cypress-beamed, 30-foot high ceiling and elevator doors of polished brass.[12]

The DuPont officially opened on October 22, 1939, when downtown Miami appeared as a sort of teenager coming out of his clothes during a sudden growth spurt. The new, extravagant landmark gave Miami a big-city look with a small-town feel. Over time, though, Miami would grow into itself. Developments had gone up piecemeal as the city grew so that the downtown area quickly gave way to residential neighborhoods like Riverside, Shenandoah and Citrus Grove. Like Garfield's European immigrants, the families that settled in these neighborhoods did so to improve their lot in life.

Pete Williams was an all-state tailback for Miami High in the early 1940s and he later starred at the Naval Academy. His family's path to Miami was probably the most typical of all. In such cases, Miami was a refuge for those caught in a South still feeling the ravages of the Civil War and Reconstruction.

Williams' father, Ernest, was born in 1891 in the East Tennessee town of Wartburg, a German settlement. His mother, Edith, was part of the Kreis family, which owned a large tract of land near the confluence of the Tennessee River. Her grandfather, Harmon, also fought in the Civil War, but on the Union side, which was not all that unusual in fractured East Tennessee. He'd often entertain youngsters by swinging his old cavalry sword about his head, his grey mustache flailing along with it.

Edith graduated from Johnson City Teachers College and found work in Wartburg where she met Ernest who became the Superintendent of Schools in Morgan County.

"Before that, he had a horse and he got the mail route in Morgan County and he realized that he had the best jobs in Morgan County and they weren't anything to brag about, that there wasn't any future there," Williams explained.

"So the Kreis family and Daddy's family, the Williams, many of them went west—Arkansas and Texas. I guess those were the two places that seemed like you could succeed at. Daddy went to Texas to see what there was there. Matter of fact, he didn't have any money to get there so he ho-bo'd on the railroad to go out there and look at it and thought seriously about it. Came back, and a lot of the families had come to Florida to look at Florida and everything. So Daddy came down to Florida and he loved this place. So maybe the following year, he went up and got my mother and my brother and sister, and they came down."

Pete, who was born in Miami a few years after the family resettled, speaks with the gentle, rolling accent of old-time Miamians, one that is fast disappearing from the now cosmopolitan metropolis. It's more of a lilt than a drawl. A little bit slow, a little bit slurred, it says to people, "We're a little bit different down here," and can be summed up in the pronunciation of the town itself: "Miam-ah."

Williams and other kids could bicycle down streets of modest single-story homes and bungalows that were designed with double-hung sash windows to provide what comfort they could during Miami's challenging summer weather. The summer was also when mosquitoes swarmed in from the Everglades like locusts. But if you were born there, you got used to it all.

The DuPont Building rises above Flagler Street, a symbol of the new Miami, shortly after its official opening in 1939. HistoryMiami.

Don Gately, writing for the website *HubPages*, recalled his Miami childhood idyllically. "Mangoes grew everywhere," he noted. "The good ones were called 'Hadens' and the not-so-good ones we called 'turpentines.' Avocados were also around. And there were guavas, and kumquats and sour oranges with thick skins. You could usually find something to pick off a tree and eat if you were hungry enough."[13]

Another account waxed romantically over "the sounds of the palms rustling when the balmy breezes pass through them, the smell of the night blooming jasmine and the salty air and the moonlight reflecting off the dew on the grass like diamonds."

As in Garfield, there was a great deal of familiarity between the residents. Community spirit helped those affected by the Depression, like Jack Pepper's family, left needy after Jack's father, John, was killed in an automobile accident in 1929. Jack was just seven at the time.

"My dad had a very good job. He was head of the Chamber of Commerce in Miami and he was on his way to a convention in Boston when he was killed," Pepper explained. "My mother got all this insurance money but it was in 1929 and all the money went into the bank and of course the banks closed and she lost it all. All of a sudden my brother was born in 1930 and here she was with four kids."

Fortunately, Pepper's mom, Rose, had an older sister in Missouri who was the vice president of a bank. She sent $100 a month for about two years. Rose Pepper learned shorthand and become a secretary.

"Thank goodness for her older sister," Pepper said. "That's what we lived on . . . $100 a month and we managed. We didn't know we were poor. Everybody around us was in the same boat so we didn't know any different. We weren't starving. We had a lot of hand-me-down clothes. We'd go to church every Sunday and people would bring their clothes in that their kids had outgrown and they'd say stitch it and you took it home. That's the way it was back in those days. There was a lot a lot of swapping and trading going on."

In fact, Pepper's mom was acquainted with Davey Eldredge's mom so that Pepper, who was roughly the same size, got some of Eldredge's hand-me-downs. "I was thrilled to get David Eldredge's clothes, I'll tell you that," Pepper said.

Like Pepper, classmate Bob Sims largely grew up in a one-parent household. His parents met in Wichita Falls, Texas. His father was a wildcatter. His mother was a Miami native and they moved back when he was three. His father built a grocery store out of a truckload of wood he hauled back from Perrine, Florida, and called it the Log Cabin.

"We felt the Depression but it was more my mother and father. What did I know?" Sims explained. "When I was in the third grade, the big boys used to walk barefooted. They were sort of a rough bunch. So I wanted to go barefoot and my mother said, 'Over my dead body. If I have to scrub floors you'll never go barefoot.'"

A local radio program that came on the air every Tuesday night, featuring a down and out family talking about their plight. Sims' mom would faithfully call in, offering two or three bags of groceries each week. But the store couldn't sustain itself.

"Everything was on credit. My dad just didn't have any more to restock, so he couldn't pay the bank and went bankrupt. He was too nice to try to collect his money and she was raising Hell with him. One day I just saw him with a suitcase and he just walked off. I was ten years old," Sims recalled.

While his mother took in roomers, Sims chipped in by getting a *Miami Herald* paper route. A hard worker, he'd get up at 3:30 a.m. each morning. By his teenage years he had built up his route to 600 customers and was the *Herald's* top salesman making $16 a month. "That's how I paid for my car," he said. "The payment was $6 dollars a week. Gas was cheap and I didn't have liability insurance . . . not required."

Sims saw his father only once after he left the family. He was in the 11th grade, delivering papers when he ran into him.

"He was really in rough shape," Sims said. "He didn't have the money to get glasses so he couldn't see very well. I said, 'Hey Dad, this is Bob, your son.' He only had 50 cents in his

Flagler Street hums with weekend shoppers and traffic in this photo taken shortly before the city's street-cars were replaced with buses. It was the place to see and be seen.

pocket and he offered it to me. I said, 'Dad I don't need it but he wanted me to take it. My mother . . . she had nothing to do with him."

Hard times didn't preclude fun. Downtown Miami was just a bus ride or bicycle trip away, and it was a wonderland. Kids gathered at Bayfront Park, also called Pigeon Park for obvious reasons. Flagler Street's sidewalks teemed with people. It was a place to see and be seen. The Olympia Theatre, with its wondrous ceiling decorated with the moon and stars, was Miami's first air-conditioned building. The Walgreens Drug Store was a modern marvel. And then there was Burdine's, the most fashionable department store in the South, its floors filled with the latest styles.

"My mother worked at Burdine's selling children's shoes," recalled Bonnie Sims. "Every once in a while, she'd be working on a Saturday and I'd get on the trolley car from Nineteenth Street where we lived. I'd go down and have lunch with her. You weren't afraid to do that. And I'd sit with her at the coffee shop or at the counter and have a malted milk. It was lovely."

As the Christmas season of 1939 approached, Cecil R. Warren wrote of Miami's shopping district as if it were London's Oxford Street:

> *Miami's streets—forgathering place of the world's great crossroads of two continents, seething with America-on-holiday in the winter and slowed to tropical tempo in the summer, have . . . in the few short years of their existence . . . attained high rank among the best-known town thoroughfares of the globe.*

An early photograph of Abraham Lincoln School No. 6, which served as Garfield's high school. The building was too small to accommodate all four grades.
Courtesy Garfield Historical Society.

An aerial view of Miami High School shows its expanse, including a separate gym and practice field.
Miahi, 1940

Cosmopolites now say "Flagler and Miami" with the same glibness with which they speak of 42nd and Broadway, Unter den Linden or Rue de la Paix. It may be doubted if the famed thoroughfares with which Miami streets may vie, with all their years of history, have seen such kaleidoscopic changes as those Miami streets have witnessed in the less than half a century that they have been in existence.[14]

If one didn't want to visit downtown, there was Miami Beach, where a kid like Bob Sims, who was hardly from a wealthy family, could relax and play where it takes dollars to frolic today.

"Every Sunday afternoon, by the (future site of the) Fontainebleau Hotel and at night, you could have a bonfire because there was nothing else around except the Firestone estate," he said. "I had a portable radio. It weighed about 50 pounds, with the batteries in it. We parked on Ocean Drive, then walk over a sandy area and some scrub brush and then get to the regular beach. We'd meet up there and have a good time . . . swim some . . . different girls, different fellas."

It wasn't the brickyard, that's for sure.

The contrast between the two high schools was just as striking. Garfield used Abraham Lincoln No. 6, built as an elementary school, for its high school, perfectly described by Walter Young as "an oversized cheesebox." It was No. 6 School, because it was the sixth school built in Garfield, in 1917, after they leveled a large glacial slope called Watermelon Hill. Garfield's high school-aged students attended classes at either Passaic or Hackensack High School at the time until, in 1919, four rooms on the second level of No. 6 were designated as the high school department. The first graduating class numbered 24 in 1923, but the school population grew quickly as it took in children from Lodi, Wallington, East Paterson and Saddle River (now Saddle Brook). At one point, school days had to be staggered in two sessions to accommodate everyone until the classes were split, with freshmen and sophomores moved to Christopher Columbus No. 8 School a mile away. No. 6 didn't even have a gymnasium. The basketball team played its games at No. 8 while gym classes trudged a few blocks over to the gym at old No. 1 School, the boys ogling the girls in their bloomers.

Facilities were so sparse that Garfield lost its Middle States accreditation for a time in the early 40s. But Garfield was nevertheless a solid school with dedicated teachers and students who could receive a well-rounded, foundational education if they applied themselves. In addition to athletics, extra-curricular activities included: a school play, a well-read school newspaper, *The Quill*, a huge glee club and a newly formed marching band, attired in sharp purple uniforms (which got rave reviews for its halftime performances). The students were like those anywhere else. In 1939, they listed Glenn Miller as their favorite orchestra, Bing Crosby as their favorite vocalist, Spencer Tracy and Bette Davis as their favorite actor and actress, *Wuthering Heights* as their favorite movie, and Hit Parade as their favorite radio program. Favorite type of girl was "feminine." Favorite type of boy was "athletic."[15]

There were five programs of study: a commercial curriculum, a general curriculum, a classical curriculum, a technical curriculum and a normal curriculum for those interested in a teaching career. Students enrolled in the latter three were the most likely to attend college. Of the 84 graduates in the January 1940 class, only 20 were from those programs. Collegiate education simply wasn't a priority among the immigrant community.

Miami High School's magnificent auditorium was home to the Miami Opera Company. The school's other appointments were similarly lavish. Hoit Collection.

Going to university was never within their grasp—or even vision. Supporting the family, however, was. The emphasis was on finding a good job. Many students dropped out of school as early as the fifth grade and went to work, in part to contribute to the family's coffers, especially during the Depression. But, again, those were desperate times.

In Miami, most of the jobs were white collar and, at the time the second high school was planned, the economy was booming. Delayed by the great hurricane of 1926, Miami High went up a year later at an estimated total cost of $1.5 million (around $21.4 million today). Designed by the Pittsburgh architectural firm of Kiehnal and Elliot in the Mediterranean Revival style so popular in Coral Gables at the time, it was a magnificent structure with wings, courtyards, a separate gymnasium and athletic field spread out over 10 acres. It would have swallowed up No. 6 School. In the days before air conditioning, the design of the school opened it up to the breezes. One former student described it as "delightful."

Among the features of the 600-foot-long main building were 79 classrooms and labs, four shops, including an innovative one for auto mechanics, two study halls seating 250 students each and a cafeteria seating 690. A gorgeously appointed auditorium seated 1,290 and was the home of the Miami Opera Company until it built its own house. A separate assembly hall seated 234. The school featured a spacious library with decorative steel roof trusses. Heavy oak front doors, with hinges of wrought iron opened onto a main hallway inspired by the Alhambra palace in Spain. It was lined with terrazzo tiles and lit by wrought iron lanterns and chandeliers. Its red roof was lined with Spanish tile imported from Cuba. It was arguably the handsomest—if not most opulent—high school campus in the nation.[16]

When Principal W.R. Thomas addressed the student body at the dedication ceremony, he told them: "You have the finest school building anywhere and the best facilities and equipment. You must live up to it. You must be the best."[17]

Every new class heard the same challenge and, for the most part, responded. Among the esteemed graduates who passed through those halls before 1939 were bandleader/actor Desi Arnaz (Class of '34), one-time Wimbledon champion Gardnar Mulloy (Class of '33) and former *Washington Post* publisher Phillip Graham (Class of '31). The list includes the former governor of New Hampshire Meldrim Thomson Jr. (Class of '30) and former Florida senator George Smathers (Class of '34) and Charles "Bebe" Rebozo (Class of '30), later the trusted confidante of President Richard Nixon. Actress Veronica Lake, sex siren of the 40s, didn't graduate a Stingaree but was at the school during the 1939 school year when she was known as Constance Keane.

In some cases, Miami High could be intimidating. Lorraine Shaffer (née Hammer) moved to Miami from East McKeesport, Pennsylvania, a town so small that the grammar school, junior high school and high school were housed in the same building. She remembered the day her parents dropped off her and her brother Harry for their first day at Miami High, pulling in front of the sprawling complex.

"That huge, monumental building just scared the puddin' out of me," she admitted. "But I fell in love with the place."

In Pennsylvania, Lorraine was being trained as a dancer and was so accomplished that she had been to New York with her instructor for three summers. She thought she was giving that all up when she moved. The reverse was true. Among the myriad Miami High programs was a huge drama department that put on semiannual musicals that played to sellout crowds. Spurred on by her drama teacher, a Mrs. Williams, Hammer became locally famous and graduated as Most Talented.

"It was such a huge, huge place and nothing stopped us from doing what we wanted to do," she said. "The football team was excelling while we were excelling at the other end of the spectrum."

Outside of athletics, in the 1939-1940 school year alone, the music department swept first-division honors in every category at the state competition, including the marching and concert bands and the boys and girls glee clubs. One soloist, Helen Bennett, won a scholarship to Stetson University for her performance. During that school year, the band played in front of a combined audience of 150,000. Meanwhile, the bi-weekly *Miami High Times* earned All-America honors from the National School Press Association as well as the Columbia University High School Journalism Award. The Pan American Club hosted the First National Convention to which clubs from all over the United States sent 150 delegates. There were clubs for everything with active memberships.

Likewise, the curriculum was large and varied with programs in commerce and math, arts and science, music, languages and social sciences. The emphasis was on preparing students for college and a good many graduates went on to pursue higher education.

There was plenty to do. The Student Council sponsored dances every afternoon in one of the courtyards, as described in the *Miahi* yearbook: "At these affairs, the whole student body, sophomores to seniors, shake off the worries of the past week and really cut a rug. Here, to the whang (sic) of a good old jook organ, many a prize-winning jitterbug is born."[18]

Part of the crowd of 21,000 that took in the annual game between rivals Miami and Edison at the Orange Bowl. Miami News.

Afterwards, the party would often move across Flagler Street to the Orange Royal, where the jukebox played, and the ice cream sodas went down easy. The driving age was 16 and a lot of kids were able to afford cars, "jalopies," mostly.

Of course, there was no bigger event at Miami High than a Stingaree football game, and much of the city joined in. In 1939, five high schools served students in Miami and Miami Beach but the Stingarees regularly only faced one of them—Edison High School. The game, among the most anticipated sporting events of the year, was usually played on Thanksgiving Day when social events were typically planned around it.

The rivalry began in 1925 when Edison was known as Dade County Agricultural School, or, less formally, Lemon City High. The North Miami school soon outgrew its agricultural designation and in October of 1931 solicited suggestions for a new name. When the inventor died that month, it became Edison High School. What didn't change was Miami High's dominance on the football field. Up until 1939, Edison had managed not one victory and two frustrating ties. Stingaree fans loved to play up the jinx angle.

No matter what team the Stings played, game day was a happening, especially after the Miami High moved into the Orange Bowl, where attractive coeds sold programs, pennants and canes for the Student Council, and concessionaires roamed the stands.

The sounds of Miami High football were many—the booming voice of Coach Jesse Yarborough, the grunts of the players, the muffled smacks of the pads, the whoosh of Davey Eldredge as he turned the corner. But there was one distinct sound that literally rang out above all—the cow bell. A single one might mimic the lazy cadence of the dairy farms that encircled the Miami area. Thousands together would be more like a buffalo stampede, under which many opponents found themselves when they came up against the Stingarees in the Orange Bowl. With each Miami score, the big oval would reverberate with the darned things, which is to say it shook often.

Jack Pepper, a high school junior in 1939, took that a step further.

"Somebody had a horn that came off of an old LaSalle but it worked by vacuum of the exhaust so to blow it you had to suck on it," Pepper explained. "It was a long damn horn. I could only suck about two seconds worth but it was a really loud horn, I'll tell you that."

In 1939, the cities' mayors were so unalike and yet so similar. When they posed for a picture on the field at half-time of the Health Bowl, they were a striking pair. Miami mayor Everest G. Sewell was in his third separate term. He was 65 years old and would be dead of a heart attack

Three-time Miami Mayor Everett G. Sewell with his somewhat eccentric look. HistoryMiami.

within four months. Garfield Mayor John M. Gabriel was 29, the picture of youth, known everywhere as the "Boy Mayor."

They shared, however, the same enthusiasm for their cities with a carnival man's flair. Sewell was as Miami pioneer. He arrived with the crew his brother John brought to start clearing the land and within a few weeks the brothers established the first store north of the Miami River. Sewell did more than just see Miami's potential as the Magic City. Sewell made sure the nation was aware of it.

In 1911, as the city marked its 15th anniversary with a gala celebration, Sewell, at the cost of $7,500, brought in stunt pilot Howard Gill for a fly-over in a genuine Wright Brothers biplane and even ventured out onto its wing in flight. When first elected president of the Chamber of Commerce in 1916, Sewell used modern public relations strategies and made frequent visits to New York to spotlight his city's benefits and did as much as anyone to start the flood of tourism.

"He was a gung-ho, non-stop promoting kind of a guy," said Miami historian Paul George. "He looked eccentric, like an early version of Tom Wolfe, the writer, with a walking stick and sometimes the white outfits, the hats. He had a big knot on the back of his neck and he had his hair come down the back to cover it up."

Sewell, though, always carried himself with an "air of dignity,"[19] and, as the leading vote getter in Miami's city commissioner elections, served three terms as mayor, from 1927 to 1929, from 1933 to 1935 and from 1939 until his death. Politics was no picnic in Miami. Sewell was driven out of office in 1935 under attacks of cronyism and corruption by the short-lived *Miami Tribune*, Moses Annenberg's crusading tabloid. "Windy Ev," as the *Tribune* mocked him, nevertheless outlasted the paper. It folded in 1937, and Sewell was returned to office in a special election in 1939 after the *Miami News'* Pulitzer prize-winning campaign recalled the entire slate of city commissioners the *Tribune* had endorsed.

Sewell had his challenges. Gambling, racketeering and prohibition liquor found their way into the tourist trade, all with the tacit approval of the city leaders. That changed when Al Capone, lured by the racing tracks and prize fights, bought a mansion on Palm Island in 1928 and used it as his alibi for the St. Valentine's Massacre the following year, all the while buying into Miami's illegal gambling and drinking establishments. Sewell tried running him out of town but it took Capone's conviction in 1934, with his trip to Alcatraz, to make that happen. Nevertheless, organized crime entrenched itself in Miami in his absence and when he was released on November 16, 1939, Capone returned permanently to Miami where he died eight years later.

A month later, three days before the Garfield-Miami game, J. Edgar Hoover announced that his FBI agents were conducting a "bird dog" investigation of crime and corruption in Miami and Miami Beach with Sewell's full approval.

"All you have to do is walk down certain streets to see them," Hoover said of what he called, "notorious hoodlums."[20]

Crime operated on a smaller scale in Garfield yet, for its size, its crime density was actually higher. Its presence, in many ways, was what propelled Gabriel into the mayor's office. It arrived, according to Howard Lanza, with the Sicilian immigrants, who quickly established underground syndicates. A sub-culture formed, and Garfield gained a reputation as a haven for small-time hoods, an image only enhanced during the Prohibition years.

Speakeasies flourished, a couple of them allegedly frequented by Babe Ruth. Illegal stills (as many as 80) were set up and their dankness hung over the city. There are stories, though unverified, that pipes running under the Passaic River were used to move the bootleg liquor to Passaic, where it was bottled and boxed. Federal agents occasionally made raids, with the operators trying to escape out cellar windows. In one such raid on a 1,500-gallon still on Jewell Street in 1926, prohibition agents discovered and destroyed $30,000 worth of liquor and equipment.[21]

Operating a still had its other dangers. In 1929, Frank Soriano died of body burns when his Harrison Avenue still exploded. That same year, fumes emanating from their small garage still killed Samuel Sherman and Hyman Schwartz. Another still blew up and rocked the walls of a nearby hall where the mayor was addressing a reform group on the problem.

Among Garfield's gangland murders was the 1929 demise of hijacker James Lemmo, shot five times out of a speeding sedan as he walked out of a barbershop on the corner of Lanza Avenue and Scudder Street. Lemmo had reportedly been shaking down the shooter, Frank Caltabellotta. In 1930, bootlegger Peter Currealo was gunned down in front of Venice Gardens, a restaurant. In 1932, Garfield thug Peter Sorrento, variously described by the *Jersey Journal*, as a "hijacker, chiseler, silk thief and stool pigeon," was found stuffed into the rumble seat of his brother's car with 12 bullets in his brain.[22] Later that same year, William Schlegel, a 20-year-old gas station attendant, was hit and killed with a hail of 18 slugs from a sawed off shotgun while fixing a punctured tire. It was a case of mistaken identity. The gunman was after racketeer Edmund "Whitey" Adamchesky, who had been cooperating with police.[23] Similarly, in 1933, Stephen Rocco, 24, murdered Frank Del Donna because he believed Del Donna had tipped off federal agents.

Garfield officials sometimes had dirty hands. In 1927, Helen Moro, wife of councilman Jack Moro, was arrested on bootlegging charges.[24] When ex-fire chief Louis Marzitelli was arrested in a raid on a still in 1931, he claimed he was there merely to repair the still. He was told that made him just as guilty.[25]

Even after the end of prohibition in 1934, the criminal element remained. The problem in Garfield, unlike Miami, was that the lure of fast cash was attracting the city's youth and driving the juvenile delinquency rate among the highest in the state. It wasn't really addressed until Gabriel's mayoral campaign in 1937.

Gabriel, the son of Hungarian immigrants, played football for Garfield High in the mid-20s and later at Drexel University, where he studied with Thomas Perrapato, younger brother of then-mayor Anthony Perrapato and then-police chief Nicholas Perrapato. The Perrapatos had quite the dynasty going. Gabriel graduated in 1932 with a degree in civil engineering but with the Depression in full swing, there weren't many civil engineering jobs to be had. He taught first at Garfield Night School while he attained his teaching requirements at Montclair State College. With Lodi opening its own high school, Gabriel was able to land a job there as a chemistry teacher. A go-getter, he entered politics three years later and was elected to the city council out of the Fourth Ward.

John Gabriel, Garfield's 29-year-old "Boy Mayor."
Courtesy Garfield Historical Society.

He was the underdog in the 1937 mayoral race against Republican incumbent Charles Bleasby, a popular physician who was hailed by *The Herald News* as the best mayor Garfield ever had.[26] Bleasby had, in fact, effectively reduced taxes and was re-elected twice. But Bleasby's downfall came after a feud with power-broker Gotthold "Gufty" Rose. The Second Ward leaned Republican, but when Bleasby refused to cooperate with Rose, Rose refused in kind to deliver votes to Bleasby (despite a last-minute appeal). In two previous elections, Bleasby had carried the ward by over 800 votes. This time, his margin was just 228. Gabriel, meanwhile, rode an overwhelming 700-vote advantage in the largely Eastern European Fourth Ward to what *The Herald-News* called, "one of the greatest upheavals in the history of Garfield politics."[27]

Gabriel had campaigned on a promise to combat juvenile delinquency. His slogan was "out of the poolroom and into the schoolroom," and after he took office, he made good on it.

He held up the football team as an example of his accomplishments with the youth of Garfield and of the benefits of staying in school. He developed a personal relationship with many of the players, and made it a point to call each of them into his office to discuss their lives and to offer advice. Gabriel started the junior safety patrol, which won a national award in Washington and established Camp Garfield for the city's underprivileged kids. At the time, it was the only municipally run camp in the state.

"It was all Gabriel's doing," Howard Lanza said. "He truly cared about the kids."

Gabriel's Juvenile Commission set about saving kids who were otherwise earmarked for trouble. Instead of sending juvenile offenders off to reform school or jail, they were brought before the Commission and counseled and a program was set up for them.

In 1940, after attracting nationwide publicity with the football team, Gabriel was the subject of a syndicated Sunday magazine feature written by Dick McCann for the *New York Herald-Tribune*. Perhaps McCann, who had been fascinated by Gabriel as one of the Health Bowl organizers, went slightly over the top in his heroic portrayal, but not by all that much if you ask those who remember the Boy Mayor.

The piece was sensationally titled, "The Boy Who Cleaned Up Hell's Graveyard" and called Garfield a dumping ground for bodies: "the last stop on Gangland's one-way ride."

"Kids would stand on street corners and openly gape at the loudly dressed mobsters as they stepped from elegant limousines," McCann wrote. "The big-time hoodlums were heroes to the boys of Garfield . . . prohibition was gone but the scars were still there. The first ugly days of the Depression made matters worse and mobs of petty thieves roamed the neighborhood . . . and scores of boys were sent off to state institutions, snarling and swearing to come back and, 'get even with you coppers.'"

Gabriel told McCann that he and his young friends, disgusted with the city establishment's ineffective response to the youth problem, hatched the idea of getting into government at a local dance.

"I guess there never was such a setting for a political coup before," he said. "There was a hillbilly band thumping out the music good and fast and the girls fretfully tapped time as we fellows hunched around a table and plotted to take over the city government. One girl was more impatient than the others. She didn't want to be a wallflower all night so she snatched up her purse, jingling with her 'mad money' and stomped out of the hall. She was my date.

"I wasn't all that chivalrous, I know, but we simply forgot all about the dance, we got so wrapped up in this idea of governing the city ourselves."

By 1939, when Gabriel was re-elected in a landslide, Garfield had one of the youngest municipal governments in the country. He appointed 36 officials averaging 30 years of age, who were approved by a city council with half of its eight members under 30. "People used to kid me for running Boys Town," he told the *Associated Press*. "But I laughed and said, Father Flanagan is doing all right with Boys Town in Nebraska.[28] Gabriel's programs worked, all grounded in a philosophy explained to McCann: "There's no such thing as a bad boy. He isn't born bad. He may grow bad . . . you see, we are not so much interested in what he did as why he did it."

McCann's lengthy feature concluded by telling the story of one of Gabriel's old childhood pals who had joined a gang after high school. He'd been released from the Ohio State Penitentiary and wanted Gabriel to pull some strings to get his driver's license back.

McCann quotes Gabriel's answer: "Look, Tom. I never thought I'd ever talk this way to you—and I'm not liking it. But I won't help you get your license back. I'll go even further. I'm going to ask you to leave town and never come back. Times have changed, Tom. You don't fit in here anymore. I'd get you a job but you know as well as I do that you don't want a job. So here, take this and get out of town."

According to McCann, the man took the bill that Gabriel had pressed into his palm. Then turned around one last time as he was leaving and said:

"Listen, Johnny, all I've got to say is this. I have been reading about what you have done here and if somebody had done the same when you and I was (sic) kids you wouldn't be telling me to get out of your house."[29]

McCann's account read like an Edgar G. Robinson-James Cagney movie script. But in Garfield, it wasn't the only thing that mimicked fantasy. One only had to look out on the high school football field.

FOUR

THE COACHES

ARGAUER

It's easy to imagine Emma Argauer frantically searching the crowded deck of the *Kaiserin Auguste Victoria* as it steamed toward New York Harbor on a rainy Saturday morning in August of 1906. The family's nine-day voyage from gritty Hamburg to a new start in America was nearing its end, and her six-year-old son had disappeared from sight.

"Artur? Wo bist du!" she cried out, with her other two other children by her side. Not that Emma was unaccustomed to such shenanigans.

Arthur Carl Maximilian Argauer had always found mischief, and that didn't end on a ship full of wonders for him and his older siblings, Oscar and Ella. That said, they were crossing the ocean on the largest liner then in existence, no place for a little lost boy. Emma's fright escalated by the second.

Suddenly, the chubby-legged kindchen appeared and embraced his mother's leg. Her heart back in place, Emma let out a reproving sigh and wagged her finger.

"Du bist ein kleiner Teufel," she gently scolded him, calling him a little devil, as he smiled back. She couldn't be angry for long, certainly not at this moment. Instead, she palmed the boy's face and extended her arm toward the remarkable scene off the bow. A shower had just cleared and the sun was shining on the distant Statue of Liberty, its copper just beginning to yield to a patina green. The fidgety youngster didn't know it, but America, with all of its promise, awaited him. And few would exploit its vaunted potentialities as would Art Argauer: coach, educator, Renaissance Man—or as the headstone in East Ridgelawn Cemetery simply defines him—"humanitarian."

Yet, when Argauer died in 1986, few realized he was a German immigrant. He'd become an institution in New Jersey and left a legacy that still endures at Tusculum College in Tennessee. And he did it through the most American of sports, football.

Arthur's destiny was sealed when his father, Charles, decided to leave Germany. Charles graduated from the University of Stuttgart then studied fashion design in Paris, London and Berlin. The Argauers eventually settled in Rixdorf, near the perpetually disputed border with Denmark. Soon, though, Charles sensed the beginnings of Europe's impending strife. Frictions over Morocco increased between Kaiser Wilhelm and French Premier Rouvier. Britain's Royal Navy unveiled the *H.M.S. Dreadnought*, a battleship with an unprecedented array of big guns. Germany answered with plans to build two dreadnoughts and one battle cruiser per year. Charles Argauer responded by taking his family to America.

Charles, a respected tailor, had been intrigued by the country since a visit to San Francisco as a 15-year-old in 1888. He chose the East Coast, where he'd live among other expats in Carlstadt, New Jersey, known as that "pretty little German village on the hill."

The Argauers weren't typical turn-of-the-century immigrants. Charles was neither tired nor poor nor wretched, and the "huddled" masses meant nothing until his son coached football. Charles' skill with needle, thread and tape measure well suited the numerous textile mills then populating the Passaic River. Furthermore, his excellent English (he also spoke French) was a distinct advantage for setting up a clothier business catering to affluent clients.

Carlstadt was a perfect choice as the family's new home, not only because it was home to so many in his profession that it had at the time been known as "Tailor Town." Perched above the New Jersey Meadowlands, where the area's two NFL teams today share MetLife Stadium, Carlstadt made for an easy transition from Deutschland to Amerika.

Even its history was transcendent. In 1851, Dr. Carl Klein led the Freethinkers, a set of German socialists, in staking out the land for themselves. The old story is that Carl somehow managed to remain the town's namesake, even after he had absconded with the treasury. Another story, however, is much kinder to the good doctor—one of a broken man leaving town after discovering his wife's affair, and that it was she who fled with the funds. In any case, Klein supposedly rests (uneasily) in an unmarked grave in a Staten Island cemetery.

The Freethinkers were an industrious ilk that valued hard work and, above all, education. Yet, they thought little of religion. Oppressive clerics had chased them out of Germany. In the original articles of incorporation of the founding German Democratic Land Corporation, it was stipulated that no religious worship would be permitted within the village's boundaries.

But as more devout Germans made Carlstadt their home, the German Evangelical Church (later the First Presbyterian) was built on aptly-named Division Street, with all houses of worship built only on one side of it. The Freethinkers barely tolerated the Evangelicals but downright disdained the Catholics, who built their church on the East Rutherford side of the border.

By the time the Argauers moved into their house on Fourth Street, religious denizens outnumbered the secular, although the town remained predominantly German. It was a pleasant town and soon took on the semblance of a suburb, with neatly kept homes lining dirt and, later, paved roads. A trolley ran down Hackensack Street, the main thoroughfare. Carlstadt was the first town in the county to install gas lamps for artificial street lighting.

Education remained a focus in Carlstadt, so Arthur received a solid one for the era. The teaching of both English and German was still mandatory in Carlstadt, and he excelled at both, as well as in his other classes. It was when school was out, however, that Art could best satisfy his curiosity.

The waterways of the Meadowlands were yet to be polluted by decades of indiscriminate dumping of hazardous waste by more than 100 companies (if not a few corpses by the region's infamous criminal element).

The Meadowlands Art Argauer knew were more reminiscent of colonial times when white cedars afforded hiding places for pirates, when fish, turtles and crabs flourished in the wetlands. Art and his siblings, Oscar and Ella, lived a short walk from a view down acres of flat marshland meandering into the river, then dissolving into the horizon of Manhattan's skyline. In an age when church steeples towered over most towns, the Argauer kids marveled at the construction of the soon-to-be 11-story Metropolitan Life Insurance Company Tower. They lived within a mile of the creek, their swimming hole. Art and his older brother, Oscar, hunted muskrats. They fished and crabbed and played fetch with their dog, which provided them all the protection they'd ever need—including from their father.

If discipline needed to be dispensed at the end of a strap, still a common remunerator for childhood sins in those days, the dog had to be locked up first, or he'd charge fiercely to their rescue. Often, it seemed, Arthur and the dog were partners in crime. Once, Arthur returned home from the creek with a basket of crabs, which he carelessly set in the sink, from which they made their escape. His mother's blood-curdling screams summoned him from his room back to the kitchen, only to see the crabs scuttling all over the floor. The dog barked wildly and snapped at the trespassers, adding to the mayhem.

Arthur's punishment was to eat his breakfast standing up the next morning. That hardly deterred his adventurous streak. A couple of weeks later, he returned home to show his mother an old tin can full of colorful snakes. Wriggling and writhing, they were taken back to their natural habitat by order of Emma Argauer.

As the family moved up the White Trolley line, the young Argauer attended grammar schools in Carlstadt, Rutherford, East Rutherford and Passaic. It seemed his entire life embraced new experiences. He'd try his hand at everything—from manual labor to gourmet cooking.

Though a good student, Argauer didn't graduate elementary school. As World War I broke out, the 14-year-old dropped out of the eighth grade and, whether out of boredom or impatience, went to work. Certainly it wasn't at the urging of his father, who had made the most of his educational opportunities in Europe. But there was no reasoning with his headstrong son, who was already growing from a stubby boy into a strapping young man.

Hard work added to his frame. In the days before weight training, it was the best way for athletes to develop strength. Think of Red Grange hauling ice back in Wheaton, Illinois. Argauer had already been earning money working on a farm on the weekends. He then became a carpenter's helper, a steamfitter, and a laborer at Forstmann Woolens, where he likely had toiled beside many of his future players' parents. He was a "roller" at Athenia Steel, then worked for a wholesale cleaner and dyer and, finally, in his father's tailor shop. Just before the Armistice was signed, he joined the merchant marine, a naturalized U.S. citizen willing to join the fight against Germany.

By that time, his father was well established as the leading tailor in the recently incorporated city of Clifton. To own an Argauer-crafted suit of Fortsmann wool was a fashion statement. Argauer could have joined his father in the business after working in the shop for a couple of years. Eventually, it might have been renamed Argauer & Son, a fixture on 720 Main Avenue. But that would not happen.

Argauer had no intention of pursuing a high school education. Instead, it pursued him. Clifton High School fielded baseball, basketball and track teams for the 1920-21 school year.

Students who played their football on the sandlots were denied requests to the Board of Education to fund a team were made. But, led by a red-haired kid named Milt Sutter, they tried again in the summer of 1921. Sutter circulated a petition that was signed by every boy in the school, and to add some gravitas to the effort, they enlisted a physical education teacher, Carlton V. Palmer, to present their proposal to the Board.

Palmer was "a very aggressive fellow" according to Sutter in a newspaper interview shortly before he died at age 95. Palmer offered to coach the team and wriggled $300 out of the Board for equipment and uniforms.[1]

The petition had worked, just not according to the students' plans. Palmer had been an assistant coach under the innovative Dan McGugin at Vanderbilt, and he saw this as an opportunity to coach at the high school level. But Palmer would not be satisfied leading a rag-tag group of kids who'd never played organized football and who didn't know a single wing from a turkey leg. Instead, he began to round up older players who had never attended or finished high school. As there was not an age restriction at the time, when the boys showed up for the first practice, they were thrown in with some men five years their senior.

"They were not in school," Sutter said. "I don't know what the arrangements were, but they came back to class and attended like everyone else. It got so that we kids who started this movement weren't going to be allowed to play because of the players he picked up."[2]

Palmer searched farms and in factories far and wide for the guys who would carry his team. He found 18-year-old Vince Chimenti, one of his backfield stars, in Brooklyn. Twenty-year-old Ray Bednarcik, another ball carrier, came out of the silk mill. Bulky 19-year-old William Ziegler, who'd become the bulwark of the offensive line at center, was working on the railroad. And then, one day, on Ziegler's tip, Palmer walked into the Argauer tailor shop on 720 Main Avenue on the corner of Clifton Avenue. He didn't want a suit. He wanted the tailor's apprentice son, and, while he wanted him for Clifton High, it was a day that, in changing the course of Art Argauer's life, forever changed the destiny of Garfield High School football.

Palmer chatted with Art about football but also argued the importance of earning a diploma. His pitch must have also impressed Charles Argauer, who knew the value of an education from his schooling in Europe.

Art Argauer never forgot that fateful day. He'd eventually follow Palmer to MacKenzie School in Monroe, New York, and then to Tusculum College in Tennessee. The same arguments that Palmer made to him, Argauer would use to assemble his football teams at Garfield.

For now, stronger and wiser than most of his classmates, he threw himself into athletics. By the end of his freshman year, he'd earn letters in four sports. His work in the mills put muscle on a frame that was built low to the ground, with thunderous thighs. The physique ideally suited him for both lugging the football and wearing the tools of ignorance as a catcher on the baseball team. Those thick legs could move, as well. In baseball, he stole 38 bases to set a state record. When he could, he'd hop on the bus with the track team to run sprints or throw the discus. He was the North Jersey champion in the 100-yard dash. Basketball was perhaps his weakest sport, although he'd end up coaching the sport and winning numerous titles at Garfield.

Sutter, the kid who got the football team started in the first place, did manage to earn a starting position at quarterback, which wasn't the feature position it is today. Still, the quarterback called all the plays. With Argauer, Chimenti and Bednarcik in his backfield, he didn't call his own number that often. It was literally men against boys when Clifton took the field.

"Ziegler could block like nobody's business," Sutter said. "It really wasn't fair. We were playing against 15- and 16-year-old kids with men."[3]

That 1921 season opened as a curiosity at Doherty Oval, the baseball stadium that was home to the Doherty Silk Sox, run by the Doherty Silk Mill. City fathers gathered in their top hats, and a school band belted out "rage and dirges" to take up the time waiting for the late arrival of the Butler High School team bus.

"Old man Jupiter Pluvius tried hard to put a crimp in the festivities," wrote the *Passaic Daily Herald*, noting how showers were dampening the occasion. But none of it bothered the anxious boys about to take the field for Clifton.[4]

Argauer would score the first touchdown in school history on a simple one-yard plunge behind Ziegler, who was nicknamed "Arbuckle" because his heft was reminiscent of the famous silent film actor of the era. When Butler completed its first forward pass of the day, Argauer was there to knock the receiver down cold. "This type of tackling," the *Daily Herald* predicted, "bids well for the future." The final whistle blew as darkness was falling just when a Clifton touchdown made the final score, 46-0.[5]

The next week, Clifton beat Emerson, 32-0. For the season, the Clifton Maroon and Gray outscored opponents, 215-46. The only loss in eight games was a forfeit against Pingry Prep, the feeder school for Princeton University. Palmer pulled his team off the field when it was losing, 20-7, because he didn't think Clifton was getting a fair shake from the officials, but the Mustangs were getting a dose of their own medicine from the more experienced Pingry team. "Pingry outclassed us," Sutter would say. "I swore they put soap on the uniforms."[6]

If Argauer needed any example of how exciting this could all be, it came in the fifth game of the season when Clifton, the small town, upset Hackensack, the big city, 21-14. That night, Palmer hired a brass band. What seemed like the entire student population did a snake dance down Main Avenue, past the Argauer tailor shop, and then on to the high school, where it lit a bonfire.[7]

"Take an old-fashioned country fair, and magnify it by 100," a passage in the Clifton High yearbook describes. "Add the noise of an old-fashioned Fourth of July with the colors of a three-ringed circus, and more excitement than a Wall Street explosion. This will give you a plain idea of the night after the Hackensack football game."[8]

Palmer moved on after that season to do relief work in Poland, but Clifton was just as formidable in 1922 under Clifford Hurlburt, who'd come down from Springfield, Massachusetts. While perennial power Rutherford was awarded the Class A state championship, Clifton put together an undefeated season as Argauer bid for All State honors. Clifton finished the season 9-0 by outscoring opponents, 140-31, including a 63-0 destruction of Hempstead, Long Island, led by Argauer's four touchdowns, and a 21-2 win over a highly regarded New Brunswick team late in the season, which was regarded as a claim on the state title.

"Whirlwind smashes through the outside of tackle which have characterized practically all of Clifton's earlier victories this year again paved the way to success," Michael Shershin of the *Daily Herald* observed with awe. "With astounding speed and behind a wall of human flesh consisting of some five or six interferes, Captain Quinlan tore across the New Brunswick flanks time and time again. Then, when New Brunswick began to check this attack, Ray Bednarcik, the sturdy, hard running quarterback and Chimenti or Argauer, quite something of battering rams, diverted the drive to New Brunswick's midsection with devastating destruction."[9]

Art Argauer in his Clifton football uniform.
Passaic Daily Herald.

The final two games of the '22 season had to have left a lasting impression on Argauer, each in its own way. Fresh off the win in New Brunswick, Clifton traveled to Newark for a game against Orange, where it slogged through not only a muddy field obscuring the chalk lines but also some questionable officiating, according to some accounts. Only two penalties were called against Orange by the referee identified as Schneider, even as several Clifton players, including Chimenti, had been knocked out of the fray.

Trailing, 13-12, late in the game, Argauer intercepted a pass at the Clifton 20, got ahead of the entire Orange team and was well on his way to an 80-yard go-ahead touchdown. As he eyed the end zone, though, the referee was whistling the play dead. Argauer stopped and turned around. Orange, the ref said, was offside on the play. Clifton, he said, could not decline the penalty.

Still, Clifton gained possession again, and was threatening at the Orange 20 with about 3:00 left in the game when Orange supporters spilled onto the field to demand Schneider end the game because of darkness. And that's exactly what he did. Clifton apparently had lost its first game ever to a high school team.

Lesson about to be learned. If things appear to be out of your control on the field, control can be regained off the field, at least in those days. Clifton's principal, Walter Nutt, protested the game that night and Walter Short, head of the state association, ruled it "No Game."

Witnesses were called into a hearing. Schneider explained the confusion at the end of the game. He said he had heard someone tell him "Time up" when he was really being told "Time out," so he picked up the ball and ran off to the field house. Such was the chaotic, often comic, state of high school sports at the time.

With its perfect record restored, Nutt sent a telegram to Short, making a claim on the Class A title and challenging any team in New Jersey to prove otherwise.[10] When that challenge went unanswered, Hurlburt turned to his Massachusetts connections and set up a home-and-home series with undefeated state champion Norwood High. Norwood would come to Clifton first.

This would be Argauer's first exposure to the thrill of intersectional play. Norwood was treated as royal visitors by the city of Clifton after arriving by steamer from Fall River to New York. The papers hyped the game all week. Clifton won the game, 13-10, with the *Daily Herald* describing Argauer as a "diamond under the light." His touchdown run, which came early in the second quarter, was no ordinary play. In fact, it may have sowed the seed for the play that gave Garfield a 13-0 lead in Miami 17 years later, the Naked Reverse where Walter Young sprang John Grembowitz.

The 1923 Clifton High football team. Art Argauer is holding the football in the front row.
Clifton High School.

From the Norwood 20, Argauer was to run a routine off-tackle slant to the right side. But Norwood had shifted its defense in that direction, leaving Clifton unable to set up the double team and trap blocks that made that play the basis of any single-wing attack. Seeing that, Argauer reversed his field, hiding behind the mass of humanity along the line, and when he swung to the left side, he was fully undetected.

Recounted the *Daily Herald*: "The run was a complete surprise to everyone, especially to Argauer's teammates who wondered where he had gone to. He crossed the line all by his lonesome."[11]

Although it hadn't been set up that way on the blackboard, it was a classic misdirection play. Argauer could see how running several off-tackle plays to that side had influenced Norwood's defense. Deception had as much of a role as power in an effective offense, especially on scoring plays.

Not all of Argauer's instructive memories came on the football field. He'd learn another hard lesson on the hardwood, where he played guard on the Clifton team that nearly upset Passaic High School's Wonder Team. The coach of that team, Professor Ernest Blood, is in the Basketball Hall of Fame. His scholarly demeanor was partly offset by the pet bear cub he kept as a courtside mascot. His charges won renown across the nation for a winning streak that reached a still-standing record 159 over five seasons before Hackensack ended it on a sawdust-strewn court in February, 1925—after Blood had left the school.

The streak could very well have ended two seasons earlier when Passaic escaped with a 36-34 win over Clifton in a game expected to be so lopsided that only a gaggle of spectators showed up to watch at the Paterson Armory. Passaic had beaten Englewood, 133-18, and Ocean City, 109-16 earlier that season and, three weeks earlier, chalked up win No. 103 over Clifton, 67-29.

Passaic was missing two starters in the rematch but, after jumping out to a 21-4 lead, another win seemed assured. Then the tide turned.

According to *Daily Herald* writer George H. Greenfield, "Passaic's morale was completely destroyed, crushed, and swept away by the onrushing Maroon and Gray cohorts of Coach (Harry) Collester. With visions of a possible victory over the far-famed Wonder Team before their eyes, they made shots they had never made before, played a floor game that they never dreamed themselves capable of, and, in general, proceeded to throw a monkey wrench into the Passaic machine."[12]

Led by Joe Tarris and two of Argauer's football teammates, Bednarcik and Chimenti, Clifton held a 34-33 lead with one minute left. Or was it really a minute? Stories persist that the time remaining was closer to 10 seconds, and that the timekeeper—from Passaic—had a slow hand on the clock. Bednarcik missed a layup that would have iced it, and, just before the final whistle sounded, Passaic's Mike Hamas made a basket and a free throw to keep the Wonder Team's streak alive.[13]

Argauer would always contend that Clifton "was robbed."

Elected captain of the 1923 football team, Argauer's leadership skills were fast emerging. "Only a man of Argauer's playing ability and caliber could endeavor such a task," the Clifton paper crowed. Mighty Rutherford was Clifton's first opponent that year and that's where Clifton's unbeaten record against high school teams ended in front of a crowd of 3,500. Still, Argauer stood out in the 16-6 loss.

"Captain Argauer, Clifton's sensational quarterback, again proved himself a remarkable player," the *Daily Herald* said. "He consistently gained ground for Clifton and as a bulwark on defense, both in the line as well as in open field plays. He made more tackles than any two members of the Clifton team and proved the all-around star of the day."[14]

The loss would be Argauer's last at Clifton. The Mustangs, as they would be known, won the remainder of their games in 1923 before Carlton Palmer came back into his life.

Palmer was recruiting a team again, now as the head coach of the MacKenzie School, an all-boys prep school in bucolic Orange County, New York. Situated on Lake Walton, the school boasted of alumni in all the Ivy League schools and of a 40-acre ball field, both of which attracted Argauer.

By that time, Argaeur's interests had extended beyond sports. He acted in the school play and was elected class president. The lure of working under his first mentor again sealed his decision. At MacKenzie, he would also join Clifton teammate Chimenti and Emil "Jerry" Bilas, a player from neighboring Garfield.

The Jersey guys provided MacKenzie with an undefeated season, including a win over Bordentown Military Academy played before 3,500 fans in Clifton. But, at 24, Argauer had finally used up his high school eligibility. By now set on becoming a teacher and coach, he spent the next year at the Savage School of Physical Education, which was eventually absorbed by New York University. There, he met a former Garfield High football player named Al Del Greco. Del Greco would go on to play influential roles during the course of Argauer's coaching tenure at Garfield, but all off the field. Blessed with preternatural wit, he pursued journalism after Savage. By 1930, Del Greco was sports editor of the *Bergen Evening Record*. He'd often use his pen to needle his old classmate. He once revealed that Argauer wore dentures. Yet, he also came to Argaurer's defense when merited. The writers all loved Argauer.

Fate intervened yet again for Argauer when Palmer left MacKenzie to take the head coach's job at Tusculum College in 1926, just in time to re-recruit Argauer. Argauer starred for him in football, where he attracted some attention from major college scouts, but, by then, he was more interested in his long-term prospects as a coach and mentor.

A letter home from Palmer to the Clifton newspaper made clear where Argauer was heading.

"Art is doing fine in his studies and is proving an especially likeable teacher in physical training. He is making great strides in many ways. Dr. Rankin (dean of the school) told me the other day of how different Art is from so many of the other northern boys, that he is more interested in his studies, gets better grades and is more gentlemanly."

Palmer, as a matter of fact, remained one of the biggest influences in Argauer's life. He eventually left coaching to become a highly successful art broker in Atlanta. Here was a man who studied in American and European universities, traveled to 42 foreign countries, including a trek, by camel, across the Arabian Desert from Aleppo in Syria to Baghdad in Iraq and served with the Polish Army in the Russian campaign. Palmer studied music in Germany, coached athletics at Vanderbilt and Tusculum, taught at the University of Alabama and lectured on art throughout the United States. He was the Renaissance man Argauer modeled himself after. While Argauer remained in the coaching profession his entire life, he appreciated what life offered beyond athletics. He was more than a football coach in that respect. He was an educator.

In that letter to Clifton, Palmer added that Argauer was going to coach the Doak High School basketball team in his spare time and it was there that he won his first championship as a coach. Doak wanted him to remain in Tennessee, but Argauer, as usual, was on the move. He earned his bachelor's and Masters degrees at Columbia University, where he first met coach Lou Little, his frequent sounding board. He began teaching at Montclair Academy in 1928 and, a year later, he landed at Hannah Penn Junior High School in York, Pennsylvania. Naturally, he coached the football team to its best record ever.

The timing was perfect. As Argauer was building his resume in Pennsylvania, the Garfield High School football team was destroying its coaches' reputation in New Jersey.

YARBOROUGH

There can be a no more apt senior citation than the one that appeared under the coy countenance of Jesse Hardin Yarborough in the 1926 edition of the *Cestrian*, the yearbook of Chester High School in South Carolina:

Mule
Football '24, '25, '26; Track '25; President Junior Class
Some things start small and grow big
Mule is noted for a great many things, being most noted for his ability to play football. He believes in having a good time and is a great lover of the more beautiful things of life (girls). You never see him worrying over anything for he says, "Worrying may spoil my good looks."[15]

Those off-hand musings turned out to be eerily prescient. Jesse—pronounced "Jess"—was nothing if not tenacious. The Mule nickname stuck with him throughout his life. His home-spun humor could be both disarming and caustic. As for starting small and growing big, Yarborough seemed destined to rise from his sleepy southern town to the bright lights of Miami, and then on as a mover and shaker in Florida.

The Yarborough family's roots ran deep in the red-clay soil of South Carolina's Piedmont region, and as far back as the Revolutionary War. Jesse's Virginia-born great-great grandfather, William Yarborough, was awarded land for his service with the South Carolina troops arrayed against Lord Cornwallis during his "winter of discontent" before his surrender of British forces at Yorktown. William became a planter in what was called the Fairfield District, a rolling land of "pines, ponds and pastures," whose fertile valleys were well suited for growing cotton and small grains. William's son, Henry, had acquired up to 26 slaves by the time of his death in 1853, leaving several to his son, William Burns—Jesse's grandfather—who marched off to war with Company F of the 12th South Carolina regiment, also known as Means Light Infantry. He was wounded at Second Manassas, surrendered at Appomattox, then happily reunited with his wife, Lizzie, and their six children, including Jesse's father, James Henry Yarborough.

Through him, Jesse Yarborough received an eye-witness appreciation of what Southerners preferred to call the War of Northern Aggression. His father was a self-described "tousled-head, freckle-faced" boy of nine years when General William T. Sherman's troops, madly intent on wreaking havoc on the birthplace of secession, crossed the Broad River at Freshley's Ferry and reached the Yarborough plantation at Jenkinsville. James Henry's memory of the event was clear when, in June of 1938, W.W. Dixon interviewed him for the Federal Writers Project of the Work Progress Administration.

As the Union Army moved up from Columbia through the Fairfield District it left behind a trail of smoke pluming from burning farm buildings. The area was rich with provisions, only to be raided and carted away by the advancing Yankees. James Henry recalled the Bluecoats as they "confiscated everything, such as corn, wheat, oats, peas, fodder, hay, and all smokehouse supplies.

"I fought like fury to retain about a pack of corn-on-the-cob that the Yankees' horses had left in a trough unconsumed. I remember, too, how grief stricken I was when a Yankee soldier killed my little pet dog," he went on. "He had a gun with a bayonet fixed on the muzzle. He began teasing me about the corn. The little dog ran between my legs and growled and barked at the soldiers whereupon with an oath the soldier unfeelingly ran the bayonet through the neck of the faithful little dog and killed him."[16]

The father's return, as welcome as it was, did little to improve the welfare of the family, which would grow to include two post-war children and suffer the death of an infant. James Henry described his father as "a lover of nature, stars, flowers, birds, and trees. He was full of sentiment and high ideals, but he was not very practical in looking after and increasing his substance of material things."[17]

After graduating from Furman University, James Henry spent a year teaching in Leon, Texas. According to his daughter, Hattie, he then studied law and was admitted to the bar, before, Hattie said, "he decided he would rather save a man before he got in trouble than to try and save him from prison after he got in trouble." So, he instead decided to attend the Baptist Seminary in Louisville, Kentucky, and then returned to settle in Chester County, just north of Fairfield, where he set out to preach.

In 1891, he married the daughter of one of his deacons, Lily Inez Harden, whose family was one of the most prominent in Chester County. Jesse was the seventh of their eight children, born in 1906. When James Henry retired from the active ministry in 1926, leaving it to "younger men," he was elected probate judge of Chester County and ran unopposed until his death in 1944 to be succeeded by his daughter, Hattie, affectionately known as "Mrs. Hattie." Together, they held the position for 40 years.

Between his roles as minister and judge, James Henry married hundreds of couples. He was the picture of a Southern gentleman, tall with a wisp of hair and a cotton-white beard. He was exceedingly proud of his children, and he'd later dote on his grandchildren, slipping them money at each visit. When he died, the *Chester News* eulogized that he "enjoyed the warm friendship of thousands of people" and that "his friendly disposition, his kindly words will cause hundreds to revere his name."[18]

Similarly, when Hattie passed away in 1973, the same paper paid tribute to her as a grand old lady, "the type of woman who if she liked you, let everyone know it. If you did something she didn't like, she didn't mince words with you but would be straightforward, shooting from the hip. How many people have been there to bear the sting of one of her lectures? How many more people have been there to be flattered by the love and attention she gave so freely?"[19]

All of James Henry's children earned college degrees: three boys from Clemson and five girls from Limestone College. All found success in life.

Jesse was the mischievous one. As the second youngest, he enjoyed a natural dispensation, which he would exploit. Always curious, one family story had it that he would wrap himself in a carpet to eavesdrop on adult conversations. "He was the 'bad boy' of the family, smoking behind the barn, always doing something crazy as a kid," said his daughter Louise. "His sisters would give him a hard time but my dad was always the one that was very special and well-loved."

Most of James Henry's time was devoted to preaching when Jesse was young. The family lived on farms, at first in Front Lawn, about 20 miles east of Chester and then in Baton Rouge, about 13 miles west. They were typical of the area, with fields cleared of yellow pine, oak, hickory, elm and black gum trees. Chester itself was—and still is—a typical southern town. Up on "The Hill," historical structures still tower over the town: a Confederate monument, erected in 1905, a Romanesque Revival city hall from 1890, a Greek revival bank from 1919 converted to a Masonic Temple in 1942, a city jail from 1914 and a country courthouse that dates back to 1852, all part of Jesse Yarborough's youth.

The football team, known as the Red Cyclones, played its games at the Chester County Fairgrounds, and, while the Red Cyclones never won a championship, Mule was good enough to attract the attention of Clemson College, which was then an all-male agricultural and military school.

His older brother James majored in veterinary medicine at Clemson and eventually practiced in Miami. Jesse majored in agricultural chemistry, was elected president of the junior class and, while he excelled on the football field, he didn't neglect his studies to the point where he had hard choices to make over what career path to pursue.

While at Clemson, Yarborough met perhaps the biggest influences of his life in football: coach Josh Cody. Everyone on campus called Cody "Big Man" during his four years at Clemson, which coincided with Yarborough's time there. He stood 6-foot-2 and weighed over 230 pounds, monster dimensions for his playing days at Vanderbilt (1914-1916 and again in 1919 after a two-year stint as an Army lieutenant in World War I).

Cody held 13 varsity letters in football, basketball, baseball and track with the Commodores. However, it was in football where he most excelled, named to three All America teams as a two-way tackle. Extremely athletic and nimble for his size, Cody occasionally played in the backfield and once dropkicked a 45-yard field goal. In his four years playing for coach Dan McGugin, Vandy scored 1,099 points in 35 games.

A teammate once said of him: "He would tell the running backs on which side of him to go, and you could depend on him to take out two men as needed. He was the best football player I've ever seen."

Cody tutored Yarborough at his old position and got the best out of him. "Mule" was more of a horse than mule by his senior year, filling out to 190 pounds and sporting a full head of hair with an iron-jawed expression. There were nothing but superlatives for his play as he earned All State honors from the *Greenville News*, leading *the Tigers* to an 8-2 record, with the only losses coming against powerful Tennessee and Florida, with the sensational Clyde Crabtree, his future assistant coach, dominating the game. When Clemson opened with a victory over Wofford, the *Greenville News* called Yarborough Cody's greatest lineman. Under the heading "Fierce Tiger" and below Yarborough's mug shot, the paper boasted of Mule's, "wonderful game," and that, "his tackling was as fierce as anything ever seen on Riggs Field."[20] Clemson's school paper, *The Tiger*, chimed in: "Mule Yarborough was the big gun of the day. This big tackle broke through the Terrier ranks many times during the four heated sessions of play and smeared the Wofford backs for loss before they could move it of their tracks. The Mule reinforced his bid for fame by his wariness in recovering two blocked punts, each of which resulted in a touchdown for the Tigers."[21]

After Yarborough helped Clemson avoid an upset against the Citadel, the *News* crowed, "Mule Yarborough played one of the greatest games of his career. Mule seems to rise to high planes when he meets the Citadel for it was last year that he entered the hall of fame when he did so well against the Charleston Cadets. (He) should rate among the best tackles ever appearing in the South if he keeps up this present pace."[22]

Against North Carolina State, Yarborough was alert enough to notice the football graze off a Wolfpack player who was attempting to down a punt. He scooped it up and went 30 yards for a touchdown, prompting the Greenville *News* to write: "Mule Yarborough, who has been a brilliant performer at tackle for the Tigers, got his chance for glory this afternoon. And he made the most of it."[23]

"Yarborough was everywhere in the game," observed *The Tiger*.[24]

The next week, he scored again when he returned his own punt block 30 yards in a 75-0 rout of Newberry as *The Tiger* waxed effusively: "Mule Yarborough again asserted his supremacy over the opposition by crashing through the defense on many occasions to bring the ball carrier down for big losses."[25]

Even after Tennessee dumped Clemson, *The Tiger* praised him. "Yarborough turned in another great performance," it noted.[26]

Yarborough's and Cody's Clemson careers ended after the Tigers defeated arch-rival Furman to win the South Carolina state championship. The day before that game, Cody accepted McGugin's offer to join him as an assistant coach at Vanderbilt, with the assumption that he would eventually succeed the "old man" upon his retirement. Rumors of his departure had surfaced two years earlier, when the Clemson cadets took up a collection and bought him a Buick. Touched by the gesture, Cody decided to stay.

Not this time. Yarborough reportedly gave a most heartfelt tribute to Cody at the post-season banquet. He and his coach remained close until Cody died of a heart attack in 1961. He looked up to Cody as a father figure and Cody considered him as a son. When Yarborough asked him for his recommendation when he applied for the Miami High School job in 1932, Cody replied (in the one letter Yarborough saved throughout his life): "I have just written (Principal) Mr. Thomas a strong letter of recommendation. There are some people whom it is hard for me to recommend. You are one whom it is always a pleasure to recommend. I really let out on you this time."[27]

Jesse Yarborough at Clemson.
Greenville News.

Later, during Cody's years as head coach at the University of Florida, it was twice rumored he was bringing Yarborough on as an assistant, although it never progressed beyond that stage. Everyone knew how tight they were and how Yarborough modeled himself after his mentor.

Cody was widely hailed as a man of principle. He valued character, loyalty and respect. He treated his players as though they were his sons, yet never fully appreciated the influence a coach could have on players' lives. In 1958, he demonstrated those principles as the athletic director of Temple University. The Owls' basketball team, with three black players in its starting five, was scheduled to play an NCAA tournament game in segregated Charlotte. In a move not necessarily expected of a Tennessee-born farm boy, Cody made clear that if the players were separated by race, the team would not make the trip. The team stayed together and ended up third in the nation after a one-point semifinal loss to eventual champion Kentucky. Two weeks earlier, the Owls played a game at Wake Forest where their three black players were the first to ever play on the court. The game was not only played without incident, but, also, the three received a nice ovation during player introductions.

Yarborough's style may have differed slightly but he was, just like Cody, exceedingly loyal to his players. "Honest and fearless with all the courage of his convictions," Scoop Latimer of the *Greenville News* called him.[28] And, before the game against Garfield in 1939, the *Newark Evening News* profiled him as a "hard driver but well liked."

"Husky in stature and possessor of a somber, serious disposition, Coach Yarborough seldom cracks a smile when on the football field. Although he keeps his boys keyed to the proper pitch at all times, both physically and mentally, and does not tolerate any horseplay, he is idolized by his players," the paper noted.[29]

Fresh out of Clemson, Yarborough considered a position at the Swift Company in Jacksonville before accepting the head coach's job at Summerlin Institute in Bartow, Florida. There, in transforming a team that had won only two games the previous year to one that lost only three, the "great lover of the beautiful things of life" met the pretty daughter of General Albert Blanding. At 6-3, the imposing general stared eye-to-eye at Yarborough as he asked for Louise's hand in marriage. Fort Blanding would be named after Yarborough's esteemed father-in-law. Anyone from Florida who enlisted in the Army during World War II was initiated into the service there.

Yarborough, according to the *Chester News*, was about to resign at Summerlin and find a job in industry—a coach's salary was hardly sufficient to support his new wife—when fate stepped in. Miami High School was in need of a football coach.[30]

FIVE

THE SPORT

On the day in 1906 that young Art Argauer arrived in America, newsboys hawked *The New York Times* in Manhattan's bustling financial district, not far from where his boat was docked. The sports page in that's day's edition featured an ad for *Spalding's Official Foot Ball Guide*, explaining the "New Foot Ball Rules." The sport was changing and, while six-year-old Arthur had no idea at the time, it would take forward-thinking men like him to complete the transition.

The year was a critical one for football, as the very existence of the game was being threatened. It had become too dangerous, in many ways resembling more a street fight than an athletic contest. President Theodore Roosevelt had won the Nobel Peace Prize in 1905 for his role in ending the Russo-Japanese War. Now, he used his negotiating skills to save a sport that, in a way, mimicked warfare a bit too closely.

During the Civil War, young men marched naively, if lustily, off to battle under the banners of their home states, dreaming of glory amid fraternal camaraderie. In a way, competitive sports, and specifically football, filled the need for such *élan* and gallantry once peace was achieved.

The sport seemed to fit perfectly an American model of "Muscular Christianity" combining strength, character and virtue and, as first played by elite Eastern (and mostly) Ivy League schools, it was one way to prepare future leaders along with a military bent.

Some of football's foundational tactics, in fact, were cribbed from Napoleonic military manuals. The concept of massing men against a fixed point was identical. Line 'em up in tight formations and mow 'em down. It was a grisly affair. And, like war, there were fatalities. In 1905 alone, college football experienced 18 deaths and 105 serious injuries.

The period's most infamous formation—the Flying Wedge—was, in fact, devised by an ardent student of military history. Lorin F. Deland, who had observed his first football game only two years earlier, immediately recognized the connection to the gridiron. He applied Principle Number One of Napoleon's art of war to a football play that he drew up and offered to Harvard, hoping to aid the Crimson's often fruitless efforts to defeat Yale. It was basically an onside kick, except in those days, the ball didn't have to travel 10 yards. Once the ball was touched, the kicking team could recover immediately and charge at the opposition behind Deland's phalanx, combining mass and momentum and turning flesh into a battering ram against flesh. Harvard unveiled it at the start of the second half of the 1892 meeting between the rivals at Hampden Park in Springfield, Massachusetts. In calling for rules changes a year later, *The New York Times* summed up the brutality in a sarcasm-laced editorial:

> *About half a dozen big healthy youths in the prime of life form a V about twenty yards from the opposing line and, at a given start signal, start on a dead run with the intention of mowing down one man—the one picked out to make the play against—so that the youth with the ball can find a convenient hole in the line to force his way through. Think of it—half a ton of bone and muscle coming into collision with a man weighing 160 or 170 pounds. What is the result? The victim is generally sent sprawling with his nose broken or his chest crushed and if the man with the ball gets through the line for 10 or 20 yards the critics all exclaim, "What a grand play!"*[1]

Indeed, upon seeing Harvard use the Flying Wedge for the first time, the *Boston Herald* described it as, "a play that sent football men . . . into raptures."[2] It also sent several players to the hospital. Still, Deland's innovation proved so popular that other momentum plays such as Penn's famed "Guards Back" were devised for use on the line of scrimmage. Some called for players to interlock arms and some fitted their jerseys with leather straps for a teammate to latch on to. Often, ball carriers were simply tossed across the line. In turn, defensive tactics were devised allowing body upon body to pile on and crush the ball carrier. To add injury to injury, whatever rules aimed at player safety were stretched. With eye-gouging, hitting below the belt, elbowing, kicking and the like, football was nothing more than sanctioned assault and battery. As Yale's 1893 football season was about to begin, *The New York Times* pondered what horrible injuries lay ahead:

> *Every wind that blows from the east will bring us the sound of cracking arms and also ribs. This will be the news from New Haven until a few days before the final game Then we shall learn that centre (sic) rush has lost thirty pounds in three days and is going into a decline; that right guard's ears have been sewed on just for this occasion, and are likely to fall off at any moment, leaving him unable to hear the signals; that left tackle is playing with a wooden leg; that right end has heart disease; that quarter back's arms have both been broken and have not knit yet; that one of the half backs cannot see and that the full-back has water on his kicking kneecap.*
>
> *Nevertheless, we shall go to see the game and there we shall behold these utterly demolished young men stagger upon the field.*[3]

A rules committee headed by Walter Camp, the "Father of American Football," outlawed momentum plays that year. But the savagery continued nonetheless, with Camp, the most influential figure in the game, not particularly interested in reforming the sport. By 1905, many progressives sought to outlaw the sport altogether. Harvard president Charles W. Eliot, a pacifist who abhorred football's military overtones, led the movement. With the sport he loved threatened, Roosevelt followed the suggestion of a friend and took action.

The old Rough Rider was a football fan since he saw his first game as a Harvard freshman in 1876. He was among those who felt that the nation was being feminized and that manly pursuits were essential in establishing a more vigorous identity that would frame America as a world leader. A decade earlier, Roosevelt had written to Camp that a leader "can't be efficient unless he is manly" and that "I would a hundred fold rather keep the game as it is now with the brutality, than give it up."[4] In 1900, he wrote an essay for *St. Nicholas Magazine*, titled "What we can expect of the American Boy," in which he advocated football as training for life with its "excellent effect in increased manliness."

A boy, he wrote, should "bear himself well in manly exercise and to develop his body— and therefore, to a certain extent, his character—in the rough sports which call for pluck, endurance and physical address. The boy "cannot do good work if he is not strong and does not try with his whole heart and soul to count in any contest. . . . In short, in life, as in a football game, the principle to follow is: hit the line hard; don't foul and don't shirk, but hit the line hard!"[5]

Indeed, the sport had grown wildly by then. By the late 1880s, the game had spread to colleges in the South and by the turn of the century, high schools began to field teams, beginning with private New England schools. Roosevelt saw it as an essential part of the educational process for boys going forward.

He did, however, have a pragmatic side. The game needed to be reformed or risk extinction. Two days after his son, 130-pound Teddy Jr., proudly broke his nose in a pileup as the Harvard freshmen played Yale, Roosevelt waved his big stick and called the representatives of college football's three powers—Yale, Harvard and Princeton—to the White House for a summit. "Football is on trial," he told the men. Roosevelt's biggest concerns were with what would be called "cheap shots." He saw intentionally injuring an opponent as a weakness in character. He would not allow Eliot and the others to "emasculate football", but he pushed the groups, which included Camp, to "minimize the danger" and come up with something. Please.[6]

As Roosevelt huddled with college football's brain trust, the brutal 1905 season—what the *Chicago Tribune* called a "death harvest"—was just getting underway.[7] In November, the nation was particularly appalled by the death of Union College halfback Harold Moore, who suffered a cerebral hemorrhage after being kneed in the head on a late hit. Columbia, Northwestern and Duke dropped their programs around Thanksgiving. Eliot warned Harvard was next, which would have been football's death knell. In January, 1906, two rival committees joined to draw up the new set of rules.

That committee, which was to evolve into the NCAA, abolished mass formations altogether, created a neutral zone at the line of scrimmage and doubled the first down distance to 10 yards to be gained in three downs and—most important—legalized the forward pass.

They couldn't legislate violence out of the game. Eleven deaths were reported for each of the next two seasons and the number spiked to 26 in 1916 as participation in the game grew. But as an unintended consequence, the new rules set football on an irreversible course into the modern era. Football became a more ordered sport and less a free-for-all. Strategies, too, evolved. The cerebral coach was as important as the bulky lineman. As Argauer stepped off the gangplank into a new country, his future profession was taking shape to suit men like him.

Pioneers stepped forward. In 1907, Glenn Scobey "Pop" Warner, coach of the Carlisle Indian School where Jim Thorpe began his athletic career that year, adjusted to the new rules by inventing a new formation that became known as the single wing. The earliest formations post-rules changes arrayed the backfield in the shape of a Y. But, since it was now illegal for an offensive player to push along a teammate, Warner moved the pusher a yard behind the line of scrimmage to be in position to open a hole for the ball carrier.

While football certainly had other visionaries, including Amos Alonzo Stagg, Fielding Yost and John Heisman, Warner's single wing was the genesis of every formation to the present day. The double wing, the Notre Dame box, the short punt formation and others were all spun off its template. Even the T-formation that supplanted it in the late 40s can trace its genesis to Warner's first sketches. The single wing is still played by certain high schools such as Xavier in New York City and Apopka in Florida, allowing undermanned teams the opportunity to compete because their whole is greater than the sum of their parts.

With the single wing's advent, football became a more spectacular and interesting sport to watch, and many would argue far higher up the Darwinian chain than its rugby scrum origins. There was beauty in on offense that relied on a synchronized, team-oriented philos-ophy where precision and vision were as important as brawn. Several plays could be run from the same formation and deception became a big part of the game. Reverses took advantage of defensive pursuit. The spinner play, where the back took the snap and twirled, either handing off to a man coming around him, or keeping it himself, was a wonderful-looking staple of any game plan. Ultimately, though, while the single wing was not as violent as the old mass formations, it still relied on power.

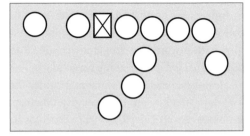

The single wing formation as played at Garfield High School with an unbalanced line to the right. Note the "wingback" behind the right end and how such a strong side made for power runs and the opportunity to spring reverses.

Seven men toed the line of scrimmage, usually in an unbalanced formation—four flanking the center to one side, two to the other, creating a strong side and a weak side, although some single wing offenses operated from a balanced line. In both variations, four men comprised the backfield and three were in position to take the direct snap from center as a quarterback does in a modern shotgun formation. Usually, it went to the tailback, the most skilled player on the field with his ability to run, pass or kick (i.e., the triple threat back). And, once that snap was made, it set into motion a set choreography intended to spring the ball carrier loose, based on double team and trap blocks, often employing a pulling guard from the weak side. The Green Bay Packers' power sweep, under Vince Lombardi, was its latter-day successor, utilizing linemen as the primary interference instead of backs. Bill Walsh, the 49ers' Hall of Fame coach, even mused about trying it, if not for the drawback of getting his Hall of Fame quarterback mauled.

"I've reflected on the single wing," he once said. "Those blocking schemes would just chew up NFL defenses. You could double-team every hole and trap at every hole. You'd have six men blocking three. Plus you'd have the power for the sweeps. Joe Montana might be able to play tailback, to run and pass, but you wouldn't let him do it unless you had another Joe Montana to spell him."[8]

Other formations sprouted from the single wing including the double wing and the Notre Dame box, all with their devotees. Miami High School played the short punt formation because

Jesse Yarborough played it under Josh Cody who played it under Dan McGugin who played it under Fritz Chrysler. It featured a balanced line with two backs situated behind and between the guards and tackles. The tailback was two yards further back with the fullback as he would be in the single wing. It was, theoretically, less predictable and better suited to passing.

Viewed from the perspective of today's modern day spread offenses, the direct snap offenses of the pre-war era hardly look like wide-open attacks. But, where offenses once progressed inch by inch, the single wing and its variations sought to isolate a ball carrier in the open field. Big plays could happen once the blocking freed a runner beyond the point of attack. The defensive end was the key. He was responsible for keeping the runner from getting to the outside, but often he wasn't quick enough to pull it off. If he were to move too far to the sideline, however, the defensive end could allow the runner to cut back inside him for a potentially big gain. Thus, the breakaway threat was born. The term "climax runner," entered the sport's lexicon. Red Grange, the "Galloping Ghost" from Illinois, emerged as one of the heroes of the 1920s, sports' so-called "Golden Age."

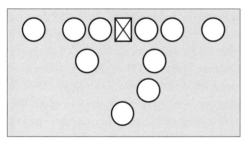

The short punt formation as played at Miami High School. Note the balanced line, the absence of a wingback and that the tailback is set further back from center than in the single wing.

Another revolutionary set of rule changes in 1912, which created four downs to pick up a first down, changed the value of a touchdown from five to six points and reduced the playing field from 110 yards to 100, with 10-yard end zones, brought more boys out for the sport at the grass roots level. First generation immigrant kids, like those in Garfield, took to football naturally, both as a way of expressing their Americanism and as a release of energy. Big, strong farm boys in the South and Midwest made for ideal players. With the growth of leisure time, a fan base grew and spread as an explosion of media coverage turned football into a sport for the masses.

The game as it was played in 1939 was still in an evolutionary phase. It was still largely played on the ground. Forward passes were used more as a deceptive tactic or out of desperation late in the game. New Jersey high school rules, for instance, limited passing to behind five yards of the line of scrimmage. The tactics were based on field position. A team gained a huge advantage with a good punter, because an exchange of punts could yield a gain between 20 and 40 yards. Teams sometimes punted on third down in order to pin a team in. Kicking field goals was difficult, so teams almost always went for it on fourth down when deep in enemy territory. Fewer drives inside the 20 were sustained. That's why scores were generally low (except, of course, in the case of gross mismatches).

It was also very much a game of leverage and technique. Blocking was more highly prized and constantly drilled. Defensive linemen got as low as they could in four point stances and sprung into the men in front of them, aiming for the midsection and driving up into the chin. While timing and coordination were essential, there were fewer shifts and stunts. It was mostly a matter of beating your man.

And, since players played both ways, on offense and defense, there was very little specialization.

"In that era, it was a simpler game," Al Kachadurian explained. "You learned how to tackle and you learned how to block. Those were the two essential things and if you couldn't do them, you weren't a football player. In that era you had to do both. So there was a beauty to it. Today, if you are very fast, you might be a running back. But you would not have been out there in that era if you couldn't make a tackle or know how to block. I admire the players today—they are bigger, stronger, faster, no question about it—but there was also an intrinsic beauty to our game."

The dangers of the sport still loomed, as they do in today's game. In 1929, they hit close to Garfield. The Comets, as they were called then, had just been beaten by Passaic's crack team. Hackensack was Passaic's next opponent. Passaic won easily, 30-6, but, in the closing moments of the game, tragedy struck. Thomas "Tabby" O'Shea, 19-year-old star of Passaic's football and basketball teams, had played what the *Passaic Daily News* called "a

Thomas O'Shea.
Passaic Daily News.

splendid game."[9] He'd scored one touchdown on a long passing play and was in on tackle after tackle on defense. After the last Passaic touchdown, O'Shea sprinted down the field to cover the kickoff as part of a three-man wall that met the Hackensack player head-on. O'Shea fell back, with the others on top of him, with a groan.

Coach Ray Pickett rushed onto the field as O'Shea lay on the ground.

"How do you feel, Tabby?" he asked.

"I'm all right, coach, but there's no feeling in my arms," O'Shea said.[10]

They carried him off the field and a doctor was summoned from the Hackensack grandstands. Medical personnel and ambulances were not yet routinely stationed at high school games. The ambulance was called after the doctor determined he was badly injured. X-rays showed cracked vertebrae, and O'Shea was operated on immediately and the surgery appeared to be successful. When he was first admitted to the hospital, he could move only one toe. After surgery, the feeling in his entire left side returned. He even joked with teammates and remarked about Fordham's win over NYU. The next day, O'Shea was dead.

At first, Passaic High School cancelled the remainder of its football season until O'Shea's mother, Julia, requested they play the games.

"There is nothing essentially wrong with football," she told Principal A.D. Arnold. "Accidents sometimes occur and no better memorial could be made for my son than to have his teammates carry on to a state championship."[11]

That's how it was with the players, too. They relished the glory and played the game because it was tough, despite the dangers.

"We were kids," Kachadurian explained. "When you're sixteen or seventeen, you just learn your plays, go out on the field, bang each other around and break your nose and loosen your teeth. But we loved it. When you're a kid, who cares anyway? When you're sixteen or seventeen years old and the cheerleaders are cheering and girls in the stands are yelling your name, you think you're a big wheel. Oh yes . . . you can't replace that."

The high school football player was truly a big deal in the 1930s. In 1937, an estimated 120,000 fans jammed Chicago's Soldier Field to watch Bill DeCorrevont, then considered high school football's greatest player ever, lead Austin of the Public League over Leo of the Catholic League, 26-0, for the city championship. And while that crowd may not have been the norm, the numbers elsewhere were still impressive. High school football was packing them in.

In Miami, the Stingarees were as popular as the University of Miami, both on the sports pages and at the turnstiles. In New Jersey, the dense population centers in the north allowed for many high schools to field great teams and accumulate great followings. Rutgers and Princeton didn't excite many fans statewide and few had the cash or the cars to travel to see the Giants at the Polo Grounds. But most anyone could take in a local high school game by walking, catching a bus or hitching a ride And, if the team was in contention for a state title, the entire community got behind it. And they did so in throngs. Minor league professional teams such as the Clifton Wessingtons, Passaic Red Devils and Paterson Panthers all played to decent crowds on Sundays. But nothing matched the excitement of high school football.

On Thanksgiving Day 1939, an estimated 200,000 fans attended 51 games across the state of New Jersey. That same year, Garfield and Bloomfield, Nutley and East Orange drew a combined 34,000 for their showdown games, three days apart and no doubt with some crossover spectators.[12] The *Nutley Sun's* Walt Maloney remarked on the phenomenon:

> If some bluenose doesn't come up with the cry of commercialism or over-emphasis on schoolboy football, we'll be surprised. The crowd of 18,000 which jammed Foley Field to see Bloomfield and Garfield tangle and the 15,000 who watched the E.O.-Raiders clash Tuesday were amazing tributes to the popularity of school football in the state. The four schools salted away more cash than they are likely to see for quite a while. There is more enthusiasm over school grid elevens in this area than is found in other states. It's hard to find a reason.[13]

Well, there was one. Gambling. No one hid it. The papers gave odds on high school games and talked about how certain fan bases had either won or lost a bunch.

"Plenty of iron men will change hands today at the Garfield-Passaic football game," Art McMahon wrote in his Sportsman's Corner column for *The Herald-News* in 1937. "Even the high school students are wagering their soda and lollipop money."[14]

Al Del Greco described a scene at the 1938 Garfield-Bloomfield game that played out in full view of the Bloomfield police:

> "I'll bet $50 Garfield wins," said a fan, waving a bill.
> "It's a bet," said the Bloomfield man. "And if you boys have any more to bet, just bring it down."
> In one small group, something like $400 was bet on the result of the tussle. There must have been thousands of dollars on the tiff. While Garfield High fans are accustomed to betting on the team, even they were amazed at the open transactions under the nose of John Law."
> After one of Ted Ciesla's neat runbacks after receiving a punt, Benny Babula kissed him.
> "The wrong guy is kissing him," said the big bowling alley man from Garfield. 'I should be kissing him."

Del Greco concluded:

> *I don't suppose there's any way to stop the betting. If the 'Alumni' want to declare them-*
> *selves in on a win streak, there's nothing much authorities can do about the matter. But*
> *the coaches must be careful to see the bettors are kept on the sidelines and in no way come*
> *into contact with the athletes.*[15]

Art Argauer certainly shielded his players from those elements. Nevertheless, he was keenly aware of the point spread. A year earlier, when Garfield lost a close one to Bloomfield, Walter Young remembered how badly Argauer felt because he'd let the bettors down. Columnists like Del Greco, McMahon and Jack Bell in Miami were key to keeping the interest high. They wrote as often and as passionately about the high school teams as they did about the pros, and, in North Jersey—with so much interest in the Yankees, Dodgers and Giants—that was saying a lot.

They mostly wrote in a folksy, slangy manner as if they were the readers' buddies. Jack Bell, for instance, called himself their "Cousin Jack." Often times, they had been athletes themselves. McMahon was a good football player for East Rutherford. Paul Horowitz of the *Newark Evening News* was named MVP of the Syracuse University baseball team. Del Greco had a particular fondness for Garfield. It was his alma mater. He was one of the Lodi kids who attended the school, which gave him insight into what Argauer and the Boilermakers were up against. He even played for Garfield in the mid 1920s and would poke fun at those bench-sitting days:

> *I will not go into details about my offensive ability. Old 21—you outsiders know*
> *nothing about that gem. It went like this. The quarterback would pivot, fake the ball to*
> *both the halfbacks and finally run back and flip a ball into the end zone. My assignment*
> *on the play was to stay close to the coach on the sidelines and give the signal for the play*
> *whenever he thought it was opportune.*
>
> *Frank Romaglia, our star booter at the time, was always deeply appreciative of the part*
> *I played. He always said,*
>
> *"Now look, when the play starts, get out of the way so you won't get hurt."*[16]

Del Greco and McMahon both published their picks in Friday's paper. Del Greco once picked Englewood to beat Hackensack, 18-0, prompting and angry group of 300 Hackensack students to march to the *Bergen Record* offices, disrupting traffic along the way. The mob forced its way through the doors and wasn't happy to learn the target of its wrath wasn't there. They ended up hurling tomatoes against the wall of the sports department and breaking a typewriter anyway.

Englewood won, 26-7, no doubt to Del Greco's extreme delight.

"Prejudice swayed my good old Fascist horse sense in the Englewood-Hackensack game," he wrote afterwards. "As an old, loyal Hackensack fan I couldn't see Englewood beating Hackensack by more than 18-0. The margin of difference was 21 points. My apologies to Englewood High School. They were better than I figured. Frankly, I over-rated Hackensack."[17]

Both McMahon and Horowitz needled Del Greco in their papers. Horowitz said he was swearing off tomato juice. McMahon said the fans of the teams *The Herald News* covered were more cultured:

Once Garfield students held an auto parade in front of the family homestead when the Boilermakers had gone against Friday's forecast. There were torchlights, sirens and three long boos for McMahon but McMahon was over at the Chowder and Marching Club and didn't appreciate the scorn.

Lyndhurst held a band concert out in front of the dwelling after it has beaten Rutherford but the Golden Bear has a brand new musical unit and was probably just seeking an excuse to practice. And next time, fellows, see if you can get in that, 'So Red the Rose' number. I like that.[18]

The writers generally liked the coaches, even if they occasionally ribbed them. The coaches, in turn, respected the writers. Bell, a World War I veteran who lost an arm at the head of a machine gun unit, held a weekly Thursday night barbeque at his house. All of Miami high school coaches attended, including friendly rivals Jesse Yarborough, whom Bell dubbed, "The Cunnel,"—Colonel pronounced with a Southern drawl—and Ed Parnell, dubbed "Pop." There was a mutual trust there. The coaches didn't mind going off the record with information. The writers could be critical but never petty. Usually, they came to the coach's defense, especially if someone's job might be at stake.

By the 1930s, the scholastic scene offered plenty of writing material. High school football began when the students put together informal teams. Then the schools ran them as part of the educational experience, eventually leading to the formation of leagues and state organizations. Now, almost every high school was fielding a football team, not just in New Jersey and Florida but also across the country. Ultimately, writers, coaches, players and bettors craved championships and not all of them were settled on the field. Garfield and Miami played for the "mythical" national championship but at least they played. Other mythical champions were simply chosen and while they weren't sending in the unicorns, it was often a flight of fancy to conjure up a winner. Basically, a mythical championship was one determined either by acclimation or in games not sanctioned by a league or governing body such as a state association.

The idea started in 1897 when Madison High School, in Wisconsin, offered to take on all comers for the United States championship. North Tonowanda, New York, recognized as the top team in the Northeast, accepted the challenge and, on Christmas Day in Detroit, Madison won, 14-0. In 1902, Hyde Park, Illinois, having outscored four opponents, 231-0, issued a challenge to any Eastern team with enough guts. Poor Brooklyn Prep stuck its neck out and was decapitated. In a game played at the University of Chicago's Marshall Field, the home team won, 105-0, reaffirming the dominance of the more open brand of football played by Western high school teams at the time. College football's popularity exploded through inter-sectional play in the 1920s and the high schools followed suit. Travel was seen as part of the educational experience. There were over 30 so-called national championship games played through 1939 and scores more intersectional games without the designation, including those between all-star teams, often for charity.[19]

But not every great team played in those postseason games. Some were prohibited by state organizations. Others simply chose not to extend their seasons. Could not one of those teams be the best? But how to figure them in? There were enough arguments—and even a few bare knuckle brawls—when it came to choosing a state champion. To come up with one supreme team by comparing teams that faced varied forms of competition and played under different age was close to impossible.

They tried, anyway.

In 1927, the National Sports News Service began to study state polls, consult sports editors, consider the strength and reputation of various programs and name a national champ. With a name like the National Sports News Service, it sounded like a large bureau with offices around the country. It was, rather, a one-man operation.

Art Johlfs was a high school official and coach in Minnesota. He was obsessed with high school sports. So he took it upon himself to determine the best team in the country. Sports editors, all doing their best to boost their local team, mailed him clips that he kept in paper bags. He'd sort through them all, man the phones and coronate a champ. Evidently, though, he either wasn't that high on East Coast or West Coast football. From 1927 through 1946, all of his selections came from the Midwest, South or Southwest.

In 1939, at least three teams were designated national champs by someone and another claimed the title for itself. Garfield and Miami had the imprimatur of the National Sports Council but it wasn't the only national championship game played that year. The Louisiana Sports Authority, which ran the Sugar Bowl game, staged its second annual—and final—national championship game in Baton Rouge on December 30 as a run up to the Sugar Bowl.

A year earlier, the LSA brought New Britain, Connecticut and DuPont Manual from Louisville down. They were both unbeaten and they put on a fantastic battle before the Kentucky team prevailed, 28-20. Johlfs followed with his own endorsement of Manual as well. But the next year, the LSA went the austere route. After considering teams like Cathedral High School in Springfield, Massachusetts, where future Heisman Trophy winner Angelo Bertelli starred, and Kingsport, Tennessee, where Bobby Cifers set the national high school scoring record, it settled on Pine Bluff, Arkansas, High School against hometown Baton Rouge High School. It was less costly to put on. But it could be looked at as more of a regional championship than a national one.

Pine Bluff had the Hutson twins, Rob and Ray, younger brothers of the great receiver Don Hutson, who by then had begun his Hall of Fame career with the Green Bay Packers. Baton Rouge had a back named Sulcer Harris, who'd go on to star at LSU. But in the end, it wasn't much of a contest. The Pine Bluff Zebras cruised to a 26-0 victory as the Hutsons scored all the touchdowns.

Pine Bluff was crowned a national champ but when comparing the LSA game to the Miami game, it really doesn't stack up well. First off, neither team came in with an unblemished record. Pine Bluff had played a 6-6 tie with Hope in a mud-marred game. Meanwhile, there was no reason Baton Rouge should have even played for a national championship. The Golden Bulldogs forfeited five of their 10 wins for using three ineligible players, albeit unwittingly, in addition to losing, 18-14, on the road to Jackson, Mississippi, which, a month later, was dumped by Miami High, 27-0. Miami could have claimed superiority over Pine Bluff as well. The Stinagrees whipped a previously undefeated Pine Bluff team, 33-7, in Miami the previous season.

Like Garfield, Pine Bluff always considered itself the national champion and celebrated the 75th anniversary of the game in 2014. Furthermore, the players on both teams probably had no idea there was another national championship game that year.

Johlfs, meanwhile, spurned both Garfield and Pine Bluff. He chose Washington High School of Massillon, Ohio. Ah, Massillon. The name just sounded like a football dynasty, one that should be supported by Doric Columns and protected by warriors in fiery chariots. What's more, the team was led by the equal of Alexander in football terms—Paul Brown.

Brown played for Massillon from 1923-1925, then at Miami University of Ohio, the so-called "Cradle of Coaches." He took over at his high school alma mater in 1932. In the eight years he spent there before leaving to take the Ohio State reins, the Tigers compiled a record of 80-8-2, won five Ohio state championships and were named NSNS champion four times, including 1939.

During that season, Massillon went 10-0 and outscored its outmatched opponents, 460-25, playing before average crowds of 17,000. Its closest win came against archrival Canton McKinley, 20-6, on Thanksgiving Day. Brown, however, eschewed post-season games of any kind. The LSA briefly mentioned Massillon as a candidate for its game but that was more wishful thinking.

"Our record speaks for itself," Brown said as the 1939 season was winding down. "Most of the schools that are being named as possible opponents for our team in a post-season game have had the opportunity in the past to get on our schedule. If they didn't avail themselves of that chance I see no reason why we have to prolong our season in order to accommodate them now."

Brown would never have taken his team south in any case because he always had a handful of black players on the squad, including, in 1939, the great Horace Gillom, with whom Brown would be reunited at Cleveland after he helped reintegrate pro football in 1946—three years before Jackie Robinson played for the Brooklyn Dodgers.

Massillon could have played in something called the Buckeye Bowl in 1939, presumably for the Ohio state championship, but again, stayed with its no post-season game policy. Instead, Toledo Waite defeated Portsmouth, 9-7, on a 40-yard field goal with 32 seconds remaining. Waite coach Jack Mollenkopf, of Purdue fame, claimed the national championship on that basis. Brown no doubt had a chuckle over that and, to end the chatter from upstate, arranged to take on Waite the next year. They met at Massillon's Tiger Stadium on a rainy November night. Massillon was on a 30-game winning streak, Waite on an 18-game tear. Massillon won, 28-0. The Tigers outscored their foes, 477-6 in that, Brown's final season.

Could Miami or Garfield taken the Tigers? It would have been quite the challenge but no doubt worth the argument.

SIX

THE BEGINNING

The pre-war years were a golden age for high school football in America, well before big money ruled sports, when the schoolboys captivated both small communities and entire states, and shared the headlines with the colleges and pros. The tiniest town could take on the biggest city. All that was needed was a coach with guile or a triple threat tailback with ability. Have them both, and you have the makings of a championship team. Garfield and Miami had them both . . . and more.

Coaches Art Argauer and Jesse Yarborough both played and learned the sport during its formative years. Their football backgrounds were similar and their intelligence, knowledge of human nature and personalities led them easily into coaching. While they may have been separated in age by six years, they each carefully and purposefully took their programs to new heights. They and their programs travelled similar roads.

Miami High football dates back to 1911 and 1912, when students teamed up once in each of those years to take on the Miami Military Athletic Association. Both games were played on Thanksgiving Day, and in both contests, the older MMAA team won, 10-3, in 1911 and, 12-0, in 1912. Both teams would appear a motley crew, with thrown-together, rag-tag uniforms and no helmets. The Miami Metropolis promised that the high school boys were working on a secret play called the Biscayne Fadaway (sic) for the 1911 game, which went for naught and faded away from all future playbooks.[1] After the 1912 game, so did Miami High football for another nine years.

With no other area high schools fielding football teams at the time, Miami High would not again compete in the sport until 1921-22 when it took on, and twice defeated, the local American Legion Post, 12-6, and 6-0. The next season, Miami faced scholastic opposition for the first time with a colorful roster that included "Bozo" Rezeau, the brothers "Little Bush" and "Big Bush" Warman and "Froggy" Buchanan at quarterback. Not yet carrying the Stingarees name, Miami opened by routing West Palm Beach, 31-0, and the Florida State School for Deaf and Dumb, 52-0. Through six games, the navy-blue and old-gold outscored the opposition, 233-13, seemingly a bit ahead of themselves for a team playing its first year of varsity football. There was even talk of challenging Scott High of Toledo for the national championship. That was before the squad, amid all sorts of fanfare, left to play Gainesville High for the state title—and returned with a stinging 58-0 defeat.

The sport was still taking shape and teams improvised. Until the new high school opened with a field behind it in 1928, the Stingarees played most of their home games at Royal Palm Park. It was a scenic venue, right in front of the Royal Palm Hotel—perhaps a bit too scenic. Until finally felled in 1925, a pair of palm trees sat at one end, still within the playing field, and players simply navigated around them. Pads were not required gear and players commonly played without headgear, a trend that continued into the 1930s. In fact, Miami's Dick Plasman went on to play for the Chicago Bears and Cardinals, where he went down in history in 1947—and with a hole in his head to show for it—as the last man in the NFL to compete without a helmet.

Despite its awkward beginnings, Miami High football kept winning. From 1922 to 1935, the Stingarees compiled 14 straight winning seasons under a top-notch set of head coaches. In 1926, sports columnist Jack Bell, then working for the *Miami Herald,* put Principal W.R. Thomas onto Tommy McCann, his fellow University of Illinois alum. When McCann left to coach baseball and basketball at the University of Miami following the 1927 season, Don McCallister, his fraternity brother at Illinois, succeeded him. It was McCallister who first took the Stingarees from the state to the national stage.

McCallister was a teammate of Red Grange at Illinois—although he sat the bench his entire time and never earned a letter. He was, however, a brilliant student of the game who, as McCann, learned under highly regarded Illini coach Bob Zuppke. Although not much was expected of the 1928 Stingarees, McCallister whipped them into shape and led them to a surprising 5-2-2 record. That season, the state's larger schools formed the Big Ten Conference after the state athletic association stopped naming champions of its own. There was one problem. The conference ended up accepting two more teams so that the Big Ten actually became the Inflated 12. The schedule didn't permit any more than a handful of games against each other, so the league decided to use the Dickinson System (explained in Chapter 11) to determine its champion.

In 1929, that became problematic. Miami and Lakeland didn't face each other during the regular season, but both teams finished conference play undefeated with one tie. The Dickinson System favored Lakeland by mere percentage points, and the Dreadnaughts rested on their laurels, refusing to meet Miami's challenge to decide the championship on the field. The Stingarees, in turn, claimed the state title on the basis of the vacated challenge, huffing that the Dreadnaughts indeed dreaded Miami. But McCallister took it further. He issued a challenge to Charlotte High School to settle the championship of the South, an offer quickly accepted by the North Carolinians.

On December 14, the two southern giants squared off against each other at Madison Square Garden Stadium, an octagon-shaped outdoor wooden arena built by promoter extraordinaire Tex Rickard to stage prize fights. Miami prevailed, 12-7. McCallister kept thinking big. He already had two teams eager to come to Miami for another intersectional game. Stivers High School from Dayton, Ohio, was claiming the national championship and Salem High in Massachusetts was claiming the eastern title. After the players voted to play another game, Salem got the nod. Miami officials considered the suburban Boston team a better draw. The Stingarees won again, 7-6, as 10,000 flocked to Miami Field—next to the future site of the Orange Bowl—for the Christmas Day game.

Miami had achieved immediate, nationwide recognition. Before the game, Jack Bell suggested that the Stingarees were playing to prove the merit of southern high school football and, in that respect, Miami did more in one game than it had achieved in its entire, albeit brief, history. The school netted $5,000 for the two intersectional games, and the Miami Beach Chamber of Commerce suggested that $1,500 go to McCallister, the man responsible not only for building a great team, but also for pushing the idea of intersectional, post-season play. Miami, seeing the value in dollars to its program and realizing the interest of teams across the country, adopted the Christmas game as annual event. Stivers got its shot the next year and returned to Dayton an 18-0 loser.

McCallister left for Waite High School in Toledo after guiding Miami to an 11-0 record in 1930, as the Stingarees shared the conference title with Lakeland. He was replaced by yet another Illinois man, Fred Major, who spent one season at the Stingaree helm, a season that shook up Miami High football forever.

By 1931, the Tampa-area members of the Big Ten were getting a bit envious of Miami's national profile. The Stingarees, they thought, were getting a bit too big for their football britches. There was already a rivalry between the two coastal hubs, and the tension came to a head when once-beaten Hillsborough visited unbeaten Miami for a pivotal Armistice Day contest that was to settle the Big Ten race. The Stingarees trailed for the first time all year but rallied in the fourth quarter to win, 11-7. Hell broke loose after the aforementioned Plasman kicked the go-ahead field goal, which Hillsborough insisted was wide. Their complaints, however, had to compete with the histrionics of hundreds of Miami fans that ran onto the field in jubilation. Officials cleared the field but not the visitors' minds. According to Jack Bell's story in the *Herald*: "The Tampa boys also objected to some of the decisions of the officials but they forgot themselves at times in their eagerness to win and used tactics which could not be overlooked."[2]

Hillsborough coach Willard Johnson was incensed at the lopsided number of penalties called in Miami's favor. He protested the game on the basis of incompetent officiating and claimed that Miami High had been using "outside influences" to gain an unfair advantage for years.

"I have no quarrel with coach Fred Major or his players," Johnson told the *Tampa Tribune*. "His boys played clean, hard football. The officiating, however, is a different matter. I do not accuse the officials of being openly dishonest. It seems to me they instinctively feel forced to favor the Miami teams. And when they got on the field this feeling, a hangover from former regimes at Miami associated itself."[3]

Johnson wasn't the first or last coach to complain about home cooking, but he went further than most by announcing Hillsborough was breaking off all athletic relations with Miami. Then, 12 days after the game, Miami officials were summoned to Orlando to explain themselves to representatives of the other Big Ten schools. They found themselves in a kangaroo court. The Jacksonville schools were always neutral toward the Stingarees, but the Gulf Coast schools banded together and introduced a measure that would suspend Miami from the conference for one year.

The Miami contingent, led by Principal Thomas, Major and James J. Marshall, chairman of the Dade County School Board, had its own side of the story. They contended that Hillsborough was the cause of the game getting out of control. They presented affidavits from witnesses complaining of Johnson's wild sideline behavior. Indeed, the coach admitted to using profanity but, instead of siding with the Miamians, the other schools accused them of making personal attacks on Johnson. The Miamians also pointed out that Johnson had objected beforehand to almost every official proposed for the game until only a few remained and Dick Hunt, normally a linesman, was forced to act as referee. Hunt also stood by most of the calls that were made. None of that mattered. After six hours of arguments, the body went into executive session. After another hour, it emerged with its decision. By a unanimous vote of the other eight schools represented at the meeting, the game was ruled no contest because of incompetent officiating. The proposal to suspend Miami was voted down but Miami received a strong reprimand:

"This body vindicates Coach Fred Major and his Miami team of any unsportsmanlike conduct in the protested game. However, this body goes on record as criticizing the conduct of Miami High School, its officials, its attitude and its apparent willingness to allow outside agencies to influence its athletic activities for the past four years."

In his column for the *Herald*, Jack Bell said plainly that Miami was dealing with a "stacked deck," that a previous meeting to which Miami was not invited was the "real business session." He wrote: "Last year there was a request, so I was told at the time, from the head of one of the biggest Big Ten schools, to do something to handicap the Miami athletic teams. This man's argument was that Miami gets so much good material the school should, in some manner, be handicapped. There was no action on his proposal. Now action has been taken."[4]

Marshall responded with a strong statement. He charged that the truth was "so far removed from any of the accusations made that no intelligent person can reach any conclusion than that the decision was made before the charges were invented.

"The findings in this case disclose such a lack of sportsmanship and common decency among the controlling authorities in the conference, both in the manner of bringing the charges and in defense of one of the indefensible acts of its members that I have advised Mr. Thomas to suspend relations with the association and announce our withdrawal from its influence . . . I am not willing to subject students of this county to the jurisdiction and decisions of men guided buy such principles."[5]

That is exactly what Miami High School did. Rather than appeal the decision, Johnson suggested to Thomas and Major: "Boys, let's wash our hands of our persecutors." The Stingarees announced they would leave the Big Ten after the Thanksgiving game against Orlando. Thomas said they were already looking to teams out of Florida to fill out future schedules. "Hooray," Bell wrote. The biggest high school league in Florida had actually booted the Stingarees into a future of regional and national prominence.[6]

The Big Ten decision had one other fateful consequence. Fred Major was not a well man. Two years earlier, he was forced to resign as head baseball coach at the University of Kentucky with a case of tuberculosis and now it was recurring. Doctors told him he'd have to give up his job one more time. He wasn't even able to coach in the Christmas game against Chicago's Harrison Tech.

"They told Freddy about it Saturday, the doctors," wrote Bell, who was a boyhood chum of Major back in Illinois. "He isn't in any grave danger now; it's merely the result of a strain that is too great . . . Freddy must get rest and quiet until he is out of danger. The memorable trip to Orlando a few weeks back —to defend Miami High School against the attack of the West Coast clique of coaches—was the blow that hurt. The coach, none too strong, made the long trip, sat through a strenuous seven-hour session and came back to Miami—all in one day. He hasn't been strong since that trip."[7]

Major headed back to Champaign, Illinois, to convalesce. He'd eventually return to Miami in 1936 to coach Ponce de Leon High School, but his brief stint as the Stingarees' mentor was over. The school had to embark on another coaching search.

Miami considered yet another Illini product, Major's younger brother Jim, who was coaching high school ball outside St. Louis. But after pouring through 50 applications, Principal Thomas narrowed the list to three and recommended to the school board Edward Lomas Wright, who went simply by "E.L." or his nickname, "Puss." Wright was a pure-bred Southerner with membership in the Sons of the American Revolution. He played football at Wofford College and for the prior two years had built an impressive record at Rock Hill High School in South Carolina, losing just twice, including the 1931 state title game, 14-6, to Orangeburg. Wright was considered not just a good football coach but also a builder of young men. His character was above reproach.

There was some question whether Wright would accept the $1,750 maximum salary set by the board, but, after visiting with Miami officials, everything seemed in order, and he was officially appointed athletic director and football coach. That was June 8. On June 25, R.C. Burts, Superintendent of Rock Hill High School, announced that Wright would be remaining there in spite of Miami's "flattering" offer.[8]

"That's funny," Thomas told Frank Godwin of the *Miami News*. "I can't understand what could've happened to make him change his mind. Why, it was only a few days ago that I received a letter from him that hinted of nothing but pleasure at the prospect."[9]

Godwin speculated that Rock Hill made an even more flattering counter offer but Wright never explained himself. A year later, he left Rock Hill to coach at Oak Ridge Military Institute, where he remained for just a short time before going into the insurance business. He returned to education as the Superintendent of Richland County District 2 in South Carolina, remaining in that position until his death in 1985. A middle school there is named in his honor.

Wright's snub left Miami with little time to fill the position and that worked to the advantage of Thomas' second choice. Jesse H. Yarborough had just finished a successful first season coaching at Summerlin Institute and was back home on the family farm in Chester, South Carolina, not far from Rock Hill. On July 8, the *Miami News* reported through "reliable sources" that Thomas had recommended Yarborough to the board and, on July 17, the *Greenville News* reported exclusively that "Mule" had been appointed head coach and director of physical education, news that had to have been leaked by Yarborough himself.[10, 11] But, as Miami discovered with Wright, appointments aren't always final, which is probably why the board refrained from making an official announcement this time.

Then, four days after that item appeared in the Greenville paper, Yarborough sent a telegram: "Am sorry to advise it will be impossible for me to accept your offer as coach at Miami High school as the salary is not sufficient to warrant my acceptance."

If it was a ploy, it worked, and not for the last time in Yarborough's career. After further negotiation, Yarborough finally accepted the position on July 23, roughly a month after E.L. Wright bailed out. He was 25 years old.

Yarborough came to Miami's attention via the recommendation of his coach at Clemson, Josh Cody, who in turn secured the endorsement of the great Dan McGugin, who had coached Cody at Vanderbilt. Aside from being a brilliant football strategist, McGugin is famous for one particular pre-game pep talk before his Commodores took on powerful Michigan in 1922.

"Out there lie the bones of your grandfathers," he said, pointing toward the direction of a military cemetery near the campus. "And down on that field are the grandsons of the Yankee soldiers who put them there."

Ironically, McGugin had not only played for Michigan, his father had fought in the Union Army. It was Michigan coach Fielding Yost whose father fought for the Confederacy. But McGugin wasn't going to let that complicate an inspiring pep talk. The game, unlike the Civil War, ended in a tie, a moral victory for the South.[12]

In Yarborough's case, he would be fully armed at Miami. It had to be one of the most attractive high school coaching jobs in the country. He was taking over a well-supported program with national aspirations and first class facilities. Over the next decade, he would use those advantages to take the program to new heights.

Football was king at Miami, and there was nothing Yarborough desired that he would not receive. Unlike most of his contemporaries who coached at least one additional sport, Yarborough coached just one. He was athletic director, of course, but that only enabled him to funnel even more resources to football. For a few years, the school didn't even field a baseball team, until Jack Bell convinced Yarborough to let him coach the squad. In the early 1940s, that program eventually produced Al Rosen, future third baseman for the Cleveland Indians. Rosen's family moved from Spartanburg, South Carolina, to Miami when Al was 18 months old in the hope the climate would help heal the child's severe asthma. But even Rosen played football for the Stingarees, asthma and all.

At Miami, Yarborough built a system enviable to any coach. Although the city's junior high schools did not field football teams, the sport was part of their physical education program. Teachers such as Clarence Drepperd at Shenandoah Junior High introduced students to the game's nuances. Yarborough eventually started an intramural program in the late winter in which junior high kids entering high school in the fall (and even current high schoolers not yet on the team) could showcase their skills. Varsity players coached those teams and reported back to him. Spring practice followed the intramural season and the intramural standouts could be invited to participate in those sessions as Yarborough searched for new gems. Yarborough was an early adopter of an emerging technology: game films. He arranged that his players' final class period was a mandatory study hall. What they studied, of course, was football. That's when the team reviewed the films and went over the game plan.

Virtually anyone with athletic ability wanted to play for the Stingarees. They were heroes to kids growing up all over Miami. "Miami High was it," said 1939 starting halfback Harvey Comfort. "When I finally got a uniform, I thought I'd gone to heaven." Pete Williams, who starred on Miami's 1942 team, tagged along with his brother to every game at the Orange Bowl. He also remembers how he attended his first game at Moore Park.

"It was when I was six or seven years old," he said. "There were wooden bleachers on two sides, and a six-foot chain link fence that they put up temporarily to keep people out. My brother and all of his friends—he was eight years older than me —took me along. He took me along on everything . . . got me exposed to everything. Made me want more and more. They didn't have any money to buy tickets and they weren't going to buy tickets anyway.

Jesse Yarborough in 1933.
Miami High School.

"Inside of the fence was a security patrol," Williams went on. "Outside of the fence was a whole bunch of teenagers trying to figure out how to get in. They were trying to knock the fence down and go over the top. So my brother told me: 'Pete, now you stay here, and don't worry about all of our friends going down the fence thirty or forty yards. You stay right here and I'm going to pick you up and throw you over the fence.' He said: 'Now when you get over there, you land, you just run, get up in the stands and sit beside somebody. You're young. Nobody will think anything about it. When they come looking for you, they will think you belong to this couple.'"

As the teenagers attempted to knock down the fence, security spotted them. It created the perfect diversion. Williams' brother tossed him over the fence.

"He told me: 'I'll be in there eventually and I'll find you and sure enough, after awhile, he came up into the stands. I don't know how he got in but he did," Williams said. "Once I got in, well, those guys on the field were my idols."

School districting wasn't in force at the time, so junior high graduates had their pick of high schools: Miami, Edison in the northern part of the city, Ponce de Leon in Coral Gables and Andrew Jackson in the Allapattah neighborhood. Yarborough didn't recruit. He didn't have to. The kids who started playing against each other on the sandlots generally stuck together—and went to Miami.

Yarborough also had the benefit of top-notch assistant coaches. Clyde Crabtree was his right-hand man, in charge of the backs. Crabtree was known as Cannonball when he played for the University of Florida Gators (and against Yarborough) from 1927 to 1929. The native of Cicero, Illinois weighed just 143 pounds in his playing days and was once allegedly carried 30 yards by Bronco Nagurski in his one season in the NFL. But once he got loose—and he got loose often—he was amazing to watch. Florida's Charlie Bachman later called him the greatest back he'd ever coached.

"If Crabtree were performing today before national television audiences, he'd be the rave of the country," Bachman gushed in a 1957 interview. "Such coordination I've never seen in an individual. And versatility, too. He could stop and go without breaking speed. He could pass with either hand. He could punt—on the dead run—with either foot. And if you gave him running room, he could get you a touchdown through several teams put together."[13]

Crabtree tended to develop backs out of his own mold. There were a few bigger guys like Bill Carey and Lefty Schemer, but it was the Davey Eldredge-type scatback that best fit Miami's short punt offense. There was a succession of those backs—one grooming the next— that continued even after Crabtree left to coach West Palm Beach at the end of the 1939 season. Pete Williams remembered his turn, how he idolized Bruce Smith and Arnold Tucker before he got to high school himself and how Tucker, one day, took him aside when he was one of six "snotty-nosed kids" having trouble running a trap play correctly.

"Why he picked me, I don't know, but he did," Williams said. "He said, 'Let me show you. When you get the ball, you do such and such and such and such; and I went to the front of the group. The coach said, 'O.K., you guys look—now he knows what he's doing.' No one knew that Arnold had given me the secret to it. And somebody gave him the secret before. We all passed it down."

It was that sort of continuity that gave Yarborough the confidence to keep upgrading the schedule year after year. Free of Big Ten commitments, the Stingarees scheduled four of nine regular season games against out-of-state opponents in 1932 and 1933, six of 10 in 1934, seven of nine in 1935 and 1936. In 1939, Garfield made New Jersey the sixteenth state on Miami's intersectional list. Such a regional schedule would have been hardly tenable had the Stingarees traveled to out-of-town games, which was seldom the case. In the three seasons after the Orange Bowl was built, Miami played just two games a year on the road. Out-of-state teams were happy to play in Miami first because it was Miami and secondly because it included a usually-hefty gate for the visiting school. By playing between eight and nine home games a year, the Stingaree program was one of the few entities with a steady income stream during Depression years.

They also knew how to work their home field advantages. They were impervious to the heat, and were buoyed by loud, enthusiastic fans. To opponents, it was usually the most anticipated road trip of the year, and the Stingarees made sure to be hospitable hosts. Walter Bell, who played for Lanier High in Macon for coach Selby Buck, a Miami High graduate, noted how there was one "very big" out-of-town game:

> Miami High, in the Orange Bowl. That was the big one! Before every out of town game, a travel squad list of the players that were to make the trip was posted in the locker room. It was sad indeed and a bitter disappointment when one's name did not appear on the list. The coaches did try to reward as many players as possible by taking them on the Miami trip.
>
> "A travel squad was posted in the locker room indicating three teams would make the trip, a total of 33 players plus equipment managers, a business manager and a few others. I will never forget the feeling of exuberance as Daddy dropped me off at the train station. After all, I was 16 and I had been to Florida only once.
>
> "We were greeted at the train station by an entourage of smiling, cheering and beautiful girls from Miami High. What class! You would have thought we were visiting foreign dignitaries. They took us on a tour of the city, had a party for us, a special breakfast and gave us a key to the city. We were treated like royalty. Miami always had a good football team and maybe they felt sorry for us. I felt like a little lamb."[14]

It was more than just Southern hospitality. If opponents felt like little lambs, that's just how the Stingarees wanted it. That would only make the slaughter easier. Overwhelm them with tropical sights and sounds, soften them up, and force them to think about anything but football. It all played to Miami's advantage. From Yarborough's first year through 1939, the Stingarees were 59-16-4 during the regular season.

Garfield had no such advantages. In 1919, with a bunch of high school kids borrowed equipment, they beat a team from No. 4 School, 13-0. By the time the players were issued official purple and gold uniforms for the 1922 season, high school football was pretty well established in New Jersey, which was unfortunate for the team they called the Comets. Garfield lost its first-ever two games by a combined score of 108-0 to Englewood and Ridgefield Park, quarterbacked by Ozzie Nelson, of Ozzie and Harriet fame. Somehow, the Comets managed to win two games that first season, by finding a team even less equipped and beating

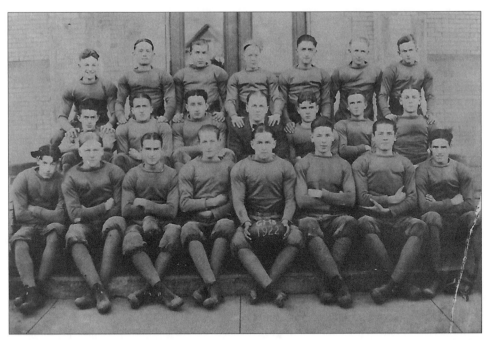

Garfield High School's 1922 football team in its new uniforms. It was Garfield's first season against high school competition. Courtesy Garfield Historical Society.

Hasbrouck Heights twice. Garfield's home field suited its record as well. *The Bergen Record* did not exaggerate when it described the sorry state of Belmont Oval in 1924:

> *"Nestled in the heart of a hill, studded with the remnants of tin cans, the relics of a goat's recent dinner, the Garfield gridiron presented an aspect to the spectator's eye which was entirely in keeping with the dull grey clouds which overhung the field . . .rough to the extent of being almost shell-ridden and muddy for no apparent reason."*[15]

Conditions didn't improve much at the forlorn field, which remained Garfield's practice home into the 1940s. Fortunately, Garfield's squad did improve. The lumps taken in 1922 paid off in experience two years later when Garfield, behind local legends John Hollis, Sam Sebo, John Micklus, Stan Piela and Jerry Bilas (Argauer's future MacKenzie Prep teammate), went 7-0-2 to share the Bergen County Interscholastic League championship.

Quickly, the city went wild over football. When the Comets traveled to play Ridgefield Park, which had trounced them to the tune of 79-0 two years earlier, they were accompanied by 1,500 fans, including the mayor and city council. The caravan consisted of 250 automobiles, fire trucks and open flatbed lumber trucks rigged with rope and stakes to hold the sliding benches. The passengers were jostled as badly as the players were in the game. Ridgefield Park, the defending state Class B champion, considered Garfield "meat," according to the *Passaic Daily News*. But after Garfield held four times from its one-foot line late in the fourth quarter to preserve a 0-0 tie, the paper proclaimed that Garfield "put itself on the state football map."[16]

"The scoreless tie was hailed with glee by the hundreds of Garfield rooters while Coach Carl Erikson and his warriors departed from the field with the conviction that the day had been a total failure," the *Bergen Record* exclaimed, adding: "The (Garfield) delegation, which stood three and four deep for the entire length of the battleground, was colorfully bedecked with pennants and large banners. Aided by numerous mechanical devices they accorded their team a huge ovation and found little difficulty in eclipsing the home team rooters in the matter of cheering."[17]

They all returned, horns blowing the entire way home, confident that Garfield was on its way to becoming a state power. Sebo was the biggest source of the optimism. He was Garfield's first superstar and a star-crossed one at that. A towheaded fireplug, just 5-7, 160 pounds, Sebo was the consummate Garfield player. His parents, Alex and Madeline Dzikowski (Sam shortened the name when he entered school to make it easier to pronounce) were poor Polish immigrants, and Sam found work to contribute to the household. He put in overnight shifts at the woolen mills; he worked on the city snow plows and at the water works. But, while he was often late to practice, he didn't give up football. He treated it as a job, a means to get ahead.

"There was always something driving him on," recalled Al Del Greco, his Garfield team-mate. "Everything that Sam did was done with intense concentration."[18]

It all paid off in a full scholarship and an otherwise unaffordable college education at Syracuse where he starred not only on the gridiron but also on the baseball diamond and even in the boxing ring. Late in his senior season, he was kicked in the chest in a game at Nebraska and, although he played in the final two games, his lungs never recovered. In 1930, his first year out of college, he joined the ill-fated Newark Tornadoes of the early NFL, to supplement his part-time salary as Art Argauer's assistant at Garfield. He also took courses in law school. When the *Bergen Record* published a picture of the Garfield coaching staff that year, he looked unwell, even aged. In 1932, doctors told Sebo he had tuberculosis.

To convalesce, Sebo moved to the Trudeau Institute sanatorium, located in the Adirondacks in Saranac Lake, New York. Somewhat improved, he then lived with college friends in Little Valley, New York, where he helped coach the local high school football team. He died there of a heart attack in 1933 just as he began as a sportswriter for the local paper. He had just been asked to select the college All America team for NBC by famed radio man Lowell Thomas. It was released a week before his death in December. Thomas introduced it by saying "It's an All-American team by a boy with an All-American spirit."

Sam had wanted to get back to work to help his brother, Joey, pay for college. Joey, like Sam, had gone to Syracuse on a football scholarship; but, after Sam became ill, Joey relented to his mother's pleas to quit the

Sammy Sebo.

The Onandanga (Syracuse University's 1930 yearbook, 1930).

sport. Sam had hoped to return to Garfield for Christmas, then head west to live on a ranch. His demise was sudden and unexpected.

Sebo's father was said to have paced the floor all night when he got the news. He told the *Record*, "He say he come home for Christmas. Look how he come home."[19]

All of Garfield mourned and, for as long as people remembered him, he remained an example in town of perseverance and hard work.

Sebo was part of Garfield's second straight co-conference championship team in 1925. Another winning season followed, but Garfield suffered through the loss of coach Guy Moore to Ramsey after the 1926 season, and fortunes ebbed again. The *Bergen Record* dubbed the 1928 edition of the Purple and Gold the "Scoreless Wonders" after they were blanked in their first nine games.

The coach of this hapless bunch was a reluctant Chick DeVito, who had been Moore's assistant. DeVito would make his mark at the school, but as the Boilermakers' baseball coach, eventually inducted into the GHS Hall of Fame with the ballfield named in his honor. DeVito conceded that X's and O's of football were like a foreign language to him, told school officials so, and even pleaded to quit several times. They wouldn't let him. Instead, for the 1929 season, they gave him a co-coach in Pete Tengi, who played on some good Garfield teams in the mid 20s, and then at Syracuse. Tengi handled most of the strategy, and DeVito provided the motivation.

For the first three weeks, it was to no avail. Garfield returned to its scoreless ways as the losing streak extended to 12 games. Now the Comets were to face Tenafly, one of the best teams in the county and a contender for Class B state honors. What got into Garfield when the teams met at scraggly Belmont Oval, few could figure. But with Garfield unleashing an aerial attack, the home team sprang what was called the biggest upset in the state, 13-6.

"It was the sweetest victory the kids ever won," said DeVito, whose team was suddenly and unexpectedly in the running for the Bergen County Interscholastic League championship when it followed up with a 21-0 win over Lyndhurst. Now, *Bergen Record* columnist James R. Sutphen wrote glowingly of DeVito: "His football ability is not great by any means but his personality and his energy is mammoth and this may be one of the reasons that Garfield has finally been able to produce something that at least resembles a football team."

The papers hyped the next week's matchup against powerful Bogota. Could Garfield do it? That would be a resounding 'no.' DeVito's team was sent back to Earth with a 26-0 shellacking. It then tied two of its last four games, to finish 2-5-2 but in spite of the improvement from 1928, Garfield's Board of Education Commissioner, Henry F. Buonocore had seen enough. "Garfield's poor record on the gridiron justifies the expense of hiring a new coach," he declared.

DeVito was relieved. Tengi was angry. He launched into a defense of the status quo with an interesting argument—that emphasizing football victories would come at the expense of academics.

"This attitude is to be deplored," Tengi said. "The boys are coming to high school for an education and not to learn how to play football so that they will give their hearts for dear old Siwash when they go to college. It is a sad state of affairs. Suppose the paid coach doesn't turn out a winning team? Will the school then have spring training for its football team?"

It was an interesting question. The young man about to apply for the job was soon thinking that very thing. Art Argauer was coaching at Hannah Penn Junior Hugh School in York

Pennsylvania when he ran into the *Bergen Record*'s Al Del Greco, his old classmate at the Savage School.

"I'm doing really well there," he told Del Greco. "But I would like to coach in Bergen County. Do you know of any place where they need a coach?"

"Garfield," Del Greco said. "They want a winning team in the worst way. Go and speak to Henry Buonocore, president of the Board of Education."

That was on a Friday. Argauer got the job on Monday. It was another happenstance guiding Garfield's fortune. Yet, there was another reason Argauer wanted to return to New Jersey. In May, he was married to Florence Harris, who, at 19, was 11 years his junior and she wanted to remain in New Jersey. They had met at a masquerade dance. Florence was wearing a Bali costume. He took her for a few spins around the dance floor, trying to avoid her toes, and proposed on the spot. "What kind of nut is this guy?" Florence asked the proprietor. A persistent one. They were perfect for each other. She was

Art Argauer in 1934. Newark Public Library (NJ) Newark News Archives.

an accomplished pianist. He loved listening to music. She hated cooking. He loved to dabble in the kitchen. He had no real family in America (neither his brother nor sister had children). She came from a big family and, when they couldn't have children, he treated her nephews and nieces as his own. In Art's life, she was the center that always held.

Over the next decade, Argauer would prove the wisdom of Buonocore's snap decision. Unlike Yarborough at Miami, the situation he inherited was far from ideal. The 30-year-old coach had to deal not only with football-related problems but also with outside issues and influences. He did it by rising above it all, selling himself to his boys and erecting a stubborn blockade against anyone and anything that would work against his teams. He was the ultimate authority. It would not have worked any other way.

Argauer put his imprint on the school quickly in each of the sports he was hired to coach. His 1930 football team opened with an upset win over defending Class B state champion Dover and went on to a 7-2 record and Garfield's first outright Bergen County Interscholastic League title. His 1930-31 basketball team won its first 22 games and, while upset in the third round of the state tournament, was invited to the prestigious Eastern States Tournament in Glens Falls, New York, where it made it to the championship game before losing to Hun, a New Jersey prep school. He was changing the culture of Garfield High School sports, right down to the nickname.

Argauer really didn't like the Comets moniker. Hackensack High School called itself the same, and he didn't like sharing. In that era, it was customary for players to print their favorite college team on their hip pads. When the 1931 team got together for the first time, there stood Purdue fan Larry Grinch with BOILERMAKERS on his equipment. It was, to Argauer, a sign from God.

"I'm not the Pope," Argauer said. "But I christen you all Boilermakers."

The new mascot fit the blue-collar city well, even if there wasn't a boiler plant in all of Garfield. Argauer liked the hard work implications of the name and, while it took years for the papers to stop calling them the Comets, by 1939, the Boilermaker nickname was firmly established.

Now that his teams were associated with factories, he had to get them out of the factories. Andy "Shang" Kmetz, who starred in both football and basketball for Argauer, was a perfect example. Kmetz was one of those would-be dropouts. He was typical of many Garfield youths who would leave school periodically to work and help support the family. In his case, it was a Slovak immigrant household with six children, headed by his father Michael, a pipefitter, and his mother Anna, who worked as a mail carrier.

One day, they answered a knock on the front door of the house on Summit Avenue. It was Argauer, neatly dressed and polite as could be with Sammy Sebo, his assistant coach, in tow. They were there to encourage the parents to keep their son enrolled at Garfield. Argauer explained just how much college cost and that football could earn him a college scholarship. 'Why, just look at Sammy Sebo here,' he might have crowed.' Sebo, why don't you tell these wonderful people how you are already taking classes at New Jersey Law School' he might have ad-libbed.

Perhaps Michael and Anna Kmetz didn't understand all the words. Andy would have to translate. But they could relate to Sebo. And there was something about Argauer that parents could trust. Argauer could remember when Carlton Palmer walked into his father's tailor shop in 1921. It was a scene he would repeat many times over the years with similar success. It certainly worked out for Kmetz. A plow-horse type of runner, he would go on to challenge Hackensack's Chubby Parcells—Bill Parcells' father—for the Bergen County scoring title. He got his high school diploma.

Argauer, in return, helped Kmetz in many ways. He introduced him to Ida Krug, the class valedictorian, to help him with his French homework, and saw to it Kmetz earned his diploma and helped him get admitted to Tusculum College. The tutoring sessions sparked romance. After college, Andy Kmetz married Ida and returned to Garfield, where he served briefly as an assistant coach for Argauer before getting the head coaching position at Hasbrouck Heights High School in 1939. Before retiring in 1955 (he was denied a $500 raise by the Board of Education), he amassed 100 career wins, just 13 fewer than his mentor, whom he'd join in the New Jersey coaches Hall of Fame. One of his players described him as a fair-minded disciplinarian who made a total commitment to his players. In other words, he was an Argauer disciple.

Kmetz may have been one of the most successful of Argauer's projects but he wasn't the only one. According to Del Greco, Argauer talked at least three other players into staying on the 1930 team. As Del Greco explained it, these were boys who would "ordinarily be simply lounging around, out of work. "He believes that being exposed to education may aid them," Del Greco wrote. "Besides, they help his football team."

Eventually, Argauer's persuasiveness would become the stuff of legends. There were stories that he would drag kids out of factories, even that he trekked to the coal mines of Pennsylvania in search of brawny bodies. No proof of that exists but, even as hyperbole, they speak both to Argauer's determination and mystique. It all, of course, began with his first Garfield team. As the 1930 season approached, observers expected Argauer to make some progress with the purple and gold. Still, even Del Greco couldn't get himself to predict his alma mater would open the season by beating Dover, even with his old friend at the helm.

"The only difference with Garfield this year and the past two seasons is that it has a new coach. There is no reason to believe that the team will do anything except dirty their uniforms. Coach Argauer hasn't much to work with." A mournful headline previewed Garfield's season: "Fast Attack is Only Hope of Garfield." The article noted how light the team was in the britches. Everyone, it seemed then, sold Argauer short.

Dover came into the season as the defending state Class B champs with a 9-1 record in 1929. Garfield hadn't scored on the Tigers in two seasons. Dover may have lost the core of that championship team but Garfield's 21-13 victory was a statement nevertheless. Kmetz, the player Argauer talked back into school, was the hero. He threw a 10-yard pass to Joey Sebo, Sammy's brother, for the first Garfield touchdown scored under Argauer. Later, he returned a kick 80 yards for a touchdown in what the *Bergen Record* called a brilliant piece of open field running.

The *Dover Advance* complained about sloppy play on both sides, calling it a "typical opening game with fumbles, mixed signals and a general impression of being much at sea apparent." No matter. Garfield had scored more points in one game than it did the entire 1928 season. Gushed the *Record*, "Garfield's exhibition is rated as one of the best in four years and much of the credit for the change can justly be given to its new mentor, Artie Argauer, who has whipped together a fine eleven out of material that looked far from promising at the onset of the season."

That season was soon highlighted by Garfield's first-ever, outright league championship, albeit in the five-team Bergen County loop. After Garfield put up a fight but fell, 18-6, against a very good Passaic squad, the Comets, as they were then known, destroyed Ramsey, 39-6, edged Tenafly, 6-0, and, then, sparked by Kmetz' 60-yard interception return, blanked Bogota, 14-0, in a showdown of league leaders, and clinched the title when Joey Sebo dropkicked a 25-yard field goal with three minutes left to play to beat underdog East Rutherford, 9-7.

It wasn't the first dramatic field goal in Garfield history. Bilas dropkicked a 30-yard field goal with 40 seconds left in a game to give Garfield a share of the 1924 league title. It also wouldn't be the last. Somewhere in Clifton, 10-year-old Benny Babula was waiting to make history.

Garfield's only other loss came in the final game of the year, 12-7, against St. Cecilia's, which was capping off its best season until a stocky Italian kid from Brooklyn took over the reins. It's the school where Vince Lombardi cut his coaching teeth, beginning as an assistant in 1939, the same year Argauer took his Boilermakers to Miami.

"While the bouquets are being passed out, hand one to Coach Artie Argauer," Del Greco wrote. "He took the squad when its morale was at a low ebb. The boys weren't interested in football and wouldn't turn out. In his first season, he captured a championship. That's not good, it's perfect."

Argauer, though, had more ambitious plans in mind. Garfield began to dominate the Bergen County Interscholastic League in every sport, including five under Argauer in basketball. After winning another league football championship in 1934, Garfield heard the complaints of the other league members and left, with Argauer continually upgrading an independent schedule.

Like Yarborough in Miami, Argauer was looking for more.

SEVEN

THE TEAMS

BOILERMAKERS

The freshmen trying out for football at Garfield High in 1936 were understandably nervous. Standing on the sidelines for the opening practice, many had struggled to even pull on their pads for the first time, never mind being thrown into the maelstrom of a full-fledged scrimmage. Now, wearing rag-tag uniforms with wide-eyed faces, they were about to be taken under the wing of Art Argauer. They knew, from both Argauer's reputation and his stoic countenance that they were not going to be coddled.

Football, after all, was a natural pastime in Garfield. Kids were drawn to it. In an age where no one was handed anything and where a guy often had to "put up his dukes," Argauer expected his players already hardened and ready to rumble. As one formed by the same mold, he would refine their rough edges with discipline and technique. But their inherent toughness would remain intact.

These freshmen gazed in wonder at Garfield's three All State players: Jules Koshlap, Jim Schwartzinger and Steve Szot. Brawny, seasoned and mature, all three would go on to play for big-time college football programs. To the freshmen, they epitomized real football players, oozing self-confidence just by stretching, alone. But now, Argauer was calling one of the freshmen onto the field for an intrasquad scrimmage against these monsters.

Benny Babula was about to announce his presence.

Most everyone heard talk about a hotshot kid Argauer was bringing over from Clifton. But the varsity players figured he'd be just another freshman who would pass through what amounted to an initiation ritual: the first practice. They would welcome the green newcomers by showing them what life would be like on the suicide squad—the kids who, in effect, were sacrificed as tackling fodder. But Babula, they would soon understand, was not going to be pushed around for fun.

Argauer put Babula on kickoff coverage, tooted his whistle and eagerly eyed his prize recruit as he took off from the line. The kick sailed down the field and, with it, so did Babula, right under the chin of the unsuspecting receiver, knocking him dizzy. The varsity man lay flat on the ground blinking his eyes to clear his head. As the coaches tended to him, Koshlap and the others asked themselves, "Who is this kid?"

Bronislaw was his Christian name. Roughly translated from Polish it means "glorious defender." In English, he was Benjamin, Benny to most, and simply Ben to his teammates. Over the next four years, most everyone around Garfield would know this name. If there were a Mount Rushmore of Garfield High School athletes, Babula's would have been the first face chiseled into it. In later years, Boilermakers Wayne Chrebet, Luis Castillo and Miles Austin all had notable NFL careers, but none was as accomplished or as celebrated a high school player as Benny Babula.

Maybe Art Argauer couldn't have foreseen that grand a high school career for Babula, even as his prized freshman smashed headlong into the upperclassman in that initial scrimmage. But Argauer certainly supposed he could be that sort of player to build a team around. Otherwise, he wouldn't have recruited him from outside Garfield's borders.

Yes. Arguably the school's greatest football player ever came from Clifton. He was within sight of Garfield, surely, just a glance across the Passaic River near the Dundee Dam on Trimble Avenue. But Clifton High, where his brother and sister had studied, didn't have a prayer of enrolling him once Art Argauer heard about the big bruiser. Even in his early youth, Babula had his way with the neighborhood kids in pick-up games on the dusty empty lots near his home. And so Argauer, himself a Clifton High legend, exploited a loophole to make Benny a Boilermaker.

It was a delicious coincidence that Babula's mother, Tekla, came to the United States on the same vessel, the *Kaiserin Auguste Victoria*, that brought Argauer to America six years earlier. Benny had his mother's features and his father's drive. Shortly after arriving in New York in 1912, Michał Babula took a bride and opened a butcher shop in Passaic that he quickly converted into a wholesale meat distribution business. He ran the business out of Garfield and owned a couple of other Garfield properties to rent, including one on River Drive. That became Benny Babula's "official" residence and, while it was sometimes questioned, it was never challenged—not even by Clifton High coach Al Lesko, who couldn't have supplied Babula with as strong a supporting cast. Lesko no doubt swallowed hard and winced every time Garfield beat up his team.

In any case, Argauer wouldn't have dwelled on it too much. Not all New Jersey towns had their own high schools. And those that did not typically sent their students to schools in neighboring towns. Lodi, for instance, sent kids to Garfield until it built its high school in 1931. Stanley Piela, later the Lodi football coach, was among the great Lodi athletes who played for Garfield in the 1920s. Wallington sent kids to Garfield, East Rutherford and Lodi at different times in the 1930s. Koshlop lived in Wallington. In 1937, the three Szot brothers, attended Garfield, East Rutherford and Lodi, respectively.

Babula started out playing tackle. That's where he made his first varsity debut in a 67-0 rout of Port Jervis in the opening game of the '36 season. It acclimated him to the *Sturm und Drang* of the trenches. But when Koshlap was hurt in the second game of the season, Argauer worked all week converting him to fullback. Over his high school career, Babula became a wonder, as good a triple-threat tailback as there was in high school football at the time. Flinging the ball with a three-quarter delivery, he could hit receivers far down the field. Some of his punts carried 60 yards in a day when field position was even more of a premium than in today's game. But what Babula did best was run.

"He would carry two or three guys on his back and keep moving," teammate Angelo Miranda said in a 1999 interview. "His legs were like pistons. I never saw anyone like him."[1]

After Babula split time in the backfield with fellow All Stater Ted Ciesla on the 1938 state championship team, Argauer built the 1939 offense exclusively around Babula and dared opponents to stop the off-tackle smash. Behind precision blocking, Babula would roar around the end and lower his shoulder. Then the "fun" began for defenders. He was big—6-1, 194 pounds as a senior. But, because his legs kept churning, he was nearly impossible for a single player to restrain. He had the ability to cut sharply without losing momentum, but he was at his best as a north-south runner. He didn't have breakaway speed, but he had huge strides that picked up yards in a flash. He owned a devastating stiff-arm and enviable balance to keep him on his feet.

"We knew where they were going to go and we'd move guys into those holes to stop him," said Al Kacahadurian, who played against Garfield for Paterson Eastside High. "It didn't matter. He ran over us anyway."

Ernie Accorsi, the former general manager of the Giants, watched the film of the 1939 Garfield-Passaic game in which Babula rushed for 193 yards. His scouting report is filled with superlatives.

"What was amazing to me was that obviously Babula was going to carry the ball on virtually every play with very few reverses or much deception and they still couldn't stop him," Accorsi noted. "His explosive takeoff—he was at his top speed on the second step—and his powerful and quick strike force made it impossible for the defense to stop him at first contact.

"He was into the second level with suddenness and broke tackle after tackle, especially arm tackles. He almost always had to be gang tackled to get him down. When he did run wide he looked like the fastest player on the field, and I loved the way he would give the tackler a leg, then take it away or stop to make the tackler miss him then run by him.

"His vision, size, long strides, speed and most of all striking, lightning-like power basically made him unstoppable and, realizing he was essentially the sole target by the defense, made it all the more impressive. Despite the three quarter arm delivery common in those days (even Sammy Baugh delivered the ball in that manner) he threw the ball with accuracy. And how about his endurance? He did everything. What a player."

Babula was the Golden Boy before there was Paul Hornung. He had the same dashing looks with wavy golden locks and a square jaw. When he returned an interception 90 yards for a touchdown in his senior year, Kachadurian, the quarterback who threw it, said his teammates were too much in awe to tackle him.

"Benny Babula scared the hell out of everybody. Even the name scared us," Kachadurian said, remembering it all over 75 years later. "He was about 6-1, I guess, with broad shoulders. No facemask. You could see his features. And he was handsome, like Flash Gordon. I think we all stood aside and said, 'Let him go, look how good he looks.' "

Babula knew it, too. He was supremely confident and impervious to pressure.

"Every time he was in a game, I was confident we would win it," Miranda said. "All of our opponents knew it, too. But to us he was just Ben, the greatest teammate you could have."

Babula, at least in high school, didn't crave publicity. Although later in life, he would light up any room he walked into, his personality wasn't yet made for the spotlight. His teammates liked to kid him about his naivety. Once, the players were handed an incomplete season schedule. Next to one of the weeks, it read, "Pending."

Benny Babula in his gold Garfield jersey. Newark Public Library (NJ) Newark News Photo Archives.

Benny and Violet outside Garfield High. Newark Sunday Call.

"Where the heck is Pending?" Babula asked, filling the locker room with howls.

The ironic truth was that Babula wasn't all that crazy about football. He enjoyed the camaraderie with his teammates as well as the satisfaction of accomplishment that football offered. His favorite sport, however, was baseball, and he dreamed of a career as a power-hitting outfielder in the majors.

"Football's silly to me. It's a wearing game," he told Willie Klein of the *Newark Star-Ledger* in 1939. "It's not that I'm afraid of injuries. I am solidly built and plenty rugged. I'm not so easy to hurt. But somehow football doesn't click with me. I guess if I quit football, I would miss it."[2]

That same article disclosed a few other things about Babula. His favorite subject was chemistry, and he liked to tinker in the lab. His least favorite was French. Klein's feature included another revelation: "It's not generally known but Benny, the cynosure of all feminine eyes at Garfield has a steady girlfriend. She's Violet Frankovic, also a student. They've known each other for years."[3]

Over 75 years later, Violet—who had gone on to marry Joseph Kolbek, a Garfielder six years her elder—recollected her time with Benny with a laugh. The papers, she said, embellished their relationship as papers did then. They hardly interacted at school, she said, only to wave at each other, but they did date after she had obviously caught Babula's eye. Violet, attractive and three years younger than Benny, was just 15 when they started to date. Her father, Butch Frankovic, head of the Garfield Indians Athletic Club, was understandably

John Grembowitz

protective, but Benny, she said, "was a perfect gentleman" who adhered to her father's rules.

"He treated me very well, he took me to such nice places," Violet said. "Benny had a way of getting a date. He would say, 'Violet, how would you like to go to Asbury Park for the day?' and I would say 'lovely.' 'I'll pick you up nine o'clock on Saturday,' he'd say. All of our dates were all day on Saturdays. So we went to Asbury Park, and we went on the merry-go-round and he bought me some taffy to take home. And then the next date was: 'How would you like to go to Palisades Park?' Also on Saturday.

"We went on a couple of rides there, and I didn't even tell my father we were going on the Ferris wheel," she said. "We stopped at the games. It was three balls for a quarter and, naturally, he hit all three balls and we came home with a stuffed animal. He always got me home by suppertime."

Babula always picked up Violet in his DeSoto. Only two players on the team had cars. Benny's family was more well-off than the rest, but he didn't flaunt it. No one was jealous; Babula always put his teammates above himself.

"Me rated with the best backs in New Jersey school football history? Aw, I'm not so hot," he told Klein.[4]

Besides, Babula's teammates were pretty hot themselves. In 1939, Babula ran for more than 880 yards, passed for more than 400 and scored 118 points, not including the Miami game—the highest among New Jersey Group 4 players in the regular season. Without him, Garfield would not have played for a national championship. But Garfield was far from a one-man team.

John Grembowitz was born in Passaic and was in school there when, in 1929, his father Frank was killed in a car crash, leaving their Prohibition-era soft drink business to his mother, Katarzyna. That same year, Joseph Klecha lost his wife Maryana to cancer, leaving the widower with four kids. He was also a beverage distributor and, in 1932, he and Katarzyna married and had a son, Frank. John and his sister Mildred became step-siblings. John would now have two older siblings (Michael and Ed) and two younger ones (Stanley and Sally), making it a yours, mine and ours arrangement.

Prohibition ended in 1933, and Joseph Klecha opened one of the scores of taverns that suddenly proliferated in Garfield. It was on Ray Street, a short walk from the Forstmann plant and up the street from St. Stan's Church. Butcher shops framed the block and a bakery was across the street, making Ray Street a bit of a commercial hub. A lot of passersby were thirsty. Klecha's Tavern did a good business.

"He was a friendly, jovial happy go lucky guy, my Dad," Sally said of her father. "He'd sing, tell jokes, make music. Everybody called him Mr. Klecha. He always wore a white shirt behind the bar and my mom made sure they were always washed and ironed. We were a very happy family. There was a lot of togetherness."

The tavern was out front, and the family lived in the back with a little flower garden in the backyard that Katarzyna kept. The boys shared a room and beds—and work. Running a tavern wasn't easy, and everybody chipped in. The boys washed and dried dishes and glassware and hauled around boxes of stock. Their chores had to be done before football practice.

John and his brothers liked to fish and would occasionally take Sally and little Frank along to their favorite spot under a big oak tree by the Passaic River. "He was so nice to me and so handsome," Sally recalled. "He was very outgoing and he had a lot of girlfriends."

Sally attended St. Stan's, where stern nuns presided in the classroom. John and his brothers attended nearby Washington Irving School No. 4, where teachers changed the original spelling of his name (Grembowiec) to a more phonetic Grembowitz. St. Stan's had a gym in the old church building where Johnny held court, playing basketball and the like. But his strength, quickness and smarts suited him for football above all the other sports and having older brothers accelerated his learning curve.

Ed was a fairly talented football player, as well, so one can imagine Art Argauer's glee when Ed told him about his kid brother, a year younger than him. Grembowitz and Benny Babula were the only two freshmen to play in varsity games in 1936 and became good friends. Babula would often drive by the tavern and the two would head out together.

Grembowitz had both classroom and football smarts. On the field, he had a knack for sorting out a play, which is why he was able to move seamlessly between the line and back-field whenever Argauer needed him. He combined his great instincts with a tremendous first step. He was fearsome as a pulling guard, and on defense he had great closing speed that enabled him to run down ball carriers otherwise headed for big plays.

"There was no question that Johnny Grembowitz had something special," Walter Young remembered. "He was just a little different than all the rest of the kids on the team. I think it had to do with his intelligence, I think it was just a notch higher than most of the kids on the team. And he played with extreme confidence."

Both Babula and Grembowitz were named to the 1939 All-State team along with a third, more unassuming player, who made honorable mention. Walter Young wasn't a typical Garfield boy in that his parents weren't from Italy or Eastern Europe. They were German immigrants from what would later become the German Democratic Republic, or communist East Germany. Young's father, Martin, was one of five boys, two of whom would be killed in World War I. His parents owned a small farm—cows, chickens, and earth crops—but it was to be passed to the oldest son and that wasn't Martin. Martin was a loom fixer (mechanic at the nearby woolen plant) and, when work was tight, he received a letter from America from his brother, Franz, who worked at Botany Worsted Mills in Passaic. Botany, a German-owned company, hired mostly Eastern Europeans for its less-skilled jobs, and Germans for managerial and technical positions. All of Botany's looms were German-made, and its main-tenance manuals were in German, which made Martin a superb candidate for employment.

So, Martin Jung (the name was Anglicized to Young upon arrival) left his family in order to provide for it. As with many others, he never again saw his parents.

Two of Martin and Ida Young's children were born in Germany: Elsie in 1910 and Curt in 1913, with whom Ida was pregnant when Martin sailed to America. For two years, he sent money home, a few dollars at a time.

"I have a postal card that my father wrote to my mother," Walter Young said. "I smile over that card because I recognize that my father was a typical, stiff-necked German man. I loved him deeply, deeply. He wrote to my mother, he sent her some money, twenty dollars. He wanted her to keep it to buy a ticket. "Dear Ida—it's as if he was talking to a strange person, there was no feeling of 'My beloved Ida'—then, 'I hope everything is OK, you know I'm working hard. Say hello to my children . . .' Nothing about 'I miss you.' It was just stiff and cold . . . incredible."

But that hard exterior betrayed his father's actual feelings. While Martin was in America, little Elsie contracted scarlet fever and died. Ida was devastated in her grief and unable to send immediate word to her husband. Forced to leave Elsie behind in her churchyard grave, she and Curt would join him in New Jersey. Curt celebrated his first birthday on the ship. At first they rented rooms in Passaic. Then, when Martin saved enough from his earnings, they bought a two-family house in the Plauderville section of Garfield, on Bergen Street. That's where Rudolph, in 1919, and Walter, in 1922, were born. Their father, though, never forgot his first-born. If ever Elsa's name would come up at the dinner table, this stoic German who believed that emotion was not permitted, became silent, Walter remembered. He never knew his sister but through his father's teary eyes.

The Young family lived in the upper two floors of the house on Bergen Street. It was a typical Garfield arrangement: two bedrooms, a living room, a kitchen without appliances and a half-bathroom. Heat generated from a coal-burning stove in the kitchen. Walter and his brother Rudy shared a third-floor room, oppressively hot in the summer and, in the winter, nearly as cold as beyond its walls. Their mother heated bricks and placed them underneath their featherbed.

"We told stories, made mischief but slept in a very warm bed," Walter said with a grin.

Out front, Walter's "Papa," as he was called, built a retaining wall about three feet high, and, behind it, planted a sour cherry tree the boys were forbidden to climb. There was one enticing branch which could be reached with a jump from the retaining wall, and, naturally, they would swing and horse around on it. It was all innocent fun.

Martin Young was often out of work and he brooded over it. He was a proud and frugal man. Instead of wasting a nickel for bus fare, he walked the two miles each way to the Botany factory. One hot summer day, Walter craved an ice cream cone from the grocery store/ butcher shop on the corner. He asked his father for five cents and, after much pleading, his father reached into his pocket and pulled out the only nickel he had on him. Walter, with holes in both pockets, cleverly stored the coin in his mouth and sprinted across the unpaved street. Too eager to get to the store, he tripped in a gully and swallowed the nickel. His disappointment, he remembered, was "beyond measure."

The proprietor of that butcher shop soon found Walter rather troublesome. As with many in Garfield, Ida Young sought work outside the home. She found it washing clothes and cleaning house for a well-do-to Passaic family, the Prescotts. Heirs to an empire built on stove polish, they were so prominent that one of the local telephone exchanges was named after them. Without that household job, the Youngs would have defaulted on their mortgage. Ida was a fantastic worker and the Prescotts, as kind as they were, often gave her hand-me-downs from their son, James Jr., for her boys. Once, Walter received a fine shirt that he ripped playing football with his friends. Another time, when he was about 10, he got a golf club and some balls.

"This was like Christmas for me," he remembered. "These things we did not ever have an opportunity to see, much less own one. So when I got it, I showed all my buddies and we walked down to the corner. That's where the children in the neighborhood came together, right in front of the grocery store and the bus stop."

Young wanted to show everyone how to hit a golf ball so he put it on the ground with the store behind him. Unfortunately, Young wasn't familiar with hitting down on the ball to create loft so when he smacked it with a mighty cut, it ricocheted off the curb, back over his head and into the store window with glass shattering everywhere. The butcher ran out, but Walter wasn't there. He had already picked up his club and started to run. He dashed straight up Midland Avenue past the Pump House and then up the hill into "Guinea Heights."

"There were no homes built there yet. I am up on the top of that hill crying and I am afraid to go home," he explained. "I am up there for hours; that's how big of a disaster it was for me. 'What is my mother going to say? What will she think of me?' I ultimately have to go home. My mother is crying. The butcher already knew that I did it from other kids that were there. What drama something like this was to this little kid. But it had a reasonably good ending. The butcher had insurance. There was no way that my mother and father could have afforded to replace that window. I don't remember if I kept the golf club. I never played often enough later in life to be good at golf."

That same butcher figured into another of young Walter's adventures. Like many "house-rich, cash-poor" Garfield homeowners, the Youngs took in boarders. One was a smoker, which fascinated Walter. He offered the boy a few puffs just as Ida Young was getting off at the bus stop on her way home from the Prescotts. She saw Walter with the cigarette in his mouth.

"Who gave you that?" she asked angrily.

Walter stammered.

"The butcher."

That night, Ida dragged her son along to visit one of her lady friends down the block. As they passed the store, the butcher said, politely, "Good evening, Mrs. Young." That set her off. Turning abruptly, she admonished the man. "Why did you give my son a cigarette?" The butcher said he didn't. Ida pressed Walter: "Did he give you a cigarette?"

"Yes," Walter answered.

It wasn't until a couple of blocks later, after his mother had walked off in a huff, that he fessed up.

"I still have the dread of having lied to my mother," he flinchingly recalled. "It was such a life-changing event that, even when I tell you the story now, I feel like I felt as a kid, almost 85 years ago."

Walter grew up in the New Apostolic Church, a strict chiliastic Protestant sect that flourished in Germany. Young's parents were devout and, as such, his guilt would have been profound. In fact, one of the most traumatic episodes of his childhood came while walking home from the church in Clifton with his Sunday school attendance card, which recorded attendance with a gold star for being on-time, and a blue star for tardiness. A dreaded red star

Walter Young

meant no attendance. Walter's card was full of gold stars, and he treasured it. The route home, however, took him over the Dundee Canal and the Passaic River. He and Rudy always leaned over and spit down from the bridges. As Walter did so, his attendance card fell into the Passaic River. He could have cried.

The church almost prevented Young from playing football. Most Garfield boys played football and baseball on the many empty lots around the city, which made for a lot of skinned knees and scar tissue—not a bad preparation for further athletic endeavors. Walter and his brother were no different and, since Rudy was older, Walter often went up against older kids. He was big for his age and he could tell he was cut out for football. At the time, he was attending No. 8 School, where the high school team's locker room was a short walk to the practice field at Belmont Oval. He looked out the window one afternoon and saw the Boilermakers boarding the team bus, resplendent in their purple jerseys. That's when he promised himself to try out for football.

"I looked at those kids and I wanted to be one of them so bad, you couldn't believe it," he said. "I overcame all the obstacles put in my way; my mother didn't want it, my father didn't want it, my brothers didn't care. They didn't play. Above all, the church was not in favor of it. But I was determined and I never quit getting after something. It was my target. I wanted to be like those kids with clean uniforms, purple and gold. I could hardly wait to get these shoulder pads. Wow, I was going to be a football player."

Young became a football player and a good one, good enough to start varsity as a sophomore and to make several all-star teams as a senior. The end position was the key to stopping the outside running plays that most teams ran. It required discipline and cleverness. Young never made the same mistake twice and, for all of his good nature, he was competitive, tough, and trustworthy.

Young was also a good student and enrolled in the technical program, considered at the time one of the most advanced academic programs at Garfield. One of his best friends was

Walter Bradenahl. They attended Sunday school together at the New Apostolic Church. Walter was born in Mannheim, Germany, and the Bradenahls came over from Berlin in 1927. The two Walters were an interesting pair together. Young was tall and well-built and Bradenahl was on the frail side. As friends, they did all the typical boy things together. Bradenahl was less inclined to rough-housing and sports, but Young appreciated the discussions they often had.

"He had a brain that was most unusual. He was the smartest kid in the school," Young recalled.

Bradenahl was an only child who worshipped his father, Walter Sr. The father ruled the roost. Young remembers how his friend would say: "My father is going to do this, my father is going to do that." Meanwhile, Bradenahl's mother, Frieda, was someone Young called, "a typical German housewife who relied totally on her husband. What he said was Gospel."

Young and Bradenahl were in the same civics class as sophomores. That's when he noticed a change in his friend's demeanor and attitude.

"There would be a discussion on world affairs and he would challenge the teacher on which system was better, the Nazi system or the U.S. system," Young said. "There would be this real vigorous discussion . . . no anger . . . but a real good debate and then on the way home, I would tell Walter: 'You've got to slow down.' But he never did."

Bradenahl's father could not find a job in his field, engineering. At the same time, he was receiving letters from Germany extolling the virtues of national socialism, urging him to return and promising him work. The elder Bradenahl swallowed the propaganda littering those missives. He fell victim to age-old, scapegoat anti-semitism, blamed the Jews for controlling everything in the United States, including his own lot. A decision was made. The Bradenahl family was returning to Germany.

"His father was taken in, completely and totally . . . and really, what does a kid know?" Young asked. "It was clear that they talked about it at great length in their home. I know for a fact that his mother did not resist her husband's plan to return to Germany. She might well have been homesick, and the idea of returning to Berlin might have been appealing. And Berlin at that time was a tremendous city and a great city to live in. All of Germany was spotless . . . until the bombs started to fall."

Bradenahl tried to persuade Young to move his family back to the Fatherland as well.

"I did not really know what Nazi meant, other than what we talked about in high school when we discussed world affairs," Young said. "I knew there was this upset in Europe but nobody knew what the extent was. My mother had a brother in Germany and they would be very intrigued when a letter would come in. But it was more normal things. I don't remember any discussion in our family concerning the heroics of Germany versus the United States. My father and mother were not influenced. There was no evidence, and we never discussed it, although I don't know what they talked about amongst themselves."

In preparation for the move, the Bradenahls left Garfield for Linden, New Jersey. Young would receive two last letters from his friend, one from Linden and the other from the United States Lines ship taking them back, each one indicating a deep descent into Nazi groupthink and a naive unawareness of what lie ahead.

The first, dated June 8, 1938, written with a fountain pen in neat script on graph paper, bragged that Linden High was "100 percent better" than Garfield High with more activities and better mechanical drawing equipment. He complained he never could draw a straight line with some of the T-squares Garfield stocked and, whatever supplies there were, were shared. He also asked Walter for a favor: to tell "little Lisa" not to forget him and to write. He lamented that he cried when forced to return a pet dog just one week after getting it from a neighborhood family.

Then, the letter grew disturbing:

> *Now the most important thing. I am leaving for Germany in a few weeks. And before I regretfully bid farewell to this "glorious land of the free and the brave" to this "God's own country" and this earthly paradise, I will come to visit you. We've sold most of our furniture and we're staying in Hitler's land "of oppressed souls and medieval persecutions" where people starve so badly that they win Olympic Games and vote 99.08 % for their leader and build their own vacation ships (workers' contributions built two large liners for service in the "Strength through Joy" movement.) I will probably serve in Mad-man Hitler's bloody horde of sadistic, blood-man murderers who eat fried Jews' noses for breakfast. I will join the Hitler Youth, then the Arbeits Deinst (sic)[Arbeitsdienst, or Reich Labor Service], then the Army. Though I must first complete my education. How I will miss our glorious freedom, our happiness and prosperity . . . No, I'm afraid we, having been reared under tyrannical Prussians, are too far gone to appreciate the wonderful circumstances under which we might exist but our terrible and mystifying affliction bids us leave all blessings behind us for that "dark pit of rejuvenated Medieval outrages." Ah, me!*[5]

The letter continued for two more pages. With a less sarcastic tone, Bradenahl outlined the reasons they had to leave, that his father's foreign accent rendered him unemployable in American offices and that he had no future himself in an America with "no pull."

"What was left for me? The CCC, the WPA or street digging. No, my lad, I'm shooting high," he wrote.

Germany, Bradenahl told his friend, needed engineers and its government agencies ruled that factories hire a workforce comprised of both young and old. Workers could retire at 60 on a government pension.

> *But then those poor souls don't have our wonderful freedom: we have only 11 million unemployed and only 80 per cent of our people are mentally below normal (I quote an American doctor), we only have a few hundred sex crimes a year and we only execute about 1,000 a year (it could be a lot worse, couldn't it?) But maybe my wit is rather caustic—let it ride.*[6]

Then Bradenahl instructed Young to tell his Garfield classmates he'll be visiting them one last time, "particularly my wonderful history class—boy what arguments, but I always came out on top."

He signed it, "Mit Deutschen Grusse (with German greetings), Walter Bradenahl," and added, "Remind Lisa that I still exist."

Bradenahl never made it back to Garfield. His next letter was dated June 16, eight days after the first. He was on board a ship of the United States Lines on his way to Germany. He joked about how his handwriting was crooked because of the ship's movement and said his family should have taken a German boat. He wrote about watching movies and playing shuffleboard and ping pong. He ended, "until the next letter then, I am, Yours Truly, Heil Hitler, Walter Bradenahl."[7]

Young never heard from his friend again. He tucked the letters away and thought often of him.

Walter's best friend on the football team was Jack Boyle, the left guard. Boyle's father, Francis, was a first-generation Irish American, who, like many Irishman, went into police work. At 21, he was one of the first officers of Garfield's police force after it was formed in 1908. He quickly rose up the ranks. In 1915, he was awarded the Wood Mcclave heroism medal for single-handedly thwarting four burglars as they tried to break into a store. He was captain of detectives during the turbulent 1920s, including the textile strike of 1926 and was deputy police chief when he died in office in 1940. Jack was with Young in the technical program at the high school. He was, Young said, "a scholar."

He was also someone of character. Harry Berenson was a small Jewish boy whose

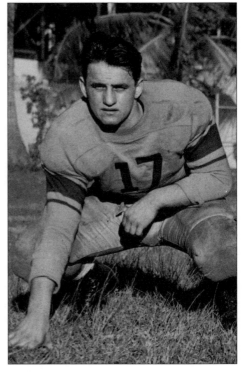

John Orlovsky

father, Sam, owned the dry goods store on Passaic Street, around the corner from the Boyles. There were few Jews attending Garfield at the time, and his slight build made him a target for bullies—until Jack Boyle stepped in. Boyle told anyone who wanted to pick on Berenson that he'd have to go through him first. That ended it. Nobody messed around with Jack and as such, he was an ideal Argauer player. He became a starter in 1938 and never relinquished the job.

Miranda, the left tackle, was a tough, stout Italian American. He never came out of a game his entire high school career. Maybe it was because he was the second-youngest of six sons, but Miranda was used to doing the dirty work of straight-ahead blocking on offense and run-plugging on defense. He and center Pete Yura were newcomers to the starting lineup in 1939, but were always strengths from the season's first game. As the center in the single wing, Yura's responsibilities went beyond those of a modern center, including long-snapping on every down. He had long legs providing a wide base, and he was seldom moved. There was very little penetration into the Garfield backfield.

Bill Wagnecz and Joe Tripoli began the 1939 season as starters at right end and right tackle, respectively. Ed Hintenberger and Alex Yoda eventually moved ahead of them on the depth chart, although Wagnecz and Tripoli still saw considerable playing time. Argauer liked to substitute liberally to keep his team fresh and to prepare for injuries. That's how young Steve Noviczky, a baby-faced freshman and a future Garfield High Hall of Famer, broke in at right guard, replacing Grembowitz when he was moved into the backfield for injuries there.

Tripoli was a giant of a kid—6-feet-1 and a team-high 205 pounds—who had just moved to Garfield from Montvale, where he won the Bergen County discus championship for Park

Ray Butts

Wally Tabaka

Ridge High School. He was from an affluent family. His father had a seat on the New York Stock Exchange, but, shortly after the crash, he suffered a heart attack and died. That left Joe the only male in the family, with six older sisters. He was living with his mother and over-protective grandmother, who insisted he not participate in after-school activities. That led to some heated arguments and resulted in Joe's mother, Frances, moving to Garfield to live with Joe's sister Marianna and her husband Santo D'Amico.

Tripoli had a car and, at times, he'd be asked to babysit his four-year-old niece Rosalyn D'Amico and he'd bring her to practice. She became the unofficial mascot of the team, playing off to the side as the boys went through their paces. Those days were among her earliest memories. So was the time when Tripoli was driving home and his car stalled out on the middle of the railroad tracks. Luckily, he got it started before a train came rolling by.

The Garfield backfield was deep behind Babula with Wally Tabaka, Ray Butts and John Orlovsky in the other starting spots. Tabaka was the next-best runner and a threat as a return man. He was the shortest player in the starting lineup at 5-7, but he was sturdy 170 pounds. He ran low to the ground and was hard to knock down. He had also had guts to try, in an ever-innocent way, to move in on Benny's girl, Violet.

"One day I was walking home and all of a sudden there is Wally and he is walking with me," she remembered. "We started having a very nice conversation about our classes and about our teachers and we did that for over a week. Then Wally said, 'Violet, I won't be walking with you for a while now because we have football practice. But I have something for you.'"

Tabaka took off his varsity letter. Violet said she couldn't take it. He insisted. She took it home and put it in the drawer.

"I never told my father about it," she said.

Ray Butts was an inch taller than Babula and just as heavy. He was primarily the blocking back, although he had huge hands that made him a receiving threat. He started at end but was moved into the backfield to fill a need. Butts was the youngest of nine children by four years, 20 years younger than his oldest sister Irene. In fact, two years after Ray was born in 1920, his sister had a son, Ken Marek, who starred for Garfield just after Ray graduated.

Butts, however, didn't come from the biggest family among his teammates. Reserve back Al Kazaren was one of 10 children. It wasn't uncommon. Neither was losing parents. Kazaren lost his father at age nine, while Ray's father, born Andrew Bucz, was a bus mechanic who was left with a house full of kids, including 10-year-old Ray, when his wife, Catherina, died of intestinal cancer in 1932. It was tough supporting the children still living at home. Like many teammates, Butts usually ate his lunch at the hot dog cart that was parked outside the high school. It was all he could afford—hardly a nutritional training table.

John Orlovsky, the youngest of four brothers, was raised without a father. His mother, a native of Russia, could not spell well, so the family's surname was listed differently on each of her four childrens' birth certificates. At 5-9, 185, Orlovsky was a very tough inside runner who constantly had to battle through a chronic shoulder injury. Like Tabaka, was very good on spinner plays out of the single wing.

What all team members shared was an admiration for their coach. Walter Young said it "bordered on hero worship."

"Every once in a while you run into someone who affects your life. Coach Argauer affected my life," Young said emphatically. "There were things he demanded that were absolutely the way it should be. What he did, how he represented himself . . . he was above reproach."

Before each game, the players would go into his office, one by one, and he would tape their knees and ankles himself, all the while talking softly and calmingly. He'd remind the player of his responsibilities and emphasize the little things he needed to remember. He was meticulous in that respect. Similarly, he was a big proponent of game films. A camera buff himself, he enlisted another enthusiast from Garfield, Michael Rayhack, to take the pictures. Rayhack even experimented with color photography. It could be said that Argauer gave him his start on his career. When World War II broke out, Rayhack joined the Signal Corps as a photographer and took a famous shot of General Douglas MacArthur aboard a destroyer. After the war, he became one of the top cameramen in the early days of television and worked on such shows as the Phil Silvers Show, the Avengers, Shari Lewis and Lamb Chop. Argauer knew talent when he saw it.

"Coach Argauer worked at a game plan all the time," his assistant coach, Joe Cody, said when the team celebrated its 50th reunion in 1989. "He never left anything to chance. The man was a master of psychology and could sell the players anything he wanted. He was a coach way ahead of his time. He even installed a special play for every game which he guaranteed would win a game if needed."[8]

Babula, at that same reunion, recalled one particular Argauer ploy before a big game against Bloomfield.

"He was so shrewd in getting you up for a game," he said. "He chased everyone but the regulars out of the locker room. He said, 'I'm going to give you guys a pill which you can't tell anyone about. It'll make tigers out of you. After you take this I want you to make sure you don't hit anyone too hard because you may hurt them.'

A kneeling Art Argauer in his coaching togs at Passaic Stadium.
Courtesy Angelo Miranda collection.

"I guess we bought his story because after swallowing the candy pills, we held Bloomfield to minus yardage and won, 18-0."[9]

Argauer didn't tolerate misbehavior. Get caught smoking and drinking and you'd find yourself benched, then off the team. "He said thing like, 'keep yourself clean,'" Young recalled.

Practices were practically as hard as games. He didn't lay off the contact. He presided over them with a rolled-up piece of cardboard. Mess up an assignment, and the player would find himself getting slapped on the hindquarters. That led to a memorable incident. When Argauer's mother, Emma, heard that he was swatting his boys, she marched down to Belmont Oval and scolded him in front of the team. If anyone found it amusing, they didn't laugh.

"We dared not," Young said.

Later in his career, the cardboard became a wooden paddle. He called it the "board of education."

There were always lessons to be learned. One day, Steve Novizcky wasn't at practice. That was a no-no with Argauer. He asked the team where he was. Someone piped up, "He's home coach. Mr. Novizcky won't let him go to practice until he's finished painting the house."

Argauer thought for moment. He put the equipment on the side and gathered the team together. They all walked over to the Novizcky house on Willard Street, grabbed paint brushes and finished the job.

Art and Florence never had children of their own, so his players were his family. In 1946, he had proudly collected 3,000 letters from former players filling him in on their progress in college or the military. In a community where college educations weren't highly prized or easily afforded, Argauer, as someone who came by his education by chance, valued it.

"Argauer was a great believer in college and worked very hard to get us in," said Bill Librera, Babula's backup, who pursued a career in education.[10]

"If it wasn't for football, none of us would have been able to afford to go. We owe a lot to Art Argauer. There is not one single thing that I could think of that would be negative about Coach Argauer," Young said. "He wanted the best kids on his team, he wanted to win, but that is what every coach wants. As far as his actions, he was absolutely above board."

After being with Argauer since their freshman years, the seniors on the 1939 team were ready for anything.

Stingarees

He was a scrawny but scrappy 14-year-old when he walked up to an unsuspecting Jesse Yarborough in the Miami High gym. It was December of 1935. His husky brother, Knox, was the captain of the Stingaree football team, eventually bound for All Southern honors and stardom at the University of Georgia. The coach had seen the youngster around, but he was hardly prepared for what Davey Eldredge was about to pronounce.

"Some day, I'm going to be a better football player than Knox," he predicted matter-of-factly.[11] Yarborough chuckled. 'Confident young man,' he must have thought. Four years later, the kid was right. Davey Eldredge turned out to be a better football player than almost any Yarborough had ever coached. He epitomized Stingaree football—small, smart and swift—and was the perfectly cast for the Orange Bowl lights. The field was his stage, and he dazzled on it. He brought the crowd to its feet every time he touched the football, always a threat to go all the way. Arguably, there wasn't a more exciting high school player in the nation.

As a 5-feet-11, 151-pound senior, he was "Li'l Davey" the giant killer. To television viewers in the 1960s, he would have looked as innocent as Dennis the Menace—until he strapped on the leather helmet, glared at the opposition and started his engine. *Miami Daily News* sports editor Jack Bell called him "a galloping waif," while the *Associated Press* was already comparing his explosiveness to that of the great Red Grange.

"He could almost be standing still, then go 'whoosh' and blow past you better than anyone else I've seen," said his teammate, Harvey Comfort. "He could really turn on the steam."

Davey Eldredge.
Miami Senior High School.

The one characteristic Davey shared with his brother Knox was competitiveness. Knox famously started a bench-clearing brawl during Georgia's 1939 game against NYU at Yankee Stadium after colliding with a Violet player on an incomplete pass. Depending on which newspaper reported it—north or south—either Eldredge responded to a punch thrown by NYU's Joe Frank, or he struck the first blow with a forearm to the face. In any case, the scuffle sparked a Civil War in The Bronx.

"It was plain that they held the NYU players personally responsible for Sherman's march and the undoubted evils of the reconstruction period," joked Tommy Holmes of the *Brooklyn Eagle.*[12]

The younger Eldredge possessed the same type of fighting spirit, inherited from both sides of the Mason Dixon line. His mother, Jennie Belle Turner, was from one of the most prominent families in Tuscaloosa, Alabama. Her maternal second great grand-father, Uriah Farmer, was among the region's pioneer planters. Davey's paternal lineage included three Mayflower passengers while another ancestor, Samuel Smith, was a renowned sea captain in Wellfleet, Massachusetts. His namesake grandson, Samuel Eldredge, moved to the Orlando, Florida, area and married Mary Stewart, the daughter of David Bradwell Stewart, one of the first orange growers in Florida. They were Davey Eldredge's grandparents and among the first settlers of Apopka, Florida. In 1895, the "Great Freeze" wiped out the orange crop and, with it, the Eldredges' budding family fortune. That set the then seven-year old Alfred Stewart Eldredge, Davey's father, on a self-made course.

Samuel, having turned from citrus growing into storekeeping, hoped his son would follow him into the merchant business, but Alfred, known better as "Red," held loftier ambitions. Saving enough by working in his father's store, he entered the Georgia Military Academy in College Park, Georgia, where he excelled academically, became a crack marksman, and played centerfield on the school's championship baseball team. He earned admission into Georgia Tech, and, in 1908, played "scrub" football under the great John W. Heisman, sacrificing his body three times a week to prepare the varsity for games.[13]

Married a year later to Jennie Belle, Red Eldredge returned to Apopka and was eventually appointed livestock inspector. He led a successful tick eradication campaign by forcing wary cattle farmers to participate in the controversial practice of cattle dipping, often at his own peril from anti-dipping associations that were known to shoot officers and dynamite dipping vats. Surviving that, he served as city clerk and tax collector until 1917, when he homesteaded

120 acres of land known as Mill Creek Island. Eldredge made a success of it, fighting off bears with an appetite for his hogs. He later credited the invaluable help of a young black man, Ed Johnson, whom the family took in and treated like a son, an arrangement practically unheard of in the segregated South. But there he was, in now-lost family photos.

Alfred Turner Eldredge was born in 1910, William "Knox" in 1915 and David Cameron in 1921, by which time their father had moved the family to Miami, where he was elected city and county purchasing agent. It gave him standing in the community and allowed the Eldredges to live comparatively well during the Depression. They even had a summer cottage at Black Mountain, North Carolina.

His parents divorced in 1937 and, in 1939, Davey was living with his mother on the first floor of the Ruth Apartments, a small complex she managed in the Shenandoah neighborhood, not far from Miami High School. By then, older brother Alfred had been married six years to the former Mary Candler, granddaughter of Asa Candler, the Coca-Cola magnate and, with Knox off at Georgia, Jennie doted on her youngest child, the bright and energetic Davey.

Davey's mother was active in Miami society as a member of the Brookfellows Literary Guild, the Miami Women's Club, the Dade County League of Women Voters, the Florida Army of Democratic Women and the Southern Cross Chapter of the United Daughters of the Confederacy, of which she was president in 1932. As a boy, Davey would tag along at some of the events and was exposed to history, reading and music. Unlike his on-the-field personality, he was rather gentle and soft-spoken, and he made friends easily at Miami High, where he participated in three sports: football, basketball and track. He was active in the Key Club service organization, elected vice president of his junior class and voted most popular. In short, he was a model student, described by Jesse Yarborough as "orderly, courteous, very cooperative, level-headed and above all a very good student." [14]

Granted, the coach could have said the same thing about practically any of his players, who, for the most part, had solid upbringings and socio-economic advantages over their Garfield brethren.

Halfback Harvey Comfort, for instance, led a rather comfortable lifestyle, untouched by the Depression although not by tragedy. His great uncle was Walter R. Comfort. The "R" was for Rockefeller, his mother's prodigiously successful family. The Comforts were among the earliest settlers of Newburgh, New York, and Walter made use of the sprawling dairy lands of Orange County to build a fortune in the ice cream business.

By the 1900s, Comfort was among the wealthiest men in New York. He soon saw an opportunity to expand his empire in the untapped, yet high-potential city of Miami. He and candy manufacturer John C. Huyler realized that the black muck soils of the Everglades were ideal for growing the sugar cane essential to both industries, and they partnered in scooping up 12,000 acres adjacent to what was then Miami's municipal border. While their sugar cane visions never materialized, the land only soared in value. In 1917, the construction of the Comfort Canal drained 1,000 acres of Everglades that was used for farming and cattle ranching. When the land boom of the early 1920s hit, Comfort turned a nice profit by selling off 50 acres to Detroit developer J.A. Campbell, who, in turn, named the tract Comfort Gardens and subdivided it, touting it as one of the most desirable spots in Miami.

There, at the corner of Seventh Street and 34th Avenue (at the edge of busy Little Havana today), Walter's brother—and Harvey's grandfather—Harvey Daniel Comfort (all the Comforts shared in Walter's success) set up a small farm. It wasn't until Harvey was seven

years old, however, that he got to Miami. His father, Harvey
Harrison Comfort, had remained in Orange County as an execu-
tive with the original ice cream company, and, in 1927, his mother
Grace died of pneumonia. Not long after, the Comforts' home in
Newburgh burned down, and Harvey's father moved the family
in with his parents in Miami.

Harvey's grandfather put him to work, feeding the farm's 300
chickens and milking the two cows. Harvey became so accomplished he could hit a target by squirting from 20 feet away. Stored
in stainless steel containers, the milk had an added benefit.

"I'd reach in there at the top and pull off the cream," Comfort
said. "I drank more cream than you wouldn't believe. About 45
minutes before I left for a football game, I'd drink a pint of it. I had
more good energy. I felt like I was cheating on those guys."

Harvey Comfort.

The Comforts' cow pasture also provided Harvey with his first football playing field. On
Sundays, he started playing with a bunch of friends who, dodging the cow flops, called themselves the "Shit Kickers." Future Miami High teammate Jay Kendrick was one of the gang
and the games soon included a few Miami High players as well. The games were so good that
passers-by would often pull over their cars and watch.

Kendrick, the other "Shit Kicker," was a naturally-gifted lineman, a 225-pound strongman
with a chest that measured 46½ inches when he later enlisted in the Army. If Eldredge was
the offensive MVP, Kendrick was that on defense. No offensive lineman could handle him.
He could break up plays in the backfield just by tossing his man aside. Even in high school,
he had a deep voice, adding to the intimidation any opponent might feel.

"He was Mr. Special," Harvey Comfort marveled. "He was so strong, a different guy than
anybody else. He could grab anybody and pick him up by the back of the shoulders and throw
them around like a tin can."

Family lore had it that Kendrick's maternal family, the Chandlers, ended up in Miami
from South Georgia, because someone stole the family's dog. Chandler supposedly got on his
horse with his shotgun and tracked the thief all the way to Miami. Once he got there, he liked
it and sent for the rest of the family. That's where Lucile Chandler, Jay's mother, was born in
1901. Jay's father, John Pike Kendrick, was another transplanted South Georgian. Looking
for adventure, Kendrick joined the Army and was part of the chase for Pancho Villa on the
Mexican border, followed by a stint in World War I. He was back in Miami in 1920, when he
married Lucile. Jay was born a year later.

The Kendricks opened a butcher shop/grocery store that did well enough for them to
afford some land near Fort Myers. Unable to pay the taxes on it during the Depression, they
lost it. Still, John Kendrick kept the store open and won a contract to supply all the greyhound
tracks with meat for the dogs. There was always something cooking on the stove in the store,
and their son Jay ate well—and grew well.

At Miami High, Kendrick became best friends with another brawny youngster. Mike
Osceola was the second great-grandson of the first Seminole chief Osceola, nicknamed
the "Swamp Fox" for his daring raids on U.S. troops during the Indian Wars of the 1830s.
Captured under a white flag and sent to Fort Moultrie prison, the chief died there of malaria
in 1838, a hero to his people.

A century later, Mike Osceola wasn't a hero to his people, at least not in 1937, when he was the first Seminole to enroll in a public school, Miami High. The tribe resented him for it, but he proudly defied them. His father, Chief William McKinley Osceola, believed that public education was the right path for future Seminole generations.

Born in the Everglades, Mike lived in a hut until he was 10 years old when his family moved to open a trading post at Musa Isle, a tourist area just outside Miami on the Tamiami Trail. A man-child at 13, he wrestled his first alligator on a dare at a family wedding, and he was soon entertaining visitors to the trading post by throwing around 225 pounders. He became so adept that he toured up and down the East Coast during the summer months, nearly losing his head to one of the reptiles in a Niagara Falls exhibition in 1937. "I must have touched his tongue because his mouth snapped nearly shut," he explained.

Mike had been encouraged by his father to learn the "white man's" language and customs from an early age and taught him English out of a Sears Roebuck catalogue. Still, at 16, on his first day of school at Miami High, he had only a rudimentary knowledge of grammar and mathematics. He nevertheless worked hard with his tutors, including Jesse Yarborough, who took a genuine interest in him. So did track coach Pete Tulley, who attempted, unsuccessfully, to teach him the mechanics of the javelin throw. Undeterred, Mike brought the javelin back to the Everglades one weekend, so he could learn the art of spear hunting from fellow Seminoles. When he returned, he beat his previous best by 40 feet and became a champion, earning himself the nickname "Big Mike."

"From then on, I gave up coaching," Tulley joked.[15]

Yarborough did not. He turned the alligator wrestler into a football lineman. The hardest part was encouraging his aggression. Osceola was concerned that he'd hurt someone. Yarborough really helped him along, though and the two remained close always.

Osceola played in 1938 and again in 1940, when he really excelled. But, for some reason, he played only one game in 1939. He was mentioned in pre-season stories and was included in the team picture taken before the season but seems to have been ineligible, perhaps academically. In any case, he and Kendrick made quite the pair as they palled around with each other. Osceola even taught Kendrick the fine art of gator wrestling. They would strap a medium-sized specimen onto their bicycle handle bars and ride to one of the downtown theatres, where they would wrestle it onstage and get into the feature for free, according to Kendrick's son, Bill. He didn't know what they did with the gator in the meantime.

A number of other Miami players also had interesting family backgrounds but, for the most part, their fathers held down white-collar jobs. Tackle Dick Fauth's father, Christian, was a German immigrant who became one of Miami's leading furniture dealers. Tackle Henry Washington's father, Raoul, was in the U.S. diplomatic corps, the vice consul to Cuba. Red Mathews' father, Thomas, sold insurance. Tackle Doug Craven's father, William, born in England, was the valet for Edmond A. Guggenheim and worked to keep the copper magnate in trim on his business trips to South America. Later, Craven became the chief steward on Guggenheim's yacht, the job that took him to Miami, where he opened a boat shop. Doug, born in Brooklyn in 1921, lived briefly in East Rutherford before the family moved to Florida. Had they not, he probably would have played on the line against Garfield for East Rutherford High School. Square-jawed, Craven had rugged good looks and was a top-notch jitter-bugger and not unpopular with the girls.

Three Stingarees lost their fathers in their youth. For glue-fingered end Charlie Burrus and

Mike Osceola, Stingaree lineman, in a publicity photo explaining football to members of his Seminole tribe in native dress at the practice field outside Miami High School.
Courtesy Larry "Mike" Osceola estate.

Paul Lewis, a reserve in 1939 (but a future Hall of Fame center), it could not have been more traumatic.

Burrus had just turned eight when his father Wendell Searcy, an insurance agent, moved the family from Tampa to Miami in November, 1927. A month later, he told his wife, Dorothy, he needed to travel to Jacksonville for a business opportunity. Once there, however, he told his roommate he expected never to see his wife and four children again and walked out with an empty glass and a bottle of mercury bichloride tablets. Despondent over his health and finances, Burrus was intent on poisoning himself. The roommate notified authorities, who found the 36-year-old man near death. His wife rushed to his bedside, where he was thought to be recovering. He died five days later.

Four years later, Dorothy remarried James Alva Hearn, a successful building contractor who provided Charley and his siblings a comfortable home life.

Paul Louis' father, Louis Louis, had come to Miami from Key West with his father, Adolph, in 1923 and established A. Louis and Sons, a men's clothier. The store had just been moved into more elegant quarters on Flagler Street when Louis Louis took a revolver and fired a shot into his chest. Although friends noted he seemed nervous for weeks, no motive for the suicide was established. The business was in sound financial condition. Paul Louis was just six years old. He was raised by his mother, Ruth, who also took over the store's operation.

As Harvey Comfort did with his cow pasture buddies, Paul Louis started playing football with a neighborhood team called the 29th Street Bonecrushers. He developed the ability to make the center snap, and Yarborough quickly added him to the varsity roster as a 10th grader. His teammates nicknamed him "A-Loo" after the name of the men's shop.

Lineman Gilbert Wilson, whom they called "Pretty Boy" as the best-looking guy in the school, was born in Chicago and christened Gilbert Cleary Hayes. His father, Curtis Franklin Hayes, a railroad worker, was crushed to death in an accident when Gilbert was just six years old. Gilbert's mother, Felicia, remarried a Scot, John J. Wilson, who gave the children his name as the family resettled in Miami. Wilson was hard man and Gilbert often accepted his stepfather's strict admonitions to protect his younger sister, Donelda. But there was one dictate he could not accept. When John Wilson prohibited his stepson from playing football at Miami High, Gilbert disobeyed him. He still worked in Wilson's stonemason business but sneaked around him and managed to make every practice and game. John Wilson didn't find out until Gilbert joined the team for a late-season road trip to Atlanta. He at last relented after watching Gilbert play in a game. Blessed with natural strength inherited from his natural father, Gilbert was one of the Stingarees' best blocking linemen.

Sophomore back Gene Autrey (no relation to the singer/songwriter/actor) suffered the loss of a parent in a different way. His parents divorced shortly after they moved to Miami from Athens, Georgia, and he spent much of his youth in foster homes until reuniting with his mother and two siblings.

Reserve back Pericles Nichols, who was called "Percolator" because he stuttered, was the son of a builder, Gus Nichols, a Greek immigrant. Nichols, like Craven, was among those players raised in Miami's outskirts. He, Red Mathews and Levin Rollins were all Alabama-born. Rollins' father, Levin Sr., was one of 15 children, the son of a Dothan, Alabama judge. A train conductor who operated on some of the same tracks his father once helped lay, Levin Sr. moved the family to Miami after some time in the Panama City, Florida, area. George Rogers had just moved down from Ocala. And Harvey James arrived at Miami High after the school year started in 1939. James was from Savannah, Georgia and quickly earned the nickname "Geechee" after the distinct dialect spoken in the low country.

James' reputation preceded him, athletically and as a troublemaker. His father, William, was never in his life. When Harvey's mother, Catherine, became pregnant with him in 1919, nine years after their second son was born, William reacted by walking out on the family. The athletic Harvey ended up under the wing of several Savannah coaches who looked after him but, for some reason, they couldn't keep him on the straight and narrow. Harvey had a difficult time at Benedictine Military Academy, where he would not be harnessed by the tight reins held by the Catholic monks. Although he starred on the football and baseball teams as a center and catcher, respectively, he was eventually expelled for unspecified bad behavior. His mother then sent Harvey off to live with a family she knew in Miami, the Melchings. Jesse Yarborough, no doubt, was delighted.

Jason Koesy's father, Szilard, emigrated with his family from Hungary when he was 12 and settled in Cleveland, eventually marrying an Ohio farm girl before moving to Florida. Szilard Koesy worked in real estate until the market went bust, then for Florida Power & Light. The Koesys first lived in a two-story building on 15th Street and, while Szilard was at work, Lola, his wife, ran a small grocery store on the first floor. The shelves were stacked with canned goods in front of bushels of fresh produce. The store also stocked meat, butter and eggs. By 1939, they had closed the store and moved to a fourth home in the Citrus Grove neighborhood while Szilard worked for the city of Miami as clerk in the water works department.

"During the Depression, he had a steady job," explained Jason's younger brother, Calvin. "It didn't pay very much but we stuck together as a family. We had meals together every night as a family; we were all together around the table, Dad was a good father authority, he made us kids toe the line. And we kind of managed to get through the tough times. Every one of my brothers and sisters graduated from college."

As the family eventually grew to include seven children (Barbara, the youngest, was born in 1934), Jason, the oldest, was left in charge of the rest when his parents were away.

"We respected him and we did what he said," Calvin noted. "I can never remember him getting into trouble and he was an A-student in high school. When I came along four years later, the teachers would tell me, 'I remember Jason. I hope you can do as well as he did.'"

Koesy did have a brush with trouble, and it almost cost Miami High its best passer. The Koesys always had a Fourth of July celebration and would send away to Ohio for fireworks. When Jason was 14, he paused to see if a firecracker fuse was lit. It exploded in his hands but he somehow escaped serious injury. Spared, Koesy saw considerable playing time for the Stingarees beginning as a sophomore in 1937. But he played the same quarterback position as Eldredge did and played less than he would have otherwise.

They were, to say the least, a disparate bunch, bound by a common cause. Just as their Boilermaker counterparts, the Stingarees revered their coach. Jesse Yarborough may have had a softer exterior than Art Argauer but he was, without question, the boss.

Arnold Tucker, the great Army quarterback who played for Yarborough in 1941, said that Yarborough, "was not rough or mean but was very exacting in his communicating what he wanted from his players. I'd like to use the word disciplinarian but he didn't really discipline his players, he was more exact, with determination . . . drive, give your best. He demanded the best of an individual."

"When he walked into the room, everyone stood at attention," Harvey Comfort explained. "He wasn't a badass. He was a gentleman. But he was very regimented. You either did it his way or you didn't do it. He just made it a point that, 'this is what you were going to do.'"

A perfect example was the few times the Stingarees travelled to away games. Before each of those trips, Yarborough held a team meeting to make clear what was expected of each player; that they were representing Miami High. For starters, everyone was required to travel in jacket and tie. He didn't want anyone blowing his nose in public or walking around with a toothpick in his mouth. Above all, no one could be caught smoking, even though, like Art Argauer, Yarborough enjoyed his Chesterfields and attempted to hide that vice from his team.

In *The Stingaree Century*, his history of Miami High, author Howard Kleinberg quotes several players. They paint the picture of a master psychologist.

Bruce Smith, a star on the 1941 team and, later a Navy Rear Admiral, noted that Yarborough prepared his players not just for football but also for life, "for living properly and studying." He could be intimidating, but Smith noted he knew how to handle different personalities. He'd shout at those who needed it, and let up on those who wouldn't react well.

John Oakley, a sophomore on the 1939 team, recalled an incident a year later in this excerpt from *The Stingaree Century*:

> *"We were up in Jacksonville for a game and I was roomed with Bruce Smith," he said. "I had a tendency to smoke now and then and there comes a knock on the door. I flipped*

the cigarette in the toilet and flushed it. In walks Yarborough and he asks: 'Who's smoking in here?' No one said anything. But he knew Bruce didn't smoke, so when we got back to Miami, Yarborough told me to report the next morning at 8 am. He didn't say why, but I knew. He ran my butt off that morning. The next year, we're up in Jacksonville again and on the train going up, Yarborough comes up to me. 'Oakley,' he said, 'I had a dream last night. I dreamed that I walked into your room and caught you smoking.' I said, 'Coach, that wasn't a dream, that was a nightmare.'[16]

Drinking, naturally, was forbidden. According to Bruce Smith, Yarborough made it seem that just one drink made you a drunkard. Yarborough also tried, with less success, to keep a handle on his players' relationships with the fairer sex, even though dates usually consisted of innocent trips downtown, sometimes on bikes. When his players flirted with girls in the courtyards after school, he'd tell them, "Stop seeing those gulls," in his South Carolina drawl. Autrey said he got the first sex lecture of his life from Yarborough. "He'd start off by telling us we'd be better off by not fooling around," Autrey recollected.[17]

Not many of the Stingarees had steady girlfriends, but Levin Rollins and Harvey Comfort were the exceptions. They both ended up marrying their younger high school sweethearts. Comfort remembered how he fell for Jeanne Shaffer when she sang for him. "I liked what I saw," Comfort said with a laugh. "When you were on the Miami High football team, that was something. It paid with the girls." There were a few other privileges, as well. They could, for example, work in the cafeteria and lunch for free. But that meant they had to work. No one loafed.

Likewise, Yarborough's practices were no picnic. In 1939, his home was about a mile from the Stingarees' spacious practice field behind the school. When the wind was right, his family could hear his booming voice barking instructions with the occasional admonition. If a player got out of line or messed up an assignment, he'd get a swift boot in the backside. To play football in Miami, a player had to be in shape. Yarborough made sure of that. He took wind sprints one step further. Each player had to pair up with someone his size. He would put his partner on his shoulders and run the 120-yard length of the field. Then he'd climb onto his partner's shoulders for the return trip.

He also had a way of thinning out the herd. In *The Stingaree Century*, Kleinberg recounts Autrey's typical experience after going out for football. With only so many practice uniforms to go around, the newcomers dressed in shorts, held blocking dummies and observed. Several quit out of boredom. "If you stood there long enough," Autry said, "Yarborough would say: 'Go ahead, son, go get a uniform.'"[18] That was just the beginning of it. Every newbie would be thrown onto defense to see if they could stand up to the pounding.

If you made it, though, there was nothing like being a Stingaree.

"No one had it better than us. We were surrounded by class people with first-class facilities. Everything was top drawer," Comfort said. "I got everything I ever wanted out of it."

Well, almost, anyway.

EIGHT

THE SCOURGE

On a sweltering St. Stephen's Day in 1932, the Toledo Waite High School football team smuggled an uninvited guest into Miami's Moore Park, where the Indians were taking on Miami High in the Stingarees' annual Christmas game. Floyd Wright, hidden under a tarpaulin, lay flat on the hot metal roof of a bus parked behind the end zone. From that bizarre vantage, he watched his teammates play on a field where he could not.

Floyd Wright was Waite's All City tackle. He was everything you'd want in a football player: mean, sinewy, fast and strong, destined for enshrinement in the school's Hall of Fame. But Floyd Wright wasn't everything they wanted in a football player below Mason and Dixon's line of scrimmage. Floyd Wright lacked one thing. He wasn't white. In Miami, Jim Crow picked the sides, strictly by race, which is why Wright was forced to watch his teammates that day, not from the back of the bus, but hidden atop it.

Either way, it stung the soul.

Segregation. It was the flip side to Miami's Song of Paradise. If slavery was the Peculiar Institution, Jim Crow was its grandson, a different way to continue the subjugation. Fueled by the bitterness of Reconstruction that persisted in the memory of many Southerners, the system was still a couple of generations away from being dragged—kicking and screaming—to its demise. It was fervently alive in Miami when, in 1929, the Stingarees first invited a northern team down for Christmas and Salem High from Massachusetts began a tradition that lasted into the war years. In 1932, Waite was the first northern visitor to run up against another tradition, Dixie's most stringent.

"Things were that way in the South back then," said Wright's teammate, Jim Thayer, in a 1979 interview with the *Toledo Blade*. "Floyd couldn't play but we got him in on top of the bus and he watched the game from there."[1]

Why Wright even accompanied the team to Miami under such circumstances is an unanswered question. Waite's coach, Don McCallister, was all too aware of what awaited a black player in the South. He brought national prominence to the Stingarees as their coach from

1928 to 1930, and he would have known he couldn't run interference for Wright across the color line. But the Illinois native, undoubtedly, was sympathetic. His brother, Frank, was an attorney for the Civil Liberties Union and would be part of the defense of the Scottsboro boys, nine African American teenagers accused of raping two white women on a train in Alabama in 1931. Apparently, Miami authorities had not asked if there were "Negroes" on the Waite team. Perhaps they assumed their former coach would tacitly understand. In any event, McCallister didn't volunteer that information.

Wright's name, however, appeared in the list of 20 travelling players McCallister provided to the Toledo papers and he practiced with the team in Toledo before the trip. It seemed clear that McCallister had intended Wright to play.

"Watch 'em. There's a charge for you." McCallister said to the Toledo writers as they watched Wright and the others practice. "If these boys go like that against Miami Monday afternoon we'll have some chance."[2]

When Waite's special rail car crossed the Ohio River into Kentucky—reversing the old path of the Underground Railroad—things had to have changed for Wright. With stops in Chattanooga, Atlanta and Jacksonville, he certainly would have attracted attention, especially when McCallister hustled his players out of the train car for calisthenics. Who knows what Wright was thinking as his gaze fixed on chain gangs of black prisoners toiling along the tracks in Georgia, until, finally, the team pulled into Miami on Christmas Day, a day before the game? It wasn't until then, it seems, that Wright's status was settled.

The only clue of what had transpired was an innocuous mention by Frank Buckley in his game-day story in the *Toledo News-Bee*. Buried near the bottom was McCallister's announcement of one change to his starting lineup, "sending Toughie Lorencz" to left tackle, yet making no mention that he was replacing Wright.[3] In fact, not a word was written about it in any publication, not even in the cheerful account of the trip that appeared in the Waite High yearbook:

> *Good morning, ladies and gentlemen. Here we are in sunny Florida on this beautiful December morning just off the coast at Miami in a forty-foot fishing boat. All around are boys fishing or lying about lazily, beautiful specimens of manhood who are here as a reward for their unequaled success in football. They have just yesterday won their twelfth straight victory, beating the mighty Miami eleven. Twenty strong, clean young men with their coach Don McCallister, a sturdy Southerner himself and Frank Pauly, his assistant, are here representing Waite High School and the whole East Side in Toledo, through whose whole-hearted support they have been able to achieve the mythical National Football Championship.[4]*

Guaranteed, Wright was not among those lounging about on the fishing boat. He wouldn't have been allowed to enjoy this or any other excursion with his teammates. McCallister used his Miami connections to house him with a black family. But in one respect, as humiliating as it may have been for Wright on top of that bus, his coach and teammates had achieved a small victory by smuggling him inside the gates of the stadium, where no black man was permitted, even as a spectator.

Wright watched his teammates fight back in the second half to post a 13-7 win over a Miami team that lost its star, Dick Plasman, to an injury early in the game. That made

Floyd Wright strikes a mean pose among his Waite High School teammates.
Courtesy Howard Wright

headlines. Nowhere was it mentioned that Waite was also missing a key player. When the Waite team headed back to Ohio, the experience was forgotten by most everyone but Floyd Wright. It would shape the rest of his inspirational life.

The last member of the Wright family to have left the state of Florida was Floyd Wright's grandfather, a slave. At the end of the Civil War, he had simply walked off the plantation that had once "owned" him and kept walking until he got to Paris, Tennessee, in the northwest corner of the state. There, he claimed his 40 acres and a mule from confiscated Confederate land, which is still in the family to this day. If a Wright ever complained about walking anywhere, he or she would be humbled by the story that "Great Granddaddy" had trudged across three states.

Floyd Wright enjoyed another great season as a senior and was considered for a scholarship by Ohio State if he could get his grades up. Instead, he married and soon had a son to support. Professional football was out of the question because, from 1933 through 1946, National Football League owners had a "gentleman's" agreement against signing black players. He played a little semipro ball but gave it up because he couldn't afford to get hurt, working three jobs at a bakery, foundry and dairy (where they feared black hands would contaminate the milk). Nevertheless, Wright persisted, performing each job with dignity, impressing each boss with his work ethic and skill. As wife Elinora would tell the children, "the only thing we have is our honor." When Wright left after 25 years, the dairy owner wrote in his recommendation, "Here's a man who worked for me 25 years, was late not one day and was only out sick two days and that is when a family member passed away. Just an outstanding worker."

It was 1939, in November, when their second son was born. As a 13-year-old, Ernie Wright was a self-described "fat" kid when he came home from Toledo Scott High School one day and proudly said, 'Hey Pop, I made the football team—I made the freshman team."

Floyd Wright scowled. "What's a freshman team? No son of mine is going to play freshman football. If you're going to play football, I'm going to show you how to play football." The son nodded, unaware of what lay in store for him. He'd find out the next day when Floyd, home for dinner between jobs, looked at him and said, "Let's go to the backyard."

It had rained most of the day and Elinora Wright looked nervously out the bay window at the scene in the muddy yard. Floyd was still in his work shoes, and his pants were covered with flour from the bakery. Ernie had never played a down of football in his life, so when his father ordered him to get into a football position, he attempted a pathetic three-point stance. Floyd grumbled, then positioned his son's hips correctly and worked on his balance and leverage.

Then he told him, "O.K., now come off the line and hit me."

Floyd Wright was in his thirties, still a physical specimen, hardened by the all the arduous labor over the years. So, when Ernie came out of his stance, ever so tentatively, he was rocked by a vicious forearm to his chest. And it happened over and over. The father and son practiced like this every day. Ernie would return home with his football gear on from team practice . . . for a more brutal practice with Pop.

"My Dad told us this story over and over," said Howard Wright, Ernie's son. "It was a year of torture. But my grandfather insisted, 'no son of mine is not going to be great.' My grandfather had a short temper, a grumpy disposition. He was quintessentially tough on his son, beyond demanding, quick to critique and slow to praise. This was tough love—to harden his son, to steel him. If he was going to do something, he was going to do it the best."

Four years later, Ernie Wright was recruited by Woody Hayes to play football for the Ohio State Buckeyes. He turned into one of the best defensive ends in the American Football League with the Los Angeles/San Diego Chargers and Cincinnati Bengals. He ended a 13-year professional career in 1972 after the NFL-AFL merger.

Howard Wright, Floyd's grandson, starred on the basketball team at Stanford University and made it to the National Basketball Association. Ernie Wright died of leukemia in 2007, but the foundation he established, the Pro Kids Golf and Learning Academy, now run by Howard, has helped thousands of inner-city kids in San Diego.

"My father did not become Ernie Wright until he put his fingers in the mud in the back yard," Howard said. "And what Floyd Ambriss Wright did was make sure that no son of his would have to sit on the periphery of anything in his life.

"My grandfather was pained his entire life by not getting the chance to get off the top of that bus and get onto that field," Howard Wright went on. "He was in an internal straight-jacket of the hatred, disdain and bitterness of that day in Miami and, instead of having that engulf him, he injected it into his son to make him something to be proud of and change the entire arc of our family for generations. He channeled all that rage and all of his ability into a 13-year-old child and that 13-year-old child went on to play for Woody Hayes and then 13 years in the NFL. You can't make that up.

"Signing up to be a Wright man is not an easy thing," Howard said. "But the more I understand the sacrifice of my grandfather, the more I see why you have to put your hands in the mud."

When Floyd Wright's sons pulled him out of his home in Toledo to live in California, he went to work for McDonnell Douglas, where he sealed and tested aircraft windows. "Only one job this time," laughed Howard, who spent summers with his grandparents. He remembers his grandfather every time he looks outside an airplane window.

"He went to work at five and got home at two-thirty and he would come back to the house and would go play golf on these terrible public golf courses that I have to say, provided me with some of the sweetest moments of my life. I saw a much softer side of the product," he laughed.

"Even when my father was in his fifties, I could still see the deference and respect for the man sitting on the other side of the Thanksgiving table," he said. "It was reverence; that what it was. It was a thank you that my father could never voice or narrate properly. You just felt it.

"My father was always the alpha man in the room. Guys wanted to be with him and talk football, ladies wanted to be around him. But I noticed even at a young age, the axis of power. When my grandfather walked in the room the conversation either started or it stopped and gravitated to what Grandpa wanted."

Floyd Wright wasn't the last black football player who suffered such Jim Crow indignities in Miami. He was followed by Clint Williams of Elmira (New York) High School in 1935, Lew Pope of Oak Park (Illinois) High School in 1937 and Richard Stevenson of McKeesport (Pennsylvania) High School in 1938. None of them accompanied their teams to Miami, although each story has a different nuance.

Lew Pope. 1938 Tabula.

Clint Williams played on Elmira's undefeated 1935 and 1936 teams. Early in the 1935 season, he replaced one of the team's starting end due to an injury and never came out of the lineup—until, of course, the Miami game. Against rival Union-Endicott, Elmira's closest of the year, Williams scooped up a blocked punt and ran it across the goal line for the winning touchdown.

While the Toledo press ignored the Floyd Wright affair, Williams' plight was well covered by the *Elmira Star-Gazette*. Coach Art Hirst had initially requested the paper not report Williams' impending dilemma. However, once Elmira accepted the invitation to play the winner of the Miami-Edison game, Williams' mother, Mabel, issued a statement that the family would not permit their son to make the trip—that the "racial prejudices" of the South would make the trip "unwise and embarrassing" for her son.[5]

Williams was immediately praised for taking one for the team. "Here is the case of a proud mother who realizes that a sacrifice must be made, not only for her son, but also to forestall any embarrassing situation for his team and clear the situation up for a public asked to help send the team South," Ed Van Dyke wrote in his Fan Fare column.

Van Dyke added: "The colored race, seemingly, understands the situation of racial prejudice in the South better than the whites of Elmira. And so Clint knew from the outset that if EHS was invited South that he could not go. But he played his hardest throughout the rest of the season—and played with a smile. He knew that the feeling of the South could not be changed. But he stuck to his guns for the sake of his team and his mates. I think Elmira should be proud, both of Clinton Williams and his parents."[6]

The team and the city rallied around Williams. The committee charged with raising funds for the trip gave Williams the same amount of spending money allotted to those players travelling to Florida. The team vowed to win the game for him and, at a banquet held in the team's honor before it departed for Miami, Williams was introduced as "the man of the hour."[7]

Williams, at first, wise-cracked and laughed bravely with his teammates at the train station. But, when it was time to leave the train, he threw his arms around team captain Bill Wescott and sobbed as the rest of travelling party furtively turned away. "Everyone felt so helpless, unable to think what could be said," Van Dyke reported.

"Boys, that's tough," Van Dyke quoted Wescott saying after Williams had gone. "We have to bring that football back to Clint."[8]

When the team arrived in Miami, Hirst lamented the absence of Williams in an *Associated Press* story.

"The only thing is our line will be lightened considerably by not having our Negro left end, Clinton Williams, with us. We thought it inadvisable to bring him south," he said.[9]

But neither the *Miami News* nor the *Miami Herald* mentioned Williams. In fact, the *Herald* ran a picture of the team sent from Elmira. Williams was conspicuously absent from the 18 players shown. It is also notable that, next to a feature on the team written for the *News* by Van Dyke (also omitting mention of Williams) was a story—on Booker T. Washington (Miami's high school for African Americans) playing Stanton of Jacksonville for the "Negro high school football championship of the state" at the "Negro city ballpark."

Elmira, as it turned out, kept its promise to Williams and thumped Miami, 13-0. Williams was there to greet his teammates when they pulled back into Elmira, and the *Star-Gazette* captured his handshake with Wescott, both of them smiling. Williams was officially presented with the game ball at the team banquet, where he wore his letterman sweater under his jacket. It was reported, rather euphemistically, that Williams was "unable to travel to Florida."[10]

The next time a black player was "unable to travel to Florida," it kicked up a serious debate. Lew Pope, nicknamed the "Ebony Streak," was the backfield star of Oak Park High School, Suburban League champions of Chicago. But, instead of Pope sacrificing for his teammates by remaining home, many thought that his teammates should have sacrificed for Pope by refusing to make the trip.

Although black families were a minority, Oak Park was, for its era, a progressive enclave. Its clubs and civic organizations hosted black performing artists and intellectuals from the Harlem Renaissance, including Zora Neale Hurston, Paul Robeson and, later, Langston Hughes.

Pope's maternal grandparents, Thurman and Eliza Martin, were the first black residents and homeowners in the east section of Oak Park, moving there from Missouri. Thurman opened an excavating business and, after Pope's parents divorced, he and his mother moved in with them.

Pope was one of the few African Americans at Oak Park High School. He was a popular student and admired for his prowess on the football and basketball teams. Little did Miami High know when it extended the invitation, that the Huskies' key player was black. It's also not clear whether Pope's mother, Leva, like Mabel Williams, would not allow him to make the trip. Apparently, though, coach Glenn Holmes tried to make arrangements to bring him to Miami even if he couldn't suit up.

Holmes accepted the bid on November 30 and, two days later, the *Miami News* ran an *International News Service* wire story headlined, *Negro Back at Oak Park Out of Game*. The short article mentioned that some of Pope's teammates had been insisting that he accompany them on the trip and quoted Principal H.R. McDaniel, who said, "I'm sorry about the development at Miami. Pope is a fine student and a good player."[11]

That dismissal sparked outrage. Oak Park's newspaper, *Oak Leaves*, received several letters denouncing the school's decision to accept the invitation without Pope:

> *"Is justice of higher value than school prestige? I am sure Oak Park people feel that it is and that they would rather see their school team stay at home than to countenance an insult to one of their boys, Lew Pope, and to his race."*
>
> —*Joseph Golden*

> *"Not only is this a great injustice to this fine athlete, but it places our high school in the class of those who are narrowed by racial prejudice. It makes us a party to the display of that prejudice."*
>
> —*E.L. Kimball*

> *"He had a large share in bringing to Oak Park its 1937 Suburban League championship. Are the local lads going to do the right thing by Pope?"*
>
> —*Harold W. Flitcraft*[12]

The *Chicago Defender*, the city's African American newspaper, insisted that Holmes cancel the game, "rather than yield to southern prejudice."

"In the first place, Holmes should never have been permitted to schedule the game knowing that Lew Pope or any other player who is not white would not be allowed to play," the paper said. "Holmes, who says he values the services of Pope very highly, doesn't make any hit with the sport-loving public when he bows to the prejudices of the south which seemingly wants a team its school can ship and bars crack players on the ground that they are not white. Let them keep their confounded nastiness down in Florida, Mississippi, Georgia or any other part of the south. Don't bring it up here and don't allow them to sow their seeds or race prejudice up here."[13]

An editorial in the *Defender*'s December 18 edition, went further, claiming, "The South won another victory over the North when Coach Glenn Holmes and Principal M.R. McDaniel of the Oak Park High School meekly and unmanly submitted to the demand," adding that they "are willing to sacrifice Pope on the altar of race prejudice rather than uphold a respectable principle."

The paper mocked Holmes' efforts to take Pope along "in some other capacity," suggesting that he "may go as a mascot dressed in a red cap and green suit, which will serve to appease the Southerners and further humiliate Pope." It claimed that a Miami official offered to furnish Pope with a jackass to "ride between the halves and amuse the crowd," but that Pope "would have to leave during play because Negroes are not permitted to witness white football games down here."[14]

Warren Stevens, sports editor of *Oak Leaves*, presented both arguments as he pondered this "problem of ethics:"

> *Judging from letters to* Oak Leaves *and casual conversations about town, many village people think that the local school should have refused the game immediately after any*

question of racial discrimination was suggested. Such action would be in keeping with the fair and liberal attitude traditional to the community.

On the other hand, the attitude of school authorities is understandable. A team of champions in all senses of the word sought a post-season game. It was offered a place in the most desirable high school classic in the country, a sort of prep Rose Bowl game. To accept, understanding the social tradition of the southern states, meant doing an injustice to one player. To refuse, according to the generally accepted point of view, would have been in some sense an injustice to the other ten youths.

The Gordian knot of racial relationships is not easily undone but one thing is certain. Lew Pope, a fine manly young athlete who refuses to mope or pout at the rebuffs of fate, has the sympathy of the whole community. He has had to absorb more than his share of punishment all season; one more blow will scarcely break his spirit.[15]

Pope saw his teammates off on their Greyhound bus. After receiving a standing ovation, he read the play-by-play of the 6-6 tie from the stage of the junior high school as details of the game—as well as his teammates' salutations—were relayed back from Miami. In 1996, he was interviewed for a segment of *Legends of Our Time*.

"I just wanted to be big about it . . . to be more honorable about it . . . and not hold it against the team," he said. "I knew that was the way of life. I wasn't any stranger to the customs of the South."[16]

Dr. Percy Julian, an African American research chemist who pioneered the synthesis of medicinal drugs from plants, wrote a letter to the editor of *Oak Leaves* that ran just before the game. In it, he asked the young men fortunate enough to represent Oak Park in Miami not to quickly forget the "unpleasant" affair:

Miami is after all so tempting a land of sunshine and adventure for our high school youth that we can hardly expect them not to choke down their sentimental attachment to this negro comrade and choose this "glorious" respite from the biting winds of Lake Michigan . . . After the game and the excitement of your trip are over, some of you, I hope, as a result of this experience, will begin to see the obvious conflict between your elders' social preachments and your social practices. You will realize that your high school teachers—despite their attempts at rationalization—have officially paid tribute to the teaching of hate in our schools. You will realize the lonely road [to] which Pope has been condemned by this and similar decisions to travel.[17]

A year later, there was little social consciousness displayed when McKeesport High School received its invitation. Richard Stevenson started at tackle for that team and played quarterback the next season. He had been abandoned by his father at birth and raised by his mother, who came to every game he played as the Tigers won the Western Pennsylvania Athletic League's 1938 championship and a bid to the Miami game. But, even though Stevenson was a star player like Williams and Pope, no word of protest was written when Stevenson was not included to make the trip, He simply didn't go, and that was that. In a 50-year anniversary story in the *Pittsburgh Post-Gazette*, Falco Corrozzo said his absence was sorely missed in the 21-14 loss.[18]

According to Stevenson's daughter, Iris Nimmo, McKeesport's coach felt so badly about leaving him behind that he bought him a new suit. Whenever Stevenson talked about it later in life, he said McKeesport would have won the game if he'd played. Like Floyd Wright and Clint Williams, who played football at Howard University and became a councilman in East Orange, New Jersey, Stevenson used the experience to harden himself. He proudly joined the Army in World War II and had a career as a welder in the Naval shipyard in Norfolk, Virginia.

"He had such a strong personality and was so outspoken that, when he couldn't get a promotion, he just took early retirement. He was just sick of it. He had enough so he left," his daughter explained. "After that he drove a school bus for three years. He made every child on that bus behave but he was so sweet and tenderhearted that they always gave him Valentine's candy."

Had any of those teams refused to play without their African Americans, it would have been groundbreaking. College teams had set the precedent and would continue to do so. Boston College, for instance, had Lou Montgomery out of Brockton, Massachusetts. He was among the top scorers in New England high school football in 1936, and was the first black athlete to wear a Boston College uniform. He excelled, as expected, on the freshman team in 1937.

The following year—his first on the varsity squad—Montgomery was nailed to the bench by Gil Dobie, described by the *Baltimore Afro-American* as a "Jim Crowish" coach, and, who also favored more of a plodding offense that didn't suit Montgomery's skills.[19]

Boston College fired Dobie after that season and replaced him with the soon-to-be legendary Frank Leahy. Leahy unleashed Montgomery as a junior in 1939 and his swivel hips and breakaway speed soon earned him the nicknames "Lightning Lou" and "Hula Lou." Yet, in order to defer to Southern customs, Boston College kept Montgomery out of games against Florida and Auburn, even though they were played at home. Administrators agreed to a clause in the contracts that allowed Southern schools to cancel games without financial penalty should Montgomery play.

When the Eagles were invited to the Cotton Bowl against Clemson, there was little question about what Boston College would do. It would take the path of least resistance.

"In view of the general attitude toward Negroes in Texas, it was deemed advisable that Montgomery refrain from playing. We conferred with Boston College officials and Montgomery will come to Texas with the team but will not play," snooted Curtis Stanford, president of the Cotton Bowl Athletic Association.[20]

Montgomery, understandably, declined to accompany the team as some sort of bystander. The next season, although banned from playing, he travelled with the team a second time to New Orleans for the Sugar Bowl against Tennessee. There, he was the houseguest of Olympic sprinter Ralf Metclafe. Instead of playing in the Sugar Bowl—which Boston College won, 19-13—he appeared in what was called the Chocolate Bowl as a guest player for the Independent Football League All Stars against the Baton Rouge Patriots, champions of the local Negro League. He was then "magnanimously" allowed to watch the Sugar Bowl from the press box. In all, Montgomery was held out of six games in his college career, and his playing time was limited in others in order to get his replacements ready.

As it turns out, there isn't one known instance of any team balking at Southern demands to excluding black players in the pre-war years. Three different books claim that New Jersey's Paterson Eastside High School, in a vote of players, refused a Florida invitation in 1941 because of a ban against Larry Doby, who eventually broke the American League color line with the Cleveland Indians. But according to Al Kachadurian, Eastside's captain that year, Eastside never even received an invitation, let alone conduct a player vote.

"We didn't have any money to make any trips to Florida," he explained. "Football season ended. We played basketball."

Kachadurian couldn't answer how his team would have voted. Neither could Walter Young when asked whether Garfield's players would have gone to Miami if it meant leaving a black teammate behind.

"What might have happened if we were faced with it, I obviously don't have the answer for that. It just simply wasn't an issue with us. We never talked about it," Young said. "As far as a black player being on our team, I can tell you with the greatest of sincerity I cannot begin to imagine that would have been a problem with our coach or with our guys."

Garfield had a tiny black population, but the black kids preferred baseball over football. The Garfield Colored Giants were formed during the 30s and played in integrated semi-pro leagues. Three black kids, John Logan, Pervis Buggs and Obey Peay, played on Chick DeVito's 1940 baseball team alongside several football stars such as Ray Butts, Al Yoda, Bill Librera and Bill Wagnecz. Later, they formed the core of a Garfield Colored Giants team that won championships after the war.

Art McMahon reported that DeVito used to rub the heads of his black players for luck, just as Miami's Stingarees rubbed the heads of two young black "mascots" when they rushed out of the tunnel and onto the field in 1937. As abhorrent as that may sound, it was a common superstition.

That's not to say that New Jersey didn't have its problems with race. Doby, for instance, often "got a little extra" from opponents after the whistle according to Kachadurian. Doby, he said, wouldn't react in the heat of the moment. "He'd simply come at them harder the next play."

Then there was Robert L. Carter, who came at "them" just as hard in a different way. East Orange High School's swimming pool was effectively segregated. White students used the pool during gym class and after school. The black students' pool time was limited to Fridays after school, alternating between boys and girls each week. Afterwards, the pool would be drained, cleaned and refilled for the white students when they returned Monday so they wouldn't have to swim in the same water.

Carter was a frail, 16-year-old, but he was armed with a powerful resource. A recent test case from the New Jersey Supreme Court required that all public school facilities available to white students also be available to black students. Carter knew this, and would enforce it. During the last part of each gym class, white students were taken to swim and the black kids were left behind to play in the gym. But Carter would have none of this. One day, he climbed down into the pool before the white students went in. With Carter alone in the water, the white boys refused to swim. Carter was later threatened with expulsion by the gym teacher, who feared he would lose his job over Carter's refusal to abide by the Jim Crowish rules. Yet, Carter persisted. He attempted to enlist other black students in his protest. No one did.

"It was a difficult, emotional effort for me," Carter wrote in his autobiography, *A Matter of Law*. "I could not swim at the time, but at every gym class, choked up and near tears in emotion and defiance, I would get in that pool at its shallow end and cling to the side until the period ended."[21]

Rather than integrate the pool, East Orange stubbornly closed it to everyone—including its championship swim team—by filling it with concrete and converting it to a facility for the marching band. Carter graduated at age 16 and later was right-hand man to Thurgood

Marshall during the historic 1954 Brown vs. Board of Education decision that abolished segregation in public schools.

The difference in the South was that Doby and Carter would not have had the opportunity to make their stands there. Miami was no exception. Raymond Mohl titled his book on Miami's post-war civil rights movement "*South of the South.*" In some ways, it really was.

Barely into its third decade of existence, Miami had established itself as so hostile to blacks that, after the 1926 hurricane, the *Chicago Defender* reveled in the storm's destruction as an act of God's vengeance. In an editorial headlined "THE FORBIDDEN CITY," the *Defender* called Miami a modern day Sodom and Gomorrah:

> *Miami—the fairest of playgrounds for white people in the South—is for us the city of the damned. It is in Miami that justice is unknown. It is in Miami that a black man is shot down for speaking to a black woman if a white man happens to desire her. It is in Miami that white men assault chauffeurs who dare to drive certain cars on the streets. It is in Miami that you cannot sit in streetcars. It is in Miami that only cooks and maidservants may enter hotels, and they through back doors. It is in Miami that only white people may sue in courts. It is in Miami that only we are forbidden the chance to employ our talents to earn the food necessary to health. It is in Miami that a black man's life is not regarded as highly as that of a black dog.*
> *And it is in Miami that the storm took its greatest toll.*[21]

The roots of Miami's repressive past were planted shortly after the city was incorporated in 1896 and after the city's blacks had served their useful purpose. Of the 368 voters in the incorporation election, 162 were blacks, most of them Bahamians employed by Henry Flagler to clear land for his Florida East Coast Railway. They worked side-by-side with whites and lived among them in tent cities.

Incorporation was important to the Flagler organization, so to ensure it would pass and to guarantee the election of its slate of candidates, it registered black workers immediately before the election. Blacks loyal to the railroad thereby assured the two-thirds majority needed for passage. Soon, however, their contribution was forgotten. Within a few years, Miami was as societally backward in its views surrounding race as any other city in the South. Blacks were excluded by state statute from voting in Democratic primaries, effectively disenfranchising them. Restrictive zoning laws prohibited the sale of land to blacks outside of "Colored Town," in the northwest sector, which comprised about 15 percent of Miami's original environs.

Sociologist Ira de Augustine Reid published "*The Negro Immigrant*" in 1939. Years earlier, he had interviewed a Bahamian who had arrived in Miami around 1910. Her description of her welcome is chilling:

> *Having passed the immigration and customs examiners, I took a carriage for what the driver called "Nigger Town." This was the first time I had heard that opprobrious epithet employed. . . . I was vividly irked no little. Arriving in Colored Town, I alighted from the carriage in front of an unpainted, poorly-ventilated rooming house where I paid $2.00 for a week's lodging. Already, I was rapidly becoming disillusioned. How unlike the land where I was born.*

There colored men were addressed as gentlemen; here, as "niggers." There policemen were dressed in immaculate uniforms, carried no deadly weapon, save a billy; here, shirt-sleeved officers of the law carried pistols, smoked and chewed tobacco on duty. Colored Miami certainly was not the Miami of which I had heard. It was a filthy backyard to the Magic City.[23]

Colored Town soon became overcrowded with row upon row of ramshackle shotgun houses. In 1920, social workers discovered 100 families living on one block. A single lot with nine cottages was found on another block. Running water or indoor plumbing were rare. Disease spread rapidly. In the 1930s, the black population of Miami was stricken with tuberculosis at four times the rate of whites. While the national illiteracy rate in 1930 was 11.3 percent among blacks 10 and older, it stood at an infinitesimal 0.3 percent for the corresponding white population.

The *Miami Tribune*, in a 1937 article on slum rents, described the squalor of a typical duplex:

Each structure contains six rooms, three on each side for each family.

Fronting directly on what would be the curbline if the street were paved, each duplex has a narrow porch approached by steps at the sides.

The front door opens into the unpainted interior, where the first room contains a double bed, dresser and chair. The furniture of the second room, immediately behind the first, consists solely of a large bed. The kitchen is even smaller than the other two rooms and contains an oil stove, a table and three chairs. A doorway beside the stove forms the entrance to a cell-like room equipped with a wash basin in one corner and a toilet enclosed in separate wooden walls. The only window in the kitchen is at the rear, looking out on a back yard that extends approximately 15 feet to the front porch of an identical house. Although the duplex is the most common type of dwelling in the negro section, the buildings throughout the area are of infinite variety, ranging from miniature shacks constructed of sheets of "tar paper" to a handful of elaborate stucco houses, surrounded by hedges and small lawns that appear at rare intervals among the mass of frame tenements.

Most of the houses are so close together that the occupants of one easily could shake hands with their next door neighbors by reaching from a window. Dogs saunter over the hardpacked earth between the houses, playing with shreds of burlap or sniffing around piles of debris and kindling in backyards where wash tubs lean against the houses. Makeshift garbage cans and barrels with broken staves form gateposts for some of the dwellings. Mouldering in plots of yellow grass and decking the curblines of rocky side streets, heaps of weatherbeaten trash wait to be removed. The bulk of these trash piles consist of rusty pieces of metal, wads of paper, artificial straw, tin cans, grass cuttings and tree trimmings. In the teeming business section, the gutters are filled with scraps of paper, dust and pieces of cardboard.[24]

To ensure Miami's black population remained marginalized, law enforcement engaged in systemic oppression. In 1908, Don Hardie campaigned for sheriff of Dade County, promising to arrest suspicious characters first—and let them explain after. Once elected, Hardie announced he would make use of "nigger hounds" to track down black suspects.[25]

Boys scamper down an alley through rows of shotgun houses in this early 1930s view of Colored Town.
Miami Dade Public Library, Romer Collection.

But Hardie wasn't the most notorious of Miami lawmen. That dubious honor would go to Police Chief H. Leslie Quigg, an amateur boxer, celebrated hypnotist, ventriloquist—and Ku Klux Klansman. Actually, Quigg was never seen in his white hood but, when asked in the 30s if he was a KKK member, he responded with, "No comment." No matter. His actions and those of his force had already answered that question.

Quigg first came to power in 1921, when appointed police chief without any police experience. He stocked the force with brutish outsiders from the Georgia hills with predictable results that came to light in a Dade County Grand Jury report on police brutality in 1928.

Three years earlier, Harry Kier, a 30-year-old bellhop at the El Commodore Hotel, died while in police custody after being arrested on charges by a white female guest of making improper advances on her teenage daughter. In actuality, he had merely been relaying a message from a white guest who wanted to meet the girl. According to testimony, Quigg ordered three of his men to "beat the hell out of him" then to run him out of town. One of the patrolmen, Thomas Nasworth, took it a step further. Kier was driven to the outskirts of town, where Nasworth shot him repeatedly, wounding his partner A.M. Tibbets with a stray shot. Kier was left for dead and Quigg was left with a dilemma. He chose to orchestrate a cover-up. The grand jury saw through it, and in 1928 indicted Quigg and the three policemen for First Degree Murder. The two arresting officers at the hotel, William Beechey and E.W. Pierce, turned state's evidence. Quigg spent three months behind bars awaiting trial and, in a typical case of Southern white justice, was acquitted along with his three men.

Despite the acquittals, city manager Welton A. Snow found the Grand Jury report rather persuasive. It included testimonies from 300 witnesses alleging police brutality that included the use of a crude electric chair to coax confessions, and the case of a suspected black car thief who had the soles of his feet beaten with a copper-bound ruler for ninety minutes. The Grand Jury deemed Quigg "wholly unfit for the office" and that, under Quigg, the police department had become a "militant, tyrannical group that follows standards foreign," using "underworld alliances, summary executions, revival of the tortures of the Middle Ages and despotism of such nature as to destroy the freedom of our citizens."[26]

Snow took their advice. He dismissed Quigg, who nevertheless retained his supporters. In 1936, he narrowly lost an election for Dade County Sheriff. Campaign literature from the race boasted that the "acute Negro problem . . . demands the strict supervision of a man so notably master of the racial situation as (Quigg) demonstrated he was, during his long reign as Miami's protector." Quigg would wait only a few months before he reigned again. In May 1937, police chief J.B. Rowland was dismissed amid controversy and Quigg re-appointed as if his past actions meant nothing. The *Miami Tribune* described the ebullient scene: "In an office packed with the cheering rank and file of the police department, packed so tightly they threatened to crush the huge floral tribute they carried with them, H. Leslie Quigg took office as Miami's chief of police."[27]

Doubtlessly emboldened by Quigg's return, the force returned to its old ways, as evidenced by an incident in November of 1937. Twelve-year-old Willie lived with his mother in the Miami Beach home where she was employed as caretaker. On a mid-afternoon Saturday, he boarded a streetcar to visit his aunt in Colored Town. He got off at a stop outside the district, and walked west on Eighth Street toward his aunt's home.

Suddenly, a squad car pulled up to him.

"Boy," said one of the two officers. "How fast can you get to Niggertown?"

"Pretty fast, I guess," Willie said nervously.

"Get going," came the order.

Willie began to run as the car trailed him all the way until he crossed the railroad tracks into the black neighborhood.[28]

Willis Murray taught in the Dade County school system for 30 years. He grew up in Colored Town and, in a 2007 interview for Florida International University's Oral History Project, recalled the dangers of "trespassing" in the "white" areas.

"All of the necessities that we needed, grocery stores, any of the necessities that we needed, we had them in a smaller scale in the community where we lived," he explained. "Our parents taught us how to maneuver. We knew that we were supposed to stay in the community where we lived. We knew not to go out of that community, because if we went out of that community, we would be in trouble. The police would pick you up. At times, they would use whips to beat you, and our parents taught us not to be caught especially in those communities after six o'clock in the afternoon."[29]

Quigg remained popular in Miami throughout his 92-year life. He served two terms as a city commissioner, collected a monthly police pension of $85 and, later in life, received a cushy job as dock master at the Coconut Grove yacht basin. A 1954 profile in the *Miami Daily News* noted that, "many of the qualities that got him in trouble in his life are qualities considered virtues. . . . He is blunt, outspoken, stubborn, brave and tremendously loyal to his friends."[30]

The Ku Klux Klan came riding—literally—into town in 1921 (the same year Quigg first took over the police force), with a single-file parade of 200 men after the main streets were cleared by a Miami motorcycle policeman and a blast of a hunter's horn. A year later, it brazenly conducted an initiation rite for 335 new Klansmen on the grounds of the Miami Country Club. By 1925, the John B. Gordon Chapter boasted of 1,500 members and maintained a respectable office not far from downtown. It was, for the most part, an acceptable part of the community. In 1927, for instance, the Klan Circus opened for a nine-day stand in February, featuring the Flying Cordobas acrobatic team and the Riding Waltons, bare-back "riders of renown."[31]

The Miami Klan promoted itself as a law-and-order organization and even offered itself as an ancillary police force, an offer which, amazingly, was refused. In 1937, it raided and ransacked the LaPaloma night club, reportedly roughing up both male and female employees in the name of civil decency. They then alighted the requisite cross out front. Al Youst, the joint's gangster owner-operator, claimed that $360 and a watch had been stolen, a charge that offended Captain George J. Garcia, grand dragon of the Florida KKK.

"Ku Klux Klans do not steal," he told the *Associated Press*. "Some of the best people in Miami are members of the Klan."[32]

Of that, the *New York Times* had no doubt.

"Although unwilling openly to condone the Klan's stand, Miami business and professional leaders—many of whom wear the hood and robe on meeting nights—are secretly supporting the drive to exterminate those elements which have been brought millions of dollars pouring in during the past," the paper said.[33]

The prevailing rationale was that, so long as the Klan "behaved itself," they were perfectly acceptable as an American institution. This attitude was clearly articulated in a 1939 *Miami Herald* editorial:

> The Ku Klux Klan has been a unique factor in certain episodes of the United States. In many parts of the South it did serve a useful purpose following the Civil War but as is so often the case, a worthy idea and need may gradually develop abuses under bad leadership and the good may be replaced by evil and harmful. Thus it has been with the Klan. May the "revitalized" organization, if it is to ride again, be restrained to the channels of the legal and proper, avoid intolerance and lawlessness (and) become truly American.[34]

Indeed, that was the KKK party line. A month before the Garfield team checked into Miami's Alcazar Hotel, so, too, had the newly installed Imperial Wizard, J.A. Colescott, an Army lieutenant in World War I and a veterinarian from Indiana. The Klan was holding a reorganization meeting in Miami, and Colescott was interviewed in one of the hotel rooms the Boilermakers would occupy. As he looked out the window onto Biscayne Boulevard, he promised a kinder, gentler Klan—delusional, if not bizarre.

"The Klan never was intended to be an 'anti' organization—anti-Catholic, anti-Jewish or anti-anything else—but only pro-American," Colescott claimed.[35]

Miami's white citizenry, in general, turned a jaundiced eye toward the black population, even though it was paradoxically capable of warm personal relationships and kindness with and toward its black brethren. Still, stereotypes prevailed, and not only in Miami. Papers across the country typically noted if a player were a "Negro," or employed language insinuating a person's race, such as a "dusky ball carrier." Such racist epithets were on display when the *Miami Herald* ran a poll to determine the 1939 Florida Sports Oddity Award. Two stories garnered the most votes. Harvey Comfort, during pre-season punting practice, had knocked a bird out of the sky, "colder than an air-conditioned mackerel." Then there was a "Delray Beach darkie" who landed a 30-pound bass that would have been six pounds heavier than the existing world record had he not weighed "the monster" on a grocery store scale before cooking it for supper.[36]

Racial prejudice proved to be stubborn. Pete Williams' father was an example. An outstanding man in every other way, he had an ingrained mindset surrounding race reflective of the culture in which he grew up.

"My father was a strong segregationist," Williams explained. "He didn't believe in treating them badly. He just didn't want them around. Let them go somewhere else. Don't come here."

Williams didn't play against an African American until Penn State came to Navy for a scrimmage. Playing safety, Williams came up and laid a clean hit on the man near the sideline that injured his ankle.

"So I wrote him and told him that I competed against a black guy for the first time," Williams said. "Daddy got the biggest kick out of that; that I had hurt this black guy, and I felt ashamed or embarrassed or something. To me it was a game of sport and I had respect for the other guys. I didn't want to hurt them. I wanted to win but I had no meanness toward them."

When Lorraine Shaffer's family, the Hammers, moved to Miami from Pennsylvania, they temporarily lived with her father's cousin, whom she reviled.

"My parents were not prejudicial. Back in my old town there was a black family named Rogers that lived on the wrong side of the tracks. Their boy stole a bicycle. Dad was a very nice man and he called the father of this boy," she recalled. "He said, 'I realize that things are really bad for you. I have another bike that I can give to you and don't tell him where it came from. Just tell him it was a gift.'

"My parents bought a home the first week we moved, but we didn't have any place to stay at first, so we stayed with this cousin," Shaffer continued. "He was on his third or fourth wife and he was a drinker. I told my father, 'Daddy, I don't want to move down there if he is going to be down there; he scares me.' It turned out he was a member of the Ku Klux Klan. When he saw a black person, he would roll down the window and yell at them to get off the street."

Children weaned on such prejudice might have felt it was normal at the time, but there must have been many who, later in life, pained to recollect their acts of cruelty during their youth. Jack Pepper was one. He explained that he has always regretted what he and his friends did for fun at the expense of black Miamians.

"I hate to recall some of these things that we did," he said. "One of the guys had a convertible. We went to an orange grove. We filled a basket full of hard green oranges and then we drove through Colored Town and threw them at the people. I've often thought: How could I have done that? My mother had four kids. I was religious. We went to church."

Such paradoxes were striking. Blacks were banned from even *attending* white athletic events. Yet, in 1937, the city somehow issued a permit for Moore Park to the Ku Klux Klan for its minting of 125 inductees. Three blazing crosses stood on the Miami Stingarees' old home field. A degree of outrage did ensue, yet city fathers passed the buck. City manager A.D.G.

Bloodworth and Recreation Director Earnie Seiler both asserted they were unaware it was a Klan function when issued the permit, which they claimed was applied for by an organization calling itself the "American Club." Bloodworth, however, admitted he was approached by an unnamed courthouse official to get a permit for "a little initiation." It was unlikely they assumed it was for the Boy Scouts.

Two years later, in 1939, Jack Bell considered the absurdity of Miami's whites-only spectator laws. His tone was typically condescending for the time but, his motives seemed well-intended:

> Is there any reason, I wonder, why Miami should continue to lead the South in bigotry, relative to attendance at our sports events by Negroes? Is there any reason why Negroes who love football should not be permitted to sit in a special section at Burdine Stadium? Why is it permissible for white patrons to go and watch the Negro baseball clubs but not for Negroes to come to Miami Field?
>
> Miami's silly ban on Negro rooting sections when white teams play grew out of an equally silly fuss downtown several years ago, in which a Negro orchestra was the innocent focal point. Since that time the tension has gradually lifted. White patrons attend Negro fights in large numbers. We go up to watch the Ethiopian Clowns play baseball; better ball, by the way, than we see at Miami Field.
>
> I have never known the true Southern gentleman to show intolerance toward his Negro neighbors. Rather has it been a willingness to help, to advise, to care for. There may be other cities in which Negroes aren't permitted to see white athletic teams at play but I don't know of one. I do know that special bleachers for them are provided through most of the South.
>
> We've plenty of room at the stadium, with 5,000 end zone seats sittin' (sic) there unused. Why not rope off a section of them for our Negro sports lovers?[37]

Somehow, Colored Town managed to flourish in many ways and produced distinguished leaders in every field. Top line black artists such as Cab Calloway, Lena Horne, Billie Holiday and Count Basie performed at the Lyric Theatre, the Cotton Club, the Rockland Palace and the Harlem Square Club, all within blocks of each other on Second Avenue, which became known as Little Broadway, rivaling Harlem in offering fantastic black entertainment. They were often joined in jamming sessions by white artists such as Gene Krupa and the Dorsey Brothers. The restaurants had hour-long waits and on Saturday nights, the Mount Zion Church offered sweet potato pies, barbequed ribs and fish sandwiches. White customers flocked there as well.[38]

Although Booker T. Washington High School was dwarfed by the splendor of Miami High, it was erected at roughly the same time. Criticized an unnecessary expenditure of $306,000, it was bombed during construction, after which guards were deployed to protect workers. Nevertheless, it became one of the finest black high schools in the South after its delayed opening in 1927, with a facility that would have been the envy of Garfield.

Despite receiving scant coverage in the mainstream press, the school's football team, known as the Tornadoes, was undefeated from 1934 to 1940 and consistently competed for state and national "Negro" championships. Players like Stanley Strachan and the Ingraham brothers, Chris and Bernard—the sons of Bahamians who arrived in Miami at the turn of the century—starred. They later suited up for the Florida A&M Rattlers, the premier Negro college football program in the country. Coach William "Big Bill" Bell not only recruited the best black talent in Florida, but also opened a pipeline to the best black players out of Ohio high schools.

In that respect, Miami High's nose was cut off to spite its face. Imagine the force the Stingarees would have been had they fielded the black players starring for the Tornadoes? Bernard Ingraham, known as "Jitterbug" for his broken-field running, was clocked in 10 seconds flat when he ran against the great Jesse Owens in a 100-yard exhibition race in 1940. Davey Eldredge ran it in 10.1 seconds when he won the Florida state high school championship that same spring. They would have formed an amazing backfield together.

In 1939, Miami encountered an important crossroads in race relations. In January, a 34-year-old undertaker named Samuel Solomon formed the Negro Citizens Services League, starting out with just 13 members. When he launched a voter registration drive which reached 1,800 assignees, he alarmed many white officials and led to dramatic consequences when, in May, the city held a special primary for a recall election that would sweep E.G. Sewell back into the mayor's office. The John B. Gordon klavern of the Ku Klux Klan naturally wasn't going to stand for Solomon's new voting bloc and was determined to employ the tactics of intimidation and terror that were still effective weapons in Florida. Only two days earlier, it was business as usual in Daytona when the victim's brothers lynched a black taxi driver who had accidentally run over and killed a 12-year-old boy. But the Miami KKK was in for a surprise.

The night before the election, hooded Klansmen brazenly roared across the tracks and down Little Broadway in a 75-car caravan. Leading the sinister spectacle was a pick-up truck hauling 25 crosses, each one laid down and set ablaze at one-block intervals. One Klansman in a black hood dangled a noose out of a passenger window, while others passed cards spelling out in red letters:

> *Respectable Negro citizens are not voting tomorrow. Niggers! Stay away from the polls.*
> *KKK*

Klansmen climaxed the hateful night—arguably the darkest in the city's history—by stringing up a noosed effigy from a lamppost at the edge of Colored Town. Klansmen attached a sign that read: THIS NIGGER VOTED.

Willis Murray recalled the night vividly.

"Just about dusk, we looked down the street and we saw the Klan . . . white sheets on, (standing) on the hoods and the running board of the cars," he said. "Our parents always taught us that if the Klan came through, to come in the house. We didn't have electric lights; we had the oil lamps. They would put out the oil lamps, pull the curtains down and we would all get down on the floor. And we were taught that just like you were taught a (fire) drill in school."[39]

All this was done with typical impunity and cowardice. The Klansmen took pains to cover their license plates, even though none of Quigg's policemen were in sight. But, this time, the reaction of the citizens of Colored Town was not typical. Signals of a defiance had already appeared at Booker T. Washington High. One of the candidates, John T. Christiansen, who owned the Miami Ice Cream and Dairy Company, had proclaimed in the papers that he didn't need or want the "Negro" vote. So the students strung a sign across the cafeteria:

"Christenson does not want out our VOTES. We don't want his ICE CREAM!" Everyone joined in a boycott.[40] Further emboldened, the residents of Colored Town emerged to confront the hooded mob and run them back across the tracks.

"The Negroes were so angered by the demonstration that they followed the 75 Klan cars through the streets, ripping down the flaming crosses . . . tearing up the leaflets and threatening to drag the Klansmen from the cars," Solomon told the *Pittsburgh Courier*, that city's black newspaper. "The next morning they rushed to the polls so fast that there were long lines waiting. Several hundred had voted a few hours after the doors opened."[41]

As many as 1,500 black voters headed to the Fire House to cast ballots, undoubtedly driven to the polls by the Klan's night ride. After voting, one black preacher paused outside the polling place beaming with satisfaction and pride. A policeman told him to move along.

"You see those white men standing over there?" he said, pointing across the street. "They are awful mad about this voting."

"Yes and you see that long line of Negroes standing over there?" the minister replied, pointing to the fire house. "Well, they're mighty mad themselves."[42]

The nation's black press hailed the new bravado. "The old Ku Klux Klan intimidation and terror no longer scares the New Negro," the *Courier* proclaimed in an editorial.[43]

"This is indeed good news," the *Chicago Defender* agreed. "For in it we can see the awakening of the new South; the advent of a new, aggressive type of black man who will not be intimidated by bed sheets or lynch ropes."[44]

Perhaps that night and the election turnout in 1939 was a first step toward racial equality in Miami, yet it would still be decades to see any major progress.

In December, when Garfield's Boilermakers disembarked their train, they would be shown a white-washed Miami for the next two weeks—from the attractions they visited, to the restaurants they patronized, to the spectators they played before in the Orange Bowl. Seventy-five years later, Walter Young couldn't remember seeing any black people, not that he gave it much thought at the time.

But maybe, on an unseen level, Miami was just slightly different in 1939 than it was when Floyd Wright hid under that tarp and on top of that bus. Wright's defiance was alive in the hearts of the residents of Colored Town.

NINE

THE 1937 STINGAREES

It was a steamy, blistering and stultifying August afternoon—just the way Jesse Yarborough liked it for the first day of football practice. He'd even assembled the team a few days early in 1937, perhaps because of the hard work ahead and perhaps out of anticipation for a new era.

The season would be a crossroads for Miami High football. The Stingarees were on the brink of a golden age that would continue into the war years. They would continue to play the best teams Yarborough could find. With 10 games against top teams from seven different states, it was arguably the most difficult schedule in the country.

And the seniors of 1939—Davey Eldredge, Jay Kendrick, Jason Koesy among others—were sophomores, full of promise and confidence. At least that was true of Eldredge, just out of Shenandoah Junior High School, as he walked through the Gothic front portals of Miami High for the first time as a student.

But there was something else wonderfully new about that season, something that would transform the entire program. Roddy Burdine Stadium, more commonly known as the Orange Bowl, gave the Stings not only a home field but also a home-field advantage. The festive atmosphere made Friday night a happening. In those early years, Miami High games were as big a draw as anything else in town.

By the mid-30s, the city had outgrown rickety Moore Park, and its 9,000 bench seats that barely accommodated high school crowds. Miami's sporting set had long been clamoring for a new stadium to rival the best in the nation and to draw more attention—that is dollars—to South Florida. The University of Miami Hurricanes needed a proper home to compete with the big schools throughout the South . . . and Earnie Seiler needed a place to realize his vision.

Seiler would become a Miami institution, as unique as Art Deco and firmly dedicated to his adopted city. Known eventually as the Mad Genius, Seiler was now in his prodigal years, and the Orange Bowl his baby. Seiler created the concept of the grand halftime spectacular long before the Super Bowl made halftime must-see TV. Each New Year's, the Orange Bowl took it well beyond marching bands and, by the late 50s, splashed it across the nation's TV sets in living color. Anything went even though most anything could go wrong at any minute. Seiler was a born showman.

He had arrived in Miami in the early 20s, fresh from the dusty plains of Oklahoma where, as a single wing quarterback for Oklahoma A&M (later Oklahoma State) he filled out his moleskin uniform with 160 pounds of lean muscle and sinew. With a receding hairline and blue eyes that often pierced through cigar smoke, Seiler could fast-talk his way into nearly anything he desired. And promoting Miami was at the top of that list.

It all began when Seiler, in a pinch, coached parts of the 1924 and 1925 football seasons at Miami High after future Florida coach Dick Stanley resigned abruptly and took an assistant's job at the University of Havana. Already, Seiler had a flair for the dramatic, a gift for the creative and a knack for success. Those palm trees on the gridiron at Royal Palm Park? Seiler tried getting around them by laying out the field on the bias but still couldn't find enough open ground for an obstacle-free playing surface. The park was owned by the Florida East Coast Railway Company and when he beseeched Henry Flagler's successors to fell a few troublesome palms, he was told he had a better chance of pushing one of the railroad's locomotives out of Miami station. Although they would be taken down a year later, the answer at the time was a flat no.

No matter. Seiler soon developed plans for a particular palm that sat at the 20-yard line, about 15 yards in from the sideline. If it had to be there, why not make use of it? So, on the opening kickoff of the big game against rival West Palm Beach, Seiler sprung his version of the old Biscayne Fadeaway. He could have called it the Biscayne Hideaway. Miami High's first superstar, Warner Mizell, the future Georgia Tech All American, received the ball while Seiler's speediest back, Ray Carter, scrunched himself up behind the trunk of the tree.

Mizell, obstructed by a wall of blockers, headed for the palm, where he lateraled to Carter and simultaneously flung off his leather helmet. The Stingarees yelled "Ball" as if for a fumble and the West Palm Beach players joined the pileup in the frantic battle for the supposed pigskin, complete with the scrum's requisite eye gouging and arm-wrenching.

In a 1972 interview with *Sports Illustrated*'s John Underwood, Seiler described what happened next.

> *"I had told Carter to count five, then come out the other way and run like hell,"* he explained. *"I counted myself: 'one, two, three, four . . . five.' No Carter. For a second I was afraid he wasn't coming out. 'Gawdamighty, he can't count!' Finally he did, and nobody saw him except one official who followed him down the field the entire 80 yards.*
>
> *"Boy, what a rhubarb. The Palm Beach coach came screaming across the field, followed closely by a couple hundred Palm Beach fans. 'I protest, I protest,' he yelled. His face was red as a beet. 'It's against the rules,' he yelled. I was very calm. I said, 'Show me in the book where it says you can't have a palm tree on the football field.'"*[1]

Seiler's brilliance didn't always play to the Stingarees' advantage. He had devised a clever system to sidestep the no-coaching-from-the-sideline rule by lining up three buckets. Depending on which one he tipped over, the quarterback would call for a run, pass or punt. Once, with Miami closing in on a touchdown, he accidentally kicked over the punt bucket and his player obediently kicked the ball out of the end zone and through the window of the building across the street.

"We had to stop the game and send a man to Burdine's to buy another ball," he told Underwood.[2]

Alas, coaching couldn't fence in Seiler's expansive imagination. He needed something bigger and grander than X's and O's. And so, after taking up a position as Miami's recreation director, the self-described "dreamer" manifested his creativity in what became not just a Miami fixture but also an American one. A group of Miami businessmen were convinced that hosting a post-season game would be a wonderful way to stimulate tourism. Seiler envisioned a tropical alternative to the Rose Bowl and the perfect boost for a fast-growing city still lacking a major league franchise. The Orange Bowl game was born.

The first, played in 1933, was dubbed the Palm Festival, matching the hometown Hurricanes against Manhattan College. Seiler, a one-man bowl committee, guaranteed the Jaspers $3,000 and, when ticket sales came up short and Manhattan threatened to return home, he named the chief of police his finance chairman. The chief then turned to notorious local bookmaker Acey Deucey to top up the difference. It was the shadiest deal involving Manhattan since Peter Minuit took the island from the Indians for 60 Dutch guilders.

Seiler nearly got run over waving people in from the street to fill the bleachers. The Jaspers were heavy favorites, so much so that Seiler had printed "Congratulations Manhattan" posters for the post-game party.[3] To trim expenses, he had the Manhattan team sail down from New York by boat. Half the players got seasick, and the underdog Hurricanes won, 7-0.

What Seiler really needed for the Orange Bowl was an actual Orange Bowl. For a decade many had been lobbying for a steel-and-concrete home stadium for the venue—but until 1936, to no avail. As Miami News columnist Jack Bell lamented:

> Here we are in this, the greatest winter resort city in this, the richest nation in the world. Men come here and build beautiful hotels, marvelous racetracks, long rows of costly cabanas, exclusive bath clubs along the ocean. We cater to the wealth of darn near half the nation during the winter season—and then we've got to say to the director of athletics at Texas Christian or Marquette or Tennessee, 'you see, we've only a little old wooden stand and we can't pay more than expenses for your trip here—but listen, we'll show you a marvelous time; shows, sightseeing, swimming, everything. You'll LOVE it.'
>
> The worst part of it is, we're telling the truth.[4]

In 1934, Miami settled for a temporary wooden structure, a literal hand-me-down that was built with the lumber left over from the American Legion parade grandstands. Seiler bought them—on credit—for $1,000 and had them hauled over from Biscayne Boulevard to form a giant "U."

Seating 5,000, Miami Stadium or the "Wooden Bowl," was erected in about a month near the baseball and softball diamonds on Miami Field, in time to host the 1935 Orange Bowl between Bucknell and Miami.

A state-of-the-art facility it was not. When Seiler hoodwinked sportscasting giant Ted Husing into lending his dulcet tones to the microphone at the '37 Orange Bowl (he'd eventually become the voice of the New Year's classic), Husing took a gander around the ramshackle press box and scoffed: "This thing is more suited to broadcasting a *bleeping* cockfight than a football game."[5]

Not everyone backed the idea. One women's group, the Riverside Improvement Association, was highly displeased. Their small neighborhood was a collection of lovely homes, which they felt were under siege. Football was bad enough, but English Cycle races were also planned for the stadium. Huffed one RIA member: "Well, if you insist on putting up that stadium here, just go ahead and do it! But don't be surprised if it goes up in smoke."[6]

To her chagrin, the only smoke she would see would be wafting from Seiler's celebratory 10-cent stogie. And, she hadn't seen anything yet.

The makeshift stadium still left Miami woefully ill-equipped for a city its size. Plenty of New Jersey high schools had concrete grandstands that could seat as many spectators and Orlando, a city with less than 22 per cent of Miami's population, had planned to construct an 8,900-seat concrete stadium that would one day be home to the Citrus Bowl. Orlando tapped federal funds. Seiler and city officials drew from the same well. Their benefactor was picked from the alphabet soup of agencies created by FDR's New Deal: the Public Works Administration (PWA). The PWA was not to be confused with the Works Progress Administration (WPA), which was more of a work relief organization. The PWA had a billion-dollar budget to pour into big projects in mostly urban areas, aimed at stimulating construction and economic growth. Among them were the Bay Bridge in San Francisco, the Triborough Bridge in New York and the Grand Coulee Dam in Washington State. The PWA solicited proposals for projects and, by late 1935, Miami was eager to submit one.

As it happened, an old frat buddy of Seiler's, Charley Gaines, was a PWA board member and a man Seiler described as adept at "getting money out of pigeon holes and into circu-lation."[7] So, without contacting him first, Seiler made a beeline to Washington, D.C. and ambushed Gaines at the Mayflower Hotel. Gaines was pleasantly surprised by what he assumed was a chance meeting, and they drank to old times, as old frat boys are wont to do. Seiler sprung it on him after the first round. He confessed he needed money for his stadium.

Gaines sighed. It seemed everyone wanted cash for pet projects. Still, he thought Seiler might be on to something, and he consulted postmaster general James A. Farley, the man for whom New York City's grand main post office was named two years earlier. Meanwhile, Seiler learned that Farley was an alumnus—and enthusiastic booster—of Catholic University, which was having an outstanding season. Seiler may not have been familiar with Catholic, but he was a big fan of miracles. He suggested that Catholic be invited to play in that year's Orange Bowl. With that, the federal cash register drawer rolled open. Ding.[8]

"You gotta use what ya got," Seiler told the *News/Sun-Sentinel* in a 1984 interview.[9]

The problem was that the funding couldn't finance his stadium, at least not yet. By Miami law, the plan required approval by the city's 8,000 "freeholders", or landowners. That's when Bell's typewriter really got clicking.

"Let's get to the polls Wednesday," he implored. "No one interested in the furtherance of football here can oppose the plan whereby we get 45 per cent of this stadium as an outright gift from the government and pay the rest back out of stadium profits over a 25-year period. That's like waking up and finding a $250,000 structure built overnight . . . give this city that stadium and watch us travel."[10]

So, on October 7, 1936, a referendum was put to vote on whether Miami should issue revenue certificates for the stadium. It seemed a great deal for the city. The certificates would be issued for $162,000 with the PWA financing the entire project with an outright grant of $112,000 and a four-percent interest loan of $112,000. The *Miami News* reported that the certificates would be entirely self-liquidating and could not be charged against the taxing power. The debt "would be retired over 25 years from the gross revenues of the stadium and in the end Miami would have a fine stadium that could not otherwise be duplicated at anywhere near such a low cost to the city."[11]

But, not so fast. The balloting turned into a complete snafu. To pass, the referendum required 51 per cent of qualified freeholders to vote, but only 2,533 out of the total 8,000 actually cast ballots, with 2,209 in favor. City officials failed to properly register freeholders, and many were turned away, even though they had certificates signed by the city clerk validating them as property owners. Crowds of irate citizens stormed the office of City Clerk Frank Reilly, but to no avail. The project seemed doomed—and well it might have been—if not for the shepherding of Colonel Horatio B. Hackett, next in command to Harold Ickes, FDR's Secretary of the Interior, the PWA's parent organization.

Hackett was one of the most respected and admired men in Washington, if not the country. The son of a captain in the 81st Pennsylvania Volunteers, he entered West Point in 1904 and starred as the quarterback of the varsity football team in his plebe year. "Dumpy," as he was known, also captained the baseball team, played hockey and ran track, winning the maximum eight letters. Hackett was superintendent of construction for a Chicago architect firm, D.H. Burnham and Company, when the United States entered World War I. He re-enlisted in the Army as a Lieutenant Colonel and headed overseas with the 124th Field Artillery. Badly wounded in the face, he somehow survived. In his war diary, "The Cannoneers Have Hairy Ears," Robert J. Casey wrote of his gumption:

> The Colonel was almost dead from loss of blood when he reached a dressing station but was pulled through by a remarkable constitution plus a miracle. He was taken to a Paris hospital where strips of his shinbone were grafted onto his jaw. For two years his jaws were wired together and he lived on liquids and pastes administered through a hole by the extraction of his front teeth. He recovered completely.[12]

Needless to say, if you needed something done, it was valuable to have the indefatigable Hackett on your side. After Seiler and Gaines settled their gentleman's agreement, it was Hackett who went down to Miami to assess the possibilities to ensure the project was viable, and not a white elephant. Hackett was a college football referee on the side, and Seiler cleverly invited him to serve as the field judge for the game as Farley's beloved Catholic U. beat Ole Miss, 20-19. Huddling with Miami officials at that contest, Hackett assured them they had a worthy project, but that they would need to reduce the amount of capital requested. He had stepped in to save the project in Washington after the aborted referendum vote. In doing so, he created a situation which allowed the city to go to circuit court to rule the vote "no contest".

A second vote was scheduled for December 4. This time, the required number of freeholders showed up and passed the measure by a whopping 22-1 majority. Miami Stadium hosted the last three games of its two-year existence, Miami High's Christmas Day game against New Britain, Connecticut, the 1937 Orange Bowl between Duquesne and Mississippi State and an exhibition game between the professional Boston Shamrocks and New York Yankees.

In the meantime, officials had to figure out where to build the new palace. Jack Bell favored a site along scenic Coral Way out by the Rickenbacker Causeway, but the PWA stipulated

Roddy Burdine Stadium, aka the Orange Bowl, under construction in 1937. Note the track being built for cycle races.

that football had to have been played previously on the site. At first, the city commissioners selected Moore Park before Hackett insisted on locating the edifice at Miami Field, where the wooden stands were being torn down, right in the backyard of the ladies of the Riverside Improvement Association.

As the steel skeleton took shape, the concrete poured and the big light towers were erected, the city commissioned a brass plaque designating the stadium as the "Roddy Burdine Orange Bowl" in honor of the recently departed sports-minded department store magnate. The playing field, a magnificent carpet of green, grew in by the end of summer and when Ponce de Leon and Edison High met on a Thursday night in late September to open up the place, Miamians had a modern marvel, what they felt was the best stadium of its kind in the country.

Painted white, the two single-deck grandstands were uniquely designed as sweeping arcs, effectively making the rows of seats curved to afford better viewing angles. The arrangement was a stark departure from the monotonous layout of typical stadiums of the era.. The eight light towers were 110 feet high, each with 124 1500-watt lamps putting out 33,000 lumens. They were engineered so the light rays from the north and south towers met 50 feet above the field to diffuse the light, creating a softer illumination and reduced glare for both players and spectators. As for the playing field, a spread of lush Bermuda rolled down from a depth of six inches. A crown was set at nine inches in the field's center for effective drainage, mitigating original concerns that the low-lying site might turn into the Okefenokee Swamp on rainy days. From his press box vantage point on opening night, Jack Bell gushed:

The Roddy Burdine Stadium is more than rows of seats supported by steel girders. It is a thing of beauty, a structure built with an eye for attractive design as well as adaptability.

No stadium in America of this size gives you the impression of soft, curving outlines, of gracefulness . . . stadia, on the whole, do not impress one as having any great beauty. They're tossed together so fans can be accommodated. So it does seem we've accomplished something here. And when the whole project is completed, when the shrubs and foliage are in place, the bougainvillea climbs the walls and the fruit-bearing trees are planted—well, then we've "got something."[13]

The city commissioners insisted on a high degree of decorum. They banned the sale of alcohol. Females would not be permitted to work as concessionaires and would be limited to selling programs and souvenirs. There was just one glitch on opening night. A bank of lights blacked out in the fourth quarter. But, by Miami High's first scheduled game two weeks later, and, barring this, it was a marvel.

The Stingarees eased into their new home. They were coming off a 5-5 season in 1936, their first non-winning campaign ever and one that ended when they were routed, 32-13, by New Britain on Christmas Day. Still, only twice did they lose by more than a touchdown, and they were the first team since 1933 to beat Boys High of Atlanta. Yarborough lost numerous players from that roster, including Steamboat Bill Carey, his prize runner, now at the University of Florida. When the "Cunnel" returned from Josh Cody's coaching school to begin practices, he wasn't optimistic.

"We've a hard schedule and a lot of green boys," he moaned. "So there's much work to be done. I reckon we're going to lose a lot of our games this fall but we'll work hard and try to keep the scores low."[14]

What Yarborough didn't let on was that he had his biggest team in terms of weight since he came to Miami and, while he was losing almost his entire backfield, he had promising options. "Power and possibilities" was how the *Miami Daily News* put it when previewing the season.[15] Yarborough, who always trained his linemen for speed, was moving three starters from the line to the backfield, including the inestimable Milton "Lefty" Schemer, his All City end from the previous year and his 1937 captain by unanimous vote.

Schemer, the son of an Orthodox rabbi, was as much of a character as had ever passed through Miami Senior High's hallowed halls. He had bushy black hair and deep-set eyes, was thickly built and low to the ground, yet extremely nimble and athletic. And, to boot, he was a regular chatterbox. Yarborough once kidded he handed the signal calling assignment to Schemer because he had no other choice.

"The darned kid talks too much anyway he'll probably chatter in the huddle and bother the signal caller," he rationalized with his typical humor. "So if we let him call 'em, he'll be the only one talking."[16]

Everybody loved the colorful Lefty. He entered Miami in mid-semester his sophomore year, "a bow-legged kid who didn't know what it was all about," wrote Jack Bell, who also happened to be his baseball coach. The natural athlete immediately made coach Clyde Crabtree's basketball team and ended up captaining football, basketball and baseball while winning 10 letters. He played everything, everywhere. In 1937, he won the city badminton championship while still in school "just to see if he could do it" and played in the highly competitive Inter City Softball League. His team won the city and state championships and participated in the national tournament in Chicago, causing him to miss the Stingarees' first football workouts. He also missed classwork. When he returned from the tournament he walked into the instructor's classroom. The teacher expected an excuse and a request for a pass. He was astonished at what he heard instead.

"I've been absent several days," Schemer told him. "When do you want me to start making up that work? I'm ready any time."

Bell gave him a job working nights at the *Daily News* indexing the greyhound charts. It was dull and tedious, but Schemer turned it into a science by analyzing past performances.

"He never quits: he never knows when he's licked; he never does anything in half-hearted fashion," Bell wrote when Schemer won the Sigma Nu Trophy as Miami High's top athlete in 1938. "He's a fighting, talkative, boisterous kid with the fire of athletic genius in his makeup.[17]

"Perhaps you get the impression I think he's tops.

"I do."[18]

True to Bell's faith in him, Schemer became a Miami sports legend. He played just a year of football at the University of Miami before leaving college for a professional baseball career. Then known as "Mike", he had a couple of stints with the New York Giants to become Miami High's first major leaguer (Al Rosen was the second).

Yarborough had an extra week before the season began, a good thing because of Schemer's absence and his re-arranged lineup. There were signs he was becoming increasingly pleased and pulling out of his pre-season doldrums. For one thing, he gave the team a Saturday off after the first four workouts.

"Nothing unusual," he told the newsmen.

"But those who know him well know that the colonel wouldn't hesitate to book a stiff session if he thought things weren't shaping up so well," noted the *Miami Herald*.

When Yarborough made his final cuts, the *Herald* said it left him with "28 huskies" with the roster listing 16 lineman, a number of them able to play two or three positions, and 12 backs, a number of them able to move back to the line. With two weeks to go, Schemer scored five touchdowns in an intra-squad scrimmage, further brightening Yarborough's outlook. But the schedule was Miami's toughest ever, 10 games against teams from seven different states, made somewhat easier by eight home games. The only road trips were the opener at Robert E. Lee of Jacksonville, the Stings' former Big Ten rival, and the Oct. 22 game against rugged Boys High of Atlanta.

ROBERT E. LEE: QUAGMIRED

For now, Yarborough was baiting the trap, rambling on as quickly as Schemer, as he laid out the case for concern to his buddy Jack Bell:

> We're going into the season with two ends and a tackle in the backfield and we've got to open away from home in Jacksonville against that Lee team. Remember that little (Virgil) Dingman kid? Well, he's littler, faster, tougher and harder to get your hands on than ever.
>
> (We're) big which goes against them until they learn how to play football. Lee has had a game and we're green hands. We've not lost in Florida for five years—or is it six? Anyway, it's a lot of responsibility to put on a green team, away from home, with two ends and a tackle in the backfield.

You know that's an awful risk to take. Playin' the first one away from home with two ends and a tackle carryin' the ball. Will they carry the ball or will they forget and start playin' two ends and a tackle?

What'll happen, I don't know. If we can stop Dingman, we might win it. If we can get off to a good start—play good ball in the first quarter—we might be all right—if we can stop Dingman and if our two ends and a tackle will carry the ball.[19]

They didn't get off to a good start, and they didn't exactly stop Dingman, who carried 16 times, averaging seven yards a pop. But what the Stingarees couldn't stop, the weather did. Cawthon Field wasn't just muddy. It was under water in places, turning the game into more of a sloppy tug of war than anything else. The home team dominated field position, but that didn't matter if it couldn't push something over the goal line, and the only team to do that was Miami, thanks to Schemer.

Opportunism carried the day and, after an exchange of two poor punts by Dingman, the Stingarees found themselves literally wading deep into Lee territory late in the second quarter. Starting at the Generals' 29, Schemer splashed ahead for three, then six yards and when Johnny Reid slipped out into the flat, Schemer surprised the defense by sloshing to his right and flinging the wet ball with his distinctive crooked arm delivery, sending Reid down to the one. It was then when Schemer, in his own unique way, really took charge. The season before, the Stingarees had made a habit of marching up and down the field only to come up empty. So Schemer, for the benefit of the entire huddle, gave a pep talk to himself.

"Now see here, Lefty," he said. "All last year when you was up there in the line playing end, the team would get down here ready to score and them backs could never get it across. You used to give 'em hell cause we didn't score. Now you're back here Lefty—just remember that—and you gotta score or you ain't no better than they were."[20]

With that, Schemer broke the huddle, took the direct snap and plunged across for the touchdown, sliding through the mud face first. His pass attempt for the extra point was incomplete to Reid, but the 6-0 margin held up when the dangerous Dingman, within sight of the goal line, was piled up at the Miami 15 as the clock ran out. The narrow win kept alive the Stingarees' streak of not having lost to a Florida team since 1928.

"I am well pleased," Yarborough said from under the dripping brim of his soggy hat.[21]

He would stay that way for the next three weeks.

Savannah: Lefty Gets Loose

The Stingarees' Burdine Stadium debut brought Savannah High School to town, a year after the Georgians defeated Miami, 7-6, at home. A back named Jimmy Tuten ran over them in that one and he was back in Savannah's deceptive double wing attack. Clyde Crabtree scouted the Blue Devils in a 7-6 loss to Boys High and came back with the view that Savannah should have beaten the Atlanta boys. The papers warned of how sharp the Georgians looked when they paused to practice in Daytona on the way down to Miami.

"One tough team," Crabtree reported.

Unlike many of Miami's future games at Burdine Stadium, the first game was an afternoon contest. The Stingarees were decked out in their finest—blue jerseys, gold numbers, silver satin pants with blue inserts—but what should have been a sparkling afternoon turned dreary. The game was played under what the *Miami Herald* called "leaden skies" as pre-game rains held the attendance down to a hardy 3,070, a gathering made to look even smaller by the spacious stands of their new surroundings.[22]

Those fans, however, were not disappointed. Schemer would not allow that. From the opening kickoff, which he returned 23 yards, Schemer was a one-man highlight reel. He gained 207 yards on 20 carries and accounted for 264 of Miami's 333 total yards, a percentage that would have been higher had Yarborough not sent the second team in for the last quarter. Schemer's biggest gain, a 73-yard gallop on a cutback to the outside, even went for naught. Well ahead of the pursuing Blue Devils, he tripped and fell at the five-yard line then pounded the ground in disgust from his knees. It was the final play of the first half.

"The mighty captain of the Stingarees strode back and forth on the stadium gridiron like a giant colossus, felling all who stepped into his path," wrote the *Herald*'s Les Barnhill.

"Lefty ran those Georgians until their tongues hung out and their sides ached," the *Miami Tribune* crowed. "Power plunges into the line; long sweeps around the ends; zigzagging runs through a field dotted with enemy players. It all looked the same to Lefty."

Jack Bell remembered something Yarborough had told him a few weeks earlier: "I'm the craziest coach in football. I've had an All Southern back out here for three years and have been wasting him at end."[23] Then, with Schemer on the sidelines, Yarborough got a sneak peek at a future All Southern back. He already had his eye on Lefty's successor in the line of great Stingaree runners. Now, with the game under control, he put him to the test.

"Eldredge," he drawled. "You're in."

The blonde kid, who had promised his coach he'd be better than his big brother, sprinted onto the field, along with Jason Koesy, another '39 mainstay, to make good on his word. One play after Koesy completed his first pass as a Stingaree, Eldredge took the snap deep in the short punt formation and, like a bolt, hit the middle of the line, knifing past the center for the first TD of his high school career. It made the final score 18-0. The sequence wasn't lost on Barnhill, who wrote, "The game proved that Coaches Yarborough and Clyde Crabtree have substitutes that can fit into the scoring machinery almost as well as the originals."[24]

SPARTANBURG: TURNING ON THE LIGHTS

The third game—the Stings' Orange Bowl debut under the lights—produced more of the same: more pre-game angst over the opposition, more rain and more Schemer. Red Dobson brought his undefeated Spartanburg team down from South Carolina and, with sheets of rain soaking 7,370 attendees, they returned with a 19-7 loss. Outweighed, the visitors couldn't contain Schemer, who gained 148 yards from scrimmage. But they did provide Yarborough, who had been bragging that his team would win easily, with some anxious moments. The Spartans likely would have won the game save for an egregiously poor officiating error.

Spartanburg was ahead, 7-6, when, with the rain coming down in full force, its punter, George Spillers, put his foot into one that came down around midfield. Schemer opted not to field the wet ball and, instead of letting it roll dead, a Spartanburg player downed it—or so it appeared to everyone except Miami's Johnny Reid. He swooped in, scooped up the ball and sprinted 54 yards into the end zone. Players on both teams stood dumbfounded, assuming the ball was dead. But it wasn't, at least not according to the officiating crew, and Miami had the lead back. Dobson screamed out his bewildered displeasure from the sidelines to no avail. As Bell explained it in his story, the field judge was supposed to raise his hand to signify a dead ball, at which point the ref was supposed to blow his whistle.

"The official was slow or the referee didn't see him or the official was relying on a fine point in the rules," Bell wrote. "Anyway, there were the Stingarees with a gift touchdown—an' hit a' rainin' like all gitout."[25]

Such gaffes were not uncommon, and when Sonny Leatherman intercepted what would have been a Spartanburg go-ahead TD pass in the fourth quarter, the Stingarees were able to drive for a final score. It made the Miami victory seem far bigger than it was actually was.

Boys: Scared Stiff

So, it was on to Atlanta, the second and final road trip of the season, against Shorty Doyal's Purple Hurricanes of Boys High. Yarborough and Doyal were two of the best high school coaches in the South, having built their programs into arguably the best in their respective states, although Tech High—Doyal's alma mater—certainly had a valid claim as well. Boys and Tech shared the same brick building and their annual game, often the *de facto* state championship, was the biggest sporting event in Georgia, with the possible exception of Georgia Tech and Georgia's annual gridiron argument. That included that fledgling little Masters Invitational that Bobby Jones organized on his new golf course in Augusta.

The rivalry's ferocity is today on full display in the Atlanta History Center. In the run-up to the game, several Tech High students, under cover of darkness, rigged up a metal "Tech" placard below the American flag outside the schools' shared entrance. They greased the pole to make sure the sign could not be taken down. And it wasn't. It was shot down, gangster style. A Boys High student emptied his 12-guage shotgun at it from a rumble seat as his accomplice drove by. The battered sign is now a museum piece.

To a Miami Stingaree, the rivalry with Boys couldn't possibly match the rivalry with Edison. But the Boys-Miami rivalry, begun on Thanksgiving Day rivalry in 1932, was still huge and, this year, the Atlanta lads were spoiling for revenge. The year before, the Stingarees had lifted themselves from the malaise of a mediocre season to stun Shorty's team, 7-0. Schemer out-jumped three defenders to haul in the decisive TD pass in the fourth quarter to snap Boys' 33-game unbeaten streak, including combined 23-0-1 seasons in '34 and '35. The Purple Hurricanes were just 3-2 coming into the game, and Yarborough had to start worrying about overconfidence after a terrible Tuesday practice session. The team would leave by train for the Friday night game in two days. It was a short workweek.

"The boys seem to think they're too good to be beaten," he said. "They'd better get it out of their heads."

The coach was singing a different tune, as they say, a couple of days later.

"The boys know them Geo'gia boys are tough. I've got to give 'em enough confidence to feel maybe we can win—by one touchdown. That'll be plenty. It's just another tough ballgame and I've just got to trust to the Gods . . . and Lefty Schemer," Yarborough said.

The game was played at Ponce de Leon Park, home of the minor league Atlanta Crackers. For the first time all season, the Stingarees didn't play in the rain. Instead, the problem was the temperature, which dipped into the 30s by game time. While that may not be Green Bay in January, to the sun-tanned Miamians, it was the Arctic. For once, the defense bottled up Schemer's runs but not his arm, and the Stingarees led, 18-2, heading into the fourth quarter. While his players may not have felt overconfident, Yarborough seemed to have been, sending his half-frozen reserves in off the bench.

From the opposite sideline, Shorty Doyal sensed an opportunity and rallied his team. The Purples nearly pulled off a next-to-impossible comeback for their lanky coach. It would be Eldredge's worst performance in a Miami uniform. First, he was called for 15-yard penalty that set up the Purple Hurricane's first touchdown. Then came the kickoff. It fell out of the cold night air and handcuffed him and, as he tried to reel in the bouncing ball just in front of his goal line, it slipped back into the end zone. Now he had problems. He couldn't just let the ball go or Boys would have recovered for a touchdown, so he scrambled and recovered it but was tackled before he could even get back on his feet.

The officials ruled it a safety. In their view, Eldredge had booted it into the end zone while desperately attempting to pick it up. Yarborough watched Eldredge's football *faux pas* with folded arms. He had seen it differently. He claimed the ball hit his player's shoulder, not his foot, arguing that the correct ruling should have been a touchback.

"The impetus was from the kickoff," he pleaded. But the officials weren't buying it.

Rebuffed by the ref, Yarborough had had enough. Doyal wasn't going to have this one on him. The first team had been sitting on the bench keeping warm, but Yarborough was sending them back into the game—and the home team captured the momentum. Somehow, the Stingarees managed to stop Boys on downs at the 12 before the Atlantans' Dan Greer outran the entire Miami team on a 60-yard punt return, with the PAT making it 18-17. Only the clock saved Miami. There was time for just one play from scrimmage. The Stingarees ran it before skulking off the field a fortunate lot.

"They won after playing some of the shoddiest ball a Stingaree team has ever displayed," Bell wrote.[26] Close call or not, the Stings were 4-0. But the schedule was relentlessly daunting. And it would soon catch up with them.

MALE: PASSED OVER

Male High, not to be confused with Boys High, had been trying to set up a game against Miami for four years. The Louisville, Kentucky school was established in 1856, the first high school west of the Allegheny Mountains. It started playing football in 1893, and its rivalry with Manual, the team that would win the LSA National Championship Game in 1938, is one of the oldest and most intense in the country. Today, Male is the third-winningest high school program in the U.S.

The 1937 season was the last at Male for coach James Wallace "Wally" Butts. Butts was known as the Little Round Man. Unlike Shorty Doyal, who was long, Butts was truly little and round. He stood a squat 5-foot-6 with several more pounds than his 155 playing weight at Mercer University, but with the same oversized forearms he had developed laboring as a bricklayer. He was described as someone with "the face of a cherub and the spirit of a hungry lion", and he stalked the sidelines as if he were caged, barking orders, often laced with colorful language he wouldn't dare use at home. His players loved that fire—so long as it wasn't directed at them.

No high school, even Male, was going to hold the ambitious Butts for long. After the '37 season, he left Louisville to take a job as line coach at the University of Georgia. In another year, he was starting a 21-year career as the head coach in Athens, where he won four SEC titles, went 5-2-1 in bowl games and won two national championships, one with Heisman Trophy winner Frank Sinkwich in 1942, the other with All American Charlie Trippi in 1946.

Butts coached through the 1960 season, a year after Fran Tarkenton led the Bulldogs to Butts' last title. He served as athletic director for three more seasons before his career came crashing down under a cloud of controversy, the merits of which are still being debated today. In March 1963, the *Saturday Evening Post* accused Butts of fixing a game with Alabama's Bear Bryant. It alleged that Butts supplied Bryant with Georgia's plays and formations 10 days before the '62 season opener between the Bulldogs and Crimson Tide at Legion Field. The point spread was 17. Bama won, 35-0.

The piece, penned by freelance writer Frank Graham Jr., was titled, "The Story of A College Football Fix", and it shook the sport to its foundation. It was based on information sold to the magazine by an Atlanta insurance agent, George Burnett, who claimed he was accidentally cross-connected to a phone conversation between the two Southern legends. Once he realized who was on the line, he took notes detailing the incriminating offer from Butts. After the rout took place, he said he felt obligated to take the story to the *Post*.

Of course, accusing Southern college football coaches at that time was paramount to disparaging Stonewall Jackson during the Civil War. Both coaches sued for libel, and Butts was awarded $3.06 million by an Atlanta jury. He eventually collected $460,00, while Bryant settled out of court for $300,000. In his autobiography, Bryant said the incident had "taken 10 years off my life."[27]

Bear, nevertheless, managed to come out of it unscathed, but Butts was out of a job, and the *Post* soon folded, partly under the weight of the judgment. At least Butts was eventually inducted into the College Football Hall of Fame, but it came in 1997, nine years after his death, when his contributions to the development of the passing game could no longer go unacknowledged. Not only was he an innovator of pass patterns at a time when most teams threw out of desperation or as a surprise, but he was also an astute and pioneering teacher of the mechanics of throwing a football when others overlooked that critical aspect of the game.

Frank Leahy called Butts "football's finest passing coach" while Tarkenton once said Butts "knew more football than any man I ever knew." When Trippi got to the pros, he remarked: "I could tell immediately they didn't know half as much about the passing game as Coach Butts."[28] And so, it was at Male in 1937 when Yarborough "butted heads" with the Little Round Man for the only time.

The Miami coach knew it would be the toughest game on his super-tough schedule. Male came in at 8-0, including what was considered an upset 28-0 win over Nashville Central the week before. The Stings' 4-0 mark was impressive, but there were dodgy moments in each of the last two games. Yarborough thought he had to come up with a wrinkle. He got it when the Stingarees stayed in Atlanta a day to watch Georgia Tech host Auburn. Auburn used a five-man line to befuddle the favored Ramblin' Wrecks in a 21-0 rout and Yarborough, after mulling it over with Crabtree on the train ride home, installed the new defense at his first practice of the week.

In theory, it should have worked. By dropping a defender off the standard six-man line in what was then called a "backer-upper" position, it should have given the Stings added defense against Butts' sophisticated pass patterns. Yarborough and the Stingarees would be on the other end of that equation against Garfield. Sometimes, things don't turn out the way you draw them up. This was such a game, and it was a wild one. In an age when Woody

Hayes-style football was the norm, Miami and Male filled the night air with an unheard-of 44 passes. And, when Butts entered an aerial dogfight, he usually shot down his opponent.

The Stingarees' hopes for an unbeaten season, the *Miami Tribune* wrote, were "snowed under by as bewildering a barrage of passes as this city has seen in many a moon," noting that the visitors "threw everything but the arc lights" at Miami.[29] Butts' Bulldogs intercepted six of the Stingarees' 26 pass attempts and ran back one of Schemer's tries 67 yards for a TD. Three other Male TDs came on passes, two of which could have been intercepted by Miami defenders. Another was set up by a pass completion. Butts emptied his bench in the fourth quarter, his team having scored in every period. Male went home with a 35-7 win after Miami had opened the scoring in the first quarter.

It was as sound a defeat as Yarborough ever experienced, and as he headed toward the handshake with Butts, he knew it.

"Well, at least we stopped you pretty well with the five-man line," he told him. "I figured we'd spring that on you; mess up all your assignments and keep you guessing."

Butts chuckled to himself.

"Why, the five-man line wasn't new to us," he said, out-drawling Yarborough as well. "We've played against it—and used it—for a couple of years."

"Oh," Yarborough said in disappointment.

"The truth of the game is this," Butts said. "That was the best line we faced this year. Miami had the best team we played. Do you realize what a game it would have been if your boys had knocked down those first two touchdown passes?"

"Yeah," Yarborough admitted glumly. "I realize."[30]

Male went on to wrap up a 12-0 season with a 25-20 win in its big game with Manual. Any hope Miami had of being touted as the Southland's best team was gone. Maybe that's why Yarborough began to fix one eye on the future.

Interestingly, the biggest revelation in preparation for the Male game had been the 200-pound 15-year old tackle Jay Kendrick.

In a story headlined, "Young Tackle Injects Fire In Stingarees," the *Miami News* noted in midweek that the big sophomore, "all but wrecked the varsity in scrimmage and forced the regulars playing opposite him to scrap from being run out of the park."

"So outstanding was the reserve's play that Coach Jesse Yarborough had him running at left tackle on the first team before the afternoon was over."

Kendrick did not start against Male, but he played very well when he was in the game and acquired a bruised shoulder as a badge of honor. Yarborough had seen enough of him to know he would mature into a good one. So, he continued to work Kendrick and Levin Rollins, another promising sophomore, with the first team at practice.

TUSCALOOSA: DAVEY BREAKS OUT

For now, Yarborough's biggest problem was figuring out how to keep his workhorse, Schemer, from breaking down with half a season remaining. Davey Eldredge had lost another costly fumble in the Male game, but there was enough raw talent there to balance the sophomore's growing pains. Whether Yarborough knew it or not, Tuscaloosa, the upcoming opponent, was the ancestral home of Eldredge's mother, Jennie Belle Turner. It was a good enough week as any to put some faith in Eldredge and loosen his leash.

The Black Bears of Tuscaloosa High were another formidable opponent. They were bringing a 5-1 record into the game having outscored opponents, 152-34, and had an offense based on deception with a lot of spinners and misdirection. Even so, Yarborough decided to stay with his five-man line while he worked to try to correct the mistakes his pass defenders made against Male. He even pressed assistant coach Clyde Crabtree into unlimbering his throwing arm against the first team defense, while, on offense, Yarborough installed a few new plays, hoping to spring Eldredge's speed.

Both bore fruit in the 26-7 win. The Black Bears would complete just three of 17 passes, none against the first team, while young Eldredge would give the 3,562 paying customers a glimpse of his future brilliance.

With Miami up, 13-0, Yarborough unveiled the sophomore to start the second half, and Eldredge promptly zipped around his right end for 21 yards. Then, in a nifty piece of broken field running, he went 12 yards to skip across the goal line. For the first time, reporters for both the *News* and *Herald* wrote him up as "Li'l Davey," such a nickname being a sure sign of stardom.

The question, "What will we do if they stop Schemer?" isn't the perplexing problem it once was in Miami High's football camp," wrote the *Miami News*. "The Stingarees coaches have a ready answer, discovered last week against Tuscaloosa and brought home even more forcefully in practice for the annual battle with Macon's Lanier High.

"The answer is David Eldredge, 135-pound giant killer."[31]

After averaging more than 10 yards a carry against the Alabamans—more than Schemer, the *News* noted—Eldredge would get his first career start against Lanier, yet another unbeaten team (7-0-1 on the year and unbeaten in 18 straight).

"Li'l David, the surest tackler in the backfield, was running wild again in practice against the reserves," the *News* continued. "He darted off tackle, swept the ends and broke through small holes in the line to reel off brilliant gains."[32]

Over at the *Herald*, they exalted how Eldredge had broken out of his "slump" and was displaying the potential he'd shown in spring practice. A lot was expected of him, but those expectations would have to wait another year.

LANIER: POETIC INJUSTICE

Selby Buck, the old Miami High standout, brought his bruising Lanier Poets back to his hometown. They sure didn't hit like Poets and late in the game—a 6-0 Lanier win—they unloaded on Eldredge, leaving him dazed and disoriented on the ground. Even though Eldredge left the game and was hospitalized for observation, the head injury was first reported as not serious. In midweek, doctors told Eldredge's family it would be wise for him not to play football the rest of the season. Miami would miss the breakaway element Eldredge brought to the attack and, just as important, his ability to break down opposing attacks with his speed from his safety position.

Four games remained, all against teams with undefeated records. Shenandoah High School was coming down from Iowa, followed by the annual bloodletting on Thanksgiving against Edison, certain of beating the Stings for once. Then there was the Kiwanis Charity Game for underprivileged children against Knoxville City, which was laying a claim to a national championship, before the season's end on Christmas night against Lewis Pope's Oak Park teammates.

SHENANDOAH: YARBOROUGH GETS HIS RESPONSE

The Iowans, as it turned out, didn't offer much competition. They were a late add-on to the schedule before the season began, and Yarborough wasn't sure they were in the same class. The contract offered the Mustangs the full guarantee only if they were undefeated, a condition barely met by tying Red Oak, 6-6, in their last conference game to split the Hawkeye Six championship and to save themselves a $100 stipend.

Shenandoah hadn't lost since 1935, a streak of 19 straight games, but they hadn't played a team like Miami, or one so motivated. Disgusted by the Stingarees' lackluster effort against Lanier, Yarborough and Crabtree sat the team down in front of the movie projector and pointed out "glaring faults" and "deplorable blocking and tackling." The poor Mustangs were going to be victims of circumstance against a much bigger and more-skilled Miami team that had just been called out by its coach.

Everyone could see it coming. Even Shenandoah principal B.V. Guernsey predicted a four-touchdown defeat, two for the warm climate, and two for the long trip. He turned out to be quite a soothsayer. Outweighed by 20 pounds per man, and playing under the lights for the first time, the visitors were jittery from the start. When their fullback, Otis McCrary, fumbled on the first play of the game, Miami turned that into a touchdown, added another before the first quarter was over, then two more when the reserves came in for the last quarter. The crowd of 5,418 mercifully cheered when Shenandoah made its initial first down in the third quarter and cheered even more forcibly when Koesy put on an Eldredge-like show in the second half. After Schemer gained 108 yards from scrimmage and took a seat, Koesy completed the 26-0 rout. He tacked on 63 yards, completed some nice passes and returned a punt 41 yards, giving Yarborough even more hope for coming seasons.

EDISON: MIND GAMES

The annual Edison-Miami game was the biggest sporting event in Miami. It was a one-sided rivalry. From when they first met in 1925, Edison, the former agricultural school, had managed just one tie in the series, as hard as it tried and as intensely its fans rooted. Jesse Yarborough loved to crow about his dominance over Edison coach Ed Parnell, although they were always good friends.

In the 1950s, long after they last faced each other, Parnell recounted one particular example of how far Yarborough would go to continue the Stingarees' unbeaten streak. One year, Parnell maintained, Yarborough was having a hard time getting his boys up for the game. The night before, Parnell claimed, Yarborough circled back to the locker room after practice and found an extra uniform, which he stuffed and then strung up on the flagpole in front of Miami High, then painted the front doors of the school in Edison red and white. The following morning, Parnell said, Yarborough dragged his team to the decadent scene.

"Look what those Edisons did to me, your head coach. And look what they did to our beautiful school."

Thus aroused, the Stingarees won going away.

"Jess may deny it," Parnell said. "But to this day, I say that's what he did to get his boys up. And you know what made it worse? He convinced everyone we did it and the Edison student council had to come out and take the paint off Miami High's doors."[33]

Whether that tale was true, Yarborough could never deny using psychological ploys in the intra-city feud.

In '37, the breather of a game against Shenandoah came at a great time in the Miami schedule. While Miami played on Friday night, the Red Raiders lay in waiting with a week off before the annual Thanksgiving Day grudge match. With Edison so well rested, the Stings could not have afforded another physical contest like Male or Lanier. Yarborough was able to empty his bench against Shenandoah in what amounted to a perfect tune up.

Miami's bitter rivals had sewn up the Big Ten Conference championship two weeks earlier against Andrew Jackson to go to 7-0 on the season. The game was to settle the unofficial city and state championships with the winner hosting the annual Christmas Day game, not that the two teams needed extra motivation.

Hyped Jack Bell, "These lads down on the stadium green will be playing far beyond their normal "Best." This is THE game. This is the biggest, most dramatic football struggle Miami has ever seen."[34]

The Red Raiders and their fans were certain they would finally take down the Stings after 13 years of frustration—or at least they had their fingers crossed. The only game they hadn't lost was the 12-12 tie in 1935. Even that felt like loss, because they had blown a late lead. Naturally, talk of "this is the year" began while Edison was piling up the wins and picked up steam during the off week with nothing to focus on but the promising prospect of their rivals.

Under the headline, "STINGAREES DUE TO LOSE, SAYS EDISON," the *Miami News* wrote, "There is a feeling at Miami Edison that "der tag" is about at hand. Nothing expressed openly would give that impression but the very action of the Cardinals on the practice field would indicate confidence that the day is almost here when Edison will score its first victory over Miami High."[35]

Yarborough loved seeing that one. There wasn't a better way to fire up his boys. Edison cocky? Have they considered the comparative strength of the schedules? It wasn't until Miami left the Big Ten that it was recognized nationally. But, as fans started to snap up advance tickets in droves to signal a record crowd, some people were buying in. The doubt even extended to one of the Stingarees' student managers, Gilbert Snyder, who was heard to whisper under his breath how Edison would win, 6-0.

The teams began to prepare in earnest. Two days after the easy win over Shenandoah, Yarborough ordered a Sunday practice and got the week rolling with a bit of psychological warfare. It was a masterful example of how to manipulate an opponent.

"No matter how good Edison is, they know we have the good old jinx on them," he said in the *Miami Tribune*. "You can tell Parnell and his team that I consider that jinx worth three touchdowns. But don't forget to make Edison the favorite. That is the way we want to go into the game."[36]

Even the week off seemed to work against Edison, because the Red Raiders consumed mental and emotional energy over-thinking the game. They took Yarborough's bait. On Tuesday, Parnell had to put them through a high intensity 45-minute scrimmage to burn off some steam.

"I think they'll come through for the school," Pops told the *Herald* inside the gates of a practice that was closed to the general public. "They're the best balanced team I ever coached and I think have a better chance to beat Miami than any Edison team ever had."

Try as he might, however, Parnell couldn't resist responding to Yarborough's boasts. "This Miami High jinx is a lot of bunk," the Edison coach barked back. "Until three years ago there was no doubt that Miami High had the best teams but since that time the picture has changed. The two teams are evenly matched again this year as to weight and reserves. Again I say they will have to show me that the Stingarees can beat the Red Raiders." Line coach Dale "Muddy" Waters chimed in, "I see no reason in the world why the Red Raiders should not win."[37]

Yarborough was winning the battle of the bulletin board. It seemed as though he had managed to transfer all the pressure to his opponent. His team worked hard all week, but they were a lot looser. Lefty Schemer placed a bet: he'd give up his best shirt and pair of shoes if Miami lost, and would buy a new suit if Miami won. Sonny Leatherman, meanwhile, was taking no chances. A senior, he'd never played against Edison due to ill-timed bouts of the flu his sophomore and junior years. He was taking cold shots all week. The day before the game, he locked himself into his room at sundown, "so that nothing could happen to keep me out of the game."[38]

Meanwhile, Youell Lester "Just Call him Joe" Crum had extra motivation. He had transferred to Miami from Edison, where he had been the starting center the year before. He did so in midterm, right after the football season, because Parnell told him he'd never make it as an end, which was where Yarborough was playing him now. Like Leatherman, nothing was going to keep him out of this game. He was playing with a broken nose and a special helmet to protect it and was hearing from Edison's Lemon City campus that the Red Raiders planned to add to his injuries.

The game was getting a lot of action. Bookies loved it. Miami backers were laying 6-5 odds on their Stingarees and, while optimistic Edison fans were taking them, the smart money began to shift toward Miami as the week went on. In fact, a poll taken inside the *Herald* sports department, where they had seen both teams in action, overwhelmingly favored the Stings. The easier prediction was that the city was going nuts over the game.

Turkey dinners were gobbled down early, well before the 3 p.m. kickoff time, and prime parking spots on the dirt lots outside the stadium went fast. Side streets soon filled up, and residents made a few bucks parking cars on their lawns. The pay lots on West Flagler Street, two miles away, started doing a brisk business.

"The uproar of frenzied cheering could be heard for blocks away from the stadium," Henry Cavendish wrote on the front page of the *Herald* the next day. "There didn't seem to be any rhyme nor reason for it—just high school football fans gone immodestly berserk for the moment."

Cavendish made note of a one-legged peanut vendor who hawked his wares for five cents a bag and high school coeds who sold programs for 10 cents. Business was good. The steady stream of fans didn't stop until after the kickoff.[39]

In all, 18,403 turned Roddy Burdine Stadium into exactly what Earnie Seiler, Horatio Hackett and Jack Bell had intended—a place that rocked with an electric atmosphere that validated their faith in the ambitious project and marked Miami as a sports town. It was the largest crowd to have witnessed a high school football game in Florida until that time and the second-biggest football crowd of the year in the state of Florida, about 1,500 fewer fans than the annual Florida-Georgia game drew. It was the first event to really light up the Orange Bowl, which would see so many more great ones over the years, from national championships to Super Bowls, until meeting the wrecking ball in 2008.

If only the game itself measured up. Miami's 28-0 win was a resounding retort to all the Edison speculation. The Red Raiders would dejectedly leave the field grumbling how Miami always seems to play its best game of the season against them and how they had peaked too early.

"The score was 28-0 but it might just have well been 10 or 20 times that amount," *Miami Tribune* writer Herbert Cormack penned. "It wasn't so much that Miami High had a great team. It has but not 28 points greater than the Cardinals. It was just that Edison, knowing it had never beaten Miami High before, kept in its mind that it is inferior to Miami High."[40]

"We played the game 1,000 times in our minds before we got to it and then we were worn out," sighed slump-shouldered quarterback Lloyd Sheehan, loathe to admit that Yarborough had gotten under the Red Raiders' skin and into their heads.[41]

Yarborough's game plan was meant to exploit the Red Raiders' over-aggressiveness with quick openers, misdirection and trap plays that kept springing runners out of the backfield. Edison had no answer for Lefty Schemer. Jack Bell called it his greatest game ever. And as the game went on, Edison didn't even have an answer for Joe Crum. The erstwhile Red Raider had been begging Yarborough to figure out a way to get him a touchdown. The coach gladly complied. Early in the third quarter, Johnny Reid called the play drawn up to do just that. It was a double slap at Edison. The game was being played under interscholastic rules, which Edison had been using all year. Miami played under collegiate rules, which didn't allow passes to be thrown within five yards of the line of scrimmage. Naturally, Yarborough found a way to take advantage of the rule with Crum the beneficiary.

All Crum had to do was to prevent his body language from giving it away as he emerged from the huddle. As Reid took the snap and headed toward his right, Crum looked like part of the blocking pattern. At that point, he slipped into the flat as Reid pulled up and hit him for the six points. The Stingarees mercilessly hurled barbs across the line of scrimmage. "What do you think of Joe Crum now?" they barked. Crum, who had been hearing all week from his old teammates, simply sank to his knees.

"I guess I showed him," he said of Parnell.[42]

They also showed Gilbert Snyder. The manager who predicted an Edison victory was banned from the team bus back to the high school. He had to walk. It isn't known whether he hitched a ride with the throngs of Miami supporters who headed up Flagler Street in their automobiles, honking their horns. A cop at the Second Avenue intersection, probably an Edison grad, handed out tickets for disturbing the peace and was booed by sympathetic crowds on the sidewalk, only adding to the deafening din.

Edison's explanation was that it was too up for the game. But the real lesson was that the two rivals' seasons couldn't be compared on records alone, not when Miami was playing some of the best teams in the South. Jimmy Ellenberg, the former Stingaree star who was assisting Yarborough as a volunteer coach, nailed it.

"Just say it's a tough, tough league that Miami High plays in," said Ellenberg, the former Stingaree. "What do those Big Ten champions feel like now?"[43]

KNOXVILLE: A HARD LESSON

Of course, the answer would be apparent to Ellenberg and his Stingaree brethren in seven days when the cleat, so to speak, was on the other foot. As the Stingarees basked in their victory with a "Bring on Knoxville" attitude, a letdown was inevitable and the Trojans of

Knoxville City High weren't coming to town for just another game. They believed that if they knocked off a program like Miami to cap off an undefeated season, they should be considered national champions. Still, the Stings, who had lost just 13-6 to Knoxville the previous season, were not unaccustomed to facing top teams. They eased into their practice sessions without much urgency but were said to have retained their fine edge while doing little hard work.

Yarborough excused what may have come across as a lax attitude, with a final jab at Parnell and Co.

"You can talk all you want about the boys gritting their teeth and murdering each other in practice," he said. "Miami Edison was like that in practice last week but not on the field. Our boys are playing around now but they'll be ready Thursday night."[44]

Jack Bell agreed. He gave the Tennessee team its due but he still couldn't see how the Miamians could fail to put up a fight:

> There's a game worth more than you're asked to pay for it. The boys from the Smokies have one of the South's finest. They've ridden roughshod over all the opposition this fall, as they did here last year. (Johnnie) Butler, the flaming halfback, has been the terror of the gridiron for two years. He will be winding up his brilliant prep career here tomorrow night, probably to go into Tennessee as a pupil of Major Bob Neyland.
>
> The Miami team is better than that of last year, however. These Stingarees were as good as they come in the Thanksgiving game. They had snap and poise and rhythm—and drive. Last year's club was more or less a misfit crew. This team, with a big, fast line and the best backs we've had in 10 years isn't going to lose by any big margin to any team. I know, you've got to throw out that Macon High game; but think of what the Stingarees of Thanksgiving day would have done to Macon! Or should we forget it?[45]

The answer: they should have forgotten it. It was less like the Macon loss than that 34-7 beating that Male administered. Knoxville may have come down with a traveling squad of just 17 players, but, as coach Wilson Collins said, they were making no alibis. On what was described as the chilliest football night of the year in Miami, Butler, the Trojans' All Southern back, led them to 21 first downs and a 25-0 rout. It was, the *News* said, "a rollicking, surging display of rhythm and speed."[46]

He could have added brute strength for the Trojans outweighed the Stingarees up and down the lineup and sent the vaunted Schemer to Jackson Hospital with a rib injury.

Knoxville wasn't picked by the as the national champion that year—Austin of Chicago was—but that was Art Johlfs' subjective opinion. Miami could have helped settle that argument. Austin was the first choice for the annual Christmas game. The school from the Windy City's far West Side featured "Wild" Bill DeCorrevont, the high school sensation of the nation, and had drawn those astounding 120,000 people to Soldier Field for the city championship game against Catholic League champ Leo.

Described as the "most talked-about high school star that ever came down the pike," DeCorrevont produced points like Chicago produced gangsters. He scored seven TDs in the opening game against Marshall High that included runs of 50, 33, 29 and 26. In a 93-0 rout of McKinley, he scored on nine of his 10 carries. In all, DeCorrevont had scored 34 touchdowns in nine games to be the nation's leading scorer at any level—high school, college or professional. Yarborough could only imagine the gate receipts if the Midwest phenom were to grace Burdine Stadium.

A call to Austin coach Bill Heiland the night of the Leo game seemed to confirm the Chicago school's interest. Heiland asked for a $3,000 guarantee with an option of 30 per cent of the gross gate. Jimmy Segreti of the *Chicago Tribune* promised DeCorrevont would fill every seat in the stadium. Meanwhile, Heiland wired the *Miami Herald* that there was "a possibility of playing at Miami." So sure was the *Herald* that DeCorrevont was headed its way that it ran a picture of him under the headline, "Can Stingarees' Stop Him?"

One problem. Austin had agreed a year earlier to a post-season game in Memphis on December 11. While it was reported that both Heiland and DeCorrevont preferred a trip to Miami—why wouldn't they?—school officials ultimately decided to both honor their original commitment and play just the one post-season game. It was anticlimactic. Wild Bill fractured his collarbone after scoring in the first half and the game drew just 5,000 fans.

OAK PARK: ANTICLIMAX

Disappointed, Miami cast its sights to the Chicago suburbs for Austin's replacement. Among the 62 other applicants, undefeated Oak Park had been the backup plan all along and Bell, trying to ameliorate the sting of missing out on Wild Bill, claimed it was a better team than Austin and had played a much tougher schedule. The Huskies came cheaper too, for a $1,800 guarantee.

Yarborough moved the game under the lights for the first time in the Christmas series, and the papers predicted a wide-open contest. The Stingarees were supposed to come out throwing, the papers said, and Oak Park, even without Pope, the "Ebony Streak," had a formidable offense. But the most that was written of the 6-6 tie was that it was a hard-fought game.

Played before 8,600, it was the final high school appearance for Schemer, who was recovering just fine from his bruised rib caused by big Jay Kendrick falling on his ankle during practice. Even hobbled, Lefty accounted for Miami's six points with a second-quarter touchdown pass to Reid. Schemer briefly left the game shaken up but, after Oak Park tied the game by taking advantage of an interception, Schemer returned and shut off the Huskies' final scoring threat with an interception, his last bit of Stingaree heroism.

All in all, it was a pretty successful season considering the 10-game gauntlet that Yarborough scheduled for his boys. The combined record of Miami's opponents for the season was 80-24-5. The Stingarees faced unbeaten teams eight times, including in their last five games. Four of their opponents finished the season unbeaten. No other team in the country was tested as much, and nothing could have better prepared the underclassmen. In May, Schemer walked up to the stage in the high school's grand auditorium to accept the Sigma Nu Trophy. Davey Eldredge was among those giving him the biggest ovation a Sigma Nu winner had ever received. As he cheered for Lefty, Eldredge remembered watching his brother accept the same award two years earlier.

He thought to himself, "Someday."

TEN

THE 1937 BOILERMAKERS

His name was John DaGrosa, better known as "Ox," and he was a sure sign of Art Argauer's apprehension as the 1937 football season approached. Argauer had leveraged his way into a new contract at Garfield after feigning a move to Lyndhurst. So, committed, he was getting on with his grand plan to establish Garfield as a perennial state power. The first part was to pack the schedule with heavyweights. Gone were five teams whom the Boilermakers outscored by a combined 203-7. The stronger teams remained. The '37 opponents included Passaic and Bloomfield, which shared the '36 state title; unbeaten Carteret, the defending Central Jersey Group 3 champ; Dickinson of Jersey City, among the favorites for state laurels in '37; and Irvington, which would be one of the surprise teams of the year.

Next, and more onerous, of course, was building a team to rival the competition. The '37 season, as it turned out, provided the growing pains. Argauer's biggest challenge was replacing his ambidextrous triple-threat back, Jules Koshlap, now a Georgetown Hoya. Broad-shouldered Frank "Sully" Socha, the team captain, would be shifted from his end spot and would shore up the running game, but his shelf life was expiring. He would turn 20 and became ineligible after six games. It was a common Depression-era problem with so many boys dropping in and out of school to take jobs and help buck up the family finances. Then there was sophomore Benny Babula, coaxed out of Clifton and slipped into the lineup as a freshman. He was just growing into his body.

In all, after collecting the uniforms from his '36 edition, Argauer felt he had enough young talent to keep the momentum of his program moving forward—so long as he remained at Garfield. But September arrived quickly and caught the Boilermakers off-guard. Most teams look good in pads during the first days of practice, and the word was that Garfield had another strong team. The first newspaper reports touted the 14 lettermen among 45 candidates reporting. The Boilermakers, the papers noted, would feature a quick backfield and a veteran line. But with just two weeks left before powerful Dickinson called to start the season, the coach soon started biting his nails again. It was a habit he started after he quit smoking, which happened after he nearly burned down his father's tailor shop with a lit butt.

Argauer's subs had outplayed his first team in an intra-squad scrimmage, and that is how Ox DaGrosa entered the picture—out of the coach's desperation. Ox was a football pioneer. He developed the five-man defensive line as Lou Little's assistant at Georgetown, then moved on to Temple before landing a spot as a Philadelphia Eagles assistant. In addition, he founded the American Football Institute, a think tank that examined the weighty issues of the sport, conducted coaching clinics and viewed the game through a scientific lens. He delivered lectures across the country to coaching groups and the like.

DaGrosa had been a tackle on Colgate's undefeated 1925 team and was one of the best blockers in the country, a player who gave no quarter. Think Vince Lombardi. He could have come out of the same mold. After World War II, DaGrosa would complain that America was going soft, which pretty well summed up his philosophy: "Football during peacetime is the closest thing to the science of war and it is a game we must know because who wants to lose a war?"[1] Ox was an impressive-looking individual and, while mild-mannered, he exuded gravitas, especially when speaking to high school football players. He had a square head and a barrel chest. His gruff voice gave his words a subliminal resonance. Equipped with a law degree from Georgetown, he could be persuasive. Later, as the Pennsylvania State Boxing Commissioner, Ox would cajole Rocky Marciano and Jersey Joe Walcott into staging their 1950 title fight in Philadelphia. Five years before that, as the head coach at Holy Cross, he cajoled enough recruits into attending the Jesuit school in Worcester that his squad made it to the Orange Bowl, where it lost a thriller to the Miami Hurricanes on New Year's Day.

Wally Carew, in his book, *A Farewell to Glory,* describes how DaGrosa snatched away star end Tom Kelleher just after he'd supposedly committed to Penn. Ox paid a visit to Kelleher's dad, and by the time the son got home DaGrosa had delivered his pitch perfectly and was filling out dad's favorite easy chair in the family living room. "Sit down and listen to what he says about the value of Catholic education," Mr. Kelleher told him. DaGrosa, despite his Italian surname, wasn't Roman Catholic. Rather, he was "a card-carrying Mason," which would have rendered him *persona non grata* to any Catholic school kid who read the "Examination of Conscience," that little blue handbook cataloging sins, both venial and mortal. The Masons were marginalized as a dangerous "secret society" and were perceived as a hostile element to the Catholic faith. As any of the nuns at St. Stan's in Garfield would warn their pupils, join them and you were signing on with the devil for an eternity in hell.

At Holy Cross, the Jesuits (an order known for modernizing the church and for its high-minded pedagogy) offered DaGrosa a form of absolution, so long as he preached the gridiron gospel of the Purple Crusaders. "He was a golden orator," Kelleher marveled. "He could have two hands full of turds, and after he was through talking, you would be bidding for it."[2]

In other words, Penn, with its Ivy-clad Protestant underpinnings, didn't stand a chance against Ox's proselytizing. Kelleher enrolled at Holy Cross. And so, it was that Argauer gathered his boys around DaGrosa, hoping he could whip the lethargy out of them with his stentorian rhetoric. According to Joe Lovas, *The Herald-News* reporter (and Garfield grad) who was on hand for the clinic, Ox emphasized two blocks—the shoulder block and the crab crawl (down on all fours, a technique since banned because it targeted the knees). Additionally, Lovas wrote that DaGrosa "gave the Boilermakers plays with which he said the best colleges in the country score touchdowns if executed correctly. As several of the plays called for passes, DaGrosa was doubtful if the Boilermakers had a passer equal to the task," Lovas wrote. "But after witnessing Benny Babula peg the pigskin with perfect shoots, he replied that the Comet back was as good a passer—if not better—than some of the professionals and also college stars."[3]

It was a prescient observation by DaGrosa, who, alas, was unable to stir up Argauer's charges, silver tongue or no silver tongue. Two days after being tutored by Ox, the Boilermakers were gored in a scrimmage by a strong Columbia High team from South Orange and Maplewood. It was less that DaGrosa's words fell on deaf ears than on bodies not quite ready for the rigors of an elite schedule. It was only a 14-6 scrimmage loss, but it felt much worse to the head coach.

"We'll be lucky to win two games this season," Argauer groused to Art McMahon of *The Herald-News*. "The line is weak while the backfield is slow and lacks the brains of last year's backfield. I need a first-string center and I'm praying that another end is found. The guards failed to give the ball carrier any interference and the blocking of the entire front wall was bad. Four of the regular linemen have charley horses and sprained ankles and the backfield is also crippled. What I need is another Koshlap to direct the team on the field."[4]

DICKINSON: ONE THAT GOT AWAY

Argauer didn't catch any breaks or sympathy from the writers. They had previously been accustomed to a lot of good-natured give-and-take with Argauer, but now they were making a plaything of his misery. "Coach Art Argauer is facing a perplexing problem, wondering as to what the showing of his team will be against Dickinson," the *Bergen Record* noted. "His eleven, a team that early in the season showed so much promise of becoming great, has suddenly made a turn almost overnight in the opposite direction. . . . The performance of the Boilermaker machine in the last few days of scrimmaging was miserable."[5] Over at *The Herald-News*, McMahon warned:

> There is nothing phony about the tears Art Argauer is shedding as he regards his squad and the schedule it faces. He had faint hopes of unappreciated strength until he saw Columbia push his pupils around last Saturday. Now he is convinced that there is no Koshlap hiding on the squad. Graduation put a big dent in his squad and the magic Argauer wand that annually waved over some obscure youth and transformed him into a first-class player hasn't had an effect as yet. Garfield's best bet is Benny Babula, a snappy passer. . . . It isn't a very pleasant outlook for Argauer but I'll help him along—I'll pick Dickinson to score a 13-0 victory.[6]

Garfield alum Al Del Greco piled on in his Friday prediction column in the *Record*:

> Art Argauer has so many crying towels in practice that reporters can't get near him. This is a very strange condition. Considering the fact Garfield has turned out good clubs year after year and Argauer may be justified in mourning, one weak vote for Dickinson to win, 6-0.[7]

In any case, the Dickinson Hilltoppers appeared to be a poor matchup for the Boilermakers. Garfield's weakness was Dickinson's strength: up front. The Hudson County team's forward line averaged 190 pounds, huge for the era, and featured Coach Charlie Witkowski's brother Johnny (nickname "Bullet") at end. But while Witkowski grabbed most of the pre-season headlines, it was another Hilltopper who would be voted New Jersey's High School Athlete of the Year.

Al Blozis was actually born in Garfield, in a heavily mortgaged house his parents bought at the edge of the Heights on Malcolm Avenue. His father Anthony, a Lithuanian immigrant, moved the family to the Bronx before the growing boy reached school age, then back across the Hudson to North Bergen after Al graduated from St. Luke's elementary school. North Bergen didn't have a high school, so its kids attended Memorial in neighboring West New York. But just as Babula lived in Clifton and matriculated at Garfield, Blozis found his way to Dickinson, with its the towering edifice overlooking New York Harbor on Bergen Hill. "If only they'd stayed in Garfield," Argauer must have sighed as he took in the sight of the 6-foot-4, 225-pound tackle destined to join Koshlap at Georgetown in a year. There, he'd grow two inches and put on 20 more pounds to become a mainstay on the Hoyas' line. His biggest impact, though, was as an NCAA champion shot putter. He was dubbed the "Human Howitzer" because of the force with which the shot put left his hand, which was how he came to the attention of New York Giants head coach Steve Owen. Owen couldn't help but marvel at Blozis' raw strength as he witnessed him set the world indoor shot put record at Madison Square Garden. It was as if Blozis was taking part in a modern-day scouting combine, except Owen, to his delight, was the only scout in attendance. "What a pair of shoulders," Owen raved to his wife. "Look at the size of that fellow. Look at how he moves. See what muscle control he has."[8]

Owen didn't have to watch Blozis play football. He knew exceptional natural talent when he saw it. The Giants drafted him in 1942. Blozis soon made All Pro, standing out even more conspicuously in a league depleted by war enlistments. Soon, he got antsy to join the soldiers in the fight but, to his dismay, he was denied by the very thing that made him so special on the gridiron—his size. At 6-6, he exceeded the height limit. He was too tall for military transports.

Naturally, that didn't stop him. In 1943, Blozis somehow managed to convince the Army to accept him and, then, to move him out of his desk job at Walter Reed Hospital. He ultimately secured an infantry commission at Fort Benning, where he wowed the brass by setting the Army's hand grenade throwing record at 94 yards, 2 feet, 6.5 inches.

With three games left in the 1944 season, he was permitted to rejoin the Giants. Then, in a matter of weeks, Second Lieutenant Blozis was off to Europe with the 28th Infantry Division. He finally saw combat in the Vosges Mountains of France, a conflict known as the "other Battle of the Bulge." When, as platoon leader, he found his men surrounded and cut off near the little village of Pairis, he deployed his sergeant with a small patrol to probe the German lines and determine their strength. According to *The Jersey Journal*, a dispatch from the 28th Infantry described what happened next:

> *The patrol ran into German fire and shortly after some of the men staggered back to their company—without the sergeant and one other man. As the day wore on and dusk approached there was still no sign of them so Lieutenant Blozis set out after them alone. Wading through snowdrifts up to his hips and wind-driven flurries that obscured his vision, he made his way toward the German lines. The last his men saw, he was working his way through a snow-filled draw, his big body moving carefully through the scanty brush. A short time later there was the hoarse, hard sound of a machine gun. Lieutenant Blozis did not come back."[9]*

That was January 25, 1945. Blozis' body was not recovered until April—one week before the German surrender. His No. 32 jersey was the first of 12 retired by the Giants. Blozis was wearing Dickinson's maroon jersey No. 17 when, in 1937, he hopped off the team bus at Passaic Stadium to face Garfield. The Boilermakers had prevailed, 13-6, a year earlier and Dickinson was eager to display its potential state championship credentials against a reputable program before 3,500 mostly-hostile witnesses.

They began early with a touchdown catch from "Bullet" Witkowski. Blozis extended his massive wingspan in front of Babula as the Boilermaker stepped into a punt, or, more precisely, into Blozis. The big Hilltopper engulfed the ball and remained on his feet throughout. As the football wobbled away from him, he nimbly scooped it up in one continuous motion and sprinted 35 yards for Dickinson's second score. The rout was on. The 26-0 defeat was Argauer's worst since Garfield's 1-7 season in 1931, his only losing season.

Del Greco drew his poison pen from the ink well:

> Art Argauer won't shed crocodile tears this year to deceive the writers and coaches. No sir, he won't go into any locker rooms and squirt water in his eyes to simulate grief. . . . His tears will be the real thing. Dickinson batted his boys around 26 to 0. . . . 'Inexperience lost for Garfield,' remarked one die-hard. 'Yeah,' said one wag. 'But those four touchdowns and two extra points had something to do with it.'[10]

Lovas made a couple of interesting—and rather optimistic—observations in his account of the game, beginning with his thoughts on Babula's first varsity start. Allowing that Babula didn't have Koshlap's "football mind," he nevertheless was impressed by the sophomore's off tackle bursts and predicted that he should shape up as a "brilliant ball carrier" before the season was over.

The second insight was about senior Carmine Perrapato, who had inherited the play-calling duties from Koshlap—to Lovas' dismay. Bemoaning Garfield's "lack of a competent field general," Lovas charged Perrapato with "poor quarterbacking" because he called his own number too often. "Unless Carmine Perrapato sacrifices the glory of scoring a touchdown. . . . Garfield will find it tough to score."

Still, Lovas wrote, Perrapato "should develop into a fine signal-caller. He shows aggressiveness, something which the 1937 edition lacks."[11]

That tenacity would figure large later in the season. But, for now, Argauer could not have been more disgusted, having seen his squad tossed around and outmuscled in successive weeks. If there had been one unwavering trait of his Garfield boys since he took over, it was toughness. But Argauer now wasn't seeing it, mentally or physically. The only exception came at the game's end, when his players objected to Dickinson making off with the game ball and nearly sparked a brawl before the coaches broke things up.

"Art Argauer is today wondering just how bad his Garfield High School football team is," the *Bergen Record* wrote. "And although Argauer's moans might have been exaggerated, there is no doubt that the 1937 edition of the Comet football team lacks brains, polish and deception."

IRVINGTON AND PASSAIC: THE SKID CONTINUES

Two games later, they were also without a victory. Although they showed some signs of improvement in a 12-6 loss to a heavy Irvington team, their play still begged *The Herald-News* to ask what was on most observers' minds: "Is Garfield's football power fading? That is the question Comet supporters are still unable to answer following the Boilermakers' second straight defeat Saturday, the first time in years an Argauer-coached eleven has dropped successive games."[12]

Traditional rival Passaic made it three. Ray Pickett's squad put up two goal-line stands to preserve a 14-0 victory in a violent game that saw the Indians' Joe Gyorgydeak ejected for landing a retaliatory uppercut to the chin of a Garfield player and Perrapato carried off the field on a stretcher, to be lost for the next two weeks with a leg injury.

"The Boilermakers won't draw a dime at their home games for the rest of the season; their fans don't go in for losing clubs," Del Greco chided.[13]

EAST RUTHERFORD. CARTERET: SOCHA TAKES OVER

Del Greco knew of what he spoke. He played on mediocre Garfield clubs in the mid-1920s. And Argauer certainly knew the dire meaning of poor attendance. Gate receipts, at the time, yielded the bulk of funding for football programs. The schools negotiated the portion of the gate the visitor would keep, and, the better the team, the more the road team could command.

But the Boilermakers wouldn't be able to disprove Del Greco's home attendance theory for a while. The next four games were all on the road, a chance for the Boilermakers to regain some prestige. The next three opponents—like the first three—were undefeated. They would face East Rutherford, Carteret and Bloomfield, the most imposing of them all. A lot was at stake. The Boilermakers somehow had to make something happen quickly, for the good of the program that season . . . and even beyond. Curiously, Del Greco grew more optimistic the week before the East Rutherford game. No doubt, Argauer had been whispering in his ear.

> Hold onto your hats. This will be a whale of a game from start to finish. Despite the fact that East Rutherford has been tearing around impressively and Garfield has been bounced around like the Giants, I'll take the Alma Mater, 12-0. That means Garfield.[14]

The next three games would be Socha's last as a Boilermaker and he let his team know how much they would miss him by reviving the season almost single-handedly. Against East Rutherford, he continually pounded the line for gains of eight and 10 yards and scored two second-half TDs in a 19-7 win and followed that up with another invaluable performance against Carteret.

Today, Carteret is one of New Jersey's legendary high school programs. It began in 1925 under a female head coach, Sally McCarthy, who admittedly knew very little football. She retired nonetheless with a 4-2 record after one season and was an enthusiastic spectator when, in, 1926, a freshman by the name of Joe Medwick, entered the high school. He'd acquire his more descriptive nickname of "Ducky" years after graduation.

As left fielder with the St. Louis Cardinals' Gashouse Gang, Medwick won the National League Triple Crown in 1937 (he's still the last to do so) and was named the league's MVP, nosing out the Cubs' Gabby Hartnett by two votes. The scant margin was a sign of the animosity that existed between the baseball writers and Medwick—not that the writers were unique in that regard. Just about everyone, opponents and teammates alike, disliked the combative (to put it euphemistically) Ducky.

When Medwick retired in 1948—only to wait 20 more years before the writers allowed him into the Hall of Fame—a former teammate snarled, "when he dies, half the National League will go to his wake to make sure that Son of a Bitch is dead."

No doubt, Medwick picked up some of those hard-knock lessons on the Carteret High School football field, where he was called "Muscles" or the "'Hammerin' Hungarian." Medwick's 19 touchdowns co-led the state his senior year, when the Ramblers went 8-1 and won the Class B Central New Jersey title. Medwick was such a force on the gridiron that he could have achieved his dream of playing football for Notre Dame, but he turned down a scholarship offer from Knute Rockne to play baseball, hitting .419 in his rookie season in the minors. So much for waking up the echoes in South Bend.

Just after the 1937 season ended, Medwick, the newly minted NL MVP, spoke before a group of New Jersey coaches, telling them he owed more than he could "ever repay" to his high school football and baseball coach, Frank McCarthy. According to Gene Hampson of the *Plainfield Courier-News*, McCarthy—as Argauer had done with several Garfield kids— persuaded Medwick to go back to school and convinced his family of the merits of a high school degree over the boy's factory job. Once Medwick re-enrolled, McCarthy spent hours tutoring him.

"The Jersey ace insisted that he never would have made the big time but for his high school experience and the attention gained there," Hampson wrote.[15]

Ten years after Medwick, Carteret's star came from an entirely different galaxy. Diminutive tailback Doug King was less of a Hammerin' Hungarian and more of a Slippery Scot. He mostly relied on speed and elusiveness to score a state-high 52 points through the first four weeks of the season. And, as King frequently flitted across the goal line, the Rambler defense stingily defended it. They were undefeated, untied and un-scored upon in their first five games.

The Ramblers knew Garfield was a step up in class, the toughest team on their schedule. As for Garfield, it was anxious to finally beat a highly ranked squad regardless of class. It was a suddenly confident Boilermaker team that looked forward to this test. Garfield "has appeared to have hit its stride," warned the *Newark News* in previewing the game[16] while the *Independent Press* of Bloomfield was more blunt in its assessment.

"Carteret's teams are usually powerful but dumb," it claimed, perhaps with Medwick in mind. "So don't count it as an upset if Art Argauer's boys use the game as a tuneup for the (Bloomfield) Bengal fray next week."[17]

If Garfield was hitting its stride, Socha was setting the pace. He punished the lighter Carteret line and opened the scoring with a 17-yard run–the first of his two TDs. And, when speedy Ted Ciesla got outside later in the first quarter, Socha took out two Rambler defenders to lead his teammate on an 81-yard dash. On defense, Socha continually threw aside blockers and dragged down the prolific King to hold him off the scoreboard in a 19-13 win that was undoubtedly Garfield's finest of the year.

BLOOMFIELD: NOT QUITE READY

Suddenly, the Boilermakers were considered potential spoilers as they readied for their annual meeting with rival Bloomfield.

Bloomfield had not lost since Garfield turned the trick in the 1934 season opener. Since that day, coach Bill Foley never took Art Argauer's team for granted. The defeat still sat on the Irishman's stomach like an ill-recommended greasy-spoon special. Their annual battle of wits always drew big crowds—and big bets—especially since Garfield seemed always capable of springing an upset.

What made it more dangerous was that Bloomfield was ripe for an ever-looming letdown. A week earlier, the Bengals won a battle of the unbeaten against Dickinson on a muddy Foley Field. Blozis blocked a punt that was returned for Dickinson's only touchdown, but the big tackle struggled on defense, consistently falling for the Bengals' trap plays on the slippery turf. A rain-drenched crowd of 15,000—including Argauer and his entire team—witnessed the 12-7 Bloomfield victory.

By then, the only blemish on Bloomfield's season was an 0-0 tie with Belleville in Week 2, attributed by Foley to the inexperience of his play callers. So here they were, Garfield and Bloomfield each coming into the game playing their best football of the season. Those same fans Del Greco claimed the Boilermakers risked losing after their 0-3 start were now back on the bandwagon, according to *The Herald-News*.

> *Garfield's Boilermakers are hungry for victory over the Bengals. Comet supporters, always loyal to the last ditch, are confident of a triumph and are willing to be their last greenback on the outcome. But Boilermaker backers want more than the 2-3 odds that Bloomfield fans are giving and with plenty of money to exchange hands if the odds go to 2-1 or higher.[18]*

Neither Del Greco nor McMahon were ready to hop on with them to predict a Garfield win. Each put their unique spin on setting up another Boilermaker letdown, starting with McMahon:

> *Bloomfield last felt the sting of defeat in 1934 when Garfield pulled a stunning upset in the opening game of the season. There is only a light hope of a Boilermaker triumph this year for the Bengals take a particular delight in spanking Garfield for that brazen defeat and the strong desire for revenge permits no relaxation or over confidence on Bloomfield's part. But when Brown beats Columbia, I guess nothing is impossible.[19]*
>
> *It has been definitely established at long last that all horses have four legs but not all four legs have horses. Garfield will make it interesting but Bloomfield doesn't frighten easily. A swell spot for an upset but common sense demands, Bloomfield, 14, Garfield 0.[20]*

Del Greco teased his old friend:

> *Garfield is getting a sweet guarantee for this ball game. So the only thing it can lose are Artie Argauer's false teeth. (You didn't know that, did you?). Bloomfield will win, of course, but Garfield will be shooting all day long for the burden of proof, whatever that means, rests with the Bengals. I've been trying to tell you that the score will be 27-6. And why should that score be burning in my head?[21]*

McMahon, as it turned out, was closer to what eventually happened. The Boilermakers lost, 19-0, but they did make it more than interesting for the 8,000 in attendance, trailing just 7-0 going into the fourth quarter before Babula left with an ankle injury and the Garfield passing game closed down. The Bengals caught a break when Socha mishandled a snap from center that led to Bloomfield's first touchdown in the opening period. Garfield twice moved deep into Bloomfield territory but lost the ball on downs each time. Finally, Bloomfield's two stars, Stan Krivik and Bill Geyer, scored fourth-period touchdowns, Krivik after a long drive against a tired Garfield line and Geyer on a 55-yard run off fake punt when Wally Tabaka slipped trying to make the tackle.

Still, Socha played heroically in his final game while Ciesla, the junior, repeatedly darted through Bloomfield's front wall behind Socha's interference. On one occasion, Socha, from his own end zone, unleashed an 80-yard punt over the heads of the Bloomfield safeties. Two years later, Socha and Ciesla were teammates at Washington and Lee.

The Independent Press of Bloomfield noted that Foley's team was caught in between two more important games on its schedule, but the writer also saw something in Garfield that made him think that the next couple of years might yield different results when the rivals would meet:

> *The Bloomfield Bengals maintained their unbeaten record Saturday at the expense of Art Argauer's Garfield club, 19-0 but looked sluggish doing it. The Bengals appeared as if they knew they were going to win and were saving their energy for tomorrow's game with Irvington. This attitude was to be expected in the lull between the climax games with Dickinson and Irvington. Garfield, on the other hand, was a better ballclub against Bloomfield than it was against Carteret. According to the program, Art is going to have a whopper of a club next year and the year after. Most of the boys who played against the Bengals will be there again next season and some more of them will be back for two . . . The victory was the 43rd in the last 46 starts and inasmuch as Garfield was the only team to defeat the Bengals during the stretch the game meant something. Regardless of the final Colliton rating of Garfield, Art Argauer has a good ball club and one that could cause trouble with any opponent. The statistics of the game show that Garfield rushed the ball just as many times as the Bengals did although their yardage was only about one-quarter as good, they passed 10 more times and punted one more time than the Bengals. It's been many a day since any club has done that to Bloomfield.[22]*

ASBURY PARK: ONLY IN AN EMERGENCY

The moral victory left Garfield hollow nonetheless. At 2-4, the main thing left to salvage over the last three games was a winning record. Asbury Park, Union Hill and Clifton were all beatable. Then there was the continued seasoning of the underclassmen. If there were a benefit to losing Socha for the final three games, it was that Babula and Ciesla would gain more experience carrying the football. For the time being, however, the papers wondered how Garfield could possibly replace its captain and chief signal-caller. The answer was Perrapato, whose over-aggressive play-calling Lovas questioned in the loss to Passaic. After being carried off the field in that game, the senior returned to play sparing minutes against Bloomfield and was now ready to reclaim his place in the starting lineup as the play-caller.

The Perrapato family comprised Garfield's ruling class. Carmine's father was Nicholas Perrapato, the police chief. His uncle was Anthony Perrapato, the former mayor. Another uncle, Thomas, was on the Board of Education. Grandfather Carmine, from Sala Consilina, Italy, owned a saloon next to the railroad tracks, where a number of Perrapatos took their first breaths of life in an upstairs bedroom. Being born a Perrapato gave you certain privileges in Garfield and Carmine may have felt slightly entitled.

Most expected a sure Garfield win. *The Bergen Record* predicted it would be by a two-touchdown margin. But a funny thing happened when the Boilermakers headed down the shore.

Ordinarily, Asbury Park High School presented the most picturesque site for a football game anywhere in New Jersey. The arched grandstand soared in front of the neoclassical high school building on the south branch of tranquil Deal Lake with the salt-traced winds adding to the seaside atmosphere.

But these weren't just ocean breezes coming off the Atlantic some 10 blocks East. Winds were whipping across the open expanse of the playing field at about 20 miles per hour, making the running game imperative, the passing game dicey.

Argauer had the heavier team anyway. The conditions only made him more determined to stick to the ground game. A year earlier, the Boilermakers were burned for putting the ball in the air when Koshlap's third-quarter pass for Perrapato was intercepted and returned 43 yards for a touchdown by Wilbur Schaefer. It was, in fact, the only time in his high school career that Koshlap threw what is today called a "pick-six." That was not going to happen this week, if Argauer could help it. And, he usually could.

At first, the winds blew Garfield's way. With the wind at his back, Ciesla, punting from his 48-yard line in the first quarter, used the coffin corner to pin Asbury Park in at its one-yard line. Facing into that same wind, Asbury's Park's Charlie Prout had his punt knocked down at the Blue Bishop 24. Perrapato eventually knifed in from the one for the touchdown, but the wind blew his point-after attempt wide of the goalpost.

Argauer took the air out of the football and played field position into the fourth quarter, often punting on third down to let his defense hold. The Boilermakers were now playing stiff into the wind after the teams exchanged sides for the final time. Midway through the quarter, they were inside Asbury Park territory when Argauer called over to Young on the sidelines. Young recalled the fateful moment:

"He never called me Walter. He called me Youngie. He said, "Go in and you tell Perry, 'No passes, no more passes, only in an extreme emergency.'"

Young relayed the message to Perrapato. The senior stared at the sophomore as if he was questioning his authority. "This is an emergency," he snapped back.

Perrapato called a pass play for Babula to look for him in the flat. Babula faded back but found himself under a heavy rush. His tossed the ball haphazardly and, as Schaefer had done a year earlier, Maury Klitzman came out of nowhere to feast upon the bone just tossed his way. He picked off the pass and, behind three blockers, galloped 60 yards for a touchdown, whistling past the red-faced Argauer on his way.

Ernie Davenport came on to do what Perrapato couldn't—navigate the wind currents by kicking the extra point. Thanks to a fumbled punt, Garfield had a final chance to win in the final minute. They had three cracks to run the ball in from the Asbury Park one but failed before Babula's fourth down pass thudded into the end zone turf. Ed Hill of the *Asbury Park Press* chalked up the Blue Bishops' 7-6 win to Garfield's brain freeze, which had nothing to do with the town's famous boardwalk ice cream:

Secretly, Bob Heiusel expected the Blue Bishops to take a trimming at the Deal Lake Stadium and everybody in the ballpark agreed with this view until Garfield's football brains went with the brisk northwest wind, which swept the Deal Lake field. Six points ahead and needing only six minutes of safe playing to sew up the decision, Garfield tossed caution aside and tried an unnecessary forward pass.[23]

It was a quiet group of Boilermakers that climbed onto the bus for the long ride back home. The defeat assured them of a losing season. Argauer-coached teams had fumbled away apparent victories before, but never like this. The coach took his usual spot in the front seat of the bus next to assistant Joe Cody. Walter Young, the innocent messenger in the tragedy, did a double take as he walked by.

"We lost. Coach cried, the only time in my life I saw him cry," Young said. "And you never saw such a desolate bunch of kids in all your life."

UNION HILL: COUNTING TO 21

The following Saturday, the Boilermakers were to host Union Hill from Hudson County. A cold downpour, which suited the Boilermaker mood, quickly turned playing fields into quagmires to force the postponement of the entire high school slate. The game was moved to Tuesday and played before a sparse crowd of 900. Those diehards were unaware they were witnessing the start of something big.

This time, Argauer made sure his team kept the ball on the still-muddy ground, and with not much left to lose except the rest of his temper, he started a squad of underclassmen. Perrapato, notably, was on the bench. Union Hill controlled the game at the start and after being stopped on downs inside the Garfield five, took advantage of a Babula fumble for a 7-0 halftime lead. Argauer had seen enough. He couldn't stand losing. He put all his regulars back into the game.

Now Garfield's first-string line took over. The visitors had just three second-half possessions as the Boilermakers slammed them with off-tackle runs and fooled them with reverses. On the first play from scrimmage after intermission, Ciesla's interception put Garfield at the Union Hill 35 and the Boilermakers cashed in to tie the game. Perrapato, who had defied the "only in an emergency" directive, would redeem himself. Sort of.

On fourth down from the six-yard line, Perrapato called for a lateral to Ciesla. It wasn't a clean exchange. The ball ended up on the ground. But Ciesla recovered it on the four and went in. Then Perrapato got even bolder. He faked the placement and Ciesla, the holder, stood up and hit Young in the end zone for the tying point. Argauer had to chuckle underneath his austere exterior, and the Boilermakers finished off their opponents by overpowering them. Late in the game, Babula capped off an 88-yard drive by going in from the eight. Young's placement made it a 14-7 final.

It was neither thought to be a great win nor an easy one. It definitely was not considered an upset. Union Hill had a fine back in Charley Coniglio and had won three straight games, including what the *Jersey Journal* called the upset of the year a week earlier over Dickinson, the team that smashed Garfield in the opening game. But, as Al Del Greco pointed out in picking his "Alma' Mammy" by a 19-0 score, Union Hill was "plenty banged up" from its momentous victory of the previous week.[24]

What no one knew then was that the victory would become the first in a 21-game winning streak that would take the Boilermakers through Miami.

CLIFTON: WAIT TIL NEXT YEAR

The following week, Garfield renewed its rivalry with Clifton after a 10-year layoff and closed out its season at Wessington Stadium, where Argauer once starred, with a 7-2 win over the Mustangs.

The game was notable for its sloppiness. The field was a mess and penalties kept stalling Garfield drives. But it was also notable for a couple of other reasons. While senior workhorse John Zecker scored the only touchdown, Babula was the obvious star against the hometown team he had snubbed by attending Garfield. He kept ripping off 15- and 20-yard gains in a preview of the next two years. The only touchdown was prophetic, as well. *The Bergen Record* called it the best play Garfield ran all season and it would become a staple of the Garfield game plan, a 35-yard hook and lateral to Zecker after Young "sat" in the flat for a five-yard completion.

Garfield finished the season with a 4-5 record. It was both a profound disappointment and a call to arms for the next two years. Argauer was in no mood to be optimistic about just his second losing season since he took over in 1930, but he very well should have been.

Of the Boilermakers' five setbacks in their upgraded schedule, only Asbury Park could have been considered a bad loss. The other four teams had five losses combined with Irvington losing only to Bloomfield, Dickinson losing only to Bloomfield and Union Hill and Passaic losing only to Dickinson and hated rival Rutherford on Thanksgiving Day. Even that awful scrimmage against Columbia didn't look so bad in hindsight. Columbia finished a second straight unbeaten season having been scored upon only once all year. The Cougars finished second to Bloomfield in the state rankings, leaving coach Phil Marvel to grouse that there shouldn't be any rankings at all.

And then there was the relative inexperience of the squad that fueled optimism surrounding the future. Garfield's starting lineup had featured five sophomore starters— Babula, Tabaka, Orlovsky in the backfield, Grembowitz and Young on the line. Young took over at left end for the second game when Socha was moved into the backfield. He'd stay there for the next 27 games. They provided the core for the '39 team. More immediately, with Ciesla and tackle Bernie Pirog returning for one more season, the '38 team looked pretty strong, too. *The Independent Press* was right.

But it wasn't until after the Boilermakers had put away the pads that their hidden potential became evident. The week after the Garfield scare, Bloomfield destroyed powerful Irvington, 34-0, to start a remarkable four-game stretch in which they outscored teams, 162-8. The Bengals took on a challenge from unbeaten New Brunswick in a December post-season game and overwhelmed them, 54-0, to finish another year as undisputed state champs.

"The battle resembled a track meet," Gus Falzer wrote in the *Newark Sunday Call*. "The Bengals just opened a zipper up the Zebras' hide and knocked the stuffing out of them."[25]

Bus Bowen of *The Sunday Times* of New Brunswick said Bloomfield could beat Rutgers.[26] Fordham coach Jim Crowley, who was in the stands watching four future Rams on the Bengals, would have agreed. He called Bill Foley's team the best he'd ever seen at the high school level.

"I'd like to have the Bloomfield varsity intact at Fordham next year," he crowed.[27]

New Brunswick, with All Stater Andy Beno at quarterback, had already accepted an invitation to play Miami Edison in Florida on Dec 17. It was not even close as the Zebras shook off the Bloomfield loss to whip Edison, 25-0. As a basis of comparison, Edison had lost to

Miami High, 28-0. In other words, Bloomfield could certainly make a strong claim as the best team in the nation.

There were rumors of a post-season game against Chicago's Austin High and its megastar Bill DeCorrevant, but nothing came of it. Argauer would have been one of Bloomfield's biggest supporters in that argument. In a sporting gesture before the New Brunswick game, he had loaned Foley the Boilermakers' coats so the Bengals were decked out in Garfield colors on the chilly sideline.

In a way, it was symbolic of the transfer of power that was to come. There soon would be no need for Ox DaGrosa pep talks.

ELEVEN

THE SYSTEM

Walter E. Short was the Kenesaw Mountain Landis of the New Jersey State Interscholastic Athletic Association. Some writers dubbed him Sir Walter the Great, while others called him The Little King. He reigned as NJSIAA Executive Secretary from 1915 to 1958, often as the sole and final arbiter of all issues and disputes concerning New Jersey high school sports.

Short was, in a word, short—in height—but most certainly not in stature. At 5-feet-4, he was a pint-sized dynamo, plucky enough to play college football at Western Maryland, brainy enough to pivot into a career in education, first teaching mathematics, history and physical education and eventually coaching three sports.

At Rahway High School (about 12 miles southwest of Newark, and 21 miles southwest of Garfield), Short's unbeaten 1911 Indians outscored the opposition, 224-12. That was one year before Gus Falzer of the *Newark Sunday Call* answered the call of fans, parents, players and coaches by naming his unofficial but widely hailed state champion. Rahway won Falzer's crown in 1914, by outscoring foes, 197-13, in another unbeaten campaign. Short molded that team into a giant killer at a school with a male population of just 97.

Short left the Union County school in 1916 to become the director of athletics for the Newark public schools. Two years later, he conceived the idea of a state-wide organization to oversee interscholastic competition. Short called an organizational meeting that drew 50 representatives from 21 schools. He formed the organizing committee with Falzer and Earl C. MacArthur from Peddie, a distinguished prep school in Hightstown, New Jersey. They handed Short unbridled control and, as *Newark Star-Ledger* writer Sid Dorfman later noted, he was off and running before the meeting ended. He never looked back.

Short once bluntly proffered how to gain consensus at the NJSIAA annual meetings: let me decide, and that, simply, will be the consensus. Then there was another, likely more sure-fire tactic, if ever actually employed, to smooth over controversy: "Open up the bar and get the athletic directors up to the rail. Then, if you've got some controversial rule you want passed, you know they'll never leave the bar until the meeting is over. If you have to, close the door so they can't get out."[1]

Short first collided with Garfield High's interests in 1924, the first year it was eligible for an NJSIAA state championship consideration. At the time, the NJSIAA awarded Class A (large schools) and Class B (smaller schools) championships in North, Central and South sections, as well as an overall titleist. But there was no formalized system in place. The awards were essentially based on arbitrary decisions carried out by Short's hand-picked Selection Committee.

Garfield, playing in Class B, went 7-0-2 in 1924, playing two scoreless ties, including one with defending Class B state champion Ridgefield Park. When the teams met in the sixth week of the season, the assumption up north was that they were playing for both the Bergen County Interscholastic League and Class B state titles.

Walter E. Short, "The Little King." Newark Public Library.

After the deadlock—thanks to that notable Garfield goal line stand—talk stirred of a post-season rematch to settle things. But Ridgefield Park went on to absorb a 38-0 loss against Newark Central, generally considered the best team in the state. Even though Central was in Class A, the lopsided defeat virtually eliminated Ridgefield Park from championship consideration in Class B and, at the same time, reflected poorly by comparison on Garfield.

The day before the NJSIAA met to pick its champs, Wendell Merrill of the *Passaic Daily News* warned in his column that Garfield needed to send a representative if it hoped to have its case considered. The Committee set aside time to hear arguments from the respective teams but, for some reason, Coach Guy Moore deemed it unnecessary. He should have become alarmed when, two weeks previously, Short had been quoted pronouncing Rahway—his old team—as the best Class B team he'd seen, despite the fact that he nor any other Committee member had actually seen the Purple and Gold in action.[2]

In any case, Short's opinion clearly carried a lot of weight. Rahway, with a tougher schedule and a formidable reputation up and down the state, got the nod. Garfield was completely snubbed; three other teams, including Cliffside Park, also from Bergen County, received more votes than it did.

Garfield's strongest argument was that the Committee's indecisiveness—evidenced by its inability to choose between Newark Central and Asbury Park in Class A—justified a post-season title game between those teams. Central was considered the better team, but Asbury Park was undefeated in New Jersey (it had lost a post-season game to Salem, Massachusetts). In his defense, Short held that any undefeated team must be given a chance to play for a championship (Central ended up swamping the shore squad, 39-0). Undefeated Garfield wondered why its post-season fate wasn't considered with the same rubric.

Wrote Merrill: "In awarding the Class B championship to Rahway High School, in face of Garfield's unbeaten record (the NJSIAA) proved that it is a body governed by politics and not by the spirit of fair play? How can these men expect to instruct scholars in the art of playing fair when they do not practice such a doctrine themselves?"[3] Moore challenged Rahway to a game, but there was little motivation for Rahway, so the matter was permanently closed. But Garfield didn't forget.

Short's dictatorial tricks were also on full display when he set up the New Jersey high school basketball tournament. He didn't use brackets. He'd re-pair each round any way he pleased. Sometimes his fast and loose style backfired. In 1931, Garfield's undefeated regular season included its first-ever win over Passaic High School, successor to the Wonder Teams. Professor Ernest Blood had already left the hilltop school but the Passaic Indians were still a power. Everyone clamored for a rematch. So did Short, but not yet. Instead of staging a third-round collision between the two, Short eyed the big—and high-revenue—gate a Passaic-Garfield semifinal would yield. Say this for Short. He wasn't playing favorites when he instead pitted his old school, Rahway, against Garfield and Passaic against Thomas Jefferson of Elizabeth. Ironically, the two underdogs won and the rematch between Garfield and Passaic never took place.

There was nothing more contentious, however, than how New Jersey named its state champs in football. As more schools fielded teams following World War I, the thirst to be recognized as a football powerhouse was unslakable—for players, coaches, parents and, of course, for legions of fans. But the season's path leading to a state championship played by two teams of undisputed merit was a circuitous and nettlesome one indeed. How were they to rate teams, big and small, from different sections of the state when they seldom shared common opponents, let alone played head-to-head?

Short's solution was to institute the Dickinson System, the brainchild of University of Illinois economics professor Frank G. Dickinson. Between 1926 and 1940, college football used the Dickinson System to crown its national champion. It wasn't very complicated. At least it didn't start out that way. Teams winning a majority of their games were classified as first division teams. Those which did not were second division teams. The plan awarded 30 points for beating a first division team, 22½ points for tying one and 15 for losing to one. Against second division teams, the points were 20 for a win, 15 for a tie and 10 for a loss. The final ranking was calculated by dividing the total point tally by the number of games played.

It was a salve meant to heal sore wounds. Who could argue with a concrete formula? While it might have looked good on paper, its application was untenable in New Jersey's messy landscape of high school football. The state effectively had a multi-tiered system of football teams because schools had been originally split by male population into Class A and B and then, further, into Groups One, Two, Three and Four. The Dickinson System wouldn't work in this environment. For instance, if Team One stacked its schedule with so-called weak sisters, it would qualify as an A team whereas Team Two could beat Team One but have a losing record against strong opponents. Wins over Team One would still carry more weight than wins over Team Two.

Discrepancies like these sometimes became problematic. Often, post-season clashes were proposed to settle the argument. Coach Bill Foley's Bloomfield teams, who dominated in the 1930s, were particularly eager to take on all comers in unofficial championship showdowns. Three times the Bengals played such games for charity, winning against Collingswood and New Brunswick, tying Rutherford.

Over the years, the Dickinson System took a few scattered potshots. But, in 1936, it was hit by a barrage of grapeshot and canister. It wasn't exactly Frank Dickinson's fault. His system become a modified Dickinson at best, with tweaks that took into account games between Groups and Sections, a clause that required a loser to win so many games before the winner received full credit and another "discretion clause" that gave the eight-member selection committee wiggle room in choosing the ultimate champs.

Short called the selection meeting for the Princeton room of Trenton's stately Stacy-Trent Hotel, famous for its oysters and clams. By the end of the marathon night, one could smell something fishy.

In Group Four, comprising the largest schools, Passaic had completed an unbeaten and untied season, its first ever under coach Ray Pickett. Only a tie with Dickinson marred mighty Bloomfield's season. Passaic had a higher Dickinson rating, but the final arguments weren't in. Foley took the floor first. Al Del Greco summarized his argument with the following points:

> *(1) Bloomfield plays nine Class A teams while Passaic plays five. (2) Four of his boys were hurt for the Dickinson game. (3) It's 'doggy-dog' (sic) football in Essex County and everyone wants to beat Bloomfield. (4) Bloomfield should have beaten Garfield by a larger score than Passaic (both were 7-0 verdicts) but the officials were blind and (5) he knew the committee would weigh all the facts.[4]*

Pickett was next.

"I felt ashamed to talk after listening to [Bloomfield Coach] Foley," Pickett told Del Greco. He told the Committee that Rutherford, supposedly one of its smaller school pushovers, was far better than Bloomfield's competition, that Passaic had its own injuries and that it was 'doggy-dog' football everywhere "these days."[5]

Dogs were also eating dogs in the smoke-filled back rooms of the NJSIAA. Unbeknownst to everyone but the Committee, a special meeting had been called prior to the proceedings to determine the point value of Bloomfield's season-ending 21-0 Thanksgiving Day win over Montclair. Montclair finished the season 4-3-1. Adhering to the Dickinson System, teams had to win more than 50 percent of their games to be considered Class A. The three wins and tie made four. But the Committee, invoking the discretionary clause, chose to overlook the rule to reach what it called a "common sense verdict."

It deemed Montclair a Class A team, making Bloomfield's win worth 10 more points. The teams finished within a point of each other (Passaic 24.3, Bloomfield 23.6) and, according to the NJSIAA's guidelines, that meant sharing the title. Since North Jersey Group Four was considered the strongest in the state, they shared the mythical state championship as well. Pickett was peeved at what he perceived as a manipulation of the system. He was in no mood for joking when Foley approached him later with a cat-that-ate-the-canary look.

"Come here Ray," Foley said. "Now about that post-season game. It will draw 10,000 on the worst day of the year and maybe 20,000."[6]

Pickett turned him down flat. He didn't think his team needed to play for the outright title. He felt it had been stolen from his boys. He pointed out how Bloomfield would have been awarded the championship outright had Passaic's Augie Lio not kicked an unheard-of 45-yard field goal to beat Rutherford, 3-0, on Thanksgiving Day.

Lio, it should be noted, went on to make All-America at Georgetown then play in the NFL for the Lions and Eagles before ending up as the sports editor of *The Herald-News*. He missed two field goals in the last scoreless tie in NFL history. But he would never have traded those for the one that beat Rutherford. When his father died, he placed that game ball in his coffin.

As it turned out, Lio's miracle field goal did figure into another NJSIAA decision. It cost Rutherford the North Group Three championship after it was determined that the Bulldogs would share it with Dover. Ridgefield Park, the third team up for consideration, had been whipped, 24-0, by Rutherford. When the Dickinson points were tallied, the Parkers were third. Rutherford was less than a point ahead of Dover, thus co-champion. But in studying the math, one of the sports writers detected that Ridgefield Park had not been awarded full points for its win over Bogota. The recount gave the outright championship to the Parkers. Apparently it was not one of those "common sense verdicts." But it was one of five decisions reversed by the Committee during the six-hour marathon meeting.

Pickett was white-hot as he made his way back home through the Jersey backwoods on pitch-black Route 206. His fellow Passaic County coaches concurred and threatened to drop out of the NJSIAA, as a few Hudson County schools had already done. Hudson County schools believed they traditionally got the proverbial Short end of the stick.

Under the headline, "Comedy of Errors," Paul Horowitz of the *Newark Evening News* wrote that the Committee had been "overwhelmed by the complexities of the system."[7]

In calling for Passaic and Rutherford to leave the organization, Art McMahon of *The Herald-News* wrote, "It is like the dead man beating against the slab of his tomb to assail the smug, self-satisfied members of the Executive Committee of the New Jersey State Interscholastic Athletic Association. They must have blossomed under the water of criticism for their only answer to an attack is a polite smile, a shuffling of papers and a weary, "Shall we go on, gentlemen?"

To McMahon it was simple.

"Passaic beat Garfield. Garfield beat Dickinson. Dickinson tied Bloomfield. Under any system but the Krazyhat, that should eliminate Bloomfield."[8]

It was a mess. But Short tried to defend the outcome.

"We started out to adhere to a system but the schools themselves create impossible situations by their schedules. The remedy will come only when the schools either play teams in their own class or take the consequences," he explained.[9]

Knowing better, Short promised to take a closer look at the selection process. By then he was the director of the Health and Physical Education Department of the Trenton public school system. He turned to J. Whitney Colliton, a mathematics teacher at Trenton Central High School, to come up with a more palatable formula.

Colliton was an interesting man. Despite his distinguished-sounding name, his life was far from the cliché of a brainy, understated and self-effacing mathematician. Born and raised in Newfane, New York, not far from Niagara Falls, Colliton was an intercollegiate champion quarter miler at Lafayette College, where he was smitten by a pretty ingénue from Easton, 11 years his younger. He married Mildred Naomi Paul at the college on Christmas Day, 1907. She was one week shy of her 17th birthday. Their daughter, Marguerite Joyce, was born in 1912 and they moved into a spacious red-brick home on Sanhican Creek in Trenton. But that's about as far as Colliton's picture-perfect life went.

In those days, nothing titillated newspaper readers, or sold more copies, than a good old divorce scandal, especially if it involved adultery. And this particular case had all the classic ingredients: Colliton was a well-respected member of the community, his wife was attractive, flirtatious and a bit of a celebrity. Imaginations ran wild as the math teacher found his private life splashed on the front pages of Trenton's papers.

Since 1935, a message, in bright capital letters, has welcomed drivers crossing the bridge connecting Trenton, New Jersey and Pennsylvania. It reads: "Trenton Makes, The World

Takes." In 1915, the restless Mildred Colliton wanted to know what that world was like. In effect, that world took her away from her husband.

Mildred had appeared in plays "and attained considerable fame" according to the *Trenton Times*, while a student at Randolph-Macon Women's College in Virginia. Her theatrical desires were never tempered. She wrote to the Fox Corporation for a position in films, and neglected to describe herself as married. She sent a photo, won a tryout and signed a contract. That found her leaving her three-year-old daughter behind with J. Whitney and sailing off to Jamaica, where, for the next five months, she was involved in the filming of *A Daughter of the Gods*, playing a sea nymph.[10]

Now lost, *A Daughter of the Gods* was an historic production, the first-ever with a $1 million budget. It was also the first-ever with a nude scene, featuring lead actress Annette Kellerman cavorting under a waterfall, her long hair barely concealing her ample breasts.

Mildred returned to Trenton with her wanderlust unsatiated. In 1917, she sued J. Whitney for divorce for "disregarding his marriage vows." The stage was set for drama as Mildred climbed onto the witness stand before a packed courtroom. She testified that, upon a visit from her cousin, Pearl Myers, a co-respondent in the case, her husband invited Myers to sit on his lap after she complained of being cold. And there, said Mrs. Colliton, Myers remained for 90 minutes.

"She thought nothing of the occurrence, the little daughter of the Collitons being present," *The Trenton Times* reported.[11]

But then, according to the plaintiff, the threesome retired to the same bed and, upon being awakened by alleged pillow talk, she found her husband and cousin embracing.

Amid the hushes of the audience, Miss Myers rushed out of the courtroom with Mrs. Colliton dramatically in pursuit. But when the cousin returned the next day, she testified that Colliton did not sleep in the same bed but in an adjoining room. At the same time, Colliton testified that he had kissed Miss Myers, but only out of friendship.

The judge, branding the charges as a "monumental and infamous falsehood," dismissed the petition. The marriage lasted until 1922 when J. Whitney sued for divorce on the grounds of desertion. The judge agreed, noting that Mildred was unable to accept the "prosaic" life of a high school math professor.[12]

According to Colliton's testimony, problems began even before Mildred sailed off to Jamaica. A boarder came into their midst, he said, and Colliton found a "mushy letter" to his wife. The boarder left. After Jamaica, Mrs. Colliton agreed to her husband's request to abandon her screen career but pursued, instead, a desire to become an automobile saleswoman. Her husband contended she became romantically involved with her boss, a W.S. Johnston. It was a suspicion he developed after they made an overnight trip to Baltimore together.

Colliton asserted that he wife walked out on him in October, 1917, just before she filed for divorce and that he returned home that day to discover most of the furniture removed. He shadowed his wife's new abode and late at night, accosted Johnston.

According to the newspaper, Colliton "administered a sound thrashing to the automobile man."

"She loved other men and a different kind of life that I afforded her," Colliton explained on the stand. "She liked the sporty and fast life which she could not get with a school professor and she was in love not only with Mr. Johnston, her employer, but with others. She was a pretty woman and attractive to the men."

Colliton remarried, to 19-year-old Evelyn Day in 1925, and returned to a relatively milque-toast lifestyle, out of the public eye until 1936 when Walter Short tasked him with replacing the unpopular Dickinson System. Colliton's system, which bore his name, outlived him by two decades. It was used in New Jersey until the 1970s when the state introduced sectional playoffs.

The math teacher accepted Short's challenge eagerly by obtaining the records of every Jersey high school football team for the four previous seasons. To Colliton, it was all about strength of schedule. He put every team in nine different groups, from A, the strongest, to J, the weakest, then determined the odds of a team in a higher group defeating one in a lower group.

His point system threw out the discredited Dickinson rule giving a Group Four school less credit for defeating a Group Three School even if that Group Three School were strong. He simply tossed school enrollment as a factor altogether. His system also dismissed margins of victory as a factor, thus preventing teams from running up scores to manufacture points. Under the Colliton System, an A team defeating another A team earned 100 points and earned 90 points for defeating a B team, and so on, until a win over a J team earned 20 points. A game's losing team received half the points it would have received had it won the game. In that way, Colliton gave an A team more credit for losing to a team in its division than beating one in the G, H or J divisions.

Additionally, the rankings changed on a week-to-week rolling basis for the current season. And, while the assigning of teams to groups was somewhat arbitrary and, in some cases judgment calls, few could argue with the math once schools had been assigned to their division. Convinced of its logic, the NJSIAA announced in October, 1937, it was switching to the Colliton System, although not in absolute terms. It still reserved the final decision for the Executive Committee. Colliton's chart was a guide.

There was less controversy in 1937 when Bloomfield affirmed Colliton's ranking as the state's No. 1 team by swamping New Brunswick in its post-season challenge game. In only two of nine cases did the committee vary from the rankings and in each of those, it awarded co-championships. The main carping came from Columbia coach Phil Marvel who felt the margin of victory should be taken into consideration. His team handily won seven games, tied one, and ended up in a tie for fourth place in Group 4 North.

"True, some malcontents spoke rather sharply, but the system by and large, seems to be just about the fairest yet compiled," Short wrote. "The end justified the means with plenty to spare. There were but nineteen so-called upsets in 499 schoolboy football games last fall with Colliton's higher-ranked elevens winning in 96 per cent of the contests."[13]

The bottom line was that Colliton's system afforded the astute coach the opportunity to fill his schedule with higher-ranked teams to improve his own team's ranking. Schedules were generally arranged a year in advance and because the rankings were based on the previous four years, a sound template had been set. Of course, Arthur Argauer was nothing if not astute, and his 1938 and 1939 schedules appeared to have been based on how opponents had fared over those previous four years. There were several teams worthy of being named champions. Garfield rose above them all. Arguer made the Colliton System work for him, while others had not.

If Walter E. Short owed Garfield a debt from '24 or '31, it was handsomely repaid when he handed Colliton the ball.

TWELVE

THE 1938 BOILERMAKERS

Two sports dynasties ruled over the 1930s in the New York metropolitan area.

In the Bronx, the Yankees rolled to four consecutive World Series championships from 1936 through 1939, led first by Lou Gehrig and then by the young Joe DiMaggio. It was an iconic run and part of a streak during which the franchise won seven of eight American League pennants. The Yanks, though, were mere Carringtons when measured against the Mings of Bloomfield High School football. From 1933 to 1937, the Bengals of coach Bill Foley won five straight New Jersey state championships, six if you count 1932 when Dickinson was forced to abdicate for using an ineligible player. Over that span, Foley's teams scored 1,301 points and allowed 61. In 1933, with the great Ed Berlinski paving the way, they smashed the opposition, 351-6. That lone TD, scored by Nutley, was the only time any team crossed the Bengals' 25-yard line the entire season. Two years later, the Bengals went through the season without being scored upon, while racking up 206 points of their own.

Foley wasn't above a little gamesmanship and politicking, and he ducked no one. In '34, Bloomfield settled all arguments by beating South Jersey's best team, Collingswood, 14-7, in a post-season charity game. In '37, when the New Brunswick Zebras posed a challenge out of Central Jersey, the Bengals walloped them, 54-0, in another post-season contest. In 1935, the NJSIAA named Bloomfield and Phillipsburg co-champions of the state, but *The Jersey Journal* actually gave its statewide trophy to the team from the banks of the Delaware. Foley asked for a post-season showdown. Phillipsburg declined. So Foley scheduled the Stateliners for Bloomfield's opening game in 1936. The Bengals romped, 52-0.

After Foley coached the Bengals to state championships in basketball and baseball that year, Bloomfield named the stadium after him, an honor usually reserved for coaches when they're either retired or dead. Foley was a living legend still in the middle of his career.

Foley was born in 1890 in the seafaring town of Gloucester, Massachusetts, where he likely could have followed the career path of his father, William Sr., a man with salt water in his veins. Raised in Nova Scotia, where his Irish immigrant father and grandfather were both shoemakers, William Sr. was drawn to the sea. By the time he made his way to Gloucester, he had attained the prestigious rank of master mariner, which qualified him to captain a vessel of any size anywhere in the world. The younger Foley certainly would have looked the part had he followed his father to sea. His ruddy complexion appeared as if lashed over the years by the Atlantic's harsh, salt winds. But, following the advice of his father, he enrolled at the Massachusetts State Teachers College and Normal School in Salem.

Somehow, Foley's first job out of college found him in a place that could not have been more unlike briny Gloucester or puritanical Salem—Goldfield, Nevada, a boomtown 186 miles north of Las Vegas that exploded into the state's largest city shortly after its founding in 1902. The arrival of the Earp brothers, Wyatt and Virgil in 1904, gave Goldfield authenticity as a Wild West outpost, although Wyatt didn't stay long, and Virgil took his last breath in Goldfield a year later.

It was left to another historical character to leave a more lasting impression on the town. Tex Rickard was the first of the great fight promoters, and it was Goldfield that gave him his start before Miami eventually delivered his demise with his death there in 1929. While Goldfield's desert yielded $88 million in minerals from 1904 to 1918, the wealth wasn't ploughed back into the town by any means. Except for a few permanent structures such as the high school, the entire place looked as though it could have—and should have—been swept away by a stiff wind. For a time, it was nothing more than a collection of tents, shacks and lean-tos, separated by dirt roads, dotted by opium dens and houses of ill repute, fouled by sewage and decaying animals and totally lacking in moral rectitude. A visitor once called it, "Dante's inferno with the lid off."[1]

Rickard was a Texas gambler who'd lost everything chasing gold strikes in Alaska, where he had one stroke of luck—a friendship with Wyatt Earp that led him to Goldfield. Goldfield was the perfect place for a risk-taking man in his mid-30s who had big dreams and the will to see them through. He opened a saloon, one of 53 in town, although none could compare to Rickard's Northern Saloon and Gambling Casino. To slake the thirst of the miners, he employed 80 bartenders. To entertain them, he staged the first of his many extravaganzas—the world lightweight championship fight in a 7,000-seat wooden stadium he slapped up in a flood wash on the edge of town.[2]

The combatants, for a then-record purse of $32,000 in gold, were Joe Gans, the first black man ever to hold a world title, and Danish-born, Chicago-bred Oscar Matthew "Battling" Nelson, the inspiration for Jack London's *The Abysmal Brute*. And he was. Nelson broke every rule in the Marquess of Queensberry's book. He was still pounding the more gentlemanly Gans with low blows in the 42nd round when the referee finally disqualified him. With Rickard hyping the race angle, the bout was a tremendous success. It drew spectators from as far away as Maine and filled the arena to capacity with gate receipts of $70,000. Rickard was dubbed the "Fight Master."

Those were the glory days for Goldfield. By the time Foley dusted himself off at the train station with playbooks in hand, Goldfield was in decline. Its ore deposits were too shallow and the process of extracting them too expensive. The prospectors' sons Foley coached often played without shoes and travelled as far as 100 miles for away games. Foley was in the middle of nowhere with nowhere to go.

One fortuitous day, a book salesmen passed through Goldfield and told Foley about a high school in New Jersey that needed a stenography and typewriting teacher. And—by the way—the position included heading up the physical education classes and coaching the school's football, basketball and baseball teams, all fully equipped with shoes. Next thing, Foley was leaving the Godforsaken Nevada town to begin a teaching and coaching career in Bloomfield. That was 1915. Three years later, he won the first of his state championships in basketball, a mere prelude to the eight he won on the football field.

Shaped no doubt by Gloucester and Goldfield, the rugged Foley had a hands-on style that demanded excellence, particularly in the fundamentals. He often jumped into the middle of a practice session to demonstrate a blocking or tackling technique and he went at it full-speed. He once broke a leg while demonstrating proper guard play and was still cussing when they slid him into the back of the ambulance.[3]

Bloomfield coach Bill Foley, the man Art Argauer most wanted to beat. And he did. Courtesy Bloomfield High School.

While he was one of the earliest and most successful proponents of the innovative T-formation, Foley didn't care much for trick plays. Opponents didn't have to do much advance scouting. They knew what they were getting from Bloomfield: straight-ahead football with a heavy dose of off-tackle smashes and quick openers.

While he led them to titles, Foley's players also revered their gruff coach for his character and conduct far from playing fields. Take the story of George Buttinghausen. The star of the 1918 basketball champs as well as an outstanding gridder, Buttinghausen spent 10 years in a plaster cast after injuring his back in a college game. Disabled but determined to work, Buttinghausen answered a newspaper job listing for salesmen for a product known as the Master Bake Pot. He got the job, and Foley did the legwork for him on his own time, pressing arms and knocking on doors. How many Master Bake Pots found their way into North Jersey kitchens was never recorded, but so many were sold that the owner of the patent sold the business to Buttinghausen for a song. Buttinghausen eventually recovered and built the business into a success, never forgetting what Foley had done for him.[4]

Garfield was everything like Bloomfield and nothing like Bloomfield. In the 30s, Bloomfield was surrounded by the urban streets of Newark, the wealthy avenues of commuter town Glen Ridge, Montclair's cultural sites, and Clifton's verdant farm fields. It possessed characteristics of all these towns. Its similarity to Garfield was in its inhabitants. Garfield had Polack Valley, Bloomfield had Polack Hill, the neighborhood around St. Valentine (Walenty in Polish) Church, which quite naturally sloped toward the Bengals' home field. The Hill was where the former coach of Goldfield High School mined his talent. The rugged immigrants must have reminded Foley of the Portuguese and Italians who manned the fishing boats of Gloucester. He had a special affinity for them. While the press sometimes called his teams "Foley's Fighting Irishman," Foley knew a pierogi from a pasty.

There was one instance when Foley was unhappy with his team's play at halftime of a 1933 game. He appealed to the boys from Polack Hill. When the team trudged into the small locker room, shoulders slumped, silent except for the clanking of their cleats, they were anticipating a full broadside from the coach. Instead, Foley broke the suspense with a question.

"How many Poles on this team?" he asked, knowing they made up about half his roster. Hands went up. "All right. Your mothers and fathers came over here to give you a better chance. Go out and show 'em what you can do."

Foley started the second half with an entirely Polish lineup that furiously scored three touchdowns to put the game away. Even Casimir Pulaski would have beamed with native pride.[5]

In many similar ways, Foley and Art Argauer, 10 years his junior, were cut from the same coaching cloth and, as their rivalry grew, so did their mutual respect. Argauer looked at Foley as the man he had to beat. If his program were to achieve state recognition, it would have to prove itself against Bloomfield. In 1933, Foley consented to give him a game. Although the Boilermakers lost, 25-0, to Foley's powerhouse, the *Bergen Record* complimented the underdogs for playing brilliant ball and *The Herald-News* suggested that if Garfield had gotten a few more breaks and not attempted so many "frenzied" passes, the result would have been a lot closer.

Garfield went on to win the Bergen County Interscholastic League title that year, but Argauer was outgrowing such quaint prizes. He was ambitious for bigger goals and keeping his mind on one thing, a return match with Bloomfield in 1934. Everything Argauer did in preparation for the '34 season pointed to one game—Bloomfield—and everything seemed to be lining up for an upset.

Argauer started organizing pre-season football practices to begin July 30, shortly after the high school baseball season ended. The blazing sun built stamina. Repetitive signal drills hammered Argauer's single wing plays into their brains. Meanwhile, Foley wouldn't see his team until September. The Bengals were also basking in sunshine, but theirs was that of their 1933 championship. They weren't sweating it out, at least not on the practice field.

Secondly, with Bloomfield scheduled for the traditional opening week of the season, Argauer added an early tune-up game against Ridgefield Park, a strong Bergen County team. Besides working out any kinks, it would add to the impression, especially in Bloomfield's mind, that Garfield was the better-prepared team. Argauer cleverly played his first team in just the first and fourth quarters, the better to save them for Bloomfield, and watched with great satisfaction as the Boilermakers rolled to a 26-0 victory in the mud of Clifton's Wessington Stadium, his semi-pro stomping ground.

Now it just so happened that Garfield was going to be the first team to play Bloomfield in its newly built concrete stadium, the future Foley Field. But if the Bengals had thought of the Boilermakers as some sort of Homecoming treat, they were getting a few butterflies after reading about Garfield's opening performance.

Suddenly, the papers were pointing to the distinct possibility of the Foleymen losing for the first time since Dickinson drilled them, 32-0, in the penultimate game of the 1932 season.

Garfield had almost its entire team back from 1933, including backfield flash John "Rabbit" Veleber, so nicknamed because he was low to the ground with a great change of pace that made him appear to hop. There was also ace passer Matty Malkiewicz, future Fordham star Bill Hintenberger, whose brother Ed started on the 1939 team, and burly tackle Joe Cody, a Lodi kid who would be Argauer's assistant coach in 1939. Berlinski wasn't the only Bloomfield star who had graduated. Only a handful of lettermen were returning. Dick Wilcox of *The Herald-News* saw the possibilities:

> *Like a girl of sixteen at her first real party, Garfield High School faces its big moment this afternoon at the Bloomfield High School Field when it battles for statewide recognition with Bill Foley's Bloomfield Bengals the stumbling block in its path . . . a veteran team in midseason form because of its intensive training practically all summer, is hot.*[6]

Wilcox went on, noting that Garfield had "a score to settle." Foley recognized the developing media narrative but he wasn't sure how to play the game-before-the-game in the press.

On the one hand, he pretended not to be overly impressed after scouting Garfield's demolition of Ridgefield Park. According to Al Del Greco in the *Record*, "Bill Foley, a rough, tough Irishman from Bloomfield, gathered the boys around him at the Wessington Stadium in Clifton last week, dangled his legs over a seat and said Garfield's strong line was in for a bit of a surprise. He didn't mention the backs—maybe he figures Garfield will play with only seven men."[7]

At the same time, Foley was poor-mouthing his team's 1934 prospects right up until the day before the game. That day, according to Ed Hill of the *Asbury Park Press,* Foley was scheduled to give a chalk talk on defense at the NJSIAA coaches' pre-season meeting. But when it was his turn to speak, he begged off, saying he had so little defense on his 1934 team, it wasn't worth discussing.

"With the material I've got this year, about all I can do is to tell my linemen to get down in a sprinter's starting position. Then I can blindfold them, place my foot in spots peculiarly suited for such action and hope that they'll upset the interference and nail the ball carrier before they realize what happened," Foley said with a glint of Irish mischief in his eye. Foley's fellow coaches guffawed at his false modesty. Hill supplied the ultimate punch line:

> *Less than 24 hours later, Bloomfield went out to dedicate a new stadium. Garfield, soundly trounced the year before, had been chosen to make the sacrifice. Forty minutes later the Bengals had been nailed to the cross, 6 to 0, and Foley's remarks of the previous night added an authentic touch to the picture.*[8]

The stunning victory was one of Argauer's finest moments. It turned the series into a rivalry minted over just two years. The Garfield coach had cooked up a strategy for the Bengals without revealing a hint of it against Ridgefield Park. He wasn't going to take Bloomfield's bruisers head-on, at least not for the entire game. He devised a wide-open game plan to exploit Bloomfield's inexperience and a weakness in the middle of the defense. Those "frenzied" passes of the previous season now fell into the hands of receivers. Bloomfield, not even close to mid-season form, couldn't keep up the pace.

Although the Bengals had the better of the play in the first half, amassing eight first downs to Garfield's two, it amounted to nothing more than a 0-0 score and a fidgety crowd of 5,000 onlookers. Argauer knew he had the Bengals where he wanted them, that they'd already worn themselves out against his well-conditioned boys. That's when he unleashed his passing attack. A tired team is always a disorganized team. Argauer sent five eligible receivers into the Bloomfield backfield, enough to scramble even a modern pass defense.

Everyone was stunned. Irvington coach Bill Matthews, one of many curious coaches in the crowd, told Paul Horowitz of the *Newark Evening News* that the Bengals were now "vulnerable." Charlie Gieske, the assistant coach at Newark East Side, Bloomfield's next opponent, blamed conditioning.

"I was completely surprised in that second half to note the marked letdown of the Bloomfield players," he declared. "They hit hard and effectively in the first two periods but they appeared to be out of condition and weary in the closing quarters. I've never seen a team of Foley-coached players before that showed any signs of wear and tear after a game as this one did today."[9]

Even the wet weather helped Garfield when it scored the only touchdown of the game. Punting on third down, Bloomfield's Addie Worthington couldn't handle the snap from center and the slippery football went through his hands. When he picked it up, he should have immediately fallen to set up fourth down. Instead, he tried to kick it again and Freddie Shupack was on him to block it at the Bengal 20 yard-line.

A couple of pass completions, one on a pretty leaping catch by Rabbit Veleber, put Garfield at Bloomfield's goal line where, on third down, Malkiewicz got behind Cody on the left side and knifed under a pile of tumbling players to score. The touchdown held up. Bloomfield was beaten.

The newspapermen tracked down Argauer amid the post-game din. The beaming coach didn't have much to say, only, "I'm tickled pink." Meanwhile, a grumpy Foley obliged the scribes. He blamed his team's inexperience for the loss and didn't mention his leaky pass defense. He said there should have been eight men on the line when Malkiewicz scored. There were only six.

"If that isn't dumb football, well I just don't know the game I guess," he said.[10] He would set out to correct that at the first practice of the week.

Delirious Garfield fans stormed the field to topple the goal posts. Bloomfield fans rushed out and tried to prevent the desecration of their new football palace. The opposing mobs started throwing punches, and the cops rushed in to break up the erupting melee. The next day's *Bergen Record* told the story with a hyperbolic lede:

> *Garfield's aerial bombs exploded the Bloomfield Football Empire. Champion last year but Saturday afternoon only a faint shadow of a once mighty machine, Bill Foley's club staggered about in a daze as the Bergen gridders toyed with it in the second half.*
>
> *Pushed all over the field in the first half by a heavier line, Garfield made its rivals look positively ridiculous in the second half with its wide open game which clicked amazingly well.*[11]

Garfield didn't get the chance to enjoy the win that long. Its status as a contender for the state championship was brief. The next week, the Boilermakers lost to Ray Pickett's Passaic Indians by the same 6-0 score by which they defeated Bloomfield. The two tough games took their toll injury-wise, and a depleted Garfield squad became Phillipsburg's 14th straight victim the week after that. Garfield, though, wouldn't lose again that season, leaving them 1-2 against three of the best teams in the state. But neither would Bloomfield. Foley plugged up the holes and closed things out with another state championship, beating Collingswood on a cold December Saturday and disappointing unbeaten Passaic, which wanted its own shot at the Bengals. After all, the Indians beat Garfield and Bloomfield didn't.

By then, however, Bloomfield's fans regarded the opening-day loss to Garfield as some sort of fluke never to be repeated.

"The point now raised is that Garfield should never have beaten this Bloomfield eleven," Arthur Rhodes crowed in the *Bloomfield Mail,* calling any criticism of the Bengals' championship season, "the equivalent to saying that an elevator is inconsistent because it stopped at every floor but the first."[12]

There had been some thought of a post-season rematch with Garfield, but Foley didn't see any need for it, other than to help fill Garfield's coffers. Foley had already snatched a measure of revenge, anyway. Those pre-season practices Argauer used to prepare for Bloomfield? Foley led the effort to abolish them and the state authorities complied, ordering that, in the future, workouts could not start before September 1. Foley contended that the Garfield loss had nothing to do with his thinking (that he didn't want football interfering with the baseball season). No one really believed him, but it didn't matter. It just further fueled his rivalry with Argauer.[13]

Bloomfield resumed its edge over Garfield, atoning for the '34 miscue with a decisive 25-0 win in 1935. In 1936, the Bengals escaped with a 7-0 win in a game where Garfield ace Jules Koshlap fumbled going into the end zone, when a poor punt out of Garfield's end zone went out of bounds at the 12 to set up the only touchdown. Bloomfield's 19-0 win followed in 1937.

Now that the 1938 season had arrived, Argauer felt again that Bloomfield could be had. This time, it wasn't hinged on early preparation or special game plans. For the first time, Argauer simply knew he had the better team—even if the papers didn't. They gave him his due but he expected Bloomfield to continue to coast toward another title. Foley was losing a lot of talent from the team he called his best ever, but those conditioned to Bloomfield's perennial excellence ignored that fact. It would be as it always was—like the latest model Buick Special rolling off a rejiggered assembly line. There'd be some changes but, under the hood, the Bengals would still purr when Foley hit the gas pedal. So they thought.

Coaches know better, though. They know how to evaluate their talent and, when that talent had been superior, as it had been at Bloomfield for so many years, any drop-off is obvious. Foley knew the dynasty was about to run its course with such a young team. And Argauer could sense that his program was poised to ascend. He had drawn a road map to his first state championship, and it went straight down Broad Street in Bloomfield, right past now-named Foley Field, where he had slapped that not-yet-repeated loss on the Bengals four years earlier.

Never before did Argauer field as powerful and as deep a backfield, with eight capable performers giving him two complete sets of backs. Benny Babula was stronger from a summer of hauling sides of beef from his father's delivery truck and wiser after the educational season of 1937. He was ready to ramp up his piston-like running style and become Argauer's hammer.

Ted Ciesla was eagerly anticipating his senior season. Smaller but quicker than Babula, he ran with a sense of joy and freedom. His breakaway speed provided a separate element

Garfield backfield members Ted Ciesla, John Zecker and John Orlovsky charge the camera. The Herald-News.

from Babula's power, giving Argauer the freedom to rotate them in and out of the backfield or play them together.

Seniors John Zecker (they called him Buck and his younger brother Half a Buck) and Ed Klecha, John Grembowitz' step brother, were sturdy blockers. Sophomore John Orlovsky and junior Wally Tabaka had gotten their share of seasoning in 1937 and were perfect understudies.

There would be two additions to the previous year's roster. Charlie Herk, a starter on the 1936 team, had dropped out of school in '37 but had re-enrolled. And Argauer was delighted when he got his first look at freshman Johnny Sekanics, maybe even faster than Ciesla and, at 175 pounds, definitely bigger. Sekanics already appeared polished beyond his years to make Argauer think he now had a triple-threat back. Though he would require nurturing and even taming, with so much talent in the backfield, Argauer had the luxury of bringing Sekanics along slowly and unleashing him on the opposition at critical times.

The line wasn't as much of a powerhouse yet benefitted from experience. Young, Grembowitz, Bernie Pirog and Coleman Szely had played every game the previous season.

Argauer plotted out the schedule with the Colliton rankings in mind, with games against three of the seven teams in Group A and two of the five other teams in Group B. The first three opponents, Dickinson, Irvington and Passaic, had been among the strongest programs in the state over the previous five seasons. Three straight wins would mean a ton of ranking points. But the biggest game of all would be the sixth of the season, at Bloomfield.

Argauer was convinced he had something special after a scrimmage with Columbia, which had driven him to despair a year earlier. This time, Garfield overpowered Phil Marvel's Gems, opening huge gaps in the defense, with Babula running effortlessly. The word spread across North Jersey. Argauer, for once, cast aside his characteristic modesty. He openly pronounced this team his best ever.

"We're not looking forward to an undefeated season but if injuries stay away from our camp, we should compile an enviable mark," he said. "The fight shown by the rookies is really encouraging and if they keep up the fine work, we'll be heard of."[14]

Art McMahon of *The Herald-News* was suitably impressed, but he was also aware of Garfield's history as an underachiever. The '34 team fizzled immediately after it upset Bloomfield. The '36 team, with an All-State triple-threat back in Koshlap and all state center in Steve Szot, failed to live up to pre-season expectations.

There was always a bunch of characters, some of them shady, some of them gamblers, hanging around the team. Then there were the meddlesome alumni who felt it was their right to stick their noses into the coach's playbook. In 1931, for instance, Argauer moved his captain, Frank Zavada, from the backfield to the line to plug a hole. Outsiders kept telling

Zavada and his father that Argauer had listened to a minor school official that Zavada was more valuable on the line. Zavada's father forced him to quit. A year later, Zavada asked back on the team. Argauer denied anyone had influenced his decision the previous year.

"If such a thing happened," Argauer declared, "it was nothing more than coincidence. I get plenty of unsolicited advice from the sidelines. I listen to it politely but pay no attention to it. I'm running the team and only when I feel a change is needed is one made. Nobody has ever dictated to me and nobody will so long as I am coach."[15]

While other coaches contended with such external pressures and distractions off the field, it seemed more heightened in Garfield. So, McMahon felt he needed to add a disclaimer to his analysis of the upcoming '38 season:

> *This is straight stuff from the bullpen. Garfield has a championship or near-championship team this fall. Class sticks out all over it. Benny Babula, a big back, is All State timber. It looks like the finest club Garfield has had in years.*
>
> *Of course it may wind up a dud. The kids out that way get big heads in an awful hurry. A coaches' problem is always tougher because of the Saturday Night quarterbacks.*[16]

"Art won't be re-elected as president of the Crying Towel Association if this keeps up," warned Al Del Greco in the *Record*. Then he picked Dickinson to win the game.[17] It would take a lot of convincing to secure the sportswriters' backing. A mere string of early wins wasn't going to be nearly enough.

DICKINSON: BENNY GETS GOING

Roosevelt Stadium in Jersey City—where Jackie Robinson would make his minor league debut 12 years later—still had its new-car smell when the Boilermakers opened their 1938 season. With its imposing art deco façade trimmed in brown, the stadium sat isolated at Droyer's Point on Newark Bay on the expansive former site of the Jersey City Airport, encircled by sweeping concrete promenades and framed by fountains. It was Boss Frank Hague's pride and joy when he opened it a year earlier, featuring Saturday high school football doubleheaders. But it hadn't yet seen anything like the show Babula was about to put on.

Dickinson didn't have Al Blozis or Bullet Witkowski, but, when the Hilltoppers scored first—following a missed field goal attempt by Herk—it seemed as if they were to about to pick up where their 1937 26-0 win left off. That was before Babula stepped on the field and delighted the 5,000 fans, most of whom had motored down the Belleville Turnpike from Garfield. Argauer alternated his backs, so Babula played about half the game. Yet, he gained 85 yards in his limited playing time and scored two touchdowns (including the equalizer) in a 19-6 win.

On one off-tackle smash, Babula displayed his trademark running style when he broke off to the right, cut beautifully to his left against the pursuit and entered the end zone in a trot. *The Jersey Journal* noted that he seemed to have four blockers facing him on each play, but Grembowitz (on the line) and Zecker (in the backfield) provided a good degree of menacing interference.[18]

Ciesla, meanwhile, deftly evaded five tacklers as he scored the final touchdown from 15 yards out. And Sekanics, the freshman, set up one of the touchdowns with an interception. *The Herald-News* complimented Pirog, Young and Jack Boyle for their blocking. It had no choice than to admit that the Garfield offense was a beast. But that's not what the paper focused on in its analysis of the relatively easy victory.

> Despite the easy triumph, the chatter appears to be over-enthusiastic. True, the Boilermakers did display plenty of power, probably more than any other Comet eleven in an opening contest but one thing which stood out, even above the victory, was Garfield's weak defense.
>
> Dickinson, especially Ralph Pompilano, ripped through the Boilermakers forward wall for repeated gains, which should quiet any talk of a title and unless Argauer can correct the weaknesses, Garfield may be in for a fall.[19]

IRVINGTON: IMPROVEMENT NEEDED

The paper followed that up with another admonition, as Garfield prepared to meet Irvington in its home opener at Passaic Stadium.

> A serious situation does confront the Garfield coach. Boys on the squad, following Saturday's triumph, started talking of capturing the state title and, unless the chatter can be stopped, overconfidence may bring about the downfall of the team.[20]

Argauer was still upbeat. Why not? He told the writers he would iron out the defensive wrinkles revealed against Dickinson and bragged about the devastating and precise blocking his team exhibited—not only at the line, but also downfield. He had the makings of a machine. Even *The Herald-News* had to concede that the blocking looked as if it was up to Bloomfield's usual standards.

It was, again, an impressive offensive performance against another team that outweighed the Boilermakers by a large margin. Ciesla and Babula were a one-two punch, as Argauer delighted in splitting the game between them. The slippery Ciesla started the scoring when he picked up a crazily bouncing punt and zipped up the sideline. He sidestepped tackler after tackler and, when it seemed as though the two Camptowners had an angle on him, Herk came up fast and snowplowed them away to allow Ciesla to finish off a 65-yard TD return. Ciesla started a second drive as Garfield moved from midfield to the 20. There, Babula replaced him, carried three straight times, and registered the second score.

An apparent TD by Babula was called back for holding, one of four major penalties on the Boilermakers. But, in the fourth quarter, with Garfield protecting a 12-7 lead, Babula followed his blockers off right tackle, reversed his field and fended off Hank Przybylowski with a stiff arm at midfield. The remainder of the 80 yards was clear sailing, and Babula scored his fourth TD of the season standing up.

Boyle, Orlovsky and Zecker drew praise for their blocking. It seemed the Boilermakers were two- and three-deep at each offensive position. One longtime football writer noted of Babula: "I've watched plenty of teams play and plenty of players in the last fifteen years. Benny Babula of Garfield is the best boy I've seen in the last fifteen years. He has all the earmarks of New Jersey's finest back."

But even Argauer began to fret about the soft spot in the middle of his line, which Irvington exploited to score twice in the 19-13 victory. Ray Pickett, coach of Passaic, the next opponent, was in the crowd, and *The Herald-News* noted that he was wearing "a broad smile" envisioning a victory for his Indians.

> *The Hilltop pilot saw that Garfield's defense was weak, especially in the center of the line . . . the two guard positions are troubling Coach Art Argauer and he is likely to shift his line a bit on defense for Saturday's contest.*[21]

PASSAIC: PROVING THEMSELVES

Bloomfield may have been the team Garfield loved most to beat, but Passaic was the team Garfield loved most to hate. As McMahon said, beating Bloomfield was a matter of prestige; beating Passaic was a matter of pride.

Just across the river from each other, and sharing the same home stadium, their annual meeting was often preceded by rumbles that landed opposing fans in jail. Garfield had beaten the Indians only once before (in 1933), so Passaic was ever confident. Early in the week, Passaic supporters had slipped across and painted "26-0"—their prediction of the final score—on Garfield's high school building. That inspired Garfield fan Emanuel Lauritano to write to McMahon.

"The reason Passaic put green paint (Passaic's colors were red and blue) on the Garfield school is that the painters are cheap," Lauritano charged. "They have no sportsmanship at all. That score, 26-0, they painted on the school will be the score Garfield will win by to show Passaic it is cheap."[22]

McMahon, meanwhile, was suggesting that the Irvington game might indicate that Garfield "is easy to score on and not the hot-shot football power it was reported." He admitted his scouting intelligence was second-hand, but still asserted that the Boilermakers were almost as weak defensively as they were strong offensively.

"The idea is to score more points than the other fellow, of course, and so far Garfield has done that," he wrote. "The gander of that formula is in the sooner-or-later misfire of the attack. Some observers have an idea that it will happen Saturday."[23]

McMahon, though, wondered if Passaic could corral Garfield's biggest threat. "If you stop Benny Babula, the sideline coaches say, you will stop Garfield," he wrote. "However, it will take a Four Power Conference in Munich to stop him if he continues those antelope runs he made against Dickinson and Irvington."[24]

Other than trying to figure out how to stop Babula—and Ciesla, for that matter—Pickett's biggest problem was that his team had yet to play a game. There was an illness in his family when schedules were being drawn up, and he never was able to secure opponents the first two weeks. This put him at a severe disadvantage as he put his very thin and green line on the field.

"If we had scheduled Garfield for at least three weeks from Saturday, we would beat them," Pickett purported, which sounded as though he was readying an excuse. "But as things stand now, it's going to be a tough battle. My boys are confident—not overconfident—but just enough to seriously think they'll win."[25]

Pickett called the Boilermakers "impressive but not overwhelming" even though his team would cram all week for this not overwhelming opponent. He practiced at Passaic Stadium behind locked doors and drawn curtains while Argauer, at wide-open Belmont Oval, had the usual throng of onlookers, including, presumably, a Passaic spy or two. There was talk of the "jitters" in Garfield's camp because of how Passaic had brought them down after their win over Bloomfield in '34. The coach, though, could feel there was something different about this group. McMahon, pondering his pick, thought likewise:

> *Passaic wants to win this one real hard. Garfield is always eager to beat Passaic and with everybody ready to concede it the state title, is especially keen about a triumph tomorrow. Garfield has Babula, the antelope. Passaic has (Joe) Gyorgydeak, the man mountain. I have a headache. Those two tough games Garfield has packed under its belt, opposed to a raw, inexperienced Passaic line facing a major test its first time out may tell the story.*
> *Garfield 13, Passaic 6.[26]*

Anticipation mounted from Monday on. On game day, *The Herald-News'* front page spelled out just how big a game it was in the world of North Jersey sports:

> *The Yanks are battling the Cubs in the third game of the World Series and Columbia's Sid Luckman is rifling passes through the Army's best football defense but this section's average high school grid fan is coldly indifferent.*
> *He has too much to worry about in his own backyard this afternoon.[27]*

Indeed, it became a perfect autumn afternoon as a restless crowd of 8,000 descended upon the stadium by the river. A creative bunch of Garfield fans set the tone by carrying a coffin labeled, "Passaic," onto the field, with placards that lamented, "He was a good fellow" and "Buried in 1938." Passaic fans hissed.

Adrenaline over-brimmed on the sidelines as well, and then on to the field on the opening kickoff. Zecker took it for Garfield and accelerated up the field but Pickett's boys, so charged up for their first live action against a hated rival, charged down wildly like hounds on the hunt. Five Passaic players swarmed Zecker, and the ball came loose. Passaic had it. Off-balance from the early body blow, Garfield's defense yielded a long first down, then the game's first touchdown on Joe Zabawa's plunge through the line.

At that point, everyone—from Coach Pickett to the boys on press row to the more fickle Garfield fans—was thinking that another Boilermaker flameout was imminent. But Garfield had recovered from an early touchdown to beat Dickinson and it would turn out to be the start of a new character trend that became a Boilermaker trademark under Argauer.

The physical tenor of the game now favored Garfield. Four Passaic starters left the game with injuries. With a decimated backfield, the Indians gained just one more first down the rest of the game. Outweighed by both the Dickinson and Irvington lines, the Boilermakers' front wall took over against the smaller, less experienced Passaic line. No soft spots appeared in the middle or anywhere else.

Argauer continued to split the game between his backfield combinations. With Babula on the bench, Ciesla got free for a couple of big gainers and Orlovsky scored his first varsity touchdown on a nice spinner play through "scythe-like" blocking. Babula, playing the middle two quarters, was unstoppable and scored the winning touchdown after having an earlier one nullified for clipping. The 12-6 final score, according to the *Bergen Record*, did not tell the story of a one-sided game.

The prickly Pickett, nevertheless, decided to cover Garfield's victory with sour grapes. He proposed a post-season rematch for charity in December.

"I think we could beat them if we played again," he told Al Del Greco. "We lost our key men in the backfield early in the contest . . . When they went out our chances were erased."

Del Greco suggested that Picket should have retreated "gracefully as possible into a cave" but that if he intended to get a rise out of Argauer, he succeeded.

"No, positively no," Argauer screamed. "I wanted a post-season game two years ago when we were licked and Passaic refused. My answer is, 'no.' "[28]

Argauer could have also pointed out that Pickett had also turned down Bill Foley's offer to settle the state championship in 1936. Meanwhile, as Del Greco, the old Garfield alum, took Argauer's side against Pickett, he ended that same column by predicting that Garfield would be knocked off before the season ended. He was obviously unconvinced of Garfield's new resiliency. He was both emphatic and long-winded on the subject:

> *East Rutherford might not do it. Bloomfield might not. But somewhere along the line, Swellheaditis will knock the Purple and Gold for a loop.*
>
> *Garfield boys, and this goes back to the days when girls wore hoop skirts, always were good scrappers. If they lost, they came back for more with head bloody but unbowed, etc. etc. But there's one thing about Garfield teams: THEY CAN'T STAND SUCCESS.*
>
> *Just now the folks are with the club 1,000 percent. But let the boys make one more step toward the diadem or whatever it is that champions get and the olde, olde, olde quarter-backs from the faculty and the olde, olde, olde second string bums among the Alumni will be telling the boys that (hah, hah) 'is that how Coach Argauer is telling you to block! My boy, take a gander at an old master.'*
>
> *That is about to fall on Garfield's neck. Argauer might be interested in train schedules after the game.*[29]

An old second-string bum himself, Del Greco knew from whence he wrote—his seat on the Garfield bench, where he had witnessed the attempted manipulations and machinations of the peanut gallery. But that's the mindset Argauer had to prevent from getting through to his team. And little did Del Greco know that his players were beginning to trust their coach so completely that they could begin to tune out the outside interference. He had become a father figure because of his earnest interest in every one of his players, his desire to see to it they got into college, or into a good job, and his ability to steer them clear of trouble.

Besides, Argauer's master plan was working. Three weeks into the season, Garfield was already the frontrunner for the state title by dint of the totally unexpected. Bloomfield had played three games and tied two of them (Nutley and Belleville). The scoreless opener against a strong Nutley team wasn't all that alarming. Nutley hadn't lost in 12 games since it last played Bloomfield. But Nutley also had two touchdowns called back for what many felt were questionable penalties. Then Bloomfield took the field for its second game and was held to another scoreless tie by neighboring Belleville.

"What's the matter with Bloomfield this season?" Frank Fagan of the *Newark Star-Eagle* asked in his lede paragraph and Bill Foley supplied a surprising answer.

"It is no surprise to me that we were tied by Nutley and Belleville. I'm surprised they did not win," he said. "We may lose a couple of ball games this season and then again we might go right on and clean up the slate."[30]

Foley's boys rebounded to pound Newark South Side, 36-0, in their season's third game, but it was clear the state championship race would not easily be handed to Bloomfield for a sixth consecutive year. Of all the challengers, Garfield had the clearest path, provided Del Greco wasn't right. And he almost was.

East Rutherford: Night Sweats

East Rutherford was next on the schedule. The Wildcats were the only opponents remaining from Garfield's Bergen County Interscholastic League days. Following Bloomfield and Passaic, it was Garfield's third-biggest rivalry and it was a contentious one, spiced by the in-between town of Wallington, which sent its mostly Polish students to either high school, depending on the year. Jules Koshlap, Babula's predecessor and a future All American at Georgetown, was a Wallington student.

The eruption of brawls, both on the field and in the stands, became common when these teams played, starting in 1925 when police were forced to pull their revolvers after a Garfield rooter came out of the stands to attack an East Rutherford player.[31] Now, with Garfield attracting so much publicity, and with East Rutherford tabbed as an easy touch by the press, coach Jimmy Mahon had his team primed.

The game was the first of two consecutive home tilts Argauer scheduled for Friday night at Passaic Stadium. Mahon's team had gone to the air to beat Clifton the previous week and it again appeared to be a great strategy, with Garfield defenders apt to lose the ball in the lights, even if it was white-coated and acquired specially for the game.

While there were reports that Argauer was suffering sleepless nights over East Rutherford, for some inscrutable reason he seemed to take the matchup lightly. He planned to start what Art McMahon of *The Herald-News* called his "Crying Squad," comprised, McMahon noted, "of boys who bleated their protests when they spent the whole of last Saturday warming their pants on the hard bench."[32]

It was the first night high school game played at Passaic Stadium and the first of any kind since the NFL's New York Giants beat the Clifton Wessingtons three years earlier. It wasn't the best lighting. Rented from a Paterson company for $90, the portable light towers squatted only 32 feet high and produced 52,000 candle-watts of illumination. The fans loved it, though. Around 7,000 turned out, not counting the youngsters who exploited the dimming twilight to scamper inconspicuously over the fences. Traffic backed up for miles into Wallington, the common access from both towns.

They almost went home stunned. Mahon's boys completely snuffed out Garfield's vaunted off-tackle smash, led by Walter Szot, whose brother Steve was an All-Stater for Garfield in 1937. The Boilermakers offense threatened only once when Tabaka, on a pass from Babula, was stymied a foot from the goal line on the last play of the half.

Garfield's win hinged on two spectacular special team returns. Johnny Sekanics, the slippery freshman, ran back the opening kickoff 65 yards, scooping up the football after Ciesla muffed it. He headed up the middle, then cut to the right sideline. His speed was too much for anyone on the East Rutherford team. Then, after East Rutherford tied the score at 6-6 with an impressive drive, Ciesla scored the go-ahead TD in the 13-6 win with a 55-yard punt return in the third quarter. Four defenders surrounded Ciesla after he received the ball, but he lowered his shoulder and ducked underneath them, breaking tackles as he went.

The victory was still a victory, but the doubters once again emerged, starting with Argauer, himself, who admitted: "We can't begin to hope for victory over Bloomfield if my club plays like this. That East Rutherford line was magnificent."

"Tired and lucky," was how Joe Lovas of *The Herald-News* described the Boilermakers as they headed toward the bus.[33]

Ray Pickett, who was in the crowd, agreed. "Either East Rutherford is very good or we are bad," he said. McMahon, who had seen plenty of the rivalry when he played for East Rutherford, lamented his *alma mater*'s close call:

> *There's a growing suspicion that Garfield isn't the high-powered football machine the headlines have been claiming. East Rutherford last night won everything but the decision. The Wildcats out-gamed, outplayed and outfought the Boilermakers and still lost.*

He didn't spare Babula, either:

> *Benny Babula still has to prove that he is a great football player. He pussyfooted last night. He was hit so hard that he began to slow up even before enemy hands were placed on him.*[34]

Interestingly enough, Argauer hated playing at night, despite the game netting his program $2,000. His players complained they lost ball carriers in the shadows. "I don't like it at all," he moaned. "It will be the last we'll play if I have anything to say about it."[35] He did. He moved next Friday night's scheduled game against Carteret to Saturday afternoon.

No sooner had the Boilermakers read of their imminent demise than their state championship stock got an unexpected boost. Once-beaten, once-tied Paterson Central, a solid team with a pair of standout backs in Gabe Mosca and Ray Stanczak and an All-State tackle in Al Rotella, walked into Foley Field and did what only Garfield had done there before—beat Bloomfield. In fact, they did what no team had done since the 1932 season, score more than one TD against the Bengals in a 20-14 stunner. The win was forfeited late in the season when Mosca was judged to be overage and ineligible. But, for now, it stood. The ever-reverential papers had been writing that Bloomfield reclaimed its stride by whipping Newark South Side the previous week, but Central did not conspire in any Bloomfield rebound.

"I have been telling the boys right along that we did not have the stuff this year," Foley lamented. "I had been hoping for the best but I knew that the first good team that we met would raise the dickens and Paterson Central was that team. We have no alibis. They did it with the little football and we may lose a couple of more games unless the team takes a brace."[36]

CARTERET: EASY DOES IT

The Boilermakers were eager to make good on Foley's prediction two weeks later at Foley Field. First, however, they would need to deal with Carteret, which still fielded the talented Doug King. *The Herald-News* reminded them of the danger of looking ahead by warning that "unless the Boilermakers rid themselves of the cockiness which has been evident the past few games, there'll be plenty of gloom in the Bergen city."[37]

Del Greco and McMahon both picked Garfield, albeit with reservations—"when have the boys had it easy this year?" McMahon asked.[38]

For once, they did, busting out for a pair of fourth quarter touchdowns by Ciesla and Babula (on the play following his own interception) to turn the game into a 20-0 rout. Argauer played his reserves freely and it was finally Bloomfield week.

BLOOMFIELD: QUIETING THE SKEPTICS

When the season began, Argauer likely had expected he'd have to muster up confidence in his team to have a chance at beating the Bengals. After all, the Boilermakers hadn't even scored a point on Bloomfield since that game in 1934. Now, he was letting on he was uncomfortable about his team being the favorite, as if it could diminish his team's underdog scrappiness. It was probably a ploy.

"Argauer is confident his team has the ability to knock off Bloomfield, but he fears the youngsters may be awed by the name 'Bloomfield,' which to them symbolizes tremendous football power," Paul Horowitz of the *Newark Evening News* reported from a Belmont Oval practice session. "The defeat of the Bengals by Paterson Central two weeks ago helps the morale of the local gridders for now they know Bloomfield isn't entirely invulnerable."[39]

Maybe not. Yet, as a 2-1-2 team, Bloomfield nevertheless held enormous sway. A big win over Dickinson the previous week had the Bengals growling again, the papers observed. McMahon reported that the smart money favored Bloomfield. Then there was that proverbial monkey perennially perched upon Garfield's back. As *The Herald-News* declared:

> Garfield's state title hopes will either soar to the highest level of the season or be smashed into a thousand pieces. But Garfield supporters have their fingers crossed. For years, in important clashes, Garfield teams have been known to "apple up" and they fear the same thing might happen tomorrow. However, the 1938 edition has done thing no other Boilermaker eleven has done in the past. That is, to spot the opposition a touchdown and come back to win.[40]

On Tuesday, Argauer spirited away from the spying eyes at unshielded Belmont Oval and held a secret scrimmage in South Orange against Seton Hall Prep, (which did not participate in the NJSIAA and used several over-age players who "prepped" there for a year before attending college). He was thrilled with the result, even if the Pony Pirates, employing Bloomfield's T-formation, matched the Boilermakers' four touchdowns. Argauer installed several "trick plays" which were carried out flawlessly. Also, aware of Central's effective passing game against Bloomfield, Argauer had Babula firing the ball downfield all day long.[41]

The quick opener was a staple of Bloomfield's offense. It was tailor-made to exploit Garfield's perceived weakness up the middle. But Argauer used the scrimmage to shift the personnel in his 6-3-2 formation. He moved Herk from fullback to left end and Grembowitz into a starting role at right guard in place of his stepbrother, Ed Klecha. Argauer promoted Emil Bazarnicki, a hefty senior, to the other guard spot and together they flanked Pete Zak, who had been a consistently strong performer on the nose. None of these altered positions were revealed in the Bloomfield game program.

"We really went to town offensively," Argauer crowed afterwards. "If the boys play against Bloomfield as they did against Seton Hall Prep our chances of victory are brighter."[42]

At the same time, *The Herald-News* dispatched Lovas to Bloomfield's practice session, where he interviewed Foley.

"I've stopped thinking out loud when asked to make predictions," Foley told the reporter. "I've got a lot of guys named Joe playing varsity ball for me who had no license getting a uniform when they first came out for football. They've been substitutes for the past two years and when I lost most of last season's eleven, I had to insert them into the varsity lineup."

Even so, Foley was hoping to play the opportunist against Garfield, aware that the Boilermakers weren't converting on all of their chances because of mistakes and penalties.

"The boys tell me Argauer has a fine squad at Garfield this season," he said. "They've been rolling up many first downs and few touchdowns. They can chalk up all the first downs but if they fail to score early, they'll probably be so tired that my boys may turn a break into a touchdown and a victory. I'm polishing up my defense and we'll be more than ready for Garfield."[43]

The *Star-Eagle* took it even further with a headline that shouted, "Bengals Have Plan To Stop Babula, Garfield Star." The paper's Frank Fagan noted how New Brunswick's Andy Beno came into the previous year's post-season showdown "expected to roam the chalk lines at will and leave the Bengals flabbergasted." But Beno was bottled up as Bloomfield penetrated New Brunswick's blocking schemes and got to him before he could get going. Perhaps Bloomfield could repeat the accomplishment against Babula.[44]

Foley also had one big addition to his lineup in Johnny Edack, a starter in the '37 backfield who had missed the first five games after appendicitis surgery two months earlier. He'd return as the Bengals' signal caller. When Lovas caught up with him, Edack gave him the Bloomfield players' view of the tussle. It seemed to be in line with what Eddie Berlinski reported back on the Boilermakers after he scouted the Passaic game for Foley: "good but not good enough to beat Bloomfield."[45]

"They all feel that Garfield will be beaten and from what I've seen of them in four games, I think we can defeat them," Edack disclosed. "They've got only two good boys in the backfield in Babula and Ciesla."[46]

If that was what Foley was telling his team, he was severely underestimating Garfield's backfield depth. In fact, Argauer was starting Sekanics with the first team because Bloomfield's defensive weakness was at the perimeters of the front line. If the speedy Sekanics could turn the corner, Argauer figured he would be off and running.

A gray morning unfolded into a beautiful October afternoon as 13,500 passed through Foley Field's gates. Bloomfield's cheerleading crew trotted out a funeral director's pet deer as a mascot, presumably a nod to Garfield's wing-footed backs. Likely recollecting the brawl following the '34 game, Garfield boosters barked a chant of "We Want the Goalposts." Bloomfield had no counter, neither from its fans nor or from the team. The Boilermakers didn't "apple up," shrink in awe or suffer from hubris. They simply dominated. The only part of Argauer's plan that went awry was starting Sekanics. He had an early fumble and Babula was in the game after five minutes. It didn't matter.

While Bloomfield's terrific left end, Joe Duckworth, made 26 tackles, including one that left Babula sprawled on the ground requiring the team doctor's attention, Garfield totaled 166 yards rushing, and Babula outgained the entire Bengals team on his own, 78-66, foiling whatever plan Foley had devised to shut him down. Grembowitz played a tremendous defensive game in his new and permanent starting role. The Bengals never crossed Garfield's 30-yard line. Garfield had too much depth and showed no weaknesses, dominating the kicking and return games as they had all season.

It was Babula's coffin corner punting that started things off, pinning Bloomfield inside its 20 on four straight possessions. On the fourth, Ray Butts downed Babula's punt on the Bloomfield one. When Sam Zahnle punted from his own end zone after the Bengals' three-and-out, Ciesla took it at midfield and raced to the 24. From there, Babula took off on a patented run off-tackle through a hole that Willie Klein of the *Newark Ledger* said was "wide enough to accommodate *The Normandie*."[47] Babula reversed his field twice as he knifed his way through the secondary. He fought off two defenders with stiff-arms at the five before hurtling into the end zone for the only touchdown Garfield needed.

The Boilermakers closed out the scoring in the final period. Bloomfield, still within six points, was finally putting a drive together behind the improved signal calling of Edack, who entered the game in the third quarter. They had a first down at Garfield's 42, when a pass from Tom Adams went through Jack Biglin's fingertips. An alert Ciesla took the ball off his shoelaces before it could hit the ground and dashed 75 yards for the score that effectively iced the game. Babula finished it off with a dazzling 70-yard punt return through a lane, wrote Gus Falzer of the *Newark Sunday Call* "no bigger than a bowling alley."[48]

This time, with a 19-0 Garfield victory, there wasn't anything for the press to criticize, no cause for Argauer angst. "Art Argauer probably got his first good night's sleep Saturday. He was the happiest man in the world after the game was over," Lovas wrote.[49] The *Bergen Record* grudgingly admitted, "The team has more power than generally given credit for and its victory . . . was impressive."[50]

"There is no use waiting until Thanksgiving Day to decide New Jersey's Group Four football champion," Fagan wrote in his follow-up story in the *Star-Eagle*. "The New Jersey State Interscholastic Athletic Association might as well hand the bunting over to Garfield High School's gridders and concentrate on other groups. Garfield today is by far the outstanding major high school eleven in the state."[51]

Now it was up to J. Whitney Colliton's formula. By extrapolating his point figures, Garfield seemed assured of finishing on top if it could win its final three games against Asbury Park, Paterson Eastside and Clifton. It would be considered the strong favorite in all three games. At the same time the Boilermakers were defeating Bloomfield, other developments worked miraculously in their favor. It was a perfect day for Garfield as most of the previously unbeaten contenders fell like dominoes.

Ferris of Jersey City had a line that averaged over 200 pounds per man (TCU, the No. 1 college team in the country, tipped the scales at 212 pounds each). But Thomas Jefferson of Elizabeth destroyed its hopes of bringing a rare state title to Hudson County. New Brunswick, generally regarded as the state's second-best team in 1937, fell to unbeaten Woodbridge. Nutley lost for the first time in 13 games to East Orange. Columbia, Garfield's scrimmage partner, was stunned by Montclair. Once-tied Paterson Eastside lost to Passaic. Down in South Jersey, Atlantic City bowed to Vineland and Collingswood, the only team to beat Vineland, was upset by Woodrow Wilson of Camden. That left Garfield, Thomas Jefferson and Woodbridge with the only realistic chances for the title.

The Elizabeth team was 4-0-1 with a 7-7 tie against New Brunswick marring its record. Before the previous weekend, John J. Hall, sports columnist for the *Elizabeth Daily Journal*, had laid out a scenario in which he predicted that the two teams would meet again in a post-season contest with the state title on the line. And he was sure that Jefferson, "the better team," would prevail the second time. Of course, Hall had Elizabeth knocking off Ferris and Garfield losing to Bloomfield, he reasoned, because "Garfield hasn't fared on the toughest competition." Garfield, "which has had nothing but clear sailing, is due for a rocky afternoon," he predicted.[52] Two conspicuous oversights existed within Hall's hypothesis; first, that Garfield had taken on some tough competition so far in the season and, second, that Garfield had cruised past Bloomfield like a super-charged eight-cylinder Duesenberg.

Hall can be forgiven for his parochial prognostication, although he neglected to mention Woodbridge, which turned back New Brunswick, 7-0. The surprising victory moved the Barrons to 5-0 on the year. While the strength of their schedule couldn't compare to that of Garfield's, talk of post-season matchup started to percolate around the Middlesex County burb. With an off-week coming up, Woodbridge fans began rooting for an Asbury Park upset.

ASBURY PARK: JUST WIN, BABY

Garfield came out of its big win at Foley Field determined to finish out the season the right way. When Argauer asked his players if they wanted a day off, they chose to get right back on the practice field to prep for Asbury Park. "No swelled heads here," Argauer told *The Herald-News.*[53]

Everyone, however, was shocked when the Colliton Ratings were released for the first time that Thursday. Despite its one tie with New Brunswick, Thomas Jefferson was ranked No. 1, with 592 points to Garfield's 587 and 576 for Woodbridge in third. The professor tried to explain that his rankings were "strictly tentative" because the value of a victory changed as teams' strengths fluctuated. The explanation was merely academic and, to most observers, must have seemed downright erroneous, since Garfield had already beaten four of the top 11 teams in Colliton's final 1937 rankings. In any case, one could reasonably argue that the Colliton System began its second season 0-1.

Walter Short stepped in to calm the chattering masses, pointing out that Jefferson might be "King for a Day," considering that its last two games were against out-of-state teams and would be weighted less.

All Garfield could do was to keep winning and, for once, it had little trouble with Asbury Park. The Blue Bishops had lost only once, to Thomas Jefferson, but they came into Passaic Stadium with a banged-up backfield. Argauer, who had lost Orlovsky for the season to a separated shoulder in the Bloomfield game, started Babula and Ciesla in the same backfield for the first time. The Boilermakers outclassed the visitors with a second straight 19-0 win. When Asbury Park came out in a seven-man line, Ciesla, calling the signals, went to the air and Babula completed 10-of-16 passes, including eight in a row and two for TDs, one to Ciesla. Grembowitz played another stellar game on defense. Asbury Park picked up only two non-penalty first downs. Meanwhile, those kings for a day in Elizabeth were summarily dethroned. Paterson Eastside, Garfield's next opponent, played them to a scoreless tie, effectively snuffing out the Jeffs' title hopes.

"It was a story of overconfidence and desperation," Chris Zusi wrote in the *Daily Journal.* "All they had ... were their newspaper clippings."[54]

Garfield, too, endeavored to contain its confidence. With Elizabeth's loss and their win over Asbury Park, it topped the Colliton Rankings again. But there was another group that awarded state championships—the New Jersey Interscholastic Bureau, which had been using its own points system since 1929 in conjunction with *The Jersey Journal*. When the *Journal*, which claimed to be near perfect, released its figures for the first time that week, Woodbridge led with 80 points to 78.53 for Garfield. That gave Woodbridge supporters—who felt trapped in Garfield's shadow—some hope.

George Molnar, sports editor of the weekly *Woodbridge Leader Journal*, mockingly wrote of the attention the Barrons finally received:

> *After several stinging blasts by this column, Newark sports writers finally awoke to the fact that we have a good football team in Woodbridge. Several of the scribes took afternoons off and invaded the Barron camp to see the inner workings of Nick Prisco's mighty eleven. The boys showed the welcome visitors a few of their trick plays and you should have seen those wrinkled brows and heard those sighs of 'oohs' and 'ahs.*[55]

Gene Pinter, sports editor of *The New Brunswick Home News*, reported in his column that Prisco had begun to hint that he'd be open to a post-season playoff. Pinter suggested newly constructed Rutgers Stadium as the venue.[56]

PATERSON EASTSIDE: BOO

There never was much enthusiasm for such a game in Garfield, considering its commanding lead in Colliton points. Argauer wasn't about to distract his team from the upcoming task of playing Paterson Eastside, which had demonstrated its capability to upset in its tie with Thomas Jefferson a week earlier. He even put the team through a hard scrimmage early in the week.

The Ghosts or Undertakers—so named because the school was built on the grounds of an old cemetery—knew they were playing the state's top-ranked team for the second straight week. Bob Whiting of the *Paterson Morning Call* dubbed them a "small but sturdy" band of giant killers. Eastside had allowed only two teams to score on it all year but was nursing several injuries after its tough battle in Elizabeth.[57]

More than 7,000 fans overflowed Paterson's Baeurle Stadium, which proved to be somewhat of a home-field advantage to Eastside. The teams hadn't met since 1933, and the Boilermakers were unfamiliar with the layout of the playing field, which had three yards of cinder track in play along each sideline. Early in the first quarter, for instance, Sekanics was in the clear up the left sideline, but he cut back into the pursuit, thinking the cinders were out of bounds.

That set the tone for a very scary game on the old graveyard. Only the speed of Sekanics prevented Eastside's 135-pound flash, Lou Cuccinello, to score from his own 19-yard line. As it was, the 55-yard run set up a touchdown pass from Bob Smith to Americo Zoccalillo deep in the right corner of the end zone. The Eastside portion of the crowd, about 4,000, went berserk. It was the first TD Garfield had allowed in four games.

Once again, the Boilermakers were forced to come back from an early deficit, this time 7-0, and, again, they proved their championship mettle with some luck and some heads-up play by Grembowitz. The Babula-Ciesla tandem advanced the ball from Garfield 35 to the Eastside four-yard line in nine running plays. On fourth down, Babula went off right tackle on the first play of the second quarter but fumbled over the goal line. Fans of both teams stood in anticipatory silence as the referee pulled players off the pile and it was Grembowitz, playing another brilliant game, who was clutching the football at the bottom of the heap. Babula's kick tied the game.

A leg injury sidelined Cuccinello and helped stall the Eastside attack the rest of the game and in the third period, Garfield went to the air to set up the winning score. Young caught a pass from Babula in the flat and on Garfield's patented hook-and-lateral play, dished off to Ciesla for 25 yards. Another pass from Babula to Grembowitz was good for another 30. Babula, again on fourth down, went off right end at the five-yard line. He shook off tacklers and with Frank Fournier wrapped around his waist at the goal line, shrugged him off with a final stiff arm. Garfield was threatening at the Eastside four when the game ended, 13-7.

CLIFTON: WRAPPING IT UP

Only the Thanksgiving morning game with Clifton remained, that is, if there were to be no post-season meeting with Woodbridge. While the Boilermakers were battling Eastside, the Barrons were trouncing a weak St. Mary's team from Perth Amboy, 38-0. While Garfield was idle the next Saturday, Woodbridge posted its fourth straight shutout against Perth Amboy High School, another weak opponent, 13-0, breaking an eight-year losing streak.

Now, the post-season banter began in earnest. The *Leader Journal* reported that Argauer and Prisco had chatted about a game, and that both Foley Field and Newark Schools Stadium were interested in hosting it. The Garfield Board of Education had tentatively agreed to the arrangement. With Garfield kicking off against Clifton in the morning, Argauer planned to attend the Woodbridge-South River game in the afternoon and then render a decision. Wrote Molnar in the Thanksgiving Eve paper:

> Of course the real question is, "Will the Garfielders accept the challenge?" They will be rated state champs and the Barrons can hurl all the challenges they please. Garfield does not have to play us.
>
> But, knowing that Garfield is a sports-loving town, I am inclined to believe that they will accept. I hope they do because I feel that the game will be a thriller. And the Barrons will win. But won't that put a pretty crimp into the Colliton system? We all know that the Colliton mathematicians are definitely on the Garfield side of the fence while sports writers believe Woodbridge has the better team.[58]

By "sports writers," Molnar meant those at *The Jersey Journal*. But even they would have to reconsider their rankings. The only crimp existing was South River on Thanksgiving Day. The largely under-rated team had some strong motivations as well. It veritably slid over the Barrons on a sleet-covered field and won the game on a blocked punt in the third quarter.

Garfield had already coasted past Clifton, 19-0. The Mustangs were held to 18 yards rushing while Babula ran for 122. Ciesla, in his last high school game, scored a pair of touchdowns, one on a pass from Babula.

Later, when Argauer left the South River field, he was confident that all the arguments had been settled, although there was one last bid for a state championship game from Vineland, the top Colliton point-getter in South Jersey. But Vineland's record was marred by a 9-0 loss to Collingwood and Argauer saw little to gain by playing them. The challenge died there. After a rebuilding program that began in 1930, the Boilermakers had battled through persistent doubt and their own stubborn legacy of underachievement. At last, they would be state champions.

So confident was everyone that Garfield would finish on top that the Boilermakers' post-season banquet was scheduled for the night of the NJSIAA meeting, where coaches pleaded their cases. Over 500 revelers seated around round tables trimmed in white in the big ballroom at Donohue's Restaurant in Mountain View. The owner, Jimmie Donohue, also had a hotel in Garfield known as the Black Sea. Babe Ruth discovered it in the 20s and it became one of his favorite hangouts. He kept a room on the third floor known as the Throne Room, painted blood red with a view of the Passaic River.[59] The Bambino was only too happy to serve as a guest speaker at the Boilermaker banquet. He turned from the dais to where the team was seated.

"How do you boys like to be state champions?' he asked them. They just smiled nervously. Then he turned to the audience. "How do you people like these boys to be state champions?" and the room exploded.[60]

Frank Dunham, sports editor of the previously reticent *The Jersey Journal,* presented the newspaper's state championship trophy, handsomely crested with a gold football. Bill Foley, who had been accustomed to accepting it year after year, was in attendance to congratulate his coaching rival. Everyone was now singing Argauer's praises, including the *Newark Sunday Call:*

> Followers of the Garfield High School football eleven clamored for a state championship grid team this year. They got it. Now they're calling Coach Arthur Argauer a "miracle man."[61]

Argauer deferred the plaudits to his boys. "From team spirit developed other important factors, like blocking," he said. "The boys blocked for each other. The backs ran hard and savagely to help the ball carrying back and the lines hit for keeps on every play. They really deserve a lot of credit, those linemen, because they made the big holes for the backs to gallop through."[62]

Babula and Ciesla finished near the top of the state's scoring list, and along with Grembowitz, Herk and Pirog, they all made numerous all-state teams. Curiously, Garfield didn't have a player on the New Jersey Scholastic Sports Writers Association's first team. The voting was held at the NJSIAA meeting the night of Garfield's banquet, where all the North Jersey writers who would have voted for Garfield's players chose to chow down instead.

Just as curiously, Frank Fagan at the *Star-Eagle* selected Ciesla over Babula for his first team. It was yet another public pronouncement of the nagging perception that Babula lacked desire.

"From the stands, it appears Ciesla is all heart and soul in football and it is known that Babula is not exactly in love with the game," Fagan wrote. "Ciesla is the driving, smashing back, good for what yardage you need on third down. Babula, it is true, was one of the state's high scorers but he is not a very fast starter and only good blocking enabled him to go as far as he did."[63]

Regardless, Babula and the Boilermakers were beginning to attract national attention. They were about to pick up their hardware when Del Greco reported that Argauer was holding indoor football practices in hopes of playing in an unnamed bowl game. A year later, Argauer revealed the team had been invited to play in Florida against either Robert E. Lee of Jacksonville—Miami High's rival—or against a team of local All Stars. The players, Argauer said, voted against going. Norwalk, Connecticut played the All Stars instead.

Under the headline "'Let Them Eat Cake' Is Command In Garfield," The Herald-News *pictures Coleman Szely, John Polcari, Ted Ciesla and Ed Klecha chowing down on ice cream and cakes as reward for completing an unbeaten season against Clifton.* The Herald-News.

Argauer turned his attention to his basketball team, but he was already fretting over the loss of eight starters in 1939. "My team is going to be hit pretty hard next year," he cried. Fittingly, Argauer, who knew beating Bloomfield was pivotal to his title hopes, was invited to the Bloomfield Fifth Quarter Club's "Win, Lose or Draw" banquet. It was a rare "Lose" year. The booster club had a tradition of inviting the coaches of the teams that conquered Bloomfield during the season. The last person invited was Argauer, in 1934. Bill Foley, conquered not just in battle but also in the war, paid Argauer a tribute along with a warning.

"Uneasy is the head that wears the crown," he said.

THIRTEEN

THE 1938 STINGAREES

Jesse Yarborough had just finished riding herd on his team through another scalding September practice session. A cap perched on his head. He tugged at the towel draped around his neck. He was bare-chested for effect, even though his Clemson lineman's physique had slipped south a tad.

He headed off the big practice field toward his office, satisfied with the day's work. The newspapermen had emerged from the sparse shade of a few stray palm trees and trailed him, eager to scribble down the "Colonel's" take on the upcoming 1938 season. He was obliging, or, more accurately, charming them. As he spun his words, exhausted players, trying not to look so, participated in the day's final ritual across the field from the interview scrum. Yarborough had left it to assistant coach Clyde Crabtree to put the squad through those universally despised wind-sprints designed to sap any little remaining energy from burning legs and aching lungs. It's how the Stingarees developed their immunity to the heat and humidity as visiting teams hit their thresholds of tolerance. Fight through the urge to quit. Make 'em think you enjoy it.

Suddenly, Yarborough halted an answer in mid-sentence and wheeled around, letting go a rebel yell of a shriek that announced to all he wasn't pleased with those infernal wind sprints. A "wild yell ripping the quiet afternoon," Jack Bell called it.

He turned back with a sly smile and a wink.

"You gotta let 'em know you're watching them all the time," he told the newsmen.

"But you weren't," Bell protested.

"Shhh. Not so loud," Yarborough chortled. "I make 'em think I can see with my ears."[1]

The performance was directed as much to the reporters as it was to his players. Yarborough knew how to make an impression, and he wanted them to know that nothing could escape his attention this year, and that this team, perhaps his best ever, was all-in. What Yarborough saw, he liked. There was size and there was depth. "I don't reckon we'll play a game this year we don't think—before it starts—we'll win," he cracked.

The reporters wanted more. He gave it to them. Heck, he said, he had to actually take it easy on his players for their own good.

"We don't scrimmage more than two or three times a week; those kids are so big and tough and hit each other so hard I'm afraid we'll be crippled before the season starts," he chuffed.[2]

They laughed at the homespun hyperbole and spread the narrative. Lefty Schemer had graduated, but Yarborough still had talent on every unit. Ever since 80 candidates turned out for spring practice, he was over the Miami moon about his team's prospects. In interview after interview, he was as contentedly confident as if he were relaxing back home watching the cows graze on the family farm in Chester. At least that is how the *Miami News'* Luther Voltz had described him when he found him alone in his office that August:

> Col. Jesse Hardin Yarborough is quite complacent these days. He lolls in a big chair, his feet propped on a table and munches on a bushel of peanuts, boiled South Carolina style, figuring all is right with the world.
>
> The colonel wouldn't want the boys to hear it but he will confess to his cronies in the sitting-around room at the University Club that his Miami High Stingarees will be very hard to get along with on the football field this fall. To use an oft-uttered phrase: The colonel's got 'em.[3]

He had them all right, especially along the line, the foundation of any great team. Burly All State guard Joe Sansone, with his pile-driving legs, 200-pound Gene Ellenson, rated among the best tackles in Florida, and Joe Crum, at end, anchored an experienced front wall while Jay Kendrick, a young Samson, was ready for a breakout year. The backfield was loaded as well. Captain Johnny Reid was back to call the signals with Davey Eldredge, the best of the runners, Jason Koesy, the best of the passers and Reddic Harris and Roy Bass, the best of the blockers. Eldredge was to alternate with Oscar Dubriel, who performed admirably in '37 after being plucked out of gym class. Alwin Carter, who had performed so well after Eldredge was injured, was yet another option.

There was plenty of competition, a coach's best friend. Yarborough could always use demotion from the starting lineup as a powerful motivating factor. On the line, Doug Craven, Levin Rollins and Gilbert Wilson were showing plenty of promise. In the backfield, J.B. Moore was looking like a find. So was a tenth-grader by the name of Harvey Comfort, who impressed Yarborough in spring practice. And, if that weren't enough, two new players with varsity experience transferred to Miami High: Roy Maupin, an end from Marist High in Atlanta, and redheaded Bobby Mathews from Sylacauga, Alabama.

When the *Miami Herald* previewed the season, Luther Evans looked to FDR's festive 1932 campaign song for his lede:

> *"Happy Days"*
>
> That's the theme song out at Miami High where the Stingarees, although facing the Southland's toughest schedule, from Goldie Goldstein, executive manager, to Coach Jesse Yarborough are confident they'll tackle the opposition with the best all-around club ever to represent the Blue and Gold.

For even Yarborough, who usually carries a face as stern as a Puritan father, can't keep a cheerful grin from creeping across his pan when he watches his charges hustle in practice.[4]

As usual, the Stingarees were thinking national championship if they could get through their 10-game schedule undefeated, a daunting but seemingly doable challenge that would begin immediately.

KNOXVILLE: FUMBLING ONE AWAY

The first game was against Knoxville, the team that proclaimed itself national champion after dealing the Stingarees a 25-0 defeat the previous year. This time, the game was on the road and, after two straight home defeats against Knoxville, the Stingarees were determined to repay the debt. Yarborough boarded an Eastern Airlines plane to Tennessee (the athletic department's budget was that impressive) to scout the Trojans' 31-0 win against outmatched Bradley County. He found them formidable, despite the loss of seven starters, including Johnny Butler, now doing his running across town for the Tennessee Vols' freshman team.

Yarborough caught up to Knoxville coach Wilson Collins on the field afterwards and marveled, "Why, they look even bigger than they did last year, Wilson."

"They aren't so big," Collins replied. "Those shoulder pads just make them appear larger than they really are."[5]

Suitably impressed, but armed with information, Yarborough got back to Miami in time to see his B team take on Fort Lauderdale's varsity. The game, while it wouldn't count on Miami's record, offered some basis of comparison, given that the Flying L's had played a 12-12 tie with Bradley County, the team Yarborough witnessed Knoxville destroy. And it wasn't exactly a B team that Yarborough was fielding. The backfield featured Eldredge and Dubriel. The line had varsity first-teamers Kendrick and Butch Miles. That the Stingarees could manage just a 13-13 tie was rather curious. Just as curious—and costly—was Yarborough's decision to play Miles, who broke his collarbone, the second of two setbacks leading up to the Knoxville game. The first occurred the previous Wednesday when Alwin Carter was declared academically ineligible. Koesy, too, was now nursing a bruised knee. Yarborough's "Puritan" visage returned as he considered ways to reshuffle his lineup.

The road trip, in any case, was a fantastic one for a team unaccustomed to making them, and there was no shortage of fanfare at the sendoff. The marching band was out on the platform at the Seaboard station in Allapattah where 24 players boarded the train Wednesday night. Coeds waved pennants, cheerleaders went through the team cheers and everyone expected the Stings to return home with a win. Yarborough even turned to a fan before he climbed on board. "Bet on my kids if you're going to put any money on the game," he winked, pre-dating Joe Namath's Miami Super Bowl guarantee by a little over 30 years.[6]

After Collins' Knoxville team had been fêted on its trips to Miami, he planned to show the visitors a "grand time" with a program that seemed to steal every minute of the Stings' time. They arrived on the L&N Railway around 11:00 Thursday night and were whisked to the landmark Hotel Farragut for a good night's sleep. The morning of the game began with a special chapel program at Knoxville High. They had planned to take a quick tour of Smokey Mountain National Park but Yarborough called it off, preferring to postpone the hoopla until after the fray.

A dance was scheduled for that night and a visit to two-year-old Norris Dam, the first major project of the Tennessee Valley Authority, was scheduled for Saturday morning. That afternoon, the team would take in the Saturday game at Shields-Watkins Field between Clemson, their coach's *alma mater*, and the powerful Tennessee Volunteers of Major (not yet General) Bob Neyland. Even Knoxville's stores greeted the Floridians in style. Merchants trimmed their shops in Miami colors. Woodruff's appliance store on Gary Street, flashed a "WELCOME MIAMI STINGAREES" message in its ad in the *Knoxville News-Sentinel* for the Bendix Home Laundry, the first automatic washing machine ever made. The modern marvel, it said, "does all the disagreeable work without attention. Bendix washes the clothes, gives them three separate fresh water rinses, spins them damp-dry, then shuts off . . . all automatically."

Why, a housewife's hands never touches water and the clothes come out "ready for the line." Unfortunately, the automatic dryer had yet to be invented.[7]

"The welcome extended by the people of Knoxville and East Tennessee may have to make up for our welcome on the field," Collins said sheepishly. "Frankly, I doubt that we shall give them as close a game as they are expecting since the Stingarees outweigh us so badly. Their experience, too, is going to tell, but maybe it will be a game they can enjoy."[8]

They did not enjoy it.

The Stingarees lived up to their pre-game expectations by outgaining the hosts, 174-39. They were not expected to lose seven fumbles and have two punts blocked. Knoxville's 19-7 victory even had *News-Sentinel* correspondent Harold Harris writing apologetically, "Knoxville fans agreed that, but for the breaks which went against them, the powerful Stingarees would surely have won."[9]

Collins called the Miami line the hardest charging his team had faced in some time. He said the Stingaree backs were hard to stop. That is, of course, when they weren't stopping themselves by dropping the ball. At first, Knoxville took advantage of field position to open the scoring in the second quarter, marching just 28 yards after Reid's punt went out of bounds. Miami's line failed to stop Joe Fritz on third down from the one and it was 7-0. The Stingarees appeared to have survived a blocked punt when they took over on downs at their five-yard line. But Eldredge, who had his problems holding onto the football as a sophomore, fumbled on the first play from scrimmage. That turned into a 13-0 deficit when Tiger Roberts scored for Knoxville from the one.

Eldredge began to compensate for his mistake in the fourth quarter. Alternating passes with shifty runs, he sparked a long, steady drive and scored standing up on an off-tackle play from the 10. He was fielding a punt later in the quarter with Miami within a touchdown. But Fritts launched the kick high into the lights at Caswell Field and Eldredge lost sight of it. It bounced off him at the 25 and rolled all the way to the five where the Trojans recovered again. A second Fritts touchdown clinched the Knoxville win. Eldredge left the field in a bad mood. He just couldn't cure himself of his bout with of fumbleitis.

"Breaks are part of the game," Yarborough said. "Knoxville played a fine game and by their heads-up play they deserved to win."[10]

ROBERT E. LEE: THERE GOES FLORIDA

Yarborough played down the defeat, even though it just about killed any chance for a mythical Southern championship. It could easily be rationalized. It was Miami's first game, Knoxville's third. Even the inimitable Neyland and Clemson coach Jess Neeley, who scouted the game for potential talent, had been impressed by the Stingarees, calling Miami's line the speediest high school unit they'd ever seen. Just clean up the turnovers and all would be fine. The Stings historically rebounded strongly after defeats, which Miamians expected them to do yet again. After all, that next game was at home against a Florida foe, Robert E. Lee of Jacksonville, and the Stingarees hadn't lost to an in-state school in 10 years.

The Generals, though, had not been pushovers. They had stayed within a touchdown of Miami the three previous years, including the '37 mud bath, and they weren't heading down the Florida East Coast Railway as any sort of get-well gift. They had rolled over their first two opponents by a combined 74-0 score. The *Florida Times-Union* wrote they were bringing a "now-or-never attitude" to the game, confident, the paper said, that "they'll be the ones to hand the Miamians their first defeat at the hands of a Florida rival since 1928."[11]

Crabtree vouched for Lee's strength. He scouted the Generals' 33-0 rout of Gainesville on the way to Knoxville and, when he caught up to the team, he brought ominous reviews. Lee's line was small but quick, he reported, and 186-pound Maxwell Partin, who shifted between end and tailback, was exceptional, a worthy successor to the slippery Dingman.

The practices were hard, despite the Stings' added injury problems with center Peter Schaefer out with a knee injury (Kendrick would be shifted to his spot) and Crum hobbled but available. Old "Cannonball" Crabtree suited up to impersonate Partin against the first team defense and had a field day getting around the ends.

"That's what you can expect Saturday," the former Florida flash told them. "And this Partin is faster than I am."[12]

Aside from stopping Partin, Yarborough's biggest problem was Eldredge. His was fleet-footed and impossibly agile. But, his hands? He just couldn't stop fumbling the football. Even in practice. With Dubriel looking sharp, Yarborough made the decision. Dubriel would start. Eldredge would come into the game as a substitute. For a kid as competitive as Eldredge, it stung like a Miami sunburn.

In spite of the issues, Yarborough sounded confident: "Tell 'em we're going to war out there," he blustered in the Jacksonville paper.[13] But did he mean it? The visitors did. Conditions were perfect for the 3:30 kickoff at Burdine Stadium. The Stingarees were not. Eldredge and Company fumbled seven more times, losing four of them. This time, the turnovers didn't lead to points. They just allowed the Generals to control the game. Partin was as hard to corral as Crabtree had been in practice. In the first half, playing end, he gained some nice yardage on a couple of reverses. In the second half, at tailback, he set up and scored the game's only touchdown. The vaunted Miami line was outplayed. The quicker Generals set them up on trap plays and Partin ran through some big holes. Miami's offense was no better. Lee's front stuffed the running game.

It wasn't until after Partin's third-quarter score that the now-desperate Stingarees showed any life. After stopping Lee on their 12-yard line, Yarborough sent Koesy into the game late and he completed pass after pass, mostly to Reid. Miami was at the Generals' 29 with time enough for one last play, trailing 6-0. Eldredge worked his way out of the backfield and was at the one-yard line with his back to the goal when Koesy let loose a pass that could have tied the game.

The crowd of 3,300 stood and watched the ball hang in the air. But Eldredge, perhaps thinking about the move he'd have to make to score, failed to secure the ball and the game was over when the ball hit the grass. The Stingarees were 0-2 and Eldredge was marked with butterfingers. It wasn't supposed to be this way.

Miami hadn't lost to a Florida team since Thanksgiving Day, 1928, when Lakeland came down from Central Florida and won by a 13-7 score. In all probability, the Stingarees, who had fumbled away the Southern championship in Knoxville, had lost their long-held claim on the state championship, unless Lee fell apart—and that didn't seem likely. In two games, the entire season outlook changed. No, things were hardly as merry on the practice field as when Yarborough bantered with the writers before the season. First, the fumbling needed to stop. Crabtree went over films of the Lee game and was certain he found the problem when he called his backs into the room.

Mike Osceola rushes upfield in a staged publicity shot.
Courtesy Estate of Mike Osceola.

"Our backs were trying too hard to fight for yardage after they were tackled," he explained. "Instead of relaxing and covering up when it was certain that they would be downed, they kept squirming and inviting second and third defensive players to hit them and the shock was just too great. One of the boys (presumably Eldredge) was trying to change the ball to the arm away from the tackler just as he was hit but I don't think he will be doing it any more."[14]

Yarborough entered the darkened room and interrupted the film session with a special announcement. Anyone who fumbled in the next game against Nashville Central would take an immediate seat on the bench. He also planned one change in the lineup with Charlie Burrus making his first start as the blocking back. Eldredge was starting the game on the sidelines.

As for his underachieving line, changes were coming, one by necessity with Ellenson spraining his ankle. To underscore the point, Yarborough was starting at one tackle his personal project, the sophomore Seminole Larry "Mike" Osceola, who had played in just one game before in his life. At the other tackle, Dick Fauth was coming up from the B Team after Roy Risgby, who started for the injured Schaefer against Lee, was benched for poor play. Crum, who played crummy against Lee, was to start the game on the bench behind Damon Bates. Even Jack Bell called out Crum in the paper.

"If Joe Crum doesn't snap out of it and play better ball than he did last week he's due for a kick in the pants from us truly," he wrote.[15]

Miamians were justifiably angry over the team's performance. The Stingarees had not been 0-2 since 1924. In fact, it was the only other time a Miami team ever had a losing record at any point in the season. Its worst overall record was 5-5, in 1936.

Nashville Central: Back on Track

Fortunately for the Stings, Nashville Central wasn't arriving as a powerhouse. Yarborough put Central on the schedule after it finished as runner-up for its city title in 1937. But with only two returning starters and 10 lettermen, Central came into Miami on a two-game losing streak after starting off with a pair of wins. A fed-up Yarborough put the Stingarees through a few hard practices. The visitors were going to catch the Stingarees at the wrong time. It all worked in Miami's favor, even Yarborough's promise to yank the first man who fumbled out of the game. Sure enough, Reddic Harris fumbled three plays after the opening kickoff, and that gave Eldredge his chance to get back on the field. In fact, the officials had barely finished pulling players off the pile before Eldredge was sprinting onto the field to play defense past the dejected Harris as he hung his head.

Li'l Davey didn't disappoint. The first time he touched the ball on one of those punt receptions he'd been fumbling, he brought the ball back to Miami's 48. Here, Yarborough's new line configuration opened a huge gap on the right side. Osceola cleared his man, and Eldredge zipped around him, never to be touched en route to a 58-yard touchdown. That was one way to avoid fumbling. Never let them catch you.

Luther Evans of the *Miami Herald* was thrilled.

"Zigging and zagging, the Stingaree speed merchant baffled the frantic backs and toyed with the safety man to go across the goal, slightly tired but unmarked after running 58 three-footers," he wrote.[16]

Eldredge repeated the feat twice more, from 18 yards out and from 48, with all three of his TDs behind the blocks of Osceola, who had an entire cheering section on hand from the Seminole tribe. It was 25-0 at halftime when Yarborough called off the dogs and played his reserves in the entire second half. The 25-7 victory certainly took the pressure off the team and, specifically, its star running back. The *Miami News* called the game a "personal triumph" for Eldredge.[17]

It was just the beginning. Yarborough alertly changed the emphasis from power to speed, utilizing outside runs and quick openers. It takes a great coach and the right talent to pull that off, but Miami soon hit its stride. Eldredge, finally free of worry about fumbling, began to run less tentatively. The offensive line, which returned the injured Ellensen and Schaefer at tackle, became more versatile and, with Osceola emerging, deeper than ever.

Savannah: Davey's Torch Dance

Winless Savannah was next to visit Miami that Friday night, but the Blue Jackets were doomed from the start. The stage was set for a crowd-pleasing show at Burdine Stadium, including halftime, which Earnie Seiler would have been proud to produce. Frances Mary Walker, Miami High's "shapely 16-year-old drum major," led the band out while twirling a flaming torch. The crowd loved it when the stadium lights were extinguished to "make the spectacle more impressive."[18]

Miss Walker was almost the biggest hit of the night. Almost. Eldredge was the main attraction. The papers now began to give him star billing again. With his socks rolled down above his high-tops, his chinstrap tight under his jaw, Eldredge looked every bit the football hero. His white jersey with the satiny-gold numerals shined in the Orange Bowl lights as brightly as Miss Walker's torch.

The *Miami News* said Eldredge was in his "best form," that he "ran with all the finesse of a great back. He was fast, had a sweet change of pace, and followed his interference and when finally on his own he was a hard hombre to render horizontal."[19]

"Li'l David has winged feet and Lawd, Lawd, how he can run," raved *Miami Herald* sports editor Everett Clay.[20]

Today, a 14-0 final score may not seem like a rout. This was. At least it was written up that way. And it happened as quickly as the churning of Eldredge's legs. Both touchdowns came in the first half before Yarborough emptied his bench. After Koesy and Burrus combined for a 21-yard pass completion to the Savannah 12, Eldredge darted around a block by Harris and was across the goal line almost before the visitors could react. Harris scored the second touchdown after Eldredge brought the crowd to its feet with a few more dazzling runs. Kendrick almost single-handedly shut down the Blue Jacket running game inside. Said the *News*:

> So neatly did everything work that Savannah appeared bewildered and did nothing soon thereafter to dispel such belief.[21]

ANDREW JACKSON: PARTIAL PAYBACK

The Stingarees' 0-2 start had nearly been forgotten along with Eldredge's fumble problems and the next week's game provided some measure of revenge. It was the second of Miami's two 1938 road trips, this time to Jacksonville to play Andrew Jackson and it was a chance to atone somewhat for the loss to Jacksonville's other high school, Robert E. Lee. What's more, Jackson was 3-1-1 in four contests and would play Lee later in the year. An impressive Stingaree win, combined with a Jackson win over Lee, could allow Miami to claim another state championship.

The Stingarees and Tigers had not played since their post-season meeting on New Year's Day, 1935, a Kiwanis Charity Game with the state championship at stake. Miami, which was twice tied and once-beaten that year, handed Jackson its only loss of the year, 7-6, when Norman Pate, the Stingarees' All-Southern quarterback, called for a pass on fourth-and-four from the Miami 44 and completed it to keep the winning touchdown drive going. Eldredge's brother Knox sent a perfect drop kick through for the point-after to give the "gallant" Stings the much-lauded victory.

"For five years I've been trying to get them to play us," explained Yarborough, back in sardonic humor. "But they have always turned thumbs down on the idea before this year. Gee! They must have a great team or they wouldn't be playing us at all."[22]

Before turning his full attention to Jackson, though, Yarborough had one other matter. His B Team was traveling to take on Fort Myers Junior High, a game that oddly turned into one of the most important of the year. The JV Stings blasted their younger opponents, 40-0, but that wasn't the point. Harvey Comfort, who first impressed during intramurals, then in spring practice, did everything for Miami. He showed what the *Fort Myers News-Press* called "shifty speed" in running for two scores and showed off his arm to JV coach Pete Tulley by throwing for two long TD strikes to Bucket Barnes and J.B. Moore, both of whom would start on the 1939 team. Tulley brought back such glowing reports that Yarborough immediately promoted Comfort to the varsity and made him part of the 30-player party headed to Jacksonville.[23]

Comfort didn't get into the varsity game in Jacksonville. After all, he hadn't practiced with the big squad all year. But he did stand closely by Yarborough to watch and learn. The Stingarees won, 12-7, in a hard-fought battle witnessed by 5,000 fans. The home team held Eldredge relatively in check, limiting him to 65 yards, but Reid took over as the featured attraction by throwing one TD pass to the revitalized Crum before taking it over from the one-yard line for Miami's second score. It was Miami's first win over a winning team and lifted the Stings over .500, where they would stay the rest of the season.

LANIER: POETIC JUSTICE

Miami was off the next week as Sea Biscuit and War Admiral dueled in their historic match race at Pimlico that Tuesday. That gave Yarborough time to plan a new look for the next opponent, Lanier of Macon, on Armistice Night. Injury-riddled Lanier was 0-4-3 and had scored just 13 points all season. But Selby Buck's team had won the Georgia state title and bullied the Stingarees a year earlier. The Maconites and Knoxville were the only two teams to hold advantages over Miami in their all-time series, and the Stingarees were hungry for payback. Yarborough also figured it was the perfect time to give Comfort his first start with an extra week of practice against a weaker opponent.

Comfort was ecstatic. He knew how rare it was to be promoted from the B team, and he didn't miss his opening during the off week by excelling in a series of hard scrimmages, proving he could play with the big boys. Yarborough and Crabtree delighted in Comfort's unique running style, low to the ground and with power. And he didn't fumble. And Comfort wouldn't be the only Sting making his starting debut against the Poets. He'd run alongside Pericles Nichols, who was also promoted to the starting lineup after an impressive debut on both offense and defense in Jacksonville.

"These backs. Along with Li'l David Eldredge, have begun to show themselves and they'll be mighty hard to stop Friday night," Yarborough crowed.[24]

Yarborough, as they say, had more depth than he knew what to do with. In fact, the *Miami News* ran a picture the day of the game with three rows of four backs stacked up on each other, smiling from inside their leather helmets. The same could be said for his line. Butch Miles was returning from his broken collarbone, but he couldn't break into the starting lineup the way Jay Kendrick had been opening holes and clogging the middle.

It was all too much for the Poets. Oscar Dubriel had run back the opening kickoff to the Miami 18-yard line and had barely caught his breath, when he took the direct snap on the first play from scrimmage and followed his blocking around the right end. He turned the corner, shrugged one defender off his hips and romped 72 yards to a score. Then, Eldredge entered the game and, after a punt, made good on his first carry, slipping into the open between right guard and tackle, and sprinting into the end zone on another 72-yard TD run. Lanier was as dazed as a prizefighter stumbling in the ring, but with no referee to call off the brutal pounding. Reid scored three times, and Ellensen blocked a punt for another TD in the 38-6 rout.

The Stingarees were peaking. Yet, there was one problem. Lime burns. Of all the hazards of the football field, the most hazardous was sometimes the field itself. When unslaked or "quick" lime was used to mark the lines, any contact with moisture—rain or even sweat—set off a chemical reaction that could cause, at worst, second-degree burns, sometimes right through the uniform. Precautions weren't always taken and a careless workman could cause unintended agony. When it happened at a Clemson-Wake Forest game in 1936, *Greenville News* sports editor Scoop Latimer, Yarborough's old friend, called it "tantamount to criminal negligence."[25] Nevertheless, instances of quick lime burns from football fields persisted into the 1960s.

The grounds crew used such untreated lime for the Lanier game with 12 Miami players developing painful blisters, four of them serious. At first, there were doubts that Joe Sansone, Roy Bass, Kendrick and Crum could play against the high-flying Pine Bluff Zebras, the defending Arkansas state champs. They all ended up making it.

PINE BLUFF: NO CONTEST

The game was originally scheduled for Saturday afternoon but was moved under the lights to drive up ticket sales. Pine Bluff's celebrated passing attack was the top attraction. Coach Allen Dunaway had been throwing it out of a double wing attack since before he coached Don Hutson, among the greatest of all NFL receivers in 1930. Now, he had Hutson's two brothers, Robert and Raymond, in his backfield. The Stings didn't face the double wing often, so Yarborough enlisted his predecessor at Miami, Fred Major, to aid the preparations since Major was running the same offense at Ponce de Leon.

The Zebras threw it all right. Everett Payne lofted 33 passes into the night air, completing 13 for 179 yards, with most of them in comeback mode. The Stingarees dominated the lighter visitors in a 33-7 win that included Eldredge's 96-yard interception return, another highlight reel play, had there been those back then. Eldredge neatly cut in front of the pass at the four and was up to the Pine Bluff 40 before any Zebra had an angle on him. He seemed to be hemmed in at the 29 but cut back and picked up the blocking of Crum and Rigsby and coasted in from there.

Pine Bluff, which would win the Louisiana Sports Authority's version of the national championship game the next season, hardly looked the part. Luther Evans closed his game story in the *Miami Herald* with a derisive kicker:

And now we have seen football as they play it in the Southwest.[26]

Ouch.

EDISON: THE JINX CONTINUES

Now, local fans were going to see how football was played in Miami. The week of the Edison-Miami game had finally arrived and, once again, Cardinal fans were certain this was their year—certain, but still nervous.

The usual back-and-forth banter had actually started before the season. A new state rule prohibited teams from practicing before September 1 (not including spring practice), and both coaches accused each other of breaking it. Pop Parnell admitted there were a few players on his practice field, but it was none of his concern if they wanted to break in new shoes. Colonel Yarborough said there wasn't a coach in sight when a few of the Stingarees were seen kicking it around.[27]

Because the University of Miami was playing Bucknell in the Orange Bowl on Thanksgiving Day (the high schools ended up outdrawing the Hurricanes by 3,000 fans), the Edison-Miami grudge match was scheduled for Wednesday night, depriving the teams of sufficient preparation time. The Cardinals, or Red Raiders as they were sometimes called, had won six straight games since being thumped, 14-0, by Jackson of Jacksonville, the only common opponent. In all, Edison was 7-1, Miami 5-2. As usual, the city championship was on the line, as was the privilege of hosting the annual Christmas game on December 26. The Stingarees were 8-5 favorites, although *Herald* sports editor Everett Clay noted that the "smart boys" were taking Edison with seven points. He had his doubts.

> *Possibly it is not as much a question of Miami High beating Edison as it is a question of the Red Raiders beating themselves. For the Edisons seem to choke up every time they step on the same football field with Miami High. There is no particular reason for this tension as the Red Raiders are usually the better ball club and figure to win with little trouble. Something always seems to catch the Edison boys in the pit of the stomach when they see those terrible Stingarees rushing down on them.[28]*

Bell, at the rival *News*, pooh-poohed Clay's theory—especially the bit about Edison's historical strength. And, for once, Edison did not quiver at the sight of navy blue and gold. The Red Raiders outplayed Miami. They outfought Miami. They outgained Miami. They did everything . . . but outscore Miami. If there were anything more frustrating than the previous season's unexpected rout at Stingaree hands, it was the 6-6 tie that captivated the crowd of 16,647 that night.

Reid got the Stingarees out in front in the opening minutes. On third and four from the Edison 45, he drifted back to his right as Crum sprinted up the south sideline. The Miami captain's heave pierced through the light beams slanting through the night. With every fan on his or her feet, the ball looped into Crum's outstretched hands then was clutched to his chest at the 17. Crum, the ex-Edison player who had so delighted in crushing his former team the year before, had seemingly begun another rout as he scampered into the end zone. Even when the Cardinal line smothered what turned out to be the critical extra point try, the Stingaree cheering section remained smug. At that point, it seemed as if the familiar script would play out again.

Instead, they spent most of the remaining play with lumps in their throats, as their team staved off Edison threats. Parnell's boys marched to the Miami 17, the 20 and the 19 only to be repelled each time, twice by batted-down fourth down passes and a third time by a Harris interception. But Edison, led by triple-threat back Red Bogart, kept battling.

Finally, down to one of their last chances in the fourth quarter, the Red Raiders sustained a drive. Bogart's passes found their mark, and a halfback, Wallace Seekins, fought his way from the five to the goal line, where the football was knocked loose and fell into the end zone. For once, Edison was spared another heartache. Pahokee Smith, a lineman who played his heart out during the game, pounced on the football to tie the game.

Out came Carleton Lowe, one of the most sure-footed kickers in the state, with a chance to put Edison ahead. But point-after conversions were no sure thing in those days, more like 50-50 propositions at best. Lowe, who was playing despite a dislocated hand, didn't get enough foot into it and the ball fell short of the cross bar. Later, in the Edison dressing room, Lowe buried his face in a towel and sobbed.

"I guess I flunked out," he said. "I just wasn't any good."[29]

It could have been worse. Miami summoned up one last drive that ended on the Edison 14 when the big red clock struck zero. Miami's stunned fans calmed fast-beating hearts. Edison fans stormed the entrance to the locker room to congratulate their team. It was as if the Cardinals had won, only they hadn't. When Yarborough met Parnell at the middle of the field after the final whistle, he said, "Shake hands with the luckiest guy in town."

"By Johnnies, I don't know what to say," Parnell told the writers. The scribes did. When they got to their typewriters, they sang the praises of Bogart, who ran and passed the Stingarees silly. Wrote Bell:

> That 6-6 score goes into the record book but someday we'll be tellin' our grandchildren about the night Red Bogart put on the greatest exhibition ever seen in this Miami-Edison football classic. Once in a long time you see a flaming, inspired boy down there leading his team with force that will not be denied. And when you do see such a boy you don't forget.[30]

Parnell outcoached Yarborough in this one. Edison's offense normally operated out of the Notre Dame box but Pop surprised Miami by alternating between the single and double wing. Edison kept attacking off the weak side of the formation, another changeup. The Stingaree line was supposed to have a big advantage, but Parnell played his tackles inside the Miami ends to stuff the middle runs that the Stingarees ran wild with in previous years. That left Edison's two ends on islands, so to speak, but the gamble paid off.

Of course, it settled nothing, least of all who would host the Christmas game. When the teams had played to a 12-12 tie in 1935, they reached a compromise that sent Miami into the Christmas game on the basis of its stronger overall record and the fact that it had established the classic. Edison would receive 25 percent of the gate receipts. This time, it wasn't so simple. Clay immediately began to call for the teams to play a Christmas rematch instead of inviting a team from elsewhere:

> Forget all this business of an unbeaten, untied, unscored-on Northern high school team and an intersectional game. Miami High and Miami Edison are the teams folks want to see play again, not Miami High and Flap Stop, Ind., or Miami Edison and Mouth Wash, Mass.[31]

Yarborough suggested playing in two weeks on December 9. Parnell demurred because his team was traveling to Greenwood, Mississippi, for a December 2 game and would be at a disadvantage. Clay persisted in the Sunday editions of the *Herald*. He included letters supporting his position from Frank B. Walton, president of the Edison student body and Joe Sansone, the Miami guard who was president of the senior class. Below the column he ran a ballot, which was worded to produce his desired outcome. He could have been a modern pollster.

The ballot offered readers two options: to be in favor of Edison and Miami playing off on December 26, or to not play off the tie at all. The option to play the game on an earlier date with the winner hosting an intersectional opponent December 26 was conspicuously absent. Given just the two choices, readership, not unsurprisingly, voted unanimously in favor of a playoff. Clay attended a meeting to decide the matter and spilled the mailed-in ballots onto the table. They ended up filed in the trash. The rematch was scheduled for Wednesday, December 19, a week before Christmas. Yarborough and Parnell would jointly choose the opponent.

Clay was unhappy. He called it a "big mistake." The decision to play on the 19th, Clay wrote, "completely ignores the wishes of the students of the two schools, as well as everybody else in town."[32]

Clay pointed out that Edison, if it won the playoff, would be playing its twelfth game of the season. Miami would be playing its eleventh. That's too many for high school kids, he argued. But, while Yarborough and Miami Principal W.R. Thomas were amenable to a Christmas rematch, not so Parnell. Edison had never hosted the Christmas game, because it had never defeated Miami. He wanted to give his kids that chance. And, so it was settled, with 40 percent of the proceeds to go to the libraries of both schools, 10 percent to charity and half to feed underprivileged children.

BOYS: SHORTY COMES UP SHORT

Until then, both teams had big games in a matter of days. For the Stings, it was the Kiwanis-sponsored game against Boys High, their second-best rival. Shorty Doyal was bringing his Purple Hurricanes into their season finale at 7-2-2 with similar results against Knoxville, Savannah and Lanier so the game was rated a toss-up. Perhaps a letdown would have been natural for Miami, caught in between its two games against Edison. But Miami dispatched the Atlantans with surprising ease. Eldredge gained most of the yards and Harris scored all the touchdowns in a 19-0 rout. Edison's trip to Mississippi produced a 19-19 tie with Greenwood the next night. Then, over the next long 18 days, everyone's attention turned to the playoff.

EDISON: THE GRUDGE BOWL

Yes, everyone's attention was on the playoff, except for Everett Clay. His focus was riveted on changing the game to Christmas time. In a last-ditch column written for the December 6 editions, Clay cited numerous conflicts that would keep attendance down on December 19. Merchants kept stores open late for Christmas shoppers, and there was a Rachmaninoff concert in the Miami Edison Auditorium. Clay pleaded for school administrators to get involved. It was no use.[33] On Thursday of that week, feelers were sent to McKeesport, Pennsylvania, High, Peabody, Massachusetts and East High of Chicago. On Friday, Yarborough and Parnell decided on the Pennsylvanians.

The newspaper ads called it the "Grudge Bowl."

Edison was a narrow 6-5 favorite. In a way, Miami had the advantage. Edison had caught them by surprise in the first game. Now the Stingarees could scheme for Bogart. "Miami High has the motion pictures of that last game and they'll be a big help," Parnell said apprehensively. "They know just how we were running those weak side plays that gained so much ground."[34]

Yarborough let on that he was shifting his lineup. Sansone, the All Southern lineman who had played a linebacker, in the first meeting, was moved back to his regular position. Kendrick was moved to tackle. On offense, Comfort was worked in to work spinner plays. Otherwise, both camps were shrouded in secrecy. Rumors of scheme changes and new formations swirled. Word was that Miami was installing new passing plays, and that Parnell had even more surprises in store for Miami.

It all added up to little. The game came down to trench warfare. Outplayed in the first game, Miami's line, led by Sansone, took over. The rumored new pass plays were unnecessary, as the Stingarees dominated in the running game with 247 yards. And yet, Miami eked out just a 7-6 win on the margin of Shaffer's extra point on the first TD of the game. Jack Rice took the kick after Edison answered Miami's first touchdown, yet did no better than Lowe in the first game. Luther Voltz suggested in the *Miami News* that there was something to the jinx since Edison had scored seven touchdowns in the 16 games and had never converted for the point-after.[35]

Where Edison deserved a better fate in the first game, Miami was the superior team and deserved this win. "They're tough when they're aroused," an Edison coach told Voltz. "If they would play the football they're capable of for 60 minutes, there's not a high school team in America able to stand up against them."[36]

MCKEESPORT: A STRANGE FINALE

Pennsylvania's McKeesport High School would test that theory. The Tigers, a.k.a. the Tubers, were Class AA (large schools) champions of the Western Pennsylvania Interscholastic Athletic League. The city, with a gritty population of over 55,000 at the time, was situated at the confluence of the Monongahela and Youghiogheny Rivers, a suburb of Pittsburgh. The National Tube Works factory employed the majority of residents, and their kids had the built-in toughness to be expected from the sons of steelworkers. They usually followed their fathers to the blast furnaces soon after graduation. The environment quite naturally forged high school football players as its factories did steel girders. Football was—and still is—a religion in Western Pennsylvania, and winning the WPIAL was and still is a massive accomplishment.

McKeesport had lost only to Paul Brown's powerhouse Massillon in the second game of the season but had not lost to a Pennsylvania opponent in three years. They were led by stocky fullback Casey Ploszay, who had scored 129 points on the season, including three touchdowns in the 38-20 WPIAL championship game win over Johnstown. Ploszay did everything for the Tubers—run, pass and punt.

Just as a few other teams that had come to Miami, McKeesport would not be at full strength. It had to leave behind its sturdy left guard, Richard Stevenson, due to the segregation laws. The Tubers, also like previous visitors, were at another disadvantage. The heat. When McKeesport's husky cigar-smoking coach, Jack Tinson, stepped off the train, he was wearing an overcoat, suit coat and vest. He quickly stripped them off and wiped his brow.

"Does it stay this hot down here?" he asked. "I've been perspiring ever since we crossed the state line."[37]

The Miamians shrugged. It was only 75 degrees. The city was in the midst of a cold snap. But Tinson had a point. His team was hardly able to practice because of snow storms in Pennsylvania. He would try to whip them into shape in three days' time, but he couldn't push them too far.

The Stingarees had been working hard in what seemed like cool conditions. Yarborough put them through three strenuous scrimmages. The day before the game, he announced his captain and alternate captain for next season in a vote of the team. Davey Eldredge would take over for John Reid and lead the team onto the field. Jay Kendrick would take over for Joe Sansone. They would be the only underclassmen to start the game.

It was, as Jack Bell wrote, a "queer" game.[38] Maybe the season was just one game too long. The game drew just 5,490 spectators and the two teams traded mistakes, including the one that gave the Stingarees a 19-13 win, their first in the Christmas series since 1932.

As time wound down, the score was even. Ploszay stood in his own end zone, apparently set to punt. But the play was a fake, a rather knuckle-headed decision. The snap, which was supposed to have gone to the up-back, rolled back to the McKeesport captain, who was aware that, if he couldn't get out of the end zone, Miami would score a safety. So, with the gold-clad Stingarees closing in on him, Ploszay blindly threw a pass into the air. The duck fell into the hands of Miami tackle Gene Ellerson, a senior who had never touched the football before in his entire high school career. He stumbled inside the one-yard line, and Oscar Dubriel took it in for the win from there.

Eldredge's debut as Stingaree captain started well when he dashed 55 yards for the first TD of the game in the first quarter. It was just like most of the other big plays he broke off, a sweep around left end, a neat cutback to the center, where he picked up a wall of blockers and an unabated gallop to the end zone with Crum wiping out the last potential tackler with a nasty rolling block.

But Davey was also called on for pass interference to set up the first touchdown and was caught napping on a bullet pass by Ploszay that pulled McKeesport even early in the fourth quarter.

It had been that kind of year for Eldredge, although brilliance mostly outshone the negative, as it did for Miami in general. No, the Stingarees couldn't claim a national title or even the Southern championship. They barely won the championship of the city. Yet Yarborough called it his best team yet and with all the seniors being lost, he wasn't sure whether the '39 team would be able to surpass it.

"That closes just about the greatest season Miami has had in the last 10 years," Bell wrote.[39]

Just wait until the next three.

FOURTEEN

THE CAUSE

On a muggy July night in 1939, a special passenger car glided along the rails, pulled by the diesel engine of the Southern Railroad's Royal Palm from Rome, Georgia, toward Florida. Final destination: Miami.

On board were 30 fidgety young boys returning from Camp Cloudmont, their summer oasis in the Smokey Mountains. They played the usual games and engaged in the usual horse-play. But this wasn't an ordinary excursion. They were suspected carriers of the poliomyelitis virus. In 1939, it made them virtual pariahs. If there were an official disease of the Depression, it was infantile paralysis. With all of the era's woes and maladies, nothing was as depressing as the scourge that preyed upon society's most vulnerable—its young.

The boys aboard the Royal Palm escaped that fate. None fell to polio's grip. They were, nevertheless, still victims of the fear and panic that spread across America in the 1930s. After the first and biggest of the polio epidemics hit in 1916 (27,000 cases and 6,000 deaths nation-wide) another wave of outbreaks swept across the country in the 30s, in summer's wake, as always. A child's seemingly innocuous summer cold triggered shudders of dread. That's how the virus first revealed itself, before attacking the body's central nervous system, withering and contorting muscles, rendering a perfectly healthy youngster to irreparable illness in a matter of days.

Treating polio's worst cases was almost as chilling as the condition itself. The iron lung was a monstrous contraption. Its vacuum pumps belched out a monotonous beat. But, as morbid as it looked and as frightening as it sounded, it was the only way to keep patients alive. Polio fatalities typically occurred from suffocation as muscles around the lungs failed to support breathing. There was always hope that victims could one day escape their life-saving prison. Most did not.

The disease was easily misunderstood. It was contagious—that much was known. But, until the 1950s, how it was transmitted remained a mystery. This unknown created paranoia. The response was isolation. Community swimming pools were drained. Movie theatres were closed. Schools were shut down. Movements were restricted. During the 1916 epidemic, the state of Pennsylvania barred all under the age of 16 entry from New Jersey and New York.[1]

The year 1939 saw six serious outbreaks in different parts of the nation with no single state escaping the disease completely. Dr. Thomas Parran, at the time the Surgeon General of the United States, alarmingly warned that if infantile paralysis were not controlled, it threatened to "wipe out all our gains in preventative medicine and make us a nation of cripples within two generations."

By contrast, few would consider Camp Cloudmont, run by a generous Miamian, C.W. "Doc" Abele, anything but the picture of adolescent health. Each summer, hundreds of boys made the trek to Mentone, Alabama, for a month of fresh air and fun. Many were the sons of doctors, lawyers and city officials, "the wealthy and moderately wealthy," as one newspaper put it.[2] Society notes in the papers happily announced that so-and-so, the son of Mr. and Mrs. so-and-so, was attending Camp Cloudmont, perhaps while the parents whisked away on a European vacation. There, atop scenic Lookout Mountain, the boys swam, fished, hiked, learned archery, played ball and experienced the vacation that most American kids of the day could only have imagined.

In late July of 1939, polio intruded upon that idyllic scene. Camper Preston Bird, Jr., 15-year-old son of the mayor of Homestead, Florida, complained of a sore throat. Two days later, he died in a Chattanooga hospital. A day after that, Robert Shearer, the 12-year-old son of the late Marine Corps Major Thomas R. "Bull" Shearer, was hospitalized with similar symptoms. When the cause of young Bird's death was listed as "acute anterior poliomyelitis," camp officials had no choice but to impose quarantine conditions. Back home, terrified parents feared for their boys' safety and, in some cases, pleaded for their release.

Miami itself had never experienced a major polio outbreak, but it was very familiar with Fred Snite. With the possible exception of President Franklin D. Roosevelt, Snite was the face of polio in the United States. And his face was all the public ever saw, its image reflected in the mirror of his iron lung. Roosevelt sought to hide his infirmity but Snite was more than willing to display his condition as a hopeful warrior and a symbol of the Depression's tenacious, down-but-not-out attitude.

Snite contracted the disease at the age of 25, a "personable young man with a fondness for sports, a lively interest in young ladies and a wholesome respect for a good time," according to his biography, *The Man in the Iron Lung*.[3] It was 1936 and he and his family were in China on a world cruise prior to entering business with his wealthy father, Fred Sr. It started as what appeared as a common cold but when Snite attempted to fill a glass with water, the glass fell and shattered on the floor—fumbled by Snite's suddenly numb right arm. Snite was fortunate he was in Peiping (now Beijing) at the time. The city's medical college was a gift of the Rockefeller Foundation, and its hospital, where the diagnosis of polio was made, housed the only iron lung in China.

Snite's father spared no expense to bring him back to the States, a 21-day journey from Peiping back home to Chicago. When his ship docked in San Francisco, it made nationwide news. So did his June,1939, trip to the shrine to Our Lady of Lourdes in France where he bathed in its frigid waters hoping for a miracle. When it wasn't bestowed, he accepted his fate readily, explaining he had "received a greater grace than a cure from Our Lady."[4]

Snite spent winters at the family's place in Miami Beach, making the trip from Chicago in a specially constructed trailer. He married two months after his trip to Lourdes, had three daughters (patients could spend brief periods outside their iron lungs). He even became a champion bridge player (nurses held his hand of playing cards in front of his mirror). A huge football fan, Snite attended almost every home game he could at his alma mater, Notre Dame. The stadium's most resounding cheers exploded not when the Fighting Irish took the field but, rather, when Snite and his iron lung were rolled into his customary spot in the stands directly behind the goal posts. Grantland Rice—the legendary sportswriter who made famous the "The Four Horsemen of Notre Dame"—dubbed him the "Fifth Horseman." Everyone knew about the "Boiler Kid," as he loved being called. He'd live 18 years in his iron lung before his body gave out in 1954.

While Miamians admired Snite's pluck, the Cloudmont affair was another issue indeed. The idea of infected boys carrying the polio virus home spread alarm across the city, and hundreds of residents besieged the office of Mayor E.G. Sewell. At first, Sewell considered holding the boys in a segregated camp at the city farm at Opa Locka. But, at a hastily called meeting, Miami health director Dr. George N. MacDonnell assured the City Commission it would be perfectly safe to quarantine the boys inside their homes—provided their parents signed statements promising the quarantine would be strictly enforced.[5]

Traveling with the boys on the Royal Palm, Dr. Walter Jones telegrammed Sewell with word that he'd examined the 18 Miami boys on board and found them all in good health, adding that Bird's polio diagnosis seemed questionable to him and that Shearer hadn't necessarily been diagnosed with polio at all (he did, eventually, recover). In closing, Jones advised Sewell to, "Ameliorate public opinion as you can."[6]

Sewell knew he had to avoid a crisis. His first responsibility was the safety of Miamians. As a three-term mayor, he had the trust of the community. However, as a pioneer businessman and the man responsible for turning Miami into a resort city through an innovative public relations campaign, Sewell was also aware of greater consequences. The tourist season would start in a couple of months. The income it generated enabled the city to recover from the Depression more quickly than industrial cities or agricultural areas. He needed to avoid the national publicity that a polio scare would ignite.

At least Sewell could be reasonably certain that the boys posed no real health threat to the city's residents. Popular wisdom at the time assured him of that. For instance, from the state capitol in Tallahassee, home of another set of Cloudmont campers, a local health officer, Dr. L.J. Graves, reassured the public there existed no danger of the disease spreading even if the boys were infected. That was true, but not because of Graves' rationale. He claimed there would be no danger "as long as the isolation rule was followed rigidly," that, "the only known way that infantile paralysis germs were transmitted was through secretions from the nose and mouth of an affected person."[7] It was an unfortunate misconception. Later, it was learned the virus was contracted only through the mouth by contact with contaminated food and water. Before then, polio outbreaks were managed in the same way as influenza was contained.

In any case, Sewell issued a statement meant to allay his constituents' fears. Public concerns, he argued, were fomented by "gross exaggerations" and that the people of Miami were becoming "unduly alarmed."[8] At the same time, he exhibited the proper vigilance. City Manager A.E. Fuller stationed policemen outside the front door of each home—and not out of a lack of sympathy. Fuller's own son was a Cloudmont camper, and he chose to keep him there until the camp quarantine lifted. Meanwhile, in Miami, the boys and their families were kept virtually under house arrest. Similarly, up the coast at Delray Beach, a local outcry followed word that 15-year-old camper Van Cason had already returned with the Miami boys. The *Palm Beach Post* reported that "indignation ebbed and flowed with the unauthorized arrival." Police Chief Al Nelson employed two extra officers to keep a 24-hour patrol outside the Cason house, but it wasn't until Cason's father was included in the quarantine that "public fear was quieted."[9]

Two days after the Miami boys were isolated, the Chattanooga hospital treating Shearer reported that his condition was improving. But the resultant calm lasted no more than a week when nine-year-old camper Jimmy Best began showing polio symptoms after he returned to Orlando. The next day, young Best was placed in an iron lung rushed to him from Jacksonville. So much for gross exaggerations. Best, as it turned out, was the last Cloudmont victim and he did survive. Eventually, the furor died down. The supposed two-week contagious period expired. The quarantine ended, the Cloudmont boys returned to school, and Miami returned to its business at hand, including the Stingaree football team and the upcoming '39 season.

Emotions were no less jittery in Northern New Jersey when polio surfaced there. Garfield's biggest brush with the disease came four years earlier. In September of 1935, an 11-year-old girl became the first fatality in a series of polio cases that kept popping up around Bergen County. At first, officials downplayed the situation. They told the *Bergen Record* that the number of cases had already begun to wane and would continue to do so as the weather cooled.[10] Then, a weekend outbreak of five new cases, including two in Garfield, "surprised" medical officials, bringing the county total up to 37.[11]

The count soon reached 40. And all hell broke loose.

East Rutherford convened an emergency joint meeting of the Boards of Health and Education on the eve of the scheduled opening day of school. The next morning, September 6, fire stations across the borough sounded the no-school siren, commonly used on snow days, ostensibly locking up every borough kid. For the next 10 days, all under 17 were not permitted to attend cinemas, Boy Scout meetings, Sunday School or "any other places where children congregate." The library closed, and the high school swimming pool was emptied, cleaned and disinfected.[12] Although police kept guard at every public place, kids managed to sneak past them into the local movie theatre, oblivious to any danger without knowing there really wasn't any danger—at least not from one another. Borough officials did not see it that way.

"If it continues these children will be subject to quarantine even after the date of September 16," chided an angry Henry Herr, Health Secretary. "The board will apply this drastic action if this carelessness persists."

School opened as scheduled in neighboring Rutherford, but students were sent home after a special mid-day assembly. They were forbidden to leave the borough for a 10-day period and, when school re-opened, they were required to present a certificate signed by parents, vouching that the pupil would not leave town from September 6 to September 16. Even teachers were banned beyond Rutherford's borders.[13]

In upscale Allendale, Harry I. Hand, president of the Board of Education, casually averred that neighboring towns "have gone panicky" over the threat. A couple of days later—after four more county cases— Allendale, too, was in panic mode. All schools were closed.[14]

Garfield was a rare exception. Even after a fourth case was reported in the city, schools remained open on the advice of school physician Dr. Ross Vilardo, who told the Board of Ed that any epidemic "could be checked more easily with the children in school than at play on the streets." He did not view the situation as alarming.[15] This, of course, suited Art Argauer just fine. With school open, so was football practice. It's not that Argauer was callous to the crisis but, ever the competitor, he couldn't help thinking that his team might be the indirect benefactor of the unfortunate situation.

Garfield had just outgrown and dropped out of the Bergen County Interscholastic League. Argauer upgraded the schedule with the likes of traditional state power Rutherford, slated as the opening-day opposition. Now, due to the polio scare, Rutherford's practices were suspended. Garfield's were not. As it was, Rutherford's players worked around the Board of Ed edict by practicing on their own for 10 days while the local P.D. conveniently looked the other way.[16] But when the Bulldogs finally opened official practices under coach Eddie Tryon, it left him with just 12 days to prepare his team for the Boilermakers. Tryon wasn't sure that was enough time.

"Naturally, I want to play this game but if the boys cannot get into shape or learn their signals by the end of the week, it would be silly to play the game," Tryon said. "However, I believe we will be able to go through with the game."[17]

Tryon had starred at Colgate and had been Argauer's teammate with the Clifton Wessingtons. They'd opposed each other before as basketball coaches but never across the football sidelines. Although the schools had previously met only once, in 1925, the game already felt rivalrous. Argauer, pessimistic at first, was feeling better about his team as his uninterrupted workouts continued. So were the papers. On the day before the game, *The Herald-News* installed Garfield as the favorite.[18]

During that week, however, four more polio cases erupted in Garfield, bringing the total in the city to nine. On Friday, seven-year-old James Scaglione died of lobar pneumonia after his release from Bergen Pines Hospital, the disease having left him with "a badly crippled left leg and other infirmities," according to reports.[19] With that, the Rutherford Boards of Education and Health ordered Tryon to cancel the next day's game. Although the game was being played in Rutherford, officials feared that the "congestion" caused by hundreds of visiting Garfield fans might "aggravate conditions."[20] They could not have possibly aggravated conditions, of course, but the order certainly aggravated Argauer.

"I am astounded by Tryon's action," Argauer told the *Bergen Record*. "He certainly knew there was infantile paralysis in Garfield earlier in the week. This last minute action is a great inconvenience to Garfield followers unaware of the cancellation who will take the trip to Rutherford."[21] Perhaps Argauer felt that the Bulldogs were ducking his team. A couple of days later, he claimed he understood the Rutherford action and offered to play the Bulldogs on Election Day. The game never took place, and Garfield and Rutherford never met on the gridiron again.

Between 1935 and 1939, efforts to fight polio mobilized into concerted nationwide movements, culminating in Miami and Garfield Highs meeting to benefit the National Foundation for Infantile Paralysis (NFIP) on Christmas night. So, where a polio scare squashed a potential rivalry with Rutherford, the anti-polio campaign presented the Boilermakers with the biggest game in their history.

President Roosevelt was largely responsible. Stricken with polio (some now claim it was actually Guillain-Barré syndrome) in 1921, FDR became the champion of the fight to eradicate it. His "state of war" against polio had existed since 1934 when the first of an annual series of "birthday balls" raised funds for Warm Springs. After finding some relief in its waters, he purchased the Georgia spa and clinic for $200,000 and turned into a world class treatment facility.

In 1938, Roosevelt expanded his birthday balls into the National Foundation for Infantile Paralysis, forerunner of the March of Dimes. The NFIP organized state and county committees that raised funds to fight the disease. Of each dollar collected, 50 cents was earmarked for local expenditure, and 50 cents was donated to the NFIP to support scientific research, public education, epidemic control and treatment. Radio personality Eddie Cantor used his show to promote the drive. In late January, in an allusion to "The March of Time" newsreels, Cantor suggested that listeners contribute their loose change and create "a march of dimes to reach all the way to the White House." Flooded with thousands of jingling envelopes addressed by kids in scrawling penmanship, the campaign raised $1.8 million through September of 1939, $268,000 of it in dimes.

Meanwhile, in the late fall of 1937, two sports columnists, Bob Considine and Tom Wrigley, began to kick around ways in which the sports world could tackle polio. Their efforts began sporadically until, in 1938, the National Sports Council (NSC) was officially inaugurated among America's leading sports editors, columnists and commentators. Grantland Rice volunteered as chairman. Collaborating with the NIPF, the NSC encouraged local high schools, colleges and sports organizations to stage athletic events across the country as NSC benefits, with 10 percent of the gate going toward the charity. In the fall of '39, the NSC sought to step up its philanthropic efforts and hatched the idea of playing a national championship high school football game in Miami to kick off the 1940 campaign with the biggest splash yet.

"The sports world will not offer a more thrilling a sight than of strong and healthy and quick young boys spending their Christmas night on the field in the battle for the Tiny Tims of today," it said in the official Health Bowl program. "They will play so others may walk. This is truly a great occasion."[22]

The publicity campaign for the game hit its stride in November, even before the teams were set and, to connect the dots between the disease and high school football, the NSC issued a press release picked up by papers nationally, highlighting five high school gridders who were fighting the disease. The author of that press release didn't have to look far to find a connection to the upcoming game. Charley Moon was the starting halfback for the McKeesport Tigers when they faced Miami in the 1938 Christmas game. He injured his back and had to be carried off the field that night but, by the start of the 1939 season, he was fully recovered.

Under a hot sun in the second game of the year, Moon suddenly, in the second half, had difficulty moving his leg. He even asked for someone else to handle his usual punting duties. Moon stayed in the rest of the game but the fans in the stands could tell something was amiss. Later, back home, Moon's legs buckled under him. He was taken to a hospital where he spent the next three weeks until a diagnosis of infantile paralysis was made. The next 18 months were spent at the Pennsylvania State Hospital for Crippled Children. Moon's condition didn't require the use of an iron lung but when he finally left the hospital he was on crutches, his legs hobbled by braces.[23]

Despite the doctors' prognoses, he was lucky enough to walk again after a five-year fight. It was through the efforts of a trainer named Nick Stack, a lay minister who devoted his career to rehabbing the crippled victims through exercise and massage. Moon devoted himself to a strenuous daily regimen of back bands and pushups as if he was training to take the field and, actually, he was. He returned to the McKeesport's War Memorial Field McKeesport in 1944 to take his momentous walk at halftime of a Tubers game.[24]

In Iowa, star tailback George Lee Harris was preparing for Avoca High's championship game against Oakland when he was suddenly brought down. At first, it was thought to be a case of spinal meningitis until doctors at Jennie Edmundson Hospital in Council Bluffs made the correct diagnosis.[25] The game that night was immediately cancelled, and Harris was confined. He would soon to be joined by his sister Nadine. Seeking healthier spaces, their mother moved the family to Newport Beach, California, where Harris completed high school, married and led a normal life until his death in 1982.

In Colorado, Bill Stevens, left end for Greeley High School, was stricken before the season's first game. He was rushed to an iron lung in Denver, escorted 64 miles by state highway patrolmen.[26] Stevens, in Snite-like fashion, maintained his good humor throughout.

"I'll be way over weight when I get out of this thing and I'll have to work like the dickens to get in shape for hockey and basketball," he said after being placed inside. The iron lung aided in the youth's recovery and in May of 1940, he was released. Upon visiting his high school, he glanced at some passing girls in the hall. "You've got some good looking new girls and the old ones are getting better looking," he quipped.[27]

Ten years later, Stevens married one: librarian Helen Jane Macy. Unable to walk up the three flights of stairs at the courthouse, due to polio's lasting effect on his legs, Stevens was married on the courthouse lawn.[28] He outlived Helen by 15 years and died in 1980.

Like Moon, Jimmy Colton played high football in suburban Pittsburgh, at Mars High School. Colton became ill while en route with the team to Oil City for a game and he was transported to Pittsburgh Children's Hospital. His father, James Sr., admitted, "The iron lung saved my boy's life. He can only breathe three minutes at a time without the respirator."

Colton's high school diploma was delivered to him while in his iron lung and a special radio broadcast of the ceremony was arranged for him. Student after student stepped up to the microphone to send greetings. "Guess I made it anyhow, eh?" he said, as the Mars School Board president made the presentation.[29]

Colton's condition seemed to be improving. He could soon spend nine minutes out of the iron lung and then, a full hour twice daily. His father visited him twice a day to talk sports. "I may not see the football games this year but I'm going to beat this thing yet," he said on his one year "anniversary" in the hospital. The newspaper photo showed him drinking a "toast" through a straw. "Everybody's been wonderful to me and it makes it a lot easier when you know people are pulling for you," he said.[30]

Colton received a visit from the singing cowboy, Gene Autry. Several Pittsburgh Pirates stopped by as well. On his birthday in June of 1941, he fulfilled a prediction by making it to Forbes Field to take in a game in his iron lung. Back at the hospital, he said it "wasn't so bad" after that because he could close his eyes and imagine he was at the ballpark while he listened to the games on radio.[31] But as his two-year anniversary passed, a kidney infection had doctors worried. The optimistic boy assured his parents: "I'm all right. I'll be at Pitt Stadium Saturday." But he never made it to Pitt's game against Purdue. After two years and eight days in his iron lung, Colton lapsed into a coma and died of uremia at 4:35 p.m. as his beloved Pirates were closing out the season a few blocks away at Forbes Field.

"White-clad nurses moved silently about, taking down the high school diploma and the autographed pictures that hung on the wall," the *Pittsburgh Press* reported. "For 18-year-old Jimmy Colton, Pittsburgh's "boiler kid" was dead.[32]

"The end came rather unexpectedly for the lad whose courageous smile and love of life had won him many new friends and hundreds of sympathizers," wrote the *Pittsburgh Post-Gazette*. Ironically, the Mars schools had been shut down for two weeks because of a polio scare.[33]

If anything could be more tragic than Colton's story, it was Jules Yon's. Jules was a skinny 15-year-old sophomore with bright red hair who wanted nothing more than to suit up in a royal blue Atlantic City High football uniform. He wouldn't make the first team, but he did make the roster as a scrub, which made him exceedingly proud and his doting mother exceedingly nervous.

Jules was the second child of Clayton and Marthe Yon, three years younger than his sister Antoinette, together the products of a love story that began in France during World War I. Clayton served with the ambulance corps with the American army of occupation in Mulhouse, Alsace-Lorraine. As he drove the ambulance, a fetching maid caught his eye. He courted Marthe Hetzel amid the chaos of war and, after being mustered out of the army, Yon returned to France to marry her. They initially settled in Atlantic City, where his family owned the Hotel Flanders (St. James Place on the Monopoly Board.)

Business, however, turned sour. Yon, together with his brother, Arthur, and sister, Jane, declared bankruptcy in 1938, listing liabilities of $331,000 and assets of only $60. They lost the hotel and were reduced to operating it as paid employees, board included.[34] Still, the family remained relatively happy, despite the indignities surrounding their insolvency.

Similarly, Jules was happily warming the bench when the Atlantic City Vikings, having just suffered their only loss of the season against powerful Vineland, visited Camden on November 11, the seventh week of the season. It was so late in the year that few were concerned about the polio scare that had closed Camden schools for two weeks in September. Camden, the South Jersey home of Campbell's Soup, across the river from Philadelphia, had experienced the most serious outbreak in the state. Some 32 cases and 10 deaths were reported in the Camden Municipal hospital. But, as the month ended with the advent of cooler weather, Camden city health director Arthur L. Stone announced that the disease had run its course.[35]

The weather on November 11 defied the forecast of cool temperatures and rain. Morning clouds yielded to sunshine, and it was a comfortable 48 degrees by kickoff in Camden—not that it mattered. Somehow, somewhere, Jules Yon contracted the polio virus, perhaps through a sip of water. By the time he boarded the team bus after Atlantic City's 12-7 win, the virus was already carrying out its grim work. Four days later, Yon was placed in an outmoded, primitive iron lung, the only one in Atlantic City Municipal Hospital. The community rallied around the youngster and, with the American Legion leading the drive, the hospital purchased a new one.[36]

The hospital's regulations were unusually stringent. Inside, he was confined to an isolation ward, where only masked doctors and nurses had access. Marthe Yon was permitted physical contact with her son only once—when he was first admitted. Jules' iron lung was situated by a second-story window, and a special platform was erected outside of it. That's how visitors saw him, but, even so, indirectly through a reflected image of his face; a mirror had been rigged above his head to afford that view. Marthe Yon climbed that platform every day. It must have felt like some sort of gallows. There she sat, so long as daylight lasted, speaking to her son through the window as he gazed back into the mirror, smiling to her as much as he could muster. She barely ate. She hardly slept.

"All knew of the daily visit of Mrs. Yon to the hospital where her son lay encased in the iron lung," they wrote in the *Atlantic City Press*. "Through freezing weather, snow or rain, Mrs. Yon could be found at his window, mutely pouring out her love for the son she could no longer help."[37]

Jessie Smail, Jules' cousin, was 10 at the time. She still can't forget the visits she made to the hospital with her father, Clayton Yon's brother, Arthur.

"It was haunting. It really was," she remembers. "You could see his face in the mirror, that's all you could see. When the breathing was right, he could speak, weakly. I have claustrophobia, so the thought of him in that iron lung would give me goose bumps."

According to Jessie, there was never any hope that Jules would recover.

"No. Not really. Everybody knew it was just a matter of time," she said. "Stop and think. Is it crueler to keep them in an iron lung or is it crueler to give up hope? That's the dilemma the entire family faced."

As the weeks passed, Yon took in Christmas gifts from classmates and celebrated his birthday in February. Two fundraising efforts raised enough money to arrange for him to be moved to the Betty Bacharach Home for Afflicted Children in nearby Longport, where he could receive visitors and at least bring some comfort to Marthe. But those generous contributions would ultimately be used for a memorial fund. On March 25, Jules broke out into convulsions and, finally, his heart gave out.

"The entire community was relieved when he showed slight signs of rallying," the *Atlantic City Press* reported. "But the gains were few and brief in nature of late, not even the mechanical lung could sustain life and shortly after 1 o'clock yesterday, doctors pronounced the youth dead."[38]

Marthe Yon was seized by hysterics and collapsed when she heard the news. Her husband feared she might make an attempt to take her life, so he and a friend, Spurgeon Cross, kept watch throughout the rest of the day and into the night. Cross returned home in the morning, and Yon briefly left the apartment to run an errand. He was gone less than 10 minutes but, when he came back, the door, to his horror, was locked. His mind raced, fixed on his greatest fear. He screamed for his wife. With only painful silence in return, he kicked in the door. In those few minutes of not being watched, Marthe had bolted the door, threw a bed sheet over a steam pipe, fashioned a noose around her neck and stepped from a chair, hanging herself in Room 105 of the Flanders Hotel.

The *Philadelphia Inquirer* recounted the tragedy this way:

> *The child she had reared to manhood's threshold was life itself to Mrs. Marthe Yon.*
> *During the months he spent in an iron lung fighting a valiant but hopeless fight against infantile paralysis, that life had become a succession of alternate hopes and fears. And when the boy Jules died yesterday—he was only 16, too young to die—there was nothing left.*[39]

Yon, the World War I ambulance driver, frantically cut his wife down and tried to revive her. A doctor, arriving later, attempted to administer Adrenaline to no avail. The double funeral took place two days later. At 10 o'clock, the doors of the funeral home were opened to a steady stream of mourners who passed in front of the two open caskets, laid side-by-side. Behind Jules' coffin was a huge blue floral display in blue and white, Atlantic City High

School colors. His football teammates served as pallbearers as the bodies were laid to rest in Greenwood Cemetery. In his eulogy, Rev. Harold G. Gaunt paid tribute to Jules' courage and spoke of Marthe as a "lasting example of mother love and devotion" who died of a broken heart.[40]

Their tombstone is inscribed in French:

> *Car vois-tu chaque jour je t'aime d'avantage. Aujourd'hui plus qu'heir et bien moins que demain.*

Roughly translated, it declares: "Because, you see, I love you more every day. Today more than yesterday and much less than tomorrow."

Those tomorrows were why they played the game.

FIFTEEN

THE 1939 STINGAREES

It was early September, 1939, the first day of football practice. In Miami, that meant sweltering conditions. Shirts were optional. Jesse Yarborough was walking around bare-chested.

A *Miami Herald* photographer was on hand to stage a picture of Davey Eldredge and his "winged feet." Clad in a skimpy pair of shorts, the camera snapped away as Eldredge tucked the football into a taut right arm, muscles straining. He flashed a six-pack and a snarl, daring any imaginary tackler to take him down. It could have been a poster for American boyhood, what Teddy Roosevelt meant when he instructed the nation's youth to: "Hit the line hard; don't foul and don't shirk, but hit the line hard!" It should have been a warning sign of what Miami's upcoming opponents would be up against. With Eldredge in the backfield, the season held unlimited possibilities. But that's not quite the picture that both the *News* and *Herald* were painting of the Stingarees that September. Rather, they questioned whether Eldredge, winged feet and all, would be a one-man team.

Exactly one year earlier, Yarborough had barely contained his excitement over his talent-laden 1938 roster. Even after it finished the season with one tie and two losses, including the Stings' first defeat to a Florida team in 10 years, he considered it to be his best team ever. Now, he was almost conceding to the press that his current edition couldn't compare. These Stingarees were as green and thin as an Everglades reed. All eleven players who started the last two games of the '38 season had graduated, including All Southern guard Joe Sansone. Yarborough might be able to cobble together a starting team. But, what about the reserves? Woe was Miami High.

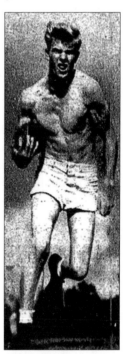

Davey Eldredge shows off his "winged feet" at a pre-season workout, a preview of things to come.
The Miami Herald.

The 1939 Miami High School Stingarees. Note how the uniform numbers followed in direct order.
1940 Mahai yearbook.

At least that's the line the coach was feeding the press, which had been busy trying to sort through a bunch of Stingaree-related malarkey since February. That's when rumors—initiated by Yarborough—began to make the rounds. The Colonel was said to be ready to skedaddle out of town to take a job as an assistant to his old Clemson mentor, Josh Cody, at the University of Florida, where several of Yarborough's players were on the Gators' freshman team.

In February, Yarborough divulged to reporters he had been offered "a very attractive position" by Florida, and the suspense hung in the humid air for a month.[1] First, Everett Clay wrote that it was a cinch Yarborough was taking the job, then wrote that he wasn't.[2] All through Miami's spring practices, the Stingarees weren't sure who their coach would be come fall when the season kicked off against Robert E. Lee. But Yarborough and his wife Louise were expecting a baby in September and were building a new house closer to the high school. That should have been the giveaway that Yarborough wasn't thinking about going anywhere. Yarborough, as Art Argauer had done in Garfield, was simply acquiring more leverage just in case a college head coach job appeared down the road.

Assistant Clyde Crabtree came much closer to leaving. He was officially offered the head coaching position at Savannah High School, one of the best jobs in Georgia. He turned it down in May after unsuccessfully reaching favorable financial terms.[3] Finally, there was a second report that Yarborough was a candidate for City of Miami Recreation Director, a position vacated by Earnie Seiler when he moved to his full-time, longtime position as director of the Orange Bowl. By August, everything was status quo, even Yarborough's trademark wit. After moving up the opening practice to August 28, he apologetically explained to Jack Bell, "the boys are so sorry this year we've got to do a lot of work."[4]

All the while, Yarborough worked on his erratic golf game—a natural lefty who played righty—he managed to break 90 several times at Miami Springs. Meanwhile, he awaited the birth of a second child, Jesse Hardin Yarborough Jr., who likely announced himself (in characteristic Yarborough fashion) with a hearty scream at Jackson Memorial Hospital on the morning of September 8. When the robust youngster weighed in at 11¾ pounds the *Miami News* facetiously conjectured that he was already enrolled for the 1959 football season at Clemson.

"Father is so pleased he can hardly shout, all of which has pleased the Miami football squad no end," the *News* joked.[5]

Life, in general, was swell. Yarborough was relaxed. And, since he helped create the news, he could easily ignore it. Better to temper expectations anyway.

"Miami, Edison to be weaker than in '38," blared the first *Miami News* headline of the season,[6] and the *Miami Herald* agreed: "The Stingarees are a big question mark."[7]

But as practices continued, leading up to the October 9 season opener in Jacksonville, there was reason to think all the hand-wringing was overblown. Eldredge, coming off a great 1939 track season, looked more mature and more explosive. Jay Kendrick was throwing people around like Kewpie dolls. If the forward line wasn't as big, it was quicker, the better to pull and get out in front of Eldredge's runs as he raced around the corner.

Jason Koesy, the team's best passer from the year before, looked good, and stocky Harvey Comfort benefitted from his sophomore year of seasoning and was shaping up as the team's best power runner. The Stingarees always seemed to have one or two transfer students come onto the team. This year they were fullback George Rogers from Ocala High, where he was a two-year starter, and a Harvey James, the kid who'd been kicked out of Benedictine Military Academy in Savannah, where he played center. He wouldn't as yet be eligible.

Red Mathews and Pericles Nichols had seen at least some varsity action in the backfield. On the line, Charlie Burrus, the state champion in the quarter mile, Levin Rollins, Dick Fauth, Doug Craven, Gilbert Wilson and Mike Osceola had seen considerable playing time, although Osceola, as it turned out, would appear in but one game all season. Still, the situation was hardly as dire as it may once have appeared.

ROBERT E. LEE: THE TEST

If the Stingarees could avenge the previous year's stinging defeat to Lee in their first game, everything else could fall into place. The Generals, in the opener, and Boys High, in the finale, were looking like the strongest teams on the regular season schedule. Every other repeat opponent looked weaker this year, especially Knoxville, the only other team to beat them in '38. Spartanburg was back on the schedule and Jackson High of Mississippi was new, a wild card.

Lee, riding the state's longest win streak at 12 games, was expected to repeat as Big Ten champion. It still had Maxwell Partin, the hard-running hero of last year's upset win. The Stingarees were underdogs for the first time in at least a decade as they climbed onto the team bus for the long trip up US 1.

Yarborough scouted Lee's opening game against Gainesville, a 52-12 rout, and came away thinking the Generals were just as powerful as they were the previous season. In turn, Lee's coach, Warren Kirkham, scouted the Miami B Team's 13-12 loss to the Miami Beach varsity, but there wasn't a lot to be culled beyond Miami's basic formations. Learning his lesson from the previous year, Yarborough didn't play his starting eleven. In fact, it was hard to even keep track of who was who as Yarborough constantly shuttled players on and off the field. Luther Evans of the *Herald* wrote that Yarborough was so loose with the lineups, he twice tried to send manager Goldie Goldstein into the game.[8] At least a few varsity players got in, including Koesy, who scored both touchdowns for the Stingarees and showed off that strong throwing arm.

Kirkham returned to Jacksonville disappointed. The Stingarees had made no determined effort to win the game, he lamented, and he was unable to get a line on them. The *Florida Times-Union* of Jacksonville noted that Lee had six returning starters to Miami's three. The home team outweighed the visitors by 11 pounds a man, but the paper warned that Eldredge was shaping up as Miami's most dangerous ball carrier in years.

"A swarm of angry Miami High Stingarees, on vengeance bent," was how the *Times-Union* described the invaders, predicting another tight contest.[9] It was right on both counts. An overflow crowd of 8,000 fans saw one of the best battles of the season.

Miami crossed midfield only once in the first half on a Levin Rollins interception just before intermission. As the two bands entertained at halftime, Yarborough made a few adjustments and the Stingarees began to control play.

Late in the third quarter, Miami got as far as the Lee seven where the home team took over on downs. But the Stingarees forced a punt that slid off the side of Partin's foot and wobbled out of bounds at the 31. The Stingarees surprised the Generals on the very next play. Burrus had hauled in a long pass from Eldredge on the previous series and now the big end with the great hands struck again. Expecting a run, Lee allowed Burrus to slip down the right side-line and Harvey Comfort's pass led him perfectly so that Burrus never had to break stride. He pulled the ball in over his shoulder at the nine and continued into the end zone. Bucket Barnes came on to kick the extra point.

Lee would not come close to tying the score. Kendrick, playing tackle on defense, led the Miami forward wall, and kept slicing through to bring down Partin before he could get going. Eldredge, though kept in check on the scoreboard, finished the night with 96 yards on the ground. His three pass completions netted the Stings 84 yards.

Maybe it wasn't a dominating performance, at least on offense, but it came against the defending state champs. Still, the Stingarees remained a mystery in the media's eyes. Depth was still an issue. Yarborough used just 16 players in all, including seven backs, and claimed not to have found any capable reserves. The *Miami News* was impressed to a point but wondered:

> The seven backs used against Lee all are small but proved themselves exceedingly tough on the defensive. It appears just a question of how they will stand up under the pounding of a long, hard schedule.[10]

Yarborough played along.

"We were lucky to beat Lee. It was really an upset," he said. "And now we have to play a team which probably is stronger than Lee. Knoxville, you know, has beaten us three years running."[11]

Knoxville: Maybe They Aren't All That Bad

Yarborough blew a significant amount of smoke toward the Smokies. Knoxville was fortunate when it beat Miami at home the previous year but most of that team had graduated. The Trojans had already played four games and lost them all by a combined score of 48-13. They had suffered their first defeat against Morristown in 14 years, and were dumped, 20-0, by Boys High of Atlanta in a game that Crabtree scouted.

The first four tailbacks on coach Wilson Collins' depth chart were injured and, with so many scrubs in the defensive backfield, he was worried about his team's poor tackling. Against Eldredge, that could mean a long night.

"We're just weak on defense. We're going to do some intensive drilling in tackling before we start down to Miami," he said.[12]

Miami fans should have been anticipating a rout. They weren't. Luther Evans wrote in the

Jesse Yarborough waits to send his first team back into the game against Knoxville High. Front, left to right: Charlie Burrus, Davey Eldredge. Doug Craven, Bucket Barnes, Pericles Nichols, Gilbert Wilson, Levin Rollins and Jay Kendrick. Harvey Comfort standing behind them. MIAHI 1940.

Herald that the Stingarees had a lot to overcome Knoxville's mastery over them, a Friday the 13th jinx and "the skepticism of the home fans to their ability."

Evans, though, added that Miami, "rated as one of the weakest elevens in recent Miami High history are confident—not cocky—that they'll overcome the invading Trojans.

Even Yarborough was "a bit" optimistic, Evans noted.

"I don't know if the kids played over their heads against Lee but if they keep that spirit and put up that tough a defense tonight and from here on, we're going to win a lot of ball games," the coach said.[13]

The week's practice sessions did not go well. They certainly weren't as crisp as Yarborough would have liked. Comfort, too, was hobbled by a "charley horse."

Still, Jack Bell showed some confidence by picking them to win: "Sticking to the Stingarees because despite their inexperience they seem to have some fire and color. And they've one of the South's sweeties in Li'l David Eldredge."[14]

It was still hot—84 degrees even in the evening—giving the home team one more advantage as 12,000 fans basked in the moonlight. It didn't take long before those cowbells started clanging, or, as Bell put it: "Almost before you could settle in your seat and say, 'I wonder how the devil these Stingarees ever beat Lee High last week?'"[15]

Seven plays, 54 yards, that's all it took. It wasn't necessarily poor tackling by Knoxville because you can't tackle what you can't see. Comfort had a 20-yard gain on a neat end-around and Eldredge accounted for the other 30 of the 54 yards, including the last 10 yards on off-tackle slant.

Knoxville had the ball for just two plays after the touchdown before Eldredge recovered a fumble at the Trojan 35. On the fourth play, Eldredge ran a delay out of the backfield and breezed through a big hole created by Kendrick and center Levin Rollins up the middle.

There he showed off his great vision and cutback ability by veering to his left. He reached the end zone without being touched for his second TD.

All night long, there was nothing the Trojans could do to stop Eldredge, Comfort or Koesy. Comfort took care of the entire third TD march with runs of 37, 5 and 15 yards while Koesy ripped off runs of 75 and 64 yards before being pulled down short of the end zone both times by Knoxville's Jim Phillips. The Stingarees rushed for a combined 340 yards and threw for 69 more, including a 27-yard TD pass from Eldredge to sub-back Pericles Nichols and a 26-yard pass from Eldredge to Koesy, who scored from the one on the next play.

Eldredge, though, was the star of stars, even though Yarborough mercifully took him out of the game for long stretches.

"You've got to toss the bouquets to this Eldredge kid, of course," Bell wrote. "He's so far superior to these other backs around here he seems misplaced. He does things you don't see on a high school gridiron. He's as fast as the wind, whirls and twists with all the finesse of (Tennessee Heisman candidate George) Cafego and is slippery as a Miami Beach jewelry thief."[16]

All of the offensive fireworks obscured the brilliance of Miami's second straight shutout. Their defensive quickness limited the Trojans to 90 yards. Knoxville crossed into Miami territory just once, in the third period, and lost the ball on an interception after reaching the 32. Collins said his team was beat by the heat and the opponent.

"It was the hottest weather we have experienced on our three trips to Florida," he said. "They would have beaten us anyway but the weather seemed to wilt our boys. At halftime, they were completely exhausted."[17]

It was also time to start reassessing this Miami team.

"And the Stingarees?" Bell wrote. "Well, they aren't big as last year or as famous. But last night they put one of the most colorful and scrapping teams on the field local Miami High fans have seen in 10 years."[18]

They were off and running.

SAVANNAH: WAKE-UP CALL

By now, the newspapers were catching on, even if they were a bit surprised. In advance of the Savannah game for the *Miami Herald*, Luther Evans wrote that "the unbeaten, untied and unscored upon Miami High Stingarees, who figured to lose games right and left this season, will go after their third straight triumph." Evans was now talking about a forward wall that "knocks down opponents like bowling pins" and "a quartet of jack rabbits in its backfield," including Eldredge with his "twinkling toes and greased hips."[19]

Perhaps the Stingarees were reading their press clippings. Yarborough was so displeased with the level of blocking in practice, he put the team through a two-hour full contact scrimmage just two days before the contest, which had moved from Saturday afternoon to Saturday evening. Every home game would now be played under the lights.

Savannah was, as Knoxville before it, winless in four games and not apt to put up much of a fight. But the Blue Jackets were coming off a scoreless tie against favored Richmond Academy and Yarborough was worried about Eldredge, who had broken a finger in the Robert E. Lee game. Fullback Rogers had a bruised shoulder and Burrus was slowed by a sore knee.

"We'll need to be in crack shape against Savannah," Yarborough declared in his cautious mode. "Our boys have been playing over their heads so far, I think. I'm scared to death thinking what will happen to them when they come back to Earth. I only hope Savannah isn't taken too lightly. The Georgians have one of the best teams in their state. And we've never had a picnic with them. You can take the scores in past games as an example. We've never defeated them by more than 14-0."[20]

They were not in crack shape, although injuries weren't a factor. Eldredge even started the game. Sluggishness was the problem.

It started out fine. Just as the previous week, the Stingarees struck suddenly. Kendrick put his man on the ground with a crushing block and Koesy broke into the open and sailed through the secondary. This time, he wasn't brought down. The play went for 46 yards and a touchdown.

But, just as Yarborough warned, the Blue Jackets were not to be underestimated. Miami's defense put up little resistance as Savannah immediately drove 58 yards to the Miami two— the first team to get that far all year. But, instead of taking four cracks at a Miami line that was buckling, Savannah tried a risky lateral play. The ball sifted through the hands of Johnson Way and bounced crazily back to the 20, where a swarm of Stingarees pursued it before Koesy pressed it against his chest to end the threat.

Miami would botch its own scoring opportunity when, on fourth-and-inches from the Savannah 12, Eldredge unwisely called a pass that fell incomplete. Soon Savannah threatened again after Comfort and Koesy ran into each other trying to field a punt. The ball skittered away and the Blue Jackets recovered at the Miami 25. The crowd of around 4,000, which had been feeling so giddy when Koesy gave Miami the early 6-0 lead, was quieted as Savannah again reached the Miami two in four plays. Inexplicably, quarterback Bob McLaurin called the same lateral play that was so disastrous the last time. It lost six yards, and Miami took the ball back on downs. Savannah, as practically every other team, lacked a capable field goal kicker.

Yarborough's frustration was palpable to anyone near the Miami locker room. If his boys weren't listening to his warning during the week, they were listening to his full-throated admonitions now. When they emerged for the second half, they were a different team, especially on the line, which finally started to make some headway.

Koesy returned an interception 28 yards on Savannah's first possession of the second half to put the Stings at the enemy 40. After scampering 22 yards around right end, Koesy faced a fourth down on Savannah's 13. There, he lifted a wonky fourth-down pass in Comfort's direction at the seven. Comfort caught it one-handedly as he fell and braced himself with the other. Miami was up by two touchdowns after the spectacular grab.

Miami scored twice more. Burrus, playing in spite of his knee injury, made a nice catch of Eldredge's running pass for a 40-yard gain before scoring from the 17 on an end around. Yarborough then sent in the reserves. Gene Bolick scored on a four-yard run to make it 26-0, but his fumble at the 19 cost Miami its shutout streak. Yarborough quickly rushed his first team on the field but Koesy, closing fast to break up a pass, inadvertently deflected the ball into the hands of a Blue Jacket receiver for the first touchdown scored against Miami. Yarborough figured he had plenty to work on after the 26-6.

ANDREW JACKSON (JACKSONVILLE): STINGIN' IN THE RAIN

The Stingarees knew they were going to pay for their first-half sloppiness. Yarborough gave them a long lecture on blocking at Monday's practice and reaffirmed his point Tuesday with films of the early struggles against Savannah.

By now, Yarborough knew what he had, a bunch of speedsters in his backfield led by the best back in the South and a line that could not only control the line of scrimmage but get out in front of running plays downfield. That quickness paid dividends on defense as well. So far no one was able to push around the Stings. Edison line coach Muddy Waters, when asked about the speed in the Miami backfield, cracked: "Why, with that blocking, Ole Aunt Kate could be scoring their touchdowns."

As Miami headed back to Jacksonville for its only other road game of the season, it sure looked like another easy victory. Andrew Jackson was 2-3, had fallen to Edison, 19-6, and had lost two starters to injury in its most recent loss to crosstown rival Julia Landon.

Yarborough, meanwhile, was getting Rogers back after missing the Savannah game and, for the first time all year, would have blocking back Charlie Fancher available. Fancher had sustained what was called a pre-season head injury (in other words a concussion). Eldredge, in addition to his broken finger, had a laceration on his other hand, but it wasn't going to sideline him. Starting end Andy Smith was recovering from a sore throat. "He lost his voice against Savannah and even a canary could have out-talked him," Yarborough joked.[21]

The Stingarees bussed up on Friday and had a workout at the stadium that night. They stayed at the grand Hotel Seminole and when they headed out of the 10-story structure for the game, they walked into a downpour that never let up. Two years previously, they had barely beaten Robert E. Lee on a muddy field. This time, it didn't matter. The first Miami touchdown was a thing of beauty in wet or dry weather. Early in the second quarter, Eldredge took the snap on an off-tackle slant and turned the left corner. The downfield blocking brought a smile to Yarborough's face as Eldredge cut to his right. Every Jackson defender with a chance at him was cut down and Eldredge, bad fingers and all, continued for a 74-yard score. These long touchdown gallops would become commonplace the remainder of the season.

Bucket Barnes came on for the extra point but missed, and that led to the first and only deficit Miami faced all regular season. Jackson punter Billy Mims got off a great boot that backed up the Stingarees inside deep in their end and, failing to pick up the first down, Miami prepared to punt. Rollins, though, had trouble snapping the wet football, and it skidded back into the end zone where Jackson's Kenneth Love fell on it for a touchdown. Mack Bishop then came on to convert the extra point that gave Jackson a 7-6 lead.

But, from that point on, it was all Miami. Eldredge sparked a late drive that took the Stings to the Jackson 14 where Yarborough sent Koesy into the game for the weary Davey. With just two seconds left in the half, Koesy circled his left end and made it all the way into the end zone. Eldredge, Koesy and Bolick, again, scored second half touchdowns as the game spun out of control. The Stingarees failed to convert on any of their PATS and left Jacksonville with a 30-6 victory.

Eldredge ran for 205 of Miami's 358 yards on the ground with Comfort adding 70 and Koesy 60. The Stingarees failed to complete any of their four pass attempts. The defense was unscored upon again (Jackson's TD came on a special teams miscue) and limited the home team to 21 yards rushing, 55 passing.

The Stingarees arrived home the next morning with a 4-0 record and a week off before Lanier came to Miami. But that Wednesday was one of the most significant days of the season. Yarborough joined Principal W.R. Thomas in a meeting at Miami City Hall where Robert J. Dill, vice chairman of the Florida division of the National Infantile Paralysis Committee, issued a proposal. He sought to turn the annual Christmas Day game at Burdine Stadium into something bigger.

Davey Eldredge and Jesse Yarborough go over the playbook before a game. Note the diagram of the short punt formation off tackle play on the chalkboard behind them. HistoryMiami Museum.

The National Sports Council had been talking with Dill's group about staging a national championship high school game. Dill was there to ask the Miamians for the use of the Orange Bowl. The group was high-powered. It also included Edison coach Ed Parnell, City Manager L.L. Lee, City Commissioner Fred Hosea, Earnie Seiler and Jack Baldwin from the Orange Bowl committee, stadium Committee Chairman A.A. Ungar, Public Welfare Director Gerald Ash, Jack Bell from the *Daily News* and George C. "Dutch" Kirkland, whose position was described in the papers as "man about town."[22]

Kirkland, who was involved in just about every sports venture in Miami, over time became known as the university's biggest football fan. A fixture at home games, he was allowed to walk up and down the sidelines, shouting: "Go get 'em Hurricanes." He remained a force of nature the rest of his life. In 1957, two years before his death at age 80, the irascible Dutch faced an assault charge for slugging a bus driver in the nose with a haymaker in dispute over a bus transfer. His lawyer said Kirkland was sorry. He would even buy the driver a new set of pants after his trousers were torn in the scuffle.[23]

Although there is no record of his vote, Kirkland undoubtedly approved of Dill's proposal, because nothing sports-related ever went ahead without him.

Theoretically, Miami and Edison Highs were relinquishing control of the game. The winner—always Miami, of course—selected its northern opponent. Now that choice would be up to a committee, although Yarborough ended up with a goodly amount of influence in the matter. It was to be an annual event, but this year, owing to limited time, the South would be represented by the winner of the November 30 game between the Miami rivals (as always).[24]

"And if Miami High goes through its season unbeaten," Dill noted, "it will have as good a claim to national honors as any team in America since it will be champion of Florida."[25]

The scene at the meeting where Miami school officials agreed to stage the annual Christmas game for the National Foundation for Infantile Paralysis. Seated, left to right, are W.R. Thomas, Miami High principal; Jesse Yarborough; A.A. Ungar, stadium committee chairman, L.L. Lee, city manager; Fred Hosea, city commissioner; Gerald Ash, director of public welfare and Jack Baldwin, Orange Bowl committee chairman. Standing are B.M. Baker, Miami Edison faculty representative; Ed Parnell, Edison coach; Robert Dill of the National Infantile Paralysis Committee; Jack Bell and Dutch Kirkland.
Miami Daily News.

It all made perfect sense, except that the entire net proceeds would go to the Infantile Paralysis Foundation, with half of that remaining in Florida. That would eliminate the home team's usual cut of the receipts, a sticky issue that seems not to have been fully addressed at the meeting.

Bell brought up another potential issue. Andrew Jackson could have a claim on the city title as well since it already defeated Edison. Once-tied but otherwise unbeaten, it might even challenge an unbeaten Miami to a game if it finished its season without a loss.[26]

LANIER: HELLO, HARVEY

Andrew Jackson's claims were of no concern to Yarborough or his team right now. Selby Buck's Lanier Poets had won three of the five previous meetings with Miami. True, they were only 4-3-1 but Yarborough scouted Lanier's 6-0 loss to Boys High in Macon and was telling everyone who'd listen that the Poets were the better team, blowing smoke again.

Yarborough, though, was particularly concerned with Lanier's 176-pound fullback Earl Dunham, whom Buck rated the best back he'd coached. Yarborough agreed. The *Macon Telegraph* trumped up the Boys game as a showdown for All-State honors between Dunham and Boys' Al Berman. Berman had the nickname "Hitler," unusual for a Jewish boy out of Atlanta (and one he undoubtedly dropped in the coming years). Dunham, who would make the athletic hall of fame at the University of South Carolina (where he was a three-sport athlete and later coached), was hard to stop in the first half when Lanier dominated, less so in the second half when Boys and "Hitler" took over.[27]

In any event, Yarborough was actually quite pleased with his well-rested and eager-to-hit squad when it resumed practice on the Monday before the game. He ran a full two-hour scrimmage, just the fourth heavy contact scrimmage of the season, and called the blocking the best he'd yet witnessed.

Red Mathews, Harvey Comfort, Davey Eldredge and Jason Koesy ham it up for the camera as they leap over the Stingarees' line. Miami Daily News.

"We want to keep the boys in the same form that they are in now," he said. "A Tuesday scrimmage probably will put the finishing touches on Monday's practice."[28]

He also had a new toy to unwrap. Harvey James, "Geechee" from Savannah, had just become eligible. Although James played center when he was at Benedictine Military Academy, Yarborough put him in the backfield to lend his blocking to the attack. Buck was riding his team hard, as well, and liked what he saw from speedy Lovick Cone, who ran for three touchdowns in a scrimmage, and Wahoo Johnson, who got loose for one long run.

Yarborough was expecting the Stings' most physical game and, as his team headed for the showers after its last practice of the week, he shouted a final reminder: "You've got to stop this Dunham kid to win."[29] Saturday night brought scattered showers and two early fumbles by Eldredge, still battling his broken finger. As Luther Voltz wrote in the *News,* "There is one thing about this Stingaree football team. It never gives its followers a dull moment."[30] But there was another truism. The Stingarees always came out on top. Once they got going after a scoreless first quarter, it turned into a comparatively easy 19-0 victory. Eldredge shook off his early fumble woes and took the Stingarees on a 99-yard march after being pinned in by a nice punt. Eldredge got loose for a 43-yard run off right tackle and hit Charlie Fancher with a pass that the halfback took on the dead run 26 yards to the Lanier four. Yarborough sent Koesy into the game after the teams swapped sides and he went around right end unmolested to score on the first play of the second quarter.

The Stingarees scored early in the third quarter on just two plays. After James, the new kid, made a great catch of an Eldredge pass for a 19-yard gain, Eldredge hooked up with Burrus to get the rest of the yardage on a fingertip catch. Eldredge closed out the scoring from the Miami 44, slipping between left guard Gilbert Wilson and left tackle Dick Fauth. He made a sharp cutback and raced past the startled Poet defenders, "without so much as saying 'how-de-do,' " as Evans wrote. At first Lanier defenders began to chase the speedster, but they gave it up and simply watched him cross into the end zone for another long TD.[31]

As for big Earl Dunham, the Stingarees followed their coach's orders. The Poets threatened only once after a poor punt by Koesy set them up at the home team's 34. They got as far as the 19 where backup center Paul Louis batted down a fourth down pass.

Davey Eldredge runs away from the entire Jackson, Mississippi team en route to a 76-yard touchdown, the most sensational of his high school career. Miami High School 1940 Mahai Yearbook.

JACKSON CENTRAL: A RUN TO BE REMEMBERED

The team they doubted in the pre-season was now on the verge of tying a school record of 15 straight wins set by the '33-'34 teams, and led by All Southern back Norman Pate. Central High from Jackson was to be the first Mississippi school Miami had ever faced, and the Tigers took the game very seriously. They arrived two days before the Friday night contest to acclimate to the heat and ran into a cold snap.

Central had a 5-3 record that included an 18-14 win over Baton Rouge High School, the team that would play in the Louisiana Sports Authority's version of the national championship game. Triple-threat tailback Doug Kenna scored all three of Jackson's touchdowns that day, but he was missing this game with a knee injury. The Tigers, as most teams did, outweighed the Stings.

Jesse Yarborough put his team through another hard scrimmage on Tuesday to keep them in shape and to review some of the ball handling problems incurred against Lanier. But the game turned out to be just another (now) routine rout, a 27-0 victory. With Kenna sidelined, the Tigers, said the *Jackson Clarion-Ledger* were, "as sputtery and balky as an ancient tin lizzie."[32] And they certainly had no answer for Miami's sleek model, Davey Eldredge who pulled off what was arguably the greatest run of his high school career. Some would call it the greatest run in the short history of the Orange Bowl—as memorable as one Clyde Crabtree pulled off while at Florida.

The fourth-down play from the Miami 24 called for Eldredge to fake a punt and find a receiver on a sprint-out pass to his right, but the Central rush got on him quickly. He spun away from those defenders and faded back, edging toward the sideline as the Tigers pursued. Then, he wheeled laterally to the opposite sideline and was chased back to his own two-yard line.

For a moment, it looked as though he might be forced into the end zone for a safety but, before being pushed out of bounds, he cut up the field diagonally, dodging tacklers with jukes and moves to get back to the original line of scrimmage. On he went, "side-stepping, changing pace, squirming, twisting," wrote Luther Voltz of the *News*. When he finally broke free at midfield, he nearly fell, his legs were so weary. There, a teammate grabbed Eldredge's elbow, helping him along, and he was gone. It was a 76-yard run that must have covered at least 150 yards.

Luther Evans of the *Herald* dubbed him "dipsy-doodle David."[33] Voltz called him a "blond miniature of a red-headed ghost named Grange," the best back ever at Miami:

> There is a large blue No. 1 on Li'l David Eldredge's gold Miami High jersey—and that is quite as it should be. Of all the fine backs who have toted footballs for the Stingarees, Li'l David must be reckoned No. 1. If anyone should care to question the point he need only to ask 5,500 customers who sat in the stands last night and watched 24 weary Jackson, Miss., football players take turns chasing Li'l David's flashing legs over the turf of Roddy Burdine Stadium.[34]

Eldredge, playing less than half the game, intercepted a pass to set up a touchdown, ran 16 yards for another and threw a dandy of pass to James for one more. The Stingarees, toying with the visitors, pulled off a flea-flicker for a touchdown. Kendrick simply dominated the line of scrimmage, recovered a fumble and opened up swaths for the Miami backs. On defense, Kendrick kept penetrating to get to Jackson's backs before they could even get started. But the *Clarion-Ledger* put Miami's win down to one man.

> The Tigers and coaches joined in a unanimous wish that they get another crack at the Miami squad—without Eldredge.
> Able to check the Miami running attack, the Centralites could do little but clutch wildly at loose air whenever Eldredge shook loose into the clear and it was his performance alone which accounted for the Stingaree victory.[35]

SPARTANBURG: TURKEYS

It was Thanksgiving week in Miami. Kind of. But not really. Miami and Edison were playing their traditional game next week. On Thanksgiving. In some places. It was the year President Roosevelt moved the holiday. But not everywhere.

Ever since 1864, when Abraham Lincoln decreed it, Thanksgiving was celebrated on the last Thursday in November. In 1939, the last Thursday fell on the 30th. FDR, in an effort to stimulate the economy, lengthened the traditional Christmas shopping season for merchants by designating November 23 the national holiday. Two years later, Congress officially declared the third Thursday in November to be Thanksgiving Day.

Florida Governor Frederick Preston Cone, a Democrat but hardly a staunch New Dealer, stood as one of 23 governors who kept the original date in an expression of state's rights. As soon as Cone announced his decision, Miami Mayor Sewell declared that the city would sit down to dinner with the President on November 23. Up the coast, the then-Republican stronghold of Palm Beach observed the holiday on the 30th. Likewise did Lake Worth— where it was reported that butchers had stocked a few turkeys ahead of the 23rd to take care of "defiant Democrats."[36]

Jason Koesy is taken down by the neck as he picks up ground against Spartanburg. MIAHI 1940.

The problem with "Franksgiving," as it was called, was that many football schedules were set long before August, when Roosevelt changed the date. That's why Miami and Edison ended up playing on the night of November 30—Thanksgiving in Florida—and why Miami played Spartanburg on Friday night, November 23, the day after Thanksgiving in Miami and South Carolina.

Appropriately, Spartanburg was the biggest turkey on Miami High's schedule. The Crimson Tide wasn't rolling. It was trickling into the Orange Bowl with a 0-7 record and a grand total of 14 points. Yarborough's biggest challenge was to keep his team focused (Edison was on deck), so he talked about how the South Carolinians had traditionally given the Stings a good game.

They did not. To begin with, the Tide ended the chilly night with minus-11 yards and Yarborough emptied his bench down to the third string after halftime. By then, Koesy had followed superb blocks by James and Rogers, the two newcomers, into the end zone and Eldredge, entering the game in the second quarter, had enough time to rip off two long scoring jaunts of 54 and 68 yards. Billy Rentz got on the scoreboard for the subs in the second half, while three other TDs were called back for penalties, two by Gene Bolick, who had 82 yards of gains wiped out and another by Comfort. It was a 27-0 win that had the feel of a 72-0 win.

Miami had run its unbeaten streak to a record 16 games. Now, for the only team to tie them during that span.

EDISON: TOO MUCH ELDREDGE

For all that the Stingarees had done so far, their fiercest rival stood in the way of all they wanted to accomplish. Edison was the classic example of a team with nothing to lose. Edison had never beaten its hifalutin nemesis from the West Side in 17 previous tries, but was there not a better year to do it? These Stingarees had a chance to become the first undefeated, untied team in the school's glorious football history and to cap it off by playing for a national championship. However, the National Sports Council had agreed that the Edison-Miami winner would represent the South in the Health Bowl on Christmas night. Edison could spoil a lot of fans' holidays, including the game's organizers. Without Miami playing, the "national championship" concept would lose its patina of legitimacy.

Pop Parnell's team was a classic underdog by any measure. The Red Raiders were having the season Miami was supposed to have, at 4-4, with three close losses to Andrew Jackson of Miami, Robert E. Lee and Hillsborough, the Stings' old Big Ten rival. They were swamped in their most recent encounter, 27-12, by Julia Landon, the strong Jacksonville squad that would later upset Bobby Cifers and Kingsport, Tennessee. Edison's defense allowed 326 yards in that one.

Comparative scores also favored Miami. Edison beat Andrew Jackson of Jacksonville, 19-6 while Miami trounced Jackson, 30-7. Miami topped Lee, 7-0, a week before Edison lost to Lee, 7-6.

Edison was also coming off an eight-day stretch in which they played three games with another short week coming up. The Thursday game with Miami would be their fourth in 13 days, although three injured players were returning to the Lemon City lineup: Eddie Hausenbauer and Johnny McCullum to the backfield and Pahokee Smith at guard. So far, Miami had played just twice in November.

Yarborough didn't want his boys thinking numbers and odds. After all, Edison had outplayed Miami in a 6-6 tie the year before, and Miami barely won the rematch by an extra point, 7-6. These games were always hard-fought. He had an uneasy feeling and he confided as much to Bell.

"I'd give a lot if it were over and I'd feel better if Edison hadn't played that bad game against (Landon). That game means they'll come clawing at us," he said.[37]

An air of tension surrounded Miami High for the first time all year. The Stingarees never knew what to expect from their rivals. Parnell usually sprung up a surprise or two for Yarborough, as he had done the previous year by running weak side time and again. When they met two days before the game to finalize arrangements (officials, etc.) Pop played a few mind games with the Colonel.

"We've been working on a double wingback and a spread formation. We've decided we don't like our Notre Dame offense," he kidded. "I don't like it either but that spread won't work against our new 4-3-1-3 defense," Yarborough countered: "And by the way I'm going to talk on WIOD at seven-fifteen Wednesday night. I want you to listen."[38]

Jack Bell was there. He duly warned Parnell about letting his team tune in. Yarborough was known to use the airtime to poke fun at opponents to take them off their game. But Parnell countered that any trash talk would only motivate his team. "I'll be listenin' and so will all the boys. If that guy can key up my team this year, it'll be his own funeral," Parnell said.[39]

At least some Miamians sat down to their Thanksgiving dinner Thursday. As the *Miami News* put it, "Today is Thanksgiving, according to your calendar, football tradition and Gov. Fred P. Cone."

And there was no fonder tradition in Miami than the city's two big schools clashing on the gridiron. Bell set the stage, as only he could, for another nail-biter, as celebrators and non-celebrators alike picked their *Miami News* off their front porches:

> *There's no denying that Miami High's band of speed demons have won the fancy of everybody who loves football. Never has Jess Yarborough had a flock of blockers so good or backs so fast. It has been a team on fire, game after game—and fans watched in delighted amazement and ever increasing numbers.*
>
> *There's no denying Edison's drab football in a few games either. Pop Parnell's kids couldn't seem to click.*
>
> *Yes, it's Miami by three touchdowns on past performances; but if you give a point more than 7 to 5 you're crazy. I've seen Edison teams seemingly outclassed even more than this one rise up and play the Stingarees off their feet. And I've seen an Edison team which was a slight favorite go down under a four-touchdown defeat.*
>
> *Naturally you've got to string along with a Stingaree team which hasn't been beaten or tied by foes just as good or better than those who've beaten Edison. Just the same, don't ever think Pop Parnell can't key a team, for this Miami game. The old boy surely had 'em clicking for a while, didn't he? Well, now he's back with every man in perfect condition. Think he and the kids are going to fold up tonight?*
>
> *Don't be silly![40]*

A stroll down Flagler Street that morning could still get you 11-5 odds with the bookies if you liked Edison and, no doubt, there were more than a few shekels wagered by those emboldened by Bell's take. And then it was time for what the newspaper ads hailed as, "the football game you've been talking about all season."

It wasn't a record crowd, but it beat anything the University of Miami had brought into the grandstands that year. The college boys couldn't match the high schoolers for the added entertainment of their games' high jinks. As 14,685 filed into their seats, an Edison cheerleader stealthily made it up the East bleachers to the big scoreboard, where he uncovered a large sign that said, "BEAT" and pinned it in front of "MIAMI." The sight triggered a ruckus when Donald Barnhill, the Miami cheer squad leader, spotted it. Making like Davey Eldredge, he sprinted up the bleachers, nabbed the sign, cut back through Edison supporters to safety on the Miami sidelines, where he ripped it to shreds to huge cheers.

The newspapers reported that, for the first time in the series, there were no fights in the stands. Even the two bands joined together for the entertainment, creating formations in the shape of a Cardinal, and then a Stingaree, although the sand they dusted up on the pristine field gave the groundskeepers fits.

As game time approached, even during warm-ups, Edison seemed the looser team. Yarborough sensed it. He didn't scream or pull out any Rockne-esque pep talks before he sent the Stings out of the locker room for the kickoff. He calmly laid out the facts without getting into what was at stake.

"They've never beaten a Miami High team. If you go out there and play football, you can beat 'em again tonight," he said, looking each boy in the eyes as he scanned the room. "You know what you're supposed to do and if you don't you'll come out and we'll send in someone who does. Don't go out there excited and tense. It's just another football game. Walk out and win it."[41]

Like everyone else, Eldredge took it in. It was going to be his last Edison game (his concussion kept him on the sidelines as a sophomore) and he knew that Edison had mapped out a plan tailored around him. The Red Raiders had always done a good job of knocking down Miami's top threat. The year before, they countered Miami's strong inside running game by moving their tackles more inside. Whatever they had concocted this year, Eldredge also knew of his own tricks—and talents. If given just one second of hesitation by Edison defenders, he would take that inch and run it a mile. He headed determinedly onto the field with his teammates.

Indeed, the Red Raiders were loose. Prior to kickoff, they did not seem like a nervous team hoping, at best, to avoid humiliation. They bantered and joked and their relaxed body language spoke of a team that had nothing to lose. This might have been discomfiting not only to the Stings, but also to their fans. So, when Stumpy Wiggins pounced on Harvey Comfort's fumble at the Miami 49, the collective blood pressure of the Miami rooting section exploded. Frank Knuck earned Edison a first down at the Stingaree nine by skittering 17 yards and the Edison fans screamed and shouted to the depths of their lungs. Their ecstasy was short-lived. The underdogs got no further than the five. There, they tried an end-around on fourth down but big Jay Kendrick diagnosed the play and stopped Bob Kolz cold.

Edison indeed came out in a special defense designed for Eldredge. Miami had been expecting a 6-3-2 and practiced against it all week. But Parnell devised Edison a 6-2-2-1. It worked to a certain extent, but not well enough. On Miami's second play after the exchange, Eldredge was Eldredge: socks rolled down over his high tops, calves showing, fingers pointing instructions to his blockers. He had his own body language, one that gave everyone a glimpse of what he had in store—a 41-yard sprint up the sideline to midfield before he was taken out of bounds. That drive stalled but the next did not.

The second period started with Miami on its 42-yard line. Eldredge zipped through an opening at left tackle and cut to his right, toward the south stands where the Stingaree supporters sat. They were rising out of their seats now, shouting, "there he goes," as soon as he crossed the scrimmage line.

"Waving a highball to a pair of Edisons with his hips, he turned on the steam goalward," wrote the *Herald*'s Everett Clay, noting how Hausenbauer, an Edison track star, tried to cut him off only to see him streak past.

"Li'l Davey literally kicked dirt in his eyes," Clay wrote. "Incidentally, the Miami Highs got in several neat blocks during the run, although there was really little need for blocking the way Li'l David was highballing it."[42]

No one touched him on the 58-yard sprint, which Clay estimated took about six seconds. That made it six straight games in which Eldredge had at least one 50-yard run for a touchdown.

Then it happened again.

Edison had been hanging in there. Although the Red Raiders got as far as the Miami 20 only one more time—Kendrick and J.B. Moore kept busting up plays—they were keeping Eldredge in check and the game was being played between the 25-yard lines. Then, early in the fourth quarter, Eldredge found some room off left guard. Edison's defenders closed and had him surrounded. But he left them reaching and lunging with a couple of hip fakes before heading toward the south sidelines with what seemed like the entire Cardinal defense in pursuit.

Dick Fauth and Charles Washington picked off a couple of defenders with downfield blocks leaving Dub Gracy with the last chance to stop him. Eldredge cut left, then right and Gracy was on the ground. This TD run totaled 59 yards. After that, Yarborough rested Eldredge for the next week's game against Boys High and Miami closed out the 13-0 win.

Clay called Eldredge, "as fast as chained lightning and twice as powerful."[43] Bell, who had already proclaimed Eldredge the best back in the South, did so again:

> The boys from Edison should know, for they ran onto the field and played the Stingarees to a standstill—except Eldredge. They couldn't have cornered him in a telephone booth. When Li'l David wasn't in there 'twere a tie. When he was in there the very air seems tense—for they never knew when he'd get past that line of scrimmage and be long gone.[44]

"All the build-up he got from you newspaper fellows was correct. He can sure run," said Edison's Pahokee Smith.[45]

But the magnanimous Eldredge deflected the credit to his teammates. "Did you see that blocking?" Eldredge said when asked about his TD runs. "Anybody can score the way those boys iron 'em out. There is nothing to it."[46]

Perhaps he was just trying to stay on the good side of his linemen. In a display of toughness, Doug Craven, after dislocating his jaw, asked Kendrick to sock him in the kisser to put it back in. Kendrick obliged. Clay was actually watching Miami High for the first time that year. He didn't think any team in the country could beat them:

> Personally we have little doubts that the Miami Highs can knock the ears off Baltimore City College High; Billings, Mt.; Brockton Mass.; Casper, Wyo.; Garfield, N.J.; Lawrence High of Long Island; Poughkeepsie, N.Y.; Seward Park and Boys High of New York City; East High of Sioux City, Iowa or any other team that may be selected to represent the North in the Starlet Bowl.[47]

The two schools' bands stayed on the field playing until the stadium emptied. Miami's was the last to leave. Its last tune: *"Hurrah for the Blue and Gold."*

BOYS: SOUTHERN CHAMPS

Up North, they would have a heck of a time sorting through the list of those potential Miami victims mentioned by Clay. All that had been required of Miami to lock up the South's bid in the big Christmas game was to beat its crosstown rival yet again. Now, to really prove it was the best the South could offer, Miami had one more rival to beat, and doing that wasn't always easy.

Boys High was coming down from Atlanta to play in the annual Kiwanis Charity Game for the benefit of underprivileged children. Their city was already abuzz, anticipating the December 15 premiere of *Gone with the Wind,* and the Purple Hurricanes were adding to the storm of civic pride. Shorty Doyal's boys, in spite of several key injuries, were 10-0-1 on the season, their record smudged only by a 6-6 tie with Atlanta's Marist College High, a private military prep school. They had just outlasted short-lived Monroe Agricultural & Mechanical, 14-7, to claim the Georgia state title. Monroe, a vocational training school, had won the title in 1938.

Miami and Boys defeated three common opponents: Knoxville, which Boys bounced 20-0, in Tennessee and Miami trounced, 32-0, at home, Savannah, which bowed at Boys, 26-0, and in Miami, 14-0, and Lanier, shut out 6-0 by Boys at home and 19-0 by Miami on the road.

As usual, the big challenge against Boys was deciphering Doyal's formations. Shorty was a master of X's and O's. Deception and trickery were always parts of the game plan. He didn't have a breakaway threat. He lost his in the third week of the season when the soon-to-be-legendary Clint Castleberry broke his arm against Savannah. Berman (alias Hitler) was very effective but he was more of a power runner, and, with a line that averaged over 180 pounds (including 230-pound right tackle Phil Alexander, a future South Carolina Gamecock star), the Purple Hurricanes had the far-heavier squad. Jake Cox, their punter, was also a dangerous weapon.

Yarborough, though, was extremely confident after scouting Boys for the second time in their state championship game against Monroe A&M on a Friday night at Ponce de Leon Park (he'd also watched them beat Lanier while Crabtree scouted the Knoxville game). He was so confident, in fact, he was making bets in the press box. "And it will be with speed to spare," he boasted, laughing at Boys' 18-pound per man weight superiority. "Our fleet backs will outrun the Purples."

The *Associated Press* apparently agreed. The bureau's Larry Rollins penned a story singing Eldredge's praises:

> Many an Orange Bowl conversation is being broken up these days by such irrelevant remarks as:
> "By the way, did you see that kid Eldredge go to town the other night?"
> "Did I? Hadn't seen anything like that since (Red) Grange massacred Michigan! They gave him a tiny hole in the line and—whoosh!—he was the little man who wasn't there."[48]

Yet, at the same time, Yarborough spoke to Jack Bell over the phone and told him it was the best Boys team he'd ever seen. Different messages for different ears: classic Yarborough.

In any event, Yarborough's players, even the fleet backs, weren't taking any chances. Although they were off from school for Governor Cone's Thanksgiving weekend, Eldredge and Kendrick called practice on their own the day after the Edison contest and had manager Goldie Goldstein hand out the equipment. They reconvened Saturday and on Sunday, running wind sprints.

That should have pleased their coach. However, when he got back on the practice field Monday, Yarborough called it a lackadaisical effort. The cockiness he displayed in the press box in Atlanta was wholly concealed from his players.

"Boys High is the strongest team that we play this season," he told the *Miami Herald* for his boys' benefit. "They outweigh us. They have a good coach and are well drilled, experienced and fast. But my boys—for some reason—figure they are going to whip Boys High easily. And I don't know how they get that way. I hope they get that silly idea out of their heads before the Atlantans take it out of their head for them."[49]

Shorty Doyal was playing mind games with his team as well. He daily flaunted Miami's superiority over the Purples the last three seasons. And this, with the mythical championship of the South on the line, was the most important game they'd ever played against each other. Each was the best team the other had faced all season.

The Purple Hurricanes left two days before the Thursday night game and stayed overnight in Jacksonville. They left the next morning on the Florida East Coast Railway's sleek new *Henry M. Flagler,* the third trip the streamliner made. The train bolted down the Florida coast at 90 miles-per-hour and cut two hours off the normal travel time, dropping the team off in Miami at 2:00, early enough to fit in a final practice.

It must have seemed like a modern miracle to the young Atlanta passengers. The *Flagler* and the *Champion* were the locomotive answers to the Seaboard Air Line's *Silver Meteor*—the "Train of Tomorrow"—which went into service in February and began daily service to Miami the same day as its competitor. The aluminum streamliners could glide from New York to Miami in 25 hours for the price of a $25 coach ticket, cause for celebration of the first arrival of the *Flagler* and *Champion* on December 1. A bi-plane trailing smoke led the way when the big diesels rolled into the Fifth Street Station, as the Edison and Ponce de Leon High Schools played on, and the newsreel cameras filmed Mayor Sewell taking his turn at the throttle. The trains were open for inspection by awe-struck crowds for the next three hours.

Sewell expressed the hope that, "streamlined service can be extended between California and Miami, so Californians can come to Miami for the winter."

For now, the biggest attraction was the Thursday night game between Boys and Miami, as captured by Luther Evans in the *Herald.*:

> *The Southland's most bitter interstate football rivals, Miami and Boys High of Atlanta, will match talent at 8:15 today for the richest prize of their colorful seven-year series—the mythical Southern interscholastic championship.*
>
> *That's right, the two strongest high school touchdown machines on our side of the Mason-Dixon Line, both undefeated this season, will clash tonight in the Orange Bowl Stadium.*

By the end of that evening, there was no doubt which of those teams mythically ruled the South. The Stingarees treated powerful Boys High as it did most of its 1939 opponents, overwhelming the visitors with a 26-0 victory, validated by 11,166 fans.

The Stingarees dazzled Boys from their first 63-yard touchdown drive as Koesy, Moore and Eldredge worked a series of laterals that gained 36 yards before Eldredge was tripped up at the Boys 13 by a diving Loftin Smith. Changing sides for the start of the second quarter, Koesy sprinted out to his right, then stopped and whipped a pass totally across the field to a wide-open Eldredge, who tip-toed into the end zone.

Now, it was the Stings' turn to show what they could do on defense. Their remarkable record on that side of the football was always overshadowed by their offensive fireworks but, here, against a strong offensive team, they were perhaps even more impressive.

Boys took the kickoff and began a drive from midfield that reached the Miami three. No team had run one in on the Stingarees all season. But four straight cracks at the Miami line didn't gain an inch as big Jay Kendrick and J.B. Moore couldn't be budged. And that was it for the Hurricanes.

Kendrick, displaying his natural athleticism, intercepted a pass at the Boys 29, and Koesy and Eldredge combined again on the same cross-field pass for a six-yard score. Miami then added a touchdown in each of the last two periods. Eldredge on a "breathless" 33-yard sprint off left guard that Bell called his best run of the season, set up a one-yard TD run by Comfort. Then Eldredge scored his 16th touchdown of the season with an off tackle slant from the five.

A beaming Jesse Yarborough poses with his team, including Davey Eldredge with the Kiwanis Trophy, after the Stingarees clinched the mythical Southern championship against Boys High. Underprivileged kids, the beneficiaries of the charity contest, join in the celebration. Miami Daily News.

Roy White, writing in *The Atlanta Constitution,* called it an anticlimactic finale for the Purple Hurricanes who "lacked the spirit" they had in their big wins over Tech, for the city title, and Monroe A&M for the state flag. He said Boys was "greatly handicapped by the heat and unsteady footing" but acknowledged the explosiveness of Miami's quick backfield.[50] Doyal, meanwhile, would confide that his greatest game plan wouldn't be worth much against a game-breaker like Eldredge. Doyal would get his game-breaker the next two years in Castleberry. And, while Eldredge failed to get off another big touchdown run, his three-TD night was sufficient for Bell.

"Eldredge was the hero—sure! He's tops in any language," Bell wrote. "He can do the things that drive the opposition nuts! He's poison with a capital POISE (if you get my meaning)."

But Bell also acknowledged that Eldredge wasn't alone, that there was something about this 1939 team that made it stand out from previous Stingaree incarnations, no matter how great they had been. "We've had bigger teams, teams with more speedy backs, teams about which more has been written. But we've never had a group so smart, so fast and so much a team, as this one," he declared.[51]

With one game remaining in his high school career, Eldredge was the toast of Miami. Two days after the Boys game, as it named eight Stingarees to its All City first team, the *Miami News* ran a playful tribute to the young star. They'd taken a picture of Eldredge at his school desk, pencil in mouth, his mind far away, while, in a bubble, he was on his way to another touchdown, the back of his No. 1 jersey showing.

And above that:

Li'l David Eldredge Thinks It Over And Decides Algebra Isn't Much Fun
But 'Tis Pleasant To Vision Himself As Foes See Him.

The Miami Daily News *pictures Davey Eldredge daydreaming about his touchdown runs and forgetting his studies.* Miami Daily News.

Then it offered this ditty:

Gee, it's hard to get your studies
When you're thinking of your buddies
And the scampering for old Miami High
They've all helped me be elusive
And our wins have been conclusive
For we always get a touchdown when we try[52]

The Stingarees accepted the Kiwanis Cup, donated by Colonel Richard Gimbel of department store fame, and with it the championship of the South. With all the celebration going on around them, in a way it felt as though they had reached the pinnacle of the season. Even with the Health Bowl yet to be played with its national championship implications, the southern championship was always more of the carrot.

The Stingarees had reasons to feel good about themselves. Christmas was 18 days away. They didn't have to worry about the next game for a few days at least. They could just let their southern championship sink in. While the title was "mythical," few teams in the South had as strong an argument: Lanier High, of Mobile, perhaps, or Knoxville Central, the other Knoxville high school. Pine Bluff, Arkansas and Baton Rouge would play for the Louisiana Sports Authority's national championship but Pine Bluff had a tie and Baton Rouge a loss on their records.

Certainly, in the city of Miami, the locals felt they were watching the best high school football team in the south, if not in the country.

As Evans wrote in the *Herald*:

> You are welcome to bring on Seward Park or any other high school club Christmas as far as we Stingaree supporters are concerned.
> That's right we're fickle but buddy, we know a winner when we see one.[53]

Garfield, as it turned out, wasn't any other high school club.

SIXTEEN

THE 1939 BOILERMAKERS

Art Argauer had built a team and won his first state football championship. Now he had to build a program.

He would do it brick by brick, not through domination but rather through grinding. Garfield had come through a tough, but fabulously successful, 1938 season preceded by a harsh and disappointing '37 campaign. The Boilermakers had followed up a losing season with an undefeated one, but each of those seasons provided important lessons for the veterans of those campaigns.

The competition in New Jersey was stiff, and the criticisms came easily—both prime motivators at persevering not only as a good team, but more importantly, as a team that is good at winning. Recall Miami coach Jesse Yarborough and how, at the start of the 1938 season, he asserted his team would not enter a single game not believing it would win. But Miami was a different case. The Stingarees' reputation preceded them. They expected to win, because the teams before them won. They would always have believers, in and out of their—and the opponents'—locker rooms. The Garfield players' belief system was built within the walls of their locker room. Bill Parcells had a saying when he coached the Giants: "Confidence is born of demonstrated ability." He might have added: "especially under pressure or in the clutch." By 1939, the Boilermakers went into every game believing they could win no matter what.

"We had complete faith in Coach Argauer, and then there was Benny (Babula)," Walter Young recalled. "I'd say we were a tough-minded team, maybe because we didn't know any better. It was as if we'd just go out there and play, trusting what we were taught. We didn't think about it. We just played."

When 65 candidates greeted Argauer at the first practice, none of them had any inkling of spending Christmas in Miami or playing for a national championship. The Boilermakers would navigate through close calls and narrow escapes until they found themselves in the blinding Florida sunshine. All the while, they summoned an innate ability to persevere, instilled by their coach, hardened by trials even tougher than faced by the 1938 team.

Every opponent was after them. Ever since state champs were first named in 1912, only Rutherford (in 1921-22) and the Bloomfield Bengals ('33-'34, '36-'37) had repeated, so the odds were against them in the first place. For so long, it had been just a matter of toppling the Bengals. Not in 1939. There were several strong squads with legitimate title aspirations, including those not on the schedule. Unlike Bloomfield, Garfield hadn't established a mystique. People thought the Boilermakers could be had.

All of this was plain to Argauer, who tempered outside expectations while building inner confidence. Perhaps out of habit, he sang the blues after that first pre-season workout, at which Paul Horowitz of the *Newark Evening News* scoffed: "Argauer's pessimism seems to have no foundation."[1] Soon, the coach gave up the charade. Who was he fooling? Not only was his varsity coming off an undefeated 1938 season, but his JV team was as well.

"I know I have a big job ahead but I'm not letting that worry me," he told the *Newark Sunday Call* as preseason preparations were being completed. "In the group out for the varsity are many big, strong boys who played on the junior varsity team when it swept aside all opposition last year. Besides, I have many regulars from the state championship team."[2]

Benny Babula had grown in size and strength. He weighed 191 pounds now, 17 more than in 1938. At 19, he was more of a man than a boy. With Ted Ciesla graduated, Babula would pick up the rest of the workload that he split the previous year and call all signals. Wally Tabaka and John Orlovsky were also returning from the deep backfield of '38, although Johnny Sekanics, that season's freshman flash, became ineligible to play in 1939 due to poor grades. Babula's power and Sekanics' speed would have been a dizzying combination, but Argauer was a stickler for making the classroom a priority.

John Grembowitz and Young were back after starting almost every game on the line in '38. Angelo Miranda, Alex Yoda, Jack Boyle and Bill Wagnecz, who had all seen action the previous year, would join them. So would Joe Tripoli, the giant 210-pound tackle, who had just moved into town to live with his grandparents after starting the previous two seasons for Park Ridge. Pete Yura was moving up from the JV to take over at center and Ed Hintenberger, whose brother had starred for Argauer a few years earlier, looked as though he could break into the lineup at right end. That allowed lanky 6-footer Ray Butts, a starter at end for four games in '38, to move to the backfield to add his blocking prowess—with Grembowitz also available for emergency duty there.

Argauer lamented his depth. It wasn't at 1938 levels, and it showed in the annual pre-season scrimmage against Columbia. The first string, even with Babula on the sidelines with a sore leg, put together a couple of 70-yard scoring drives, but the subs stalled. Later, Babula showed off his throwing arm in a non-contact scrimmage, completing nine straight passes against a Columbia defense that knew he was passing. Columbia coach Phil Marvel marveled indeed, calling Babula, "the best pitcher in football I've ever seen."[3]

Garfield, the papers said, would be going to the air more often and with greater effect. That was one big area of improvement.

There was one change on the coaching staff. Andy Kmetz left after the 1938 season to take the head coaching job at Hasbrouck Heights. He was replaced by John Hollis, a star on the 1925 team beginning a 38-year tenure at the school. The schedule was stronger from a Colliton-System standpoint with just one key change. Argauer added Thomas Jefferson of Elizabeth, which had challenged Garfield's state supremacy through much of the 1938 season, in place of smaller Carteret. An undefeated season would not guarantee Garfield

Walter Young gets into a stance for his preseason publicity shot at Belmont Oval. Courtesy Estate of Walter Young

Ray Butts goes up for a pass at a preseason practice session at rocky Belmont Oval. Courtesy Estate of Jack Boyle.

another state title—other teams had slightly stronger schedules according to Colliton—but it would put the Boilermakers above most others.

DICKINSON: DOMINATION

Dickinson was the first to test the defending champs in the traditional season opener at Passaic Stadium. The Jersey City boys were supposed to be weak on offense, strong on defense, and they were missing two injured starters. Unlike the nail-biting 1938 meeting, however, no one was pointing out any Garfield weaknesses when the game was over.

While Al Del Greco derided Dickinson as "big and fat and greatly overrated" Garfield took full advantage, and 7,000 spectators could vouch for the Boilermakers' strength.[4] Everyone was expecting a smooth ride to another state title after the 33-0 victory, bigger than any recorded by the 1938 (20-0 over Carteret). It was the most lopsided win since the Boilermakers defeated overmatched St. Cecilia by the same 33-0 score in the final game of the 1936 season.

No sooner had those lucky fans settled into their bleacher seats than the rout began. As expected, the Boilermakers started throwing early, as two straight hook-and-lateral plays moved the ball to Dickinson's 45. Babula gained 43 yards on a couple of off-tackle smashes,

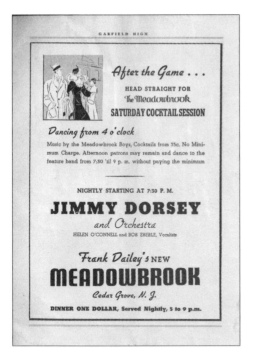

GARFIELD HIGH

After the Game . . .

HEAD STRAIGHT FOR

The Meadowbrook

SATURDAY COCKTAIL SESSION

Dancing from 4 o'clock

Music by the Meadowbrook Boys, Cocktails from 35c. No Minimum Charge. Afternoon patrons may remain and dance to the feature band from 7:30 'til 9 p. m. without paying the minimum

NIGHTLY STARTING AT 7:30 P. M.

JIMMY DORSEY
and Orchestra

HELEN O'CONNELL and BOB EBERLE, Vocalists

Frank Dailey's NEW

MEADOWBROOK
Cedar Grove, N. J.

DINNER ONE DOLLAR, Served Nightly, 5 to 9 p.m.

The inside back cover of the Garfield-Dickinson game program invites fans to drive over to Frank Dailey's Meadowbrook to dance to Jimmy Dorsey's orchestra after the game.

and then went over from the two for a TD. In six snaps, Garfield travelled 70 yards. The Hilltoppers were star-struck.

In all, Babula ran for 92 yards and two TDs and completed 7-of-11 passes with one TD. One scout told Del Greco: "No little guy on any team will drag down that Benny Babula. It takes a big, strong man. That means three of the opponents must slap him down."[5] Garfield's line held the visitors to 25 yards rushing. What's more, Argauer's fears about his depth proved to be unfounded. He substituted liberally, using his regulars only in the first and fourth quarters, and never lost momentum.

"It will take an unprecedented string of injuries to stop Garfield High School from retaining its state football championship this year," noted the *Bergen Record*. "The team is banked three deep with unlimited power in reserve."[6]

Charles Witkowski seconded that thought. He called the '39 Boilermakers the best drilled team he'd ever seen in a season opener and rated them over the '38 champs.

There was one skeptic (the usual one): Passaic coach Ray Pickett. He scouted the game and was confident he could shut down the Boilermakers, at least through the air. He'd get that chance in two weeks. First, it was Irvington's turn. The Camptowners would provide Garfield with the first test of wills when they hosted the Boilermakers at cozy Morrell Field.

IRVINGTON: SURVIVAL

Irvington had opened the season as impressively as Garfield, with a 26-0 win over Thomas Jefferson. The Jeffs, as it turned out, were not even close to their 1938 form but few guessed it at the time, given coach Frank Kirkleski's sterling reputation. He wasn't accustomed to losing big.

In any case, Irvington knew this was its chance to muscle its way to the front line as state title contenders and it could not have been more motivated. The Camptowners (Camptown was the original name of the Newark suburb) had no fear of the Boilermakers. They knew they had come close to pulling off a late comeback win the year before. They were always a challenge due to Coach Bill Matthews' unorthodox offensive formation, with an unbalanced line to one side and an unbalanced backfield to the other. They were as deceptive a team as Garfield ever played. Garfield had seen it before, of course, but playing Irvington always required a sharp week of practice and certain adjustments. The Boilermakers had not reacted well to it in the 1938 game with Irvington gaining plenty of yardage on trap plays and smashes up the middle by Polish pals, Hank Przybylowski and Johnny Kulikowski, the "Flying Skis." Both were back.

The Garfield line charges in a preseason publicity photo shot at Passaic Stadium. From left to right:
Ray Butts, Angelo Miranda, John Grembowitz, Pete Yura, Jack Boyle, Joe Tripoli and Walter Young.
Courtesy Estate of Angelo Miranda.

It was another bright, warm day. The shirt-sleeved 8,000 in attendance must have marveled at the intricate maneuvers and booming horns and drums of Irvington's 132-piece band, then at Babula's also-booming punts in warmups. He was quite a sight, exploding his thick right leg into the football, lifting off the ground with his left, his outstretched hands held high and his blonde-topped head surveying the results. He sent the ball soaring, some boots carrying 80 yards. Irvington, warming up on the side of the field where those punts rolled out, couldn't fail to notice. But the Camptowners remained undaunted, even if they had to flip back a few footballs. They planned to force Babula to punt more than a few times.

Irvington started strong. Matthews threw everything at the visitors—half-spinners, reverses and lateral pass plays. There was often no telling which back was taking the direct snap; that's how well the offense was designed and disguised. The Boilermakers were on their heels on every play as Irvington marched 79 yards for the first TD of the year against Garfield.

Steve Reckenwald, who started the game in place of Przybylowski, hit left tackle for eight yards on the first play, and, as the Camptowners kept the Boilermakers guessing, went off right tackle and into the clear. Babula made a touchdown-saving tackle at midfield. Again, it was Reckenwald for 10 more yards, but he fell to injury and was replaced by Przybylowski. Kulikowski made five yards up the middle and, when it seemed as though Irvington would simply run the Boilermakers into the ground, Przybylowski surprised them with a short pass to Charley Hedden, who raced to the one-yard line, where Wally Tabaka rushed across the field and pushed him out of bounds. The Boilermakers caught their breath and stopped one play cold. But, on the next, Kulikowski went off tackle for the touchdown. Importantly, Garfield managed to bat down the pass on the conversion try to keep the score 6-0.

Irvington's confusing offense made the Boilermakers look like 11 blind mice at the snap of the ball. Garfield fans were stunned. Irvington was not "big, fat and overrated" like Dickinson.

Winning this one would require not only Babula's best, but also pulls on the rope from several teammates. Two in particular stood out: Wally Tabaka and John Orlovsky.

The compact but elusive Tabaka took the ensuing kickoff. Garfield fans rose to their feet as he weaved through the open field to give their team great starting field position at its 40. Babula tugged his helmet over his blond locks and immediately called his own number. He hurtled across the line and, as two blue-shirted defenders darted for him, fired his right arm out at them and sent them both to the ground. Partially in the clear now, he picked up a great block by Orlovsky and, as the Garfield fans stood again and shouted, "Go, Benny, Go," he obliged them, outrunning the last safety man for a 60-yard touchdown, eating up the yards with his gigantic strides. According to Gus Falzer of the *Sunday Call,* it looked as though he were "travelling in seven-league boots."[7] One play, one touchdown. The Camptowners' shoulders slumped heavier as Orlovsky converted the place kick. Garfield led, 7-6.

Fans, sitting shoulder-to-shoulder in the late afternoon glare of the sunlight, were witnessing one of the most thrilling and most crucially contested games of the year. The grandstands at Morrell Field were so close to the field it was as if the spectators could feel the heartbeats of the players and the players, the hushed breaths of the spectators.

Now it was Irvington's turn to respond in a game of thrust and parry. Kulikowski ripped off a big run, but fumbled. Babula threw himself on the ball at Garfield's 13. Irvington forced a punt but it was unlike the bombs that launched from Babula's foot in the pre-game. It was a rare misfire, a shank, and Irvington took over 30 yards from another touchdown. Garfield was penalized 15 yards for piling-on to cut that distance in half. Backed up against its end zone, the Boilermakers' defense got even more aggressive, so Irvington burned them with more deception.

On the next play, Hal Hornish sucked Orlovsky out of position and lateraled to Przybylowski, who found open field and skirted his right end to put the gutty underdogs back up. Again, they failed to tack on the extra point. This time, Kulikowski tried kicking, but his try went wide. The half ended, 12-7, with Irvington on top and Argauer addressing his team in the dusty, stuffy locker room. Tactically, he cautioned them against over-reacting on defense. Motivationally, he reminded them how many comebacks they pulled off last year.

Irvington changed into white jerseys at halftime and, so too, its luck. Tabaka began the second half with another fine kickoff return almost to midfield, and the Boilermakers, playing with what Falzer called "smugness," pounded their way to the Irvington 18, where the Camptowners gallantly held on fourth down.[8]

With just more than a quarter to go, Irvington resorted to convention to protect the lead. It played the field position game, hoping to rely on a defense that had deprived Garfield any sustained multi-play drives. Kulikowski got off an excellent quick kick on third down, and the Boilermakers were 67 yards away from the go-ahead touchdown. Now, it was Garfield's turn to get creative. Babula faked a punt and roared around the right side for 33 yards, before three Irvington players hauled him down at the Camptowner 36. With the home team on its heels, Babula called for Garfield's pet play, the Naked Reverse, and Orlovsky gained 11 yards for another first down on the 22. Runs by Babula and Orlovsky netted seven as the third quarter ended with Garfield 15 yards from the end zone.

The teams collected themselves as they switched ends of the field. Irvington dug in, but the Garfield line's strong blocking enabled Babula to chew up seven yards to the eight for another first down. The anxious Camptowners jumped the next snap and were penalized a critical five yards for offside. Falzer described what happened next:

> *A young man answering to the name of Nickolopoulos was sent in to brace the Irvington line at the center. While he stood there in defiant attitude Mr. Babula paraded around the right end and scored.*[9]

It wasn't exactly a parade until Babula had shaken off an Irvington defender behind the line of scrimmage. One man hardly ever took down the determined Babula. Orlovsky continued his great day by adding the extra point. Garfield regained the lead, but Irvington had one last chance and was determined to make it count. The kickoff went out of bounds, so Irvington started at its 35 and Kulikowski started hitting the center of the Garfield line like a wrecking ball. A series of line bucks and a couple of pass plays put Irvington at the Garfield 20 with all the momentum on its side. Garfield was barely hanging on. The 8,000 could sense an upset in the making when, on third down, Kulikowski burst through the middle one more time to the 10.

But, as Kulikowski pulled himself up, there it was. A yellow flag. As Joe Lovas of *The Herald-News* put it, "eagle eye" umpire Frank Spotts had "spotted" a hold by Irvington's left tackle, Hal Arnold.[10] Home fans groaned as the yardage was marched off to the 35. On third-and-25, Irvington had to abandon the ground game that had advanced the ball deep into Garfield territory. The Camptowners completed two passes but came up short of the first down and Garfield managed to run the last two minutes off the clock. Two exhausted teams left the field, one in relief, the other in despair. The *Sunday Call* ran a picture of an utterly dejected Matthews, whose boys had done everything but win. Falzer empathized:

> *The team in gold held to its two-point lead for dear life up to the final whistle. You could have knocked the Irvington boys down with a crowbar, such was their chagrin, when defeat was their potion after they had come within 10 yards of conquering the state champions.*[11]

It would have been easy to chalk up the close call to Garfield's overconfidence. It wasn't. Irvington was good, tricky and inspired. It was easily the best game the Camptowners played all year. They finished with a 5-2-2 record, falling to an upset by Kearny with two scoreless ties against Bloomfield and a good Newark West Side team, eighth in the state in the final Colliton point standings. But that's the danger the Boilermakers faced every week—that an inspired opponent would elevate its game against them. But winning those games also had its benefits, as Art McMahon of *The Herald-News* noted.

> *Garfield's close rub at Irvington may encourage future Boilermaker opponents or discourage them, depending on how they prefer to accept the narrow squeak. One school will accept the 14-12 victory as proof that Garfield can be beaten when a robust offense is thrown into its teeth.*
>
> *The other and more logical school will recognize the fact that the Boilermakers beat one of the outstanding clubs of the state in Irvington and did it the hard way—by coming from behind. Pre-season dope conceded only two teams had much chance to upset Garfield. Irvington was one and Passaic the other.*

Irvington had its chance Saturday and missed by the space of a 15-yard penalty for holding. Passaic gets its opportunity this week and the Indians have a world of followers who think Ray Pickett's club has the tools necessary to manufacture a victory. The Passaic-Garfield series has seldom produced a margin larger than a single touchdown and when games are that close they belong to anybody right until the final peep of the whistle.[12]

Yes, Passaic was next. And it was anybody's game.

PASSAIC: PICKETT'S CHARGE

Like Irvington, Passaic could have a clear path to the state championship if it could pull off an upset. As Irvington before them, Passaic went into the Garfield game off an impressive win, 31-6, albeit over a mediocre Clifton team. As usual, Pickett was talking up his team's chances, although with not quite the same verve as in 1938. Inwardly, he still lamented how two of his backfield starters were knocked out of that game and how he was forced to play an inexperienced line in Passaic's first game of the season. He had been spoiling for a rematch, but didn't get it. So, here was another chance against the gold-clad rivals from across the river.

While Picket had complained before the '38 contest that his team hadn't yet played a game, he nevertheless believed Garfield had a scheduling advantage this time.

"Saturday's results were bad for us," he griped. "Garfield had a tough game and must realize that it has some weakness and can't get careless. We had an easy game and Garfield now knows we are strong. If Garfield had had an easy game and we had a tough one, it would have improved our chances."[13]

That was debatable. Argauer and the Boilermakers weren't likely to take any Passaic team lightly, especially since they knew how competitive the last game was. Both coaches soon reverted to a more cautiously optimistic tenor.

"Garfield has a tough club but if (Nick) Corrubia, my sophomore quarterback, continues to display the blocking game he showed against Clifton, the Boilermakers will be in for plenty of trouble," Pickett said.[14]

"Garfield met its toughest club Saturday," Argauer claimed. "I don't think any club will give us as much trouble as Irvington did."[15]

Pickett, as usual before the Garfield game, worked his team behind locked doors at the stadium. Argauer, too, was taking no chances this time. He had sensed that Passaic regularly spied on his workouts at wide-open Belmont Oval, so he took the unprecedented step of closing practice. He had little choice after seeing the throngs hoping to watch the Boilermakers' first workout of the week. When the team walked over from the No. 8 School locker room, they found the hill overlooking the field mobbed with spectators—in mid-afternoon. There were more there than at some high school games today.

Argauer wasn't about to open up his playbook to the nosey onlookers, so he had the entire area cleared. As the fans grumbled, he posted guards at the every entrance to ensure they couldn't return. It was futile. For the rest of the week, Argauer took the team to a field in neighboring East Paterson where he could prepare in peace.

Those drills didn't exactly go well. The first string had a difficult time working against Passaic's plays and, on Thursday, fullback Ray Butts, who had done a great job of blocking in the first two games, twisted his ankle. It was swollen so badly, Argauer doubted he could play. The inexperienced Al Kazaren took his place in practice. In addition, guard Jack Boyle had

Garfield's first stringers line up at their Belmont Oval practice field shortly before the game against
Passaic. Note the scraggly field and makeshift goalpost. The line, from left to right: Bill Wagnecz, Angelo
Miranda, John Grembowitz, Pete Yura, Jack Boyle (with a bandaged nose), Joe Tripoli and Walter Young.
The backfield: Wally Tabaka, Benny Babula, Ray Butts and John Orlovsky.
Courtesy Garfield Historical Society.

been smashed in the nose against Irvington and was having trouble breathing. Sophomore
Ted Kurgan lined up there in practice.

As the injuries kept the new whirlpool bath in the Garfield locker room whirring (the
admiring press marveled at Argauer's modern "hot water machine"), the papers trumpeted
Passaic's upset chances. *The Herald News* even noted that Garfield was coming off an unlucky
thirteenth straight win. The paper didn't explain why it wouldn't have been even unluckier when
the thirteenth win actually occurred. In any case, Passaic had more than a puncher's chance.

> *East Rutherford stopped Babula last year and there's no reason why Passaic can't turn*
> *the trick. The Indians have an experienced line composed of six veterans and a letter-*
> *man.Orlovsky and Tabaka are good ball carriers, always dangerous, but without Babula,*
> *the morale of the team is practically shot. Irvington showed that Garfield's defense can*
> *be penetrated and if Passaic gives its ball carriers any kind of blocking, speedy (Mungo)*
> *Ladyczka and (Joe) Zabawa may get off to a long run. Garfield experienced trouble*
> *beating Passaic last year when the Indians presented a green line in their opening game.*[16]

Elaborated the *Bergen Record*:

> *Realizing that Pickett has pointed his Passaic Indians for the contest, Coach Art*
> *Argauer appears a trifle worried. Then again, Argauer hasn't quite recovered from*
> *Saturday's thrilling contest with Irvington. Passaic gets its opportunity this week and the*
> *Indians have many followers who think Pickett's club has the tools necessary to manufac-*
> *ture a victory.*[17]

Both cities were on edge. Fans snapped up advance tickets at Geldzeiler's and Sidor's in
Garfield and Markey Brothers and Rutblatt's, the two sporting goods stores in Passaic. Garfield
boosters were laying odds of 7-to-5 and in some cases 2-to-1. They were getting plenty of
takers, although both McMahon and Del Greco cautiously picked Garfield to prevail by 7-0
and 13-7 scores, respectively.

Then, on Friday night, the fever pitch broke the thermometer. Some Garfield fans thought it a good idea to drive across the bridges into enemy territory and honk their horns while parading through the streets. Passaic fans were tipped off and were waiting for them with tomatoes, rotten fruit and vegetables, and, in some cases, rocks.

At Broadway and Gregory Avenue, Passaic boosters came out from between parked cars to let loose a storm of garbage down on one of the Garfield vehicles. In a pique of road rage, the incensed driver climbed out of his car and put up his dukes. Badly outnumbered, he was saved when local residents called police to the scene. His car, however, was thoroughly trashed.

Mistaken for a Boilermaker invader, an innocent bystander named Edward Baultz was driving home when he was ensnared in the melee. Brawlers stoned his car and smashed his windshield. Another Garfield contingent ran into a fusillade of refuse when it reached the intersection of Monroe and Market Streets. "It was a pleasure," a Passaic rooter told *The Herald-News*. "Them Garfields got it all right."

Passaic police protected the high school from vandalism, but some Garfield cars made it through to the Main Avenue business section where they created a ruckus and held up traffic.[18]

Dawn ushered in a nervous calm. The anticipation before the 2:30 p.m. kickoff seemed interminable, as the concrete grandstand filled up hours early. Up to 12,000 squeezed and elbowed their way through the gates. Stadium personnel were already ringing a flimsy wooden fence around the field as the teams—Passaic in red helmets, red jerseys and khaki pants, Garfield in gold helmets and jerseys, khaki pants and purple trim—trotted onto the grass to loosen up. Even the New York Giants hadn't drawn as many to Passaic Stadium when they played Argauer's Clifton Wessingtons. There was a palpable buzz in the air and, once the game started, spectators in the grandstand had to stand to get a view. It was as if it were the homily part of a high mass, except everyone fixed their gaze on the celebrants.

Argauer deferred his decision on his injured players until the warmup. Boyle had been fitted with a facemask to shield his nose—Young had been wearing one all year—and he'd start in his regular position. Butts was able to move around on his ankle but Argauer didn't want to use him the entire game. Kazaren got his first varsity start. The game wouldn't be too big for him. He was the starting third baseman on Garfield's baseball team. He had confidence in his athletic abilities.

The teams eyed each other from their halves of the field. The Boilermakers knew their opponents well, knew they had All State candidates in left guard Al Fadil and right tackle Joe Gawalis, part of what Passaic rooters were calling their Maginot Line, and a capable pass catcher in left end Dan Kuzma. The backfield featured Zabawa and Ladyczka, two kids from Passaic's heavily-Polish First Ward, just across the Passaic and Monroe Street Bridges. Some players cursed each other in their parents' native tongues. Sure, they shared deep-rooted cultural backgrounds, but the only thing they shared today was a shared ambition to topple one another.

That played out on the line where Walter Young played opposite Joe Gawalis, Passaic's captain. Gawalis was plenty tough. He reached the Golden Gloves boxing finals that year, would play football at Georgetown and was a future Marine.

"On offense, every time he came to the line, he'd whack me on the head. Boom. Boom," Young explained, still a bit peeved by the memory. "And I thought to myself, 'this has got to stop. This has got to stop.' There were no facemasks back then. So next time he came up to the line, my elbow found him right in the nose."

Stunned, Gawalis confronted Young.

"You keep hitting me on the head, there's more of this," Young warned him.

"And that ended it," Young said. "He didn't hit my head anymore."

With tensions that high, it would be as good a high school football game as one could ever see, not from offensive fireworks distinguishing great games today but, rather, from the import freighted in every snap, every contested yard. There was beauty in it, too—in the artistry of Passaic's spinners, in Ladyczka's punting form, in the precision of Garfield's blocking and, especially, in the graceful power of Babula. Even the game's violence seemed orchestrated with symphonic drama, the hits reverberating like bass drums.

There was no better example than the Babula run that helped set up the first touchdown of the game. The teams had thrown themselves up against each other for a full quarter when Garfield took over at the Passaic 46, and Babula called for the Boilermakers' patented off-tackle smash right.

With his long legs, Pete Yura took his wide stance at center and, as soon as he snapped the ball, it seemed everything was set in motion with military precision. Babula was already moving to his right and lowering his shoulders when he caught the snap chest-high, five yards deep in the backfield. John Orlovksy, the wingback, slanted toward center on the right side of the formation, did a quarter-turn and fired himself through the hole. John Grembowitz, the right guard, exploded backwards out of his stance and pulled to the right to form Babula's cordon with Wally Tabaka. Kazaren, the halfback, made a 90-degree turn out of his stance and, with Tabaka passing just behind him, laid his shoulder into the chest of Kuzma, who had penetrated upfield from his left end position.

The seal block prevented Kuzma from getting to Babula, but failed to knock him off his feet, and he pursued the play. Passaic players scattered across the ground as Babula turned the corner and tore through the hole with his great forward lean, his big strides eating up turf. Kuzma, trailing, raised his arms and considered making a dive at Babula's heels from behind, but then thought better of it. Babula, with superb field awareness, now saw he could cut back to his left. He did just that, and stiff-armed Oliver Henry to the ground while Nick Corrubia, the Passaic safety, shook himself free of Young's downfield block. Corrubia got a hold of Babula's legs next, but another patented Babula stiff arm dispatched him. Babula almost lost his balance from the hit but, just before his knee touched, he braced himself with his right hand against the ground, righting himself, and kept going. Finally, Kuzma, on a

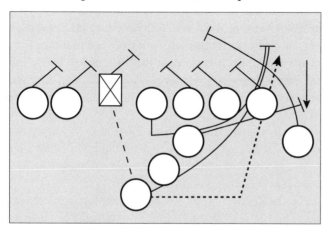

A diagram of Garfield's devastating off tackle smash. Note all the moving parts and how they formed a wall of interference for Benny Babula.

great hustle play from behind the line of scrimmage, wrangled the big man down by his neck at the Passaic 26.

The play was an amazing in several ways. It hinged on superb, choreographed blocking as well as Babula's vision, natural decision-making and, of course his power. And, it wouldn't have been stopped without Kuzma's determination. Preserved on film, one can watch it over and over in amazement to see all the pieces falling together.

If the Indians didn't know it, they did now. Babula was a horse, and that horse was determined to carry the Boilermakers the entire day. Again and again, he called his number but, even though the Indians knew he was coming, they needed three, four and sometimes five men to haul him down. As the drive continued, Babula hammered on, absorbing blows, pushing forward. He gained another 15 to the six and, on three straight off tackle smashes, the horse plowed into the end zone. Orlovsky, the kicking hero of the Irvington game, missed the extra point. 6-0 Garfield.

The lead didn't last long. Ladyczka sparked the comeback. First, he pinned the Boilermakers inside their 10 with a nice punt and, in three plays, the Passaic defense forced Garfield to punt. Babula barely got the kick off with Teddy Ryback charging him. It would have been a penalty for running into the kicker today, but no such rule existed. Ladyczka fielded the football at the Garfield 40 with running room. Sensing Bill Wagnecz coming hard to his left, he pushed off with his right foot, cut inside Wagnecz and escaped his long, futile reach. Grembowitz dove at him, but missed, and Ladyczka spun out of Orlovsky's tackle. He was finally tripped up along the left sideline at the 20 amid a cloud of red clay dust kicked up from the baseball infield.

Here, Passaic went at the middle of the Garfield defense with Zabawa carrying the ball. The Indians kept blasting away inside the five until, on fourth down, Zabawa got behind right guard Murray Friend and tunneled in under four Garfield defenders. The score remained tied at 6-6 when Fadil's kick was wide to left of the red-striped uprights, as a group of Garfield girls in bobby socks gleefully jumped up and down behind the end zone.

Both teams threatened to no avail in the remainder of the first half. Babula got loose for a couple of good gainers but Garfield lost the ball on downs at Passaic's 31 when Orlovsky came up short on a pass from Babula. Louis Bednarz, at first unable to bring down Orlovsky by the neck, pursued him a second time, finally yanking him down, with his fist clutching the back of his jersey. The Indians took over and Ladyczka hit Bednarz with a 40-yard pass play, with Grembowitz saving a touchdown by running Bednarz down at the Boilermaker 20. On the next play, Ladyczka took a handoff from Zabawa on a spinner play and got around the right side. Grembowitz, from his knees, and substitute Ted Kurgan, from behind, combined to jar the ball loose and Tabaka recovered.

The half was nearly expired when Ryback got the ball back for Passaic by recovering a Babula fumble. But Garfield stuffed Zabawa on a spinner play up the middle and with Ladyczka running an end sweep, Young forced him back into Grembowitz' grasp. The half ended with the Indians five yards short of what they used to call pay dirt.

Butts, who had entered the game for Kazaren in the second quarter, lost a fumble on Passaic's 30 after Orlovsky and Babula had done some hard running on Garfield's first possession of the third quarter. But the Boilermakers started their winning drive from their 32 on their next possession following a Ladyczka punt. It came with Argauer having scattered substitutes into his line as Kurgan, Julius Fick. Ed Leskanic and Len Macaluso all played parts.

Babula quickly hit Tabaka with a pass for a first down and, with Grembowitz and Butts laying down defenders ahead of him, gained 16 yards round his end before running into the Passaic cheerleading squad. Switching up his calls, Babula turned into lead blocker for Orlovsky on two straight runs and continued to cross up the Passaic defense with a pass to Butts who lateraled to Tabaka for 12 yards to Passaic's 17. That was enough fooling around. They instead resorted to blunt force and that meant turning the horse loose. Babula dragged four Passaic defenders for 12 yards to the five, then, on the second play of the fourth quarter, he ran an off-tackle smash to his left and followed the blocks of Orlovsky and Macaluso into the end zone. Orlovsky missed the extra point but Passaic was offside, so Babula gave it a try—but missed.

Babula inadvertently gave Passaic another chance when he tried to run with a fake punt and was stopped short of the first down at the Passaic 40. The Indians moved to the Garfield 25 on the strength of Ladyczka's arm, but he threw one pass too many when Tabaka intercepted and returned it 19 yards to the 29. Garfield could have added to its winning total but Orlovsky fumbled as he crossed the goal line. Butts ended the game with another interception of Ladyczka.

When they added up the stats, Babula had run for 193 yards, more than tripling Passaic's total. Garfield totaled 259 rushing yards to Passaic's 59, more than negating Passaic's 119-44 edge in passing yardage. Garfield finished with 15 first downs to Passaic's eight. As well as Passaic fought, it was, in the end, Babula's day and another example of him coming up big in the big games. McMahon and Del Greco agreed.

"He's the Difference," Del Greco wrote in capital letters. "Irvington looked classier than Garfield. Benny brought the Camptown team to its knees. It was Benny who beat Passaic on Saturday. Garfield High's men simply blocked and Babula ran wild. He packs tremendous power. And yet, the opponents know he's raking the ball. They're laying for him but he just can't be had."[19]

"The difference between Passaic and Garfield on Saturday was Benny Babula," McMahon wrote, as well. "It is the same difference that lifts Garfield from the ordinary football class to the first flight in New Jersey schoolboy championship ranks."[20]

The game was a win-win for Garfield, a win on the field and a win at the gate. As the home team, Garfield took in $4,237 in ticket receipts and put out about $230 in incidentals, including $70 for the rental of the stadium, to turn a profit of over $4,000. That windfall made its dispute with East Rutherford, the next opponent, rather ironic.

EAST RUTHERFORD: DAYLIGHT SAVING

The original schedule had the teams meeting under the lights at Passaic Stadium Friday night as they did the previous year. That game drew a big crowd and, as the host team, Garfield took in $2,200 and offered East Rutherford just a $15 guarantee, which the Board of Education upped to $75 after East Rutherford athletic director and coach Jimmy Mahon made a personal plea. Now, it would be East Rutherford's turn to make a box office killing.

But a week before the game, Mahon suddenly received a letter from the Garfield board announcing that night games were henceforth banned and that the game would have to be played on Saturday afternoon. "After giving due consideration to all circumstances and the danger to the health of the players, the above decision was unanimously decided upon," it said.[21]

Mahon and the East Rutherford officials were incredulous, but there was nothing they could do beyond airing their side of the story, which Mahon did by calling McMahon and Del Greco.

"When Art Argauer asked me last year to play our game at night, I told him it was all right with me if I could get the permission of my superiors," Mahon explained. "I got the permission and then asked Art if he would agree to play a night game in 1939 so that we might have a chance for a good gate. He agreed and we played."

Mahon said he double-checked with Argauer several weeks before the season began and was assured that the rematch would be played at night.

"Now, though, I get a letter from the Athletic Council informing me that night games for Garfield are banned because they are injurious to the players," Mahon went on. "Argauer says Garfield couldn't see my kids last year. As a matter of fact, it was just the opposite. Sekanics scored a touchdown (on the opening kickoff) before we could get accustomed to the lights. As it later turned out, that touchdown meant the ball game."[22]

Mahon had a point about what Al Del Greco called Garfield's "trumped-up squawk," although the lights were really quite poor. Garfield barely escaped with a 13-7 victory as East Rutherford controlled the play. A loss would have cost the Boilermakers the state championship. Argauer vowed immediately after the game that he'd never play another night game—Christmas games in Miami eventually excluded, of course. Obviously, this time, he wanted to avoid adding another variable that could affect the outcome.

East Rutherford was a tough enough opponent that always pointed to Garfield as one of the biggest games on its schedule. Paterson Central had trampled the Wildcats in their last game two weeks earlier, after East Rutherford tied rival Rutherford in their season opener, but their record hardly mattered. They historically played the Boilermakers tough.

East Rutherford was the only opponent Garfield had faced every year since the program began in 1922 and Argauer was 5-2-1 against Mahon since he took over in 1930. The 1932 contest, a 6-6 tie, erupted in fisticuffs in the fourth quarter when every man on the field squared off with an opponent as if it were a hockey game. Spectators soon rushed onto the field to join the melee, which carried on for five minutes until Passaic police broke it up. Each school considered cutting off relations with the other, but didn't. Yet, certainly some bad blood remained and now, a little more was split with Garfield's refusal to play at night.

Mahon was riled up. He prepped his team as if it were the biggest game left on the schedule. Which it was. He knew this was a perfect spot to spring an upset. The Boilermakers were coming off two intense, physical games against Irvington and Passaic. They were a little banged up, while East Rutherford, having not played the previous week, was in top shape. Plus, with Irvington and Passaic behind them, everyone was talking about how Garfield had just one big hurdle left—unbeaten Bloomfield, two games down the road.

"Everybody but Art Argauer expects his championship club to draw a breather at East Rutherford," the *Bergen Record* noted.[23] Del Greco, the Garfield alum, and McMahon, the East Rutherford graduate, made their predictions accordingly.

Del Greco:

> *The club which knocks off Garfield will be some sucker outfit, not conceded a chance. East Rutherford isn't a sucker outfit by any means but it has a whale of a chance for that Jimmy Mahon can always steam up a club which plays against Garfield. However, Benny Babula is still with the champs and I look for Garfield to win by a 20 to 7 score.*[24]

McMahon:

*Over in Garfield this is considered a breather for the hard charging Boilermakers.
And indeed, the Wildcat record for the year makes it look like one. On the chance that
East Rutherford will never roll over and play dead for an old rival like Garfield, I'll call it
respectably close. Say 19-6.[25]*

Mahon was telling people to expect an upset as the game, played at Riggin Field in East
Rutherford, neared. As with everyone else, he felt the key to beating Garfield was up-front
and, with the extra week of prep time, he worked in a new wrinkle by shifting his line to
Garfield's strong side, where Babula did his most of his running. Then, Argauer decided to
start backup Bill Librera in Babula's place along with a few other regular backups. It made no
sense. After telling his team not to take the Wildcats lightly, he was doing just that.

Librera was a capable backup who would star as Babula's successor in 1940, but this wasn't
his day. He fumbled when the Boilermakers reached midfield immediately after the opening
kickoff and, after the Boilermakers stopped three East Rutherford rushes, he fumbled
receiving the punt. The Wildcats quickly turned that into a 6-0 lead when Joe Sondey hit Ed
Subda with a two-yard scoring pass after the Boilermakers fell for a fake handoff.

Argauer left his second teamers in for one more offensive series that went nowhere and
East Rutherford was forced to punt one more time. Now Argauer sent Walter Young in off the
bench, and the gangly end came around the corner to block Subda's kick and recover on East
Rutherford's 19. Now Babula went into the game and picked up 17 yards to the two, followed
by a two-yard TD run by Tabaka. Argauer chose to run for the PAT and Babula plunged over
to make it 7-6.

For the second straight week the first half whistle saved the Boilermakers. The home team
was at the Garfield 13 when the half ended. Although the Boilermakers controlled the second
half, limiting East Rutherford to only three possessions, they scored only once, on a 15-yard
pass from Tabaka to Young, who played hero for the second time, then kicked the extra point
to boot. It also came on the play after Babula left the game with an injured leg. Mahon's game
plan didn't stop Babula completely, but it did tie him up. The Wildcat captain, Ed Bode, had
two hard tackles that sent Babula to the sidelines.

Garfield had a chance to add to its lead late but was stopped inside the one-yard line. No
one on its sideline was happy with the 14-6 win. Argauer was probably happy the game hadn't
been played the night before, if this was how things went during the day.

"I'm afraid the boys can't stand prosperity," he said. "Unless they awaken to the fact that
they can be beaten, they will be on the outside looking in when the title is handed out this
year. Of course I'm partly to blame for starting the second team against East Rutherford."

The record stood at 4-0 and the critics began to howl. It was one thing to escape with
narrow wins against state powers like Irvington and Passaic. But East Rutherford? Wrote
McMahon:

*Benny Babula is apparently All State everywhere but East Rutherford. The Wildcats
stopped him cold and just to show that it was no fluke, handcuffed him again Saturday.
East Rutherford's football camp treats the entire Garfield title unit with the same disre-
spect, as a matter of fact.*

The narrowness of Garfield's last three victories makes that November 4 tussle with Bloomfield loom very important in Art Argauer's program. The Bengals are coming on fast. They had to have something to whip Central, 19-0. That same Central team walloped East Rutherford, 34-6, just to give you a hint of its merit.

Still, unlike some, McMahon wasn't predicting doom:

Disregarding all the storm signals, I'm going to stick with Garfield to win the state title. The Boilermakers have what it takes when they are under pressure.[26]

THOMAS JEFFERSON: THE BREATHER

Before the Boilermakers got to their next pressure spot against Bloomfield, they took on Thomas Jefferson of Elizabeth, the team that briefly challenged them for state laurels the year before. The Jeffs, however, were decimated by graduation and their 1939 team was a disaster. Not expecting much competition, Argauer scheduled two scrimmages during the week, the first against Ridgefield Park, the second against Rutherford. Babula, still limping from the injury sustained against East Rutherford, was held out of both. Orlovsky threw out his shoulder making a block against Ridgefield Park and it was feared he was lost for the season. Meanwhile, Otto Durheimer, one of Babula's backups, developed pain in his side and was rushed to the hospital to have his appendix removed. It was a good thing that Elizabeth didn't offer much competition.

The game, played at Williams Field in Elizabeth, was a 26-0 rout. To replace Orlovsky, Grembowitz was moved from the line into the backfield and young Steve Noviczky got his first start at right guard. Alex Yoda, who showed power in the Passaic game, started at left guard instead of Tripoli. Babula, playing on his sore leg, ran for two TDs plus a conversion and passed to Tabaka for another score. Argauer was able to sit down his regulars in the fourth quarter and Red Barrale, who was turning 20 the day of the Bloomfield game and becoming ineligible, was given the chance to direct the team in his final game. He scored the last touchdown on a one-yard run then took off his shoulder pads seemingly for the last time.

The win allowed Argauer just a momentary pause to catch his breath before the epic clash with Bloomfield. With their fifth straight win and sixteenth overall, the Boilermakers moved past the midway point of the season. They were ranked number one in the state in both the Colliton System and by the *Jersey Journal*. With the first rankings now released, the competition for the state title was getting clearer.

Close behind Garfield in the Colliton ratings was undefeated and unscored upon East Orange, followed by Nutley, also undefeated and unscored upon, then Columbia and Bloomfield, both unbeaten. Vineland, the defending South Jersey champ that so wanted a post-season showdown with Garfield in '38, was also unbeaten and unscored upon but the Poultry Clan's schedule was working against them again, and they trailed the five North Jersey schools in points.

Vineland fared better in the *Journal's* ratings, which had it in a three-way first-place tie with Garfield and Nutley with Woodrow Wilson of Camden, yet another unbeaten team, close behind. That began to give Clan supporters hope for at least a title shot with a post-season clash.

The mish-mash would be settled somewhat in the coming week. Of the 10 unbeaten teams among state contenders, six were in action against each other. The Garfield-Bloomfield tussle

Benny Babula dives across the goal line, leaving a sprawled jumble of Thomas Jefferson defenders in his wake. Courtesy Estate of Angelo Miranda.

topped the Saturday slate with Vineland at Atlantic City the top attraction in the southern part of the state. On Tuesday, Election Day, Nutley was visiting East Orange at Ashland Stadium. Paul Horowitz speculated that the winners could be 1-2-3 in the next Colliton ratings.

BLOOMFIELD: GREEN PASTURES

Argauer and his players weren't paying much attention to Nutley or anyone else. Beating Bloomfield seemed a perfect path to repeating as state champs with Asbury Park, Paterson Eastside and Clifton closing out the schedule. And the Bengals were converting plenty of believers.

After Bloomfield's impressive win over Paterson Central, Frank Fagan of the *Newark Star Eagle* warned Garfield that Foley was "waving his magic wand" again.[27] Foley wasn't expecting much from his team before the season, especially after the Bengals were bounced around by powerful East Orange in a scrimmage. He noted his team was "younger and lighter" than any he'd coached in eight years—but he did feel it had a chance to play spoiler against the three opponents with title aspirations—Garfield, Nutley and Irvington.

By Garfield week, the Bengals had exceeded Foley's expectations. While their schedule was less stellar than Garfield's—with only Paterson Central regarded highly—Foley's reputation convinced many neutral observers that he had the makings of another state title team. Garfield, meanwhile, had its doubters, all pointing out the nail-biters the Boilermakers played against Irvington, Passaic and, especially, East Rutherford. Relying on what he heard from "scouts," Herb Kamm, the sports columnist for the *Asbury Park Press,* was the leading voice of critics calling Garfield overrated.

"The Boilermakers are a good club and they've piled up a nice stack of points already under the Colliton system," Kamm penned. "But the report is that Art Argauer's 1939 edition isn't as strong as some of the enthusiastic scribes up that way would have you believe—which may be good news to Asbury Park's gridders, who'll have the pleasure of finding out for themselves in another week come Saturday."

Kamm noted that Thomas Jefferson coach Frank Kirkleski, after his team's 26-0 loss to Garfield the week before, described the Boilermakers as the easiest team his boys had played in five weeks. It was an odd pronouncement, considering Argauer had emptied his bench in the second half and had used 32 players against the Jeffs. But there it was.

"Argauer pits his charges against Bloomfield this Saturday and the word up that way is that the Bengals are loaded for bear, eager to avenge a 19-0 setback they suffered in the clash between the bitter rivals last year. Bloomfield stands a good chance of ending Garfield's victory streak," Kamm surmised.[28]

Argauer had other concerns. There was the matter of Orlovsky's shoulder. He'd been seeing a New York orthopedic specialist who was somewhat optimistic that Orlovsky could play with a brace, but he hadn't given his final approval and Orlovsky hadn't practiced all week. And even if he had been wholly recovered, there was a chance that Librera and end Ed Hintenberger would be unavailable. Both were scheduled to report to Fort Dix the morning of the game for a week-long National Guard camp. Argauer was frantically trying to pull strings, calling "everybody but the President," noted Art McMahon. The coach couldn't figure out how Hintenberger and Librera got themselves committed anyway since each was under the 18-year age limit. "It would be funny if the threat of war kept Garfield from winning a football game," McMahon wrote.[29]

With Orlovksy's status in doubt, Argauer was trying to find a way Red Barrale could play. Barrale was turning 20 on game day, about two-and-a-half hours after kickoff, to be precise. He planned to ask for Foley's permission. Such agreements had been made in previous seasons. In the end, he thought better of it, knowing that other teams might protest Barrale's eligibility, and he didn't want to risk a prospect of forfeit.

It was also raining during the week, which curtailed practice sessions. Both Foley and Argauer claimed the weather as a disadvantage to his team. Argauer complained it was difficult to adjust his lineup for injuries and to install the five new plays he planned to unveil against Bloomfield.

Of course, even without Orlovsky and Barrale, Garfield would still have Babula, but he, too, was preoccupied. He came to practice each day worried about his mother, who was seriously ill. The *Newark Sunday Call* had put together a photo spread of Babula at home with his family, at school with his girlfriend Violet Frankovic and surrounded by adoring Garfield kids. It was to run in the paper's magazine section the day after the game. But that happy tableau was being overshadowed. When Babula left his house the morning of the game, doctors were considering whether Tillie Babula needed surgery. They decided to forgo the operation to ease Babula's mind. Still, he'd go into the biggest game of his young life knowing there was much more at stake than a football game—even if it was *the* football game of the season in New Jersey. As *The Herald-News* put it:

> As far as Garfield and Bloomfield supporters are concerned, the Nutleys, East Oranges, Columbias and the rest of the undefeated Group Four football teams might just as well take a back seat and forget about the state championship. Tomorrow, the Boilermakers

A view of the overflow crowd of 19,000 that jammed Foley Field to witness Garfeld's 18-0 win over Bloomfield. Newark Sunday Call.

and Bengals collide at Foley Field, Bloomfield in the outstanding schoolboy struggle in the state this week, publicized as the state title clash.[30]

Game day morning brought freezing temperatures to North Jersey as fans gulped down coffee and hot chocolate to brace for the contest. By 11:00 a.m., parked cars jammed the streets around Foley Field, and it was soon apparent that the crowd could exceed record proportions. When the *Newark News* reported that extra bleachers had been brought in, the paper said they were "ample enough to supply the crowd," but that was hardly the case.

Officials posted an "S.R.O" sign an hour before kickoff and, 30 minutes later, Bloomfield police closed the gates to all except advance ticket holders. They entered the stadium, passing the shutout, begrudging latecomers. More than a thousand of them, however, managed to secure vantage points from the hill outside the stadium. The entire scene pulsed with humanity and 50 Bloomfield cops circled the field to keep order. Among the throng in the wooden grandstands on Garfield's side of the field were Walter Young's father and mother, at the only football game they would ever attend. They could not believe the fuss their son and his playmates had kicked up. The crowd was estimated at 19,000, not including those outside the stadium. More eyes watched this high school game than any other before in New Jersey.

As usual, there was a lot of betting action between the grandstands. Del Greco had predicted a score of 13-6, Garfield, McMahon, 18-7, Garfield. During the week, bookies were laying odds of 8-to-5 for Garfield backers, 6-to-5 for those taking Bloomfield. With the cockiness afforded by pregame Adrenaline, and the courage provided by hip flasks, each side was settling for even money now.

Bloomfield fans started a taunt: "California, Oregon, Arizona, Texas. We play Garfield just for practice." Meanwhile, Red Simko didn't disappoint. He walked up and down in front of the Garfield stands, tossing lollipops to cheers. As he did, a helmetless Babula warmed up with punts soaring over 70 yards. The Bengals always looked intimidating. Their snappy black jerseys with red trim made them appear larger than they were—and they were large. But all eyes were on the 6-1, 190-pound Babula, who was, as always, larger than life, now appearing even more classically heroic with his curly blonde locks.

A Steve Bognar cartoon in *The Herald-News* during the week had asked, "Can the Bengals stop the Garfield terror?" and "If so . . . can they upset the Boilermakers?" Bognar also asked if Red Simko would be there to cheer on his team? The answer to the last question was yes. The answer to the first question would be no, making the second question irrelevant.

Argauer didn't have to pull strings with the National Guard. As it turned out, they were due to report Sunday, not Saturday. Even so, Orlovsky would not play. His New York doctor had fitted him for a brace. But the shoulder still needed healing and he'd have to rest two more weeks.

At last it was 2:30—game time. Bloomfield's opening kickoff, to a crescendo of cheers, bounced to Wally Tabaka, ace return man, who raced with it 18 yards before he, as he almost never did, fumbled the ball. A huge roar erupted from the Bloomfield side as kicker Bill Greenip threw himself on it at the Garfield 35. Two running plays netted a first down at Garfield's 25 and two more set up third and seven at the 22. Here, the Bengals tried to bait the Boilermakers with a misdirection play. The interference went left while Bob Kerr tried to sneak around the right side. But Young had learned his lesson from the 1937 Bloomfield game, when he had put himself out of position and got an earful about it from his coach. This time, he stayed put and threw Kerr to the ground for a five-yard loss. The Bengals then tried a fourth down pass but turned the ball over on downs.

The Boilermakers couldn't move, so Babula punted down the right sideline. Kerr neatly caught the ball on the dead run and was heading for daylight. Wagnecz, whose job, like a modern gunner, was to get up the right side as swiftly as possible, was caught flat-footed. But, out of desperation, he lunged for Kerr's arm and the ball popped loose. Jack Boyle beat Kerr to the bouncing ball for the recovery. It was a mistake on Kerr's part. He should have been carrying the ball in his outside arm.

For Garfield, it was a second bullet dodged. The third came after a fourth down try from the Boilermaker 48 when Yura's errant snap from center went over Babula's head. But two plays later, Bloomfield returned the gift. Ray Butts, who played a tremendous defensive game behind the line, recovered Francis Vesterman's fumble. The Bengals' offense would not see Garfield's side of the field again although Vesterman would curse his hands one more time when he was unable to hold on to what would have been an interception, juggling the ball and finally dropping it five yards later with an open field in front of him.

For Garfield, the uncharacteristic sloppiness of the first quarter luckily went unpunished. When the teams switched sides, Tabaka got it started with a 15-yard punt return to the Garfield 46. Babula took Yura's snap and followed his blockers around left end, where he slipped two tacklers and stiff-armed a third for 18 yards, his longest carry of the game. Now, Babula drifted to his right and, with his sidearm delivery, whipped a pass to Young, who lateraled to Tabaka for a gain to Bloomfield's 32. Babula got 10 more yards on an off-tackle smash and hit Tabaka with a pass inside the 10.

The Bengals' defense was winded, leaning over at the waist. Still, they ganged up on Babula to stop him for no gain. They would not do it twice. On the next play, the big guy went off left tackle, gave one defender a straight-arm and outran another into the end zone. He was inches short on a plunge for the extra point. The halftime whistle blew with Garfield leading, 6-0. Each team went into the lockers knowing it had a chance, but Bloomfield also knew it has squandered opportunity against a good team. Garfield could feel it was taking over the game as long as it could hold onto the ball.

Little Roy Gerritsen struts his stuff at halftime of the Garfield-Bloomfield game at Foley Field as drum majorette Margaret Hoving leads the way. The Herald-News.

Outside the locker rooms, there was quite a stir. Five-year-old Roy Gerritsen, decked out in a purple band jacket, white hat atop his head, was making his debut as the Garfield High band's tiny drum major. He marched down the middle of the field with his cut-off baton until he reached the 50-yard stripe.

There, he gave the signal for the band to come onto the field. Led by drum majorette Margaret Hoving in her smart outfit and cape, they joined him and played on. The 5-foot-7 Miss Hoving and 3-foot Roy made quite the sight as they twirled away to the music. Gerritsen's parents were a bit apprehensive as their son was about to take the field before 19,000. But he eased their fears. "Mom and Dad, you make me laugh. Why are you so nervous? I'm not," he said.[31]

Neither were the Boilermakers when they emerged from the dressing room. They would score a touchdown in each of the last two periods while completely stifling the Bengals' attack. Babula was inexorable. When Garfield marched 65 yards in the third quarter, Babula carried the ball seven consecutive times for the final 26 yards. Somewhat tired, Babula went to the air during a 60-yard fourth quarter drive, where he ate up 40 yards with two passes to Young. When the drive reached the four-yard line, Babula spread the glory. Tabaka had just let a touchdown pass slip through his fingers and, when his teammates urged Babula to score again, he instead called a play for Tabaka, who went in over left guard.

Babula injured his hip when blocked on the subsequent kickoff and stayed in the game for a few plays to shake it off. When he came off the field with 2:00 left, he received a thunderous ovation, as did Tabaka when he came out. Even the Bloomfield fans appreciated Babula's dominating performance in the 18-0 win.

When they tallied the stats, Babula, on 26 carries, had gained 106 of Garfield's 142 yards rushing and completed nine of 13 passes for 116 yards. Three of his four incompletions were drops and seven of his nine completions went for more than 10 yards, no small feat in those days. Babula also averaged 36 yards on six punts, including one that went for only 10 yards because Grembowitz backed into him. And, on one of Tabaka's punt returns, he laid out three Bengals with one block.

Bloomfield was completely shut down. Young, Noviczky, Yoda, Boyle, Grembowitz and Butts were singled out for their play. The Bengals netted 20 yards rushing after netting minus-13 yards in the second half. They didn't complete a pass in seven attempts. The only things Garfield didn't conquer were the goalposts. Those 50 Bloomfield cops prevented Garfield fans from getting close, unlike 1934 when the two fan bases did battle over them.

In his game story for the *Star-Ledger,* Sid Dorfman wrote: "It was plainly a case of too much Bennie Babula. If there was something Babula failed to do, it went by unnoticed. He was in just about every offensive play Garfield tossed at the bewildered Bengals, running, passing and kicking the Foley brigade dizzy in as great an exhibition as this season will see. It was simply Babula against Bloomfield and the All-State back collected."[32]

But was it that simple? To say that was to ignore the coaching dynamic on display between Art Argauer and Bill Foley, two masterful football strategists. In the end, the game stood out, undoubtedly, as one of Argauer's masterpieces. Argauer not only motivated his team into its finest performance, but also devised a brilliant game plan while cleverly negotiating injuries and uncertainty. For the first seven years of their rivalry, Argauer was the challenger punching above his weight. But in '38 and '39, the roles were reversed. Argauer had the better team. While on top, Foley never played chess with X's and O's. He ran his T-formation, sometimes shifting into a conventional single wing; but you either stopped it or you didn't. Then, before the 1938 game, Foley claimed he found a way to stop Babula. But couldn't.

That's not to minimize Foley's coaching brilliance. His teams were so finely tuned and so filled with "confidence born of demonstrated ability" that opponents were routinely caught up in the gears of the machinery. Argauer always looked for the monkey wrench, whether in his early preparation in 1934 or, as the favorite these last two years, to exploit Bloomfield's weaknesses.

Yes, Argauer had Babula and he was daring Bloomfield to knock him off. The papers wrote about the five new plays he would use, but he never did. As usual, everything worked off the off-tackle smash. But Argauer also tweaked the game plan to include more reliance on the passing game, which seemed to catch Bloomfield off-guard. Defensively, he stopped the Bengals cold by using four different alignments, a 6-3-2, a 5-4-2, a 5-3-2-1 and a 6-2-2-1. On passes, he dropped a lineman into coverage, a modern innovation.

He also went deep into the lineup and mixed things up, partly out of necessity due to Orlovsky's injury, and he continued to do so throughout the season. The right side of the line was totally different than on opening day. Young Steve Noviczky was at right guard, where Grembowitz had been playing, Al Yoda had played himself into a starting job at right tackle

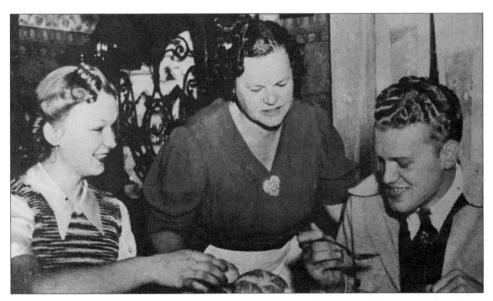

Benny Babula's mom, Tekla, serves him and sister Eva Polish specialties in one of the pictures that ran on the Newark Sunday Call's magazine photo spread. Newark Sunday Call.

and Ed Hintenberger had surpassed Bill Wagnecz at right end. Big Joe Tripoli was also moved back to the second unit with stocky Angelo Miranda changing sides from right to left tackle. Center Pete Yura and left end Walter Young were the only fixtures at their original positions.

When Babula jogged off Foley Field, passing through the phalanx of backslapping Garfield fans, many of them a little richer from his exploits, his thoughts were only of his mom.

The team bus pulled up. Babula was away from the tumult now, but, as he climbed on, Lou Miller of the *New York World-Telegram* was waiting for him.

"Ben, got a minute?" Miller asked, extending his hand.

Babula could not have put on a better show for the New York press, which had crossed the river to check him out personally. But, as Miller noted in a story that ran Tuesday, "scant light heartedness was apparent on the classic Babula features as the big Polish boy boarded the bus for home. Although he had just given one of the finest triple-threat exhibitions of the year, Benny was worried about his mother, who was ill at home."[33]

Babula, not exactly in the mood, was polite but no great interview. He did tell Miller that he might not be playing college football. Miller went on to write that Babula was haunted after every game by "his mother's anxiety." Tillie didn't want to see her boy get hurt and he was thinking of quitting the game after high school to ease her mind. Miller claimed Argauer told him so. An exaggeration? That wasn't beyond a newspaperman's desire to sell papers in the 30s, and it made the story juicier with Benny now more worried about his mother than she had ever been about him. That wasn't exaggerated.

Babula drove home from the high school as quickly as he could. It was euphoria around town as evening fell. He passed cars tooting horns, people out on Palisade Avenue walking almost above the sidewalk. Across the Ackerman Avenue Bridge he went and, when he entered the house on Trimble Avenue, his father greeted him with a huge smile and hearty handshake. All was good: his mother's condition had improved, and there was no need for an operation.

Babula could finally take in all his good fortune in one giant exhale. With his mom on the mend, things could not have been better, and the future much more promising. Babula telephoned Violet then slept well that night. The next morning, his family opened the *Newark Sunday Call* to a full-page photo spread: "Day with Ben Babula, Garfield's All State Quarterback." The captions below the glossy pictures made him blush:

> *Sort of pensive is Bashful Ben on way to school in Garfield; his "queen in calico," is Miss Violet Francovic (sic).*
>
> *Even football stars must study. Here is "Golden Boy" in classroom, absorbed in something or other.*
>
> *Then, for a hearty luncheon at home with his mother, Mrs. Michael Babula, and his sister, Eva.*
>
> *Admiring youngsters listen to Babula's explanation of how the game was won.*
>
> *On gridiron Coach Arthur Argauer points out to his ace player some new wrinkle in practice of Ben's teammates.*
>
> *Ben's on the loose—as hard to stop as a locomotive. Looks like another Garfield score.*[34]

Babula didn't like publicity, but there was no stopping the hero treatment now. It was the business of newspapers in those days. Heroes were needed and, sometimes, created. Babula came ready-wrapped. Even the New York City papers were touting Babula as the best high school player in New Jersey. And the Jersey papers agreed. Frank Fagan of the *Star-Eagle* for instance:

> *Garfield may have other challenges hurled in its direction but so long as Benny "Bingo" Babula is at large the Boilermakers have nothing to fear. It is the opinion in this corner that Garfield, with Babula going Bingo on those chalked lines whenever he desires, will come into its second New Jersey Group 4 championship.*
>
> *Babula is above the average schoolboy football player. He can do most anything on the football field and, with the expert blocking given by his teammates; he probably could make a joke out of any scholastic eleven in the state.*
>
> *Bloomfield today will tell you that Garfield, without Babula, is just another ball team (but) Argauer has a great team, even greater than the one which won the title last year.*[35]

It certainly seemed that way now, with the hardest part of the schedule behind them. Joe Lovas of *The Herald-News* wrote of "green pastures ahead," that "unless the Boilermakers suffer a severe letdown in their remaining games, they are assured of their second straight New Jersey Group Four championship."

Art McMahon concurred:

> *Garfield has only itself to worry about from now until the close of the football season. Asbury Park, Paterson Eastside and Clifton would be deep dish apple pie and ice cream after Irvington, Passaic, East Rutherford and Bloomfield.*[36]

But not everyone was thinking that way, certainly neither East Orange nor Nutley, scheduled to meet on Tuesday in the wake of all the breathless Garfield title chatter. No one could yet say with certainty that Garfield would come out on top of the Colliton rankings if it won its last three games, so both Nutley and East Orange held legitimate state title visions.

Those two Essex County communities were totally different in character. By the turn of the 20th century, East Orange had evolved into a wealthy suburb of Newark, its eastern neighbor. In the 30s, it retained those characteristics of big homes and leafy avenues with a central business district that included glitzy department stores such as B. Altman and the 10-story Hotel Suburban with a well-heeled clientele. Meanwhile, throughout its five neighborhoods, the city's demographics were a diverse mixture that included Jewish, Irish, Italian and other European ethnicities along with a growing black population that was reflected in the football roster. The city and school had made some racial progress since the swimming pool incident of 1933.

Nutley, on the far end of Essex County adjacent to Clifton, also held an equally interesting, albeit different, past. Its brownstone quarry had been a magnet for Italian immigrants, particularly from the province of Avellino. The quarry was abandoned in the late 20s, and a famed bicycle velodrome with seating for 12,000 was built there. When cycling's popularity faded, its boards were converted for midget auto racing, ignoring the safety dangers of so steeply pitched a track. They called it the "Death Bowl." Upon the third fatality of the 1939 racing season, it was closed in August.

By 1939, Italian-Americans who had originally worked in the quarry became firmly entrenched in Nutley. They had worked through earlier prejudices prohibiting them from even walking through some parts of the borough. Now, their sons comprised the vast majority of the high school's football roster. No one, not even the bluest-blooded of Nutleyites, complained.

The contrast of the two towns existed, too, between the two teams' coaches. At age 48, Nutley coach George "Chief" Stanford was one of the longest-tenured coaches in the state. He played on Newark Central's first football team in 1912 and then professionally in California and Nevada. While serving in France near the end of World War I, he received a letter from Dr. F.W. Maroney, the state supervisor of physical education, about the coaching vacancy in Nutley. Although he hadn't attended college, he got the job in 1919 after completing a physical education course. That began a fantastic 23-year coaching career that included four state championships in baseball and three in football. Stanford drilled his teams hard in fundamentals and produced quality teams year after year. His 1922 championship team was led by Frank Kirkleski, the Elizabeth coach.

East Orange coach George Shotwell was just 28. He had been an All American center at University of Pittsburgh, which dominated college football in the early part of the decade. Shotwell had a string-bean body at 159 pounds and at 6-feet, was diminutive for a center, even back then. But he was technically proficient and, in a day when every hike required a long snap, Shotwell had never flubbed a snap his entire career. He also has a very high football intelligence quotient, and was rightly known as a "keen diagnostician of plays" who was unsurpassed in that respect, according to his coach, the legendary Jock Sutherland

"I am perfectly willing to admit that Shotwell is the most remarkable center I have ever seen," Sutherland said in 1934. "If all my centers in the future are more Shotwells, I'll be satisfied."[37]

Shotwell first coached at Hazleton High School in his native Pennsylvania, where he took over a losing team and lost just three games in two seasons. In 1938, East Orange, with no shortage of funds, coaxed Shotwell to New Jersey with a $4,000 offer, a $1,400 raise. East Orange, like Hazleton, was starving for victories when Shotwell arrived. Then he went 8-1-1 in his first season and undefeated his second. A feature article in the *Star-Eagle* ranked him the No. 1 citizen in the city.[38]

Shotwell brought with him Pitt's offense, the "Sutherland Scythe," a variation on the single wing that moved the wingback further off the line of scrimmage. But he used just 10 plays. That's all East Orange needed.

Both coaches met tragic ends. Shotwell, down on his luck, was one of 30 victims in a 1981 fire at a boarding home in Keyport, N.J., that would lead to more stringent state regulations on such facilities. Stanford, the World War I veteran, re-enlisted as a captain in World War II. He died while at home on leave of a heart attack on April Fool's Day, 1943, having taken his leave of absence from Nutley the previous May.

When Stanford met Shotwell in 1939, each had arguably his strongest team ever. While the papers had hyped Garfield-Bloomfield as the game of the year, these two powerhouses were actually more evenly matched. Gus Falzer gushed, "chances are there will be more fighting there than on the West front in the European War."[39]

Nutley, led by Frank Cardinale, the state's leading scorer with 96 points, had been destroying the opposition, 176-0, in total. Their fans were already drawing comparisons with Garfield. One curious fellow reported back to *Nutley Sun* sports editor Walt Maloney from the Garfield-East Rutherford game. Babula, he said, "couldn't carry Frank Cardinale's water bucket."[40]

But after watching Babula romp over Bloomfield, Maloney wrote, "This corner must disagree with those who have been telling us that Garfield's Benny Babula is not a great back. On the basis of his performance in the Bloomfield game, we'd say that Babula is Garfield and without him the Boilermakers would be just another team. Perhaps he's not as spectacular or as fast as Nutley's Frank Cardinale but he's a 190-pound, six-foot back that any coach would like to have."[41]

Cardinale was backed up by the passing arm of halfback Motz Buel, who could also flash speed when running the ball. On defense, Rusty Rusignulo was a 5-4, 150-pound terror. Stanford already called it his best team in 21 years and that included his two unbeaten squads in the late 20s. East Orange had Bob Duffey spearheading its defense at one end and two African American backs running the ball, shifty George Bennett, a 118-pound speedster with dizzying open field moves, a scatback before the term was invented, and Ken Whitney, a strong-legged sophomore. Most, including *East Orange Record* sports columnist John Edmonston, were predicting a Nutley victory.[42] Against their only common opponent, Montclair, Nutley romped, 31-0, while East Orange won, 16-0. But East Orange defeated Nutley, 19-0, the previous year and was judged to have played stronger opposition.

As it turned out, Nutley and East Orange were plenty good, just not good enough to beat each other. A 6-6 tie knocked both teams out of the race for the state title, at least so long as the Colliton System was concerned. By anyone's educated guess, three closing wins would now give Garfield its second straight championship.

Argauer and Babula were both part of the unprecedented weekday crowd of 14,000 at concrete Ashland Stadium in East Orange, just in case the state title would be decided in a showdown with Garfield. "Post-season game?" asked Argauer, sitting directly behind the press box. "You can never tell. That's why I'm taking all these notes."

Nutley was certainly in favor of one.

Stanford told Art McMahon beforehand: "We'd be only too happy to play. Of course, if we should be beaten or even tied, there wouldn't be much of a demand for the game but the possibility has been discussed here and we're for it."[43]

McMahon also spoke to an East Orange High School official whom he didn't name but, staring at the split of possible a $10,000 gate, admitted: "We could use that money."

East Orange controlled the first half and scored. Nutley came back to gain the better of the play in the second and tied the game late in the fourth quarter. East Orange had a bit of fortune on its touchdown. On the previous play, Frank Schettino booted a field goal through the uprights, but the play was nullified when both teams were called for offsides. The groans from East Orange fans turned into cheers when Schettino faked the kick, took the direct snap, and threw for the touchdown to Whitney. Schettino's try for the extra point was blocked.

East Orange did a good job of containing Cardinale, but Buel had more success in the air and a long completion set up a 15-yard TD on the next play. Cardinale drifted back as if to pass, then cut back across the grain and beat the defense to the corner of the end zone. Nutley fans were still roaring when Carl Hagelin got ready to try the game-winning point after touchdown. He'd made 15 straight in practice before the game. But nerves got to him. He yanked the kick way left. It wasn't even close. So, the game ended with an unsatisfactory tie that made no one except Garfield very happy.

Argauer, McMahon said, could throw away his notes. There would be no post-season game. Besides, McMahon said, Argauer, "should be able to beat either Nutley or East Orange without benefit of scouting. Garfield looked two touchdowns better than both without even hiking up its pants."

As for Babula, McMahon wrote: "I don't know what he thought about it but, for one, I was convinced that he is still the best in New Jersey. Nutley's Cardinale and East Orange's Whitney are just gallant also-rans."[44]

ASBURY PARK: A REAL EMERGENCY

The bandwagon was full. Now Argauer just had to steer it home. And Asbury Park, the next opponent, had always been a prickly proposition. The Blue Bishops, after all, were the last team to beat Garfield in 1937. Down in Asbury Park, Herb Kamm, now sufficiently impressed by the Boilermakers after their demolition of Bloomfield, was writing about Garfield in "the throes of a letdown" against the 3-4 Blue Bishops, "likely to take the Bishops just a bit too lightly now that the pressure is off."[45] So while the *Bergen Record* talked about a "breather," Argauer was hyperventilating. He cautioned his team against over-confidence, not that anyone expected the Boilermakers to lay an egg.

McMahon noted that the biggest threat to a great team is from within and that Garfield was impervious to such self-sabotage.

"Part of Garfield's greatness, I think, is in the mental balance of the team," McMahon wrote. "The Boilermakers shoot at every game with grim determination that does not permit ego to ride as a passenger. The squad values the championship too highly to let thoughts of individual glory short circuit the power. Long ago Garfield had that trouble but it profited by its mistakes."[46]

McMahon picked Garfield, 19-6. Del Greco predicted that "a three or four touchdown win would not be a surprise." Garfield fans were equally confident. The Chamber of Commerce bought up and sold 3,000 tickets and set up buses to take fans to Asbury Park. It was going to be a party, which only made Argauer fret more.

"I believe the hardest part of our schedule is up ahead," he said. "There's Asbury Park this Saturday. They've been improving right along and beat a good team in Phillipsburg. They're always in top shape for Garfield. The title is no cinch by any means."[47]

The bus ride to Asbury Park took close to two hours and allowed Argauer plenty of time to revisit bad memories. At last, the bus driver made a left over the railroad tracks and pulled up in front of the sweeping white grandstand. It was an elegant, wave-like structure although the architecture was surely lost on the Boilermakers, who were squarely fixed on the football game. The Jersey shore has a different kind of cold—damper, rawer—and it was that way as the wind whistled through the tall arches of the 12-year-old stadium. Argauer glanced up at the big letters that spelled out Asbury Park Stadium. He didn't need the ocean breeze to give him the chills, just the remembrance of the heart-wrenching loss two years earlier.

"Only in an emergency."

His own words kept pounding inside his head, reminding him of his mistake by the lake. This time, Argauer was already determined not to die by the interception. The harsh conditions only reaffirmed his plans to keep the football on the ground. He had been daring against Bloomfield, and it won the day. But he would turn cautious here, and it almost cost him a loss and much more.

Argauer wasn't the only one who recalled the Boilermakers' last visit. The Bishops remembered how they had hung in there and come out on top. If they could stay close and get a break or two, they could pull off the biggest upset of the year and make their season. They believed it, because they'd done it before. And they were geared up for Babula.

The Bishops, so named because the city was named after Francis Asbury, the first bishop of the Methodist Church in America, had Garfield well scouted and were ready for the off-tackle smash and end sweep. The zeroed in on Babula, just as J. Edgar Hoover would do on a gangster. They pinned pictures of him on the bulletin board and scribbled his name on adhesive tape and affixed it to the blocking sled. And Argauer, no doubt scared off by what happened in 1937, played into their hands. His instructions to Babula might as well have been: "Only in an emergency."

While Asbury Park packed everyone in tight, Babula threw one pass the entire first half. Even after the Boilermakers reached the Bishops' 14-yard line, they stubbornly clung to the ground and lost the ball on downs. It made even less sense considering how Babula had passed Bloomfield silly the previous week when 12 of his 13 passes were on target.

Halfback Jack Netcher, an outstanding sophomore who would be voted the top high school athlete in the state two years later, shocked Garfield with a 53-yard touchdown gallop on the fifth play of the game. He burst through on an off-tackle play and with a nifty cutback, headed toward the sideline with three Boilermakers on his heels. It seemed they had a shot at bringing him down at the 16, but he simply accelerated and scored standing up. With Tony Falco's extra point, and the home team led, 7-0.

Garfield had trailed before, of course, but, this time, it seemed much more of a slog. Asbury Park was much more successful at moving the ball with Netcher and Garfield's defense stopped several drives in its own territory. But the Boilermakers, who hadn't been shut out since the 1937 Bloomfield game, needed to score. The Garfield rooters, making up

Benny Babula finally gets loose in the fourth quarter for a 20-yard gain against Asbury Park. John Grembowitz (33) is out in front of the play, looking for someone to block. Asbury Park's Jules Sagui (39) chases Babula for Asbury Park. Courtesy Estate of Angelo Miranda.

almost half the crowd, kept waiting for something to happen, as it had every game since the start of the 1938 season. They sat with elbows tucked between chins and knees. As the third quarter neared its end, Garfield's 17-game win streak seemed imperiled. That's how bottled up the Bishops had Babula. But great teams share one thing. Art McMahon wrote that the greatest threat to a great team is drawn from within; so too, the greatest strength. Garfield would get the break it needed to feed its opportunism.

The Blue Bishops were driving again at the Garfield 38 when Dick Irons came into the game for the first time. The Asbury Park captain had injured his knee at practice Wednesday and was pleading for coach Red Young to put him in the game. He got his wish, soon to be lamented by Coach Young. As Irons was being tackled on his first carry, his knee was wrenched again and he dropped the football. Garfield had it and Irons had to be carried off the field.

Finally, the Boilermakers got something out of their running game. On the last two plays of the third quarter, Babula hit the middle for 11 yards and Grembowitz got five more to the Asbury Park 46. The first two plays of the fourth quarter could have spelled disaster. Babula fumbled twice, recovering the first before teammate Len Macaluso pounced on the second for a two-yard gain. It was fourth and three. With Asbury Park keyed in on Babula, the snap went to Tabaka on a spinner play and he made the first down with two yards to spare.

The Boilermakers were still shying away from the pass, but at least they were keeping the Bishops honest by giving the ball to someone other than Babula. Now, for only the second time all game, Babula faded back to pass. Somewhat incredibly, he couldn't find an open receiver. But as the Bishops closed in on him for what looked to be a loss, he escaped and made it all the way down to the 16 before being forced out of bounds.

Babula could sense that the Bishops were on the run and he thought of a play call that was as timely as Perrapato's was disastrous back in '37. The Bishops had scouted the Boilermakers well. But they hadn't seen one particular play. Garfield had run it only once before all season.

It was the Naked Reverse.

Orlovsky had gained 11 yards on it against Passaic. If the defense bit hard, it would work for at least 10 yards. Now, with Orlovsky hurt, it was Grembowitz carrying. Sure enough, the Bishops went aggressively at Babula as he headed toward right and Grembowitz was able to turn the left corner. At the 10-yard line, he cut back toward the center of the field and twisted his way to the one-yard stripe. He fell over the goal line as he was being tackled.

Now it was a matter of kicking or running for the tying point. The wind made the choice easy and Babula wasn't going to be stopped this time. He muscled his way through the Bishops' line. It was 7-7.

A tie could have destroyed Garfield's title hopes and everything else with it. And now it looked as though the Boilermakers wouldn't even salvage that. Babula sent the kickoff intentionally out of bounds, and the Blue Bishops took over on their 35. With Netcher sparking the attack again, they picked up three first downs in succession to reach the Garfield 25. But on fourth-and-three an incomplete pass gave the Boilermakers the ball on the 26.

Grembowitz was stopped for no gain. Time was growing short. It was truly an emergency, a do-or-die moment. Babula's second pass of the entire game fell incomplete. Third-and-10. Babula faded back again and Ed Hintenberger worked his way across the middle. The pass clicked for 12 yards and a first down on the Garfield 38. The clock kept running. Babula rolled out slowly, to his right, at least 15 yards behind the line of scrimmage and stood there. He was about to throw the biggest pass of the season. Had Garfield kept grinding out the yardage, there would not have been enough time for a comeback. The Boilermakers needed a big play.

As usual, all eyes were on Babula. But none were on Bill Wagnecz, unsung, unnoticed— and uncovered. He hadn't caught a pass all season, but he was able to work his way wide open down the field. Babula spotted him and let loose with a pass that travelled an impressive 53 yards through the gusty winds. Wagnecz caught it on the run as it fell from the gray sky and made it to the 18 before he was tackled after a 44-yard gain. Babula's interception that led to defeat in '37 would be properly atoned for.

Babula and the offense now hurried down the field. He carried twice for seven yards against the softened-up defense and then . . . those Garfield fans in attendance weren't the only ones following the play with elevated blood pressures and fast-beating hearts. The game was broadcast on WCAP (for Wonder City of Asbury Park) and all of Garfield was tuned into the action as Babula drove their team down the field. But with Garfield on the 11-yard line . . . silence. Wonders ceased. The station cut out.

Thankfully, Babula did not.

As Wagnecz stepped up, so again did Hintenberger, catching another Babula bullet for a first down before being wrestled down at the one. Babula would have four cracks to win the game. The Bishops' linemen dug in, trying to get as much leverage as they could, crouched low to the ground. They stuffed Babula once. Not twice. Babula crashed over and Garfield's players had no energy left to celebrate. Although Babula was stopped on his attempted run for the extra point, it didn't matter. The game ended following the kickoff and four Asbury Park plays. That's how close the Boilermakers came to disaster and how frantic the rally had been to pull it out.

"By a snake's eyelash," McMahon wrote.[48]

Argauer knew how fortunate he had been, how he'd gotten away with one. When the final whistle sounded, he headed straight for Red Young, the Asbury Park coach, and warmly shook his hand.

"We are lucky," he told him. "I hope we never have to play an Asbury Park team like that one again. It's a great ball club you have."[49]

It truly was a great ball club in the making. Two years later, the Blue Bishops would win the state Group Four championship and be considered for the Miami game. As Garfield's 1937 loss here had been for the Boilermakers, this would be part of that 1941 Asbury Park team's foundation.

"If there is such a thing as glory in defeat, Asbury Park High School's gridmen courageously covered themselves with more than enough to overshadow the glory which went to Garfield's indomitable eleven Saturday," Kamm wrote.[50]

Indomitable, yes. That was the perfect way to describe the Boilermakers who, behind the force of Babula's will, exemplified Al Davis' "Just Win, Baby" mentality years before he dreamed it up. Indisputable, no. With two weeks remaining in the regular season, Garfield could take nothing for granted. Wrote McMahon:

> Garfield is now at that unhappy stage where danger lurks around every corner. It's a tribute when teams start pointing for you but it is tough on the nerves and fingernails. Good thing the season has only two weeks to run or half the citizens would be cutting out paper dolls for relaxation.[51]

The state title race was all the more clear now. With Nutley and East Orange having played to a tie, there were just four unbeaten and untied Group Four schools left, with Vineland, Columbia and Woodrow Wilson of Camden joining Garfield. Columbia had barely survived its toughest test of the season, 2-0, over New Brunswick and was playing East Orange for the championship of the Oranges Saturday. Woodrow Wilson played such a weak Colliton points schedule that it didn't merit discussion, but Vineland, which so badly wanted to challenge Garfield in a post-season state championship game in 1938, was having an even stronger season this year.

Vineland High School, situated about 40 miles southeast of Philadelphia, had been playing football since 1894 and was a powerhouse throughout the 1930s, especially after Nello Dallolio took over from his old coach Edwin Lowden, in 1935. Born in Bologna, Italy, Dallolio was considered the finest defensive end ever to play for Vineland and he bestowed that prowess to his teams.

"The man lived and ate football," Tony DiTomo, the signal caller on that '39 team once said. "He would even diagram plays during class."

"He made ballplayers out of people," said another former player, Jay Luisi. "He was hard on you but you were better for it."[52]

Like Dallolio, many of his players could trace their heritage to Italy. Charles K. Landis founded the town as a planned utopian farming colony in 1861, hence Vineland, and would later determine that the soil was suitable for growing grapes. In an effort to attract experienced Italian grape growers, he started an Italian language newspaper and advertised an offer of 20 acres of land, provided it be cleared and used for vineyards. Not wine. Landis insisted that Vineland be dry. But local resident Thomas Bramwell Welch perfected the process of pasteurizing grape juice that prevented fermentation from occurring and alcohol-free Welch's Grape Juice was born.

By the turn of the century, most of Vineland, and eventually up to 90 percent, was involved in the poultry industry, hence the most fantastic of nicknames, the Poultry Clan. Dr. Arthur Goldhaf, a local veterinarian, changed the industry when he developed a revolutionary small pox chicken vaccine and in 1931, the largest egg auction in the country opened in Vineland.

All these farmers' boys made awfully good football players. Led by the dynamic backfield of DiTomo and Joe Chielli, the '39 Vineland squad stormed to victories in its first seven games without allowing a single point, including its latest 42-0 romp over Bridgeton. The Poultry Clan, as it was last year, was clucking for recognition from the northern part of the state and not getting it.

Carlo Sardella, sports columnist for the *Vineland Evening Times* was among the most passionate of the screamers. He reported that a Vineland scout by the name of Joseph Z. Poke took in the Garfield-Asbury Park game and that Garfield was "lucky." He told Sardella that Garfield would score two touchdowns against Vineland but that Vineland would score four.[53]

The prospect of a Garfield-Vineland post-season showdown was first proposed in the papers a week earlier after Garfield beat Bloomfield and Nutley tied East Orange. *New Brunswick Home News* sports editor Gene Pinter said the sectional showdown would be "a natural" and suggested new Rutgers Stadium as the perfect site. Paul Horowitz of the *Newark Evening News* said simply, "the time has come."

It was hoped that a big Vineland victory against New Brunswick that week would create more momentum for a Garfield clash. In advance of that, Vineland athletic director Jack Pennino[54] on Wednesday sent Art Argauer a telegram asking if his Board of Education would sanction a post-season contest between the teams. He also wired Columbia coach Phil Marvel with a similar request but was shot down. Columbia's claim, however, had lost some luster when it barely beat New Brunswick, 2-0, scoring its safety when a New Brunswick player intercepted a pass and back into his end zone.

Argauer was hiding his cards. He had been dead-set against playing Vineland in a post-season game the previous year, since Garfield had such a large lead in Colliton points, and it seemed he would be using the same logic again.

"I don't want to commit myself," he told *The Herald-News*. "However, if Garfield is rated far above Vineland in the Colliton System (and it was at that point) and we're picked as champions, I can't see why we would need to engage in a post-season game."[55]

Still, he left the door slightly ajar by noting that the players had voted not to accept an invitation to play Robert E. Lee in Jacksonville, Florida, the year before and maybe they would feel differently this year, especially if the game were played against another New Jersey team.

"Of course, if the game is arranged, it will be played either at the Passaic School Stadium or Foley Field. I wouldn't consider any other field," he said.[56]

He also told Frank Fagan of the *Star-Eagle*: "Of course we would like to play a post-season game but wait until we have completed the season. We have two hard games coming, one with Paterson Eastside and another with Clifton. Both are apt to cause us plenty of trouble."

The reason for Argauer's caginess was hidden in a short *Associated Press* story that ran in *The Herald-News*, right next to the one on the Vineland telegram. Headlined "Miami Starlet

Bowl Tilt for High Schools", it announced that a national high school football championship was set for Christmas Day and that a committee would select the teams from across the country.

Argauer was sitting as coyly as could be in the catbird's seat. Everything was going to plan. Back in Garfield, the pride in the Boilermakers was spreading. Mayor John Gabriel announced a plan to raise $20,000 to build the team a home football stadium.

"A few years back when people spoke of Garfield they thought of crime headlines, today that think of football champs," he boasted.[57]

EASTSIDE: THE PERFECT GAME

For now, the Boilermakers were hosting Eastside at Passaic Stadium. The Ghosts were coming into the game with a 4-2-1 record, better than Asbury Park's, and they were using last week's result to convince themselves they had a chance of an upset. Indeed, Art Argauer was complaining that his team was "its own worst enemy" and, in 1938, they had to come from behind to beat Eastside, despite being heavily favored.

Eastside, however, was playing its crosstown rival, Paterson Central, five days after this game, and coach Dave Ross was having a hard time keeping his players' minds on Garfield. It was even suggested in the Paterson papers that he rest his starters against Garfield to keep them healthy, but Ross announced he would field the same starting lineup that took the field in a 7-6 win over Clifton the previous week. For once, however, the opposing team wasn't pointing to Garfield week as the biggest of the season. Eastside wasn't pinning Babula's picture to the bulletin board. They were already thinking about hitting Central's Ray Stanczak.[58]

For two years, Argauer wanted to see the game where everything clicked for an entire game. The perfect psychological conditions—including the motivation of a state title and the memory of the escape from Asbury Park—would surround this game and it didn't take long for them to prove a potent force in front of the 6,000 at Passaic Stadium.

Frank Fournier kicked off for Eastside and Babula corralled it at his 20. He headed straight for the right sideline and continued, untouched by anyone in blue and orange, until he scored the first touchdown in a 48-6 romp. Three minutes later, he bulled his way in from two yards out after completing 50 yards worth of passes on the TD drive. On the day, Babula would score four TDs and throw for another in just two quarters' worth of duty. He capped off his day when he stepped in front of Al Kachadurian's pass and sprinted 90 yards for the TD. Again, he had a clear field ahead of him, meaning he ran a total of 170 yards for two scores without being touched.

But Babula wasn't alone. Wally Tabaka had a great day running the football and on defense, while Ed Hintenberger made a spectacular TD catch when he took Babula's coffin-corner pass away from two Eastside defenders and scored after juggling the ball and holding onto it in the end zone. Garfield didn't miss a step when Argauer played his second team in the entire second and most of the third periods. Librera was sensational with a 25-yard TD strike to Ed Leskanic and, after Babula exited late in the fourth period, a 17-yard TD pass to Al Kazaren with Kazaren making a diving catch. There was more good news with the return of John Orlovsky for the first time since he had hurt his shoulder. He caught two passes and kicked two extra points. Babula was good on the other four. In all, Garfield gained 362 yards, 197 through the air. Ross waved the white towel and took his first team out of the game after it was 28-0.

When the newspapermen rushed down from the press box, they found Argauer in a decidedly upbeat mood. Beaming for once, he told them his team had played "perfect" football.

"Babula, Tabaka, Librera, Butts and Grembowitz turned in sparkling exhibitions while Leskanic, Hintenberger and Kazaren made spectacular catches of passes for touchdowns. It was the first time since the opener that I could sit back and relax," he said.[59]

Then he handed the writers the real story of the day. He was seeking an invitation to the Christmas game in Miami, "providing the arrangements are satisfactory," and had already put outside influences into action, namely Mayor John Gabriel, who in turn enlisted Governor Harry Moore.

"The way we played against Eastside today is the way I know they could play all season," he said. "This team is only just hitting its peak. I'd like to get an invitation to Miami for the boys. I think they deserve it and I also think we can make a good showing against any team in the country."[60]

There were, of course, teams in New Jersey who still thought they could make a very good showing against Garfield. Nutley was feeling chipper again after blasting Bloomfield, 32-0, behind Cardinale's four touchdowns. It equaled Bill Foley's worst loss ever. East Orange, meanwhile, did Garfield a favor while bolstering its own credentials again with a win over the previously unbeaten Columbia Gems.

Then there was Vineland, still clamoring for a post-season shot at Garfield as two of the three unbeaten and untied Group Four schools left. As Vineland fans held big signs during the New Brunswick game demanding to know why Garfield was afraid to play their team, the Poultry Clan held on for a 14-9 win, losing its unscored-upon status. The Zebras, historically one of the top programs in New Jersey, were having an off year and were beset with injuries. Nevertheless, if critics were giving Garfield credit for some of its narrow victories, Vineland deserved the benefit of the doubt in this one. Paul Horowitz took in the game at Vineland's Gittone Stadium and came away impressed by the Poultry Clan as a sure-fire title contender.

"Offensively, Vineland is every bit as good as Garfield. They have a 200-pound guard and a set of fast running backs. Garfield would win but it wouldn't be pushover," he predicted.[61]

Meanwhile, Willie Klein of the *Newark Star-Ledger* speculated that, if Garfield and Vineland did meet in the post-season, it would not be for the mythical state title. He thought it still possible that East Orange or Nutley could top the Colliton rankings.

With one game left in its season, Vineland knew it would ultimately be buried in those rankings as the latest figures were released two days before the traditional Thanksgiving Day finales. Garfield led with 680 points, East Orange was next with 618 and Passaic, beaten only by Garfield, was third with 606. Then came Nutley at 600. Vineland, incredibly, was seventh with 520 points, behind Columbia and Newark West Side. Vineland would complete its first unbeaten season since 1930 with a 39-0 rout of its longtime Turkey Day rival, Millville. Sports columnist Carlo Sardella would lament in the *Vineland Evening Times* how the big win against 2-7 Millville actually worked against the Clan.

> *The Red and Gray football warriors were progressing forward rapidly against Millville High School yesterday but were stumbling backward in a hurry as far as J.W. Colliton is concerned.*
>
> *Vineland went nowhere in a hurry after plastering Atlantic City. The triumph over the Blue and White elevated the Red and Gray into fifth place in Colliton's list among all teams*

of the state. Then Vineland beat Bridgeton and dropped down to sixth. Then Vineland had a whale of an afternoon in beating New Brunswick—and slipped to seventh. Now that Vineland beat Millville—quick, Henry, the Flit.

Post-season? Dunno yet. Art Argauer, Garfield coach is supposed to let Vineland know Monday—after his team plays Clifton High. For the sake of anyone interested in seeing that game it's to be played at Passaic. Coach Nello said today, "With a couple of days rest, I believe my team will be ready to show Garfield a trick or two."[62]

Coach Nello Dallolio would witness Garfield for himself, when the Boilermakers closed out the regular season. He said it was purely a scouting mission just in case the game came about. He wasn't driving up with a personal appeal to Argauer. But he was so itching to play the Boilermakers. The day before, he ranted to Sardella over Paul Horowitz' assertion that Garfield was a better team than Vineland.

"Just look at the records!" Dallolio bellowed, collecting his thoughts but not his temper.

"Look at the records. And tell me that Garfield is a better defensive team. I don't make it a policy to really express myself about my team but this time I'm going to. The 1939 team was the result of three years of patient building, during which we kept right on winning titles and football games and I believe it was the best in the state—bar none."[63]

He might as well have challenged Argauer to a pistol duel. Even though Argauer wouldn't give his official word until Monday, it was already looking like Miami or nothing.

"The boys would like to play in Florida and I hope we receive the bid," he told *The Herald-News* smugly. "If we don't, I doubt whether we will play a New Jersey school in a post-season game. The Colliton System places us far ahead of Vineland."[64]

CLIFTON: NOT SO-GRAND FINALE

Argauer and his team were preparing as if the Clifton game would mark the end of the season. The players presented their coach with a briefcase before the game. He invited the fathers of all his senior players to watch the game from the Passaic Stadium sidelines, and a *Herald-News* photographer was in the post-game locker room to capture Babula's "Farewell to Garfield Football" with pictures of Benny shaking hands with his father, posing with Argauer and his fellow seniors and taking his shoulder pads off for the last time.

The game turned out to be an anticlimactic end of the regular season. It was a cold, bleak afternoon and, while Clifton (winless in two years) was a game opponent, Garfield played rather uninspired football. Benny's mom, well enough to attend the game, saw her son play for the first time and was so nervous that she left the game in the third quarter and never wanted to see him play again. He scored 20 points against his actual hometown team, but Art McMahon noted he was "off stride" in his closing performance. Nello Dallolio could not have been impressed.

"He scored three Garfield touchdowns but his passing was nothing to tell the visiting firemen about. However, if Michigan's (Tom) Harmon and Iowa's (Nile) Kinnick have their sour days, Babula is entitled to one, too," McMahon wrote.

There was nothing left for Garfield to do but wait for Professor Colliton to do the math, address Vineland's challenge and await for word from Miami."[65]

The day before the Clifton game, Vineland athletic director Jack Pennino sent a telegram to Argauer requesting a visit to Garfield with other school officials on Monday to discuss the game. Argauer wired back that Garfield school officials would defer action on a post-season game until after the final Colliton ratings were released.

He then sent a four-word telegram to Pennino, "DO NOT COME MONDAY."[66]

Pennino angrily slammed down the paper. He immediately phoned Colliton who told him it was "almost certain" that Garfield would be ranked first. Pennino also claimed that Colliton told him that Vineland was the best team in the state but that its inability to schedule games against stronger North Jersey teams worked against it.

Pennino later phoned Argauer to demand an immediate answer on whether the game would be considered. Argauer agreed to "put the matter squarely up to the boys," adding that they were excited over the prospects of a Miami game. Dick McCann, secretary of the National Sports Council, had told him Friday that the Boilermakers were among the final eight teams under consideration. Argauer said he was told his chances were "excellent."

"We could play within a few weeks," Pennino countered.

Argauer hesitated.

"Our boys don't seem to favor a game with your team," he replied.

Pennino hung up the phone.[67]

Meanwhile, Argauer was telling people that the Garfield Board of Education had conducted a poll on Friday night that the team should "rest on its laurels."

Paul Horowitz told Pennino that Argauer was "pussy-footing around" and that he didn't want to play Vineland because it would hurt Garfield's chances to get the Miami bid.

Vineland, naturally, was bitterly frustrated. It felt that the system was working against it to prevent it from winning a championship on the field. Indeed, Dallolio had returned from the Garfield-Clifton game confident the Poultry Clan would beat the Boilermakers if they played.

Sardella summed up the view from Vineland in a column:

> Mebbe it's an old Chinese proverb, but someone once said, "No matter how thick your butcher slices it, it's always baloney."
>
> Arthur Argauer, coach of the undefeated, untied and so-powerful-are-we Garfield eleven, tells Jack Pennino, "We'll wait for the Colliton system."
>
> He informs a Newark sports writer, "We're considering the Starlet Bowl" and tells another sports scribbler, "My boys believe they have enough football." (But he said that before the Starlet Bowl bid came through.)
>
> When the good citizens of Garfield toss a banquet this year for their team, they should extend a cordial invitation to J. Whitney Colliton and confer upon him a varsity 'G.' He was just as important to Garfield's prestige as Benny Babula or Mr. Argauer . . .
>
> Vineland fans, you may just as well reconcile yourselves to the fact that Vineland will never reach a No. 1 rating in the state—unless the Red and Gray schedules Garfield, Rutgers, Penn, Villanova and Notre Dame together with Collingwood, Camden and Atlantic City as "breathers."
>
> All boiled down, here's the answer. Garfield is afraid of Vineland. There's no doubt about it . . . if (Argauer) thought he could lick Vineland he would go along with the post-season plans.[68]

It had nothing to do with fear, just ambivalence. Argauer's survey of his players' attitude

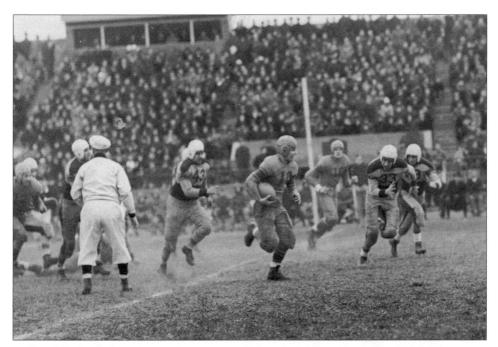

Wally Tabaka breaks loose for a good gain against Clifton. Garfield played uninspired football but won the game to complete an undefeated regular season. Courtesy Estate of Angelo Miranda.

toward a Vineland game was predictable. A Garfield football player didn't know Vineland. He knew Bloomfield and Nutley and East Orange. A team from South Jersey wants to challenge us? So far behind us in points? No need to drag ourselves onto the field in freezing weather and mud to prove a point that was already made. Tropical Miami? That was a different story. Otherwise, it was basketball season.

The next day, November 28, the NJSIAA held a preliminary meeting and made an interesting announcement that revived Vineland's hopes. The NJSIAA, which only named sectional champs, would withhold the final Colliton points standings. Garfield, as North Group Four champ, and Vineland, as South Group Four champ, would be equivalent. It was actually meant to throw cold water on the Garfield-Vineland debate but it turned out to be a futile attempt to avoid unfavorable comparisons. A few days later, Walter Short reversed the decision. Only a few teams hadn't finished their seasons. Nutley, for instance, had one more game left against Hillside. The current rankings before those games were already out and wouldn't change that much. No use trying to hide them. The papers wouldn't buy it. Even Sardella wrote it would have been locking the barn after the horse got out.

"We had thought that by keeping the point standings secret we would be acting fairly to every team in the state," Short explained. "Vineland, for instance, plays teams which cannot give it as many points as do Northern teams. Vineland may or may not be as good as the best in North Jersey. We see now there is no reason for keeping secret something everyone already knows. It would have only created bad feelings against us by the North Jersey teams."[69]

The association would release the final Colliton figures when it named champions at its regular meeting the following Monday night, December 4. Until then, the debates continued and not just in Vineland. Nutley wasn't happy, either. The Colliton system, Coach Stanford said, "does not do us justice." The Maroon Raiders were a Group Three school (enrollment under 600) and, with the exception of one game, which played a complete Group Four schedule. They could end the season unbeaten as the best Group Three school in the state and not be recognized. Of course, Coach Stanford would have been thrilled if his team were ranked above all the Group Four schools, but that obviously wasn't going to happen.

"I would not have any headaches as a coach if I was able to book enough Group Three teams to qualify Nutley for the Group Three title," he told Anthony Marenghi of the *Star-Eagle*. "It would be easier on all of us. Why, I would not even have to watch the team on Saturdays. I could scout the opponent for the following week. But what happens? Group Three schools will not play us and we have to go into the next class."

Stanford rattled off Nutley's results, noting that his team had scored in every quarter up until the East Orange game. Then he began comparing Nutley's record to Garfield's.

"Nutley beat Bloomfield by 32 to 0 and, by the way, when did any team beat the Bengals by 32 to 0? Garfield defeated Bloomfield by 18 to 0. We whipped Clifton, 41 to 0, and Garfield beat Clifton by 21 to 6 and that was after they lost six straight games.

"Now take Irvington," he went on. "Garfield practically fought a tie with Irvington. They each scored two touchdowns but Irvington lost on the two kicks for points so the score was 14 to 12. Kearny beat Irvington by 13 to 7 and we defeated Kearny by 17 to 0."

Stanford said he would welcome a post-season game, "with Garfield anytime. We certainly would consider an extra game to decide the title."[70]

Stanford would get his extra game, but not with Garfield. First, they had to beat Hillside, the only Group Three school on their schedule. They barely did when Carl Hagelin—the kid who missed what would have been the winning extra point against East Orange—booted the winning field goal in the mud late in the fourth quarter. Still unbeaten, they were invited to Florida Field in Gainesville to play Suwannee High School of Live Oak, FL on December 15. It came on December 6; two days after state champs were officially announced.

Del Greco had reported that Mayor John Gabriel was trying to convince Argauer to play Nutley in a charity game that would raise money for the new stadium project. Passaic, meanwhile, wanted a rematch. Players chanted, "Bring on Garfield" after the Indians defeated Rutherford in their annual Thanksgiving Day game. "We'd beat them if we played them again," McMahon quoted one Passaic player as saying. "They were lucky. We're hot now. We're just beginning to hit our stride." Passaic was even willing to forfeit some of its profits by offering the Boilermakers a $7,000 guarantee.[71] Del Greco further reported a plan where Garfield would play Lawrence, Long Island, with the winner to play in Miami.

Then there was Ridgefield Park, the other undefeated team besides Garfield in Bergen County but a Group Three school. Coach Carl Biggs declared his team wanted its shot at Garfield and a Bogota businessman was willing to put up a cup to go to the winner. The supporters of the 11-0 Park team were sore that Garfield was unanimously awarded the county championship trophy given annually by Congressman J. Parnell Thomas. They wrote a letter to Al Del Greco.

Dear Al: It had been brought to our attention through the medium of your paper that the Thomas Trophy awarded by J. Parnell Thomas has bestowed upon the football team of Garfield High School, your glorious and worthy Alma Mater. This said trophy signifies that Garfield has the best football team in the County of Bergen. Now, there are those of us who very strenuously object to this choice which was made, we understand, by a group of reporters who, judging by their selection, have never played football and, we might be rash enough to say, have never seen either of the two teams which were considered, in action.

In short, we undersigned think we could give Garfield the beating of its existence. Don't misunderstand. It isn't that we think Garfield hasn't a good team; it is just that our team is a hell of a lot better. We will meet them any time, any place and under any conditions they name.

Try picking a score for Garfield versus Ridgefield Park the way you make your other predictions, by comparative scores. Garfield beat East Rutherford by one touchdown; Lyndhurst beat East Rutherford by one point or one touchdown; we beat Lyndhurst by five touchdowns. And you still have the nerve to unanimously vote Garfield County champs? Do you see why we object?

If we should happen to lose to Garfield, we'll be the first ones to admit it. But 'til then we'll be the last to admit their superiority.

The letter was signed by twelve distinguished citizens of Ridgefield Park, followed by a P.S.

Don't try the argument that Babula didn't play in the East Rutherford game. We're talking about teams, not one-man teams. The Boilermakers, heh. They couldn't open a can of sardines with a pick axe.[72]

Of course, the undersigned forgot that Garfield dominated Ridgefield Park in the scrimmage where Orlovsky was hurt and Babula was sidelined. As Del Greco replied in his column, "Argauer would no more dream of playing Ridgefield Park than jumping off the Brooklyn Bridge." The Bogota businessman said he was giving his cup to the Parkers because Garfield refused to play them.[73]

Everyone wanted a piece of the Boilermakers. The Boilermakers wanted only a piece of Miami.

The Poultry Clan continued to cluck. They realized there would be no showdown with Garfield, but it wanted to play somebody, anybody. There was a rumor Vineland would play Admiral Farragut, the state prep champion. Then Vineland asked Hazleton, Pennsylvania, for a game. Hazleton said no. And, in one last hopeful gasp, the *Vineland Evening Times* claimed it was in the running for the Miami game.[74]

The paper had sent a letter to Grantland Rice, chairman of the National Sports Council, urging the selection committee to give Vineland consideration. It published a return letter from Richard McCann, NSC secretary:

"I have been instructed to inform you that the Florida State Sports Committee, which is handling the selection of the two teams . . . is giving Vineland's undefeated high school football team serious consideration. I will keep you posted on developments."

Sardella crowed in an adjacent column: "It would be a real twist of fate if Vineland, ignored by Garfield for a post-season game because Garfield was looking ahead to the Starlet Bowl, receives the invitation. Hunch: Then Garfield would accept Vineland's challenge."[75]

That was Monday. McCann had not kept the *Evening Times* posted because, on the same day, New York City's Seward Park High School was awarded the Miami bid. It was also one of two blows Garfield received before the NJSIAA officially raised Boilermaker arms in triumph that night. The *Jersey Journal*, using its own points system, which it claimed as superior, gave its trophy to East Orange, based on what it considered to be a stronger schedule. East Orange, as Nutley, would walk away with something from the season. Not Vineland. It tied for second with Garfield, small consolation to the Poultry Clan; but at least someone thought the teams were comparable.

The *Journal* had been using its system, a Dickinson modification, since 1928 and claimed that, in 11 years, there were 41 post-season matchups between New Jersey teams and that in all but one of those match-ups, the team rated higher by the Jersey City newspaper won. As with the Colliton, the system was based on comparative schedule strength but made no distinction between teams from different parts of the state—or even Vineland's two Philadelphia opponents. A team with an 8-1 record was a team with an 8-1 record. So, a win over Atlantic City was worth 100 points to Vineland, just as a win over Passaic was to Garfield. Garfield's Irvington win was worth 90 points, even though Irvington was superior to Atlantic City.

The *Journal* mocked the NJSIAA awards as "crystal ball selections" based on "absurd tabulations." The problem was that, in general, northern New Jersey teams were stronger, and the Colliton System took that into consideration. Vineland was the exception to that. It was the only southern team with a Class A Colliton rating. But Vineland was one apple placed aside a basket of oranges.[76]

Losing the *Journal* trophy after holding it in 1938 didn't mean as much to Argauer, so long as Garfield was recognized by the NJSIAA and accorded the mythical state title via the Colliton system. However, he did attend the meeting at the *Newark Evening News* auditorium with trepidation. The final tally had Garfield leading East Orange by 21 points, 649 to 628. According to a rule the NJSIAA established the previous year, teams falling within a three percent difference in points would be declared tied. Argauer was nervous that Garfield and East Orange would be declared co-champs of Group Four North Section. In the end, the NJSIAA committee gave Garfield sole ownership of the title, since East Orange had the Nutley tie on its record. Meanwhile, despite that tie, Nutley was fourth with 618 points.

Looking back, Garfield's razor-thin win in the Colliton System tally revealed just how a confluence of fortunate events had nudged fate toward Garfield's favor. Just think how, had Nutley's Cardinale not scored that late touchdown to tie East Orange, East Orange would have nosed out Garfield in points. Or, how, had Hagelin made that extra point to give Nutley a win, the Maroon Raiders would still have fallen short of Garfield. East Orange, though, had no desire to play Garfield to decide things.

The Poultry Clan, meanwhile, was still in a "fowl" mood. Vineland, with 67 fewer points than Garfield, finished sixth behind Newark West Side in the statewide Colliton standings. Even Colliton admitted it was an obvious injustice, but an unavoidable one, given Vineland's schedule. Starting the season with two Philly teams that weren't even in the system didn't help at all either.

"I agree that the geographical location of Vineland makes it impractical to schedule teams of higher ranking but it is not the fault of the system," Colliton explained. "No system can tell the comparative strength of such teams as Vineland and Garfield since they do not actually play each other, nor do they meet common opponents by which one might judge their mathematical ratio. My system tells only how strong a team is in respect to the opposition it has met."[77]

After the Seward Park bid seemingly ended Garfield's Miami dreams, Vineland took one more stab at a game. The answer was still no. To this day, however, Vineland considers itself 1939 "state" champs and lists that team among its best ever on a long list of great teams.

Accolades came to Garfield two nights later, when the team was back at Donohue's for its awards banquet, where the menu featured, fortellingly perhaps, a Florida fruit cup followed by cream of chicken a la Reine and roast Vermont turkey. The 700 guests and their cars jammed the Route 23 circle to a standstill. Some sat in the barroom with the main banquet room already packed. A band played, "Hail, Hail, the Gang's All Here" as the team strode in. Every opponent's coach attended, including Bill Foley and Ray Pickett. Every newspaper sent a representative.

The Garfield Fire Department presented the team with a shiny $400 water wagon, painted in Garfield colors, to be wheeled onto the field during timeouts. It was fitted with multiple spigots so players could drink simultaneously. Only five colleges in the country had such a contraption, the fire chief boasted. The team presented Coach Argauer with a watch and listened to speeches from Washington and Lee coach Warren Tilson, Fordham coach Jimmy Crowley and NYU coach Mal Stevens.

Letty Barbour, Garfield's teenage songstress, performed two numbers. Then Argauer addressed the parents: "I am grateful for your confidence and for having the honor and pleasure of association with your sons. The boys are champions because they are unselfish, cooperative, loyal, have team spirit and the determination to play their best under all circumstances."[78]

The Boilermakers had made it through the season with their twentieth straight win and had emerged from a barrage of obstacles with a state championship. There was a feeling of satisfaction that night. Uniforms had been put away for next season.

Or, were they?

SEVENTEEN

THE CHOICE

The ballroom in the state-of-the-art Hotel New Yorker, around the corner from Pennsylvania Station, brimmed with over 125 dignitaries, luminaries . . . and sports writers (even then, they could never pass up a free meal). It was the week before Thanksgiving in 1939, and the assembled were about to tune up their digestive tracts by taking knife and fork to some rubbery Chicken Cordon Bleu.

As they passed the celery stalks and radishes at the dais, master of ceremonies Bob Considine, syndicated columnist for the *New York Mirror*, introduced the already legendary Grantland Rice. As chairman of the National Sports Council, he would announce, in his soft but husky southern drawl, what had been agreed upon three weeks earlier in Miami: that the Orange Bowl would host the great kickoff to President Franklin D. Roosevelt's 1940 national infantile paralysis prevention drive. On Christmas night, the first annual "Starlet Bowl" would be played for the "mythical" national championship of high school football, with the expected proceeds of $60,000 dedicated to the war on polio.

"The fight against this dread sickness is the sports world's fight," Rice stated from the podium. "This year infantile paralysis struck right in our own ranks. We must do our share in stamping it out."[1]

It was an ambitious objective. The National Sports Council raised $1,000 in its first year of existence, 1938, and in 1939, boosted that total to $100,000.

"This year, with a game like the high school championship in the Orange Bowl to start it off, the men and women who are of sound limb and body might well raise the sizable fortune which the researchers need to lick the confounded bug," Considine said.[2]

"In Chicago, they raised more than $9,000 last year in pennies, nickels and dimes," added speaker Herbert J. Lorber, who directed the Second City's infantile paralysis campaign. "Surely we can afford to match their pennies with dollars to fight this great public enemy. Nobody knows where he lurks or how he attacks. Money is needed in great sums not only to combat the disease but for research work. It is fitting at this Christmas time we should not forget the Tiny Tims who need help."[3]

The summer of '39 had already brought the plight of polio victims to the sports pages when Lou Gehrig was diagnosed with amyotrophic lateral sclerosis, reported incorrectly as a form of infantile paralysis. Physicians told Gehrig's wife Eleanor that his condition was terminal but she instructed the doctors to keep that news from her husband. Lou was told, instead, that his chronic "infantile paralysis" had a 50 percent cure rate. In July, when Gehrig gave his "Luckiest Man" speech at his Yankee Stadium retirement, the public thought he still had a fighting chance. It knew little about ALS, the withering disease to which the slugger would give his name.

Then, in October, two members of the Loyola University football contracted the polio virus. Officials cancelled the team's showdown with St. Mary's, which was expected to draw more than 50,000 fans in Los Angeles. Lineman Bob Link made a full recovery. Quarterback Burch Donahue was left permanently paralyzed from the waist down.

That was what Rice referred to as "in our own ranks."

The dinner at the New Yorker effectively served to symbolically hand over Miami's annual Christmas classic to the National Sports Council. A Florida delegation, led by Governor Frederick Preston Cone, was on hand to voice its support for the event. Cone was joined by Miami City Commissioner Fred Hosea, Robert J. Dill, chairman of the Florida State Infantile Paralysis Committee, and Dr. A.F. Kasper of the Orange Bowl Committee to enthusiastically endorse the joint venture. Cone predicted that all 39,000 seats in the Orange Bowl would be filled. The Lou Gehrig Cup would be awarded to the winner. It was hoped the Iron Horse would be on hand to present it on behalf of all those in iron lungs.

Placing charitable feelings aside, Miami knew it was losing control of the game (at least in theory), yet it was also aware that the publicity value was well worth the sacrifice. Newspapers and radio stations across the country hyped the game. Being associated with FDR certainly didn't hurt. Planned as an annual event, it was the perfect lead-in to the still-burgeoning Orange Bowl game on New Year's Day. The potential for tourism dollars was clear as crystal.

The next day, wire stories heralding the "Starlet Bowl" national title game ran in almost every U.S. paper, giving several locales hope that their team might be the one selected by "a committee consisting of sports writers from across the country." That wasn't entirely true. It had already been decided that, in the interest of time, the South was to be represented by the winner of the annual Edison-Miami bloodletting, as had always been the case for the annual Miami Christmas game. So, all speculation surrounded the northern opponent. Sixty teams were said to have contacted the Committee, with the list eventually narrowed to 20.

But consider the National Sports Council members who attended that New Yorker dinner. In addition to Rice and Considine, there were John Kiernan, *The New York Times* columnist, Bill Corum, *New York Journal-American* columnist, Dan Parker, *New York Daily Mirror* sports editor, Tom Meany of the *New York World-Telegram* plus Henry McLemore and Jack Cuddy of the United Press International and Sid Feder of the Associated Press. Both wire services were based in New York. So, "The National Sports Council" at least in that November's assembly, was a bit of a misnomer, not unlike baseball's World Series. The selection of the northern team, in reality, was being made in New York and, more important, through the perspectives, biases and provincial knowledge—of New Yorkers. Any team outside of the five boroughs was at a disadvantage at the outset. As Howard Cosell would say one day, anything across the Hudson "might as well be Bridgeport."

Miami's Jesse Yarborough accompanied the Florida contingent to New York and, that night, he was already involved in negotiations to bring a Gotham representative to the Magic City. By the sound of the press release announcing a nationwide hunt for a northern opponent, one might conjure up an exciting—and very maddeningly difficult—comparison among high school football teams all over the land, those which were beginning to feed stars to some of the strongest college football programs in the country. It was 1939, and it had been decades since the Northeast had "owned" the game. What about high schools in, say, the Midwest—Wisconsin, Illinois and Indiana—or Texas and California? But, in New York, the deliberation seemed, in scope, far from national. While Art Argauer was telling Jersey writers that Garfield was interested in the Miami game, Lou Miller of the *World-Telegram*, Leo Waldman of the *Herald Tribune* and James Murphy of the *Brooklyn Eagle* wrote (based on the scuttlebutt at the dinner) that Erasmus Hall, the esteemed high school from the Flatbush section of Brooklyn, was the frontrunner.

"That became apparent last night," Miller wrote convincingly, calling it a "strong probability" that Erasmus would be playing for the national championship.

"Powerful forces," Murphy wrote, "were at work" to pull Erasmus into the matchup.[4]

"Although Erasmus Hall has not definitely been tendered the bid," Murphy wrote, "the *Brooklyn Eagle* learned today that the Buff and Blue has the inside track and victory over Boys High School's eleven Saturday in the Erasmians' final game would definitely clinch the matter."[5]

Erasmus, situated in a mostly-Jewish, middle-class neighborhood, had an "Ivy League" reputation that went a long way with the Committee. Certainly, the massive school, with its impressive corridors and stained-glass windows would have been a match for Miami High as a cathedral of learning and, with the city's longest winning streak at 12 games, it looked like a shoo-in.

Even Jack Bell, who flew to New York to cover the festivities, wrote that the "crack" Erasmus team was "commanding favor" in both New York and Miami.[6] Joe McEvoy was a tough ball carrier, Morty Rauff and Allie Goldstein could throw it and 6-foot-2 end Warren Slavin was a pure receiver who made it look easy.

One problem. Boys High. Never count out a team that's been a cross-borough rival since 1898, and one that draws 14,000 fans at its home field. And, certainly don't count out a team that was also unbeaten and tied just once in its opening game . . . and, which by the way, was the last team to beat you back in 1937. No doubt, Boys had read how Erasmus had already punched its ticket to Miami when it landed a knockout punch to its rival's chances. Waldman called it "one of the most spectacular games ever played on a local gridiron,"[7] as Boys, flashing a pretty nifty passing attack of its own, rallied for two fourth quarter touchdowns to pull out a 19-12 win, the first of many crimps put into the Committee's grand plan.

Now things were wide open. In the Tuesday editions of the *Brooklyn Eagle*, James Murphy speculated that unbeaten Seward Park from the lower East Side of Manhattan was now the Miami frontrunner—ahead of Boys, unbeaten St. Francis Prep of Brooklyn, unbeaten but tied Abraham Lincoln of Brooklyn, unbeaten Lawrence from Long Island and Garfield.

The Florida delegation, which was so impressed by the size and power of the Boys team in its win over Erasmus—"They play fine football too!" one exclaimed—was staying in town to take in Boys' last game against unbeaten but tied Lincoln, part of a doubleheader at Ebbets Field.[8]

"It is no secret that the committee favors a New York City aggregation because of the drawing value of such a representative," Murphy reported.[9]

By this time, there wasn't a single selection committee. Yet, the National Sports Council, all sportswriters, deferred to Dill's group, mostly comprising politicians and officials. The Floridians would, naturally, consult with the New Yorkers but, in the end, it was going to be Florida's choice.

Richard "Dick" McCann, a New York-based sportswriter with the Newspaper Enterprise Association, was the National Sports Council secretary. Just 29 years old (he'd be the general manager of the Washington Redskins from 1947-1962 then serve as the first director of the Pro Football Hall of Fame), he was the point person for the event and the man in charge for keeping everyone on message. Gruff in his later years, he must have been more of a soft-sell master as a young man. McCann was ever mindful of the value of keeping the entire nation interested, so he assured John Ross of the *Eagle* that no team in the country had the inside track, pointing out that even Erasmus was still a candidate, in a veiled, though comically awkward, attempt at transparency and inclusiveness.

"Why Eramus?" McCann was asked.

He thought fast.

"Columbia went to the Rose Bowl in 1934, although it was defeated once," he explained as if there was any relation.

Ross did the best he could with the information he had.

"The sponsors of the bowl game are anxious to line up a team boasting color and tradition, both of which Erasmus and Boys High possess plenty," Ross wrote. "And so, 'Who's going to the Orange Bowl?' remains a mystery. Unlike that 'Who killed Cock Robin?' business, this mystery should be cleared up by no later than December 1."[10]

As a sort of disingenuous beauty pageant judge, McCann kept telling every team that it had a great chance. But, of course, not all teams hold equal beauty. And some had little reason even to be on the stage. No one seemed, for example, to be too worried about one not-so-tiny detail. Under the rules of the New York State Board of Education, no New York state team would be allowed to make the trip. Regulations prohibited New York football teams from playing games after December 1, from playing more than seven games in a season and from travelling more than 100 miles away from home. Put in place to discourage overemphasis on sports, the rules were implemented prior to the 1938 season—after Syracuse and Elmira had played in prior Miami Christmas games.

But, while the New York State bodies approved those trips, the New York Public Schools Athletic League historically frowned on post-season contests in any sport. In 1934, the PSAL prevented James Madison from accepting an invitation to play in the Miami game. That was the first such disappointment for Madison star Marty Glickman. Two years later, in the 1936 Olympics, Glickman and Sam Stoller, both Jews, were taken off the United States 100-meter relay team just before the race to appease Adolf Hitler, already embarrassed by Jesse Owens' gold medals against his Aryan sprinters and jumpers.

In this case, everyone just assumed the Board would loosen its regulations when it came to Seward Park.

"Sweet charity can exert a powerful influence," Miller wrote in the *World-Telegram*. "It is almost certain that the necessary sanctions would be issued by the educational bodies since the entire proceeds of the big event, minus traveling expenses, would be donated to the worthy cause."[11]

Ross, however, wondered why none of the teams had, as yet, checked with the authorities in advance. It was a very good question. Ohio teams, for instance, were immediately warned by state athletic association commissioner H.R. Townsend of its rule that prohibited games after December 2, and were reminded that the penalty for a violation was suspension from the association.

Curiously, the High School Games Committee of the Public Schools Athletic League met at the Hotel Astor without even discussing the Miami situation. Everyone was kicking that can of worms down the road.

Far from New York City, the game was fueling a good deal of excitement among the nation's undefeated teams included in all the speculation. Among them:

BOYS TOWN, NEBRASKA

Father Flanagan's school appeared on the first published lists. Founded on Flanagan's premise that "there is no such thing as a bad boy," the school for homeless and abandoned boys outside Omaha was immortalized in the 1938 film, *Boys Town*, starring Spencer Tracy and Mickey Rooney. Undoubtedly, the school's mandate, spirit and scrappy football team made for a fantastic feel-good story with its against-all-odds angle.

The school was so poor, Coach Ken Corcoran explained, that all of its team's cleats and equipment had been donated.

"The boys didn't really wear football pants last fall," he said. "It was mostly adhesive tape."[12]

The team drew its players from 19 states and represented eight nationalities and, incredibly, had not been beaten in five years. It built its 35-game winning streak against bigger, more experienced players with a schedule that got tougher each year. In 1939, Boys Town was 7-0 and outscored opponents, 152-15. In the two games it played at Creighton University Stadium, it drew 20,000 spectators.

The stocky 29-year-old Corcoran—"Corky" to his 28 players—was a colorful character. He was everything to everybody at Boys Town, where he taught, served as principal (until 1938) and ran all physical education activities, even corn-husking contests. A native of Kankakee, Illinois, where he was an all-conference quarterback at St. Viator College, he built the program from scratch, teaching football to boys new to the game. One of his more interesting innovations was the "jitterbug shift" where every man seemed to be moving before the play.

"We work a long time before the boys get a play perfect but when they do, it's perfect," he said. "Maybe we have one advantage. My boys know about bad breaks and when they get them in a game they don't waste time worrying about it. You know our string of games in which the opposition went scoreless ended on an 84-yard runback of the opening kickoff for a touchdown. But our boys came back to score twice and win." [13]

That took place in the season's fifth game against then-undefeated Cathedral of Omaha, as Ben Jakowski ran for the winning points in the third quarter. Many of Boys Town's wins were close affairs, although the season ended with a 32-8 rout of Conception, Missouri.

Boys Town had played in and won a post-season contest the year before. After the filming of the popular movie, Hollywood agent Frank Orsatti organized a charity game for the school against the elite Black-Foxe Military Academy, where his son was a student. Talk about contrasts.

So, Father Flanagan's boys took their first train rides, to Los Angeles, and played before a crowd of 10,000 that included co-stars Tracy and Rooney, Clark Gable, Bing Crosby, Norma Shearer, Myrna Loy, Joe E. Brown, Don Ameche, Pat O'Brien, Robert Taylor, Wallace Beery and Shirley Temple, whose brother, George, played tackle for Black-Foxe.

With scouts from Notre Dame and USC looking on, Boys Town won, 20-12, in an entertaining game that featured plenty of razzle-dazzle on both sides. Nick Loncaric, the biggest Boys Town player at 180 pounds, scored the winning touchdown on a 73-yard pass play. *Los Angeles Times* sportswriter Carl Blume described Boys Town "rip-snortin'" football team.[14]

The game even made Hedda Hopper's must-read gossip column.

> *Once during the game, a boy came back dripping. There were no blankets handy. A friend standing by said, "Wait, I'll get you one from Blacke-Foxe." Kid stopped him by saying, "Never mind; I don't need it. I'm not a sissie." And neither were the Black-Foxe boys.*[15]

Alas, Boys Town pulled itself out of the running. After a week of speculation, Father Flanagan advised Miami organizers that the team played against smaller Class B schools in Nebraska and, with a backfield that averaged 145 pounds and a line that averaged 160, would most likely be overpowered against a team like Miami.

BROCKTON HIGH SCHOOL, MASSACHUSETTS

Brockton, known as "Shoe City" for its long history manufacturing shoes, boots and even ice skates, also had a long football tradition that began with its high school's first game in 1897. Brockton was a powerhouse throughout the 1930s, racking up four undefeated seasons that decade. The team lost only once in 45 games dating back to the 1935 season and won three straight state Class A championships from '37 through '39.

Brockton's 1939 team had a well-balanced backfield and a big line. Bernie "The Flying Frenchman" Lanoue was a shifty open field runner and big play specialist who was named co-MVP by the Massachusetts Interscholastic Sports Writers Association. At 5-foot-10, 150 pounds, he called all the plays. Billy Gold, at 210 pounds, was the pile-driving back and Jim Dodero, a 6-foot, 180-pound end was the top receiver and hardly ever missed a kick.

The only blemish on Brockton's 10-0-1 record was a 7-7 tie with Medford in the second week of the season. Brockton smashed Manchester Central, the best team in New Hampshire, 16-0, in a battle of unbeaten teams and walloped opponents by a total score of 279-21 on the season.

McCann wired for information about Brockton on November 25. Donations toward the trip started rolling in, and the Boston writers got squarely behind the Miami bid. When the New York writers came up for the Harvard-Yale game, the Boston scribes "gave them an earful" about Brockton's prowess.

There was a tough, scrappy junior high player who watched every Brockton game, waiting for his turn the following season. His name was Rocco Francis Marchegiano. In 1940, when Brockton slumped to 5-4-1, he started at center and linebacker. Marchegiano ran back an interception 65 yards for a touchdown when Brockton beat New Bedford, 26-6, and quit after that one season of high school football to find work to help support his family. Twelve years later, he KO'd Jersey Joe Walcott to win the heavyweight championship of the world. By then, he was known as Rocky Marciano, the Brockton Bomber. Today, Brockton's teams are known as the Boxers. They play in 10,000-seat Rocky Marciano Stadium.

CITY COLLEGE, BALTIMORE, MARYLAND

Had Jesse Yarborough alone been picking the opposition, deliberation would likely have begun and ended with the team from "The Castle on the Hill." Indeed, two years later, Miami invited City to the 1941 Christmas Game. The 1939 team was celebrating the 100th anniversary of the school's founding, when it was one the first high schools in the nation to field a football team. Its rivalry with Baltimore Polytechnic Institute, begun in 1889—and persisting to this day—is the second oldest in the nation. Completed in 1926, its four-story neo-Gothic structure, topped by a 150-foot tower, cost nearly three million dollars.

Harry Lawrence, who had kicked the winning field goal for Poly against City in 1926, arrived at the castle in 1934 and began an unprecedented run that included 54 straight victories through the 1941 season (and finally broken in the Miami game). The streak had reach 38 games in 1939 when City retired the *Evening Sun Trophy* after winning it five times.

When City capped off its season with a 12-0 win over Poly, Craig E. Taylor wrote in the *Sun* that the Collegians were looking for more football worlds to conquer.

> *The chance may come in the new Starlet Bowl game. While City College is opposed to post-season games as a matter of principle, it was learned after the game that the school probably would be receptive to a bid to play in the national scholastic championship game. Grantland Rice heads the committee in charge of the event. The City record will be placed before Rice.*[16]

The Collegians placed four men on the 1939 All Maryland team, three of them on the line—left end Lou Hessen, left guard Anthony Nardo and center Arthur Brandau—and one in the backfield, local legend Dick Working, a future Baltimore Colt.

LAWRENCE AND HEMPSTEAD HIGH SCHOOLS, NEW YORK

The two best teams on Long Island both finished the season without a loss. For Lawrence, it was one of four unbeaten seasons in the nine Nick Farina coached at the school. Farina, out of Steelton, Pennsylvania, starred for Bucknell in the first Orange Bowl game in 1934 before joining Lawrence. Under his stewardship, he laid the foundation of a football program that, today, is the winningest on Long Island.

At the time, Farina called the 1939 edition his best team. Led by all-county end Bob Pearsall, the Golden Tornadoes scored 135 points in winning seven games behind a line that averaged 183 pounds and a backfield near 172. With Bill Kupper and Bucky Bucchioni up front, Lawrence didn't allow a touchdown all season. The only points against were scored by Freeport when a blocked punt went through the end zone.

"If a Metropolitan team is to be invited, then by all means the bid should go to Lawrence. And by the metropolitan area we mean all of New York City, Nassau, Suffolk, New Jersey, Westchester and the neighboring counties in Connecticut," wrote Michael Lee in the *Long Island Daily Press*, noting that he was doing "everything in our power to see that they get the invitation."[17]

Hempstead was hardly mentioned as a possibility, and its coach, Joe Fay, protested that his team's candidacy was woefully underbilled. Led by Mike Kostynick, the best back on Long Island, and Ray Romano, a rugged tackle, the Tigers matched Lawrence's 7-0 record and received the Rutgers Trophy as the outstanding team on Long Island in a vote of Nassau-Suffolk coaches, polling 56 votes to Lawrence's 52. Lee, however, noted that Lawrence rolled over Hempstead when they met in a scrimmage.

Although it was reported that Lawrence obtained advance permission to make the trip to Miami, both Long Island schools ultimately would have run afoul of the New York State Board of Education ruling.

POUGHKEEPSIE HIGH SCHOOL, NEW YORK

Poughkeepsie High was another that fell under New York State BOE regulations. The Blue had won 16 straight games under coach Sam Kalloch, the longest winning streak in the state, allowing just five touchdowns over that span. Poughkeepsie, about 80 miles north of New York City, dominated football in the Hudson Valley, winning the region's mythical championship nine times from 1923 through 1939.

The Blue was simultaneously being touted for the LSA Game in Baton Rouge, but Poughkeepsie authorities had a more realistic view of their post-season chances of heading to Miami. They told the *Poughkeepsie Eagle-News* it was doubtful they would be able to obtain permission. The Blue was even unable to accept an invitation to play Malden, Massachusetts, after the regular season ended.

Poughkeepsie would also have run smack dab into Jim Crow territory on any trip South. Its star ball carrier, Don "Sandy" Greene, was black. Along with Johnny Ross and Gus Siko, he was part of a high-scoring backfield. After Green led Poughkeepsie to a come-from-behind, 26-14, victory over Newburgh (playing with an infected tooth), Tom Yates of the *Newburgh News* called him, "About the finest ball carrier you'll find in this neck of the woods. He's dynamite." The *Middletown Times-Herald* called Greene's play in a 38-6 win over Middletown, "one of the greatest exhibitions ever seen at Wilson Field. Shifty, fast and powerful he was unstoppable once he got past the line of scrimmage."[18]

The '39 team was one of nine Kalloch coached at Poughkeepsie. When he retired in 1969 after a 47-year career, Kalloch had won 64 championships in three sports. The Poughkeepsie football field was named after him in 1980.

EAST HIGH SCHOOL, SIOUX CITY, IOWA

"The corn belt is booming East High of Sioux City for Miami's Starlet Bowl," Eddie Brietz wrote in his *Associated Press* sports roundup. And, the Iowans certainly had little reason to disagree.

The Black Raiders featured Bobby Odell, a speedy six-foot halfback who won the 220-yard hurdles state championship. Odell later won fame at the University of Pennsylvania where, in 1943, he won the Maxwell Trophy and was the runner-up to Notre Dame's Angelo Bertelli in the Heisman Trophy voting. At East, Bobby, a farm boy whose brother, Howdy, had starred for Jock Sutherland at Pitt, led his team to consecutive state championships and on a 23-game winning streak. The Black Raiders were 8-0-1 in 1939, while outscoring foes, 167-24, and handing Mason City its first loss to an Iowa team in three years, 13-0. The only hiccup was a 6-6 tie with Omaha Central. In fact, only two ties with Omaha Central marred their record over the 1937-1939 period.

"There is no question that Odell is the greatest all-around back in the state," the *Des Moines Register* crowed when it named him to its all state team. "This hard-running, elusive 180-pound speedster is the best prep back turned out in Iowa since Jay Berwanger (the first Heisman winner ever) ran roughshod."[19]

No question, that an Odell-Eldredge showdown would have been a quite a spectacle.

BILLINGS HIGH SCHOOL, MONTANA

The Broncos of home-grown coach Clyde Carpenter won their second straight state title by routing Great Falls, 33-7, for their seventeenth straight win. It was Billings' fifth outright state title, their second back-to-back and the fourth under Carpenter, who starred on the 1925 team that tied Great Falls for the state championship.

"Hammerin' Herman" Frickey was Billings' big gun. Somewhat stubby at 5-foot-11, 185 pounds, Frickey combined power and breakaway speed to run away with the state scoring title with 138 points. He scored in all 10 games, including the opening week win over Casper, Wyoming, and three times in the state championship game against Great Falls, where the *Great Falls Tribune* remarked that he, "ran with the polish of a college star and the power of a locomotive."[20]

Billings was far from a one-man team, however. Cousins Herbie and Wilbert Hein made first team, All Big Six Conference, as lineman. Herbie, a glue-fingered end, formed the back end of a potent passing combination with southpaw quarterback Jack Davis, an expert field general. Playing their home games in the shadow of the Rimrocks, the Broncos rang up 270 points but allowed 92, including a 20-14 win over the Montana State freshmen that counted on their 10-0 record.

Even after playing 10 games, Billings was hungry for more. After dispatching Great Falls for the Montana title on Thanksgiving Day, Carpenter challenged any state championship team to a game but added, "frankly, we are gunning for a bid to the proposed Starlet Bowl game in Miami."[21]

Frickey went on to the University of Minnesota, where, as a sophomore, he helped the Gophers, in 1941, win a second national championship in a row. In the Little Brown Jug game against Michigan, Frickey both set up and scored the only touchdown, hauling in a 43-yard pass from Heisman Trophy winner Bruce Smith, and then scoring from two yards out after Smith left the game with an injury.

NATRONA COUNTY HIGH SCHOOL, CASPER, WYOMING

Casper opened the season with a 37-14 loss at Billings, which, on the surface would make the unbeaten Broncos the natural choice between the two. But there were extenuating circumstances in that match. The Mustangs' entire first team backfield was missing that day and, while their defense couldn't handle Frickey and Co., they grabbed the selection committee's attention by winning their last eight games, outscoring teams by a whopping margin: 239-26.

In fact, coach Okie Blanchard wired all of the Mustangs' opposing coaches, including Clyde Carpenter at Billings, soliciting words of support.

"Appreciate anything favorable you can say on behalf of our team. Bill to me the cost of your message," the telegram said.

John Powell, the coach of the Cheyenne team that lost, 32-6, to the Mustangs, obliged: "Hear you are considering Casper high school team for Health Bowl game at Miami on Christmas. They have a fine team, the strongest in Wyoming I have seen all in my 15 years as coach here. They are flashy, spectacular, powerful and well-coached. You will do well to select them."[22]

Casper even tried to schedule a rematch with Billings on an open date the weekend before Thanksgiving, even offering to pay the Broncos' expenses for the 225-mile trip. Casper had been the last team to defeat Billings before the Broncos began their 17-game winning streak in '38.

The Mustangs themselves had won 18 straight games over the '37 and '38 seasons before losing to Sheridan, 6-0, in the Wyoming state title game. They avenged that defeat, 20-6, in the final game of the 1939 season to reclaim the state championship. Casper was 30-3 over three years, with wins over teams from Nebraska, South Dakota, Utah, Texas, Colorado, Montana and Wyoming.

Casper placed five players on the first team All Wyoming with two on the second team and five more on honorable mention (i.e., the entire starting team plus one). That featured the spark plug of the offense, Vic Niethammer, who would play at Notre Dame, as well as three linemen (Stan Hendrickson, Warren Rash and Dale King) and "Shadow" Ray, picked as a first team alternate.

Had Casper played in Miami, Coach Blanchard would have been able to show off his creative "razzle dazzle" plays, which must have appeared to many as more screwball than football. The "Blanchard Nightmare" had the linemen actually turning their backs to the line of scrimmage, and, after the ball was snapped the backs formed a cluster, usually catching the defense flatfooted. Then, Niethammer would dart out with the ball. There was also a fake Nightmare where the line would snap around and face front while signals were being called.

There were reverses, triple laterals and just about anything else that came to Blanchard's mind. He unleashed a new one against Sheridan. The line made a sudden sweep to the left without the ball being snapped, forcing Sheridan to come across offside. Today, of course, it would have been a penalty against Casper for a false start.

JEANNETTE, PENNSYLVANIA

The team from the biggest glass-producing town in Pennsylvania won the coveted Western Pennsylvania Interscholastic Athletic League championship by edging previously unbeaten Ambridge, another Miami possibility. Bill Olezewski's 95-yard return of the opening kickoff stood up in a 6-0 win for Jeannette.

Jake Abraham and Johnny Marsico formed a two-pronged running attack as the Jayhawks, one of the most storied programs in the fertile football ground that is Western Pennsylvania, went 10-0 and allowed just 20 points. They dominated Johnstown, 19-0, for the right to play for the title.

Jeannette, however, never created a lot of momentum for itself and the appearance of McKeesport, another Pittsburgh-area team, in the 1938 Christmas Game worked against the Jayhawks. The Committee never contacted Jeanette after it briefly entered the picture following the Erasmus loss.

In addition, it was reported that Oak Park, Illinois, which played Miami in 1937, Dennytown and Bedford, Pennsylvania, Mount St. Michael out of the Bronx and Hackettstown, New Jersey, were "pulling strings" to win the nomination. Hackettstown was the state Group Two champion, far below Garfield in the Colliton rankings, but Joe Stanowicz was a First Team All State pick who finished the season as New Jersey's scoring leader.

Back in New York the following Saturday, the Florida delegation was among the 15,000 fans at Ebbets Field who witnessed Boys topple Lincoln, 12-7, "setting themselves up," the *Eagle* reported, "as the No. 1 local choice to go to the Orange Bowl on Christmas Day."[23] With team MVP Irwin Kolodney calling the signals, Lebowitz throwing his 220 pounds of heft and Markowitz adding his 198 against the Lincoln front wall, the *Herald-Tribune's* Waldman wrote: "It is doubtful if any team in the city could have stopped this Boys juggernaut."[24]

Perhaps.

But the Florida officials weren't convinced, or at least they felt that it didn't matter. By then, they were becoming infatuated with the rags-to-riches story of Seward Park, a tale that could be spun to hype the game, sell more tickets and, as Bob Considine put it, "buy more iron lungs."[25]

Seward Park had played only seven games and, while it played a much weaker schedule than the Brooklyn teams, it was the only unbeaten, untied team left standing within the city's boroughs. The school sat on an overcrowded, sweltering-in-the-summer, grimy-in-the-winter, corner of New York's poorest neighborhood: the old Jewish ghetto of Manhattan's Lower East Side. These football players were the underprivileged, the press releases said, the most likely to be hit by polio. They called them the Dead End Zone Kids.

Milton Gross of the *New York Post* was just one scribbler who took up their cause:

> *Miami, the travel folders relate, is a sunshine city. There are white warm sands, warm winds blowing off Biscayne Bay, tropical palm trees, orange groves and beaches where people from in state meet and speak to those from forty-seven others. Seward is situated in the lower East Side. Essex, Broome, Grand and Ludlow Streets, on which the school stands, do not have sunshine and warm sands. Ludlow Street, in fact, has pushcarts. Essex Street has delicatessen stores. All four have people and tenements far too many for the small area. When the snow falls in the winter it does not stay white for long and the sun can't shine through a tenement wall.*[26]

Yes, this was very, very far from the Sunshine State. Many of the school's kids qualified for free lunches through its lunch-card program. Halfway through the season, a thief broke into the gymnasium and stole the team's practice uniforms. For the rest of the year, the players drilled in street clothes. They didn't have a practice field nearby so, each day after school, coach Jerry Warshower shepherded them on the subway to Brooklyn, where, after an hour-long trip, they worked out on the venerable Parade Ground at Park Circle. The fare was 10 cents. The school contributed a nickel. Each player had to make up the difference, which for some was surely a handsome out-of-pocket expense.

Built on the site of the old alimony jail where Boss Tweed died and Al Smith later presided, Seward Park was a venerable institution that provided a quality education despite its claustro-phobic, cramped classrooms and relatively limited funds. If the football team wasn't winning, there was always the school play. Enrolled that year was a handsome freshman named Bernard Schwartz, who later took the stage name Tony Curtis. Estelle Scher was a junior. She played a Golden Girl as Estelle Getty. At one time or another, Eddie Cantor, Al Jolson, Zero Mostel, Walter Matthau, song writer Sammy Cahn, Jerry Stiller and Joe E. Roszawikz, better known as Joe E. Ross of Car 54 fame, walked the halls of Seward Park. So did convicted spies Julius and Ethel Rosenberg, although they didn't meet until New Year's Day, 1939, at a Young Communist League Meeting where Ethel was waiting to take the stage to sing with the choir.

They married that summer of '39. Whether the ill-fated newlyweds concerned themselves with the adventures of the Seward Park football team is unknown.

The team wasn't highly regarded when the 1939 season began with a win over defending Queens champion John Adams at Dexter Park. Student editor Seymour Weintraub described the scene in the January 1940 edition of the *Almanac*, the Seward Park yearbook:

> *It was an Indian Summer afternoon, late in September of 1939, and the thin crowd of three thousand partially filled the wooden stands at Dexter Park. The makeshift gridiron, recently a baseball diamond, had yawning cavities at the extreme ends and what had previously been a bullpen now housed forty blue jerseyed athletes. A grim figure paced in measured strides before the assembled gridders and then in a sharp, nervous voice, "Adams is big. Adams is good. Adams is smart. But Adams thinks they're facing a setup today. If they're big—we're bigger. If they're good—we're better. If they're smart—we're smarter. That crowd out there today doesn't seem to think we have a chance. Seward? Bah! But we can't lose, if we won't lose. Well, what's the answer, boys?"*
>
> *And with that, Coach Jerry Warshower strode away amid, "Yeah, we'll show 'em. So they were Queens champs, were they? They'll be chumps today! Huh! Smart are they, big are they?"*
>
> *Seward Park went out that afternoon and literally showed 'em. They outran, outgained and outplayed the doughty warriors of John Adams High School as they did every other opponent on their suicide schedule.*[27]

Weintraub, a budding Grantland Rice, eventually gave up on his dream of becoming a sportswriter and turned to the entertainment business, where, known as Sy Weintraub, he owned Panavision and produced a series of successful Tarzan movies in the late 50s and two Sherlock Holmes TV movies in the 1980s. While he may have embellished a few details back in his high school yearbook days, Weintraub perfectly captured the underdog theme of Seward Park's football warriors.

Triple-threat back John Kammerer did most of the running and most of the scoring. Weintraub waxed poetic on his exploits in the *Almanac*, describing him as, "a tousle-haired, 160-pound thunderbolt who doesn't know enough to admit when he's licked." He was, "Seward's gridiron chieftain, the ghost stepping, climax running, touchdown tycoon."[28]

He scored on a 76-yard double reverse and accounted for the two critical extra points, one on a kick, the other on a pass, as Seward Park nipped Adams, 14-12, then scored both touchdowns, one on a 63-yard burst, in a 12-0 win over Monroe the next week. It was a familiar story in a 14-12 over Curtis in the third game as Kammerer scored one TD and provided both extra points. Kammerer threw for the only touchdown when Seward defeated Stuyvesant, 6-0, in a triple header attended by 20,000 at Ebbets Field and added four touchdowns as Seward won its final three games by a combined score of 73-6.

The guy opening up most of the holes for Kammerer was 240-pound Seymour Cohen, the Seward center, who turned around and played tackle on defense, where he was an immovable object plugging the line. Jacob Fine, who had a huge interception return for a TD against Curtis, made the *Journal-American's* All City team at end, while Tony Mancuso was Kammerer's mighty-mite counterpart in the backfield. Ted Wakulinski combined with Kammerer on many pass plays.

The 1939 Seward Park High School football team, the Dead End Zone Kids. Note the ragtag look.
The Almanac, January 1940.

The Dead End Kids narrative was not exactly genuine, though. Seven Seward Park players were not from the teeming ghetto of the Lower East Side. Starting end Ruby Roth, starting tackle Dan Chertoff and starting halfback Dan Stark, plus second teamer Len Farber lived across the East River along with their coach. Hardly the Upper East Side, at least a tree—or two—grew in Brooklyn.

Warshower had arrived in 1935 to turn around a program that could barely win a game. Over that time period, wrote the *Herald-Tribune*'s Leo Waldman, Warshower "developed student interest, loyalty and material which is on a par with any other school in the city." A decade earlier, Warshower had helped Boys High to an undefeated season in 1925 and went on to win nine high school letters in football, basketball and baseball at Boys. He played all three sports at Ohio University where he made the college's Hall of Fame in basketball, and caught the eye of a few major league scouts as a catcher. Instead, he began a coaching career after graduation in 1931. The 1939 season was to be his last at Seward, but it stands as the best in the school's history.

As the final week of November arrived, there was growing optimism at Seward that the '39 football season would be extended. Miami defeated Edison on Thursday night, November 30, to clinch its spot in what was renamed the "Health Bowl" while James Murphy wondered in the *Eagle* why it was taking so long to name the northern representative.

"The committee in charge of the big intersectional fracas may be hurting its own cause by waiting too long to reach a decision," he wrote. "Practically all teams under advisement have finished their campaigns and broken training and it will take a lot of hustling to get them back in their top form. Under such circumstances, it would not be a fair test to pit such a combination against a Miami High or Miami Edison unit that has maintained strict training."[29]

On that same day, Leo Waldman, in *The Herald-Tribune*, was, for the first time, reporting that Garfield had the best chance of landing the bid.[30] But Murphy was still speculating that the choice was coming down between Seward Park and Boys, noting that Warshower had played for Boys under its current coach Wally Muller, who also developed Tony Maggio, the head coach at St. Francis Prep, which had also been considered. It was rather coincidental that by beating Erasmus, Muller and Boys had given Warshower his shot. If Erasmus had won that game, the Miami bid would, in all likelihood, have already gone to Erasmus.

Now, the publicity machine was fueling out more (false) hope, naming as "outstanding" 10 finalists in no particular order: Seward Park, Boys, City College, Billings, Brockton, Casper, Lawrence, Poughkeepsie, Sioux City and Garfield. The release said a committee including William T. Edwards, chairman of the Florida State Committee for the Celebration of the President's Birthday, Robert Dill, assistant chairman, Bob Considine, Henry McLemore of UPI and Sid Feder of AP would hand their decision to Rice and the announcement was to be made Tuesday, December 5.

Dick McCann, meanwhile, was still pumping up the hopes of any team that asked about their prospects—Vineland and Hempstead, for instance. At the same time, the New York sportswriters made a pre-emptive strike on behalf of Seward Park.

Joe Williams, perhaps the most influential sports columnist in New York City, was already appealing to Mayor Fiorello La Guardia to intervene on Seward's behalf in his column in the *World-Telegram* on Wednesday, Nov. 29. It was reprinted in the *Miami News* on Saturday, two days before the selection committee was to convene at the Columbus Hotel in Miami.

Underneath the headline, *Come on, Mr. Mayor; Give The Seward Kids a Break*, Williams wrote:

> *Down on the lower East Side of this city, in what was once the heart of the old Ghetto, stands William H. Seward High School. It seems safe to say that the per capita wealth of the fathers of the boys who attend this school is the lowest in New York. For the parents of most of its pupils, sending their sons to Seward means tremendous hardships.*
>
> *To these youngsters of the old slum area has come an incredible possibility. Their football team is wanted for a post-season contest with Miami High School in the Florida city on Christmas Day. This game, in the Orange Bowl, would be a 100 per cent benefit for the Infantile Paralysis Fund.*
>
> *But a hard-hearted Board of Education, brushing off all notions of sentiment, of human feeling for these youngsters of the sidewalks of a neighborhood of tenements, meager park spaces and education and life—joys that come the hardest way—has voted against letting the lads of Seward go to Miami.*[31]

Williams went on to say there needn't be fears about the Seward boys—"*they could take care of themselves*"—and noted that the Board had previously killed off an annual baseball game between the champions of New York and Chicago, an annual New York championship game, sponsored by the *World-Telegram* in one of the three major league parks and even nixed trips to the Penn Relays in Philadelphia.

No sensible reason for the official attitude has been advanced. The board just won't let the boys have a good time. It is up to Mayor Fiorello H. La Guardia to override the board's veto. Charity asks that this splendid football team be sent to Florida. Justice backs it up. Let's go, Mr. Mayor!³²

The column ran in New York five days before any team was to be named and in Miami two days prior. But it served a purpose—to assure the committee that the New York media would pressure La Guardia into action and that it would be a mere formality to clear the way for Seward Park. So suggested the *Miami News* in its headline over the Williams column:

Please, La Guardia, Listen To Joe; Let New York Boys Play Miami High

It was about this time that other politicians started getting involved, including New Jersey's Governor Harry Moore in support of Garfield.

Montana Governor Roy E. Ayers sent a wire to McCann that read:

Billings, Montana, high school football team now on the eligible list would like the opportunity of being considered to play the Miami high school on Christmas day in the Health Bowl game. I urge your earnest and favorable consideration of the Billings team for this contest.³³

Montana Senator James A. Murray sent another supportive telegram a few days later while Wyoming Governor Nels H. Smith put in a word for Casper:

Wyoming should be highly honored if the Casper high school squad should receive the invitation to play in the Health Bowl at Miami on Christmas day, which they would most happily accept.

Casper high school has a very colorful squad, having defeated teams from Pampa, Texas, Ogden, Utah, Curtis, Nebr.; Salt Lake City, Utah and every Wyoming team they have met in the past three years. I believe the meritorious purpose behind the health bowl would be satisfactorily served by the selection of Casper high school as the western representative.³⁴

Not all the wires were positive. According to Al Del Greco, the National Sports Council received several wires against the Garfield team on the grounds that Garfield was a gangster hotbed. They were all found to have come from Brockton, Massachusetts.³⁵

At the same time, Garfield Mayor John Gabriel and New Jersey Governor Moore were working behind the scenes. Noted Del Greco, "all eyes are on Mayor John Gabriel, the kid who played halfback on the club about twelve years ago. He's the Grand Chief Poo-bah Wire-Puller."³⁶

As everyone awaited the announcement, Ed Rosell, columnist for the *Poughkeepsee Star-Enterprise*, was playing the best hunch.

The New Yorkers do not have a record that begins to compare with Poughkeepsie's but the Seward team can be ballyhooed to the sky. With attention centered on the "gate" the committee is apt to figure that such a team would have a greater crowd appeal.³⁷

Jesse Yarborough joined the committee when it met Monday. He was being given final approval and had no problem with the decision to extend the invitation to Seward Park. They weren't trying to pick the best team, as Rosell astutely noted. They were trying to pick the best story. All those teams around the country could at least say they were considered, an honor in itself. And who was to say it wasn't still a national championship game? Seward Park was undefeated. Everyone around the table congratulated each other on the selection, toasting to the success of the game, puffing on cigars, oblivious to the problem they had just created for themselves. They proudly brought their choice to Grantland Rice.

At 10 p.m. that night, Dill phoned Warshower long distance to extend the invitation. He turned it down. Warshower knew the State Board of Education rules line by line and he knew he could not say yes without violating regulations. He was confident that an exception would be made and actually began to make plans to bring down a 40-man squad on a 12-day trip. But Seward Park still needed the approval of both the New York City and State Board of Educations with the official acceptance coming from the state. Bureaucracy works slowly. This was a way to force those sluggish boards board into action.

The National Sports Council cautiously announced that the invitation was extended and the *United Press* reported in Tuesday's papers that "only approval of the New York Board of Education was necessary" to send Seward Park south.

The jilted teams should have read the tea leaves. But in Brockton, the news came as a shock and the Boston papers screamed. The Boston-New York rivalry even extended to high school football back then.

"Judging by the success our Greater Boston elevens have had against New York opponents, Brockton is about five touchdowns better than the Sewards," Will Cloney wrote in the *Boston Herald*. "The trouble is the selection committee comes from New York."[38]

"Why Seward Park High was selected over Brockton is a question likely to go unanswered," wrote Ernest Dalton of the *Boston Globe*. "Bay State teams have always rated higher than the best New York state can produce."[39]

Dalton, boasting that "schoolboy football is really football" in Massachusetts, started his argument all the way back in 1922 when Lawrence, unbeaten in three years, challenged all comers and was embarrassed by Brockton, 57-0, with captain Donald Phillips suffering both a broken wrist and a broken leg. He mentioned Marblehead, Massachusetts, traveling to Staten Island in 1935 to take on unbeaten power Curtis and leaving with a 29-0 win. Then there was Lawrence's narrow, 6-0, win over Quincy, Massachusetts earlier in 1939 and that Quincy was a Class B team never ranked higher than 27th in Massachusetts. He could have mentioned another more direct comparison. Curtis, which was beaten by Seward Park, 14-12, went up to Manchester, N.H., and was bounced, 14-0, a week before Brockton went into Manchester and won a convincing 16-0 verdict.

Ignoring all those facts, and assuming that bureaucratic approval for Seward Park was a foregone conclusion, the Sports Council opened a ticket office in the lobby of the newly opened DuPont Building in downtown Miami Tuesday morning. But just as those first tickets were sold, Hiram Jones, the all-powerful director of physical education in the state Department of Education, instructed Seward Park Principal Robert D. Brodie, to refuse the invitation.

The *Brooklyn Eagle* reported that, since Lawrence, Long Island, fell under the same New York State prohibitions, Garfield now had the inside track, dismissing a rumor that Mayor La Guardia would step in as "highly improbable."[40] Things got more confusing the next day,

Wednesday, when Dr. Harold G. Campbell, New York City Superintendent of Schools, issued a one-paragraph statement that was also wired to Jesse Yarborough at Miami High: "We have a telegram invitation for this game. We cannot accept the invitation because it is against the State Board of Education regulations."

Warshower had also sent Yarborough his regrets, but a couple of hours later La Guardia threw himself into the picture. Letters and telegrams in support of Seward had piled up on his desk, including one from Bob Considine. Certainly all the New York City sports pages were pushing for the rules to be circumvented.

"Rules are rules of course but rules were also made to be broken in some cases," wrote Jimmy Wood, the *Brooklyn Eagle* sports editor. "In this particular case we feel that the Board of Education would please everyone interested if it took (the) rules, tied them together and gave them a long heave off the end of the first convenient dock. The cause is great enough to break any man-made rule."[41]

Either La Guardia concurred or he felt he had a winning issue. He wired Campbell, "I approve of the Seward High School football team's going to Miami. Issue necessary instructions for the trip."[42] He also sent a separate notice to Considine: "I have your telegram of December 4. Seward High football team is being granted permission to play in Miami. I have so instructed the superintendent of schools."[43]

According to Leonard Lewin of *New York Daily Mirror*, Warshower was about to walk into a meeting with his players to tell them the trip was off when someone rushed out of the coaches' office to tell him La Guardia had come through. He instead told the team that La Guardia's intervention was, "the thing we've been waiting for, although you'll have to withhold your exuberance until we get official word."

Officially, Warshower said, "as far as I'm concerned, we're still not going as I've received no official word from the board."

"But there was joy hidden in his formal statement and it didn't take much to detect it," Lewin wrote.[44]

La Guardia and Warshower may have thought things were settled, but Campbell wasn't necessarily taking the mayor's recommendation. He was busy with a budget meeting all day and was unavailable for comment. But the *Journal-American* quoted a source close to the city board who indicated Seward Park's cause was hopeless.

"The city and state boards intend to maintain their earlier stands," said the source. "Dr. Hiram Jones, director of the health and physical education division of the State Department of Education was approached by Seward's representatives in Albany today (Wednesday) but refused to waive the state rulings. Apparently, the state and city boards intend to stick together on this."[45]

When Jones was reached for comment by the *World-Telegram*, he reiterated his stand: "State regulations forbid football games after December 1. We've already turned down two other schools and can't make an exception in this case."

But the *World-Telegram*'s report went on to speculate that La Guardia may have had gone over Jones' head, as high as the governor's office. The paper quoted from a statement issued by James Kieran, the mayor's secretary. It noted that "special arrangements have been made with the state board to permit Seward Park to participate."[46]

According to Milton Gross, those "special arrangements" were interpreted by an "authoritative source" as official state action resulting from advice the mayor received that he was not in violation of state Board of Regents regulations by becoming involved. The next day, Kieran denied that state officials had been contacted.

It was a total mess.

Exactly who had the final authority, no one seemed to know. Everyone had an opinion. D. Walker Wear of the New York State Athletic Commission quoted a high official of the State Board of Regents, "I see no reason why, if the local school authorities asked for special permission, it couldn't be granted."

Organizers were running out of time.

The Florida people were demanding an answer from Campbell as to Seward's status. The National Sports Council felt that New York Governor Herbert Lehman was their last resort, that he might succeed where La Guardia failed. Grantland Rice wired the governor:

> We respectfully ask your support of Mayor La Guardia of New York City in his effort to gain the permission of the State Board of Education for Seward Park High School football team to play on Christmas Day in Miami in the Health Bowl game for the benefit of the Fight Infantile Paralysis Campaign. The entire proceeds from this game will be donated to the fight. All of New York City's sports writers join me in this game. We are most grateful for anything you may do. It is urgent that the official action be speedy.

Lehman wired back, telling Rice that if he received an invitation from Florida Governor Fred Cone, he would gladly get on board. When that telegram came from Cone, Lehman turned the telegram over to Dr. Frank P. Graves, state Commissioner of Education with his "personal recommendation" that the rules be bent for Seward Park.

That was Friday. The saga had been playing out for the entire week, organizers all the while exhausting valuable time for promotion. But most everyone in New York felt that Lehman had the final say and had saved the day. James Murphy's story in the Saturday editions of the *Brooklyn Eagle* lavished praise on both the governor and the mayor:

> Pushcart hawksters had the peddling of their wares along the East Side of Manhattan rudely disturbed today as a mighty cheer went up from the lusty lungs of the students of Seward Park High School, all obstacles having been cleared from the path that leads to the Health Bowl in Miami. The city's only undefeated and untied football team today was virtually assured the necessary sanction to combat Miami High.
>
> The strain of uncertainty had been so severe the players, the majority of whom had never been outside the confines of the city, were unable to sleep and do justice to their studies. Now they can get their natural rest and prepare for the trek to the land of sunshine to do their bit for a worthy cause. It is a well-deserved reward for a work well done.[47]

Yes, Murphy went on, the mayor's appeal to the governor had "worked like magic." Warshower re-issued the equipment and uniforms and put them through a "limbering-up session." Meanwhile, Boys coach Wally Muller, Paul Sullivan of Erasmus and Tut Maggio of St. Francis Prep all offered to help with the team's preparation. Ebbets Field and several high school fields in Brooklyn were being offered as practice sites.

"All that stands between Seward Park and Miami is the formal request to the State Board of Regents for approval and it will be forthcoming," Murphy wrote.[48]

Cue the fail horns, the sad trombones. It did not happen. Graves ended it.

The Commissioner told Lehman in yet another telegram his "hands were tied" by the state regulations. Graves said the rule, in effect since 1937, had "worked admirably in ridding the game of football of many of its abuses and of much criticism leveled at it.

"A number of high schools have asked during the past two years for exceptions to be made and have had to be refused," he wrote. "Will you please explain to Governor Cone that any exception made now would be in contravention of all that has been done and would set a precedent which would plague that state not only in this but in all matters of educational policy.

"We regret very much that we have to disappoint him."

Graves told Lehman that he deeply sympathized with his "generous wish that permission be granted. Your interest in the matter is in keeping with your well known sympathy with youth and with all good causes."

Neither Graves, nor Jones, nor Campbell, nor Lehman nor any other individual had the authority to suspend the regulation. That could only be done by vote of the Board of Regents. They had scheduled a meeting to decide the matter but not until December 15. Organizers couldn't wait. They withdrew the invitation. The entire process had been a waste of time. The matter could have been addressed earlier if there weren't so many governing bodies and so little chain of command. In Brockton, for instance, they cleared the way days before the decision was to be made, the school committee voting unanimously to accept the decision of its athletic committee. Only in New York, so the saying goes.

For the most part, the press across New York cried tears for Seward. As Bob Brumby wrote in the *Daily News*:

> An inexorable ruling prevented these boys, who overcame heart-breaking obstacles in running up an unbeaten football record, from spending sun-dappled days on the Atlantic, exploring the tropical splendors of the Southern city and contributing to a most worthy cause. We aren't criticizing the men who enforced the ruling, they had a duty to perform and did so, but we do think some elasticity should be put into the ruling. After all, the school officials are dealing in human equations, not slide rules or algebra.[49]

Said Jack Minnoch of the *Troy Record*:

> Sometimes I think the men who make such regulations can't be fathers with sons of high school age. I wonder if they're not bachelors who never enjoyed athletics as boys and are now overzealously putting pet theories to work.[50]

The *Saratogian* of prim and proper Saratoga Springs was one of the few editorial boards that approved of the outcome.

> There is good sense in those regulations, although some may complain that they are an evidence of "bureaucratic control by Albany." To that the obvious retort is that high school boys are not fit competitors for the funny "bowl" titles promoters think up. Neither by physique, training or experience are they to be compared with intercollegiate players. Even in that field, the more eminent institutions (the Ivy League schools) want no part of the bowls' dubious honors.

They stick to the quaint idea that football or any other form of competitive athletics should be a sideline in schools and colleges. When a legitimate interest is unduly prolonged so that football is played on Christmas and New Years Days, when all the ballyhoo which is natural to local rivalry is used to build up fake rivalries, it is time to call a halt.

The schools are not responsible for these ridiculous performances. Commissioner Graves believes that 90 per cent of local school men in this state want the reasonable regulations of the Regents enforced. It is hardly sensible to send New York boys traipsing off to Miami to play football in December. They might better do a little homework before the examinations begin.[51]

An ever-hopeful Art Argauer, with a hunch that Garfield would still land the bid, had been monitoring the situation to the point where he was carefully pasting clippings into his scrapbook. One column, Super Snoops, was written under the pseudonym The Phantom and provided a clear analysis of why Seward Park was chosen in the first place:

"How those folks down South fall for that word, New York," The Phantom wrote, adding that southern officials were looking for free publicity by singling out various teams throughout the country, then *"dropped the teams like a hot coal, because at all times they were determined to get a team from New York. They did not care a hoot for the team's record as long as the team hailed from the big city.*

"Who is this Seward High anyway? Well, they played seven games and happened to win all seven and we venture to say, against teams that Garfield would not even consider as worthy opponents.

"We are not bragging when we say that there is not a team in New Jersey or in the city of New York that Garfield could not lick—but those are the breaks of the game."

The same column disclosed that as late as 10 p.m. Wednesday, before La Guardia stepped in, railroad officials were calling Argauer's home to make transportation arrangements. Garfield, it said, was the next choice. But who really knew? Art McMahon of *The Herald-News* was on what turned into a working vacation in Miami, where he had a long chat with Jesse Yarborough, who he said was pulling the strings. McMahon reported that Brockton, not Garfield, was the second choice, based on his conversation. The writer urged that Boilermaker boosters send telegrams to the coach because he was getting plenty of them from Brockton.[52]

Another development occurred earlier that same Wednesday. Nutley was awarded its bid to play in the December 15 benefit game at the University of Florida in Gainesville. The appearance of one New Jersey team in the Sunshine State would further complicate matters down the road.

For now, Argauer had been patiently waiting. Basketball practice started. The season opener was December 16 against Dickinson. The gala football banquet had taken place on Thursday, when Argauer had known Seward Park was still not a sure thing. The *Star-Ledger* quoted Dick McCann that Garfield would go if Seward Park could not. Argauer was waiting for a phone call; just not for the one he got that Saturday.

It would have been easy to turn to either Garfield or Brockton at that point. Each could get to Miami in a day. But the National Sports Council was so hung up on getting New York into the game that it instead went with a contingency Joe Williams had suggested during the Seward uncertainty. It would send a metropolitan all-star team to Miami. Considine phoned Yarborough, who didn't like the idea but went along with it. Because the *World-Telegram* team was the only one to include teams from outside the city, including Garfield, those 22 players would be hastily summoned and thrown together.

Tom Fitzgerald of the *Boston Globe* asked a very good question on behalf of Brockton.

"At the risk of appearing to be a provincial sour puss, it would be nice to know just what line of reasoning the officials used in selecting an all-star group to play in a game originally exploited as a championship high school contest?"[53]

Indeed, the national championship concept was ditched, certain proof that no team outside New York City had been in the plans. Considine tried to explain the switch in his syndicated column. Lamenting that Seward Park had "suffered a mild attack of strangulation on the red tape of schoolboy athletic regulations," he called the all-star plan an "ideal solution" because six New York metropolitan area teams had "good claims" on the original invitation and they would all be represented.

As for Billings and Sioux City, Considine explained that the cost of bringing them from such distances would have cut into the proceeds going to charity:

> *New York's high school teams had the inside track in the eyes of the selection committee, chiefly because of their accessibility and the fact that between now and April Miami is mainly populated by New Yorkers.*
> *Seward Park would have drawn well, for it is as colorful as Boys Town or that team of orphans in Fort Worth. The All Met will draw even better, we think for it will appeal to Miami visitors from Westchester as well as Hester Street, from East Orange to the end of Brooklyn. The kids are a little younger than Coach Jesse Yarborough's crack Miamians but we grow 'em tough up here. Where do you think most of those Southern All Americans come from?*[54]

Joe Lovas of *The Herald-News* knew that Considine's happy talk would not resonate with the teams whose hopes were dashed so cavalierly. "You can bet your last dollar that coaches and school officials will shy (away from) the "Health Bowl" game next year—if it is held. They probably realize they were given a run-around and won't even consider a bid," he wrote.[55]

By the time Argauer got the call from McCann, he knew what was up. McCann told him that Benny Babula, who made the *World-Telegram's* first team, and John Grembowitz, who made the second, would be on the team and that he had been named to the five-man coaching staff headed by Seward Park's Jerry Warshower. Argauer, Nick Farina of Lawrence, Paul Sullivan of Erasmus Hall and George Negroni of Harrison, New York, representing Westchester County, would assist.

Babula wasn't keen on playing until he found out his pal Grembie was also selected. They all climbed into Argauer's car Monday afternoon, crossed the George Washington Bridge and headed through the snow to the Sutton Place Tennis Center, the only indoor facility that could be secured for a practice.

Every All Star but Frank Cardinale was there. He was in Florida with the Nutley team and was to meet the rest of the All Stars in Miami. Practices were arranged for the next 10 afternoons at Columbia University's Baker Field, with another evening session, if necessary, at an indoor armory. Players were expected to attend classes, although that was tough for the Jersey kids. There were even plans to take the team to spend the weekend at a country club before leaving for Miami on December 22.

"We're going down there to win. It's not going to be just a joyride," Warshower told the players.

Most of them were from the city, including Kammerer and Cohen from Seward Park. Warren Slavin and Morty Rauff represented Erasmus Hall, tackle Mel Downey, Boys, and Bill Kupper, Lawrence. Six came from New Jersey: the two Garfield boys, Cardinale, Bob Duffey from East Orange, Herb Schwartje of Dumont and Bob Forfar of Kearny.

They couldn't do much on the tennis courts, although Babula did enough to impress John Ross of the *Eagle*. Everyone looked on "in amazement," Ross wrote, as Babula "tossed the pigskin around like a baseball. If a first look means anything, then it's 'Beware Miami!'"[56]

It should have been "Beware Met All Stars" because, while the Sports Council was assuring Miami organizers there was no question with the All Stars being allowed to make the trip, Frank Graves was wiring Harold Campbell that the new plan was "in obvious violation" of state rules. Graves warned Campbell against all-star players "from public schools utilizing school equipment and supplies or any of your school teaching personnel." Campbell simply passed the message on verbatim to the schools without comment.

Graves made clear that no players could go as representative of New York public schools. If the parents approved of the trip, it was their personal business. Heartened by that detail, the Sports Council plowed ahead. The coaches' situation was a bit worrisome, but high school coaches regularly coached semi-pro teams on the weekend. Isn't this similar? Can't they volunteer to work for charity? As for the players, the Sports Council's interpretation of Graves' telegram was that they were not in violation if they were not representing their schools.

"The boys will be away on their Christmas vacation and they can do anything they please," one coach told the *Journal American*. Accordingly, the National Sports Council announced that all 22 players selected would make the trip with their parents' permission.

At the start, it was all very pleasant when everyone convened at Baker Field for the second practice. Because of the restriction on using anything issued by New York high schools, Columbia University athletic director Edward Elliot took the boys to the Lions' locker room and told them they were welcome to use any football gear that fit.

One kid picked up an old pair of shoes and asked Elliot if he could wear them.

"Nope," Elliot chuckled. "They're Sid Luckman's shoes. Nobody can fill them."

New York Yankees trainer Carl Painter had volunteered his services and all the players were asking him questions. But, soon, things were in an uproar. Grantland Rice had sent Graves a request for permission to use city-employed coaches. Those coaches were now hearing Graves' answer and it had them wondering if they were jeopardizing their careers.

"The proposed Miami game is not approved," Graves had replied. "Parents may send their boys as individuals if they choose. If any member of school teaching personnel is utilized in preparing for, or the playing of this game, it would be a violation of the regulations."[57]

Then, one of the players told the others he had been threatened by his principal, that if he participated in the game, he would not be granted a diploma. There was also a rumor that anyone who played in the game would lose his eligibility for spring sports. "In a few hours a picture of keen expectation was converted into one of panic," the *World-Telegram* noted.[58]

The second practice itself was a mess. The five coaches had met over spaghetti at Mama Leone's the night before to plot strategy and assignments, but it was going to be difficult to bring together players from so many different systems and mold them into a cohesive unit in so short a time. Again, the New York kids oohed and aahed as Babula showed off his punting leg. They all posed for pictures.

"The two all-star practices on Monday and Tuesday were terrible," Argauer told Del Greco. "New York's kids came down without any equipment. We just stood around like dunces."

As he was standing around, Argauer sidled over to Dick McCann and Robert Dill, whom Argauer had not met.

"Things don't look so hot," he told McCann.

"What about Garfield?" Dill asked.

"Garfield is ready," Argauer said. "And our Board of Education has approved the game."

"Approved the game?" said the astonished Dill, accustomed to the obstacles the New York boards were constantly laying down. "How can the Board of Education approve of a team going down there when Garfield hasn't been invited?"

"I played a hunch," Argauer said with a wink. "I asked the Board on Monday night."[59]

The practice ended at 6:30 pm. When the New York kids got home, they told their parents about the one boy whose diploma was threatened. Jittery parents jammed the switchboard at the *World-Telegram* demanding clarification. Now it seemed as though several players would quit out of fear.

No one wanted to continue the fight against Dr. Graves, certainly not the principals of the schools involved. With so much uncertainty and fear, the National Sports Council made the call to abandon the All Stars. They would be mourned by John Ross in the *Brooklyn Eagle* the next day.

> Twenty young gridders rolled out of bed this morning to find a cherished dream shattered—one that visioned them playing in Miami on Christmas Night. Little did they know yesterday, these big huskies called the Metropolitan All-Stars, that the New York State Education Commission was going to sweep down on them after almost every detail had been worked out for the glorious gridiron adventure. But today, the All Stars, like Seward Park's Dead End Kids, are saying, "Gee, it would have been swell, eh?"[60]

Now what? Well, there was always Garfield. Argauer got back to his home in Newark. McCann was on the phone. Could he meet with him and Dill at the Hotel New Yorker at 10:30 p.m.? Argauer went him one better. He roused Mayor Gabriel, three school commissioners and a Board of Education representative and took them along.

There, at the same hotel where three weeks earlier Florida officials determined that Erasmus Hall was the perfect choice, they talked things over. It wasn't a cinch. The talks lasted three hours. But, for once, McCann and Dill were dealing with officials who weren't trying to stonewall them. The Garfield party left at 2:30 a.m. with a tentative invitation from Dill.

There was one last holdup. Yarborough—even as hundreds of telegrams from Garfield reached his desk. Too small of a town, not enough drawing power. Then, when Nutley was named to play in Gainesville, he felt that another New Jersey team would gum up ticket sales even further. Yarborough was not informed of the goings-on in New York, that the Met All Stars were disbanded.

McMahon drove over to Miami High Wednesday morning and told Yarborough of Dill and McCann's late night meeting with Argauer, how Garfield was extended the invitation awaiting the coach's approval. McCann had told McMahon, while the Seward nonsense was going on, that Yarborough was making the final decision. It was McMahon who reported the previous week that Oak Park was Yarborough's second choice after Seward Park, then Lawrence, then Garfield. Yarborough, though, was under the false impression that Nutley, not Garfield, was the New Jersey state champ. McMahon set him straight.

"I don't want Garfield to think I was against it," Yarborough told McMahon. "I thought the New Jersey school was not well known. After all, the committee hopes to derive much financially from the game and a New York school would have been preferred.

"When Seward Park was refused permission to play the game, I was against the selection of the All Star team but assented to the committee's desires for a New York club. Garfield has a good club and a splendid record and I'm sure it will give us a good game."

Yarborough told McMahon that he would accept the recommendation of any team the Florida committee selected.

"Mr. Dill is returning from New York, and I expect a call from him in any minute from Washington," he said.[61]

So was Argauer. He got his call at 12:30 pm. Yarborough had agreed. Garfield was going to Miami at last. They'd gotten there by a most circuitous route. But they were going. And nothing could change that.

"I'm glad for the sake of the boys," Argauer said before ordering the equipment out of storage and calling a practice at Belmont Oval immediately after school. "It's the greatest thing that ever happened to them. All their life they'll remember this trip."[62]

Leonard Lewin of the *Daily Mirror* came the closest to summing up the zany process that finally put the bid on Garfield's doorstep:

> Well! Here we go again! This Health Bowl game situation has produced more contra-dictory communiqués than the European War, so on with No. 356, or something.
>
> Dick McCann, staff general for the Sports Council forces of the Infantile Paralysis Fund, after losing a battle for official sanction of the Metropolitan All Star team Tuesday, turned right around yesterday with a telegraphic and telephonic bombardment which culminated in the capture of the services of unbeaten Garfield, N.J.[63]

The game was saved.

At this point, everyone was too weary to complain any more, except the Brockton people. This appeared in the *Fitchburg Sentinel*:

> With all due respect to the committee picking the Christmas day opponent for Miami the champion Brockton team is the best high school team it could have picked. Brockton has won the Mass. title three years in a row and has the skill, the size and players to give any high school team in the country a battle. Evidently Miami High or the committee on selections is not looking for a real champion. Greater New York teams have always been fairly easy for Massachusetts teams.[64]

But Garfield wasn't a New York team. Even the *World-Telegram* called the Boilermakers the best high school team in the metropolitan area. Upon seeing Babula, Erasmus coach Paul Sullivan called him, "a honey of a player." The *New York Times* called him "the star of stars."

In the end, did justice prevail? Was Garfield the better choice anyway? East and Billings had their arguments. They could have maintained that Odell and Frickey were the equal to Babula. Brockton and City College could stand on their records. However, while there existed no credible comparative analysis of the relative strengths of the New York and New Jersey schools (because they crossed over to play each other so infrequently), there was one pivotal game in 1939 that would clearly finger the needle toward Garfield.

In October, Flushing High, the eventual champion of Queens, accepted a $1,000 guarantee to visit Foley Field to fill a suddenly open week on Bloomfield's calendar. The Bengals, undefeated at the time but not as powerful, trampled the Red Devils, 26-0. It was clearly a step up in class for the New Yorkers. Even the hometown paper, the *Long Island City Star-Journal*, agreed. And it had made Flushing the favorite before the game.

"We are glad we changed our mind at the last minute and went to see the Armys and Columbias scramble to a 6-6 deadlock instead," wrote columnist Bob Mann. "Probably the only thing the Red Devils were aware of today as they drilled for next Saturday's meeting with Adams was that Jersey elevens play a bigger and better brand of football. The fact that the Bloomfields had been shattered by graduation and were virtually a veteran-less team, seemed to make no difference in the final score."

The headline above Mann's column read "Stay East of Hudson Seems Good Advice."[65]

In an accompanying story, Flushing coach Bob Fulton called Bloomfield "a well-trained, physically perfect, cohesive machine." "Drilled well in the fundamentals, Bloomfield's Bengals pushed the Red Devils all over the lot. The line was vastly superior and broke through with consummate ease," the article noted. The paper also quoted an "observer" who noted: "There aren't any inflated heads around here today, the boys have been shown a vastly superior type of high school football."[66]

Flushing lost its other game against a Jersey foe later that season, 19-0. It came up against Seton Hall Prep, which, as a prep school, could play over-age players. Flushing did bounce back from the Bloomfield debacle by beating Adams the next week, 13-6. By comparison, Seward Park opened the season by edging Adams, 14-12, while Garfield dominated Bloomfield, 19-0. The scores don't offer proof, just an indication of the level of competition.

What wasn't debatable was the strength of New Jersey football. At least five other teams— Nutley, East Orange, Vineland, Passaic and possibly Columbia—could have gone down to Miami and given the Stingarees all they could have handled. Together, they would have formed a much tougher schedule than Miami played during the season. But, by now, these arguments fell moot. The Boilermakers were packing their summer clothes. The final verdict on the Boilermakers' selection would be made in Miami on Christmas Night.

Years later, Walter Young mulled back on the entire madcap escapade: "Thank you, New York State Board of Education."

For all that Garfield went through, on the field and off, both in and out of their control, it was a miracle they ended up playing in the game. The Boilermakers didn't walk through a big door with Miami on the other side. They navigated a maze, balanced on a high wire, dangled a few times and wound up on their feet.

And there was still one more miracle to come.

EIGHTEEN

THE TRIP

It was as if everyone from the city of Garfield had chipped in for an Irish Hospitals' Sweepstakes ticket and collectively hit the jackpot. Against odds that seemed just as long . . . their Boilermakers were going to Miami.

Paperboys around town delivered the glad tidings that rainy morning. *The Herald-News* screamed, "GARFIELD TO PLAY MIAMI CHRISTMAS" across its front page, pushing the war news down below the fold.

The players wore their lettermen sweaters to school, the underclassmen in purple and the seniors in white. Even the teachers had a hard time concentrating on that day's lessons. There were pats on the back for Michael Babula as he made his rounds delivering his meat. In the taverns and corner bars such as Klecha's on Ray Street, the patrons downed shots to toasts of *Na zdrowie!* (To your health!). Even the looms at the woolen mills seemed to whirr a bit more merrily. Everyone, of course, expected the Boilermakers to return a winner.

It had been a community effort, from Mayor John Gabriel's behind-the-scenes politicking to Art Argauer working his Florida connections, to ordinary citizens who deluged Jesse Yarborough's office with telegrams after Art McMahon reported that the Miami coach had the final say in the selection process. Now that Garfield finally got the nod, Hy Goldberg, the *Newark News* columnist, said that if the committee was looking for an underdog story, it wasn't getting short-changed in Garfield:

> *That's all very unfortunate but the bitter pill for Seward is ice cream for the Garfield boys. There aren't any Vanderbilts on the Garfield team. Most of these lads are just as much "Dead End Kids" as the Seward boys, even if they don't live down near the East River. They are the children of mill workers and under ordinary circumstances, trips to Florida are something they read about on the society page, if, by accident, they should happen to turn back from the sport page.[1]*

Argauer was buzzing around with preparations with the team leaving in six days on December 19. He wanted to call an immediate practice after school at half-frozen Belmont

Oval, but the rain kept the team indoors for a skull session. In the meantime, Mayor Gabriel quickly arranged for subsequent practices to be held at Passaic Stadium.

"Belmont Oval's days are over," Gabriel declared, ever hopeful that a new stadium was forthcoming. "Why should we show our worst side to the visiting newspapermen?"

Argauer had already started working with the team for its basketball season opener in three days against Dickinson in Jersey City, where footballers Ed Hintenberger, Bill Librera, John Grembowitz, John Orlovsky and Al Yoda were in the lineup that came away with a 51-35 victory. There would be another game against Kearny the night before the planned departure. They would win that, as well, but for now, football was back as the number-one focus.

The *Bergen Record*'s Al Del Greco, the old Garfield Comet, headed back to his old haunt to catch up with Argauer and the boys at No. 8 school, where team manager Louis Kral reissued uniforms and equipment amid the hubbub. Most of the players, as if on a cloud, jaunted through the raindrops up Palisade Avenue from their classrooms at No. 6 to their lockers at No. 8 and engaged in a little horseplay once they got there. Argauer, Del Greco's old Savage School classmate, was flashing an ear-to-ear smile. For once, the stern coach was letting the team have a bit of fun.

An anxious lad tugged on Del Greco's arm.

"Look, I'm an assistant manager," he said excitedly. "There are seven of us. We collect the uniforms, we clean the helmets, we sweep the floor. We see that these guys don't rob the building and are we going to Miami?"

Del Greco "took a philosophical slant" on the matter and told him, "In every life, some rain must fall."

The kid got the message.

"Nuts."

The basement room was crowded with reporters and photographers, and Argauer was multi-tasking as he pulled on his coaching togs.

"We've got 500 choice seats. The Bowl seats 30,000," he told one reporter before instructing the squad to put on their uniforms for pictures.

"There won't be time later," he explained.

He turned to William Capone, Board of Ed secretary and needlessly reminded him: "You had better take care of all the train and boat reservations."

And then to William Whitehead, president of the Board of Ed, he said: "We should order forty-four new rayon jerseys right now with yellow numbers on the purple. They'll only cost about three-fifty, and that'll give us a swell set-up. The old jerseys will go two more years."

Then he came back to the reporters, offering them a cigarette.

"They're on the desk," he said. "Honest, I think we'll play a better game than any crowd of All Stars. Of the twenty-two All Stars picked on the *World-Telly* team, only two played the double wingback system (to be used by Seward Park coach Jerry Warshower). How can you get any place that way?"

Benny Babula was in demand. A photographer asked him to pose with his coach. Babula ran his finger through his wavy blonde hair and asked for a comb.

"Thinks I got all day," the photographer whispered underneath his breath.

"Nothing the matter with your hair," Argauer told him.

"One of you fellows hold a football," the photographer said. So Wally Tabaka found one and threw it against the wall, nearly knocking out the camera.

Newark Evening News

32 ••• WEDNESDAY, DECEMBER 13, 1939

Garfield Accepts Health Bowl Bid

Brother, Can You Spare a Dime?

All-Star Team Plan Is Killed

Jersey Eleven Will Play Miami High December 25

The Newark Evening News *spreads the news of Garfield's Health Bowl selection on its lead sports page.* Newark Public Library.

"No brains," Argauer chided.

"Here, throw it right this time," he said as he tossed the football back. Tabaka caught it easily, looking the ball into his hands then sent back a low spiral that Argauer missed somewhat clumsily.

The players howled.

"Now settle down," Argauer said, getting back to business. "There are some things I want to make clear to you about this game."

The room emptied out except for the players and coaches.

"The door closed," Del Greco wrote. "And the assistant manager peered into the room through the keyhole."[2]

Garfield already rivaled the Stingarees in enthusiasm, especially after a rather depressing occurrence that took place in Miami over the past weekend. With some free time between games, Jesse Yarborough headed out for a round of golf at Miami Springs, where the $10,000 Miami Open, featuring Byron Nelson, Sam Snead, Ralph Guldahl, Jug McSpaden and Henry Picard, would be played later that week. He asked Jay Kendrick to caddie for him as he teed it up with state official E.D. Fancher, Dr. A.F. Kasper of the Orange Bowl Committee, and Milton Chapman, managing director of the Miami Biltmore Hotel, where the Missouri Tigers stayed during the Orange Bowl.

The conversation was carefree and Yarborough, after a decent front nine, was hoping to break 90 again. They were on the 11th tee, a long par four, when Chapman took a mighty cut with his driver and hit one off the club's toe. Kendrick was standing in the most unfortunate spot imaginable, at Chapman's two-o'clock (just in front and to his right). He had no time to react and the golf ball hit the star lineman just under his right eye. Blood gushed from a gash requiring three stitches at nearby Jackson Memorial Hospital. Kendrick had been one of his most durable players, and now he was injured in a freak accident. The *Miami Herald* reported that Kendrick's availability for the Christmas game wouldn't be known until his X-rays were viewed.[3] But the coach knew that, outside of Eldredge, there wasn't a more valuable member of his team than Kendrick. What he didn't know was that a big, bruising back named Benny Babula would soon be banging away at his line and that Kendrick would be needed more in this game than in any other.

The Boilermakers, meanwhile, had to make up for the week that was lost before they were finally extended the bid. They hadn't played a game in the 19 days since the anticlimactic win over Clifton. Miami, meanwhile, never broke training while playing two huge games in that span, one for the city championship against Edison, the other for the Southern championship against Boys High. In fact, while a handful of Argauer's two-sport athletes were already playing basketball, Eldredge and the other gridders who also played on Clyde Crabtree's basketball team were not going to join the cage squad until football was finished.

Of course, it could work both ways. The Stingarees had been through a long season and had gotten emotionally charged up for two championship games. This was not necessarily their biggest game. The Boilermakers were, in a way, fresh and rejuvenated. This was unquestionably their biggest game, not just of the season but of their lives.

Miami's two newspapers gave the Garfield announcement equal billing with the golf tournament and its record 217-player field, happily noting that the national championship was back on the table with the demise of the Met All Stars.

Yarborough began his preparations for the game with a light practice the same day Garfield got back to work. It was mostly a photo session. The hard practices would start the next day as he tried to gather information on Garfield. The coaches would exchange their offensive and defensive formations but not their game films. And, in that, Argauer held an advantage.

There was no way Yarborough could know anything about the strengths and weaknesses of Garfield, especially on short notice as the National Sports Council fumbled for an opponent. This left Yarborough a bit on his heels, a bit sucker-punched when it came to pre-game surveillance. Argauer, on the other hand, had a spy, of sorts. The vacationing Art McMahon attended the Stingarees' rout of Boys High. The newsman could tell Argauer not only what plays the Stingarees used but also in what circumstances they were employed. Additionally, he imparted to Argauer reconnaissance on Eldredge's play and how the Purples had strategically plotted to thwart the speedster.

McMahon's wasn't the only brain Argauer picked. Ever meticulous, he would leave no detail unattended. He phoned Charles Benson, the coach at Pompton Lakes. Benson's team had played in Clearwater, Florida, in 1938 and lost 20-6 after defeating the Floridians, 13-7, in New Jersey in 1937.

Benson's advice? Don't drink the water.

That gave Argauer an idea. Garfield operated its own artesian well water works in neighboring East Paterson, where groundwater was contained in aquifers under pressure between layers of permeable rock. Residents claimed, then as now, that there was no better drinking water in New Jersey. Maybe it was because of the exotic name "Artesian," but in any case, that was the water that would slake his players' thirsts in Miami. But, how to get it there? Ah, convenient connections, again. Mayor Gabriel's family ran a dairy farm. They would fill twelve forty-gallon stainless steel milk cans with artesian well water and load them onto the train.

Argauer would also get an idea of the strength and merits of Florida football from Nutley. On the same day the Boilermakers were back practicing, the Maroon Raiders were going through their first workout in Gainesville, where they would meet Suwannee High that Friday night. Suwannee High was out of Live Oak, a once rich cotton-producing area that was devastated by the boll weevil infestation of the 1920s. Farmers had since transitioned to growing tobacco as their main cash crop—that and high school football players. They grew them big and strong in Live Oak.

The Maroon Raiders were already in Florida when they opened the local papers and read that Garfield had been chosen for the Health Bowl. Now, they suddenly felt as though they were on the undercard. In fact, the *Florida Times-Union* reported that the entire Nutley crew was "sort of steamed" about it.

"There wasn't a boy here today who didn't believe his team could whip Garfield," the paper said.[4]

The Maroon Raiders pointed to their edge in the comparative scores against Bloomfield and Clifton and claimed that Garfield refused to play them or to even consider it. They had also been led to believe that they were a favorite—over Garfield—to play Miami.

It had been reported by Walt Maloney of the *Nutley Sun* that, according to a story in the *Washington Times-Herald* by-lined Vincent X. Flaherty, the Health Bowl committee was about to name Nutley as the northern representative before the nod went to Seward Park. Flaherty's source of information was McCann, the fast-talking guy who'd been keeping up everybody's hopes. Had Maloney known that, he might not have written that, according to the "grapevine," the bid was "as good as in Nutley coach George Stanford's hands."[5]

Disappointed by the Miami verdict, Nutley accepted readily when the invitation from the Jacksonville organizers of the Gainesville game came "like a bolt out of the blue." Nevertheless, there seemed to be a lot of envious Maroon Raiders. Garfield was stealing their thunder.

Now, as a way of building up the Gainesville game, *The Nutley Sun* was calling the Suwannee team "the most feared in Florida" and reporting that Miami had turned down a challenge to play the Green Wave. Of course, the Stingarees would have had a hard time squeezing another game into their crammed schedule, especially at the end of the year. They had little to prove playing a northern Florida club after defeating Robert E. Lee, the champion of the Big Ten, the biggest football conference in Florida.[6]

Suwanee had won all nine of its games by a combined 321-37 score and had an All Southern guard in Rudolph Fletcher. The papers hyped the game as a battle between two hard-driving fullbacks, Frank Cardinale for Nutley and Suwannee's Nicky Tsacrios, who scored 133 points to Cardinale's 132 on the season. Stanford, meanwhile, proclaimed his team "ready for any schoolboy team in the country.

"The caliber of football played by high school elevens in this state (New Jersey) I think is the best of its kind," he said. "Sure, we're going to beat them."[7]

He was right. The game wasn't close. Nutley was the superior team.

Suwannee squandered an early opportunity when Tsacrios intercepted a lateral from Motz Buel to Cardinale, only to fumble himself with a clear field ahead of him. Later, Tsacrios was hit hard while fielding a punt in the second quarter and he fumbled again at the Green Wave 19. Cardinale finished off that drive and scored again once more before the half. The heat got to Nutley in the second half—Stanford used just three subs trying to keep the slippery Tsacrios in check—but the teams played a scoreless second half and Nutley earned a 14-0 victory, as convincing as 14-0 win could be.

Charley Bozorth, writing in the *Gainesville Sun*, acknowledged it a was a one-sided contest with Nutley, "working with precision and grace that was beautiful to watch." He added: "While a power in themselves, the Suwannee eleven just couldn't cope with the faster, harder running New Jersey team."[8]

Suwannee wasn't on the same level as Miami. Anyone who'd seen both of them play agreed. But because Nutley's win reinforced the strength of New Jersey high school football, Argauer had to be heartened. New Jersey teams had now won five of the six games played against Florida squads since 1936, and McMahon reported from Miami that "cocky" Stingaree supporters were suddenly a bit jittery. Of course, that did not stop *The Sun*'s Maloney from predicting doom for Garfield based on what people were telling him down south:

> *Being a Northerner, we should say that the Boilermakers will annihilate the Stingarees but reports on Miami make us think the Floridians will be victorious next Monday night.*
>
> *Although they were crowned Northern Jersey champions and acclaimed by many as state kings, we were not overly impressed with Garfield's record during this season. Certainly, they do not rate as being one of the contenders for the national championship, which Miamians (but not Floridians) are calling this game.[9]*

It turned out to be one of the last of Garfield putdowns, at least in North Jersey. For the most part, though, everyone in New Jersey, and even the metropolitan area, wished the Boilermakers well. Lodi coach Stan Piela, who starred on Garfield's unbeaten 1924 team, even offered his team up as scrimmage fodder to Argauer the day Nutley played Suwannee. Piela knew the Boilermakers needed to knock off the cobwebs and he was happy to help his *alma mater*. "I'd like to see his boys in good shape for that Miami game," he explained. Argauer called it "a gracious move" that he "appreciated very much."

"The boys are in good condition but need some work to sharpen themselves. That long train ride to Miami isn't going to do them any good," he said, somewhat worriedly.

Of course, the Lodi boys couldn't wait. When Piela told them to prepare for the scrimmage, their faces lit up with thoughts of: "Get Babula." Big Stan quickly put a stop to that.

"Listen. If any of you boys dare to touch that big boy, I'll personally see that you're fried in the best olive oil. Let's get it straight. We're friends for a while, not enemies," he said, firmly.

"I can't imagine anything more terrible than Babula getting hurt in practice now," Del Greco wrote. "Argauer would never live it down. So don't be surprised if Benny doesn't do any running."[10]

Babula did a lot of running, in fact, and the Lodi kids never really touched him. He burst off the end for several long runs and completed a series of passes (9-of-11 in all) that left the Lodi defenders bewildered. He came out of the scrimmage unscathed. But Argauer would still be left second-guessing himself about the wisdom of accepting Piela's offer.

Early on in the scrimmage, Wally Tabaka made a cut on a field still soggy from the previous days' rain. He felt something go in his left knee and, although it wasn't terribly painful, it didn't feel right. He came off the field limping, and Argauer sent him into the grandstands next to John Grembowitz, who was sitting out the scrimmage with a staph infection on his arm. The *Bergen Record*'s Art Johnson reported that neither seemed to be serious, but Argauer wasn't going to take any more risks.[11] Only light practices were scheduled for the next three days before the long trip over the rails Tuesday. Team physician Dr. Erwin Reid would join them and try to nurse Tabaka's knee back to playing condition. Hopefully, it would respond well in the warm Florida sun.

Now, each team had a major injury concern. By Sunday, it became official that Kendrick would not be available. He was taken back into Jackson Memorial and kept in a darkened room. The injury was much more serious than it first appeared.

Yarborough couldn't believe how fortune was beginning to turn against his team.

"All year long we didn't have an injury," he lamented to Art McMahon. "Now Kendrick is out. (Henry) Washington is in Havana where his mother is ill. His father (Raoul F. Washington) is vice consul there. (Dick) Fauth has the flu and is in the hospital. That's luck for you."[12]

Yarborough, unsure of the status of Washington and Fauth, both tackles, suddenly had limited options. He decided to violate a cardinal rule of coaching. He changed three positions to replace one man. He moved Levin Rollins from center to right tackle and shifted Doug Craven from right tackle to Kendrick's spot at right guard. Then, instead of using backup center Paul Louis—a future Stingaree Hall of Famer—he moved Harvey James into the pivot spot. James had played exclusively as a blocking back his one season at Miami but had been the starting center at Benedictine Military Academy. That's also where he would make the Hall of Fame at the University of Miami and from where the Cleveland Browns would draft him.

It wasn't as if Yarborough were throwing slugs into the lineup. He knew Kendrick was a long shot anyway and, in the least, he had two weeks to practice with the new configuration. Still, Kendrick was a major loss.

Argauer had a couple of other minor concerns. Walter Young's mother balked at her son making the trip. The game was on Christmas when New Apostolic boys would be in church, not on the football field. Had Walter not had two older brothers, Argauer might have been missing his star left end, just recently named to at least one All State team. But Rudy and Curt ultimately convinced their mother to let Walter make the trip of his young life. She needn't worry about him behaving himself. That much was certain.

Babula, meanwhile, was reaching his 20th birthday on Christmas Eve. That would have made him ineligible by NJSIAA bylaws. There was a brief concern that he'd be unable to play. But the Florida age limit was 21, not 20. Three Miami players had already turned 20, Harvey James in July, Charlie Burrus in November and Bucket Barnes in December.

When Argauer informed Yarborough about Babula's age, Ole Mule said playfully, "You stick to your regulations and I'll stick to mine."[13] He wasn't serious, of course. There was no way organizers were going to disqualify one of their primary gate attractions. In fact, Argauer ended up bringing back Red Barrale, who turned overage just before the Bloomfield game.

By this time, Garfield was becoming a national story. Back home, the papers had to decide whether to spring to send someone to Florida to cover the game. Art McMahon was already in Miami for *The Herald-News*. There was no question he would remain there while Joe Lovas covered the activities in Garfield. Al Del Greco didn't get to make the trip, much to his dismay. The *Bergen Record* used anonymous "special" dispatches all week. Paul Horowitz arrived in Miami shortly after the team but he was the only Newark writer there. The *Star-Ledger* contracted *Miami Herald* sports editor Everett Clay as a stringer. The New York City papers retained some interest in the game once the Met All Stars were nixed but only the *New York Times* staffed the game.

Then there was Hardy Whritenour. Whritenour was a 17-year-old high school student who had little interest in high school. He dreamed of becoming a sportswriter and he managed to wrangle assignments covering high school games for the *Paterson News* and his hometown *Little Falls Herald*—without pay. At the dinner table he'd regale his family with tales of the games he saw and while they humored him, they really wanted him to earn his high school diploma. They thought changing schools might help so Whritenour transferred between Passaic Valley, Paterson Central and Paterson Eastside but never did graduate.

It just so happened that the Whritenours were vacationing in St. Petersburg over the 1939 Christmas holiday. Young Hardy made his way from there to Miami to cover the game. Later in life, he'd be known as Joe Whritenour. After serving as a combat correspondent for the *Stars and Stripes* during World War II, he eventually settled in as the long-time sports information director at Lehigh University. He'd type out his releases in a room with his pet parakeet, who learned to mimic the sound of his fingers pounding on the keyboard.

Meanwhile, the National Sports Council was cranking up the publicity machine after losing so much valuable time that could have been spent on promotion and ticket-selling. Its press releases, however, along with *Associated Press* wire stories, were widely picked up by newspapers around the nation, unlike the marginal attention the Louisiana game piqued.

The NSC sought to get the ball rolling just before the Seward Park announcement with a release on the game's importance as the opening salvo in the anti-polio campaign with its focus on the four high school gridders—Jules Yon, Charley Moon, Jimmy Colton and Bill Stevens—felled by the disease since the start of the 1939 season.

"More than ever before the fight against infantile paralysis is the sports world's own fight," it said.[14]

Surely, the NSC was ready to wax poetic in press releases about Seward Park but, in Garfield, it found material to spin a new narrative in two figures—Gabriel and Babula. The mayor, never camera-shy or media unfriendly, willingly participated in the publicity campaign, even if it may have given him a little more credit than he deserved. It was all for the good of the city. If they didn't know about Garfield before, they certainly knew now.

Considine promptly began working the "Boy Mayor" angle in his syndicated "On the Line" column in the *New York Daily Mirror* where he called Gabriel "the wonder boy of Jersey politics" and took one final shot at New York's regents:

> *His Garfield High School football team has been selected to play Miami High in the Health Bowl game . . . the novel part of all this is that they are actually going—a pardonable observation on our part, inasmuch as we've been enthusing in print for more than a week over this and that foe for Miami High. We wrote a piece about Seward Park, the Dead End Zone Kids, and then, when they were finally sidetracked by our charitably-minded educators, we spit on our hands and did some more literary cartwheels over the selection of the World-Telegram's All Metropolitan team. This, too, was ploughed under by our persevering pedants.*
>
> *We don't know what is the matter with New Jersey's educational fathers. They obviously don't believe that it hurts a boy to see a section of our great country that most of the kids could never hope to see: Florida. They apparently don't even think it will be harmful for the Garfield boys to stop off in Washington for a look at Congress and a trip through several of the nation's great shrines. Like Mayor La Guardia, the Jersey educators see nothing unconstitutional, or even criminal, in the kids having a great Christmas holiday.[15]*

Considine shared the story of how Gabriel drove past a Garfield practice one day and decided to have a look. The competitive juices from his football playing days at Garfield and Drexel kicked in, and he sauntered to the middle of the field where he asked Wally Tabaka to flip him the ball.

"Let me boot one," the mayor pleaded. He swung his leg mightily, too mightily, as a matter of fact. There was a loud ripping noise from the seat of his pants. Indeed, he would have been showing his own "worst side" to the newspapermen.

"Miami High gridmen are herewith warned not to be astounded if he comes tearing out of his flag-draped box on Christmas night, silk hat tucked under his arm, and tackles a touch-down-bound Miamian," Considine joked.[16]

Indeed, at one of the pre-Miami practices at Passaic Stadium, Gabriel obliged photographers by climbing back into a gold uniform—jersey number 25—and lining up for a field goal with Babula holding. It got good play across the country as papers ran the NSC press release on the boy mayor:

> Gabriel blew his horn—and the undefeated football team of Garfield High School got the bid over a score of other crack schoolboy elevens scattered through the nation.
>
> You see, Mayor Johnny Gabriel, the 29-year-old chief executive of this thriving little industrial town, made it practically a campaign issue to get this trip and game for his high school boys. He bombarded the Florida Sports committee, the National Sports Council and various noted sports writers with phone calls, telegrams, letters and personal visits seeking the bid for the boys.[17]

Of course, none of that helped until the New York State Board of Education wielded its gavel but then, as now, there was no letting the facts get in the way of a good story. And there certainly was a lot of truth in the mayor's enthusiasm for city and team.

"I just had to holler for them," Gabriel was quoted as saying. "You see, we used to have a high juvenile delinquency rating here about five years ago and I campaigned on the platform of getting the boys out of the alleys and back into the classroom. When I got into office, I told the kids that if they concentrated on athletics and studies, life would be happier and better all around. I got them to be more interested in sports because, you know, if you're playing a game you're keeping out of trouble.

"Well, it worked. The accent on athletics produced two happy results: the delinquency rate dropped and the victories rose."[18]

It also helped having a player like Benny Babula. And, with college scouts eyeing the Garfield flash, the press got busy hyping the game as a battle between the two blonde backs: Babula and Eldredge.

"There are a couple of blondes who will be preferred by the gentleman of the collegiate football scouting profession when Garfield High of New Jersey and Miami High of Florida get together in their high school clash on Christmas Day," an *Associated Press* story barked, calling each a "ball of fire" and speculating that they could even end up on the same college team.[19]

Other papers ran an NSC release that portrayed Babula as another Bill DeCorrevont, the Chicago High School sensation who attracted nationwide fame two years earlier before deciding on Northwestern:

> He's got a face like a matinee idol. He's got a powerful frame like a Tarzan. And his name sounds like a football cheer.
>
> Benny pronounces his name to rhyme with Yale's great cheer, "Boola-Boola" which is quite all right with Eastern experts because they've been pronouncing him the greatest schoolboy back in the nation.

The story added that Benny's boosters would have none of those DeCorrevont comparisons:

> *"What do you mean Bud DeCorrevont the second?" they snorted. "Benny is second to no one. He is Benny Babula the First, not Bud DeCorrevont the Second."*

Actually, the anonymous writer got that wrong. "Bud" DeCorrevont was Bill's brother, also at Northwestern. He probably took more literary license when he "quoted" Argauer regarding the college scouts:

> *They've been after him so much—at school, at practice, everywhere—that I wouldn't be surprised to see one of them pop up right in the huddle and hand him a contract to sign and a scholarship to use.*[20]

Papers everywhere began attaching Babula's name to some big-time college program: Tennessee, Notre Dame, Princeton and Georgia Tech, which was playing Missouri in the Orange Bowl New Year's Day. One story even had him heading to William and Mary with Johnny Grembowitz in a package deal. Babula himself broke the suspense while in Miami when he named Fordham as his number one choice. Eldredge, meanwhile, was said to have every college in the south on his list. He wouldn't announce his intention to attend Georgia Tech, his brother Knox's biggest rival—for quite some time.

Hyperbole or not, it all helped to focus national and local attention on the game—just as its organizers had hoped—and triggered a spike in ticket sales.

Back in Garfield, the city was planning a grand send-off Tuesday morning. Incredibly, when viewed through today's lens, there was a final matter the Boilermakers needed to tend to. The school's basketball team was scheduled to host Kearny on the eve of the Miami trip, with the Garfield squad suiting up several football players. A specter of injuries loomed.

Tabaka, naturally, didn't play on his injured knee, and Argauer kept Babula out of the lineup in the 55-30 victory. However, five other football players participated, including Orlovsky, who scored 14 points. Joe Benigno, one of the Jewell Street boys, led the Boilermakers with 15 points.

With that, Argauer and his boys hurried home to packed bags. It was an early wake-up call. John Gabriel declared December 19 a citywide holiday, and it remains one of the most spectacular days in Garfield history.

"Schools will be deserted, factories will be slowed down, shops will be shuttered and housewives will leave the breakfast dishes soaking as all of Garfield moves to Newark to cheer the boys on their way when they board the streamline special for the sunny south," trumpeted the *Associated Press*.[21] And, for once, they weren't exaggerating. Almost half the city turned out for the twelve–mile procession to Newark Penn Station to see their heroes off to Miami—more than anyone could have imagined.

An organizing committee cutting across party lines demonstrated what could be achieved with politics put aside. By 7:45 a.m., thousands were gathered around the high school on Palisade Avenue, where 15 buses, 200 private automobiles countless trucks and the pumper from Fire Company 1 were to be loaded with supporters.

One Garfield motorcycle cop, four cruisers from the Garfield police department and six more from the Bergen County police force led the entourage and cleared the way.

Banners draped across the front of the buses read: "Garfield to Miami in Fight Against Infantile Paralysis."

School was suspended for half the day, and the entire student body of the high school and elementary schools—2,800 strong—went along for the ride. Benny's sister Eva drove his girlfriend, Violet Frankovic.

The motorcade headed toward Passaic Street and crossed the Passaic River into Wallington, then on through the Carlton Hill section of Rutherford and into Lyndhurst, North Arlington, Kearny and Harrison, hugging the Passaic River bank south toward Newark, sirens and horns blaring, lights flashing. People craned from their front porches, and workers peered out of factory windows all along the way, cheering along with passers-by. The players opened their bus windows and waved back to some of the same fans who had rooted against them during the regular season. But they were New Jersey's team now.

They crossed the Central Avenue Bridge in Newark and stopped at Raymond Boulevard and Broad Street, along Military Park, where they disembarked and marched down the final few blocks to the railroad station. The purple-clad Garfield High School band, with Margaret Hoving high-stepping out in front, played Garfield's fight song. But one band wasn't enough. Joseph F. Fitzgerald, the head of the New Jersey Committee for the Celebration of the Presidents Birthday, arranged for his hometown Carteret High School band to join the party. Gabriel told the blue-cloaked Rambler band: "If our team is as good as your band, Garfield will win by a large margin."[22]

Ordinary folks off the street joined in until the throng swelled to what Newark police estimated at 10,000.

Students carrying the banners led the parade, followed by the Garfield High band. Next came Gabriel and other city officials, followed by the players and coaches, the Garfield Junior Patrol, the Carteret band, which lined either side of the entrance to the station as the players walked through and, bringing up the rear, what seemed like all of humanity.

It was a mob scene. Traffic and commerce came to a temporary halt in New Jersey's largest city but few seemed to mind. Office workers fashioned makeshift confetti and rained it down from skyscrapers. The players must have felt like Charles Lindbergh.

At Penn Station, photographers snapped pictures of Babula, in a fashionable trench coach and tie (all the boys wore their Sunday best), shaking hands with Gabriel and Argauer.

As the flashbulbs popped, reporters asked for final comments.

"Better spirit is in the team today than I've ever seen," Gabriel said. "I honestly think the team will win. By the time Babula gets through with them, he'll be All American. The most important part is they know they can't be beaten."

"We're going to do our best," Argauer promised. "The boys are in great shape physically. If we get acclimated, we're going to lick 'em."

Babula was more modest.

"I hope we win," he said. "I feel fine and so does the rest of the team."[23]

The photographers wanted to get a picture of Babula with Governor Moore but he couldn't be found. Moore had intended to deliver a prepared speech to the team just before the train pulled out. But, battling the hundreds that managed to squeeze onto the platform at Penn Station, he and Senator John G. Milton somehow got lost in the jostling throng.

Benny Babula and John Gabriel wave good bye from the back of the Vacationer *as the Garfield team pulls out of Newark Penn Station.*
Courtesy Garfield Historical Society.

They ended up on Track 3 while the team was on Track 1. In what must have seemed like a comic Laurel and Hardy short, all he could do was shout across the sets of tracks to Gabriel. The newspapers compared him to "Wrong Way" Corrigan, the aviator.

If the players weren't impressed by the pandemonium breaking out at Penn Station, then they must have been when they took in the special coach train commissioned for the trip to Florida. The original plans were for the team to journey by boat, which would be docked in Miami and also serve as the team's hotel for the week. With time running out, Garfield was instead whisked down on the Atlantic Coast Line's *Vacationer* streamliner, which had been put into service only the year before. With the massive diesel engine out front, it must have seemed to the boys that they were stepping onto a space ship.

A final photo was taken of Babula and Gabriel waving from the rear of the last car to a huge ovation from the masses sending them off. Rosalyn D'Amico, Joe Tripoli's little niece who hung out at the team practices, had a great view from atop her father's shoulders. Violet and Eva waved frantically from the middle of the mob scene, but they weren't sure if Benny saw them. They shrugged as the train powered up and chugged out of the station at 9:45 am for the 26-hour journey with brief stops in Washington, Richmond, Rocky Mount, Charleston, Savannah and Jacksonville.

Babula and Grembowitz sat together up front, across from Argauer and his wife Florence. The team saw her only at breakfast and at the Christmas Eve dinner. Most of the players looked excitedly out the train windows. Only two had ever been more than 100 miles away from home. Only a handful had even been to New York City. When the train got to Philadelphia, one of the players asked if they'd reached Miami.

"Settle down," Argauer told him. It was one of his favorite phrases.

All the while, Letty Barbour, the high school songstress, entertained the team. She went from car to car and, by all reports, never stopped singing. Just a 15-year-old, she was discovered by *Daily Mirror* radio critic Nick Kenny, who gave her the stage name of Barbour and secured a spot for her on Major Bowes' *The Original Amateur Hour* over WHN Radio in New York.

"How old are you?" the major asked her.

"Sixteen," she fibbed, blushing.

"What do you want to be when you grow up?" he said.

"Seventeen," she answered.

Whatever her age, Letty wowed Bowes with her rendition of *God Bless America* and won the segment and got a few gigs at North Jersey nightclubs. She was not just keeping the team entertained on the trip; she was to sing over the public address system, including *God Bless America*, before the game.

Inside the team's special car on the Vacationer *just before the train left the station en route to Miami. Starting linemen Pete Yura and Jack Boyle are in the front lower right. Assistant coach John Hollis beams in the upper left.* Courtesy Estate of Angelo Miranda.

The Garfield High traveling party waves goodbye to the throng of well-wishers outside Newark Penn Station. Art Argauer, Benny Babula and Mayor John Gabriel are all visible at center. Courtesy Estate of Angelo Miranda.

Born Letizia Barbato, she lived on Westminster Place at the edge of the Heights with her parents and paternal grandparents. Her father, Joseph, a real estate and insurance agent, was born in Marseille and her mother Giulia was born in Italy. Letty's mother and grandmother made their own pasta and baked bread and rolls every morning, a daily treat for Letty's friends before they walked together to school.

Apart from Letty's warbling, the trip was uneventful. But, when they pulled into Jacksonville station at 4:15 a.m., to be switched over to the Florida East Coast tracks, the Boilermakers got their first taste of Southern hospitality. J. Frank Gough greeted them to escort them on the last six-and-one-half hours of their journey.

Gough was the president of the Greater Miami Hotel Association, a rather prestigious position in a city whose economy revolved around the tourism trade. He managed the Alcazar, where the team lodged at the hotel's expense. Built in 1925 as the Miami skyline rose from the ground seemingly overnight, the Alcazar was one of the most lavishly accommodated hotels in town.

Gough, a full-fledged Irishman, was a Brooklyn native who started his hotel career in Illinois. Now he was a Miami fixture and man about town, frequently mentioned in Jack Bell's newspaper columns, mostly to poke fun at his golf game. He was one of those larger-than-life figures, perfectly suited to the hospitality industry, and he was eager to show the Boilermakers the time of their lives. He would be there at their beck and call. After flying up from Miami, Gough filled in Argauer what awaited them in Miami.

Brilliant sunshine gleamed off the *Vacationer* as it rolled the team into Miami Depot, right on time at 11:59 a.m. The station itself wasn't very impressive, unlike four-year-old Newark Penn Station, with its airy, vaulted waiting halls and neo-classical inspirations. Instead, Miami greeted visitors with an outdoor platform fronting a non-distinct wood-frame building that was built in 1912 and dwarfed by the 361-foot Dade County Courthouse as its backdrop. In later years, the city wasted little time in razing the structure, long-derided as a traffic-clogging blight on the city.

But, to the Garfield players in 1939, it was the gateway to heaven. There, at Miami's sun-drenched gates, awaited a sun-tanned welcoming committee with all the accoutrements of a momentous civic event. Mayor Sewell greeted Mayor Gabriel and Yarborough shook Argauer's hand as he got off the train. The two coaches greeted each other heartily as they met for the first time—with their reputations very much preceding them.

A Movie Tone newsreel camera and radio microphones had been set up. Argauer unabashedly stepped before them, delighting in the attention, although he might have had to jostle his way to get in front of Gabriel.

"The boys are all are in good condition. Right now they need rest," he stated authoritatively, noting that not many slept well in their seats amid the excitement of the trip.[24]

The advance publicity had the photographers scrambling for the mayor and Babula. They clamored for pictures of Babula and Eldredge—the two blonde bombers—together in the same frame. They got the photo-op their editors expected: lovely Health Bowl queen Martina Wilson posed between them. Davey represented the team with Harvey Comfort, who was to take over captain duties at halftime, a Miami Christmas game tradition. Comfort reached his hand out to Babula and got more than he expected—three of his fingers crushed by Babula's vice-like handshake. When Comfort got back to his team, he warned this guy might be a problem.

Jesse Yarborough greets Art Argauer with a handshake as the Garfield team arrives at the Florida East Coast Railway station in Miami. Courtesy Garfield High School.

"That guy better not grab my hand again 'cause I'm gonna pull it right back," Comfort said. "He's got some strong grip."

Babula, undoubtedly, was far gentler as he joined the arms of two Miami coeds who escorted him to a waiting car. They were part of Miami High's all-female reception committee, described in official dispatches as "a bevy of Miami High School's famed beauties."[25] They brought gifts of oranges, bananas and coconuts to each player.

Peeling off their overcoats to bask in the warmth of both the bevy and the climate, the Boilermakers were paraded down Flagler Street in a 50-car caravan to the sounds of the Miami High School band and the Miami Drum and Bugle Corps. Told they would be taken to the Alcazar, one puzzled player asked the coach: "Gee, are we heading for Alcatraz?"

"This seems to be the biggest thing to hit Miami," a native told McMahon. "The Orange Bowl teams arrive, they are put in a bus and taken to their hotels. This Garfield sure must be plenty of football team to earn all this."[26]

The parade swept them to the steps of the Alcazar as if by magic carpet.

The ornate lobby was bedecked in tropical motifs. It was fitted with comfortable parlor chairs around an outsized Persian rug, ringed by ferns. An expansive, towering balcony added even more grandness. Gough led them up to the tiled rooftop of the 13-story hotel—some taking the first elevator rides of their lives—where the team was treated to an opulent lunch. There they ate, hundreds of miles from frost-bitten Garfield, shaded from a blazing sun by potted palm trees, scattered around the Alcazar's novel sun-bathing compartments.

The magnificent Alcazar Hotel, the team's home in Miami, as seen from across Biscyane Boulevard.
HistoryMiami Miami News Collection.

The team hangs out in the well-appointed lobby of the Alcazar. Red Simko, the Boilermakers' head cheer-leader, can be seen in the background after hitchhiking down to Miami. Courtesy Estate of Angelo Miranda.

Looking down, they could marvel at magnificent Biscayne Boulevard, with its three sets of royal palm islands. Directly across the thoroughfare, Bayfront Park stretched out its multi-colored hues only Florida could produce, toward the city's sun-on-chrome waters. It was other-worldly. They had never been feted like this before and maybe never would be again. Years later, Garfield's starting guard, Angelo Miranda, put it in perspective.

"Going to Miami was like another part of the world. We felt like we were part of the rich, the elite, when many of us were just about penniless," he said. "A trip like this was like a fairy tale. To be put up in a hotel for two weeks, being served breakfast, lunch and dinner, was the most beautiful thing that could ever happen to us. That game gave us hope."[27]

The boys chowed down, guzzling nothing but their own water, and got their room keys, four each in two-room suites. As tired as they were from the trip, the pranks began. Being typical goofy boys, they pushed the elevator buttons to stop on every floor. And they couldn't stop phoning each other's rooms just as modern-day teens can't stop texting. They drove the hotel's telephone operators crazy.

Argauer would put a stop to that later in the week when he told the boys that the hotel charged a five-cent tax for room calls.

"My gosh, I'm bankrupt," one cried.

There was no time for a nap. Practice was next, barely four hours after their arrival. Yes, practice. Nothing like some hard work to snap their minds out of paradise. And, while some grumbled, one was surely anticipating it. Wally Tabaka had been flexing his knee with

The starting lineup poses outside the Orange Bowl. Wally Tabaka (10) is pictured with John Grembowitz (33) on the line. Tabaka would be ruled out with a knee injury. Courtesy Estate of Angelo Miranda.

Art Argauer, nattily attired in a white linen suit tailored by his father, gathers his team around him outside the Orange Bowl at the Boilermakers' first practice in Miami. Courtesy Howard Lanza.

apprehension the entire trip down and, as he stepped off the train and squinted into the sun, he hoped it would be a magical elixir that would allow him to play.

The players really felt the Miami heat for the first time when they assembled in front of the Alcazar to board the bus to practice at Miami Field, just outside the Orange Bowl. Art McMahon had forewarned them in his reports from Miami when they were still working in the New Jersey chill.

"The weather has turned unusually warm in Miami and the Boilermakers may have to steal a leaf from the books of their grid hosts and do their practicing in shorts and bathing suits," he wrote. Instead, Argauer had them in full gear, heavy woolen jerseys and all.

"Now is the time," he said, to get them accustomed to the heat.

Now was also the moment for Tabaka to finally test the knee. He went off to the side with Dr. Reid and Bill Dayton, the University of Miami trainer who had been assigned to the team. Tabaka tried to loosen it up. It didn't feel any better. He tried to push off. He couldn't. He knew what that meant, and he started to cry openly. His teammates saw him.

Reid confided to Horowitz that Tabaka was definitely out with a torn ligament although there was no official word.[28] The *Miami Herald*'s Everett Clay, freelancing for the Newark *Star-Ledger* held out hope for the readers that Garfield could "slip him" into the game for a few minutes.[29] There were also scattered reports during the week that Dayton was cautiously optimistic Tabaka might play but, after some improvement, it stiffened up again on Friday night.

Tabaka stayed in uniform and posed for pictures. It was easy to see his disappointment in those shots. Garfield would miss him. While his sidelining didn't balance the Stingarees' loss of Kendrick, the Boilermakers nevertheless relied on Tabaka's talents as a return man and as a complement to Babula in the backfield. He ran most of the Boilermakers' spinner plays and, without him, the Garfield attack would be less deceptive. As a senior, he had started every one of Garfield's 20 straight wins and was one of the team's leaders.

It was truly a misfortune.

"Everyone felt terrible for Wally, he was so well-liked by all," Young recalled all those years later. "It was the one bad thing about the trip."

Argauer already expected Tabaka not to be ready and he was prepared. The good news was that John Orlovsky was healthy again after giving his shoulder a few weeks' rest. When Orlovksy was first injured, Grembowitz came out of right guard and replaced him at right halfback. Grembowitz would now have to shift into Tabaka's left halfback spot, though more as a blocker than runner. The Miami practice was Grembowitz's first. The staph infection had kept him out of the all workouts up north.

As the sun bore down on them, some of the players tried to beg off, yet Argauer kept them for the next two hours. He didn't work them particularly hard. There were lengthy warm-up exercises and what was called a signal drill, the offense going through its plays without working against a defense. Argauer told Paul Horowitz of the *Newark News* he wanted to tire the players out so they'd get a good night's sleep.

He also told Horowitz he was more worried about overconfidence than the heat. The players, having scanned the Miami roster, were pleasantly surprised to note their light-weighted opponents. Indeed, the Stingaree backfield averaged only 146 pounds per man, 36 fewer pounds per man than Garfield's backfield, with the Boilermakers enjoying an 11-pound average edge on the line.[30]

Benny Babula gets his powerful leg into a punt during a practice session outside the Orange Bowl as a few of the locals look on and marvel. Courtesy Jack DeVries.

"Benny Babula and his mates are wondering how the Miami backs can penetrate the powerful line of the Boilermakers," Horowitz wrote.

The Boilermakers weren't permitted to practice in the stadium in order to protect the playing field. Of course, that also meant that anyone could watch their workout. And as the *Miami Herald* reported, "all eyes were on 'Boom-Boom' Benny Babula.

"The Garfield attack looked impressive," the *Herald* observed. "The big blonde runs well and can hit pass receivers both near and far downfield."

The paper called Babula the "most troublesome back" the Stingarees would see, not only in 1939 but since the 1931 Christmas game when Andy Pilney starred for Harrison Tech of Chicago before earning fame at Notre Dame.[31]

Clay, on assignment for the *Star-Ledger*, noted that the Boilermakers "moved with smoothness and snap that cause favorable comment from spectators."[32]

Babula uncorked a few long punts and the team posed for the newsreel cameras and photographers. There always seemed to be pictures to take. The starters lined up outside the Orange Bowl stands for a few group shots. Gabriel, looking snappy in a pair of white slacks, posed with the shiny new water wagon that Garfield would use for the first time. Crowed Jack Bell:

> *The boys from Garfield are with us! They're a nice looking flock of kids; big and eager, and excited as they look around Miami for the first time. And with them are quite a number of New Jersey backers just as excited and just as confident the boys will have little trouble taking the Stingarees of Miami High into camp next Monday evening.*
>
> *Garfield High comes with a great record. The boys, as they got off the train this noon and grinned happily, looked like good athletes. Perhaps there isn't a better team in the East this fall. There's no way of knowing what team, if any, is best in high school football. But this one did all asked of it, a clean record of victory no one can deny.[33]*

Back in Garfield, the excitement continued to mount. The game would be broadcast in Florida with Ted Husing at the microphone, but none of the New York stations were paying for the hook-up. *The Herald-News* announced that it would stage a play-by-play reading in Garfield's No. 8 School gymnasium. The paper assumed the cost of leasing telegraph wires from Western Union with Morse code operators at both ends transmitting the action. Advance tickets were snapped up at 15 cents each, with the proceeds going to the Garfield Athletic Association.

At least 500 fans made it down from Garfield to Miami. That's how many tickets Gabriel ordered. But, after they had been mailed to New Jersey for sale, it was quickly noticed that the seats were on Miami's side of the field.

"This would have caused a furious renewal of the War Between the States and made the Health Bowl something else," reported the wires. "But Arthur Suskind Jr. who is handling this detail of the game for the National Sports Council hurriedly wired Miami for 500 different tickets and thus made certain that the blocking and tackling will be confined to the gridiron."

The first Garfield rooters, around 250, made the trip with the team on three cars that were added to the special train. Another fan train left the next day, and still more arrived on the

Havana Express train Friday. Other stragglers travelled by car, including a few 12- and 15-car caravans. Some even made it down by thumb.

Bill Wagnecz's father, George, had just purchased a 1939-model Plymouth. He wanted to drive the family down in it but he couldn't get out of work. Instead, six family members and Bill's girlfriend (later wife) Marguerite Comment squeezed into the sedan for the three-day journey. Another uncle, John, wouldn't have fit so he took one of the chartered buses instead.

"It was myself, my mother (Julia), my older brother Ernest, my Aunt Anna and Uncle George (Roman) and their eight-year-old son, George, plus Marguerite," remembered Bill's sister, Eleanor, just eight at the time. "We all crammed in there and when I say crammed, I mean it. My mom and my aunt were a little on the heavy side. I sat on my mother's lap most of the time and my cousin sat on his mother's lap. Poor Marguerite was squeezed in between us in the back seat."

Ernest was behind the wheel most of the time but Uncle George was a bit of a back-seat driver. He got his turn in South Carolina, where a motorcycle cop noticed the New Jersey license plate and chased them down for speeding. They all had to traipse down to the police station to pay the fine. Uncle George didn't drive again—from either seat. It remained a family joke for generations.

R. Sal Barrale, clerk to the Garfield Board of Assessors and the brother of Red Barrale, was already in Florida on honeymoon with his new bride Edythe. He found out about the Garfield bid when he bought a paper in Jacksonville to shut up a pushy newsboy. The Barrales, as planned, took in the Nutley game in Gainesville before heading to Miami to catch up with the team.

Lou Mallia, 23, was temporarily unemployed. He had a '37 Pontiac sedan. He headed down with three of his buddies and, when one begged him to take his friend, he reluctantly agreed, so he crammed the car with five guys. Mallia did all the driving. He had bought a trip plan from the Continental Oil gas station to keep track of expenses, but was kind of sore when his buddies didn't pick up their share. They went straight through to Savannah before stopping to sleep and got to Miami the next day.

"When we finally got to the Alcazar, those guys were living it up," he recalled many years later.

Mallia's bunch found less luxurious quarters.

"We stayed in a so-called hotel with the bathroom down the hall. A so-called hotel," he repeated. "All they had in the room was a sink to wash your face. It may have been one or two dollars a night."

Another enterprising bunch from the Garfield Indians athletic club chipped in to buy a '31 jalopy, a wreck that guzzled gas at the rate of nine miles a gallon. They made it as far as South Carolina before blowing a tire in the middle of the night. They couldn't see, so they set one of the spares on fire in order to change the tire. Off they went once more until the car started to buck. It gave out for good in Brunswick, Georgia, where they sold it for $11 and took a bus the rest of the way.

Red Simko hitchhiked down on his own, leaving ahead of the team on Monday and arriving Friday. Garfield's top cheerleader and candyman got as far as Richmond, Virginia, where he was stranded for 10 hours before an FBI agent gave him a lift into Jacksonville. Garfield fans driving south saw him on the side of the road outside Jacksonville and took him the rest of the way. Simko said the longest ride he received was 900 miles. He bragged that the entire trip cost him $4.35.

Bunches of Garfield High students followed Simko's lead.

At one point, Gabriel was asked, "What do you think the Board of Education will do about these hitchhikers who are skipping school to see the game?"

"What do you think?" he replied with a wink and a smile. Suffice it to say the New York State Board of Education would not have approved so cavalierly.

Somewhat unfortunately for the players, most of those kids ended up freeloading at the Alcazar.

"I remember going up to our room and finding a dozen of the guys from back home in it," Bill Librera said at the team's 50th reunion. "After a while I asked them where they were staying and they said, 'With you . . . look at this room. And guys, when you go to breakfast in the morning bring us back rolls, because we're short of money.'"[34]

It wasn't as an adventurous week for the Miami players, who were all at home. The only difference for them was that they were on Christmas vacation. Yarborough held his last hard scrimmage the Friday before. He practiced every morning at 9:30 in the days leading up to the game to beat the heat, but the sessions lasted just over an hour. It had been a long season. One day the entire team met for a photo session at the school. Eldredge, Koesy, Comfort and Red Mathews posed for campy publicity shots on Miami Beach. Just in their helmets and

In a Herald-News *promotional photo, Art Argauer and the boys take in the paper's account of their trip south. Showing interest, from left to right, are Ed Hintenberger, Benny Babula, Angelo Miranda, John Orlovsky and John Grembowitz.* Courtesy Howard Lanza.

bathing trunks, they feigned to prepare to receive a hike delivered by a lovely young woman. As Jack Bell noted:

> *To Col. Jess Yarborough and his boys this Christmas day game is old stuff. They've been playing it since 1929 and are going about their job of getting ready with little fanfare. It's just another football game to them for if ever a high school team had poise it's the 1939 Stingarees.*[35]

That may have been. But, for once, the Stingarees weren't playing a team that held them in awe. What's more, they knew very little about the makeup of Garfield's team, apart from the barrage of publicity surrounding Babula and the formations Argauer sent them in an exchange with Yarborough. There was no film available and, unlike Argauer, who had Art McMahon's report from the Boys High game, Yarborough knew no one who had seen the Boilermakers in action. Interestingly, Yarborough practiced with a seven-man defensive line to stop the big back in his tracks and perhaps make up for the penetration that Kendrick would have given them. But the formation also opened his team up to reverses and end-arounds. Offensively, Miami concentrated on the passing game, perhaps rationalizing that, without Kendrick, the running game would be less effective.

Things were going just as Argauer had planned—even his late Wednesday practice, the ploy to tire his boys out. Many of them slept through breakfast the next day. They were on a tight regimen down to the minute, designed to fix their minds on the business at hand with two workouts scheduled on certain days. There were three meals a day on the roof of the Alcazar and, at one o'clock, Argauer read to them greetings and best wishes from town residents published in the *Garfield Guardian.* They returned a message that they were "striving to bring victory and glory to Garfield."

On Thursday, the team's first full day in Miami, organizers took them on a sightseeing tour of Miami Beach just before practice, where Argauer began to install a game plan geared to stopping Miami's high-flying offense. The philosophy was exactly the reverse of Jesse Yarborough's. He was bringing men up to the line to stop Babula. Argauer was moving them further back to stop Eldredge.

At the team's first practice, the papers dutifully reported that Argauer used a standard 6-2-2-1 defensive formation. That suited Argauer just fine, knowing that Yarborough would be anxious for any tidbits, and that he had no intention of sticking with a six-man line.

Paul Horowitz' story in Friday's *Newark News* offered the first hint of Argauer's real strategy.

"Pass defense was stressed in yesterday's drill, which lasted an hour and 45 minutes," Horowitz reported. "Coach Argauer believes the Southerners will fill the air with passes and he is toying with a defensive setup that probably will surprise the Miamians."

The surprise setup was a five-man line with Grembowitz as a sort of rover. Not only would this put more men in the secondary if Miami went to the air, but it would also work against Eldredge's breakaway ability.

McMahon saw that first-hand in the Boys game and again while watching the Stingarees' scrimmage the previous Friday. The description of Miami's "short punt" offense that he provided in *The Herald-News* was probably quite similar to the scouting report he gave Argauer:

The plays are diversified but the pet ground gainer is an off-tackle smash that requires breathless speed and expert blocking. Dave Eldredge is a ball of lightning and much of his success is due to the speed with which he reaches the scrimmage line. Garfield will have to keep a hair trigger defense to keep him under control.

It was useless, Argauer thought, to have an extra man at the line of scrimmage given that Eldredge did his real damage once he got past the scrimmage line. So, Argauer would array six of his men in a formation that maintained a numerical advantage over Eldredge's quick-footed downfield blockers. They were also instructed not to go at Eldredge straight on but rather at angles to limit the effectiveness of Eldredge's jukes and fakes. Here is where Grembowitz would be key. While he wasn't as fast as Eldredge, he was smart. He knew how to take away space, and he was relentless. He never gave up on a play.

As luck would have it, neither Miami paper had anyone at the Boilermakers' Thursday practice. Everyone, even Mayor Gabriel, along with his mother, whom he brought along, seemed to be at the opening of Tropical Park. That was the news of the day. Both the *News* and *Herald* relied on the daily press release, which still had Garfield in a six-man defensive line. Unless Yarborough had a spy at practice, he was unaware that Argauer was scheming otherwise. Argauer had one day to practice in relative seclusion. And since the practice was more a mental one—meticulously going over and over the new formation—he could over-look the lethargy, which was evident to observers.

As Horowitz wrote, "Two days of practice under a hot Florida sun has caused the players . . . to show signs of sluggishness."

McMahon, obviously watching the same workout, went even further.[36]

"Miami's weather has been as important as Miami's football team to Garfield High's knights of the gridiron," McMahon wrote. "Staging their second drill in this semi-tropical air, the Jersey Boilermakers plainly showed the effects of the hot sun. Here it is mid-July in Jersey and the boys just can't get football conscious. They were sluggish, peevish and out-and-out unimpressive."[37]

There was a good reason for that. Dayton was advising the Boilermakers not to swallow liquids during practice.

"No matter how much of their imported water they drink, they sweat it right out," McMahon reported. "Their blood has thinned in the normal 48-hour transition and the natural slow gait that attacks all who have trapped Florida sand in their shoes has caught up with them."[38]

That was the popular belief then. So the Boilermakers would go to their water wagon, swish their artesian well water around to wet their whistles and spit it out. Rather than combatting the dehydration with hydration, Dayton suggested that Argauer give two 10-grain salt tablets to each player after each drill.

"The salt treatment has done wonders to offset devitalization of the players in this climate," Horowitz explained, although McMahon noted sarcastically, "a glance at the Hurricane record is hardly a strong recommendation for the practice."

"Anyway," McMahon continued. "Argauer plans to try the tablets in an effort to restore some of the Jersey vim and vigor to his weary Boilermakers."

Off the practice field, the intrigue began to build between the two coaches. Argauer worried about playing at night. Remember, he had begged off a return game under the lights against East Rutherford after the nearly losing to the Wildcats in a poorly-lit night game at Passaic Stadium in 1938. He vowed at the time it would be the last night game his team would play.

Miami had a distinct advantage, of course. The Stingarees played every one of their home games and one of their two road games under the lights.

At first, Argauer asked that the game be played with a white ball. Yarborough refused to even use the white ball for just one half. The white paint made the ball too slippery, he said. Argauer's request to practice Friday night in the Orange Bowl was also turned down on grounds that the Boilermakers would rip up the playing field. He got around that by scheduling a Friday night practice at Stranahan Field in Fort Lauderdale. The people up the coast were happy to comply. Their civic rivalry with Miami was fierce and they saw this as a chance to stick it to them.

Yarborough didn't attempt to prevent that. He had other concerns that threatened the very playing of the game.

Garfield was being lodged, fed and feted in typical Miami style, all expenses paid at a total cost of $2,000, with Frank Gough's Alcazar slicing that in half by putting up the team. What were the Stingarees getting out of it? Every other Christmas game put money into the athletic department's coffers. Now they were expected to play the game for nothing—and that's not what Miami High had agreed to when Robert Dill and his group met with Miami High and Edison High authorities back in November.

According to Jack Bell, who was present at the meeting, Dill was informed that both Miami and Edison already played charity games. Edison played Greenwood, Mississippi, for the Lions Club fund and Miami played Boys High for the Kiwanis fund for underprivileged children. Miami would donate the total take of $3,231.70 for that game.

Dill was amenable, and city officials at the meeting said they would ensure the home team would receive a fair share. Dill asked Miami principal W.R. Thomas how much the Stingarees usually netted playing on Christmas.

"Anywhere from $1,500 to $3,500," Thomas said.

"Oh," Dill replied. "We won't have any trouble getting together on the matter."

As Bell noted, the Miami High officials agreed without even a handshake. "How dumb they were," Bell wrote.

At the time, no one gave it a thought; most all had assumed they had a potential gold mine in Seward Park. Whether that was true or not, Dill convinced the National Sports Council that Miamians would fill the stadium and assured the Miamians that New Yorkers would scoop up boxes at $200 apiece. Meanwhile, the press was being told that every cent of the proceeds would go to fight infantile paralysis.

It wasn't until Garfield became the opponent that Miami High was told that the state chairman of the infantile paralysis committee still assumed Miami would play *gratis*. The Miami High School athletic council hastily met and voted to request $3,000. Dill, after all, had previously told Thomas not to take less than the school would usually profit on the game.

That was, however, when Dill had dreams of an $80,000 gate. Then, when it appeared ticket sales lagged—largely due to the botched Seward Park-Met All Star affair—even a $20,000 gate seemed unlikely despite the Sports Council's best efforts to whip up interest.

So, in an all-out effort, the Sports Council began promoting the game with a special 15-minute spot on the CBS Radio Network. Featuring Kate Smith, it was aired coast-to-coast.

The papers ran pictures of Sam Snead (who had just come from behind to win the $2,500 first prize at the Miami Open) and former heavyweight champ Jack Dempsey (who ran a restaurant and bar in Miami Beach) purchasing boxes for the game. However, neither could attend: Dempsey headed to the Philippines to referee a fight and Snead went back to West Virginia with a toothache.

A ticket office was set up in the lobby level of the beautiful new DuPont Building. The window to Flagler Street was plastered with pictures of both teams. Considine had written that once word got out about Babula, "ticket sales leaped." But regular Miamians, who were being asked to attend a third straight big high school game, were more confused than enthused by the organizational mismanagement.

Now Miami High was told: "Sorry, you're not taking anything out of the pot." And, when the state infantile paralysis representative reminded the city of Miami that it had guaranteed the school $1,500, the city fathers hemmed and hawed.

"The old buck looked like a football handled by Sammy Baugh," Bell later wrote. "There were definite threats to call off the game, which I'm sure weren't as serious as they sounded."[39]

As it was since the start, no one seemed to be in charge. And that's how the matter was left as game day approached—just hanging like the moon over the horizon. Nevertheless, it remained very much on Yarborough's mind. He was, and legitimately so, annoyed.

With a Machiavellian touch, Yarborough waited until two days before the game to press the issue and threatened not to take the field unless the high school was compensated. The city of Miami now agreed to turn over to the Stingaree coffers the money it received for the stadium rental and concessions—about $1,500.

Of course, Garfield's athletic treasury wasn't profiting from the trip, either. Art McMahon estimated that the Boilermakers would have netted at least $4,000 from a post-season show-down against either Vineland, Nutley or Passaic. But he also noted that the season's profits were already at $7,000 after the big paydays against Passaic and Bloomfield.

"Coach Art Argauer and other school officials favor the Miami trip as a reward for the players," McMahon wrote when Garfield was considering its options. "They don't feel that the squad should be called upon to increase the treasury's football booty with a postseason tilt here but if the opportunity to take a pleasant journey to the land of oranges and sunshine is offered as bait, that's barking right up the palm tree."[40]

Garfield's benefits from the game came in the form of nationwide publicity and in the once-in-a-lifetime experiences of the players. Friday, three days before the game, they were treated to their most enjoyable outing of the week, a two-hour boat ride down Biscayne Bay on the *Silver Moon*. The excursion boat was famous for midnight cruises and about a month earlier, made news when Ray Hamilton, a 23-year-old visitor from Buffalo, declared, "this boat's too slow for me," and dove into the water three miles from shore. Feared drowned, he showed up at the hotel later that day. He was an expert swimmer.

There were no such theatrics on Garfield's voyage but it was quite an affair. Gabriel was on hand again and, as the ever-present photographers snapped away, he was greeted at the gangplank by the ship's captain whose boat was plastered with posters for the game. A Miami High coed awaited each player and, as a full band played away, several danced up a storm. Nearly everyone knew how to dance in those days. It was the path to romance, and they had stars in their eyes as they cruised along the bay. There's a picture of Babula and Grembowitz relaxing with the girls. They looked like movie stars at a Hollywood party.

John Gabriel shakes hands with the captain of the Silver Moon *as the team boards, drawing interest from some of the local kids.* Courtesy Estate of Angelo Miranda.

The two lovely Miami High coeds assigned to keep John Grembowitz and Benny Babula entertained on the boat trip. With Babula is Martina Wilson, the Health Bowl queen. Courtesy Estate of Angelo Miranda.

The Silver Moon, *adorned with game posters, is fully loaded with the Garfield team as it prepares to leave the dock.* Courtesy Estate of Angelo Miranda.

Angelo Miranda twirls his girl around the Silver Moon *dance floor to a live orchestra as Leonard Macaluso bashfully holds his girl close. Martina Wilson has her arms around Benny Babula in the background.* Courtesy Estate of Angelo Miranda.

Letty Barbour relaxes with Mayor John Gabriel and his mother aboard the Silver Moon *cruise.*
Courtesy Estate of Angelo Miranda.

Earlier, several Garfield players joined several Miami players in a visit to Jackson Memorial Hospital, where they were photographed visiting young polio victims and, then Jay Kendrick, who wore a huge bandage over his right eye. Argauer sent his reserves.

Back at the Alcazar, Frank Gough was fully enjoying his guests, even the moochers. He loved Letty Barbour's voice and set her up with a gig at the Eight O'clock Club on one night and to accompany the hotel band on another. One afternoon, he escorted her into the News Tower, where she wowed the staff with "South of the Border" and got her picture taken for the next day's paper.

Jack Bell called Letty "Little Personality" and noted, "blasé sportswriters, photographers and even Smiley quit her beloved switchboard, paused and listened. After she left the evening was spent in attempts to speak Mexican and wonderment that the high-salaried crew staging the infantile paralysis fund hadn't discovered Letty days agone."[41]

The Boilermakers' Friday night practice would be their best of the week. The night air was crisp. The Boilermakers reveled in it. They had finally been unshackled from the day's 85-degree heat. Even after an earlier two-hour workout under the sun at Miami Field, they were refreshed and active. They opened the windows on the bus ride up Rt. 1 to Fort Lauderdale and, when they arrived at Stranahan Field, a big crowd awaited them, anxious to confirm if Babula indeed had a frame like Tarzan. He didn't disappoint.

Wrote Horowitz: "Benny Babula's passing and kicking so impressed a small group of Fort Lauderdale residents, one was heard to remark, 'Gee! They ought to play Miami University, not Miami High.'"[42]

Similarly, the headline over McMahon's story read, "Babula's passing Makes 'em Sit Up." McMahon called it a "flashy workout" and wrote that Garfield, "found in the brisk air of this place at night the tonic it needed.[43]

"The air was sharp last night and there is no question that if the weather gods treat Garfield that way Monday, the Boilermakers' chances of victory will be enhanced," he said.

It was pretty much impossible to quantify those chances because of both the variables and the unknowns. The *Associated Press* made Garfield the favorite because of the 17-pound per-man weight advantage it took into the game. The Stingarees' backfield, with Jason Koesy, at 150 pounds and its biggest starter, was the lightest the Boilermakers had faced. Both the *Miami Herald* and *Miami News* had it too close to call. The *Bergen Record*, which did not have a man in Miami, gave the clearest insight into the locals' thought process in a story headlined "Jersey Champions Have Few Backers", which was written anonymously as a special to the paper:

> In spite of their 20-game winning streak, Garfield High School's Boilermakers will be underdogs when they oppose the Miami High Stingarees.
> Miami High School's backers are offering odds that vary from 6-5 to 8-5. Few wagers have been made.
> Except for Babula, sportswriters here haven't a high opinion of the Garfield eleven. All of them are stringing along with the Miami team. The Miami scribes figure the Stingarees will win on speed and deception.[44]

It was interesting that Argauer used a white ball that night in Fort Lauderdale. The New Jersey writers all reported that he had convinced Yarborough to approve it after the Miami coach learned that Garfield wore yellow-colored jerseys that, Argauer told him, would blend in with a regular football. Those reports were wrong. The only white ball in the game was a souvenir ball that was used for autographs. However, both Horowitz and McMahon reported that the lightweight purple jerseys Argauer had ordered had come in. Argauer said he would use them at least one period unless it was a cool evening.

"The Boilermakers have been complaining in the afternoon workouts that their suits are too heavy, the sweaters especially becoming sweat-clogged after brief periods of practice," Horowitz noted.[45]

The Fort Lauderdale excursion was noteworthy for another reason other than the cooler temperatures. Nearby was another reminder of the war in Europe. The *SS Arauca*, an unarmed Hamburg-American freighter flying the Nazi flag on its maiden voyage, was docked in Port Everglades, where it would remain for the next 20 months as Washington walked a diplomatic tightrope with Berlin.

The *Athenia*, Garfield's first connection to the war, had the unfortunate distinction of receiving the first naval shots fired in World War II. The *Arauca*'s crew watched as the first shot fired in American waters crossed its bow, a blast that could be heard up and down the South Florida coast in full view of both U.S. Coast guard and pleasure craft. In a clear violation of U.S. neutrality laws, it came as a warning shot from the British cruiser *HMS Orion*, which, in hot pursuit, had been signaling the Germans to return to international waters. Instead, Captain Frederick Stengler, choosing to outrun the Brits, steamed into Port Everglades, where hundreds had flocked to watch everything play out from shore. There, the *Orion* could still be seen, lying in wait five miles off the coast.

"I would rather run her into a beach rather than let them have her," Stengler told the newsmen who had rushed to the scene. "Port Everglades saved my ship and crew and that is important."[46]

The incident had occurred on Tuesday, while Garfield trained down to Miami. And in the days since, the ship, the captain and his crew had become the top tourist attraction in South Florida. It all created a chamber of commerce windfall and a source of pride for the people of Fort Lauderdale, accustomed to their roles as second-class citizens to Miami. Gawkers came by the thousands, while Fort Lauderdale's residents—some of whom had run gifts out to the *Orion*—brought provisions and gifts to the *Arauca* as well. The *Fort Lauderdale Daily News* quickly became infatuated by the charismatic Stengler who, the paper gushed, looked "younger than his 52 years and has impressed everyone with his sparkling personality, keen sense of humor and by his exceptionally good English."[47]

One photo showed Broward County sheriff Walter Clark lighting Stengler's cigarette. Another had Stengler decorating a Christmas tree on board the ship while the infernal Nazi flag could be seen in the photo looming over the scene, an eerie sight in retrospect. The *Daily News* conveyed Stengler's holiday wishes to the citizenry:

> *American (not Miami's) tolerance and good will to men was shown again on Christmas when Lauderdale aided in making it a better and happier day for the 52 officers and men of the German freighter* Arauca *held at bay in Port Everglades (Lauderdale, not Miami)*
>
> *And today, Capt. Frederick Stengler, skipper of the ship driven to haven here to escape the guns of the British cruiser* Orion, *asked the* Daily News *to express his thanks to local residents.*
>
> *Lauderdale residents will not be forgotten for the friendly manner in which they have come to the aid of the* Arauca's *crew and the many gifts and acts of kindness that they have showered on them to make Christmas a better season, Capt. Stengler declared.*[48]

The *Arauca* was hardly a man o' war. It was not staffed by the military, and it wasn't serving to re-supply German navy ships in the region (which is what the *Orion* had believed). It carried a load of sugar, but that's another story. Still, it was clear that South Floridians, oblivious to the horrors of the Nazi regime, had not yet taken sides in the great conflict. What's more, they basked rather blissfully in their neutrality as the *Daily News* proudly named the *Arauca* saga its best Story of 1939.

Explained staff writer John D. Lopp:

> *The game of "run shippie run" played by* Arauca *and the* Orion—*had everything. It captured the imagination of the entire world. It brought the realization of war home to the section of the western hemisphere owned and operated by these 48 United States of America. It has already made history and may make more. It brought more than 100,000 visitors to Port Everglades in 48 hours. It put Ft. Lauderdale into the headlines throughout the world. It was just plain red hot spot news—a natural from the word go.*[49]

The cruel irony of the *St. Louis* being turned away, and the *Arauca* being celebrated, was lost on everyone at the time. Close as they were to the *Arauca*, the German ship was not on the Boilermakers' sightseeing itinerary. They were taken to a jai alai fronton on Saturday, tapered down their practice and, finally, focused their attention on only two things: Christmas and the game. If the boys were homesick at any time, it was now. Knowing this, the genial Gough appeared at Saturday's dinner to invite Argauer and the team to the hotel's Christmas Eve celebration the next night. "They'll like to listen to our singing of Christmas carols," Gough said. Argauer paused and thought for a few seconds. Gough must have thought he was contemplating the offer. But Argauer had an idea. "Let *me* show you some Christmas carols," he replied. The coach huddled his boys around him and whispered the "play" to them. Gough was about to feel the full flavor of what made Garfield. He was to be given a clue as to what brought this Boilermaker team together. And it gave him goose bumps.

The Polish boys from the Valley gathered to belt out "Dzisiaj w Betlejem" (Today in Bethlehem), the Italians of the Heights sang the lullaby "Caro Gesù Bambino" and the Carpatho-Rusyns, who wouldn't celebrate until Orthodox Christmas on January 7, joined in early celebration with "Boh Predvichnyj" (God of Ages). Everyone joined, as they did from all corners of town on the playing field, in the singing of "Oh Come All Ye Faithful."

"The astonished Gough sat in wonderment," Jack Bell related in the next day's paper. "When they had finished, he got up and started away. 'Hell,' he said, over his shoulder. 'I'm going to call off that lousy show I had booked.' "[50]

Most of the Boilermakers attended church on Christmas Eve (they would go again on Christmas), the Catholic boys taking communion at the marble altar of historic Gesu Church.

There was a cool breeze off the bay Christmas Eve and, if they wanted, the boys could have imagined it was sent from home. There were good reasons to think of home that night. At Christmas Eve supper at the Alcazar, Argauer conveyed Christmas blessings he received from Monsignor Jan Wetula of St. Stan's. Then Argauer led them in a prayer for victory and followed that up with a simple message that begged for the same effort he had come to expect from them and which they always gave. McMahon wrote that Argauer delivered the plea as passionately as Knute Rockne might have.

"I want only one thing from you boys for Christmas," the coach said, looking around the room at his players who, as usual, were giving him their full attention. "Give me a victory out there tomorrow. It will be a grand present for you fellows, too, as well as for your parents, friends and thousands of followers."[51]

Back in Garfield, many of those parents, friends and followers were observing their ethnic Christmas Eve traditions. In the Italian homes of the Heights, the meal of seven fishes would be served. No day was more sacred—or as delicious. The line into Bertola's Fish Market on Harrison Avenue had stretched around the block the day before. Stuffed after the feast, many walked over to Mount Virgin Church where Father Dooling—the Irish priest in the Italian parish—celebrated Midnight Mass. There was little jingling in the collection basket. Bills went out this day.

In the Polish and Slovak homes of the Valley, mushroom soup, cabbage soup and pierogi, tenderly prepared by moms from scratch, was part of the meatless meal. According to Polish custom, the *opłatek*, or Christmas wafer, is passed around the table before the family begin their feast. A shred of the thin wafer is broken off, followed by a wish for the coming year.

It's often for health or long life. But, on Christmas Eve 1939, the biggest wish may have been for Benny and the boys to bring home a national championship, even if some parents raised eyebrows reprovingly.

NATIONAL CHAMPIONSHIP HIGH SCHOOL
FOOTBALL
GAME

Christmas Night

KICKOFF AT 8:15 P.M.
BURDINE ORANGE
BOWL STADIUM

★ ★ FIGHT ★ ★
★ INFANTILE ★
★ PARALYSIS ★

MARCH OF DIMES

MAKE RESERVATIONS NOW!
PHONE 3-3139 or 5-9690
66 N.E. 2ND AVE. Miami - GREYHOUND BUS DEPOT MIAMI BEACH

All of Garfield got behind the team as evidenced by this Christmas-themed cartoon. Portrayed, from left to right, are Art Argauer, Benny Babula, John Grembowitz, Wally Tabaka, John Orlovsky, Walter Young and Ray Butts.

Later, at a packed St. Stan's, where midnight mass traditionally opened with a rousing "Wsród Nocnej Ciszy"(In the Midst of Night's Quiet) how many thoughts wandered 1,200 miles south in anticipation of a not-so-quiet next night?

Bob Johnston may have gone a bit overboard in previewing the game for the *Bergen Sunday Star* but, then again, he probably captured the emotions of most people in Garfield when he wrote:

> *Tomorrow night our great, strong, courageous heroes from Garfield High School will open their throttle wide. They'll shove into high gear, swing into action and sail into the midsection of Miami High School's southern powerhouse. The Argauer-Babula axis will muster all forces. The two elevens will meet in the new "Health Bowl" and should treat fans to a killer-diller night of gridiron thrills unsurpassed in schoolboy football.*[52]

Back at the Alcazar, the Boilermakers were fast asleep. They would wake to a Christmas like no other.

NINETEEN

THE GAME

J ack Bell was alone at his News Tower desk in the pre-dawn hours of Christmas Day, 1939. The landmark building dominated the Miami skyline, now tinged by the last warm glimmers of a nearly full moon. Across the clutter of the newsroom, Bell searched for inspiration as he gazed out the window to the tired yet anxious city.

A block up at the Alcazar, Garfield's Boilermakers were lost in that dreamy, syrupy sleep of teenaged boys, undisturbed by the snores of the freeloading friends crashing in their rooms. In the bedrooms of their tidy and modern ranch homes, Miami's Stingarees would soon awake to gather by the tree with their families to nervously count down the hours as the holiday crept toward game time.

Bell could have easily added the final flourishes to hype that night's game. Hyperbole was a sportswriter's stock-in-trade back in the day. But he used not one word in his column to touch on football or any other sport, for that matter. Instead, Bell captured the mood of the day to come and, more precisely, of the time.

> Out across Biscayne Bay this Christmas morning, I can see only the calm resulting from the quiet of a beautiful night. 'Tis just turning light in the east as I write. There's not a sound in this great building overlooking the water. Only an occasional motor car rolls down the boulevard and even then slips along as if in stealthy apology. No boats churn the waters; no breeze whips the smooth surface into choppy ripples. All is quiet, peaceful, serene—a great city asleep after a day and a night of merry-making.
>
> This is Christmas morning.

Bell wrote on. He pecked at the keys with only his right hand; he had lost his left arm in World War I. Bell knew war—what it looked like, what it felt like, what it smelled like, and he could sense its intrusion from across the turquoise waters of Miami's beaches. He wished it would stay put and remain far from the simple joys on these shores. Joys such as high school football. But it was hard to ignore the day's headlines. They told of Hitler's Christmas

Eve visit to the Western Front where Nazi leaders warned foes that Germany would fight "to victorious end," and that "only when we have won will we be able to speak again of peace at Christmastime."[1]

That Christmas Eve, the Fuhrer strode across the frontier into France, marking the first time he had set foot on French soil since 1918 when he was a corporal with the 16th Bavarian reserve. It was an ominous moment.

Bell was looking at a nation at peace—but for how long? As Pope Pius XII prayed for a "just and honorable peace," Christmas Day began in war-torn Finland not to the sound of church bells but to bombs dropping from Russian warplanes. It seemed only America was being spared the bloodshed. Bell presumed that the world needed a miracle, the type of miracle that had occurred on that first Christmas when mankind was gifted new codes of tolerance, reason and compassion.

"All this seems so far away this morning as I watch the sun come out of the East," Bell continued. "It is far away because we in America have not lost the teaching of Jesus. The lights of our millions colored our Christmas trees yesterday while the children of Europe crept into bomb-proof cellars and no joy was in their hearts. No guns roared death in America.

"There can be no illusions after this war is over. They cannot bring to us the glorious teachings of Communism, of the new Germany, the new Japan, the new Italy. Ah no; our way may not be the perfect way but we have peace in our great nation. We've not lost our way."[2]

In 1939, that faith-based mindset was the foundation supporting a great and true sense of purpose in America and extended naturally to those young Boilermakers and Stingarees. Choices were simpler: black and white, good and evil. Bell's words are instructional. God and country provided a moral compass for a nation still eking its way out of the Depression and about to be yanked by the lapel into World War II.

There was peace, yes—for the time being. Think of those boys as they slept. At the end of this day many would have played out their most carefree moments of youth. In the fast-coming years, they would meet war as earnestly as they played that Christmas night. For now, beginning at 8:15 that evening, football was their immediate sense of purpose. Freeze those few hours, with the game going on in front of Miami's partisan fans, with thousands packing Garfield's No. 8 School to squirm, soar and scream along with the play-by-play. That is your snapshot of America at the end of 1939. That is what Bell saw from his News Tower window.

Art Argauer hadn't slept much since Christmas Eve supper with Florence and the boys before he bid the team a final good night. As he stared out his hotel window that Christmas morning, he searched not for inspiration but for reassurance. From the moment he stepped down from the *Vacationer* and faced the newsreel cameras, the immigrant tailor's son and his team had been besieged, almost as curiosities. This was his time away from the excitement; a quiet moment of reflection on what he was hoping would be his players' best Christmas ever.

He was one of the first to rise from bed at the Alcazar, carefully trying not to wake his wife. The coach was nervous. His fingernails were nubs. He could remember back to '38 when the 20-game winning streak was just starting and how the newspapermen questioned Garfield's heart, how they chided him over a "swelled head" and noted how past Boilermaker teams "appled up" in the clutch. That's how Art McMahon put it, at least. "Choked" would be today's term—and McMahon was Argauer's buddy!

Argauer didn't doubt what his team could accomplish. They had responded to pressure with four second-half comebacks during the season. They'd stepped up in big games, in front of those 19,000 in Bloomfield where they dominated their most dangerous opponent. By then, the local reporters were squeezing themselves onto the Garfield bandwagon. Argauer never asked for an apology. The newspapermen knew they were wrong about this group of players.

Vexing thoughts whirled in his mind. Would Miami's heat and humidity sap his team? He'd ordered his boys not to allow it to become a psychological advantage for the home team. They were not to show any weakness. During timeouts, no one would be allowed to take a knee. Garfield's unique water wagon could gain an edge in itself. The Stingarees were known to play mind games, always yapping about the heat during breaks. Who knows? Maybe they could look upon the curious apparatus as some sort of secret weapon.

There was, however, no margin for error. Without Benny Babula rising to the occasion, without John Grembowitz doing his job in Wally Tabaka's spot, and without significant contributions from some yet unknown and unheralded heroes, the Boilermakers were not going to dismantle the Miami machine.

Ole Mule Yarborough could not have had an easy night, either, as he readied for an opponent he never really wanted to face. In fact, he wasn't getting much sleep at all those days for a different reason: three-month-old "Buzz" was testing his lungpower through the night in the family's new house. There, early in the morning, the tree sparkled with ornaments and tinsel as 5-year-old Louise opened her gifts from Santa Claus, and then it was off to Uncle Henry's place.

Yarborough had a few things on his mind as he drank eggnog at his brother's home. His teams had lost to bigger northern visitors before and Garfield outweighed his squad significantly. If anyone could have banged heads with Babula, it would have been big Jay Kendrick. Instead, he was bandaged up in a dark room at Jackson Hospital. Doctors wouldn't even let him leave his bed. He'd have to listen to the game on the radio.

Yarborough's confidence was still high. His team had convinced him it was his best since he started coaching at Miami in 1932. He still had a quick, precision offense, with every player drilled in the short punt formation, a new look for Garfield. And he still had Eldredge, who could break a big run at any time. No one on Garfield's team could run with him.

Both coaches knew what was at stake.

Everett Clay, the *Miami Herald* sports editor who strung for the *Star-Ledger* that week, spelled it out in his lede. He simply swapped references to each team for each paper:

> *Christmas Night and the Garfield Boilermakers (Miami Stingarees)—the kids who made up their minds to become good football players, and did—are near the end of a long, tedious trail and at the end rests the swellest Christmas present in schoolboy grid circles—a respected claim to the national interscholastic championship.*
>
> *Equally as near, or as far from the lucrative prize are the Miami High Stingarees (Garfield High Boilermakers).*
>
> *Tonight, barring a tie, one of those teams is going to contain the happiest bunch of boys in all the land—for they clash in the first annual Health Bowl encounter at the Orange Bowl Stadium and to the winner goes the national title.*"[3]

In the pages of the *Miami News* Luther Voltz scribbled that the game promised, "all the components of a football thriller."

He wrote the contest would answer "an age-old question, debated ever since David upset Goliath." He went on:

> *This time it is a good little football team—Miami High—led by a good little man—Li'l David Eldredge—against a good big football team—Garfield, N.J.,—led by a good big man—Boom-Boom Benny Babula.*
>
> *The Stingarees haven't been outcharged on defense or outblocked on offense by any team they have faced. This alone has been the envy of every coach who has seen the Miami team play. The boys start blocking at the outset, never seem to tire and they haven't had a touchdown scored through them all season. The boys feel if they can shake Davey loose a couple of times they'll have the Garfield boys so busy watching him that the Miami pass offense will click.[4]*

Christmas Day dawned gloriously in Miami and, before long, the peace and serenity of which Bell lyricized was swallowed up by the bustle of a holiday just getting under way.

"The warmness in Miamians hearts today will be kept glowing throughout the holiday as Old Sol's rays do their duty," the *Miami News* wrote as it heralded the busy day.[5]

The resort city anticipated its best tourist season in years. More than two million visitors were expected over the next five months, and they were expected to inject around $200,000 into the economy.[6] As one promotional piece put it, "People are pouring in here by the hundreds. Holiday is in the air. Night spots are gay and the goose, apparently, honks high."

The *Miami Herald* called that night's game, "the day's outstanding spectator sport spectacle."[7] But on this Christmas Day, visitors as well as natives could choose from a variety of entertainment options. The Health Bowl wasn't the only game in town.

Tropical Park, which had opened in front of a record 11,431 bettors four days earlier, offered a special eight-race program, beginning with a 2 p.m. post time. At the Hollywood, West Flagler and Biscayne Kennel Clubs, the greyhounds ran at night with free transportation from downtown. More than 7,000 punters of the other sort wagered almost $4,000 at the Biscayne dog track. The Biscayne jai alai fronton turned people away after a capacity crowd of 3,301 passed through the turnstiles. The ads had boasted that Senorita Lucha Reyes, famous Mexican stage, screen and radio star, was making her American debut with an 8 p.m. concert there. And, if one just wanted to take in a movie, the satirical comedy *Ninotchka*, starring Greta Garbo and Melvyn Douglas, was opening at the Olympia on Flagler.

A complete Christmas dinner could be enjoyed at the famous 7 Seas restaurant for $1.25. For the budget-conscious, the Dinner Bell on First Street served turkey dinner with dressing and cranberry sauce for 30 cents. The feast included soup, hearts-of-lettuce salad with mayonnaise dressing, snowflake potatoes, creamed sweet peas or fresh garden string beans, homemade mincemeat or pumpkin pie, homemade biscuits and rolls, coffee or iced tea.

Garfield fans Lou Mallia, John Hilla and the Kopec brothers, the guys who had motored down in Mallia's '37 Pontiac, spent Christmas morning on Miami Beach, as did the Wagnecz contingent. A couple of Garfield buddies had jobs at the ultra-chic Roney Plaza, one as a bellhop, the other working room service. Together they conspired to smuggle the visitors into the hotel's private beach through the employee entrance.

Hilla spied the palm trees in the courtyard and quickly scaled one for its coconuts. They split them up and drank the milk. Ersatz eggnog.

"We didn't stand on ceremony. We didn't look to see if it was prohibited or not," Mallia said.

As the daytime hours passed, the Boilermaker and Stingaree players followed their pre-game routines and, in Garfield's case, it was pretty well regimented, although Babula still had college scouts buzzing around him in the lobby when he left to attend morning Mass at Gesu Church. Art McMahon saw him and Grembowitz together in one of the front pews, praying fervently for a bit of divine intervention.

The team had a light meal at 4 p.m., the players' last chance to take a drink of water. Soon after, a bus took the players on the three-mile trip to Burdine Stadium, where they clomped into the cramped visitors' locker room. Argauer had time to read a few good luck telegrams. The first was signed by the Metropolitan All Stars and coaches left behind:

BEST OF LUCK IN YOUR BATTLE AGAINST MIAMI HIGH. WE KNOW YOU'LL MAKE GREAT SHOWING FOR METROPOLITAN AREA. SCORE ONE FOR US.

Then from Dick McCann:

HERE'S HOPING SANTA HAS FILLED 33 PAIRS OF STOCKINGS WITH WINNING FOOTBALL PLAYERS. BEST OF LUCK TO YOU AND YOUR BOYS TONIGHT

And Grantland Rice:

WIN LOSE OR DRAW THEY ARE FIGHTING GALLANT FIGHT FOR WINNING CAUSE. WE THANK THEM FOR GIVING UP CHRISTMAS DAY FOR NATIONS LESS FORTUNATE YOUTH. GOD BLESS THEM ALL SINCERELY

And the sports staff of the *World-Telegram*:

WE'LL BE PULLING WITH YOU DURING YOUR GAME WITH MIAMI HIGH. WE KNOW YOU'LL BE BATTLING FOR METROPOLITAN PRESTIGE. MERRY CHRISTMAS BEFORE AND AFTER THE CONTEST

Argauer neatly tucked away the well wishes. He'd keep them as souvenirs for the rest of his life. For now, though, he had his coaching duties. At a certain point, he began to perform the tape jobs on his players, one by one, as he always had. In the case of his seniors—Babula, Grembowitz and Young among others—it would be the last time. As he wrapped ankles, the coach softly gave each player final instructions and encouragement.

It was a quintessentially perfect Miami night, with a Kodachrome dusk unfolding into moonlight and warm breezes. The temperature was 76, but Garfield welcomed even the slight drop in the mercury. A full tropical moon was equally hospitable. Everett Clay noted how there was nothing more beautiful than the way Babula's booming punts soared against the backdrop of that moon, made famous in song, an appropriate theme for the hopes of both teams.[8]

Shine on as we begin, a dream or two that may come true, when the tide comes in.

The sun had set at 5:37 p.m. and now the specially engineered arc lights shone on a pristine playing field. Bloomfield physician Maxwell E. Stone, in a letter home to the *Independent Press* described the grass "as green as an Irishman's tie on St. Patrick's Day."[9] To the Boilermakers, who practiced on the Belmont Oval rock pile and played games on Passaic Stadium's scratchy turf, it almost seemed unreal.

Of course, the entire scene could have appeared that way. The Orange Bowl did not yet have an upper deck. It was, for its time, still formidably impressive with its steel light towers rising high above the grandstands. White walls curved around the sidelines. Wooden bleachers were set up behind each end zone. The white scoreboard featured a giant clock that wound down the time in red. In the stands, the setting was almost genteel, as, according to McMahon, "Men and women sitting around in summer attire made the football picture incongruous."

The pre-game festivities featured a reminder of why the game was being played. Santa Claus posed with three crippled children. Fred Snite was set up behind one end zone in his iron lung. Originally, President Roosevelt was supposed to address the crowd through a telephone hookup at halftime, just as Lou Gehrig was supposed to present the trophy to the winning team. Neither took place, but that hardly diminished the night's drama.

The portly figure of Jersey City Mayor Frank "Boss" Hague, accompanied by an entourage of politicos, lumbered into the stadium. FBI director J. Edgar Hoover found his seat and John Gabriel took up Senator Claude Pepper's invitation to see the game from his box.

Clifton High coach Al Lesko, with his brother, was there to watch his city's greatest player star for Garfield, the team next door. And Nello Dallolio, the Vineland coach who thought that his Poultry Clan should have been playing in this game, interrupted his Florida vacation to gauge how his unbeaten South Jersey champs would have stacked up in a showdown with the Boilermakers. He was still fuming over what he deemed the injustice of the Colliton rankings and Argauer's perceived ducking of his challenge.

As Garfield fans climbed the steps, they could see a little bit of home below. Famed cheerleader Red Simko made his appearance, tossing lollipops to the Boilermaker faithful. Garfield High's cheerleaders hadn't made the trip south, so Simko borrowed a megaphone from the curious Miami High crew and performed an impromptu cheer at midfield, jumping split-legged in the air. To the Boilermakers, it had to have brought a bit of familiarity to what must have appeared to them as a most alien, if not spectacular, scene. The Stingarees, after all, were in their comfort zone; it was just another home game with cowbells ringing and Jack Pepper's rigged-up car horn screaming.

As the Boilermakers charged out through the tunnel in their bright gold uniforms emblazoned with royal-purple trim, it was their chance to contribute to the spectacle. Their fans, together with hundreds of Northern vacationers, rose in salute while respectful acknowledgment came from the Miami side. The Boilermakers then burst into the bright light of the Orange Bowl. The scene was simply exhilarating.

Lou Mallia's Garfield buddy, John Hilla, shimmies up a palm tree in search of a coconut at the Roney Plaza on Miami Beach Christmas morning, then cracks open the fruit of his labor. Courtesy Lou Mallia.

"Nothing we had ever seen before in our young lives was that magnificent," Young recalled.

Butterflies? Maybe the Boilermakers had a few. Awe? Hardly. Maybe they didn't know any better. Maybe it was the blind invincibility of youth. Maybe it was that they could always rely on the training they received from Argauer. And, maybe it was the knowledge that, in Babula, they had one of the best high school players in the nation.

In any case, the players were loose, a lot looser than their head coach. Argauer fidgeted while making pre-game small talk with Yarborough. They paused for Michael Rayhack's camera, each decked out in dark suits and wide ties—Argauer's with an abstract, circular motif. He wore a game-day suit tailored for the occasion by his father. Yarborough's trademark fedora allowed him to tower even higher over his stockier counterpart. As Rayhack's camera whirred, Argauer looked strangely ill at ease.

Not his players. They eyed the other side of the field, and observed nothing unusual—just their opponents going through structured warmups. The Stings must have seemed pretty cool, and perhaps had a calming effect on the Boilermakers. They had entered the field, as always, with surprisingly no great fanfare, and calmly carried themselves in business-like fashion before going through their pre-game routine. Their rayon jerseys were dazzling, much more dazzling than Garfield's woolen ones, which were already soaked with sweat. Miami's were white with blue and gold trim and their gold pants were satiny. The uniforms almost made their cuts seem sharper, their first moves quicker, with Eldredge the sharpest and quickest of all.

That didn't faze the Boilermakers. They were from gritty Garfield, after all, unaccustomed to the finer things. Then, as if to prove their aplomb, the Boilermaker players spontaneously huddled around a microphone at midfield and serenaded the big crowd with "Silent Night." That got a big ovation from the crowd. Everyone loved it. Between that little sideshow and Simko's lollipops, the Boilermakers were winning over Southern fans. Still partisan and certainly confident, they couldn't help, at least, being appreciative. These Garfielders were charming.

Miami's Stingarees, too, stole furtive glances at their opponents, particularly the heralded Babula, of whom they'd been hearing since Harvey Comfort's painful handshake at the train station. As they watched the Boilermakers going through their calisthenics, they had one thought. "They're big." They'd been whizzing past bigger teams all year, of course, but these guys were big *and* talented. If Garfield was facing its toughest opposition of the year, so was Miami.

The game programs went fast. They sold for 15 cents each, half as much as a turkey dinner at the Dinner Bell would have cost. The program cover announced, "NATIONAL CHAMPIONSHIP," in capital letters. Inside, Miami fans brushed up on Garfield in a short piece Art McMahon contributed.

> *Win, lose or draw, Garfield High School's football players, 33 in all, will cherish the memory of this visit to Miami. The scenic beauty of this city and the grand hospitality of the committee in charge of the game is more than Aladdin's lamp could conjure.*
>
> *Miamians tonight will see the greatest forward passer turned out of New Jersey schools in the last decade when Benny Babula begins throwing aerials. This Golden Boy, 190 pounds and 6 feet, 1 inch tall, has an unerring eye, a great sense of timing and is a smart field general. His booming punts, his tricky change of pace and his knack of shaking off tacklers have made him a unanimous all state choice by New Jersey sports writers for two years in a row.[10]*

Back in New Jersey, the doors to No. 8 School opened at 7:30. The actual high school building, No. 6 School, didn't even have a gymnasium and, since the Boilermakers played their home basketball games at No. 8, that's where *The Herald-News* arranged to set up the wire. In lieu of any live radio broadcast, it was a public relations masterstroke.

Al Mura got there early enough and paid his 15 cents admission to be donated to the Garfield High athletic program. Mura was lucky enough to stake out a spot in the gym, the better to hear Milton Deutsch read the play-by-play as it rattled across the ticker tape machine set up on the gym stage. Fans were told there would be dancing beforehand, an over-optimistic proposition. That gym was a bandbox and it didn't take long before it was bursting at the seams.

Violet Frankovic was not among the revelers. Although she was eager to get news of the game, her protective father, Butch, didn't allow her to attend. She surely would have been identified as Benny's girl and attracted unwanted attention. It would be too crowded, too unsafe, and, because her friend Edna couldn't join her—it was Christmas, after all—Butch didn't want her walking home alone in the dark. In a way, he was right. It was over-crowded. Estimates put the throng at 2,300. After the gym reached capacity, they crammed people into the hallways. When they, in turn, became swollen with fans, John Alnor, the janitor, threw open classroom doors.

The throng outside #8 School after hearing the call of Benny Babula's game-winning field goal
Courtesy of Howard Lanza.

At 7:45, 15 minutes after the doors opened and 30 minutes prior to kickoff, they were forced to cut off ticket sales. Hundreds were still in line in the 22-degree chill outside. Garfield police forced the school doors shut, but two of them were torn off their hinges as people tried to force their way inside. They could have accommodated twice as many, had there been room. Some who didn't get in stayed out in the cold, hoping they could hear the PA or at least judge the game by the crowd's reaction. Phone calls bombarded the police desk asking for the score. The telephone lines were jammed.

Anyone with an emergency that night was better off walking to headquarters to report it.

A few managed to keep informed without squeezing into the bursting school. Above Klecha's Tavern, the boys connected their crystal set to the box springs in the bed they shared with their step brother, John Grembowitz. It made for a perfect antenna. As game time approached, they were able to pull in the voice of Ted Husing describing the Orange Bowl scene via a Florida radio station.

Herb Zockell was lucky he wasn't in the gym—although he didn't think he was so lucky at first. The 11-year-old never missed a home game and, as a member of Mayor Gabriel's award-winning junior safety patrol, he was part of the honor guard that escorted the team to Newark Penn Station. His family celebrated Christmas with relatives in Clifton, and that's where the dour youngster would be—fortuitously, as it turned out.

Herb's cousin had received a radio as a Christmas gift and, as the two youngsters fiddled with the dials, they detected the scratchy sound of atmospheric skip. Ted Husing's voice came through the static. He and the Klecha family were probably the only Garfield fans to hear the broadcast.

The cover of Walter Young's game program, signed by almost every member of the Garfield traveling party. Note the "National Championship." Courtesy Estate of Walter Young.

As game time approached, the Garfield police received a call from a Michael Sabino that a bullet had just ricocheted through his kitchen on Lincoln Street. Perhaps the city's criminals weren't interested in the game or just trying to take advantage of an inattentive public. A half-hour later, a Nicholas Latoni reported his 1932 Ford sedan stolen from in front of his home on River Drive.

Back in Burdine Stadium, marching bands from four high schools—Miami, Edison, Andrew Jackson and Homestead—paraded around the field. Letty Barbour had already performed her rousing rendition of *God Bless America* over the PA. The teams lined the sidelines as the bands combined to play a snappy National Anthem. And finally, it was time for football.

The coaches agreed that the game would be played under two different sets of rules: Florida Federation rules would be used in the first half and New Jersey rules in the second. In Florida, passing was permitted from any point behind the line of scrimmage while in New Jersey, the passer had to be at least five yards behind the line. That would be a distinct advantage to the Boilermakers. Florida's rules were also more liberal regarding substitution. They allowed for the substitution of a player twice in one period. New Jersey rules did not permit re-entry of a player in the same period.

Michael Rayhack set up his camera on the sidelines to take the film that would forever preserve the game. Captain Eldredge met captains Babula and Grembowitz at midfield as referee Bill Harkness of Tennessee, dressed in a long-sleeved white shirt and blousy pants, flipped the coin into the air. Garfield called it. Miami won it. The Stingarees took the ball.

As Bobby "Red" Mathews returned the kickoff, Eldredge remained on the sidelines, his ear turned toward Yarborough above the din. As usual, the plan was for them to spend the first offensive series studying and dissecting the opponents' defense to determine what plays would work best. Since plays could not be sent in from the sidelines, it was an opportunity for the play-caller to get his coach's input. And there was indeed a surprise to behold when Argauer opened in his new Eldredge-proof scheme, a departure from the notes the sly head mentor had exchanged with Yarborough a week earlier.

On first down, Jason Koesy, who started in Eldredge's position, burst around the left side of Miami's line and gained 10. The Miami crowd roared in delight at first, then gasped. Grembowitz announced his presence early. Together with guard Jack Boyle, he ran down Koesy and threw him to the ground with a thud and a yelp. The Miami back went down in a heap and held his knee, fighting back the pain. The senior's night and high school career were over with torn cartilage. Miami, already without its best lineman, had now lost its best passer on a night it planned to pass frequently. It would be up to its best runner to carry the night. Eldredge had to go into the game immediately. He and Yarborough had just the one play to digest things.

As they helped Koesy off the field, it was apparent to all that the big Jersey kids could deliver a blow. Now Eldredge would see if Grembowitz and his teammates could catch lightning.

Eldredge would be a revelation to the Boilermakers. Years later, when his son, Davey Jr., was ready to play high school football, he'd tell him the best way for a small man not to get hurt was to do the hitting himself. Packing 141 pounds, he'd start taking it to the Boilermakers—when he wasn't running away from them.

As the trainer tended to the wincing Koesy on the sidelines, Eldredge immediately brought the crowd back to life. He raced out from his deep set in the short punt formation with surprising speed and shed two yellow-jerseyed men with surprising strength. He turned the

Davey Eldredge tries to muscle past Ray Butts as the Garfield defense closes in on him in the first half.
Courtesy Estate of Angelo Miranda.

corner and, with an economy of movement, quickly cut upfield as Garfield's defenders flailed at him. The play gained 16. This wasn't North Jersey-style football and the Boilermakers had to be shocked. They'd given up sizable chunks of yardage on back-to-back plays and Miami was nearly in their territory at the Stingaree 46. Would they test the right side of the line again? Garfield was on its high-topped heels.

Here fate intervened for the first, but not final, time. While on the sidelines for the first play, Eldredge may not have had a chance to see that Grembowitz had been moved off the line into Argauer's backfield. As he considered his next play call from the huddle, Eldredge saw Garfield in its conventional 6-3-2 and he decided to soften up the Boilermakers, who were perhaps gearing up for another run. He called a pass play. But to complete Argauer's ruse, as the Stingarees headed to the line, a Boilermaker dropped off of it, perhaps unnoticed. The 6-3-2 converted into a 5-3-2-1. There would be six players defending against the pass.

Now Eldredge leaned over from the waist, his hands outstretched, waiting for the ball. Each potential Miami ball carrier did the same. It was part of the deception of the short punt formation and it forced a defender to read other keys.

Harvey James' snap went to Eldredge but Grembowitz's instincts told him that Eldredge would not be "lugging the leather," to use the sports writing parlance of the day. Instead, Eldredge peeled back out of the formation to look for the dark blue helmet of Charlie Burrus leaking into the Garfield secondary. The ball never reached Burrus' famous sticky fingers. Grembowitz may have been more accustomed to the muscular work of the pits, but his football intelligence kicked in. He dropped back, cut across the potential receiver and snagged the football. He was tackled immediately but Miami's first foray, which had begun so threateningly, had been parried.

Was it an impetuous play call? Was Eldredge getting too greedy? Maybe. But it was also a great defensive play by the All State lineman turned linebacker. Grembowitz would not be suckered. He had turned the momentum in Garfield's favor when an early Miami score would have set a far different tone. It was just one series, but the pattern was already established: Miami would threaten. Grembowitz would step up. A Stingaree chance would be wasted with a turnover.

"Grembowitz was the only man who seemed able to control Eldredge," McMahon wrote in his account of the game. "He played a grand defensive game, this converted lineman, and when they re-tell the story of this Miami game, his name will come up in every other sentence."[11]

The faithful back at Garfield's School No. 8 would certainly hear Grembowitz's name often, as Deutsch read the plays over the loudspeaker. Now, as the fans caught their breath after Gremby's interception, it was the Boilermakers' turn with the ball. Everyone in the gym anticipated Babula's name, but the first two snaps went to Orlovsky and Grembowitz, who tore through the middle of Miami's line for a first down, attacking the spot where Kendrick usually played. Babula's first carry of the game gained four and, after the Stingarees stopped Orlovsky on a spinner play, Babula uncorked his arm for the first time. Benny started out as if he were sweeping his right end and, as Ed Hintenberger—part of the up-front blocking—peeled off into the flat, Babula flicked a pass to him with his three-quarter delivery, leading him perfectly. Orlovsky was trailing the play and Hintenberger neatly shoveled the ball to him with his left hand. Orlovsky gained an extra 10 yards before Mathews shoved him out of bounds.

Argauer smiled on the sidelines, a lot less jittery than he was before the game. He loved those hook-and-lateral plays and, with Miami stacking the line with seven men, the flat would be open. It would take longer for the Miami secondary defenders to get there.

The Boilermakers were 29 yards from the end zone and Babula, calling the plays, entrusted each one of those yards to himself. He first tried a sweep to the left side. Grembowitz eliminated James with a nice cross-body block while, with a shrug, Babula flicked one futile tackler from his ankles. Eldredge raced over from his safety spot and finally took the big man out of bounds by the hip at Miami's 17.

On the next play, Babula, stumbling and stiff-arming his way, circled back and gained eight more yards around the right side. The Stingarees weren't used to being beaten off the ball, but they dug in and began to make a stand. Three Stingarees stuffed Babula when he tried to cut back up the middle on second down. Then, when he tried to go off left tackle again, Eldredge got there quickly to collar the bigger man around the neck. So much for being "Li'l."

Now it was fourth-and-one at the eight. Babula called his own number once again, testing the right side. He skipped over one man who had penetrated the backfield, lowered his shoulders and powered through Doug Craven for five tough yards to keep the drive alive. Tripping before he could cut into an open hole, Babula lost a yard on the next play and Garfield called timeout.

Out came Garfield's water wagon for the first time. It was certainly a curiosity. Yarborough had examined it before the game and promised himself to get one. The Miami crowd buzzed and razzed as Louis Kral, the manager, pulled it behind him. The Miami school newspaper would note that Kral was big enough to play tackle.[12] He was big but he was unable to

Benny Babula crashes across the goal line for Garfield's first touchdown between Dick Fauth, hanging on his legs, Davey Eldredge and Harvey Comfort. A crushing block from John Grembowitz has Eldredge (1) on the ground. Courtesy Estate of Angelo Miranda.

participate in sports after contracting pleurisy in his youth. Too bad the Boilermakers weren't getting any benefits from the artesian well water inside. They were parched, but they dutifully spit it out after a quick swish and wiped the perspiration off their heads with towels. At least the timeout provided a breather for Babula and his teammates, if not refreshment.

When play resumed, Garfield executed a piece of single wing perfection. Babula took the snap and blasted around his left side as Grembowitz and Boyle (who kicked out from his guard position) roared out in front of him. Orlovsky provided the cross-body block on the outside defender, Brownie Brown, and Young administered the seal block on Levin Rollins. Harvey James had gotten through the backside and had a chance to take Babula down from behind around the shoulders. But Benny, sensing his proximity, reached back with his right hand and fended him off. Grembowitz lined up Eldredge in the hole and took him out with a perfect form block to the midsection, lifting Eldredge off the ground with the force of the blow. Babula fell across the goal line with Dick Fauth, the left tackle, clinging to his ankles. Flash bulbs popped in Babula's face, the historic moment captured for the next day's newspapers.

No one had done that to Miami all year. No team had scored on the ground through the Stingaree line. One of the only two touchdowns they allowed came on a deflected pass after a fumble late in the game against Savannah. The other was on a bad punt snap that Andrew Jackson recovered in the end zone. Not one team had sustained a drive against the Stingarees longer than 19 yards. This one went 54 yards—on Garfield's first possession. They were really missing Jay Kendrick.

Babula lined up to try the point-after from about the 11-yard line, but his end-over-end kick sputtered off to the right, leaving the score at 6-0. Garfield didn't threaten again the rest of the half. But Eldredge gave the Boilermakers fits. He'd spin, reverse field and flash through holes, usually to find Grembowitz taking him down in the end. All season long, once Eldredge was in the clear he was gone. Early in the second quarter, that again seemed the case, but Grembowitz took a great angle and wrapped him up, helped by reserve Julius Fick.

Somehow, Miami just couldn't dent the scoreboard. Later that same quarter, the Stingarees were at the Garfield 37 after a 17-yard run by Comfort. They were in attack mode—perhaps too much so. The snap went to Comfort, who retreated and escaped the frenzied clutches of two Garfield men. The crowd leapt to its feet screaming as Comfort leaned back and hurled one. It was silhouetted against the arc lights before Brown brought it down at the Boilermaker nine. Brown was thinking touchdown. He made a move on Pete Yura but the Boilermaker stymied him and bent him over at the waist. Bill Wagnecz, the second man in, knocked the ball loose and pounced on it. Another Miami turnover.

It wasn't the last Miami chance before the half ended. From his end zone, Babula boomed a 68-yard punt (he'd total seven punts of over 50 yards). Eldredge doubled back and returned it 27 yards to the Garfield 38, where Babula hustled up the field to make the tackle. On second and seven, the snap was wide of Eldredge and he had to chase the ball down for a 15-yard loss. Yet another missed chance. Then, a long pass intended for Andy Smith hit him squarely in the face and fell incomplete, a gaffe that must have smarted both his cheek and his ego.

The game was being played ferociously at a frenzied pace. Even with the limited padding and flimsy headgear of the day, injuries weren't all that common in the era. Both teams, for instance, had survived the year having lost but one starter. Neither injury to Garfield's Tabaka nor Miami's Kendrick had occurred in a game. But with the hitting and urgency amped up, things became dangerous. Koesy was hurt on the first play of the game and both of the Stingarees' All City ends, Charlie Burrus and J.B. Moore, were eventually lost to injuries. Garfield's Hintenberger, as well, went out with bruised ribs.

Now, close to halftime, Babula took the snap and faked a quick kick, then took off. Orlovsky, as he had done on the touchdown play, was out ahead of him but tripped and clumsily landed on his shoulder. He could feel his collarbone crack. After losing so much time during the season with a chronic shoulder injury, it was hard for Orlovsky to accept this latest setback.

That now made it two of Argauer's regular backfield men sidelined. The coach called for the next man available.

"Kazaren," he barked.

Al Kazaren was a full-time reserve who, a year earlier, played JV. Argauer always made sure he got his substitutes into action during the regular season, so Kazaren had seen some playing time. He even started the Passaic game when Ray Butts was hurting. Argauer expected his reserves to fill in admirably. It was a point of pride with the coach. Now, had Argauer not moved Grembowitz from the line to the backfield when Orlovsky was injured during the regular season, Kazaren would have started. He may have been a bit disappointed when he still didn't get the call for Tabaka, but this was his chance.

Argauer wasn't going to hide him. Kazaren was to take up all of Orlovsky's responsibilities, except for holding on placements. Every man counted in those times, whether as part of the single wing blocking or on defense. No one left the field. Kazaren' first test came only a few plays after entering the game. Eldredge attempted a pass on the final play of the first half and

Garfield Mayor John Gabriel gives announcer Ted Husing an earful about the Boilermakers' halftime lead as Miami Mayor E.G. Sewell strikes a bemused pose. Courtesy Estate of Angelo Miranda.

Kazaren was there to make the interception. It was, quite likely, a confidence booster. As the teams headed into the lockers, the restless crowd settled down. But, back in Garfield, antsy fans at School No. 8 wondered if the Garfield offense could re-ignite and if it could keep clamping down the Stingarees.

John Gabriel appeared on the field to chat with Husing and garner a little more publicity. Husing introduced Georgia Tech and Missouri, the two teams meeting in the Orange Bowl on New Year's Day, and the teams' captains addressed the crowds over the loudspeaker. Paul Christman, Missouri All-American, was among them. Little did the Georgia Tech players know, but Eldredge would be playing there next season.

The Miami High band took the field and formed a merry-go-round and then, as it played "Happy Days are Here Again," it arranged itself in the letters "FDR" in honor of the President, then "NJ" in honor of the visitors from Garfield.[13] In the locker room beneath the grandstands, the Stingarees were stunned. If they hadn't taken the game seriously, they did now. They'd trailed only once before in a game, and never in the second half.

"At that point, it sunk in," Harvey Comfort recalled years later. "They were a good team. We knew we were in a game and we really wanted to beat them."

Across the way, Argauer was not happy, despite the lead. Apart from the first possession, his offense had been stymied. The turnovers were bonuses, but how long could they expect to hold Miami in check while giving up yardage as they had? He informed his boys they were being outplayed. "Pick your skirts up and play some real football," he told them. Or lose.

The Miami High School band forms the letters "NJ" during its halftime performance.
Courtesy Estate of Angelo Miranda.

Actually, there was an apparel issue that was more serious than Argauer's quip about the skirts. Argauer had ordered lightweight purple silk jerseys for the game. They were sitting in boxes inside the locker room. There they remained. Years later, at the team's 50th anniversary reunion, players mistakenly remembered that Argauer had handed them out. Rayhack's film proved them wrong. Garfield stayed with the traditional yellow the team had worn for 20 straight wins. Was Argauer superstitious? Or did Yarborough beat him to the punch? Miami, which had nothing but lightweight gear, changed from white jerseys to navy blue. Garfield would have been unable to don darker jerseys as well. Was that why Argauer had to tell the team to stay in its woolen yellows, now heavy with sweat? It's an unanswered mystery.

The uniform change handed Miami another benefit. The football could be hidden much easier amid darker jerseys, especially during night games. With so many ball fakes, the deception of the short punt formation was enhanced.

As the second half started, the Boilermakers dug deep, perhaps heeding Argauer's message. Kazaren got into the thick of it again by returning the kickoff and Babula began to go deeper into the playbook. After finding a hole for 19 yards on first down, he called the hook-and-ladder to Young, who lateralled to the busy Kazaren while acrobatically diving forward in front to block a Stingaree. The play gained six. Babula got the first down and more up the middle then flipped a short pass in the open flat to Ray Butts, and the fullback skipped out of one tackle and fought for 14 through three other defenders. Now, Babula tried the left side himself, where Brownie Brown and Henry Washington (back from Cuba) twice stopped him for one-yard gains. Washington forced his forward progress back five yards the second time as if Babula were on a blocking sled. Now, on a huge third-down play, Babula came right back to the other side and, with Kazaren in front of him, gained 16 yards to the Miami 20 before Mathews took him out of bounds. The crowd buzzed.

The Stingarees were being set up. When Garfield scored its first touchdown, it came after a steady dose of Babula from the 29-yard line in. The Stingarees would be expecting another off-tackle run and they'd be swarming to that spot. Babula sensed it was the perfect time to spring Argauer's pet play, the Naked Reverse. To the Stingarees, it would look like the same play that Babula scored on for the first touchdown of the game, only to the other side.

A naked play is one run with practically no interference. It's a bit risky, but that would only add to the misdirection with almost everyone heading to the strong side, especially with Miami aligned in a seven-man front. Plus, the handoff would go to Grembowitz, primarily a blocking back up, but now lined up as the wingback. All he needed to do was to take one step toward the line and turn his back toward the defense. As Babula started ahead behind a cordon of blockers, the exchange was made. The fake was so good that Miami defenders kept following Babula as he lowered his shoulder into James. Grembowitz, hiding the ball, circled around the formation against the grain, unnoticed for those critical seconds. With giant strides, he raced for the far sideline and the flag (a pylon would be there now) at the corner of the end zone.

The heady Young, at left end, was now the key to the play. Eldredge, too, had been influenced by the fake at his deep safety position, but he had enough recovery speed to run Grembowitz down. His teammates, trying to scramble back after realizing they had been taken in, were being chopped down one by one. Eldredge would have the only shot at preventing the score.

Young's job had been to tap his man at the line and allow him to move inside in initial pursuit. Then he was to locate Eldredge and line him up in the open field. It was not an easy task for the 6-1 Young. The slippery Eldredge was as difficult to block as he was to tackle. Young got downfield quickly and was able to lunge at Eldredge's knees with a cross-body block as the Stingaree came across the field. Eldredge instinctively turned his body to avoid the block but it was too late. Young cut him down in a heap, getting in front of Eldredge just barely enough for the officials to let the play go without a clipping penalty. It would be another 75 years before Young could be sure he didn't get away with something.

As they did on their first possession of the game, the Boilermakers had struck on their first possession of the second half with the second rushing TD scored against Miami all year. The Orange Bowl fell silent except for the several hundred delirious Garfield rooters while, back home, pandemonium reigned above Klecha's Tavern. Rather than try another placement—keep that in mind for later—Babula took the pitch and roared through the middle of the stunned Stingarees for the third scoring run through their line. It counted for only one point and a 13-0 lead. The two-point conversion rule was decades away.

The Stingarees hadn't trailed all season, let alone by two touchdowns. Thirteen points was all Miami had allowed all year against the best teams in the South. They had shut out seven teams, including powerful Boys High of Atlanta and had gone five straight games without giving up a point. If anyone doubted Garfield belonged in this game, those voices were now muffled.

Babula came out for a breather, and even the Miami fans paid him tribute with a standing ovation. At the same time, spectators observed determination, if not desperation, in Eldredge. In his mind, he was going to bring his team back. There was still time with his big-play ability,

The moment, captured by Michael Rayhack's camera, that John Grembowitz takes the handoff from Benny Babula to score on the Naked Reverse.

Referee Bill Harkness signals for the touchdown as, somewhere in the pile of players, Davey Eldredge gives Miami its first score of the game. Mahai 1940.

After taking a pass from Benny Babula, John Grembowitz falls forward for extra yardage as he's pulled down by Irwin Sibley early in the fourth quarter. Walter Young (note the facemask) doubles back.
Courtesy Estate of Walter Young.

and the heat was certain to become a Miami ally as it had been so many times before. Garfield had to crack. So thought the Stingarees.

Argauer got aggressive. He signaled for the kickoff team to try an onside kick, but Bill Librera's surprise effort skidded out of bounds at the Miami 49—excellent field position. With Babula temporarily out of the game, Eldredge took over. On the third play of the drive, Eldredge found a hole up the middle, then instantly cut back to the left side. As Eldredge was about to break into the open, Grembowitz made his best defensive play of the day: lunging and reaching out with one hand to pull the scatback down by the sleeve of his jersey at Garfield's 26. It was one of seven tackles Grembowitz made on the drive.

Undeterred, Eldredge continued the onslaught. He dished a pass to Brown in the flat which Butts nearly intercepted but deflected to Brown for a 10-yard gain. Then Eldredge carried six straight times. Grembowitz, then Joe Tripoli, made nice tackles but Eldredge would not be denied. He was in the end zone before the exhausted Boilermakers even reacted, as he started off right tackle, then cut back slightly for the three-yard score.

It was a prompt and necessary answer to Garfield's second touchdown on a drive with only one pass attempt. But here the Stingarees made a fateful decision. Barnes was a pretty sure kicker, yet they chose to fake a kick and run it in for the extra point and not with Eldredge. Mathews took the snap. He was piled up just a foot short of the goal line. Garfield 13, Miami 6.

The Boilermakers had shown signs of wearing down on that drive. By then, Miami's psychological games were on full display.

"It's hot as hell," the Stingaree linemen groaned on cue.

"I need a drink."

"I'm sweating."

Jack Boyle thought of something clever to say. "I'm sorry I forgot to bring my winter underwear," he shot back. Not knowing what to make of that one, the Stingarees stopped chattering. The Boilermakers were still standing, as instructed, during timeouts but it was a miracle they could. Ever since their light 4 p.m. meal they were prohibited from drinking, and the two salt tablets they were instructed to take were doing what salt tablets do. The wool uniforms were not helping. It was as if they were soldiers at the battle of Gettysburg only this time, the Southerners seemed to be turning the tide.

In a way, Garfield was just trying to hold on. A 15-yard holding penalty aborted the Boilermakers' next possession and the Stingarees reached deep into Garfield territory once again—only to set them themselves up for more disappointment. Years later, Giants coach Bill Parcells, a Jersey guy who loved the ground game, proposed that three things can happen when you throw the ball and two of them are bad. Eldredge stubbornly kept trying to mix in the pass. Babula read the next one and stepped in front of the Miami receiver and nabbed it at the Boilermaker 22. Babula had just come back in for Librera before the play. For Miami, it was yet another costly turnover.

Despite the interception, the crowd still sensed a whiff of a momentum shift as the fourth quarter began. Babula tried to make something happen, flinging a pass across the middle into the hands of Miami's Gilbert Wilson. Wilson cut neatly to his left and sprinted 40 yards for a touchdown that appeared to tie the game. The cowbells rang out. Miami was taking over. At least that's what those not paying close attention might have believed. Luckily for Garfield, the head linesman, Bob Wilson, was alert. The ill-fated Brown had jumped offside— and obviously so. He was across so early and by at least a yard, he had time to try to scramble back before the snap, but to no avail. It was just one of two penalties called on Miami all night. Whether Babula thought he had a free play is unknown. In any case, the Miami TD was nullified. Garfield, however, was showing signs of fatigue. Two plays later, the Boilermakers called another timeout.

Babula picked up one more first down and sailed a long cross-field pass that Wagnecz couldn't reach. Babula punted from his 46. It was a beauty and carried through the back of the left side of the end zone for a touchback. From his 20, Eldredge gained three, upended by Butts. Until then, Garfield had at least prevented him from breaking loose. During the season, eight of his 16 touchdowns were for 50 or more yards. His longest gain so far was 17 yards on the first touchdown drive.

In other words, he was due to break one. It happened on the next play from Miami's 23.

Walter Young, playing standup left end, peeked over the Miami line for his key and began to follow the wingback to his left as Eldredge took the snap. Young's job was always to force the play back to the middle. But Garfield was light on that side and there were four blockers coming his way ahead of Eldredge. Young was taken out of the play with a perfectly executed double team to open a huge swath. Butts was, in effect, the linebacker on that side, but Gilbert Wilson, the pulling guard, nullified him. Grembowitz tried to save the day by diving over Charlie Fancher's block but he came up empty as Eldredge sailed past. Now Li'l Davey turned the corner and sped in a blur past Rayhack's camera and the hapless Garfield bench.

At that point, Eldredge really turned on the speed. Comfort always said his teammate could go "woosh" better than anyone he ever saw. Now, the Boilermakers saw and heard it for themselves.

Kazaren took a swipe at him but came up empty handed. At the 50, Eldredge found daylight under the stars and no one would be able to catch him from behind. Florida's state champion in the 220-yard dash was arguably the fastest player in the nation. He was in that most glorious of places for a breakaway back—just him, the warm air and the disappearing yard markers. The home crowd's crescendo intensified with every 10 yards of Eldredge's dash. Back in New Jersey, Herb Zockell and the Klechas listened painfully to Ted Husing's count-down, "the 30, the 20, the 10, touchdown."

When Eldredge crossed the goal line, nothing but teammates were nearby. A few turned around to form a final ring of unnecessary blockers. Comfort climbed off the turf and saw Babula watching helplessly. He grabbed his handshake nemesis by the sleeve of his jersey, jumped excitedly and pointed toward his wee teammate in the end zone. A Miami writer speculated that he was telling Benny, "that's what a real football player looks like."[14] It was more what a beautifully designed play executed perfectly looked like.

They let Bucket Barnes kick it this time, and he drilled the PAT through the middle of the goal posts. Garfield's two-touchdown lead was gone. It was 13-13. Lou Mallia, in the stands with his Garfield buddies, was already "broken hearted." Zockell, the Klechas and a school full of Garfield boosters suddenly felt almost doomed.

The Herald-News reported from School No. 8, "A pall of gloom settled over the crowd," which it said had been "downright hysterical" after Garfield went up 13-0.

"It was a football crowd, a roaring, cheering, excited, understandably partisan football crowd," the paper wrote. "It cheered Garfield High School to the echo every time the home team scored a yard or two and it cheered every time the name of Garfield High School's great Benny Babula was mentioned. It groaned every time Miami High School executed a spectac-ular play which is to say that it groaned frequently."[15]

It was groaning now. Things appeared desperate, so desperate that the injured Tabaka, who was in uniform but forbidden from entering the game by Dr. Reid, pleaded with Argauer to put him in. The coach refused.

But Garfield wasn't finished. In a strange way, the advantage was with the Boilermakers even after Miami tied the score. The Boilermakers had learned how to win games like this one. Miami was never even required to take the class. The Stingarees were accustomed to winning easily. They'd never been forced to come from behind all year, let alone finish it off. Garfield had been through several do-or-die situations already. And as Babula dropped back near his goal line on the kickoff, he knew this was just another challenge.

The Stingarees were rolling and the Garfield defense was feeling the heat. The Boilermakers needed to string together some first downs, and they hadn't done that since the first series of the third quarter. This was probably going to be their last chance to score. Otherwise, their odds of even escaping with a tie were going to be long.

Was Comfort's taunt in Babula's mind? Babula was one of two deep backs on the left side and, somewhat surprisingly, Barnes kicked it to him. It's possible Babula would have ended up with the ball on a lateral or reverse, but after gathering in the football, he quickly headed over the right side and gained a head of steam behind some good blocking. A swarm of Stingarees met him as he approached midfield but he drove through them until finally pulled down at Garfield's 48. Few plays in the game were bigger than that one. It swung field position in Garfield's favor and broke momentum. Now, even if the Boilermakers were forced to punt, Babula could pin Miami deep. But punting wasn't in Babula's plans.

Eldredge had his moment. Now it was Babula's—again. Sheer power and sheer will. That was the matchup on the first two plays with Miami ganging up to stop him for three yards each time. Now on third and four, Young slipped out into the flat to receive a Babula pass. Young tossed a lateral to Kazaren for a few extra yards and the first down.

Miami's short punt formation was supposed to be a better passing formation because it set the tailback a little deeper and afforded more pass protection than the power-based single wing. But in this game, Garfield outperformed Miami through the air. The Boilermakers threw less often but with more efficiency. The hook-and-lateral to Young was an example.

Now, from the Miami 42, Grembowitz gained a yard from the fullback position and shifted to wingback when Garfield next broke the huddle. An alert Stingaree defense might have known what was coming next. It did not. Once again, the Naked Reverse burned them. They swarmed toward Babula's side as he headed off-tackle, taken in by the play fake again. Grembowitz got away clean but this time Eldredge's speed chased him down, preventing a touchdown by forcing him out of bounds from behind, not before the pet play netted 28 yards to the Miami 14.

The Stingarees dug in. They stopped Babula twice after two-yard gains and forced a third down incompletion. It was fourth-and-six from the 10.

Babula had done much in his high school career. One thing he had never done was attempt a field goal. In fact, field goals were as scarce as snowflakes in Florida. The last one kicked at Burdine Stadium came the year before when Tennessee's Bowden Wyatt converted from 15 yards out against Oklahoma in the Orange Bowl. This was also the same end of the field from where Babula missed an extra point in the first quarter. Now he'd be 10 yards further back. The Boilermakers huddled up, all ears turned toward Babula for the play.

"Field goal," Babula said.

His teammates gulped.

Young thought, at first, he'd be kicking it. On the rare occasions when Garfield attempted a field goal, he would have tried it. Babula only kicked extra points.

"I was lousy," Young recalled years later. "But frankly we were all lousy because it was never practiced. We never stayed there and practiced kicking field goals."

But Babula's intentions were clear.

"I'm kicking this one," he said, taking on the responsibility. Young didn't protest. Benny was the boss.

"That was that," Young said.

There was one other major issue. Orlovsky was the usual holder, but he was out with that broken collarbone. So Grembowitz had to hold. As he put his knee down and awaited Yura's snap, many fans still doubted Garfield would kick. Up in the press box, the writers were certain he wouldn't.

"Fake. It's got be a fake," they said.

Grembowitz was at the Miami 22. That was the official yardage back then, although the goal posts were on the end line and it would go down as a 32-yarder today. Babula had but one thing left to do before he stepped into the kick, the same thing he had done countless times at St. Joseph Church, his home parish in Passaic.

He blessed himself.

"I was a strong believer in religion—and hoped it would go over," he would recall at the 50-year reunion. "When it went through, I knew God had answered my prayers."[16]

The kick was no thing of beauty but it was indeed granted Godspeed and accuracy as it eked over the crossbar. From the goal line, referee Harkness used only one arm to signal good. Perhaps he doubted it himself. Babula sunk to both knees in thanks to the heavens.

"It wasn't a perfect kick," McMahon wrote. "It twisted and turned uncertainly and was safe by only a yard or two."

It was perfect enough and no one on the Garfield sidelines doubted it would be.

"I knew it was over, knew Benny was a tough man under pressure, ice water in his veins," assistant coach Joe Cody said. "I'd seen him carry two and three guys over a goal line."

The Miami fans slumped. Bedlam ensued in the Garfield rooting section, where the Wagneczs sat. Mallia hugged his buddies, just as the Klecha family was doing back in Garfield. Over at No. 8 School, Deutsch cleared his throat and read the result of the kick loudly from the tickertape: "A perfect field goal," even if it wasn't that all that perfect. The place erupted, giving rise to a legend that the spontaneous jumping for joy caused a crack in the school's foundation. More likely, it kicked up a great amount of dust from the hallway floors.

When they finally calmed down, the ecstatic throng had a few more breaths to catch. Just under 2:00 remained when Babula's kickoff went out of bounds at the Miami 35. With a quick-strike offense like Miami's, that was more than enough time to win the game. On fourth down, Eldredge stopped hearts when he was able to zig zag away from a tackler in his backfield, reverse field and gain six yards for the first down. Grembowitz made the tackle yet again.

Comfort skirted his left end and got out to midfield. Garfield was barely holding on. And then, Eldredge made one last ill-fated play call, a sprint-out pass. Because New Jersey rules were in force, Eldredge would have to remain at least five yards behind the line of scrimmage so the play looked less like a run and Garfield's backs did not bite.

Also, unlike the previous plays, including Eldredge's long touchdown run, Miami didn't line up an end on the right side, so Wagnecz, in for Young at left end, had a free run into the backfield. He charged straight upfield. Comfort attempted to cut him but Wagnecz leapt over Eldredge's only blocker. He flashed in front of Eldredge's face, causing him to hurry a throw off his back foot that flew over his intended receiver. It was a great, if under-acknowledged, defensive play.

Back in coverage stood Kazaren, Orlovsky's replacement. He hardly had to move. The football floated through the arc lights, destined, it seemed, for him. "Hang on," he must have thought. Hang on, he did. He caught it at the 40 and returned it 10 yards to the 50, where he was tackled at the feet of the despondent Eldredge. Kazaren was the unsung hero that Argauer needed. It was his second interception and Garfield's fifth takeaway of the game. Losing hope, Miami rooters began to file out of the stadium as Garfield's fans remained to soak in the final seconds.

Teams didn't take a knee in victory formation in those days. Babula simply crashed the line three final times. His first-down carry was nonetheless a signature moment. He burst through the middle on a straight dive and carried three Stingarees for three yards until he gained a clinching first down with a 12-yard gain. He was a power back, and that was one last power run. He hit the line again for two and then, running easily, was brought down at the line. Babula cradled the football as if every one of his high school football memories was wrapped up inside it. The final whistle blew. There was no confetti. Except for the Garfield rooters in the stands, there was little celebration at all. That's the way things were done back then.

Players from both teams milled about the field, totally spent, and it was difficult to tell which team won. There were no theatrics, no primeval shrieks into the night. Argauer was not hoisted onto his players' shoulders and carried off the field. The Boilermakers, as proper sportsman, shook hands with the sullen Stingarees and headed back to their locker room. Even the Miami rooters rose and applauded them, while, at School No. 8, fans let out a big cheer that sounded more like relief.

By the time newsmen reached the closed doors of the Boilermaker locker room, it was a far more jubilant scene than on the field. Louis Kral tried to keep the crush of Garfield fans at bay while, inside, joy and pandemonium reigned.

Grembowitz and Young were self-appointed gatekeepers. They greeted each visitor with a slap on the back.

"We did it. We really did it."

"Didn't Ben go to town?"[17]

Mayor Gabriel had made his way down from Pepper's box. He couldn't contain himself. His little city was on the map because of the young people to whom he dedicated himself.

Argauer made a brave but vain attempt to maintain his composure as reporters moved about the room in shadows. How could he have imagined this scene, celebrating the championship of the entire United States, when he was a youngster, on board the ship that took him from Germany to his new country? He didn't even know what a football was.

Center Pete Yura was the calmest Boilermaker in the room, it was said, although he'd played one of the fiercest games. Perhaps he just had nothing left. That was the case with Babula, who said he could barely lift his legs in the final minutes. He slumped on his stool, eight pounds lighter than when he had started the game in the Miami heat. He simply stared into space, perhaps stunned by the accomplishment. When he did talk, he spoke in awe about Eldredge, the pint-sized player it took all his brawn to match.

"That Davey was the best player we ever ran up against," Babula told young Hardy Whritenour.[18] At the next locker, the gallant Grembowitz, weary from chasing and tackling the Miami mite, simply nodded in assent.

"He's better than Eddie Berlinksi of Bloomfield," Argauer chattered, rating Eldredge over the legendary back who powered the Bengals to an undefeated season in 1933. "I wouldn't want to see him against my team again."[19]

Perhaps the Miami players would have spoken just as glowingly of Grembowitz. They eventually voted him—and not Babula—on their all-opponent team. Gremby had ended Miami's first drive with an interception and, for most of the night, prevented Eldredge from running absolutely wild. His lead block on Eldredge led Babula into the end zone for the first touchdown. He scored the second on a Naked Reverse and set up the field goal on another. He even held for the field goal as an emergency replacement.

No one from Miami was doing much talking now. It was strikingly different across the way from Garfield's celebration. Players could be heard rustling and moving from outside the Stingarees' locker room, but there would be no reaction to record. Yarborough barred reporters from entering.

The Miami players were taking it hard; no one harder than Li'l Davey.

Eldredge had played valiantly. Of the Stingarees' 254 yards of rushing offense, he accounted for 190. The papers were effusive, even Garfield's hometown *Herald-News.* McMahon wrote that Babula, in spite of his great game, had been overshadowed in the battle of the blonds.

"It was little Eldredge who was the fair-haired lad . . . a heartbroken boy when the final whistle sounded but he was a hero in defeat. Missouri and Georgia Tech will not show a better ball player in their Orange Bowl game next week. Ever try catching a mouse on the kitchen with your bare hands?" McMahon asked. "That's the picture of Garfield reaching out for Eldredge."[20]

McMahon was right, but Eldredge was inconsolable. The first Miami drive of the night, so promising, ended with his interception. The last drive, as the Stingarees moved desperately on the weary Boilermakers, ended in his interception. On the night, Miami outgained Garfield, 282-230 although Garfield had the edge in first downs, 12-10. The difference was turnover ratio. Miami gave the ball up five times. Garfield didn't turn it over once. Babula's only interception was run back for a touchdown, but the points were wiped out by an offside call away from the play. Four of Miami's nine passes, many downfield, were intercepted. Only two were completed. The Boilermakers threw eight times, mostly in the flats, and completed four.

No wonder Eldredge was still lamenting the defeat decades later.

The night now belonged to the revelers—and the writers. Up the deserted grandstands clambered the ink-stained chroniclers. Soon, a frantic press box echoed with clicks and clacks of typewriter keys and the bells and swoosh of the carriages, strangely rhythmic sounds that always grew louder in syncopated creativity and urgency when there was a good story to pound out. Sportswriters were always told to "make it sing." This was an opera. The very act of producing tight copy on deadline can be considered a contest in itself—fingers keeping up with thoughts in a jumbled race that somehow managed to sort itself out at the finish line. Thoughts came more naturally in a game that wrote itself. This one did.

Babula and Eldredge ran wild. The superlatives wafted on cigarette smoke.

The *Associated Press,* noting that Garfield had won "brilliantly," called it, "one of the best matches ever seen on the Orange Bowl field."

"A frenzied crowd sat awestruck," Clay wrote in the *Star-Ledger.*[21]

McMahon began his game story: "Many a low moon will hang over Miami before football fans sit in on the equal of last night's hair-raising struggle between Garfield and Miami, a contest that raised the New Jersey school's banner aloft."[22]

"When Garfield last night won its 21st straight game, a crowd of 15,000 in the Orange Bowl saw a dazzling exhibition by two of the greatest schoolboy backs in the country," Paul Horowitz wrote. "Benny Babula of Garfield and Dave Eldredge of Miami lived up to their advance ballyhoo in every respect."[23]

In his lede, Emanuel Strauss of the *New York Times* said Garfield won with Babula, "living up to all of the praise heaped upon his head."[24]

Even Miami's student newspaper, the *Miami High Times,* gave Babula and the Boilermakers their props.

"One of the rarest of football feats executed by a truly great high school team robbed Miami High of the mythical national championship," Dale Melching wrote.

The kid reporter even managed a bit of humor:

> *Beneath a lucent moon and brilliant stars the tale of David and Goliath was re-enacted (with slight variations) in a football pageant staged by the combined casts of Garfield N.J. and Miami High Christmas night.*
>
> *David Eldredge and "Goliath" Benny Babula played their leading parts perfectly until the very end when Goliath digressed from the original story and from the viewpoint of the hometown audience spoiled the show.*[25]

Luther Voltz, tapping out the game story for the *Miami News*, described the steel stands as rocking with cheers for Babula and Eldredge as they waged "the finest personal war a Miami football audience has ever seen."[26]

Chuck Dewees wrote, also in the *Miami News*: "With all due respect to the potentialities of Georgia Tech and Missouri, if the Orange Bowl game produces more sheer thrills than last night's fray, it will have to be one of those dream games."[27]

This was one of those dream games, at least for the Boilermakers. They'd linger in Miami for a week and more. Then it was back to Garfield and the rest of their lives. This, though, was a night they'd never forget.

A magical night in the Magic City.

TWENTY

THE AFTERMATH

Benny Babula should have collapsed into his bed at the Alcazar and slept through his wake-up call. Contentedness is the surest sedative. But as he restlessly tossed and turned, he put more moves on the sheets then he had on Miami High defenders earlier that Christmas evening. His shoulder and back ached with the accumulated effect of the hits he absorbed charging the Stingaree line. The enormity of what he and his teammates had just accomplished was sinking in, and it was overwhelming.

The Garfield High School Boilermakers were national champs, and though some might dispute it, they could at least claim to be. And, so they did.

"Whether Garfield was better than teams in Chicago, Butte, San Francisco, Dallas, Los Angeles and other western points is a question that can't be answered," Art McMahon wrote in his conclusion. "Miami started out by calling the Christmas night game for the 'Mythical national championship.' In a couple of days it had dropped the 'mythical' moniker and was boldly advertising it as a national championship contest. It was Miami's brainchild and don't blame Garfield for being bashful in accepting honors thrust upon it."

McMahon noted that, at the very least, Garfield could be hailed as the bravest team in the nation:

> *The comeback was an old story to them. They had been doing it all season, often waiting for an uncomfortably long period before salting away a decision.*
>
> *They battled heat, a partisan crowd, unfamiliar nocturnal shadows and a layoff of three weeks at Miami but they conquered the greatest schoolboy team in the South and the strongest foe they've met in two years. The fact that it was facing one of the leading teams of the nation had been hammered into Garfield from the minute the Miami trip was arranged but the Jerseymen went into the Christmas night game as mentally relaxed as if they were playing the Showhank Rangers.*
>
> *The phlegmatic type makes the best athlete. Jou Louis is that way, so lacking in imagination that in less than a round he butchered Max Schmeling, who had previously punished*

Assistant coach John Hollis (center, front) poses with a group of players at the Venetian Pool. Hollis spent the rest of his life coaching and teaching physical education at the high school. Courtesy Estate of Jack Boyle.

The boys gang up to throw Art Argauer into the surf when the team spends a day at Miami Beach. Courtesy Estate of Angelo Miranda.

him brutally. Likewise, Garfield couldn't understand how a hot night, strange surroundings and a hostile crowd were supposed to impair its football efficiency.

Any team could have gone to Miami and lost. It took a good team to go down there and win. That's why this Garfield team was great, and indeed, at times Magnificent.

Well done, Boilermakers![1]

While most *Herald-News* readers agreed with McMahon, Garfield still had doubters in New Jersey, particularly in Nutley and Vineland, whose coach, Nello Dallolio, remained unconvinced. Upon his return to the South Jersey hamlet, he unabashedly told Carlo Sardella at the *Vineland Evening Times* that his Poultry Clan could have licked an all-star team drawn from both Garfield and Miami and that, if Davey Eldredge had Vineland's line been blocking for him, the result would have been different.

The Boilermakers, though, had little trouble ignoring Vineland's barrage of sour grapes. They were the kings of scholastic football and they were treated as such over their extended stay. This was what Art Argauer called the "educational" part of the trip, and while some, it was said, slipped off to be educated in nocturnal pursuits not on the coach's lesson plan, it was a grand tour indeed.

The team had to check out of the Alcazar, which was filling up with football fans from Georgia Tech and Missouri, the two Orange Bowl teams. Frank Gough gave Argauer a hearty slap on the back and wished him well, thankful that the Boilermakers had left his hotel intact. They spent the next seven nights at the Antilla Hotel in Coral Gables, which, built in the Mediterranean Revival style, was the quintessential Florida resort. There, the players had full use of the famous Venetian Pool in Coral Gables, which had been built as part of George Merrick's vision for his planned middle class utopia. It was renowned as the "world's most beautiful swimming hole," a far cry from the brickyard pond back in Garfield. With limestone outcroppings left from a quarry pit

Ray Butts, Benny Babula, Wally Tabaka and John Orlovsky relax at the Venetian Pool in Coral Gables, where the team spent an extra week. Courtesy Estate of Jack Boyle.

used for the construction of Coral Gables' earliest buildings, it resembled a Venetian lagoon. The more adventuresome Boilermakers spiraled off its high diving tower—to Argauer's dismay. There, was, after all, a basketball season waiting back home.

The players also had the use of pool at the Floridian Hotel while Argauer arranged for a condo on a side trip to Miami Beach. There, the players engaged in a bit of horseplay with their coach, ganging up on him and tossing him into the surf. For once, he cheerfully allowed it. Argauer had brought along a set of basketball uniforms, hoping to arrange a game with Miami High or any other team. His players did not share his enthusiasm for further competition in Florida and he was unsuccessful in finding an opponent. Losing to a Northern team in one sport was apparently enough.

There were bus trips to the Seminole Reservation, the Everglades and Key West. A deep sea fishing trip yielded more sea-sickened Boilermakers than fish. Theatres offered them free admission. They took in a Missouri practice on the grounds of the swanky Biltmore Hotel. They returned to the Alcazar to watch the Orange Bowl Parade from its roof and cheered when Eldredge rode past on a float that held members of the All Southern team. Eldredge, as it turned out, would have a seat on the Georgia Tech bench during the game.

The week was a social whirl. University of Miami coach Jack Harding took Garfield's eight seniors to lunch on campus, showing them "the works." Perhaps he was hoping to persuade a couple to enroll. None did, although he did lure one of Garfield's rivals, Passaic end Dan Kuzma. Miami Beach debutante Cornelia Nordyke hosted another group, while others attended a formal dance at the Coral Gables Country Club.

Lou Mallia (front) and Steve Kopec show off a couple of oranges they "liberated" from roadside groves.
Courtesy of Lou Mallia.

Players sent telegrams home. Angelo Miranda's, on New Year's Day, was typically brief:

HAVING SWELL TIME BE HOME WEDNESDAY HAPPY NEW YEAR

Newark News columnist Jimmie Ebben implored families to let the kids settle back into their old routines once they returned:

> *Friends and relatives are asked not to be too severe on the boys for several days, at least, until they get the champagne and caviar tastes out of their systems. While the squad observed rigid regulations prior to the Health Bowl kickoff, they subsequently let their hair down to the extent of consuming filet mignons smothered with lamb chops, double dip ice cream cones with sprills (old Jersey for sprinkles) and staying up on several occasions until the witching hour of midnight with a couple of pillow fights thrown in. Added to all this were ocean and pool bathing, fishing parties and sight seeing tours and other delights one associated with a tropical visit.[2]*

The week was climaxed New Year's Day at the Orange Bowl, watching Georgia Tech use its innovative offense to dazzle Missouri, although some spectators felt it didn't measure up to the excitement of the Health Bowl.

By then, Garfield rooters had made their way back home, bringing with them fresh citrus, Indian trinkets and scores of baby alligators.

Lou Mallia's ride home with his buddies was one of the more adventuresome. They detoured across the state along the Tamiami Trail and up the Gulf Coast to Tampa, where they stopped at Ringling Brothers' winter quarters. Then they headed back east through miles of orange groves, a site that proved too tempting. Mallia pulled over the Pontiac. They

The Newark Star-Ledger *announces the Boilermakers' return to New Jersey across the top of its front sports page.*

hopped the growers' roadside fences, helped themselves to Florida's finest, then stacked the orbs under the back window.

Mallia had insisted to do all the driving, having little trust in his friends. When they reached Virginia, temperatures plummeted and the roads iced up. John Hilla pleaded to take over the wheel and, for some reason, Mallia gave in. In Quantico, near the Marine barracks, they rode down a hill covered with black ice. Hilla hit the brakes and lost control, sending the car into a skid. It spun three times with the purloined oranges flying about. When the thrill ride stopped, the guys found themselves in a ditch. They gathered the oranges and other jilted stuff, got out, and found they had a damaged left front wheel. Surely, it could have been much worse.

"We didn't have the money to fix it," Mallia recalled. "We got towed to a garage and I wired home to a neighbor of mine, Danny Kowalczyk, for money to repair the wheel and to pay for the hotel we stayed in. It had a pot-bellied stove in the lobby. That's how we got warm."

All the while, the city of Garfield prepared to welcome back its heroes with the grandest celebration the city would ever see. As Argauer said: "This is something that happens once in a lifetime. A great thing for a city like Garfield, totally unknown before it came here. That victory was a swell Christmas present."[3]

A special Citizens Committee drew up elaborate plans that involved most everyone in the city. In his congratulatory wire to Argauer the day after the game, assistant principal Frank Paparozzi promised that the send-off crowd would "seem puny" compared to the welcome-home crowd. Indeed, the *Associated Press* would say that the team returned to "tumultuous

Benny Babula locks lips with his girl, Violet Frankovic, to the urging of the assembled media after returning to Newark Penn Station.

acclaim that might have evoked the envy of a Caesar"[4] while the *Star-Ledger* would compare the reception to the ones accorded doughboys returning from World War I.[5]

Aboard the *Vacationer* for the trip back to New Jersey, players slept with bags of oranges stowed above them. Their first sign of home came, as did Mallia's, in frosty Virginia, where the train was delayed for one hour and eighteen minutes to repair a busted bearing. The mishap blew out a fuse controlling the heating system, pushing the cars' temperatures to below freezing. The boys knew they weren't in Florida any more.

There was, of course, a warmer reception awaiting them in Newark—as eighteen bus-loads of students (given half the day off), scores of private cars, three fire trucks, six Bergen County police cars and the high school band headed their way. There was even a special media car for the press, complete with a ready-made story. Forget football. Romance sells.

It started the day after the game when McMahon wrote of how Babula was recovering from his aches and pains: "His cares rode with the wind when among his batch of congratulatory telegrams, he found one from his girl, Violet Frankovic."[6]

Violet and Benny's sister, Eva, once again drove together to Newark Penn Station. This time, Violet was in plain sight when her beau emerged from the train. Harry Forbes of the *New York Daily News* reported that "Benny's sweetheart" could hardly say a word when she spotted her hero.

"She didn't have to," Forbes added. "For the hug and kiss he received were much better than any wasted talk."

Mayor John Gabriel meets and greets the team as it arrives at Newark Penn Station. Note the bag of oranges brought home on the trip. Courtesy Estate of Angelo Miranda.

Forbes asked her if she were still upset at Benny for having posed with a couple of comely young ladies in Miami.

"No," Violet grinned, "the boys had to have a buildup."[7]

The *Newark Star-Ledger* described the scene in detail, although it may have taken a few dramatic liberties, according to Violet's memory years later:

> *Prominent among his well-wishers was Violet Frankovic, whom Benny blushingly admitted to be, "my girlfriend."*
>
> *Violet did not reveal the same bashfulness, welcoming the backfield star with a shower of kisses that left Benny looking like a chorus girl. Photographers, caught off guard, rushed over as Violet was finishing the romantic welcoming.*
>
> *"Let's have a shot of that," a half-dozen photographers requested of the couple. Benny just put one foot over the other and turned crimson. Violet saved the situation by obliging with another half-dozen smacks.*[8]

The images were played on the pages of the *Star-Ledger*, *The Herald-News* and the *New York Daily News*. Violet, in her sharp hat, pulled her beau closer, Benny closing his eyes to prepare for the incoming smooch.

Forbes noted that Argauer, whom he described as "a bespectacled little man" was thrust into the background. "Holding a brief case, he looked more like a college professor than the

The mob outside Garfield High School as the team's caravan through the city reaches its end.
Courtesy Estate of Angelo Miranda.

Art Argauer is the focus of attention at the Casino Grounds, where 20,000 gathered at a bonfire-lit celebration. Courtesy Estate of Angelo Miranda.

man who has brought Garfield two state championships and 21 successive victories," Forbes proffered.[9]

John Gabriel, having trained back to Garfield soon after the game, was front and center again, a pink carnation pinned to his lapel. Close by, too, were Babula's beaming parents. The Health Bowl was the first time Michael had missed one of his son's games. They stood by approvingly as Benny and Violet obliged the photographers one more time.

As the players walked from the lobby into the daylight, they were greeted with a thunderous cheer and an overture from the Garfield High School band, led by drum majorette Margaret Hoving. There were an estimated 7,500 revelers outside the station, and, as Babula emerged, waving, they broke into a spontaneous snake dance. Gabriel escorted Babula to the lead car for the caravan home but he insisted that his parents join him.

It was a boisterous ride back to Garfield. Buses and cars tooted their horns. Fire engines and police cars screeched at full blast, luring fans into the cold to cheer the Jersey conquerors. As the first cars crossed the river into Garfield at the Five Corners intersection, factory whistles from the Hammersley Plant announced the boys were home. One resident, Albert Buonocore, gave the team a 15-gun salute with his yacht gun, and the city's fire stations sounded their alarms. *The Herald-News* reported that it was an unending cacophony from then on.

Here, another 8,000 joined in for an eight-mile procession throughout the town, up into the Guinea Heights, past the fish store on Harrison Avenue, then down onto Midland Avenue, where they could catch a glimpse of Belmont Oval across the railroad tracks. They continued on through the German neighborhood on Plauderville Avenue and into the heart of Polack Valley via Lanza Avenue, where the priests and nuns at St. Stan's came out to wave. Eventually they made their way up Palisade Avenue past Holy Trinity, the Slovak Lutheran Church. Everywhere, on storefronts, factories and homes, placards hung: "Garfield Welcomes Its National Champions" and "Welcome National Champions." Someone strung up an effigy, stuffed and dressed in football gear. Across its chest hung its epitaph: "This was the Miami High School team which met Garfield."

The line stretched for two miles and took 20 minutes to pass. All along it, Garfield's proud residents applauded until the parade finally disbanded in front of Walter Young's "oversized cheese box" of a high school. But the celebration wasn't over. At 7 p.m., thousands reconvened at the high school for a torch-lit march down Palisade Avenue to what was called the Casino Grounds near the frozen brickyard pond. It was where the stadium and, later, the new high school, would eventually be built, just not as soon as everyone then thought.

A full-page ad for the Stark and Sons Coal Company ran in the papers:

> *Don't forget the HOT TIME tonight on the CASINO GROUNDS. Remember you can have a HOT TIME every night by burning StarKoal, "The Champ of American Hard Coal."*

The phrasing was cute, the invitation unnecessary. Even as the temperature dipped to thirteen degrees, well over half the town's population—20,000—turned out for the celebration, jamming the streets for blocks around. The players had to walk single file through the adoring crowd to get to the rostrum while city officials scrambled to climb over guardrails to their seats.

As the Garfield High School band played the *Star Spangled Banner*, firemen took a torch to a 40-foot wide pile of old Christmas trees that the Department of Public Works had collected.

The flames lurched one hundred feet. The seventeen-acre tract, said *The Herald-News* was illuminated into "one vast sea of faces" with many huddling near the bonfire as it blazed throughout the program, about four football fields from the main stage.

John C. Timko, chairman of the Garfield Community Council, spoke first. "The city has never witnessed and probably will never again witness a celebration of this kind," he said.[10] And he was, of course, right.

Master of Ceremonies Joseph F. Moriarty, the Superintendent of Schools, introduced Argauer, who called Babula the greatest back he'd ever had. The proud coach acknowledged his parents, Charles the tailor and Emma, who once scolded him for how he treated the boys. How they must have felt while sitting on the speakers' platform, thinking back to when they arrived in New York Harbor, hoping the best for their children.

Moriarty called on the mayor, who sprang from his seat. Gabriel told the crowd how proud he was of "my boys" and brought up John Grembowitz to ear-splitting screams. The game's hero presented the game ball to Argauer who, in turn, presented it to high school principal Nathan Lincoln.

"The memory of this occasion will be treasured long after we are all gone," Lincoln said. He, just as Timko, was correct.

William A. Whitehead, president of the Board of Education spoke, as did assistant coach John Hollis (who, as a gym teacher, would be telling Garfield students tales about the game for another 36 years). Then it was time for Babula to take the microphone. Moriarty introduced him as, "the greatest high school back in the country today."

Bashful Benny gave credit to his teammates before ending his speech by saying, "I'm thrilled by the reception and my feet are chilled."

"That's the first time Benny ever had cold feet," Moriarty quipped.[11]

Fireworks lit the sky until, at 9 p.m., the last embers of the bonfire were extinguished. Amazingly, the huge crowd was incredibly orderly. The lone item on the police blotter from that evening concerned a seventeen-year-old Josephine Knoedl, who suffered second and third-degree burns on the forehead when a woman waved a flare into her face. The woman offered to pay her $1 for her trouble but, according to the police report, she wouldn't divulge her name and made off into the night.

The accolades continued for several weeks. The SS Cyril and Methodius Church of Clifton advertised that Babula would appear, along with Violet, at its first annual minstrel show, coached by Violet's dad, Butch Frankovic and including a few numbers by Letty Barbour. The Paterson Athletic Club hosted the team at a fund-raising dinner to meet the "wonder team" that shocked Miami High. Babula collected an award as the top Polish-American high school athlete in the East and was honored as the state's outstanding high school athlete of 1939 at the Newark Athletic Club's awards dinner. NJSIAA boss Walter Short, in attendance, remarked how Babula, with his modesty, "exemplified the meaning of sportsmanship and effort in sports."

Michael Rayhack's game film, along with those of the welcome home celebration by the Ritz Theatre, played to full houses at the Ritz on Passaic Street. And Rayhack was there to show the film at a meeting of the Fifth Quarter Club, Bloomfield High's booster club, which invited coaches Art Argauer and George Stanford to the festivities. There, the two post-season conquerors of Florida teams reached a tentative agreement to open the 1940 season with a game against each other. Pressed while attending Nutley's football banquet, Bill Foley refused to say which team was better in 1939.

"They were both good," he said. "Nutley played its best game of the season against us and murdered us. I wouldn't pick Garfield over Nutley but I wouldn't pick Nutley over Garfield."[12]

When the Garfield boys returned to school, graduation was only days away for some. Schools, then, typically graduated two classes per year—in January and June.

Babula, Jack Boyle, Grembowitz, Al Kazaren, Walter Young, Pete Yura and manager Louis Kral were among the January grads. Wally Tabaka, Ray Butts, Bill Wagnesz, Chet Szawarski, Bill Orutosky and Otto Durheimer received their diplomas that summer.

While Babula had indicated he would attend Fordham, he was still looking at other colleges. His father told some at the welcome home celebration Babula was headed to Princeton. Jim Schwartzinger, Babula's teammate on the '36 team, wanted him to join him at Tennessee. Babula, Tabaka and Grembowitz took a road trip to visit Duke and William and Mary, where Grembowitz eventually enrolled. Years later, Babula lamented not going to Notre Dame and said he stayed local, "because of a girl." But he and Violet didn't remain a couple much longer, outside of a few dates such as the one at the Fabian Theatre in Paterson to see *Gone with the Wind*. Eventually, so was their romance.

Violet had been told by her friend Edna that girls were "hanging all over Benny," in the remaining school days, but she already had other pursuits, including plans to attend business school. Meanwhile, Benny enrolled in a couple of business classes at the Clifton Evening School. Art McMahon speculated that Babula actually was planning to join his father's meat distributing outfit and forgo college.

Babula complicated matters even further in February when it was learned he signed a professional baseball contract the previous spring with the Salisbury Indians, the Washington Senators' farm club in the Eastern Shore League. Babula maintained that he would not report to the club because, as a minor, he wasn't bound by the contract. The papers down there, however, were listing him as a prospect as late as March. With Argauer writing to Commissioner Keenesaw Mountain Landis, it was eventually invalidated, allowing Babula to retain his amateur status. Babula made his official commitment to Fordham in August with an announcement from Bergen County Prosecutor and Fordham alum John Breslin, but he still hoped for a baseball tryout with the New York Giants.

In June, Argauer took his '39 team to the biggest symbol of the country's isolationalism. It was Garfield Day at the New York World's Fair, a city holiday, and the boys were being given their literal last hurrahs. Schools closed and buses took children for $1 and all others for $2. New York City motorcycle police escorted the buses from the George Washington Bridge to the site of the fair in Flushing, Queens. With its futuristic Trylon, Perisphere and Helecline, the fair offered wonderful prospects for the rest of its visitors' lives, even as war was raging overseas. The Boilermakers, having accomplished great things on the gridiron, could only imagine what the world had in store for them.

The team itself left the high school at 9:45 a.m. Argauer's instructions on a handout sheet were explicit. SQUAD MUST STAY TOGETHER. His graduated seniors were still heeding him, of course. The program began with lunch for the players and guests at the YMCA Building at 2 p.m. to the sounds of the GHS Band with little Roy Gerritsen waving his baton. The team visited the National Foundation for Infantile Paralysis Exhibit at 3 p.m. and

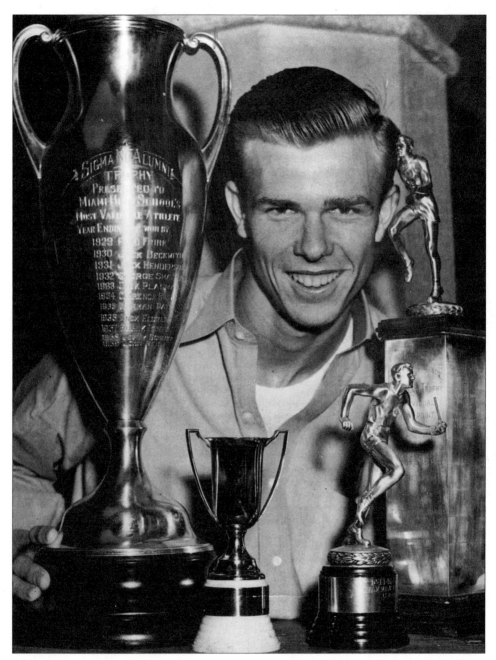

Davey Eldredge poses with the Sigma Nu trophy as the top athlete at Miami High School for 1939-40.
HistoryMiami.

proceeded to the Florida State Exhibit where Christy Walsh, representing the National Sports Council, presented certificates. In later years, when Walter Young was told that other teams claimed the 1939 national championship, his rejoinder was always: "Well, I have a certificate that says it was us and that's good enough for me."

Keith Morgan, President Roosevelt's right-hand man in the campaign against polio, served as master of ceremonies. Speeches were presented by Basil O'Conner, the NFIP president, Babula, and, of course, Mayor Gabriel. The Garfield Cadets drum and bugle corps closed things out with a stirring exhibition at 4:45 and the players had until 10:30 p.m. to meet at the buses for the ride home—their last together as a team.

"Garfield's 2,000 persons made up only a small portion of more than 50,000 at the fair grounds yesterday but as far as they were concerned nothing existed on the grounds but Garfield's own," *The Herald-News* reported.[13]

Eventually, things returned to routine in Garfield and Miami, which meant that the Miami High Stingarees were winning at everything. The papers didn't dwell on the loss to Garfield, and the Stinagrees returned to the basketball court to begin their season in earnest on January 9. With Eldredge and football teammate Andy Smith in the lineup, Miami reached the state semifinals before bowing to Robert E. Lee.

In May, Miami won the state track meet with a record number of points as Eldredge closed out his high school athletic career in style. He took the 100-yard dash, setting a meet record of 10.1 seconds and anchored the Stingarees' victorious half-mile relay team. He was second by an inch to Ray Gillis of Robert E. Lee in the 220 final and fourth in the broad jump. Then, with Harvey James at catcher and Harvey Comfort at third base, the baseball team won the Florida District 8 tournament and was upset in the state semifinals, 3-1, by Bartow in 11 innings. Eldredge collected the Sigma Nu Trophy as Miami High's top athlete and headed to graduation and the start of Georgia Tech's football practices.

Preparations for Miami's 1940 football season were already underway with intramurals and spring practice when Clyde Crabtree accepted an offer as athletic director and coach at Palm Beach High School. Then he took Jesse Yarborough's other assistant, John McDonald, with him. Yarborough apologized to the student body at a May assembly for costing them the Garfield game with his "foolish substitutions."[14] Then, as Argauer did, he made a play for more money. The "Cunnel" didn't get another job offer, though. He simply resigned, leaving the Stingaree athletic department rudderless for a few weeks until he was bumped up to $3,500 a year, coincidentally the same salary as Argauer's.

The Health Bowl initiative petered out that summer. There never was another one. Miami High felt it had been given the runaround by the Infantile Paralysis Foundation and the National Sports Council, so it reverted to independently hosting the Christmas classic. With Miami unavailable as a venue, the Council didn't have many other warm-weather options with a stadium large enough to accommodate a big crowd. Los Angeles, for instance, was too far from the NSC's base in New York. So, the idea died an unfortunate death. Great concept. Bad execution.

As Jack Bell explained, irreconcilable differences doomed any chance of a second game, even if the original had turned out to be "most colorful" of the season. Fans may not care how much the promoters bicker, he wrote, as long as the product is good. But, he added: "This game caused more ill feeling, argument, threats and down-right differences of opinion than anything ever staged in Miami."[15]

In the end, with a paid attendance of 11,041, the Health Bowl made $7,500 for the fight against polio—not a small sum, yet far below expectations. John Gabriel intimated there was a chance the Miami High team would be invited to play Garfield in Roosevelt Stadium in 1940. ("Such a game, which drew only 15,000 people in Miami, would attract 25,000 or more in the Metropolitan area," he boasted.)[16] Despite his enthusiasm, that rematch never came to pass. That was unfortunate, because both Garfield and Miami went on to continued success the next two seasons, the Stingarees the next four. They went 19-1-1 in 1940-41 and went undefeated in '42 and '43 when they snared what they missed in 1939—two national championships as determined by Art Johlfs. The only loss came against Boys High, 13-0, as the crafty Shorty Doyal befuddled Yarborough with a four-man line and Clint Castleberry put on a show, reacting to Yarborough's typical pregame braggadocio.

Miami High hosted two more Christmas games in 1940-41 and won them both, a true indication of the strength of Garfield's 1939 victory. Harvey Comfort took over as the star of the 1940 Stingarees and made the All Southern team. He didn't have Eldredge's breakaway ability but he had plenty of speed and proved a better passer and field general. Other hold-overs from the '39 team included Gilbert Wilson, Gene Bolick and Charlie Fancher. Mike Osceola, the big Seminole, returned after missing most of the 1939 season while Paul Louis blossomed into a Hall of Fame player at center along with sophomores Arnold Tucker and Bruce Smith.

As Miami considered which team might be its Christmas opponent, there were reports that Yarborough was anxious to play another New Jersey team. Nutley and Asbury Park shared the state championship but since Nutley already had accepted a bid to return to Florida to play the Jacksonville All Stars (the Maroon Raiders won that game easily, 22-7) the attention turned toward Asbury Park. But Yarborough actually had other ideas.

A week before the regular season ended, Miami officials contacted Argauer with a proposal. Arrange a post-season game with Asbury Park with the proceeds to be split three ways among Garfield, Asbury Park and Miami. The winner would be invited to the Christmas Day game, using the gate receipts to pay for the trip while the loser pocketed the cash for its troubles. Meanwhile, Miami High would profit from a game it wouldn't even play. At least that's the story Argauer told Herb Kamm of the *Asbury Park Press*.

"They still haven't gotten over the licking we gave them," Argauer claimed. "And I know that Jesse Yarborough wanted us back. He hates to lose and he probably figured his team was good enough this year to hand us a trimming. You know—revenge stuff."

Argauer told Kamm his overtures to Asbury Park were turned down and that's why Miami ended up inviting Chicago's Fenger High School.

"A return game between us would be a natural," Argauer explained. "But they insisted that we play a game up here to raise some dough and when Asbury Park refused to go along, that put both of us out of the picture."

Kamm surmised that Miami was quite certain Garfield would win.

"It's strange, though, that Miami never presented the same sort of proposition to Asbury Park and if that's the way the wind blew, Asbury Park should feel quite satisfied that the bid went to Chicago instead," Kamm wrote.[17]

Yarborough began his lobbying for Fenger as his personal choice on December 1, right after Fenger defeated Leo High for the Chicago prep championship in front of 65,000 at

Soldier Field. Fenger, set in the far south side of Chicago, boasted of a 37-game unbeaten streak. Drawing from the hardy stock of the Lithuanian neighborhood that surrounded it, Fenger fielded a team that, as Garfield did, outweighed the Stingarees by 20 pounds a man. But this time, Miami's speed and trickery prevailed. Yarborough, perhaps remembering how John Grembowitz dogged Davey Eldredge, assigned Gilbert Wilson to shadow Fenger's giant fullback, Ray Florek. Comfort scooted through the Fenger defense all night, executed a spectacular statue of liberty play with Bruce Smith and the husky Chicagoans wilted in the heat. As Eldredge shouted encouragement from the sidelines, the Stingarees ran away with a dizzying 19-0 shutout win.

The next Christmas, with a 7-7 tie against Boys the only blemish on a 9-0-1 regular season, Miami produced an even more impressive win. Baltimore City College, the same school that was up for consideration as Miami's Health Bowl opponent two years earlier, was Maryland state champs for six straight years and had a 54-game unbeaten streak against high school-age competition, losing only to Fork Union, a college prep school. Miami officials announced the choice on the evening of December 6, 1941, the last day of peace in America.

There was never any talk of cancelling the game—the entire sports world was determined to carry on after Pearl Harbor—and in spite of new wartime travel restrictions it drew over 14,126 spectators, the largest ever in Miami's Christmas series. Perhaps it was an act of defiance against the war. It was also the hottest Christmas in Miami in 25 years—85 degrees at game time—and the visitors couldn't cope. Garfield had semi-acclimated itself to the conditions by arriving a week in advance and barely made it across the finish line, exhausted but triumphant. Baltimore City arrived the day before the game and immediately began to suck wind. The Collegians had a star-studded lineup, led by future Baltimore Colt Dick Working, but, like many northern teams before them, they were up against more than just the Stingarees.

"We had been practicing in Baltimore in the freezing cold, and on frozen turf," quarterback Joe Pokorny recalled years later." The heat and the change in temperature had exhausted us."[18]

Miami won, 26-0, its biggest Christmas win ever and its second straight Christmas shutout. Arnold Tucker scored twice while Gene Autrey and Gene Bolick, holdovers from the '39 team, each crossed the goal line. The 142-pound Bolick, who was Eldredge's third-string backup, emulated Li'l Davey by leaving City tacklers grasping at air on a 67-yard touchdown run. Some, like Jack Bell, suggested that Miami could now claim the national championship even though none was officially on the line. Boys High could have made the same claim, though, when, on New Year's Day, it throttled previously unbeaten Asheville, North Carolina, 44-0, in the Milk Bowl at Ponce de Leon Park. Outweighed by 25 pounds per man, Boys got TD runs of 24, 38 and 70 yards from Castleberry, who watched the entire second half of his last high school game from the bench. Castleberry gave the game ball to a 10-year-old victim of infantile paralysis.

Johlfs did not take Bell's suggestion. He snubbed both Miami and Boys when picked the National Sports News Service national champion. He gave it to 11-0 Leo of Chicago.

Meanwhile, back in Garfield, the Boilermakers fell just short of two more state championships in 1940-41.

For Walter Young, the "serious" kid, it wasn't easy. He decided against playing college football, although he had his opportunities to do so. After graduation, he worked in one of the "few and far between" jobs at a manufacturer of scales for a few months until enrolling at the Newark College of Engineering, which didn't field a football team. His older brother, Curt, was an engineer, and he hoped he had shared his brother's aptitude for the profession.

Something else pulled him to Garfield's first game of the 1940 season: the big showdown against Nutley. Young went to Passaic Stadium alone, and, while everyone else in the crowd of 12,000 sought out the best seats available, Young arrived early, sat in the distant corner of the grandstand, hunched down, and cried.

"I don't know why. I was just overwhelmed, I suppose, watching that game and not being in it," he said.

Young's tears were symbolic. The 1939 season really ended on the day the 1940 season began. And that was even clearer when the Boilermakers lost for the first time since that 1937 game in Asbury Park, when Carmine Perrapato saw it as an emergency situation. Nutley scored twice in the first half and, after the sluggish, Babula-less offense managed a third period score, the Maroon Raiders didn't allow the Boilermakers across the 50-yard line the rest of the game. With the 13-7 victory, Nutley vainly claimed bragging rights retroactive to 1939, even if it was a tough case to make.

The 1940 Boilermakers didn't have Babula or Grembowitz or Young and the Maroon Raiders didn't have Frank Cardinale or Motz Buel. But Nutley had Carl Hagelin at end as well as Mike Ritacco, a tough runner who carried the day. Garfield did have Orlovsky, who had an intricate surgical procedure on his shoulder in the off-season and was cleared from National Guard duties at the last minute in order to play in the game. The line returned four of its seven starters—Hintenberger, Miranda, Noviczky and Yoda. Bill Librera would replace Babula as the signal-caller, and his arm was strong enough. And the flashy Johnny Sekanics, who had impressed so much as a freshman on the 1938 team, had regained his academic eligibility. He'd learned a tough lesson in 1939, allowed only to practice with the varsity and appear in junior varsity games. Back in the fold, Sekanics was being looked at as the next great Garfield back with Al Del Greco flatly saying, "they're going to forget Babula so fast it won't even be funny.

"The guy steps into big shoes," Del Greco wrote. "Boom Boom Babula was a big guy. But my operatives . . . inform me that Sekanics is simply a gifted ace. Besides all his natural ability, he's a toughie. Babula was a big, nice guy who parted his hair neatly and hitched creases in his football pants. But this Johnny is a roaring meanie. He'll run interference—Babula never could do that."[19]

It was unfair to Sekanics. He had an outstanding high school career. He just wasn't Benny. And neither was *this* Boilermaker team *that* Boilermaker team, although it didn't lose another game that season. It ran up nine straight victories and won the championship of the new Passaic Valley Conference, improving so greatly that Argauer was burning for a Nutley rematch that he didn't get.

Indeed, Nutley was upset by Hillside in the last game of the year but still came out on top of the Colliton ratings with 667 points to Garfield's 640. Asbury Park, which was dropped from Garfield's schedule because of the Boilermakers' scheduling obligations in the new PVC, was fourth with 620 points. But with Asbury Park the only undefeated team in the state, both the *Star-Ledger* and *Newark Sunday Call* ignored the Colliton standings and named the

Blue Bishops as their state champs. The *Jersey Journal* discarded its own ratings system and went along with Nutley. The controversy over state champs just wouldn't go away.

Picking up after the Nutley defeat, Garfield ran its win streak to 16 games with two games remaining in its 1941 season. Ten players remained from the 1939 roster, including linemen Hintenberger, Noviczky and Miranda, who all started the Miami game, plus Len Macaluso, Joe Lucas and Bob Schultz. It seemed they were about to lead the Boilermakers back to a state championship.

Paterson Eastside had lost to Passaic and Garfield had defeated Passaic so it seemed natural Garfield would beat Eastside. But, led by the speed of Larry Doby, who returned an interception 55 yards for a touchdown, and the power of Al Kachadurian, who had thrown that big interception to Babula two years earlier, the Ghosts pulled off a 13-0 shocker. It was the first time Garfield had been shut out since the 1937 Bloomfield game.

The Boilermakers closed out the season by routing Clifton, but were closed out themselves when the NJSIAA awarded state championships. The Colliton System placed Montclair at the top with 660 points, followed by Garfield, with 596 and Eastside, with 534, even though both Garfield and Montclair lost games to Eastside. The NJSIAA split North Jersey into two sections that year and awarded one sectional championship to Montclair and the other to Eastside over Garfield, ignoring the Colliton rankings because of the head-to-head result. So, while Garfield was considered everywhere to be one of the top three teams in the state, it was the only one left without a championship.

Still, looking back over a four-year period, the record was the best in New Jersey. The Boilermakers won 37 times and lost twice, and both losses came against state championship teams. Soon, however, that accomplishment would seem trivial.

In the summer of 1940, Argauer told McMahon, "My worries now concern things bigger than football. My sister is in Germany and I'm working day and night to get her back here. It's tough. You can't get word in or out."[20]

Miami's sense of security was also about to change. A week before Jack Pepper was to graduate in 1941, he and a friend, Os Moody, thought it a good idea to sail the Moody's father's four-mast schooner to Nassau in the Bahamas. It was an all-black crew so they had to sign on as engineer and assistant. The boat had a converted Pierce Arrow automobile engine for auxiliary power, which they used to reach the Miami sea buoy. Once there, they put the sails up and waited for the wind to take them the rest of the way. Except it didn't. They soon became becalmed—and worse.

"We cranked up the Pierce Arrow engine again and the damn thing wouldn't go," Pepper remembered, shaking his head. "We drifted for about four or five days north along the Gulf Stream. We were about 200 miles east of St. Augustine."

Moody's father, Clarence, chartered a seaplane and frantically looked for the boys. On the second day, his heart leapt as he spotted them off the coast of Daytona. The seaplane landed on the water and they rescued the boys with a rowboat.

"Then we had to fly to Nassau to clear customs," Pepper explained. "We got back to Miami on Friday at 4 p.m. and Mr. Moody took us to the hotel to get a shave and a haircut and then we went to the high school to graduate, except I had missed an exam. After the graduation, the teacher came to me and said I gave you a failing grade because you did not take the exam. I had to go to her house to take the exam."

Nothing however, was as traumatic as what the boys feared as they drifted along in the Atlantic—the reports of several German U-Boats patrolling the waters.

"We were scared to death," Pepper admitted.

The war was about to intrude on all the boys' carefree lives.

TWENTY-ONE

THE WAR

Paul Louis squinted into the sun as it levitated over the horizon at the 320th Bomb Group's airbase in Alto, Corsica. It was August 1944, and the Allied invasion of Southern France was about to get underway. The Group's fleet of B-26 Marauder medium bombers was assigned to soften up the German defenses around Toulon. The air and ground crews of the Army Air Corps stationed at Alto coined an unofficial slogan: "Too long to Toulon." They worked round-the-clock shifts: four hours on, four hours off.

Each dawn, six Marauders took off in formation from six runways and, to Louis, who was off duty that day, the combined roars of their 12 Pratt & Whitney engines somehow reminded him of the cacophony of cheers thundering at the Orange Bowl as he played center for the Miami High Stingarees. It occurred to him that the heroes here, soon to be encountering heavy enemy flak, were not being hailed by thousands of fans. The only other people watching these kids take off were a general and a few Red Cross girls. How incongruous, he thought. And how dutifully and without question had yesterday's football heroes transitioned to this greater task.

The Japanese invasion of Pearl Harbor burst the bubble in which Americans had been ensconced since Germany opened hostilities in the fall of 1939. Garfield and Miami, as everywhere, were roused from their indifference. Its young people averted their attention from the everyday in bids to protect the every day.

Bob Sims, Miami High class of 1941, was a typical example. Sims was working the night shift for the telephone company. He came home at eight in the morning that indelible Sunday, scanned the newspaper over breakfast and read that Miami would be playing Baltimore City College in the Christmas game. Then it was off to bed. He woke up at 1 p.m. The neighbors were blasting their radio. Without air conditioning, most people left their windows wide open. Naturally, the racket woke him up, so he gave up on his nap and returned to the kitchen.

"I can't sleep," Sims complained to his mother. "They've got the radio turned up so loud."

"Don't you know?" Sims' mother shrilled. "They bombed Pearl Harbor!"

"Where's Pearl Harbor?"

"Oh, it's horrible," his mother replied plaintively. "Everybody's going to have to go into the service."

Sims flew the P-38 Lightning during the war and made it back unscathed. He was one of 16 pilots who escorted Japanese envoys to the tiny, peanut-shaped island of Ie Shima on the way to Manila, where the Japanese representatives agreed to the terms of the surrender document signed on the *Battleship Missouri.*

By then, much had changed for the boys who played in the 1939 Health Bowl. As Bob Sims' mom had predicted, nearly everyone had been enlisted or drafted. World War II reshaped their lives as well as their memories. Whenever they looked back to their high school years, many did so through the smoky filter of armed conflict. It made the game more distant, and, to some, more irrelevant. When they returned, they were quick to get on with their lives, not to reminisce. It wasn't until they reached middle age that many could reflect upon their younger years.

Miami, itself, became a hub of wartime activity, with its bustling tourists replaced by a stream of military personnel. It had the climate, the flat terrain, open land and ample waterways to provide training grounds for all branches of the armed forces—and the hotel space to house them.

The U.S. Naval Air Training Command, with six training bases, was headquartered at Naval Air Station Miami at Opa-locka, which dispatched patrols to hunt German U-Boats attacking shipping vessels off the coast. The Germans reportedly landed saboteurs, and the entire state of Florida was a suspected hotbed of espionage activity. The Army Air Corps virtually took over Miami Beach, where nearly half a million men passed through its basic training and officer training centers while housed in posh, oceanfront hotels. The parks and golf courses were converted to drill fields, and a POW camp and off-shore artillery range was installed at the north end of the beach.

Garfield, too, did its patriotic duty with rationing and victory gardens while sending the majority of its young men off to war. Garfield's industry was unique; many of its factories were owned and operated by German immigrants or their descendants. The ethnic origins of the city's industrialists had been a thorny issue in the First World War. Heyden Chemical, Forstmann & Huffman, Gera Mills and Garfield Worsted mills were among those seized by the Alien Property Custodian. Julius Forstmann was forced to prove his loyalty as an American citizen before the U.S. Attorney General.

The U.S. government took less draconian measures in World War II. Nevertheless, even though Carl Edward Forstmann (running the factory after the 1939 death of his father) and Henry Hartmann (head of Hartmann Embroidery Works) were pillars of the community, their plants were under strict government scrutiny. Heyden Chemical, meanwhile, was required to submit copies of all product formulas to the government. Ironically, Hartmann manufactured the majority of uniform insignia patches for all branches of the U.S. military during the war and the Forstmann plant turned out fabric for uniforms and blankets.

Nearly all of the players on the Miami and Garfield teams of the 1939 season went to war. In all, 34 of 36 players who had started in at least one game—plus the team's managers— served during World War II. Many on both teams traded college football jerseys for military uniforms. Ex-Stingarees Jay Kendrick, Harvey Comfort and Gilbert Wilson were playing at Florida, Harvey James at Miami and Davey Eldredge at Georgia Tech. Ex-Boilermakers Benny Babula, Ed Hintenberger and Steve Noviczky were playing at Fordham, John Grembowitz at

Frank Miranda poses with his five sons, all in the service. The brothers, from left to right, Steve, Carmine, Anthony, Angelo and William. All survived the war. Courtesy Estate of Angelo Miranda.

William & Mary, Jack Boyle at Manhattan, Ray Butts at NYU and John Orlovsky at Syracuse. All served.

Comfort flew dive bombers in the Pacific. Gene Autrey flew Corsair and Hellcat fighters on 79 night combat missions over the Marshall Islands and was awarded three Distinguished Flying Crosses and 12 Air Medals. Jason Koesy flew "The Hump" as a navigator on the C-87 in the India, Burma and China theatres. Charlie Burrus eventually reached the rank of colonel and Red Mathews attained a major rank. Mathews also later served in Korea as a commander in the strategic air command.

Garfield's Bill Wagnecz, part of the 94th Fighter Squadron, First Fighter Group, won the Air Medal with two Oak Leaf Clusters escorting bomber crews in a P-38 Lightning.

Bill Wagnecz is helped out of his parachute by his crew chief after returning to his base in Italy from a mission over enemy territory. National Archives.

Alex Yoda was wounded at the Battle of the Bulge. His high school sweetheart, Helen Herina, was a nurse in General George Patton's Third Army. Their romance continued in Europe and they married soon after the war. Angelo Miranda, who trained with the ski troops, was there in the snow as well. He served along with four of his six brothers. Bill Librera earned a bronze star as an infantry man fighting in Europe and Louis Kral, the Garfield manager who couldn't play football because of pleurisy, flew more than 40 bombing missions. Joe Tripoli, the 6-foot-4 lineman, was assigned to submarine duty, of all things. Steve Noviczky served with the Army in the Pacific theatre and was part of the occupational forces in the Philippines and Japan. He would have been one of the first men onshore in the invasion of Japan had the atomic bomb not been dropped.

Levin Rollins was on a football scholarship at the University of Miami, when, in 1941, he secretly married his 17-year-old sweetheart, Jeanne Ware. He was soon called up from the National Guard and sent to Camp Blanding, from where he mailed letters back and forth to his bride. He was tired of keeping the marriage a secret so Jeanne handed her mother one of the letters and locked herself in the bathroom while she read it. Having survived that, the couple had their first child, Levin III, in 1943, before he was sent overseas.

Rollins was first wounded during the Normandy invasion. It was a horrific injury. He lost his entire triceps muscle, and was sent to recuperate at an English hospital, where the Queen Mother entertained the troops playing the piano. Patched up, he was released and rejoined his unit but, a month later, Rollins was wounded again, this time in the leg during street fighting in the German town of Aachen.

Kendrick was one of the many who found any way possible to enlist. Blind in his right eye because of the golf ball injury, he somehow passed the eye test and enlisted in the Army eight months after Pearl Harbor. He was in an infantry division that island-hopped toward the Philippines. The Army favored sending Kendrick to Officer Candidate School, and requested he sign a waiver in case he was blinded in his other eye. "The hell with that," he said, and remained an enlisted man.

Even Art McMahon, the wise-cracking sports editor of *The Herald-News*, volunteered for the Navy. He commanded one of the Tank Landing Ships (LST), the floating behemoths that brought everything from tanks, jeeps, cargo and troops directly onto the beaches. Rising to the rank of lieutenant commander, McMahon participated in the invasions of the Philippines and Borneo.

Likewise, Red Simko, Garfield's lollipop-tossing head cheerleader, joined the fight although not a young kid. Red left his job with the city recreation department to join the Army Air Corps and became one of "Steed's Flying Colts," named for Col. Thomas W. Steed, commander of the 456th Bomb Group flying out of Stornara, Italy. To his fellow crewmen on the *Galloping Ghost*, a B-24 Liberator, he wasn't Red. At 34, he was known as "Pop," one of the oldest waist gunners in the 15th Army Air Force. Simko survived more than 35 combat missions against strategic targets in German industrial centers throughout Southern Europe, keeping his younger crewmates loose with his incessant talking, and unleashing his own barrage of quips and jokes as the big bomber flew deep into enemy territory.

Crewmen loved flying with Simko. He was their lucky charm. He had his own good-luck piece, a beat-up, brown duck-billed hunting cap he purchased at Markey's Sport Shop in Passaic, the same store that sold Garfield High football tickets. He was convinced of its powers when he survived a forced landing on a B-24 training mission in a blinding storm in the Nevada mountains.

"I have never gone on a mission without this hat," he explained. "I might go off in the morning without my dog tags or other flying equipment but never without my lucky hat.

"When I forget this, I go back for it, no matter how far I walk. When we get up in the blue where it is forty-below-zero, I use a helmet and put this in my pocket. It hasn't failed me yet."

Simko could have opted out of his 35th mission against a hard target. He had a head cold. He flew anyway.

"Not me," he said. "I want them as they come. If they are rough, I take 'em that way. I guess I am a little too old for flying but I volunteered and it is what I want. If they hit you, there is always your parachute."[1]

Simko never needed his parachute, but flying a mission against a concentration of Nazi troops outside Bucharest, the *Galloping Ghost* lost one engine en route and another on the way back. It landed at an emergency field on an island near friendly territory, coming to a stop in the woods after running off the end of the landing strip. Simko received the Air Medal, "for meritorious achievement in serial flight while participating in sustained operational activities against the enemy."[2] But, just as many of his contemporaries, he never boasted about it. Even in the 1960s, no more than 20 years after the war, few knew that the little man running the Garfield recreation department and delivering "bug juice" to the playgrounds, was a decorated war hero.

So was Jack Boyle, the Garfield guard who, back in his high school days, prevented kids from bullying Harry Berenson, the little Jewish kid, whose brothers, as it turned out, were also war heroes. Boyle was playing freshman football at Manhattan College when the war broke out. After a year prepping at LaSalle Military Academy, he'd received a number of offers from bigger schools, but his father, Francis, the former police chief, died in 1940, so Boyle decided to stay close to home. He didn't take long to join the Navy after Pearl Harbor.

Jack Boyle in his Navy dress uniform portrait. Courtesy Estate of Jack Boyle.

In March of 1945, Boyle was part of the strike force on the aircraft carrier *Intrepid* as it battered Japanese military outposts in preparation for the Easter Sunday landings on Okinawa. He was flying in formation in his Corsair when his wingman was hit by Japanese anti-aircraft fire. The debris flew into the propeller of Boyle's plane, leaving him no choice but to ditch in the water. He inflated his raft and began to drift. He knew that if the current took him to shore, he would be captured by the Japanese and killed. They were not taking prisoners. Just as darkness approached, a Navy destroyer spotted Boyle's raft and brought him back to the *Intrepid* where he would be credited with shooting down a Japanese Zero fighter plane in a kamikaze attack.

Walter Young, too, yearned to be a pilot like his good friend Jack Boyle, but was rejected because of vision after enlisting. Still, the Air Corps needed kids with technical backgrounds and since Young was studying at Newark College of Engineering, he was accepted into the meteorologist program. Always thinking ahead, Young thought he could "learn something in the process," but when he entered the program, he feared he wouldn't finish it.

"I was getting involved with people who had Masters degrees or were physicists," he explained. "As we went along, we kept getting a list of kids who washed out of the program.

Walter Young, while stationed in North Africa, takes time to check out the Sphinx and pyramids. Young is the one on horseback. Courtesy Estate of Walter Young.

I went through the whole program and I finished in the middle of the class. But I didn't trust myself. I was terrified of washing out."

It was odd that an All State end on a national championship football team would lack self-confidence but that was Young—always fretting that he wasn't doing enough.

Young would serve two years in North Africa—tracking weather patterns to plan flights— and then the last half year in Germany up until the end of hostilities there. The army took advantage of his fluency in German and used him to interrogate prisoners, including the last remnants of Rommel's army. He never forgot the images of the destruction and despair in his parents' native land.

"Thousands upon thousands of young girls came in wanting to get away from the Russian army. They had nothing except the clothes on their backs. It had a tremendous effect on me . . . to think that sixty million people lost their lives in this war," Young said.

"The whole country came down," he explained. "I came into the Frankfurt area. There was no station, just walls. I went out of the train, but didn't go too far. Tracks were down. Bridges were down. All I saw was rubble."

Not everyone saw hazardous duty. Wally Tabaka even found love while stationed over-seas and married a girl from Tunis. John Gabriel, too, was married during the war, to a Garfield girl, Mary Nagel, in 1942. But the Boy Mayor was recalled from his honeymoon in Havana and was soon packing up to report to Fort Eustis, Virginia, as a second lieutenant. Gabriel actually ran the city from his post, receiving and sending back municipal documents by airmail while surviving a legal challenge from Republican councilman John Frank who claimed Gabriel had relinquished his office when he was called to active duty.

State Supreme Court Justice Joseph L. Bodine ruled that no vacancy existed, slapping Frank's hand by remarking, "I will tolerate no back-biting or sniping at men who are in the service of the United States of America."[3]

Gabriel served out the rest of his term, which ended in 1943. Several times he broke tie votes on the city council by mailing his ballot and vetoed a council vote to spend $200,000 for fire apparatus. He argued the public couldn't afford it and that the armament drive couldn't spare the materials. The council, split down the middle on party lines, re-passed the measure, 6-2—perhaps the first sign that his political career was doomed. Not that it mattered.

Gabriel, with Broadway's Red Buttons as his orderly, spent the bulk of the war as the commanding officer of three touring fundraisers, "Army Play Boy," "This is the Army," and "Winged Victory," with music by Irving Berlin and starring, among others, Karl Malden, Mario Lanza and future TV Superman George Reeves. The shows were lavish productions, featuring a cast of 300, most of them servicemen and servicewomen. Reviewers raved with patriotic fervor and Darryl Zanuck brought *Winged Victory* to the screen in 1944, directed by George Cukor.

Jesse Yarborough served as Miami's district air raid warden once the war broke out. Having graduated from Clemson with a reserve commission in the infantry, Yarborough applied for reinstatement to regular duty in April 1942 and was re-commissioned as a first lieutenant in the Army Air Corps. He graduated from officer training at Miami Beach and headed for Maxwell Field in Alabama as an administrator, which allowed him to coach the Stingarees in the last two games of the 1942 season. Back home on leave, he filled in after coach Lyles Alley himself left for the service.

Two years later, Yarborough was coaching the Maxwell Field football team, with Davey Eldredge on the team. The two made a triumphant return to the Orange Bowl when L'il Davey scored two TDs in Maxwell's 13-0 win over the Miami Naval Training Center team. Then, in 1945, Yarborough was at Mitchell Field on Long Island coaching the First Air Force football team with six NFL players on his roster. He was twice put on notice that he was to be deployed overseas but the order never came.

Eldredge, as it turned out, had the most successful college football career of all the '39 Stingarees and Boilermakers; however, just as Babula, he never achieved the heights his high school career had promised.

It was hard for Eldredge to live up to such lofty and expansive expectations. After his outstanding freshman season at Georgia Tech, for instance, Ted Husing declared on the air that Li'l Davey would "make the football fans of the nation forget Tom Harmon."[4]

The papers gushed as Eldredge impressed, first at spring practice and then in the immediate run-up to his first varsity season. He was a "darting ghost" with "swivel hips" and "harder to bring to Earth than a runaway parachute . . . darting in and out of holes no bigger than the ball he carried . . . harder to stop than a housecat with a running fit . . . sometimes looking as if he was running backwards."[5]

But Eldredge had one problem. As a sophomore on a 3-6 team, he played behind Johnny Bosch, the hero of the Ramblin' Wrecks' 1940 Orange Bowl win over Missouri. He flashed at times, including in a loss to Notre Dame and against Florida, but he was held back by his limitations as a passer. Then, as a junior, he was overshadowed by the player to whom he was often compared as a high schooler: Boys High's Clint Castleberry.

Because so many college teams were losing players to the military, eligibility rules were changed in 1942 to allow freshmen to play varsity ball just as Castleberry arrived on campus. Eldredge slipped to third on the depth chart behind Castleberry and was eventually moved from tailback to wingback in Tech's single wing attack. The Statue of Liberty play was Eldredge's specialty. He scored a 40-yard touchdown on it against Florida in a 14-7 loss to Texas in the Cotton Bowl. But Castleberry was the story of the season. He took the nation by storm and finished third in the Heisman Trophy balloting.

Perhaps Castleberry and Eldredge would have formed a dynamic backfield in 1943, but they never got the chance. Both were called to active duty from the Army Air Corps reserve that spring. A year later, Castleberry was the co-pilot on *Dream Girl*, one of two B-26 Marauders on a ferrying run up the Africa Coast. Both planes disappeared. A six-day search ended when a British RAF plane observed unidentified debris. Castleberry was reclassified from "missing" to "killed in action" although his body was never recovered. He was one of the sports world's most-mourned World War II losses.

While Eldredge served in the European theater, Babula served in the Pacific as a Naval gunnery officer on a landing ship and was awarded a purple heart after being wounded. Babula had gone to Fordham. Coach Jimmy Crowley was collecting running backs. As one of the original Four Horsemen, he had coached the legendary Seven Blocks of Granite, including one named Vince Lombardi, and was still pounding away with a powerful running game that put the Rams among the nation's best teams year after year. Babula was earmarked to take over as the backfield's big gun in 1942.

Babula received his share of hype in the New York press. He was once quoted as saying his undercut jaw came from "running the ball ferociously." Sadly, Babula's future as a big-time college back was stymied when he injured both knees playing freshman ball in 1940. He was a reserve on Fordham's 1941 and 1942 teams and perhaps his most disappointing moment came when the Rams, ranked sixth in the nation, nipped Missouri, 2-0, in a rainy, muddy Sugar Bowl game his sophomore year. The seniors on Missouri's team remembered watching Babula's big night in Miami and he was getting a lot of work leading up to the game. The writers expected him to play a major role. Yet Crowley kept him on the bench the entire game. He never again played with the brilliance he flashed at Garfield and, soon, his name would vanish from national headlines.

Soon enough, Paul Louis was back in the air after his reflective moment at the airbase. While he was co-piloting his 27th mission near the Brenner Pass straddling Italy and Austria, a German fighter came at his cockpit in a head-on attack. The B-26, once known as the Widow Maker, was going down.

The crew scrambled to get out of their flak jackets. The bombardier even crawled through Louis' legs to escape. Three crewmembers didn't make it, but Louis, along with pilot Truman Cole and the others, parachuted from the doomed bomber. Louis landed on a mountainside above the tree line, where he was nicked by German fire. He was captured when he whistled in response to one he had assumed was from a fellow crewmember. It wasn't. Unfortunately, whistles don't have German accents.

Louis was in enemy hands. Worse yet, he was a Jew in the hands of the Nazis. He had taken necessary precautions. His dog tags were marked with a "P" for Protestant.

However, from his neck hung a mezuzah, a small decorative case containing a piece of parchment inscribed with Old Testament verses and carried by many Jews as a symbol of their identity. It had been his late father's, and his mother gave it to him before he headed off to war.

As Louis and the other prisoners were sent to a POW camp in the Po Valley, they were herded into a temporary holding area in an air raid shelter. The Germans had given him chewing gum when he was captured. He thought fast, wrapping the mezuzah in one piece and sticking it to a pipe.

Taken for a Protestant, Louis was treated relatively well by his captors, despite chronic food shortages. Imprisoned with British officers, he was able to satisfy his lifelong love of books by reading theirs, including The *Complete Works of Thomas Jefferson* and The *Question Box*, by Catholic priest Bertrand L. Conway. As his obituary noted, "as he was being force marched in the dead of winter, while other prisoners carried bread, Paul carried books." In fact, Louis died listening to his wife and children read his favorite literary passages.[6]

After his first five months of captivity, Louis was shipped to Stalag 7-A, just north of Moosburg, and about 30 miles northeast of Munich. On April 29, 1945, a Sherman tank from General George S. Patton's Third Army crashed through the Stalag's front gate. Louis was liberated. But before returning Stateside, Louis and two fellow POWs—John Millihan and Jule Spach (an old VMI classmate)—slipped out of camp to see Moosburg. What they saw was completely unexpected. Staggering toward them on the street, barely able to walk, was what appeared like a group of skeletons, clad in ragged, striped outfits. They were looking straight ahead with empty eyes and a frozen countenance of horror.

"My God, what's that?" exclaimed Louis, later to find out he had encountered survivors of the nearby Dachau concentration camp.

"And we thought we had it bad," Millihan said.[7]

Louis would never forget the sight of those concentration camp survivors. Back in the States, he thought of his mezuzah. His brother-in-law was still serving in the Italian theater as the Allied forces mopped up. Louis gave his brother-in-law the location of the air raid shelter and the very spot where he'd hidden it. It was still affixed to the pipe by the chewing gum, and his brother-in-law recovered it.

Although many like Louis served, no one on Miami High's 1939 football roster was lost in the war. The 1938 team was not as fortunate. Joe Crum, the kid who transferred from Edison to play for the Stingarees, had joined the Navy two months before the Pearl Harbor attack and quickly became an accomplished Marine fighter pilot. In 1943, he was at Guadalcanal. Jack Bell, who had moved to the *Miami Herald* by then, told the story in his well-read Town Crier column (Bell, himself, spent time in Burma as a war correspondent for *The Herald*):

> "He went into the South Pacific when the going was the toughest. I know only what the boys who flew down there had to say . . . that 'Old Joe was one hell of a flier.' That's what they all said when they came back.
>
> "Joe went down trying to save a fellow flier. He saw an American surrounded, went down to his aid and the Japs hit him from behind. Joe's dad was in the last war up to his ears. Joe never missed a step in trying to win this one."[8]

Crum's body was never recovered.

In Garfield, on the corner of Midland Avenue and Marcellus Place, stands the city's war memorial inscribed with the names of those native sons who gave their lives. Garfield High

School's 1939 team contributed its share.

Stanley Saganiec was among the Boilermakers who visited the polio victims, and then Jay Kendrick, at Jackson Memorial. A ship's cook second class on PT-129, *The Artful Avenger*, he heroically manned a 20-mm gun to come to the aid of a companion boat that had suffered engine damage and was at the mercy of Japanese shore batteries off the coast of Kauwi, New Guinea. Saganiec took out, in effect, three hostile barges before being struck by enemy fire on May 7, 1944. He died of his wounds on August 5, sixteen days before his 21st birthday.

The Navy presented the Silver Star to his parents posthumously with the following citation, signed by Secretary of the Navy James Forrestal:

> *"Saganiec . . . fired his weapon with extreme accuracy to explode one of the three remaining barges, all of which were beached.*
>
> *"With flames from the first explosion spreading to the second barge, he concentrated his effective rapid fire on the third craft and nearby enemy shore batteries.*
>
> *"By his prompt action, unfaltering marksmanship and great personal valor in the face of shattering volleys from powerful Japanese guns, Saganiec contributed essentially to the destruction of three important Japanese cargo ships and his zealous devotion to duty throughout was in keeping with the highest traditions of the United States Naval Service."*[9]

Staff Sargent Valentine Maciag, son of a Garfield councilman, was killed in action in Holland in April, less than a month before V-E Day. His parents learned of his death after the war in Europe was officially over.[10] He had returned to his unit from the 185th U.S. Army General Hospital in England after recovering from shrapnel wounds received as a rifleman and second scout of his platoon in the Huertgen Forest.

"We jumped off at dawn under cover of a heavy barrage," he told the *Garfield Guardian*. "We spotted our first group of Nazis after advancing 300 yards and I killed one of them with a rifle."

Maciag's unit surprised and captured eight Germans before he was hit.

"We broke out of the woods into a clearing," he explained. "A sniper opened fire from the window of a house and was knocked out by out automatic rifleman. A barrage of 88s forced us back and I was digging a foxhole at the edge of the clearing when I was hit in the shoulder."[11]

That was November 28. Maciag was killed on April 16, two months after he turned 23. He is buried in the cemetery at Margraten.

Then, there is the sad story of Carl Raia, who, like Maciag, did not make the traveling squad for the Miami game but did star on later Garfield teams. Raia was the nephew of Lou Mallia, separated by only five years.

"I was an orphan at 23 months (both his parents died in the 1918 flu pandemic) and when my sister married my brother-in-law, he married me too," Mallia explained. "Carl and I were like brothers. They didn't have separate bedrooms back then. We slept together in the same bed . . . like brothers."

Carl was still in high school when the Japanese attacked Pearl Harbor. Mallia was in his buddy's car with another friend when they heard the news and the next morning, the three of them went to the Paterson post office to sign up for the Navy. Only one passed the eye test and was accepted.

"We went down the hall to the Marine Corps, same eye test and I was rejected," Mallia said. "That put us in a new group: the ready, willing and able group. I said if they want me in the Army they'll have to come get me and they did."

Mallia was crew chief on a B-17, but he didn't have to dodge Messerschmitts on bombing raids. He flew photographic missions in France. Meanwhile, Carl, emulating his uncle, enlisted in the Marines over his mother's wishes. He told her he would "go under a fictitious name" and became a Marine. He was eager for combat. Instead, he was stationed at the Brooklyn Navy Yard. Mallia visited him there when he was home on furlough. Raia was restive in his role.

"He was on guard duty," Mallia said. "He said: 'I've got to get the Hell out of here. I didn't join the Marines to be on guard duty.' I said, 'you've got it nice here. What are you complaining about?' "

Raia finally convinced his commanding officer to release him. He got his wish and went to the Pacific. A mortar shell killed him on Okinawa in the last stages of the fighting. Mallia was in England "entertaining the girls," as he put it, when his nephew was killed. He was consumed by guilt. All those years later, he choked up as he recounted his loss. "He joined the Marines because his uncle was in the Army," Mallia said. "He joined because of me."

John Grembowitz battled a series of injuries at William & Mary and never won a regular starting job on the line. He did, nevertheless, contribute to the Indians' 1942 season, when they were ranked No. 14 in the nation with a 9-1-1 record. The only loss was to the star-studded North Carolina Pre-Flight Cloudbusters, one of the top service teams in the country, coached by Fordham's Crowley.

Grembowitz almost had the chance to return to the same Orange Bowl field where he sparked Garfield's victory in the Health Bowl but the Orange Bowl committee snubbed William & Mary in favor of 10th-ranked Alabama. William & Mary cancelled its 1943 football season, and Grembowitz graduated with a business degree. He immediately enrolled in the Army Air Corps, eager to do his part for the war effort. On the morning of March 2, 1944, Air Cadet Grembowitz found himself in a BT-14 trainer going through landing drills at Auxiliary Field No. 9 in Cherryville, Kansas.

One air cadet encountering BT-14s for the first time described them as "extremely complicated and powerful monsters with many complexities new to us." While considered the best training aircraft available, the BT-14 was very unsteady and hard to land. If a pilot got himself too close to the ground, he could easily lose control.

With the D-Day invasion less than three months away, the Army needed pilots. It sent raw, eager kids into a literal crash course. Recruits were constantly reminded to keep their heads "out of their asses" and on a swivel because other planes could come out of nowhere with deadly consequences. By the end of the war, 15,530 young pilots were killed in some 6,500 training accidents, resulting in the loss of 7,114 aircraft—a wrenchingly astounding average of 10 deaths and 40 accidents per day.

John Grembowitz was one of those 15,530 lives lost.

That fateful day was a perfect day for flying. The ceiling was high with thin overcast and unrestricted visibility. The exercise was called "shooting hurdles," multiple touch and go landings designed to give pilots a lot of experience in a short amount of time. Planes were sent up one after another and, likewise, landed in swift succession. The BT-14 ahead of Grembowitz, piloted by Walter S. Wyckoff, was advised by the control tower to "apply throttle" and fly back around because he was too close to the aircraft that had landed ahead of him.

At that instant, Grembowitz turned on his approach leg. The official accident report suggested that Grembowitz had thought the "apply throttle" order was directed to him, so he climbed to 700 feet. As the Grembowitz plane leveled in flight, Wykoff, climbed from below. Wykoff crashed into Grembowitz in mid-air. The propeller of the Wykoff's aircraft sheared away the entire rear "empennage" section, containing the stabilizer, elevator, vertical fin and rudder of Grembowitz's plane. Grembowitz had no chance. He lost control of the plane and was killed when it knifed back to earth.

Wyckoff attempted a forced landing and crashed through some trees before impacting the ground. He received serious injuries but survived. He was just a kid who made a tragic mistake but he was so wracked by the memory of the accident, he didn't tell his family of his close call with death until the very end of his life.

Under "RESPONSIBILITY" the accident report exculpated Grembowitz of causing the crash: "It is considered the responsibility rests with A/C Wyckoff, W.S., in BT14 aircraft No.40-1208, in that he did not ascertain other aircraft in his flight path."[12] Just like that, because of a pilot error that any trainee might make under the circumstances, a promising life was snuffed out. Grembowitz was a bright and good man. Had he survived the war, he undoubtedly would have had much to contribute. "John was more than just a football star," Joe Simonaro wrote in the *Garfield Guardian*. "He was a man's man, well liked, well-mannered, well-bred.

"Johnny, as his colleagues knew him, symbolized righteousness. He was an earnest toiler . . . a firm advocate of hard work. In all instances, the more leathering the assignment, the finer results he would achieve." Art Argauer, meanwhile, called his former player, "undoubtedly one of the finest football players I ever trained . . . and he was always a gentleman."[13]

The Army never released the details of the crash to the family. A phone call delivered the grave news to Grembowitz's mother, Katarzyna, and, soon after, an army captain knocked on the door of Klecha's Tavern.

"It was such a shock," Sally Skawienski, his step-sister remembered. "All those boys were overseas and here Johnny was killed in the U.S."

His body was sent home by train in a steel casket welded shut and placed upon a bier in the Klecha family living room. Hundreds of people paid their respects to the grieving family. Flowers filled the home. The high school sent an arrangement of yellow daffodils with "GHS" in purple across a football.

"It was a very difficult time; you don't know how to handle these things; you can't eat, you can't speak, and you can't sleep," Sally said. "It was really like a blur. Somehow you live through it but Mom never forgot. He was in the prime of his life."

Among the mourners was a girlfriend named Peggy, whom Grembowitz had met in Kansas and who came all the way to New Jersey for the funeral. Perhaps the romance would have led to marriage. Florence Sluja, the girl who had studiously pasted newspaper clippings on football in a scrapbook, was there, too. There was a power failure the night of the wake and, while waiting for the lights to come back on, she met her future husband, Stanley, another of Grembowitz's step-brothers.

St. Stan's Church was just a block away. The casket was covered with an American flag, carried onto a caisson and taken there for the Requiem High Mass, celebrated by Monsignor Jan Wetula, the priest who had sent his blessings down to the team in Miami that Christmas Eve now six years before. Argauer, and any teammates still home, served as pallbearers. Those

The inscription on John Grembowitz' marker in St. Nicholas Cemetery includes his air wings.

on duty overseas were designated honorary pallbearers. That's what Grembowitz's mother requested. Benny Babula—who would soon graduate as an ensign from Fordham's naval reserve program, also carried his old teammate. Louis Kral, the team manager who pulled the water wagon, was back from Africa with 40 bombing missions under his belt.

When the mass began, the church was filled to capacity and with tears, especially when the choir sang the Polish hymn, *Serdeczna Matko (Loving Mother).*

All the mourners walked in the funeral procession, along practically the same route of the victory parade after the 1939 championship homecoming celebration. Hundreds lined the streets of the largely-Polish Fourth Ward. Neighbors came out of their homes to observe, yet, this time to bow their heads. When the caisson reached the high school, students, dismissed to pay their respects, lined up on both sides of Palisade Avenue in solemn salute.

The procession turned left on Passaic Street, but instead of making a quick right onto Midland, as the team and its entourage did on its way to Penn Station, it continued to St. Nicholas Cemetery. There, near a bank of trees along the river at the back of the cemetery, an honor guard shot off three volleys, sounding not unlike the yacht gun that welcomed the triumphant team back to Garfield. A bugler played Taps. Garfield's hero was laid to rest with his father, Frank.

The inscription at the bottom of the headstone is simple and touching, though easily overlooked by those who might walk past the grave today. Below "Cadet John" and in between the dates 1920 and 1944, his mother sent him to heaven with his set of wings.

TWENTY-TWO

EPILOGUE

In 1999, nearly 60 years after the Health Bowl was played, the owner of a dusty old garage on Main Street in Garfield was cleaning it out when he pulled the tarp off a dilapidated contraption that had been sitting unnoticed for 30 years.

When Angelo Miranda saw it, his eyes welled up with tears. It was the Boilermakers' fabled water wagon, its purple and gold paint chipped and faded. By then, many of his teammates had already passed away. The last reunion had been on the golden anniversary of the game ten years earlier. Miranda probably knew this was going to be the final tangible reminder of the event that Art Argauer promised Angelo and his teammates they would remember the rest of their lives.

The wagon, stored away as an outmoded piece of equipment in the 50s, had resurfaced once before in 1959 when Garfield sports historian Walt Popek asked Argauer if he could restore it. But after a celebrated appearance at the 1969 reunion (where Davey Eldredge and Benny Babula were reunited), it went back into storage and was forgotten—unlike the memories of the players still remaining.

So much had happened since those men were boys and now it seemed as though the trip could be appreciated even more. As was typical of that generation, they hadn't bragged about their accomplishments to their kids, who could recall few details other than that their dads won a national championship. Still, that fact seemed to be mentioned in each player's obituary. Similarly, the obits of the '39 Stingarees inevitably noted their football feats.

Alex Yoda was the first member of Garfield's 1939 squad lost after the World War II, barely 35 years old at the time. A Garfield police officer, the Boilermakers' old starting right guard was on a fishing trip when he suffered a massive heart attack at lunch, collapsing onto the table in front of his shocked friends. He left his wife Helen, the school nurse at Garfield High, and three children.

Al Kazaren and John Orlovsky also died relatively young. Kazaren, who was the vice president of personnel for the Engineering Corporation of Newark at the time, died of a heart attack at age 56 in 1977. Orlovsky, who passed on his football talents—and his bad

Angelo Miranda poses with the Garfield High water wagon when it was first presented to the team in 1939. Courtesy Estate of Angelo Miranda.

shoulder—to his sons John and Dale, was 59 when he suffered a fatal heart attack while driving his car in 1989. Dale Orlovsky remembered how broken up Argauer was at the wake.

Like Kazaren, many of the Boilermakers made good. Ted Ciesla, star of Garfield's 1938 team, had a successful college career paying baseball and football at Washington and Lee University and received his law degree from John Marshall College. He was Garfield's 37-year-old city attorney when he died of a heart attack in 1958.

Joe Tripoli held an important post with the non-profit Rand Corporation during its UFO investigation. Angelo Miranda worked for the Bergen County Board of Elections. Bill Librera coached three sports at five different high schools and retired as the athletic director of Indian Hills High School. After the war, Wally Tabaka worked for the Garfield Water Department and mounted an unsuccessful bid for mayor of Wallington, running on an unpopular platform that would have closed the saloons on Sunday. He lived in Paris for a time and returned to work as a Washington, D.C. lobbyist for the Hunt Brothers, Nelson Baker and William Herbert, who tried to corner the world silver market in 1980. Steve Noviczky spent his entire career at Uniroyal, working his way up to an executive position. Ray Butts ran a costume shop. Pete Yura moved to Bristol, Pennsylvania, where he worked in the business offices of Rohm and Haas, a chemicals manufacturer.

There were many success stories among the old Stingarees. After earning an engineering degree at the University of Florida, running back Gene Autrey served as vice president, president and chief operating officer of several Florida utilities companies and was President of the Orange Bowl Committee. Staunch lineman Gilbert Wilson obtained a law degree from Washington and Lee University and retired as a partner in the Norfolk law firm of Preston,

Wilson and Crandley in 1991. Sure-handed Charlie Burrus had a long military career and retired as an Air Force colonel.

Ace passer Jason Koesy, armed with an engineering degree from Georgia Tech, retired as Systems Director of Line Maintenance for Eastern Airlines. Pericles Nichols, the stuttering backup back, became one of South Florida's biggest builders and developers. Levin Rollins, wounded twice in World War II, couldn't help getting shot. In 1964, working as a Florida state beverage agent, he took a shotgun blast while on a routine inspection. He wisely moved to North Carolina.

Miami High's football success continued through 1965 when the National Sports News Service named the Stingarees national champs with a 12-0 record, their first unbeaten season since 1943. From 1931 through that season, Miami High was 207-57-22, an incredible .802 winning percentage. During that span, the Stingarees were named state champions 24 times and never had a losing season. Among the few disappointments was the end of their streak against Edison in 1952, when the Cardinals pulled out a 21-7 victory before 31,391 at the Orange Bowl, driving coach Ed Parnell almost to tears.

"We've experienced the tragedy of defeat so many times, it's certainly wonderful to experience the gorgeous thrill of victory," Pop said.[1]

The '65 national title turned out to be Miami's last hurrah on that scale. There was, however, one other Miami team to capture a national championship in football. *USA Today* named the Booker T. Washington Tornadoes, the formerly segregated black school, the best high school team in the country in 2013.

Today, Miami High School sits, restored to its former glory after a $55 million project, in the middle of the Little Havana neighborhood.

Garfield High finally got its own stadium in 1946 and a decade later, a high school accommodating all four classes was built alongside it. After several lean years, Boilermaker football experienced a revival in the 1960s and in 1965, Garfield won a state championship behind quarterback Kevin Rusnak, who moved on to play at Ohio State. With declining enrollment, the Boilermakers soon were unable to compete with the state's powerhouses. They have, however, produced championship teams—and NFL players such as Wayne Chrebet, Miles Austin and Luis Castillo—while competing against smaller schools in North Jersey.

JACK BOYLE

Garfield's starting right guard married Garfield High band member Irene Kral before shipping out with the Navy. She was the sister of Boilermaker manager Louis Kral, who had to prod his friend into asking her for a first date. Had she been widowed when Boyle was forced to ditch his plane at Okinawa, their eight children would never have been born.

"First and foremost, my dad was a family man. His whole life was about sacrifice and providing for his family," said his son, Brian. "He worked his way up through the telephone company from a lineman to being general manager of the whole upstate area in New York. I know he had a great time in Miami. He and Al Kazaren were very close but he never talked about the game. My father . . . when chapters closed in his life, he closed the entire book. The past didn't mean much to my Dad."

Boyle left Garfield for good shortly after the war and made his home near Utica, New York. He returned to Garfield just once, with his son Brian, to see the old sights in 1994. Irene stayed home.

"My mother wanted no part of it," Brian explained. "She didn't have many fond memories of Garfield. Her father was a Botany Mills guy, he was laid off a lot and things were rough there. She really moved on."

Jack Boyles' son, Jim, played college football on the University of Vermont's last team. His grandson, John, played for Cornell after he passed away. His granddaughter Molly, was a standout athlete at Harvard, where she threw the hammer. Boyle loved that. But after Irene passed away in 2002, he took it hard—"they were incredibly close," Brian said—and his health deteriorated.

Still, they remember Jack Boyle in Utica.

"I'm a doctor in Utica," Brian said. "I've been in practice for twenty-five years so I've taken care of a lot of the guys he worked with. As soon as they'd see my name they would always say, 'Oh your father' . . . and tell me a story. He was very well liked by those he called '"his men.'"

JAY KENDRICK

Kendrick, the victim of that errant golf ball, had a heart as big as his large frame and booming voice. Kendrick met and fell in love with a single mom, Harriet Nelson, whose husband, a clarinet player in a band, had run out on them. He had no problem adopting the son, Bill, and giving him his name.

"He was a big, gruff guy who didn't take any crap, but he was my guy. I could always depend on that man," Bill Kendrick said. "Frankly, I don't know what would have happened to me if it wasn't for him. He guided me and set me on the straight path. I was not a good student (though he eventually became an attorney). He made me learn my tables and start working. And he gave me chores to do. I took care of the yard. There was always something for me to do."

Kendrick stayed friends with Mike Osceola. Kendrick even learned the Seminole language. When Bill was a little guy, they'd all go fishing in the Everglades. Once they caught an alligator together but the hook broke before they could pull him in.

"They were a feisty pair. Dad was not one to back down and Mike neither," Bill said. "Like many Seminoles, Mike didn't have a chance. Alcohol got him. Dad was one of the first ones to go down there when he died."

Kendrick got a job as a county building inspector through Jesse Yarborough after the service and was appointed and re-elected District Constable in the 1960s. After a long life together, his wife passed away in 2009, by which time he was already experiencing dementia.

"He'd ask me where Mom was and I'd tell him she was resting," Bill said. "He broke down when he found out and he passed within four months of her death."

HARVEY JAMES

Of all those on the Miami and Garfield teams, Harvey James may have had the biggest impact on kids. James, who replaced Jay Kendrick in the starting lineup against Garfield, remembered his own travails in his long career as a coach at Edison and Norland High Schools. The kid who was booted out of Benedictine Military Academy to be set straight by Jesse Yarborough at Miami High paid extra attention to boys like himself.

"He kind of looked out for the underdog," Don Bailey, who played for James at Edison said in James' 1988 obituary. "He saw the troubled kid who had potential, and he'd try to get him involved in athletics and spend all that energy on the football field. He was really more influential to me than my own father. I was hanging out with the wrong crowd back at Edison, and I grew from a troubled boy into a man in one football season under that guy."[2]

James came into his own as an All America caliber center at the University of Miami after returning from his World War II stint in the Navy to resume his college career with the Hurricanes, playing football, baseball and basketball. He was inducted into the school's Hall of Fame in 1982.

Midway through the 1946 season, James suffered a severe foot injury that threatened his career. Trainer Bill Dayton, the same guy who prescribed those salt tablets for the Garfield team, fashioned an aluminum brace. The next week, James hobbled off the bench to inspire a comeback win over Miami of Ohio.

James was drafted by the Cleveland Browns in the All America Football Conference after coach Paul Brown was told he was the best football player in Florida, but James' pro career never got going after a training camp injury. Returning to South Florida, he married University of Miami and nationally-ranked tennis star Ruth Hulbert in 1947. James worked three jobs to provide for the family and put two kids through college. He got out of bed at three or four to deliver the *Miami Herald,* then went off to the school to teach and coach. At night, he worked as a mutual clerk at the dog track.

"He'd put us to work on the weekends. I remember waking up at five in the morning, getting into that red station wagon and delivering papers with the whole family," said his daughter, Carol Haderer.

James had a favorite saying that he no doubt picked up playing high school football. "If it hurts, rub a little dirt on it and keep going," he'd tell his players.

That kind of tough love led to an old player of his naming two-year-old thoroughbred— Harveygiechyjames—after his favorite coach.

"Like others, I was a rough kid when at Edison," Nathan Kelly said. "But Harvey worked me into a man. Harvey was able to straighten out some who needed help because he as was tough as they and, above all, he was a good man."[3]

LETTY BARBOUR

The Garfield nightingale began but never quite finished a professional singing career. Her big break came in 1945 when she signed a contract with the Henry King Orchestra, which brought her engagements at the Biltmore in New York and the Trianon and Aragaon ballrooms in Chicago. There, she also appeared with the Mitch Herth Trio at the Glass Hat where she warbled her specialties, "Sorrento" and "J'Attendrai."

Letty's voice was also heard coast-to-coast on "Two for the Show," a weekly radio program hosted by the rubber-faced Joe E. Brown and Lee Sanguinette on KMOX (with its powerful 50,000-watt, clear-channel signal) and syndicated by CBS. In 1949, Barbour was referred to, in *The Billboard* magazine, as a "five-foot two-er . . . a chirper" who was being groomed by Jimmie Martin as a "top vocalist spot on the discs."[4]

Fate intervened, however, when Letty suffered a ruptured appendix that became gangrenous.

"Her mother and I went out to Chicago and stayed with her for two or three days in the hospital and at that point when she was well enough where my mother and father insisted that she come home to fully recover, which she did," said her brother, Joe Barbato. "Then she started dating a guy from Passaic, Sol Goldberg. They married, originally against my father's

"Lovely" Letty Barbour is featured as the vocalist for Henry King's Orchestra in a 1945 advertisement that ran in the Chicago Tribune.

wishes, and her career sort of ended at that point." Letty had broken off one engagement while in Chicago. This marriage ended in divorce three years later. But Letty never resumed her career full-time, outside of a few local appearances and recording a few radio jingles including Chock Full O' Nuts coffee and Pabst Blue Ribbon beer.

Letty was married a second time to Leonard Carlucci and settled into a role as a wife and mother back in Garfield. When she died in 2004, her short obituary did not mention her singing career, only that she was a well-loved teacher's aide at No. 7 School in Garfield.

JOHN GABRIEL

John Gabriel, who, at the dedication of the new City Hall in 1941, first used the term, "City of Champions," continued to bring attention to Garfield after the trip to Miami. In 1940, the *New York Daily News* saluted Gabriel with a photo spread titled, "Progress-Town in New Jersey." In August of 1939, he had officiated at the third marriage of Olympic swim champ and Tarzan actor Johnny Weissmuller to actress Beryl Scott at the home of Garfield city official Henry Janowski. Then, in November of 1941, he was part of one of the last American feel-good stories before the bombs fell at Pearl Harbor—the Park Bench wedding—even if turned out to be not quite true.

According to the story, quartermaster Second Class Bill Langford, stationed at the Brooklyn Navy Yard, was on shore leave when, strolling in Central Park, he came across a dirty-faced, shabbily-dressed girl crying on a park bench. Josephine Phillips, 19, had left her home in Passaic several months after her father passed away when she couldn't get along with her mother, sister and brothers. She met a guy, fell in love and when she found out he was married, tried to commit suicide by drinking iodine.

She ended up in New York, broke, cold, alone distraught, riding the subways just to stay warm. The tall, sympathetic Texan struck up a conversation with her and learned that she would try to kill herself again the next morning. As it was written in the *Philadelphia Inquirer*, the sailor took her out to dinner and when she refused his offer to pay for a room, "they walked the streets all that night, talking, talking, talking . . . of what might be."[5]

They were to meet for another date the next night but Langford was suddenly and without prior warning transferred to the Philadelphia Navy Yard. The girl waited for him at the same bench, where a fellow sailor brought her a note from Langford, explaining he had shipped out, although she didn't know what to believe. Instead of her Prince Charming, she was accosted by New York's finest, arrested for vagrancy and locked up. No one believed her story until she convinced a newspaper reporter of it. Langford saw the story, got a 10-day leave and, six weeks, after their chance meeting, found her back living with a cousin in Passaic, where he proposed.

"She has a half-Nelson on my heart," he wrote to a cousin in Shreveport, Louisiana, before popping the question. "All she has to do is put on a little pressure and who knows what will happen?"

The couple told their story on the *We The People* radio show, had their pictures taken for *LIFE Magazine* and caught the interest of *Gone with the Wind* producer David O. Selznick, who bought their story for $200 and planned to make it into a movie.[6]

All they needed was someone to marry them and that someone was the ever-willing John M. Gabriel. The ceremony took place in the council chamber of the new Garfield City Hall. Wearing a peasant-style dress signifying her Polish roots and donated by a local store, Josephine choked back tears as Gabriel did the honors in front of snap-happy photographers and newsmen. When Gabriel uttered the words, "You may kiss the bride," the newlyweds went into an 11-second clinch, as timed on a reporter's stopwatch. A silver chest, a gift of Selznick's gleamed nearby as someone played Mendelssohn's recessional march on the piano accordion.

They were whisked into New York where the Hotel New Yorker provided the bridal suite. There they danced to the Benny Goodman orchestra live. The bandleader dedicated "You and I" to them as he played the melody on the keys of his licorice stick.

The *Associated Press* story recounted the wedding night, or at least its romantic ideal of it:

> *Bill carried Josephine across the threshold of their room and they walked out on the terrace and looked past the million lights of the skyscrapers at the black and white pattern of Central Park. They drank champagne and laughed and sucked lollipops they had bought on 42nd Street.*[7]

(OK, so you can't really see Central Park from the Hotel New Yorker but it sounded good anyway. At least they didn't have Red Simko tossing the lollipops.)

"He's my dream boy," Josephine whispered. "There never was a better."

Gabriel's picture ran with the story in several papers. More good ink for Garfield.

Gabriel had been touted frequently as a candidate for higher office but chose not to re-enter politics after the Army despite his obvious knack for it. Instead, he used his civil engineering degree to start a very successful and profitable construction company in addition to a real estate and insurance agency. The man excelled at anything he did.

Gabriel moved out of Garfield to the greener, more residential sections of Bergen County. In 1957, he was selected to *Sports Illustrated's* Silver All America team honoring 25 former college football players whose achievements off the field stood out 25 years after their college graduation. The list included graduates of Harvard, Yale, Princeton and both military academies. Among the honorees were Carl H. Hageman Jr., vice president of Union Carbide, Harry L. Hansen, Harvard Business School professor, Dr. Frederic T. Billings, a specialist in internal medicine, Ivan B. Williamson, athletic director at the University of Wisconsin, Ben Schwartzwalder, head football coach at Syracuse, the late William Kane, commander of the *U.S.S. Saipan* . . . and Gabriel.

"I might not play college football again," Gabriel was quoted as saying. "But I wouldn't trade the experience. Football taught me to work under pressure."[8]

In the end, his hard-driving personality—as well as his stubbornness—got the best of him.

"He was in great physical shape but like everybody in those days, he smoked, he drank his Manhattans," his son, John. Jr. explained. "And he was also stressed."

In 1965, Gabriel was finishing a round of golf with his physician at the Ridgewood Country Club when he experienced some chest pains. "John, we've got to check you out," the doctor said. "You've got to come in. I've got to see what's going on."

A couple of months later—he still hadn't visited his doctor—Gabriel was watching a crew excavate for an outdoor swimming pool at the family's new house in Washington Township, New Jersey. It was close to 90 degrees with 97 percent humidity that August day—very Miami-like—and Gabriel didn't like the pace or proficiency of the workmen. So he climbed down into the hole to show the crew how a hole should be dug. John Gabriel Jr. was home that day, about to leave for business school. He heard a commotion and when he ran out, his father was at the bottom of that hole. He had a massive heart attack and died instantly at age 54. The Boy Mayor died too young.

ART ARGAUER

Not everyone in Garfield celebrated Art Argauer after he returned with the team from Florida. During those heady days in Miami, Garfield officials promised him a raise and Argauer, figuring he'd brought about $10,000 into the athletic department treasury, asked for a $1,000 increase. The problem was, Garfield was broke, and it was refusing raise petitions from the Garfield Teachers Association at the same time. When news of Argauer's request hit the papers, he was suddenly looked at with "hardened eyes" in the hallways.

"A fellow teacher glared at me the other day as if I were one half Hitler and one half Stalin," he complained to Art McMahon.

That's when Argauer began to listen to job offers from other schools. He accepted one— from Clifford Scott, the other high school in East Orange—and in the end, the Garfield Board

Art Argauer at the desk in his den, later in life. The Health Bowl game ball is proudly displayed.
Newark Public Library, Newark News Photo Archives.

of Education came back to him with a counter-offer, which he accepted. It was the second time he had pulled such a maneuver. It happened in 1937 when he backed out of a deal with Lyndhurst High after Garfield came back after him.

After Argauer got out of the Clifford Scott contract, Al Del Greco chided Garfield officials, suggesting "the next time Argauer asks for a raise, those Garfield boys should act promptly and break into the nearest bank and settle the matter pronto. (They) must have learned by now that their coach isn't a guy who can be pushed around. He's no little political stooge, who can be kicked around by his inferiors."

But Art McMahon had a different take. Argauer, he said, "had run out of tricks." The next time, McMahon said, "Garfield can laugh at his threats to quit."

Garfield didn't laugh. When, in 1946, he received a $4,300 offer from Kearny High School (an increase of $450 over his Garfield salary), the Board of Education simply yawned and let him go.

"The small sum should not have been allowed to stand in the way. He was worth it," a *Garfield Guardian* editorial contended.

Of course, while the Boilermaker program foundered, the *Jersey Journal* was soon talking about his "wizardry" at his new post. He took over a team that hadn't won in 17 games over two years and immediately led them to a 5-5-1 season. Then, in 1948, with future New York Giant Alex Webster on his team, Argauer coached the Kardinals to an undefeated season and consideration as Miami High's opponent in what was then the Kiwanis Classic. Kingsport, Tennessee, got the bid instead. Webster considered Argauer his first great coach. Argauer wasn't done with Garfield, however. Before the 1948 began, Argauer coached the Alumni against the Boilermaker varsity at two-year-old Garfield Stadium. His players included Benny Babula, Ted Ciesla, Bill Wagnecz and many others who starred on the four teams that lost only two games between 1938 and 1941.

The coach took it as seriously as the 1934 Bloomfield game. Just as he did then, he conducted practices throughout the summer. Ciro Barcelona, the Garfield quarterback and son of Joey Harrison, the old boxer, remembered how the game went.

"They were out of football for a while but they could still play the game. Oh my goodness, they were outstanding," he said. "That year, we just started wearing mouthguards. I didn't want to wear mine. On the opening kickoff, Benny Babula ran right over me. He was like a horse. My teeth came loose in my mouth. I wore my mouthguard after that."

The high school kids absorbed a 19-6 beating and Joe Lovas, writing in *The Herald-News*, was hard on the coach he praised so lavishly back in the day. He felt Argauer had poured it on and suggested that Argauer had lost many friends for doing so. "I was once one of Argauer's biggest boosters. It came to an end Friday night," he declared.[9]

All was eventually forgiven. When Argauer returned as athletic director and football coach in 1958, Augie Lio wrote in *The Herald News*, "Garfield's Knute Rockne is back."[10]

The first game marked a happy return as the Boilermakers clipped Lodi, coached by Argauer's old assistant, Joe Cody, 14-6, but the talent pool was thin at Garfield in the 50s and even his old magic touch failed to produce a winner.

Art and Florence had no children of their own. Neither did his brother or sister. But Argauer made himself a tremendous uncle to the nieces and nephews on his wife's side.

"He was all about family," said his grand niece Linda Gale Prior. "I always thought that it was a shame that they had no children but we were the people to whom they gave their love and we were better off because of him and my Aunt. Because he had that stern face, many of the kids were afraid of him. But he was warm and wonderful under all of that."

Linda lived in Rhode Island but frequently stayed over the Argauers' house in the 60s. "I'd sleep in the den with all of his trophies and awards," she said. "I knew it was a privilege to be in there. He loved to cook and he always made me whatever I wanted—big breakfasts with pancakes, waffles and all the fixings."

Argauer always wore a big chef's hat and apron when at the grill, which probably would have had his old players howling. So would the story Linda told about when she'd leave to go home.

"We had this funny little thing we had between us," she remembered. "He always gave me a wet kiss on the cheek and would say, 'If you do not wipe it off, I will give you two dollars. So the kiss took place, the money was paid and then I would get in the car, look back at him and wipe it off. He would pretend to run after the car yelling, 'I want my money back.' "

Argauer stayed close to his players for the rest of his life and helped lots of local kids into Tusculum College, his *alma mater*. The school still gives the Art Argauer Award to its coach of the year. Garfield High named its football field after Argauer, just as it later named its gymnasium after Coach Hollis.

Unfortunately, Argauer's break with the school was not quite as gracious. In 1962, in what some might call typical Garfield fashion, the Board of Education was playing politics. There were two teachers that some on the board wanted removed. They were 62. So the Board made 62 the new mandatory retirement age.

Argauer was turning 62. He was swept out with the wash despite a slew of vocal protests. On the final day of the 1962 school year, Garfield's faculty and student body gave Argauer a "day" with an assembly in the school auditorium. A spontaneous standing ovation lasted 10 minutes as Argauer dabbed his eyes. The next evening, close to 300 Garfield students, including the entire senior class, formed a motorcade to his house in Clifton, where they filled the street and sang school songs.

"It was an impressive sight and Art's neighbors joined to make it an evening the Argauers will never forget," *The Clifton Journal* reported.

Argauer wasn't entirely through, however. Clifton hired him as the high school athletic director and after two more years, he finished there where it all started 43 years earlier, after Carlton Palmer walked into his father's tailor shop.

Argauer remains one of the most successful high school coaches in New Jersey history with a 177-67-13 record in football. In basketball, he had five Bergen County Interscholastic League championship and two Passaic Valley Conference championships before turning the reins over to John Hollis after the 1942 season. He also won five state professional titles as coach of the Clifton Wessingtons and the 1947 championship of the American Football League (not to be confused with the league that merged with the NFL) with the Clifton Rams. Add his 9-2-1 record in alumni games and his all-time football coaching record is 221-80-14.

Argauer died of a heart attack in 1986.

"He was sincere, honest and straightforward," Abner West, executive secretary of the NJSIAA said then. "You couldn't find a better guy to coach against. The game on the field was all that mattered."[11]

JESSE YARBOROUGH

Just as World War II was interceding, it seemed that the "Cunnel" was about to graduate —from high school to a big time college job. So speculated Marshall Dann of the *Detroit Free Press* after watching Miami High take apart Baltimore City College in the 1941 Christmas game. Dann was so impressed by the precision of the Stingaree attack, he wrote that Yarborough "reigned undisputed as the leading developer of high school talent in the United States.

"Miami's sports fans who confidently confess that they have the nation's outstanding high school coach in Jesse Yarborough are in a quandary over the same Mr. Yarborough's future— they both hope and fear he'll do a Paul Brown on them," Dann surmised.

Brown, of course, left Massillon for Ohio State after the 1940 season. Yarborough left Miami High, all right, but for a hitch in Uncle Sam's Army. He'd come close to moving into the college ranks after the war but fate had other plans for him, it seemed.

He was scheduled to interview for the University of Maryland coaching job and was considered among the favorites until the Terrapin brass cancelled. They had settled on a guy named Paul Bryant. The Bear had met Washington Redskins owner George Marshall at a cocktail party where Marshall offered him an assistant coaching position with his club. Bryant mentioned he was interested in a head coaching job, so Marshall put him in touch with Maryland's president and former coach Curly Byrd. Bryant was hired the day after they met.

In the meantime, University of Florida boosters began a move to bring Yarborough to Gainesville as the Gators' head coach but in January of 1946, he admitted "the irons I had in

A silver-haired Jesse Yarborough a few years before his death. This is his daughter's favorite photo of him.
Courtesy Louise Greer.

the fire are definitely cooling off."[12] A month later, Yarborough announced he was returning to Miami High as athletic director and coach.

"Jesse's finally decided, 'it's good enough for me," Principal W.R. Thomas said.[13]

Except it wasn't. In April, Yarborough abruptly resigned to accept a position as Welfare Director for the City of Miami along with its attractive $4,600 annual salary. Although he would admit, "if it wasn't for football, I'd be plowin' a mule in South Carolina," he remained in politics the remainder of his working life, never to coach again. His all-time record at Miami was 96-13-4.

"The idea of getting into something different and still being in Miami appealed to him," said his daughter Louise. "Then people started asking him to run for office and it just took off from there."

Yarborough was a natural politician with his disarming sense of humor, his smarts and his natural people instincts.

"He could tell a good joke and take a good joke," Louise said. "He had so many friends— men and women — but he had problems remembering women's names. He called them all 'Petunia.' When he died, we got fifty sympathy cards signed 'Petunia.' "

In 1949, he was elected to the Dade County Commission and in 1958 was appointed to the Dade County School Board where he took a lead role in the contentious desegregation of schools. According to his daughter, he received threatening phone calls in the middle of the night and awoke one morning to find a load of bricks dumped in the front yard.

Yarborough lost a Democratic primary race for Florida Secretary of State on 1960 but was later elected to the in the Florida House of Representatives where he served six years. He served four more years as a Public Service Commissioner until he was "soundly trounced" in a 1972 run-off, his twelfth election campaign. Naturally, he cracked a joke about the defeat as he announced his retirement from public life.

"I should have stuck to football," he said. "I'd be coaching at Notre Dame right now."[14]

Yarborough maintained a connection to football by serving as President of the Orange Bowl Committee in the 50s. All the while, he never forgot his old players. He used his position in government to help them if they needed it. He remained their beloved "Coach."

Paul Louis, for instance, became one of Florida's most-respected attorneys during a 57-year career, a "tenacious advocate who never abandoned a cause or a client," according to his 2008 obituary. In *Neil v. State*, he argued before the Supreme Court of Florida and gained a decision that ended the common practice of excluding individuals from jury panels based on race.

When Louis filled out his questionnaire after being elected to the Miami High Hall of Fame, he wrote, "Under Coach Yarborough's program, although not a natural athlete, I was able to develop my maximum potential as an athlete and student which permanently influenced my life."

Louis kept two pictures on his office wall of his two greatest influences. One was of a federal judge. The other was of Yarborough.

Ironically, the coach who was so strict about his players smoking died of emphysema in 1980 after a lifetime of smoking. He was 73. Said Ralph Davis, a friend, upon his death: "I think the biggest thing in his life was to see this group of men he coached go out over Florida and the U.S. and make such a huge success in industry, the professions and government."[15]

BENNY BABULA

Somewhat luckless in marriage and career, Babula nevertheless remained a larger-than-life character. His name is still recalled in Garfield, and it was in Miami at least through the 1960s. A member of the Garfield Cadets drum and bugle corps attended a competition there and needed a haircut. When the barber found out he was from Garfield, he sighed, "That Benny Babula was some ballplayer."

Benny Babula in a photo taken at the Boilermakers' 50-year reunion in 1989. Courtesy Estate of Angelo Miranda.

"When he walked into a room, he always got a lot of attention," remembered his niece, Kathy Otterman, Eva's daughter. "He always had a big smile, was outgoing and friendly, a life of the party type. He had a personality that made him a very likable guy."

His son, Bernard, concurred.

"You definitely knew where he was when he walked into a room," he said. "He had a very optimistic outlook on everything. He would always try to find something positive in a situation."

Babula considered an offer from the Chicago Bears (and another from the Washington Senators) after the war but there wasn't much money in pro football at the time, and it was time for these players to get on with the rest of their lives. Similarly, teammate Steve Noviczky turned down an offer from the New York Giants.

So, Babula naturally took over his father's meat distribution business and his white delivery truck could be seen at butcher shops all over town. A popular figure, he served one term as a Garfield councilman in the late 1940s.

Babula was married for the first time during his senior year at Fordham to Eileen Brown, a girl from Belleville. He was soon off to war and the marriage didn't last long after he returned. His second marriage was to Jeanne Dul, the sister of his pal and hunting companion, Dr. Emil Dul, who had starred for Argauer's teams in the mid 30s. Bernard, his only child, was born from that marriage. Lastly, he was wed to a much younger woman, a native of South America, named Carol.

Together, they opened a sandwich shop in Clifton called "Mr. and Mrs. Pastrami" and later a restaurant, "With Love." It was located in Wayne, not far from the old Donohue's, where Garfield once threw its awards banquets and where Babe Ruth addressed the Boilermakers in 1938. Bernard, played piano there. In the end, however, Benny couldn't sustain the business and had to close it.

Babula remained physically active throughout his life, although the knee injuries from his Fordham days always bothered him.

"His knees would swell up with liquid.," Bernard recalled. "He would have to have his knees injected without any Novocaine. It never stopped him. He started skiing in his 50s and he was very good, even on bad knees, but he wound up breaking his leg."

In fact, John Gabriel's son, John Jr., remembers that very event. They somehow ended up on the same chair lift and began talking. Benny said he was from Garfield. Gabriel said he was born there.

"He introduced himself as Benny Babula. I said, 'You've got to be kidding. My father was John Gabriel.'" There was laughter, amazement and whatever good stories they could get in until they reached the top.

"We got off the chair lift and I remember thinking how much he reminded me of Paul Hornung. He was still a big, handsome guy with curly hair and he said, 'C'mon, let's go right down here.' And I said, 'Ben, that's a little steep for me. I don't think I want to do that.' All right, I'll see you later,' he said and he went flying down.

"About two hours later, I was skiing a run and I see one of those sleds coming down. And I look and it's Benny in a sled. I don't know if he had a broken leg but he was certainly hurting."

Bernard recalled his father's physical strength.

"He would arm-wrestle anyone and it would stun people just how strong he was," he said. "He won a few golf championships. He loved playing golf. We were up at Stratton Mountain in Vermont and he wanted to get in a round. The pro offered to play with him and was shocked when my father beat him. As far as sports went, he excelled at whatever he picked up."

Benny would talk about the Miami game when Bernard was young, but Bernard admitted: "I was only half-listening.

"I know he brought up the fact that he had never kicked a field goal before. He also said that they were worn out and couldn't get hydrated. He said that if they actually drank the water, they would have won by a bigger margin.

"But wherever we would go, people knew. My wife once took my son to get a pair of shoes. The salesman, a young kid, knew all about him. To this day, people remember; they bring it up."

Babula saw Davey Eldredge one more time at the 1969 reunion and he was the main attraction at the team's 50-year reunion.

As he reached his 80s, Benny began to show signs of dementia. He moved back in with his second wife, Jeanne, and their son and there, as comfortable and happy as he could be, he passed away of Alzheimer's Disease in 2003. His obituary in the *Bergen Record* was strangely brief:

> *Born in Passaic, he lived here (Clifton) most of his life. Mr. Babula, a World War II lieutenant veteran, was a wholesale meat salesman in the local area for 45 years. He was a football member of the Garfield High School Hall of Fame and a member of the John Marshall Chess Club of New York City.*[16]

Who knew that he played chess?

Benny Babula was laid to rest in the Brigadier General William C. Doyle Veterans Memorial Cemetery in Wrightstown, New Jersey.

DAVEY ELDREDGE

Remembering her father, Eldredge's daughter, Jennie McCoun, described him as a "gentle soul" and, as such, it seemed life took him on a path far from what he would have made for himself. Where the "galloping waif" of the high school gridiron could always outrun the opposition, misfortune caught up to him and brought him down hard.

After returning from the war, Eldredge turned down a professional offer from the Miami Seahawks of the new All America Football Conference and transferred from Georgia Tech to join old teammate Harvey James to finish his collegiate career at the University of Miami. Eldredge played one season, in 1946, before hanging up the cleats. His best performance came in the third game of the season when he showed off the old wings from his Stingaree days and got loose for touchdown runs of 50 and 63 yards against Texas Christian.

"Spindle-hanked Davey Eldredge, a twisting, turning, darting wraith among gridiron Goliaths, had vindicated himself today after some of the sideline wisebirds had whispered the spring in his legs was gone," wrote John McMullan in the *Miami Daily News*.[17]

Eldredge helped the Hurricanes to eight wins and was named to the southern squad in the annual Blue-Gray game. A year later, he and James were named to coach the Miami freshman team, which he hoped would be the start of a long career. But it didn't work out. In 1948, Eldredge turned to another career popular with ex-athletes: politics, as campaign manager for a state senate candidate. Eldredge was a Democrat and, at the time, Southern Democrats were typically segregationists. According to his son, David Jr., it was a description that never fit him and, in he end, that incongruence contributed to his downfall. Although he was elected to the Florida State House of Representatives, he was a reluctant politician.

"He wasn't staunch by any means. They weren't his views down deep and that's not what he taught us," said the younger Eldredge, whose resemblance to his father is stunning. "In my dad's mind, the reason you kept people separate was that if you put them together, they'd get hurt. He saw the abuses that had taken place. So, being known as a segregationist from today's viewpoint . . . that's kind of a distortion of what he was."

In any event, Eldredge's mom was "torn up" by it, having taken in the black boy, Ed Johnson, all those years ago in Apopka.

"And it certainly ended my father's political career," David Jr. said. "He should have been a coach, because that's where his love was. He definitely didn't belong in the political arena. When he got out, he was probably in his forties, and he worked for a company, doing PR work and he wasn't cut out for that, either. His life was pretty much over at an early age. He just never could find his niche."

Despondent, Davey fell victim to what his son said was the end of all the Eldredge men: "untapped talent eaten up by alcohol."

Like his brothers, Al and Knox, he turned to the bottle and became an "absent" father to his two children. It led to his divorce from the former Dolores Papy, the 1946 Miami University Homecoming Queen whom he married in 1949.

"People have a lot of resources now to them care of those things but he was unable to manage his alcoholism. His last years were not pretty. He never recuperated from the divorce and his health the last three

Davey Eldredge flashes a smile during one of his terms in the Florida House of Representatives. State Library and Archives of Florida.

or four years went downhill," his son explained. "He wasn't drinking at that point but the damage had already been done. He died of kidney failure when he was 63."

There were some good times, though. Father and son bonded over football and attended all the Miami Hurricanes and Miami Dolphins games they could. After the Dolphins drafted Bob Griese, he moved in across the street from the Eldredge family.

"They all got together and played cards and Bob was very nice, very conservative," young Eldredge recalled. "As a kid, I went completely nuts. A few days after they won the Super Bowl, he and Howard Twilley came over and played basketball on my driveway. Football was my life up to that point. You just couldn't get it any better than that: tossing the football with the quarterback of the Miami Dolphins, a future Hall of Famer. That was a very wonderful time."

Davey Sr., even through his struggles, remained a kind-hearted man.

"Anybody that I'd ever talked to always asked me about him and they'd always make that comment: 'Gee, we really liked your dad. He was such a very sweet man.'" David Jr. said. "Even when he drank, he was not an angry person. He was just kind of lost . . . kind of a sad, lost person."

Davey Eldredge spent his last days in the hospital, lapsing in and out of unconsciousness. His son was a massage therapist at the time. He was rubbing his father's back because his kidneys were shutting down.

"You've got good hands, boy," Eldredge told his son, suddenly alert. He had just come out of a coma.

"What's been going on?" the younger Eldredge said.

"I've been having sweet dreams, sweet dreams of mother," he told him.

Eldredge died a day before Miami University defeated Nebraska, a 10 ½-point favorite, 31-30, for the national championship in the Orange Bowl, one of the biggest upsets to have taken place since that Christmas night in 1939.

Eldredge always remembered that night. In 1962, he challenged Dante Fascell in the Democrat Primary for the U.S. Fourth Congressional District. Fascell, who would serve a total of 19 terms in Congress, was the incumbent with the backing of President Kennedy. He won in a landslide. That night, Eldredge was asked: "Was there ever a time in your life before when you'd given everything you had, with all your power and still took a licking?

Eldredge thought for a moment.

"Yes," he replied. "There was a time. It was Christmas night of 1939 . . . a football game.

"That night, Miami High was playing for what was called the national high school championships against a team from Garfield, New Jersey. Both teams were undefeated . . . we were good and they were, too. They had us 13-0 at the half but we scored two in the second half to tie it up . . . and then their big man, a fellow named Bam Bam Babula, kicked a field goal that beat us, 16-13, in the last three minutes.

"I thought I was going to bust wide open after that but I didn't . . . I don't reckon I will now."[18]

WALTER YOUNG

Shortly after the German surrender in World War II, Walter Young's mom opened her mailbox to find a letter postmarked Berlin. It was from the mother of Walter Bradenahl, Walter's classmate, who had returned to Germany with his family while spouting Nazi slogans.

"Berlin lies in rubble. I am destitute," Frieda Bradenahl pleaded in neat German script that belied her situation. "Please send anything you can. My husband has gone mad. He is a vegetable. My son and my future lie buried on the Eastern Front."

Walter Young despaired as he held the frayed letters he had received from his friend all those years ago. In a way, they explained to him life's different pathways and how lucky he was to have been directed down his. How could a kid from Garfield High School, perhaps the smartest in his class, end up as part of Hitler's spearhead in Operation Barbarossa, only to perish in July of 1942 near the Russian village of Volokonovka?

Had Walter Bradenahl Sr. not fallen under the influence of Nazi propaganda and kept the family in Garfield, it's possible his son would have fought on the other side, the same as Young.

"My mother sent care packages to her but she never came back, it was not in the cards. We don't know what happened to her," Young said sadly. "I read this letter every year. I'm trying to figure out what Walter was thinking, why he made that mistake—he was totally brainwashed and looking forward to what he was going to do—and what would have become of him if he hadn't been."

Walter Young returned from the war, earned his degree at NCE and went back to work for Richardson Scale Company, where he had worked in the mail room right after high school graduation. There were petty jealousies from the other workers but Ingram Richardson, President of the company, saw something in Walter that he might not have seen himself. Young counted Richardson and Argauer as the two most important influences on his life and he rose to become President and CEO of Howe Richardson Scale Company, then branched out to purchase a small company, A.H. Emery with a few other associates. He built that into a thriving company and, in his nineties, was the oldest active CEO in his industry.

No one on the '39 team was as successful in business as he was, although he couldn't see that.

"Even today, that feeling is with me," he said shortly before he passed away. "What I accomplished . . . I should have been much more than I am."

Walter Young (left) and Len Macaluso show off the game ball from the Health Bowl at Garfield High's Homecoming Game in 2014. Courtesy New York Daily News.

But Walter was wrong.

The boy who collected gold stars for Sunday school attendance was guided by the tenets of the New Apostolic Church for the rest of his life, to where he became an unpaid minister. His church believes that individuals are responsible to God for their behavior. And his was exemplary. His funeral, in 2015, fit the man. The simple church was packed as Foley Field may have been in 1939 and when the entire congregation's voices lifted high in "How Great Thou Art," everyone could understand and sense Walter's life of devotion.

Stuart K. Hine, the English missionary who translated the hymn—in 1939 as a matter of fact—found particular meaning in the last verse: "When we reach that heavenly home, we will fully understand the greatness of God, and will bow in humble adoration, saying to Him, O Lord my God, how great thou art."

Walter Young believed that, and he lived in such a way to prepare for that moment. The minister at his funeral put it perfectly when he spoke of Young's "abundant life."

Similarly, when Young looked back at his Garfield High School teammates, he looked beyond the accomplishments on the field to where those accomplishments led.

"It was an interesting period in our history, there's no doubt about it, when a whole bunch of kids . . . Italians, Germans, Polish and so forth all got along so well. It can't happen anymore. It is a period long gone," he said.

"I've given a lot of credit for the success of the team to coach Argauer which he rightly deserves, of course, but you know at the same time, a bunch of the kids on that team . . . they were good students, they were bright and it always amazed me how successful some of these kids were when they grew up as men. I don't mean they became millionaires but they became good parents, raised good kids, had good jobs and made something of themselves."

"That is the true legacy of that team."

Of both teams, really. Of Boilermakers and Stingarees.

APPENDIX

GARFIELD HIGH SCHOOL FOOT BALL TEAM—NEW

GARFIELD HIGH
Starting Lineup

No.	Name	Position	Weight	Height
23	Walter Young	L.E.	170	5-9
43	Angelo Miranda	L.T.	191	5-9
30	John Boyle	L.G.	192	5-11
1	Peter Yura	C.	169	5-9
38	Steven Noviczky	R.G.	190	5-9
25	Alex Yoda	R.T.	200	6-0
8	Edward Hintenberger	R.E.	178	6-1
16	Benny Babula	Q.B.	190	6-1
17	John Orlovsky	L.H.B.	180	5-9
33	John Grembowitz	R.H.B.	180	5-10
6	Raymond Butts	F.B.	190	6-2

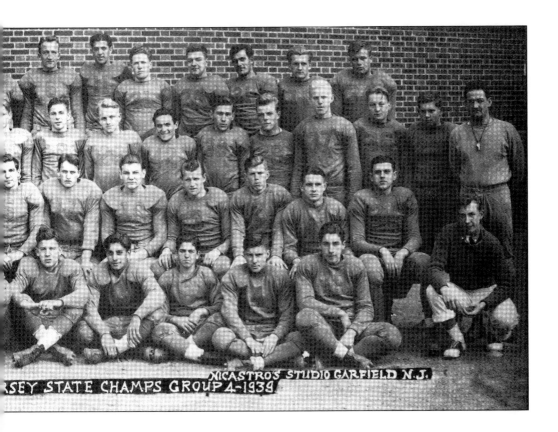

SEY STATE CHAMPS GROUP 4-1939 — NICASTRO'S STUDIO GARFIELD N.J.

MIAMI SENIOR HIGH
Starting Lineup

No.	Name	Position	Weight	Height
11	Moore, J.B.	L.E.	160	5-11
24	Fauth, Dick	L.T.	175	5-9
22	Wilson, Gilbert	L.G.	175	5-11½
16	James, Harvey	C.	174	5-9
23	Craven, Douglas	R.G.	200	6-1
25	Rollins, Levin	R.T.	162	6-4
12	Burrus, Charlie	R.E.	165	6-1
2	Koesy, Jason	Q.B.	150	5-9
10	Comfort, Harvey	L.H.B.	151	5-8
18	Mathews, Bobby	R.H.B.	141	5-8
6	Fancher, Charlie	F.B.	145	5-8

GARFIELD 1939 ROSTER

1-John Shaud
1-Pete Yura*
2-Valentine Maciag
2-Casimir Serafin
3-Lou Barcia
3-Stanley Saganiec*
4-Bill Wagnesz*
5-Julis Fick*
5-John Solarno
6-Eugene Bognar
6-Ray Butts*
7-Arthur Arts
7-Bob Schultz*
8-Ed Hintenberger*
8-Curt Echardt
9-John Gabor*
9-Sam Jenco
10-Wally Tabaka*
10-Carl Wildeman
11-Cosmo Costa
11-Bill Librera*
11-Dan Socha

12-Leonard Macaluso*
13-Edward Ochab
14-Steven Nagel
14-Bill Polcari*
15-William Orutowsky
16-Benny Babula*
17-John Orlovsky*
18-Chester Szarawski*
19-Carl Raia
20-Ted Kurgan*
21-Red Barrale*
22-Nick Geomacaco
23-Walter Young*
24-Steve Sabo*
25-Alex Yoda*
26-Otto Durheimer*
27-Herb Georgius*
28-Charles Karoly
29-Joe Tripoli*
30-Jack Boyle*
31-George Gunza
32-George Piasecki

33-John Grembowitz*
34-Joe Lucas*
35-Steve Burek*
35-William Galler
37-Andy Sudia
38-Steve Noviczky*
39-Joe Jaskot
39-Bill Orutosky*
39-John Pizzi
40-Ed Leskanic*
42-Carmine Pinto
43-Angelo Miranda*
44-Al Kazaren*
*On Miami traveling squad
HEAD COACH—Art Argauer
ASSISTANT COACH—Joe Cody
ASSISTANT COACH—John Hollis
TEAM MANAGER—Louis Kral
ASSISTANT MANAGER—Leon
   Kaminsky
ASSISTANT MANAGER—John
   Sayban

MIAMI 1939 ROSTER

0-Gene Bolick
1-Davey Eldredge
2-Jason Koesy
3-Perk Nichols
4-John Oakley
5-Billy Rentz
6-Charlie Fancher
7-Paul Louis
8-Andy Smith
9-Irwin Sibley
10-Harvey Comfort
11-J.B. Moore

12-Charlie Burrus
13-Charlie Jordan
14-Albert Anderson
15-John Williams
16-Harvey James
17-Gene Autrey
18-Bobby Mathews
19-Bucket Barnes
20-Brownis Brown
21-Bion Morgan
22-Gilbert Wilson
23-Doug Craven

24-Dick Fauth
25-Levin Rollins
26-George Rogers
27-Stanley Pyfrom
28-William Wilson
29-Henry "Charles" Washington
30-Donald Glore
31-Jay Kendrick
32-Ray Slaigh
HEAD COACH—Jesse Yarborough
ASSISTANT COACHES—Clyde
   Crabtree, John McDonald,
   Pete Tulley
TEAM MANAGER—Goldie
   Goldstein

HEALTH BOWL GAME SUMMARY
**Garfield 16, Miami 13, Orange Bowl,
December 25, 1939**
Garfield—Young, LE; Yoda, LT; Boyle, LG; Yura,
C; Noviczky, RG; Miranda, RT; Hintenberger, RE;
Babula, TB; Grembowitz, LHB; Orlovsky, RHB;
Butts, FB.
Miami—Moore, LE; Fauth, LT; G. Wilson,
LG; James, C; Craven, RG; Rollins, RT; Burrus,
RE; Koesy, TB; Comfort, LHB; Mathews, RHB;
Fancher, FB.
Score by periods
Garfield 6   0   7   3–16
Miami. 0   0   6   6–13
Scoring: (G) Babula 4 run (Babula kick failed), (G)
Grembowitz 20 run (Babula run), (M) Eldredge
2 run (Brown kick failed), (M) Eldredge 78 run
(Brown kick), Babula 22 FG.
Substitutions: (G) Wagnesz for Young, Kurgan for
Yoda, Tripoli for Miranda, Fick for Boyle, Macaluso
for Noviczky, Kazaren for Orlovsky, Librera for
Babula, Barrale for Babula. (M) Smith for Moore,
Brown for Burrus, Barnes for G. Wilson, Morgan
for Barnes, Pyfrom for Rollins, Louis for James,
Eldredge for Koesy, Nichols for Mathews, Rogers
for Fancher.
Referee: Harkness, Umpire: Cole. Head Linesman:
Wilson. Field Judge: Thompson.

HEALTH BOWL PLAY BY PLAY
**(Composite from *Star-Ledger* and
The Herald-News)**
First Quarter
Co-captains Benny Babula and Johnny Grembowitz,
of Garfield, and Captain Davey Eldredge, of Miami,
huddled with the officials for the toss of the coin.

GAME STATISTICS AS COMPILED BY THE HERALD-NEWS

Garfield		Miami
16	First Downs	13
177	Yards Gained Rushing	244
5	Yards Lost Rushing	16
10	Pass Attempts	9
6	Completed	2
0	Intercepted	4
52	Yards Gained Passing	39
224	Total Net Yards	267
5/46	Punts/Average	2/34
6	Punt Return Yardage	32
4/36	Kickoffs/Average	3/50
58	Kick Return Yardage	43
0/0	Fumbles/Lost	2/1
24	Yards Penalized	10

Individual Rushing
(M) Eldredge 23-211, Koesy 1-10, Comfort 5-26,
Mathews 2-5
(G) Babula 25-103, Grembowitz 8-60, Orlovsky
4-26, Kazaren 2-8, Young 1-6.
Individual Passing
(M) Eldredge 1-6-10-4, Comfort 1-2-29-0
(G) Babula 6-10-52-0
Individual Receiving
(M) Brown 1-29, James 1-10
(G) Butts 2-15, Young 2-12, Orlovsky 1-14,
Grembowitz 1-8

Garfield won the toss and elected to kick off to Miami. Miami elected to defend the east goal. Babula kicked to the Miamians' two. Mathews returned to the 20. Koesy swept his own left end for 10 yards, Grembowitz making a brilliant tackle to stop the elusive back. Koesy was hurt and Davey Eldredge replaced him. Eldredge electrified the crowd on the next play by whipping through left tackle for 16 yards and another first down on the Miami 46. Grembowitz intercepted Eldredge's pass on his own 46 and was nailed in his tracks.

Grembowitz and Orlovsky smashed through the center of the Miami line for a first down on the Stingarees' 43. Babula went around left end for three yards before Moore stopped him. Orlovsky gained one yard on a spinner play. Babula passed to Orlovsky for a first down on the Miami 29, Mathews forcing the Garfield back out of bounds. Babula blazed around left end for still another first down, placing the leather on the Miami 17. Babula, stumbling and stiff-arming, reached the Stingarees' nine where he was topped by Eldredge. Babula was stopped by Fancher for no gain at center. Babula, attempting to skirt left end, was smothered by half of the Florida team. Babula whipped through the right tackle for five yards and a first down on the Miami four. Babula lost a yard at the center of the line, where he was stopped by James, and the New Jersey team called timeout.

Babula roared through right tackle for a touchdown as a dozen photographers flashed bulbs in his face as he dove over the Miami line. Babula's placement was wide and the score was Garfield 6, Miami 0.

With Orlovsky holding the ball, Babula kicked off to the Miami 11. Mathews lateraled to Eldredge and he danced back to the 35, stopped by Hintenberger. Eldredge skirted left end for six. Miranda broke through and smeared Comfort for a one-yard loss. Eldredge could gain but one yard in two attempts. Eldredge punted to the New Jersey 26. Orlovsky gathered the pigskin to his chest and galloped back to his 36. On a reverse, Young picked up two yards. Babula's pass, intended for Grembowitz, was short. Babula punted beautifully to the Miami 14. Wagnesz downed the ball.

Eldredge skipped around left end for three. Eldredge, feinting as if to pass, spun around right end for five as the first quarter ended with the scored Garfield 6, Miami 0.

Second Quarter

As play resumed, Rogers plunged over center for first down on the Miami 25. Eldredge visited left tackle for five. Grembowitz halted him. The fast-stepping Miami halfback collected another first down with a brilliant 11-yard dash through left guard. He was in the clear when Fick and Grembowitz wrapped their arms around him. Wagnesz stopped Comfort for a one-yard loss but Eldredge pestered Garfield again with a six-yard excursion at right end. Comfort blazed through right guard for 17 yards, making it a first down on the Garfield 36. The entire Garfield secondary made the tackle. Garfield called time out.

Eldredge garnered three yards in two tries at left end. Grembowitz again pulled the Miamian's legs from under him. Eldredge's pass, sailing toward Brown, was blocked by Orlovsky. That is, the ball hit the Garfield player in the face. Miami was penalized five yards for excessive time out. The penalty was the first ruling by the officials.

The crowd came screaming to its feet on the next play when Comfort hurled a long, high aerial to Brown, who caught the pigskin on the Garfield nine. Brown, however, fumbled and Wagnesz recovered the leather on the Garfield nine.

Babula punted to the Miami 46 and Eldredge returned to midfield. The play was called back. Garfield was penalized to its own one-yard line. The officials ruled that the New Jersey backfield failed to come to a stop after shifting.

Babula dropped back into the end zone and booted the ball to the Miami 36. The crowd gave the 68-yard boot a reverberating roar. Eldredge returned the leather to the Garfield 38 where Babula hustled up the field to make the tackle. Mathews failed to gain at the center of the line. Eldredge fumbled and recovered. The play cost the Miamians 15 yards as Leskanic brought Eldredge down. Comfort's pass hit Smith in the face on the Garfield 14 and got away from him. Eldredge's cleats sent the ball spiraling out of bounds on the Garfield 10.

Babula danced around right end for four. The N.J. aggregation, confident and playing with the smoothness of a well-oiled machine, had more poise at this stage of the game than the Florida gridders. Garfield called time out. Babula and Orlovsky picked up five yards between them in two tries at the center of the line. Orlovsky received a resounding tackle and coach Art Argauer took him out of the encounter after suffering an injury to his collarbone. Kazaren replaced him.

Babula punted 35 yards to the Miami 46 where Young downed the kick. Eldredge's pass was intercepted by Kazaren on the Garfield 29. Smith stopped Kazaren in his tracks.. Grembowitz and Babula gained two yards at left tackle and the first half ended. The score was still Garfield 6, Miami 0.

Third Quarter

With the exception of Kazaren in the backfield and Fick at guard, Garfield's lineup appeared unchanged as the second half opened. Miami's lineup was the same which left the field at the end of the first half.

Barnes kicked off to Kazaren on Garfield's five-yard stripe and ran it back to the 17 where Brown tackled him. Babula raced around right end for 19 yards before being hauled down by Washington. Babula passed to Young, who lateraled to Kazaren. The play gained six yards. Babula dug through right guard for seven more then Benny flipped a 14-yard pass to Butts, bringing the ball to the Miami 38. On second down, Babula tried left tackle but failed to gain when Brown stopped him. Again Benny tried left tackle but Charles Washington halted him for no gain. Babula pulled the fans to their feet when a 15-yard dash around Miami's right flank, giving Garfield a first down on the Stingaree 20, where Mathews forced him out of bounds.

Garfield scored its second touchdown on the next play when Babula faked a line smash and handed the leather off to Grembowitz, who sped wide around Miami's left end to score all by himself. Babula split the middle of Miami's line for the extra point and Garfield led, 13-0.

Librera's kickoff slithered out of bounds on the Miami 49 and he replaced Babula in the Garfield lineup. Eldredge scampered four yards around right end then Comfort added four at right guard. Eldredge whipped 17 yards around left end before Grembowitz pulled him to earth. The play gave Miami a first down on the Garfield 26. Eldredge whipped a pass down the left side and Harvey James grabbed it after a Boilermaker deflected it into the air.

It was first and 10 on Garfield's 16. Eldredge went over right guard for two yards. Eldredge slipped through the same spot for five more and once again it was Grembowitz who made the tackle. Eldredge skidded off right end for four yards and a first down on the Garfield five.

Eldredge scooted off left guard to the Boilermaker two-yard marker. Tripoli made the tackle. Eldredge started off right tackle, cut back in slightly through guard to tally. Barnes replaced Wilson but instead of kicking, Red Mathews tried to burrow into the Garfield first defense but was stopped short of the added point and Garfield still led, 13-6.

Barnes kicked off to the Garfield five and Babula brought the apple back to the 25. Grembowitz picked up two yards at left guard then the Boilermakers were penalized 15 yards for unnecessary roughness, shoving the ball back to the 14. Babula tried to skirt left end but half the Miami line threw him for a three-yard loss. Babula's punt wobbled 27 yards to the Garfield 38 where Grembowitz stopped Comfort in his tracks. Garfield called time out.

Eldredge scampered 11 yards around right end behind good blocking for a first down on the Garfield 26. Kazaren made the tackle. Eldredge flipped a short pass over the middle and Babula short-circuited it, returning to the N.J. 22 as the quarter ended. Babula had shortly before the play replaced Librera. The return was seven yards.

Fourth Quarter

When play resumed, Kazaren crashed through center for three yards and on the next play Babula passed eight yards to Grembowitz, giving Garfield a first down on the Garfield 33. Babula tried another aerial but Gilbert Wilson, Miami guard, intercepted it and behind good blocking went 40 yards for a touchdown. The play was nullified, however, when an alert official spotted a Miami lineman offside and the Stingarees were penalized five yards. It was first and eight for the Garfield lads on their own 37.

Babula faiiled to gain on an end skirt and Kazaren plunged through center for three yards and it was third and one. Hampered by the heat, Garfield again called time out. Babula made it a first down with a two-yard gain at left guard. He faded swiftly and skied a long pass down the left side lines but Wagnesz could not quite make the catch. Grembowitz went over left tackle for two three-footers. Babula's pass for Young was knocked down by James. Benny sailed a beautiful 54-yard punt over the Miami goal. Officials brought it back to the 20 and it was first and 10 Miami.

Eldredge jumped over tackle for two yards, Butts making the stop. With four mates running in front of him, Eldredge skipped around left end, eluded two Garfield tacklers, had another pair of Boilermakers cut down by the interference and then pulled into the clear as the procession reached the 50-yard line. With no one between him and the goal, L'il David was a cinch. With every stride he pulled away from the gallant Garfield pursuers to score.

The run was good for 77 yards.

Barnes sailed the placement kick through the uprights and with minutes left to play the score read: Garfield 13, Miami 13.

Barnes kicked off to the Boilermakers' 13 and Babula sprinted back 31 yards to the Garfield 46. Babula got three at left tackle then found three at right tackle. Babula passed to Young who lateraled to Kazaren to give Garfield six yards and a first down on the Miami 42. Benny passes one yard to Butts. On the same reverse play that scored Garfield's second touchdown, Grembowitz raced 27 yards around left end before being knocked out of bounds on the Miami 15 by Comfort.

On second down, Babula went around right end for two yards. Babula's pass for Wagnesz across the goal line was incomplete. Babula hit left tackle for only two yards, bringing the ball to the Miami 10. Then, on fourth down, Babula dropped back and booted a perfect field goal through the posts and New Jersey led, 16-13. Benny kicked from the 22.

Only a few minutes remained and Eldredge returnd to Miami's lineup. Babula kicked out of bounds on the Miami 17 and the ball came out to the 35.

Eldredge failed to gain at left tackle. Eldredge's intended pass for Brown was knocked down by Kazaren. On a fake pass, Eldredge went six yards to the 41. One minute remained in the game. Comfort slashed around left end for a first down on the Garfield 49.

Eldredge's pass was intercepted by Kazaren and he returned to the 50. Garfield called time out. The fans began filing out of the gray steel stands. Babula carried two Stingaree tacklers 12 yards for a first down on the Boilermakers' 38. Babula's line plunge added one. Running slow and easy, Babula was stopped as the game ended.

Final score: Garfield 16, Miami 13.

GARFIELD HIGH SCHOOL 1939 GAME SUMMARIES

Garfield 33, Dickinson 0, Passaic Schools Stadium, September 30

Dickinson—Urana, LE; Michelitte, LT, Esposito, LG; Blum, C; Whelan, RG; Vogt, RT; Morschauser, RE; Milosevic, TB; Johnson, LHB; Zurawecki, RHB; Sarenson, FB.

Garfield—Young, LE; Miranda, LT; Boyle, LG; Yura, C; Grembowitz, RG; Tripoli, RT; Wagnesz, RE; Babula, TB; Tabaka, LHB; Orlovsky, RHB, Butts, FB.

Substitutions: (G) Librera, Schultz.

Score by periods

Dickinson 0   0   0   0–0
Garfield 7   6   7   13–33

Touchdowns: (G) Babula 2, Schultz, Orlovski, Tabaka. Points after touchdown: (G) Young 2, Kurgan (placements).

Referee: Kirkland. Umpire: Dupes. Head linesman: Abbott.

Garfield 14, Irvington 12, Irvington, Morrell Field, October 7

Garfield—Young, LE; Tripoli, LT; Boyle, LG; Yura, C; Grembowitz, RG; Miranda, RT; Wagnesz, RE; Babula, TB; Tabaka, LHB; Orlovsky, RHB, Butts, FB.

Irvington—Hedden, LE; Arnold, LT; Cherney, LG; Rinaldi, C; Addonizio, RG; Packin, RE; Hoffman, RE; Hornish, TB; Saymanski, LHB; Kulikowski, RHB; Reckenwald, FB.

Substitutions: (G) Yoda, Macaluso, Leskanic, Hintenberger, Kurgan, Burek, Schultz, Fick. (I) Hudak, Wassel, Prybylowski, Nickolopoulos, Smith. Sparks.

Score by periods

Garfield 7   0   0   7–14
Irvington 6   6   0   0–12

Touchdowns: (G) Babula 2, Prybylowski, Kulikowski. Points after touchdown: (G) Orlovsky 2 (placements).

Referee: Bonnel. Umpire: Sparks. Head linesman: Spence.

Garfield 12, Passaic 6, Passaic Schools Stadium, October 14

Passaic—Kuzma, LE; Fadil, LT; Anlonovsky, LG; Rybak, C; Murray Friend, RG; Gawalis, RT, Hook, RE; Corrubia, TB; Ladyczka, LHB; Henry, RHB; Zabawa, FB.

Garfield—Young, LE; Tripoli, LT; Boyle, LG; Yura, C; Grembowitz, RG; Miranda, RT; Wagnesz, RE; Babula, TB; Tabaka, LHB; Orlovsky, RHB, Kazaren, FB.

Substitutions: (G) Hintenberger, Kurgan, Yoda, Lucas, Macaluso, Fick, Leskanic, Butts. (P) Christie, Schwartz, Baker, Koselski, McCarthy, Milt Friend, Negrycz, Bednarz, Sloma.

Score by periods

Passaic 0   6   0   0–6
Garfield 6   0   0   6–12

Touchdowns: (G) Babula 2, (P) Zabawa.

Referee: Steinhilber. Umpire: Horn. Head linesman: Thompson.

Garfield 14, East Rutherford 6, Riggin Field, October 21

Garfield—Hintenberger, LE; Miranda, LT; Boyle, LG; Yura, C; Grembowitz, RG; Yoda, RT; Leskanic, RE; Librera, TB; Tabaka, LHB; Orlovsky, RHB, Kazaren, FB.

East Rutherford—Weaver, LE; Kutyniak LT; Bode, LG; Ormsby, C; Belini, RG; Sasse, RT; Sesselman, RE; Subda, TB; Sondey LHB; Dabek, RHB; Mastroianni, FB.

Score by periods

Garfield 0   7   7   0–14
East Rutherford 6   0   0   0–6

Touchdowns: (ER) Subda. (G) Tabaka, Young. Points after touchdown: (G) Young (placement), Babula (rush)

Substitutions: (G) Babula, Young, Wagnesz, Fick, Barrale, Tripoli, Noviczky, Durheimer. (ER) Markowsky, Esposito, Lampert, Wisneski.

Referee: Seigenfuse. Umpire: Springer, Head linesman: Claxton.

Garfield 26, Thomas Jefferson 0, Williams Field, October 28

Garfield—Young, LE; Miranda, LT; Boyle, LG; Yura, C; Noviczky, RG; Yoda, RT; Wagnesz, RE; Babula, TB; Grembowitz, LHB; Tabaka, RHB, Butts, FB.

Thomas Jefferson—Miller, LE; Halleck, LT; Kania, LG; Czuzak, C; Karafel, RG; Burnelsko, RT; Sadowski, RE; Van Arsdale, TB; Gervasel, LHB; Delaney, RHB; Savage, FB.

Score by periods

Garfield 0   7   13   6–26
Thomas Jefferson 0   0   0   0–0

Touchdowns: (G) Babula 2, Tabaka, Barrale. Points after touchdown: (G) Babula 2 (placements).

Substitutions: (G) Hintenberger, Kurgan, Macaluso, Lucas, Fick, Tripoli, Leskanic, Barrale, Librera, Szarawski, Kazaren, Mikulik, Schultz, Polcari, Thomas. (TJ) Peck, Wazilewski, Queen, Kindervatter, Scutro, Fletcher.

Referee: Steinhilber. Umpire: Fish. Head Linesman: Hebel.

Garfield 18, Bloomfield 0, Foley Field, November 4

Garfield—Young, LE; Miranda, LT; Boyle, LG; Yura, C; Noviczky, RG; Yoda, RT; Wagnesz, RE; Babula, TB; Tabaka, LHB; Grembowitz, RHB; Butts, FB.

Bloomfield—Landrum, LE; Johnson, LT; Lobell, LG; Greenip, C; Kochal, RG; Stevens, RT; DeLuca, RE; Kerr, TB; McGowan, LHB; Vesterman, RHB; Adams, FB.

Score by periods

Garfield 0   6   6   6–18
Bloomfield 0   0   0   0–0

Touchdowns: (G) Babula 2, Tabaka.

Substitutions: (G) Kurgan, Macaluso, Lucas, Fick, Tripoli,

Hintenberger, Leskanic, Librera, Szarawski, Kazaren, Schultz. (B) Johnson, H. Pindar, Robinson, Cosgrove, Shipley, Markowitz, Morton, Marfuggi, Cotton, Zahnle. Referee: Hyens. Umpire: Wittpenn. Head Linesman: Bonnell.

Garfield 13, Asbury Park 7, Asbury Park HS Stadium, November 11

Garfield—Young, LE; Miranda, LT; Boyle, LG; Yura, C; Noviczky, RG; Yoda, RT; Hintenberger, RE; Babula, TB; Tabaka, LHB; Grembowitz, RHB; Butts, FB.

Asbury Park—Layton, LE; O. Manger, LT; Sutphin, LG; Reichey, C; M Manger, RG; Sagui, RT; Lankenau, RE; Dugan, TB; Malta, LHB; Netcher, RHB; Falco, FB.

Score by periods

Garfield 0   0   0   13–13
Asbury Park 7   0   0   0–7

Touchdowns: (G) Grembowitz, Babula. (AP) Netcher. Points after touchdown: (G) Babula (rush), (AP) Falco (rush).

Substitutions: (G) Fick, Macaluso, Tripoli, Leskanic. (AP) Wight, Wills, Irons, Cascella, Martorella, Savoth, Palumbo.

Referee: Thompson. Umpire: Steinhilber. Head linesman: Hebel.

Garfield 48, Eastside 6, Passaic Schools Stadium, November 18

Eastside—Doby, LE; Stampone, LT; Ottavia, LG; Roughgarden, C; Contini, RG; Sorrantino, RT; Fournier, RE; Vaslos, TB; Smith, LHB; Kachadurian, RHB; Marone, FB.

Garfield—Young, LE; Miranda, LT; Boyle, LG; Yura, C; Noviczky, RG; Yoda, RT; Hintenberger, RE; Babula, TB; Tabaka, LHB; Grembowitz, RHB; Butts, FB.

Score by periods

Eastside 0   0   6   0–6
Garfield 14   0   7   27–48

Touchdowns: (E) Cleeland. (G) Babula 4, Leskanic, Hintenberger, Kazaren. Points after touchdown: (G) Babula 4 (placements). Orlovsky 2 (placements).

Substitutions: (E) Chiapelli, Suhl, Jaffee, Landi, Runz, Schneider, Fusilli, Siegal, Herring, Calvano, Peterson, Cleeland, Ordini, Arbus, Cubby, Breslin. (G) Wagnesz, Leskanic, Sudia, Saganiec, Tripoli, Kurgan, Sabo, Fick, Macaluso, Gabor, Jaskot, Luca, Serafin, Librera, Orlovsky, Kazaren, Szarawski, Schultz, Orutowsky, Polcari, Raia, Burek, Mikulik.

Referee: Schanz. Umpire: Claxton. Head Linesman: Bunn.

Garfield 21, Clifton 6, Passaic Schools Stadium, November 25

Clifton—Anderson, LE; H. Scussel, LT; Pedranti, LG; Porter, C; Peliner, RG; E. Scussel, RT; Roche, RE; Demchak, TB; Perez, LHB; Lennon, RHB; Sanicki, FB.

Garfield—Young, LE; Miranda, LT; Boyle, LG; Yura, C;

Noviczky, RG; Yoda, RT; Hintenberger, RE; Babula, TB; Tabaka, LHB; Grembowitz, RHB; Butts, FB.

Score by periods

Clifton 0   0   0   6–6
Garfield 7   7   7   0–21

Touchdowns: (C) Sanicki. (G) Babula 3. Points after touchdown: (G) Babula (placement and rush), Hintenberger (pass from Tabaka).

Substitutions: (C) Mack, Dunkersloot, Watson, Pellack, Stewart, Thoms, Zanoni, Leach, J. Pavlik. (G) Wagnesz, Leskanic, Tripoli, Kurgan, Fick, Macaluso, Lucas, Librera, Schultz, Orlovsky, Kazaren, Szarawski.

Referee: Spence. Umpire: Maroney. Head Linesman: Dupes. Field Judge: Bonnell.

MIAMI HIGH SCHOOL 1939 GAME SUMMARIES

Miami 7, Robert E. Lee 0, Municipal Stadium, October 6

Miami—Smith, LE; Craven, LT; Barnes, LG; Rollins, C; G. Wilson, RG; Kendrick, RT; Burrus, RE; Eldredge, TB; Mathews, LHB; Comfort, RHB; Rogers, FB.

Lee—Hoskinson, LE; Silverberg, LT; McRae, LG; Willingham, C; W. Raborn, RG; Platt, RT; Weaver, RE; A. Faulkner TB; Partin, LHB; J. Faulkner, RHB; George, FB.

Score by periods

Miami 0   0   7   0–7
Robert E. Lee 0   0   0   0–0

Touchdowns: (M) Burrus. Points after touchdowns: (M) Barnes (placement).

Substitutions: (M) Moore, Koesy, Nichols, Oakley. (L) Shubert, Jones, Leslie, Katz.

Referee: Finnefrock. Umpire: Barfield. Head linesman: Rahaim. Field Judge: Smith.

Miami 32, Knoxville 0, Orange Bowl, October 13

Knoxville—Lane, LE; Ledford, LT; Schriver, LG; Bailey, C; Crisp, RG; King, RT; Westbrook, RE; Ousley, TB; Hatfield, LHB; White, RHB; Phillips, FB.

Miami—Smith, LE; Fauth, LT; Barnes, LG; Rollins, C; Kendrick, RG; Craven, RT; Burrus, RE; Eldredge, TB; Koesy, LHB; Mathews, RHB; Rogers, FB.

Score by periods

Knoxville 0   0   0   0–0
Miami 14   6   6   6–32

Touchdowns: (M) Eldredge 2, Nichols, Comfort, Koesy. Points after touchdown: Barnes 2 (placements).

Substitutions: (K) Weese, Robinson, Freels, Hodges, Clarkm Hickman, Evans, Vann, Traumann. (M) Moore, Brown, Anderson, Perkins, G. Wilson, Glore, Williams, Fisher, Morgan, Pyfrom, Louis, Nichols, Oakley, Rentz. Comfort.

Referee: Harkness. Umpire: Cole. Head Linesman: Wilson. Field Judge: Thompson.

Miami 26, Savannah 6, Orange Bowl, October 20

Savannah—Hathaway, LE; Tabakian, LT; Durant, LG; R. Wood, C; Holec, RG; Cerellas, RT; Cosnahan, RE; McLauren, TB; Knudson, LHB; Hardin, RHB; Johnson, FB.

Miami—Smith, LE; Fauth, LT; Barnes, LG; Rollins, C; Kendrick, RG; Craven, RT; Moore, RE; Koesy, TB; Mathews, LHB; Comfort, RHB; Nichols, FB.

Score by periods

Savannah 0   0   0   6–6
Miami. 6   0   14   6–26

Touchdowns: (S) Griner. (M) Koesy, Comfort, Burrus, Bolick. Points after touchdowns: Koesy, Barnes (placements).

Substitutions; (S) Blake, Griner, Wade, Oliver. Shore, Holec, T. Wood, Way, Heimken, Connor. (M) Burris, Brown, Anderson, Washington, Hill, Perkins, Fisher, G. Wilson, Louis, Bolick, Oakley, Rentz, Autry, Rogers.
Refree; Harkness. Umpire: Spain. Head Linesman: Goldstein. Field Judge: Thompson.

Miami 30, Andrew Jackson (Jacksonville) 7, Municipal Stadium, October 28

Miami—Moore, LE; Fauth, LT; Barnes, LG; Rollins, C; Kendrick, RG; Craven, RT; Burrus, RE; Koesy, TB; Comfort, LHB; Rogers, RHB; Mathews, FB.

Jackson—Glenn, LE; Padgett, LT; Bishop, LG; Crosby, C; Heyn, RG; Lewis, RT; Bright, RE; Kenyon, TB; Ramsey, LHB; Cook, RHB; Alsobrook, FB.

Score by periods

Miami. 0   12   6   12–30
Jackson 0   7   0   0–7

Touchdowns: (M) Eldredge 2, Koesy 2, Bolick, Jackson. (J)Love. Point after touchdown: Bishop (placement).

Substitutions: (M) Fisher, Bolick, Nichols, Smith, Eldredge, Autrey, Washington, Brown, G. Wilson, Glore, Louis, Anderson, Pyfrom, Morgan, Rentz, Sibley, Osceola. (J) Hoffman, Bowers, Love, Zell, Williamson, Mims, Craig, Horne.
Referee: Finnefrock. Umpire: Burkhalter. Head Linesman: Lynch. Field judge: Wood.

Miami 19, Lanier 0, Orange Bowl. November 11.

Lanier—King, LE; Bryant, LT; Knight, LG; West, C; D. Johnson, RG; Thomas, RT; Corn, RE; Volk, TB; W. Johnson, LHB; Reynolds, RHB; Dunham, FB.

Miami—Moore, LE; Fauth, LT; G. Wilson, LG; Rollins, C; Kendrick, RG; Craven, RT; Burrus, RE; Eldredge, TB; Mathews, LHB; Comfort, RHB; Fancher, FB.

Score by periods

Lanier 0   0   0   0–0
Miami. 0   6   7   6–19

Touchdowns: (M) Koesy, Burrus, Eldredge. Points after touchdown: (M) Rogers (run).

Substitutions: (L) Suddath, Morris, Mueket, Connally, Cousins, Stewart, Banks, Horne, Harvey, George, Gilreath. (M) Jordan, Brown, Anderson, W. Wilson, Washington, Glore, Williams, Barnes, Morgan, Pyfrom, Saigh, Louis, Hill, Bolick, Koesy, Nichols, Oakley, Rentz, Sibley, James, Rogers.
Referee: Harkness. Umpire: Hunt. Head linesman: Goldstein. Field Judge: Seiler.

Miami 27, Jackson (Mississippi) 0, Orange Bowl, November 17

Jackson—McCaskill, LE; Cotten, LT; Dorman, LG; Gober, C; Adams, RG; Gates, RT; Moore, RE; Harper, TB; Downie, LHB; Gray, RHB; Paquette, FB.

Miami—Moore, LE; Washington, LT; G. Wilson, LG; Rollins, C; Kendrick, RG; Craven, RT; Burrus, RE; Koesy, TB; Mathews, LHB; Comfort, RHB; Nichols, FB.

Score by periods

Jackson 0   0   0   0–0
Miami. 7   6   7   7–27

Touchdowns: (M) Comfort, Eldredge 2, James. Points after touchdown: Koesy (placement), Barnes (placement), Sibley (run).

Substitutions: (J) Dockery, Shores, Post, Majors, Chastang, Aldridge, Loper, Chambers, Simmons, Black, Borchardt, Caldwell. (M) Smith, Jorda, Brown, Anderson, Fauth, W. Wilson, Glore, Williams, Morgan, Pyfrom, Saigh, Louis, Bolick, Eldredge, Oaklay, Rentz, Fancher, Sibley, James, Autrey.
Referee: Seiler. Umpire: Goldstein. Head Linesman: Thompson. Field Judge: Spain.

Miami 27, Spartanburg 0, Orange Bowl, November 24

Spartanburg—Earnhardt, LE; Debbins, LT; Gibbs, LG; Daniels, C; Cantrell, RG; Stone, RT; Smith, RE; Atwell, TB; McMillan, LHB; Tindall, RHB; Cannady, FB.

Miami—Moore, LE; Washington, LT; Morgan, LG; Rollins, C; Kendrick, RG; Craven, RT; Fauth, RE; Koesy, TB; Comfort, LHB; James, RHB; Rogers, FB.

Score by periods

Spartanburg. 0   0   0   0–0
Miami. 6   14   7   0–27

Touchdowns: (M) Eldredge 2, Koesy, Rentz. Points after touchdown: Koesy (placement).

Substitutions: (S) Wertz, C.K. Smith, Cook, Justice. (M) A. Smith, Jordan, Burrus, Brown, W. Wilson, Glore, Williams, Barnes, Morgan, G. Wilson, Pyfrom, Saigh, Bolick, Eldredge, Nichols, Oakley, Rentz, Fancher, Sibley, Autrey.
Referee: Wilson. Umpire: Cole. Head Linesman: Davis. Field Judge: Worley.

Miami 13, Edison 0, Orange Bowl, December 1

Edison—Kols, LE; O'Neil, LT; Adams, LG; Wiggins, C; Smith, RG; Netsch, RT; Gardiner, RE; Hausenbauer, TB; McCollum, LHB; Knuck, RHB; Depew, FB.

Miami—Moore, LE; Fauth, LT; G. Wilson, LG; Rollins, C; Kendrick, RG; Craven, RT; Burrus, RE; Koesy, TB; Mathews, LHB; Comfort, RHB; Fancher, FB.

Score by periods

Edison 0   0   0   0–0

Miami 0   7   0   6–13

Touchdowns: (M) Eldredge 2. Points after touchdowns: (M) Barnes (placement).

Substitutions: (E) Shuck, Powell, Snowden, Weekley, O'Noff, D. Collins, Schmidt, Pearson, Gracy, Down, Downs, Mathis, Waters. (M) Smith, Jordan, Brown, Anderson, W. Wilson, Washington, Glore, Williams, Barnes, Pyfrom, Louis, Bolick, Eldredge, Nichols, Rents, Sibley, James, Autrey, Rogers.

Referee: Harkness. Umpire: Cole. Head Linesman: Brown. Field Judge: Wilson.

Miami 26, Boys 0, Orange Bowl, December 7

Boys—J. Brown, LE; Eaves, LT; Cox, LG; Anrel, C; Jordan, RG; Alexander, RT; Conger, RE; L. Smith, TB; R. Kenerly, LHB; Jarvis, RHB; Berman, FB.

Miami—Moore, LE; Fauth, LT; G. Wilson, LG; Rollins, C; Kendrick, RG; Craven, RT; Burrus, RE; Koesy, TB; Mathews, LHB; Comfort, RHB; Fancher, FB.

Score by periods

Boys 0   0   0   0–0

Miami 0   12   7   7–26

Touchdowns: (M) Eldredge 3, Comfort. Points after touchdown: Rogers (run), Matthews (run)

Substitutions: (B) McKinney, Furchgott, Richards, N. Kenerly, Almand, DeFreese, Kenimer, Finchia, Thompson, Bailey. (M) Brown, Smith, Jordan, Washington, Anderson, W. Wilson, Glore, Barnes, Morgan, Williams, Pyfrom, Saigh, Louis, Eldredge, Bolick, Rogers, James, Nichols, Rentz, Sibley, Autrey.

Refree: Bradley. Umpire: Harkness. Head Linesman: Wilson. Field judge: Slate.

MIAMI HIGH SCHOOL CHRISTMAS RECORD (6-6-1)

1929 Miami 7, Salem, Mass. 6

1930 Miami 18, Stivers, Dayton, O. 0

1931 Harrison, Chicago, Il. 18, Miami 7

1932 Waite, Toledo, O. 13, Miami 7

1933 Miami 19, Central, Syracuse, N.Y. 7

1934 Scott, North Braddock, Pa. 26, Miami 14

1935 Elmira, N.Y. 13, Miami 0

1936 New Britain, Ct. 32, Miami 13

1937 Miami 6, Oak Park, Il. 6

1938 Miami 19, McKeesport, Pa. 13

1939 Garfield, N.J. 16, Miami 13

1940 Miami 19, Fenger, Chicago, Il. 0

1941 Miami 26, Baltimore City College, Md. 0

1939 COLLITON RANKINGS TOP 25

Garfield 649	Woodbridge 484
East Orange 628	New Brunswick 480
Nutley 618	Red Bank 460
Newark West Side 591	Orange 458
Vineland 582	Paterson Eastside 451
Passaic 570	Snyder 448
Columbia 560	Paterson Central 443
Irvington 542	Collingswood 440
Kearny 520	Trenton Central 435
Linden 510	Woodrow Wilson 415
Hillside 509	Ridgefield Park 415
Union 493	Memorial, West New York, 412
South River 490	

1939 WORLD TELEGRAM ALL STARS
The team that never made it to Miami

FIRST TEAM

ENDS
Bob Duffey, East Orange, N.J., Warren Slavin, Erasmus Hall, N.Y.

TACKLES
Henry Majlinger, Stuyvesant., N.Y. and Irv Kintisch, New Utrecht, N.Y.

GUARDS
Kenny Franklin, Valley Stream, N.Y and Bill

Kupper, Lawrence, N.Y.

CENTER
Marty Martinson, Curtis, N.Y.

QUARTERBACK
John Kamerer, Seward Park, N.Y.

HALFBACKS
Benny Babula, Garfield, N.J. and Ernie Colaneri, Harrison, N.Y.

FULLBACK
Frank Cardinale, Nutley, N.J.

SECOND TEAM

ENDS
Herb Schwartje, Dumont, N.J. and Harold Enstice, Flushing, N.Y.

TACKLES
Charlie Martus, New Rochelle, N.Y. and Melvin Downey, Boys, N.Y.

GUARDS
George Kurs, Tilden, N.Y. and John Grembowitz, Garfield, N.J.

CENTER
Seymour Cohen, Seward Park, N.Y.

BACKS
Bob Forfar, Kearny, N.J., Bill Wright, Freeport, N.Y., Vinnie Pesature, DeWitt Clinton, N.Y. and Mort Rauff, Erasmus Hall, N.Y.

1939 ALL STAR TEAMS
NEW JERSEY ALL STATE
NEW JERSEY SCHOLASTIC SPORTS WRITES ASSOCIATION
FIRST TEAM

ENDS
Bob Duffey, East Orange; **John Grembowitz, Garfield**

TACKLES
Al Rotella, Paterson Central; Joe Gawalis, Passaic

GUARDS
Carmen Scarpa, Orange; Carl Harr, Columbia

CENTER
Tex Warrington, Bordentown Military Academy

BACKS
Benny Babula, Garfield, Joe Stanowicz, Hackettstown; Joe Chielli, Vineland; Frank Cardinale, Nutley

SECOND TEAM

ENDS
Hal Thompson, Manasquan; Matt Bolger, St. Benedict's

TACKLES
Ted Otlowski, Perth Amboy; Buddy Trucano, Vinland

GUARDS
William Cherney, Irvington; Bill Nichols, Atlantic City

CENTER
Jack Ehrich, Newark West Side

BACKS
Mungo Ladyczka, Passaic; Bob Forfar, Kearny; Wasilek, Woodbridge; Baroni, Blair Academy

NEWARK EVENING NEWS (HIGH SCHOOLS ONLY)
FIRST TEAM

ENDS
Bob Duffey, East Orange; Herb Schwartje, Dumont

TACKLES
Al Rotella, Paterson Central; Joe Gawalis, Passaic

GUARDS
John Grembowitz, Garfield; Bill Nichols, Atlantic City

CENTER
Jack Ehrich, Newark West Side

BACKS
Joe Chielli, Vineland; **Benny Babula, Garfield**; Oscar Givens, Linden; Joe Stanowicz, Hackettstown

SECOND TEAM

ENDS
Walter Young, Garfield; Charley Darcy, Atlantic City

TACKLES
Buddy Trucano, Vineland; Lawrence Stevens, Bloomfield

GUARDS
Potter, Kearny; Carmen Scarpa, Orange

CENTER
Bill Leone, Camden

BACKS
Mungo Ladyczka, Passaic; Bob Forfar, Kearny; Tony Tortoretti, Newark West Side; Frank Cardinale, Nutley

NEWARK SUNDAY CALL
FIRST TEAM

ENDS
Bob Duffey, East Orange; Matt Bolger, St. Benedict's

TACKLES
Melvin Van Sant, Glen Ridge; Al Rotella, Paterson Central

GUARDS
William Cherney, Irvington; Carmen Scarpa, Orange

CENTER
Tex Warrington, Bordentown Military Academy

BACKS
Benny Babula, Garfield; Joe Stanowicz, Hackettstown; Joe Chielli, Vineland; Frank Cardinale, Nutley

SECOND TEAM

ENDS
Carl Harr Columbia; Ralph Files, East Orange

TACKLES
Ted Otlowski, Perth Amboy; Albert Loux, Peddie

GUARDS
John Grembowitz, Garfield; Beef McGoldrick, Pompton Lakes

CENTER
Jack Ehrich, Newark West Side

BACKS
George Wasilek, Woodbridge; Bob Burns, Seton Hall Prep; Mungo Ladyczka, Passaic; Bob Forfar, Kearny

NEWARK STAR-LEDGER
FIRST TEAM
ENDS
Bob Duffey, East Orange; Andy Dutch, Admiral Farragut
TACKLES
Pinder, Seton Hall Prep; Al Rotella, Paterson Central
GUARDS
Carmen Scarpa, Orange; Joe Walsh, Hun School
CENTER
Tex Warrington, Bordentown Military Academy
BACKS
Joe Chielli, Vineland; **Benny Babula, Garfield**; Benny Reiges, Bordentown Military Academy, Hughes, Seton Hall Prep
SECOND TEAM
ENDS
Matt Bolger, St. Benedict's; Charley Darcy, Atlantic City
TACKLES
Vance, Collingswood; Stawicki, Pennington
GUARDS
Denny Brown, Blair Academy; Bill Marion, Lawrenceville Prep
CENTER
Jack Ehrich, Newark West Side
BACKS
Jack Dobbins, Blair Academy; Felix Cantore, St. Peter's (New Brunswick); Oscar Givens, Linden; Joe Stanowicz, Hackettstown

TRENTON TIMES (HIGH SCHOOLS ONLY)
ENDS
Bob Duffey, East Orange; **Walter Young, Garfield**
TACKLES
Buddy Trucano, Vineland; Robert Yarnell, Rutherford;
GUARDS
Ralph Hackett, Trenton; **John Grembowitz, Garfield**
CENTER
Jack Ehrich, Newark West Side
BACKS
Benny Babula, Garfield; Joe Stanowicz, Joe Chielli, Vineland; Ray Dooney, Atlantic City; Frank Cardinale, Nutley
SECOND TEAM
ENDS
Norman Selby, Woodrow Wilson (Camden); Dick Harris, Vineland
TACKLES
Al Rotella, Paterson Central, Lawrence Stevens, Bloomfield
GUARDS
William Cherney, Irvington; Bill Nichols, Atlantic City
CENTER
Russell Best, Dover
BACKS
Joe Stanowicz, Hackettstown; Bo Robinson, Trenton; Bob Forfar, Kearny; Steve Makuka, Burlington

JERSEY JOURNAL
FIRST TEAM
ENDS
Bob Duffey, East Orange; Matt Bolger, St. Benedict's
TACKLES
Jim Kerley, Camden Catholic; Al Rotella, Paterson Central

GUARDS
Norm Hoff, Haddon Heights; Ernie Rosatti, Pennington,
CENTER
Jack Ehrich, Newark West Side
BACKS
Jack Dobbins, Blair Academy; **Benny Babula, Garfield**; Joe Chielli, Vinland; Benny Reiges, Bordentown Military Academy
SECOND TEAM
ENDS
Johnny Weiss, Snyder; Ray Holloway, Haddonfield
TACKLES
Albert Loux, Peddie; Joe Stanik, South River
GUARDS
John Grembowitz, Garfield; Pete Calcagno, St. Benedict's
CENTER
Tim Regan, St. Michael's
BACKS
Ken McKinley, Morristown School; Bob Burns, Seton Hall Prep; Don Watson, Ridgefield Park; Frank Cardinale, Nutley.

ALL BERGEN COUNTY
BERGEN RECORD
FIRST TEAM
ENDS
Herb Schwartje, Dumont; **Walter Young, Garfield**
TACKLES
Vince Korsak, Ridgefield Park; Leo Cahill, Leonia
GUARDS
John Grembowitz, Garfield; Ed Cohen, Ridgefield Park
CENTER
Bob Dorsett, Leonia
BACKS
Benny Babula, Garfield; Don Watson, Ridgefield Park; Unkie Campbell, Teaneck; Dick Carmelich, Dumont

SECOND TEAM
ENDS
Paul Melville, Ramsey; Henry Gramkow, Ridgefield Park
TACKLES
Charlie Pillon, Teaneck; Clarence Hough, Lyndhurst
GUARDS
George Chudik, Englewood; Howie Rockfort, St. Cecilia
CENTER
Ray Frichette, Ridgefield Park
BACKS
Tony Matsrionni, East Rutherford; Alex Evaskovich, Dumont; Dickie Owen, Leonia; **Wally Tabaka, Garfield**

HERALD-NEWS
FIRST TEAM
ENDS
Walter Young, Garfield; Herb Schwartje, Dumont
TACKLES
Leo Cahill, Leonia; Carmine Santoianni, Rutherford
GUARDS
Ed Cohen, Ridgefield Park; **John Grembowitz, Garfield**
CENTER
Bob Dorsett, Leonia
BACKS
Benny Babula, Garfield; Wally Tabaka, Garfield; Tony Matsrionni, East Rutherford; Don Watson, Ridgefield Park
SECOND TEAM
ENDS
Henry Gramkow, Ridgefield Park; Richard Beck, Lyndhurst
TACKLES
Clarence Hough, Lyndhurst; Steve Wagner, Lodi

GUARDS
Pete Signa, Rutherford;
George Chudik,
Englewood
CENTER
Pete Yura, Garfield
BACKS
Unkie Campbell, Teaneck;
Dick Carmelich, Dumont;
Ray Butts, Garfield; E.
Sullivan, Lyndhurst.

BERGEN SUNDAY STAR
FIRST TEAM
ENDS
Charlie Dunlap, Teaneck,
Henry Gramkow,
Ridgefield Park
TACKLES
**Angelo Miranda,
Garfield;** Rob Hufnagle,
Leonia
GUARDS
**John Grembowitz,
Garfield;** Longton,
Teaneck
CENTER
Ray Frichette, Ridgefield
Park
BACKS
Unkie Campbell, Teaneck;
Les Fletcher, Leonia;
Don Watson, Ridgefield
Park; **Benny Babula,
Garfield**
SECOND TEAM
ENDS
Herb Schwartje, Dumont;
Hasbrouck, Rutherford
TACKLES
Vince Korsak, Ridgefield
Park; Swede Maki,
Ramsey
GUARDS
Bob Dorsett, Leonia;
Livingston, Dumont
CENTER
Fabris, Hasbrouck
Heights
BACKS
Jack Steinert, Hackensack;
Ed Etaskovich, Dumont;
Dickie Owen, Leonia; Ed
Sullivan, Lyndhurst

ALL SOUTHERN
Alabama: Jenkins,
Birmingham; McCoy,
Birmingham; Godfrey, Pell
City; Mims, Sylacauga.
Arkansas: Robert Hutson,
Pine Bluff; Ray Hutson,
Pine Bluff; Hughes,
Little Rock; Warrington,
Blutheville
Georgia: Paschal, High
Tech; Dunham, Lanier;
Ryckeley, Marist;
Langford, Columbus
Florida: Partin, Robert
E. Lee; Fletcher, Live
Oak; **Davey Eldredge,
Miami;** Nuckols, Bolles
Kentucky: Kuhn,
Louisville; Freeman,
Louisville; Stephenson,
Covington; Lenabar, St.
Xavier
Louisiana: Harris, Baton
Rouge; Honn, Shreveport;
Giacone, Bogalusa;
Ghersanich, Warren
Easton
Mississippi: Lane,
Greenville; McLeod,
Laurel, Ostrom,
Greenville; White,
McComb
South Carolina: Byers,
Greenville; Bridwell,
Parker; Pate, Columbia,
Owens, Columbia
North Carolina: Brewer,
Wonston-Salem; Painter,
Asheville; Amon,
Charlotte; Carlton,
Lexington.
Tennessee: Holland,
Memphis; Cifers,
Kingsport; North, Castle
Heights, Tillett, Knoxville
Virginia: Serlich, Maury;
Doyle, Petersburg;
DeShaun, Roanoke; Parr,
Hopewell
Texas: Daniel, Bryan;
Jackson, Houston; Mercer,
Temple; Hall, Corpus
Christi

FLORIDA ALL STATE ASSOCIATED PRESS
FIRST TEAM
ENDS
Maxwell Partin, Robert
E. Lee; **Charley Burrus,
Miami**
TACKLES
Gus Kalouris, Plant;
Phonsie Howell, Live Oak
GUARDS
Pershing Scott, Landon;
Jay Kendrick, Miami
CENTER
James Hurst, Landon
BACKS
**Davey Eldredge,
Miami;** Al Faulkner,
Robert E. Lee; Nick
Tsacrios, Live Oak; Guy
Tompkins, Hillsborough
SECOND TEAM
ENDS
Gwinn Girard, St.
Petersburg; Joe Graham,
Landon
TACKLES
Dick Fauth, Miami;
Leon Joyner, Bartow
GUARDS
Bill Raborn, Robert E.
Lee; Rudolph Fletcher,
Live Oak
CENTER
Charlie Davis, Plant
BACKS
Freddie Caldwell,
Orlando; George Magee,
St. Petersburg; Jack
Hightower, Landon; Dave
Frazier, Landon

FLORIDA SPORTS WRITERS ASSOCIATION
FIRST TEAM
ENDS
Maxwell Partin, Robert E.
Lee; C.C. Wester, Ocala
TACKLES
Jay Kendrick, Miami;
Gus Kalouris, Plant
GUARDS
Pershing Scott, Landon;
Rudolph Fletcher, Live
Oak

CENTER
James Hurst, Landon
BACKS
**Davey Eldredge,
Miami,** Charles Nuckols,
Bolles; Al Faulkner,
Robert E. Lee; Guy
Tompkins, Hillsborough
SECOND TEAM
ENDS
**Charley Burrus,
Miami;** Jack Hoskinson,
Robert E. lee
TACKLES
Phonsie Howell, Live
Oak; Reggie Ausley, Ocala
GUARDS
Bill Raborn, Robert E.
Lee; Friedson, Miami
Beach
CENTER
T.R. Spicer, Ocala
BACKS
Jack Hightower, Landon;
Freddie Caldwell,
Orlando; Joe Renfro, Fort
Myers, Nick Tsacrios,
Live Oak

MIAMI ALL CITY MIAMI NEWS
FIRST TEAM
ENDS
**Charley Burrus,
Miami; J.B. Moore,
Miami**
TACKLES
**Dick Fauth, Miami,
Doug Craven, Miami**
GUARDS
Jay Kendrick, Miami;
Bill Smith, Edison
CENTER
Levin Rollins, Miami
BACKS
**Davey Eldredge,
Miami;** Jack Farley,
Miami Beach; **Harvey
Comfort, Miami;**
Curtis Barwick, Jackson
SECOND TEAM
ENDS
Bill Baker, Jackson; Bob
Kolz, Edison
TACKLES
John Netsch, Edison; Don
Baxter Jackson

GUARDS
**Gilbert Wilson,
Miami;** Ed Friedson,
Miami Beach
CENTER
Stumpy Wiggins, Edison
BACKS
Harold Lundbloom,
Jackson; **Jason Koesy,
Miami;** Billy Wilcox,
Miami Beach; **Red
Mathews, Miami**

MIAMI HERALD
FIRST TEAM
ENDS
**Charley Burrus,
Miami;** Billy Baker,
Jackson
TACKLES
Dick Fauth, Miami,
John Netsch, Edison
GUARDS
Jay Kendrick, Miami;
Ed Friedson, Miami Beach
CENTER
Levin Rollins, Miami
BACKS
Harold Lundbloom,
Jackson; **Davey
Eldredge, Miami;** Jack
Farley, Miami Beach;
Curtis Barwick, Jackson
SECOND TEAM
ENDS
J.B. Moore, Miami; Bob
Kolz, Edison
TACKLES
Doug Craven, Miami;
Carl Graf, Jackson
GUARDS
**Gilbert Wilson,
Miami;** Pahokee Smith,
Edison
CENTER
Fred Pasquerella, Jackson
BACKS
**Jason Koesy, Miami;
Harvey Comfort,
Miami;** Eddie
Hausenbauer, Edison;
Gordon Stark, Miami
Beach

GARFIELD HIGH SCHOOL RESULTS THROUGH 1941

1922 (2-6)
At Englewood, L, 29-0
At Ridgefield Park, L,
79-0
At Hasbrouck Heights,
W, 12-8
Butler, L, 6-0
East Rutherford, L, 18-3
Kearny, L, 12-0
Hasbrouck Heights, W,
6-0
Belleville, L, 6-0

1923 (3-3-1)
At Glen Ridge, L, 21-0
Tenafly, W, 13-0
Leonia, L, 12-8
Butler, W, 25-0
Ridgefield Park, L 21-0
East Rutherford, T, 0-0
Dumont, W, 12-0

1924 (7-0-2, BERGEN COUNTY LEAGUE CO-CHAMPS)
Butler, W, 25-0
East Rutherford, W, 3-0
At Westwood, W, 30-0
Clifton, T, 0-0
At Tenafly, W, 26-6
At Ridgefield Park, T, 0-0
At Dumont, W, 32-0
Leonia, W, 16-7
Newton, W, 16-7

1925 (6-3, BERGEN COUNTY LEAGUE CO-CHAMPS)
Butler, W, 25-0
At Rutherford L, 14-0
At Leonia, W, 6-0
Ridgefield Park, W, Forfeit
At Barringer, L, 10-0

Tenafly, W, 14-0
Ramsey, W, 21-0
At East Rutherford, L, 9-0
Alumni, W, 12-0
At Clifton, W, 14-3
At Newton, W, 13-0

1926 (4-3-1)
Jamaica, L, 13-0
Butler, W, 50-0
At East Rutherford, T, 6-6
At Tenafly, W, 26-0
Bogota, L, 14-13
East Rutherford, L, 6-0
At Clifton, W, 12-0
Newton, W, 35-18

1927 (2-3-3)
At Dover, W, 7-0
Dickinson, L, 12-0
At Emerson, U.C., L, 25-0
Tenafly, T, 7-7
At Clifton, W, 2-0
At Bogota, T, 0-0
Alumni, W, 13-0
East Rutherford, T, 6-6
At Newton, L, 7-0

1928 (0-8)
Dover, L, 6-0
At Passaic, L, 27-0
Emerson (U.C.), L, 6-0
East Rutherford, L, 21-0
At Tenafly, L, 32-0
At Union Hill, L, Forfeit
Bogota, L, 21-0
At West New York, L,
40-13

1929 (2-4-2)
At Dover, L, 10-0
At Passaic, L, 19-0
East Rutherford, L, 12-0
Tenafly, W, 13-6
Lyndhurst, W, 21-0
At Bogota, L, 26-0
Weehawken, T, 6-6
St. Cecilia, T, 6-6

1930 (7-2, BERGEN COUNTY LEAGUE CHAMPS)
At Dover, W, 21-13
At Passaic, L, 18-6
At Ramsey, W, 39-6
Tenafly, W, 6-0
Bogota, W, 14-0
East Rutherford, W, 9-7
At Roselle, W, 6-0
Woodrow Wilson, W,
30-0
At St. Cecilia, L, 12-6

1931 (1-7)
At Passaic, L, 14-0
Ramsey, L, 31-0
At Tenafly, L., 30-7
Bogota, L, 27-0
At Union Hill, L, 19-6
At East Rutherford, L,
20-7
Dickinson Evening, W,
14-0
St. Cecilia, L, 26-0

1932 (4-3-2)
Woodrow Wilson, W, 6-0
Passaic, T, 0-0
Dumont, W, 16-13
Bogota, T, 0-0
At Ramsey, W, 19-0
At Union Hill, W, 20-13
East Rutherford, T, 6-6
South River, L, 14-6
Tenafly, L, 19-0

1933 (6-3, BERGEN COUNTY LEAGUE CHAMPS)
Passaic, W, 6-0
At East Rutherford, L,
12-0
Eastside, W, 12-0
Bogota, W, 33-0
Ramsey, W, 12-0
At Union Hill, L, 13-7
At Bloomfield, L, 26-0
Tenafly, W, 13-0
At Dumont, W, 18-0

1934 (8-2-1, BERGEN COUNTY LEAGUE CHAMPS)
Ridgefield Park, W, 26-0
At Bloomfield, W, 6-0
At Passaic, L, 6-0
At Phillipsburg, L, 6-0
At Tenafly, T, 0-0
Bogota, W, 25-0
Union Hill, W, 13-0
At Ramsey, W, 32-0
East Rutherford, W, 20-14
Eastside, W, 19-2
Dumont, W, 52-0

1935 (6-1-1)
Dickinson, W, 18-0
At Passaic, W, 14-7
Tenafly, W, 21-0
At Bloomfield, L, 25-0
At East Rutherford, W, 39-6
Eastside, W, 19-6
St. Cecilia, W, 47-0
At Ridgefield Park, T, 6-6

1936 (7-2-1)
Port Jervis, W, 67-0
Eastside, W, 20-7
At Dickinson, W, 13-7
At Passaic, L, 7-0
East Rutherford, W, 20-0
Newark East Side, W, 29-0
At Bloomfield, L, 7-0
Asbury Park, T, 7-7
At St. Mary's, W, 54-0
St. Cecilia, W, 33-0

1937 (4-5)
Dickinson, L, 26-0
At Irvington, L, 12-6
At Passaic, L, 14-0
At East Rutherford, W, 19-7
At Carteret, W, 19-13
At Bloomfield, L, 19-0
At Asbury Park, L, 7-6
Union Hill, W, 14-7
At Clifton, W, 7-2

1938 (9-0, STATE CHAMPS)
At Dickinson, W, 19-6
Irvington, W, 19-13
At Passaic, W, 12-6
East Rutherford, W, 13-6
Carteret, W, 20-0
At Bloomfield, W, 19-0
Asbury Park, W, 19-0
Paterson Eastside, W, 13-7
At Clifton, W, 19-0

1939 (10-0, STATE CHAMPS, MYTHICAL NATIONAL CHAMPS)
Dickinson, W, 33-0
At Irvington, W, 14-12
Passaic, W, 12-6
East Rutherford, W, 14-6
Thomas Jefferson, W, 26-0
At Bloomfield, W, 18-0
At Asbury Park, W, 13-7
Paterson Eastside, W, 48-6
At Clifton, W, 21-6
At Miami, W, 16-13

1940 (9-1, PASSAIC VALLEY CONFERENCE CHAMPS)
Nutley, L, 13-7
At Dickinson, W, 12-7
Irvington, W, 6-0
At Passaic, W, 13-6
At East Rutherford, W, 13-2
Paterson Central, W, 26-6
Bloomfield, W, 33-0
At Paterson Eastside, W, 13-7
Thomas Jefferson, W, 32-7
Clifton, W, 13-7

1941 (8-1, PASSAIC VALLEY CONFERENCE CO-CHAMPS)
Dickinson, W, 13-6
At Irvington, W, 7-6

Passaic, W, 14-2
East Rutherford, W, 19-0
At Paterson Central, W, 32-0
At Bloomfield, W, 13-0
Newark West Side, W, 13-0
Paterson Eastside, L, 13-0
Clifton, W, 20-0

MIAMI HIGH SCHOOL RESULTS THROUGH 1941

1921
American Legion Post, W, 12-6

1922 (6-1)
At West Palm Beach, W, 31-0
St. Augustine School for Deaf, W, 52-0
Berean A.C., W, 31-0
Sanford, W, 40-13
West Palm Beach, W, 54-0
Plant City, W, 25-0
At Gainesville, L, 58-0

1923 (8-2-0)
YMCA, W, 16-13
Fort Lauderdale, W, 25-0
Daytona, W, 18-6
West Palm Beach, W, 14-7
At Jacksonville Duval, L, 26-0
At Sanford, L, 7-0
Ocala, W, 7-0
At West Palm Beach, W, 12-7
Gainesville, W, 16-13
Fort Lauderdale, W, 12-0

1924 (5-2-0)
Fort Lauderdale, L, 2-0
Jacksonville Duval, L, 18-0
At West Palm Beach, W, 26-0
At Seabreeze, W, 21-0
At Daytona, W, 24-0
West Palm Beach, W, 30-7
Ocala, W, 39-6

1925 (8-2-1)
Lemon City (Edison), W, 33-0
Key West, W, 50-0
Fort Lauderdale, W, 26-7
At Jacksonville Duval, L, 28-7
Hillsborough, W, 13-7
Gainesville, W, 20-7
At St. Petersburg, L, 21-0
At West Palm Beach, W, 25-7
St. Augustine, W, 58-0
Lemon City (Edison), W, 28-0
Tech High, T, 0-0

1926 (5-4)
At Key West, W, 13-0
Lemon City (Edison), W, 15-0
At Daytona Beach, L, 3-0
At Fort Lauderdale, W, 13-0
West Palm Beach, W, 14-0
St. Petersburg, L, 7-6
At Hillsborough, L, 19-0
Jacksonville Duval, W, 2-0
At Tech High, L, 27-0

1927 (6-2)
Melbourne, W, 39-0
Hillsborough, L, 18-6
Fort Lauderdale, W, 18-6
At West Palm Beach, W, 13-12
At St. Petersburg, L, 24-7
Bartow, W, 26-13
Plant City, W, 24-0
Lemon City (Edison), W 37-6

1928 (5-2-2)
Melbourne, W, 72-0
Plant, W, 13-0
Lemon City (Edison), W, 38-12
At Fort Lauderdale, T, 0-0
West Palm Beach, W, 19-3
At St. Petersburg, W, 6-0
Hillsborough, W, 13-8
Orlando, T, 6-6
Lakeland, W, 13-7

1929 (10-0-1)
Eastern United
States Champion
Fort Pierce, W, 35-0
Plant, W, 17-0
West Palm Beach, W,
13-0
Hillsborough, W, 21-6
Fort Lauderdale, W, 26-6
Andrew Jackson,
Jacksonville, T, 6-6
Lemon City (Edison), W,
24-0
Orlando, W, 33-7
R.E. Lee, Jacksonville, W,
25-7
Charlotte, W, 12-7
Salem, W, 7-6
*Last two games played at
MSG Stadium*

1930 (11-1)
Ponce de Leon, W, 13-6
Lemon City (Edison), W,
39-0
UM Freshmen, L, 12-0
West Palm Beach, W,
20-0
Plant, W, 19-6
At Fort Lauderdale, W,
27-0
At R.E. Lee, Jacksonville,
W, 20-7
Plant City, W, 38-0
Fort Myers, W, 18-6
Orlando, W, 7-0
Gainesville, W, 49-0
Dayton Stivers, W, 18-0

1931 (8-1-2)
Edison, W, 19-0
Ponce de Leon, W, 32-0
Andrew Jackson,
Jacksonville, W, 7-0
Plant, T, 0-0
Gainesville, W, 39-0
West Palm Beach, W,
18-0
Hillsborough, W, 11-7
Fort Lauderdale, T, 7-7
Fort Myers, W, 7-0
Orlando, W, 34-0
Carter Harrison Tech,
L, 18-7

1932 (8-3)
Ponce de Leon, W, 22-0
Edison, W, 12-0
Lanier, L, 21-14
At Fort Lauderdale, W,
17-0
Fort Myers, W, 29-0
Boys, L, 6-0
West Palm Beach, W,
27-0
Tech, W, 19-0
At Palmetto, W, 13-0
Miami All-Stars, W, 46-13
Waite, L, 13-7

1933 (9-2)
Fisher (Miami Beach),
W, 25-0
R.E. Lee, Jacksonville, W,
18-0
Ponce de Leon, W, 40-0
At Fort Lauderdale, W,
32-0
Spartanburg, L, 25-21
Savannah, W, 7-6
Lanier, L, 14-3
At West Palm Beach, W,
19-0
Tech High, W, 20-0
Edison, W, 6-0
Syracuse Central, W, 18-7

1934 (10-1-2)
At Tech High, T, 0-0
Ida Fisher (Miami Beach),
W, 19-0
Fort Lauderdale, W, 50-0
Spartanburg, W, 24-0
At R.E. Lee, Jacksonville,
W, 14-6
Charlotte, W, 26-0
Lanier, W, 19-0
At West Palm Beach, W,
13-0
Boys High, T, 7-7
Savannah, W, 9-0
Edison, W, 28-0
North Braddock Scott,
L, 26-13
At Andrew Jackson,
Jacksonville, W, 7-6

1935 (5-4-1)
Ramsey Tech,
Birmingham, W, 13-0
Gaffney, S.C., L, 19-18
Spartanburg, W, 21-0
At R.E. Lee, Jacksonville,
W, 6-0
Savannah, W, 19-6
At Lanier, W, 13-7
Boys High, L, 19-7
University, St. Louis, W,
21-7
Edison, T, 12-12
Elmira, L, 13-0

1936 (5-5)
At Spartanburg, W, 7-6
Edison, W, 6-0
Chester, L, 2-0
At Savannah, L, 7-6
R.E. Lee, Jacksonville, W,
20-12
Bellevue, Kentucky, W,
14-6
Lanier, L, 12-0
Boys High, W, 7-0
Knoxville, L, 13-7
New Britain, L, 32-13

1937 (7-3-1)
At R.E. Lee, Jacksonville,
W, 6-0
Savannah, W, 18-0
Spartanburg, W, 19-7
At Boys, W, 18-17
Male High, L, 34-7
Tuscaloosa, W, 26-7
Lanier, L, 6-0
Shenandoah (Iowa), W,
26-0
Edison, W, 28-0
Knoxville, L, 25-0
Oak Park, T, 6-6

1938 (8-2-1)
At Knoxville, L, 19-7
R.E. Lee, Jacksonville,
L, 6-0
Nashville Central, W,
25-7
Savannah, W, 14-0
At Andrew Jackson,
Miami, W, 12-7
Lanier, W, 38-6
Pine Bluff, W, 33-7

Edison, T, 6-6
Boys, W, 19-0
Edison, W, 7-6
McKeesport, W, 19-13

1939 (9-1)
At R.E. Lee, Jacksonville,
W, 7-0
Knoxville, W, 32-0
Savannah, W, 26-6
At Andrew Jackson,
Jacksonville, W, 30-7
Lanier, W, 19-0
Jackson, W, 27-0
Spartanburg, W, 27-0
Edison, W, 13-0
Atlanta Boys, W, 26-0
Garfield, L, 16-13

1940 (9-1)
R.E. Lee, Jacksonville, W,
26-0
Andrew Jackson, Miami,
W, 21-7
At Savannah, W, 13-0
Andrew Jackson,
Jacksonville, W, 26-6
Birmingham Ensley, W,
18-0
Kanier, W, 37-0
Greenville Parker, W,
33-4
Edison, W, 28-7
Boys, L, 13-0
Fenger, W, 19-0

1941 (10-0-1)
Ponce de Leon, W, 39-0
At R.E. Lee, Jacksonville,
W, 35-0
Andrew Jackson, Miami,
W, 35-0
Savannah, W, 34-0
Andrew Jackson,
Jacksonville, W, 39-7
Greensboro, W, 36-6
Lanier, W, 45-0
Petersburg, W, 40-0
Edison, W, 26-13
Boys, T, 7-7
Baltimore City, W, 26-0

ENDNOTES

CHAPTER TWO: THE BUBBLE

1 "Okonite worker's wife, daughter, 5, land without son," *The Herald-News*, September 15, 1939

2 Caulfield, Max. *Tomorrow Never Came*. New York: W.W. Norton & Company, p. 13

3 Allen, Tonya. "The Sinking of the S.S. Athenia." UBoat.net. March 21, 1999.

4 "Text of quiz on sinking of Athenia." *Philadelphia Inquirer* (Associated Press), September 9, 1939

5 "Mother and daughter, survivors of Athenia, learn after arrival in U.S. that boy, 10, is safe." *Tallahassee Democrat* (*Associated Press*), September 17, 1939

6 Stark, Jack. "Athenia horror told by party on Southern Cross." *The Miami Herald*, September 23, 1939

7 Theis, Grover. "Vivid rescue tale brought to Miami by Southern Cross." *Miami Daily News*, September 23, 1939

8 Ibid.

9 Okonite, Op. Cit.

10 Davis, Edward, "Athenia victims shake calm of photographer." *The Jersey Journal*, September 20, 1939

11 Mother, Op. Cit.

12 Hadley, Michael L. *Count Not The Dead, The Popular Image of the German Submarine*. Montreal: McGill-Queens University Press, p. 111

13 "'Why lie about Athenia?' Goebbels asks Churchill." *The Pittsburgh Press* (*United Press*), October 23, 1939

14 *The Herald-News*, September 5, 1939

15 Carter, Boak. "But-Says Boak ." *The Palm Beach Post*, September 9, 1939

16 Davis, Op. Cit.

17 Theis, Op. Cit.

18 "Refugee ship cruising off Daytona, Master reports." *The Miami News*, June 9, 1939

19 "On Keeping Sane." *The Miami News*, September 7, 1939

20 "Football spurs Americans to spurn European war." *Miami High Times*, October 12, 1939

CHAPTER THREE: THE CITIES

1 "Frost in Florida." *The State*, December 30, 1894.

2 Scott, William Winfield. *History of Passaic and Its Environs*, Volume 2. New York and Chicago: Lewis Historical Publishing Company, 1922.

3 "Garfield. New Jersey, City of Industrial Peace." Garfield Chamber of Commerce, 1940.

4 New Jersey Boxing Hall of Fame.

5 Ibid.

6 McMahon, Art. "Beware the murderous gleam." *The Herald-News*, February 25, 1932.

7 McMahon, Art. "Frankie Turrano's mother attacks boxing." *The Herald-News*, March 11, 1932.

8 Frazure, Hoyt and Smiley, Nixon. *Memories of old Miami*. Miami: Miami Herald, 1964.

9 George, Paul S. "Brokers, binders and builders." *The Florida Historical Quarterly*, July 1986.

10 Ballinger, Kenneth. *Miami Millions*. Miami: The Franklin Press, 1936, p. 106.

11 Runyon, Damon. "March to Florida to get underway soon." *Tampa Morning Tribune (Universal Service)*, December 14, 1929.

12 Austin, Tom. "Architectural Focus: The Alfred I. DuPont Building." *Ocean Drive Magazine*, March 15, 2012

13 Gately, Don. "Miami Memories, 1940-1952." HubPages, January 8, 2011.

14 Warren, Cecil. R. "Streets reflect character of Miami." *The Miami News*, November 28, 1939.

15 "Garfield pupils list their likes in questionnaire." *The Herald-News*. December 1, 1939.

16 Kleinberg, Howard. "*The Stingaree Century.*" Miami: Howard Kleinberg, 2003, p.91.

17 Bucks, Joan. "School withstands stormy days." *Miami Herald*. January 10, 1963.

18 "Student Council." Miami Senior High School, *Miahi, Miami*: (Miami, 1940).

19 Frazur and Smiley, Op. Cit.

20 "Miami wants FBI probe into wave of crime." *Panama City Pilot (Associated Press)*, December 22, 1939.

21 "Federal agents destroy two more distilleries in the wooden section." *Passaic Daily News*, 1926.

22 "Garfield man is victim of gang killing." *The Jersey Journal (Associated Press)*, June 21, 1922.

23 "Young Garfield hijacker 'spills the works' on Schlegel and Pelletiere murders." *The Herald-News*, July 12, 1932.

24 "Women held as bootlegger." *Plainfield Courier-News*, September 10, 1927.

25 "Former fire chief held." *Asbury Park Press (Associated Press)*, December 9, 1931.

26 "Dr. Bleasby's defeat." *The Herald-News*. November 4, 1937.

27 "Bleasby's defeat result of slight to Gotthold Rose." *The Herald-News*. November 4, 1937.

28 Glover, William. "Youth at helm in city in New Jersey." *Greensboro Daily News (Associated Press)*, February 4, 1940.

29 McCann, Richard. "The boy who cleaned up Hell's graveyard." *New York Herald-Tribune (This Week magazine)*, June 30, 1940.

CHAPTER FOUR: THE COACHES

1 DeVries, Jack. "A QB for the ages." *The Herald-News*, November 22, 2000.

2 Ibid.

3 Ibid.

4 "Clifton High School scores 46-0 win over Butler High in opening game." *Passaic Daily Herald*, October 3 1921.

5 Ibid.

6 DeVries. Op. Cit.

7 "Clifton defeats Hackensack and then celebrates." *Passaic Daily News*, October 24, 1931.

8 *The Reflector*: Clifton New Jersey: Class of 1922.

9 Shershin, Michael. "Clifton has easy time." *Passaic Daily Herald*, November 18, 1922.

10 "Hurlburt gridders challenge any team in state for title." *Passaic Daily News*, November 22, 2000.

11 "Clifton wins from Norwood." *Passaic Daily Herald*, December 4, 1922.

12 Greenfield, George. *Passaic Daily Herald*, March 1, 1923.

13 DeVris, Jack. "Clifton's basketball Hall of Famer and other tales of Mustang round ball." *Clifton Merchant Magazine*, February, 2014.

14 "Rutherford spoils Clifton's record." *Passaic Daily Herald*, September 30, 1923.

15 *Cestrian*, Chester, South Carolina: Class of 1926.

16 J.H. Yarborough oral history interview conducted by W.W. Dixon in Chester, South Carolina, 1938-06-28." From *WPA L. C. Project Writers' Unit*

17 Ibid.

18 "Rev. J.H. Yarborough died Wednesday AM." *Chester News,* April 27, 1944.

19 "A Great Lady." *Chester News and Reporter*, May 7. 1973.

20 "Fierce Tiger." *Greenville News,* September 28, 1930.

21 "Ambitious Terriers smothered by Tigers." *The Tiger,* October 1, 1930.

22 Weimer, Carl D. "Clemson barely beats Bulldogs." *Greenville News,* October 4, 1930.

23 Parker,Gene. "Powerful line and Welch in lead role." *Greenville News,* October 12, 1930.

²4 "Clemson Tiger team drives Wolfpack from door." *The Tiger*, October 16, 1930.

25 "Clemson Tiger did not show best form defeating Wofford Terriers, 30-0." *The Tiger,* October 23, 1930.

26 "Clemson licked by Neyland's Vols." *The Tiger,* November 5, 1930.

27 Cody, Josh, *Josh Cody to Jesse Yarborough, May 1, 1932*. From Jesse Yarborough estate.

28 Latimer, Scoop. "Straight from man who knows, Mule Yarborough of Miami." *Greenville News*, November 2, 1950.

29 "Miami schoolboys to stress deception." *Newark Evening News,* December 17, 1939.

30 "Yarborough goes to Miami as grid coach." *Chester News.* July 26, 1932.

CHAPTER FIVE: THE SPORT

1   "The rugby game as played now is a dangerous pastime." *New York Times,* December 2, 1893.

2   "Blue again on top." *The Sunday Herald,* November 20, 1892.

3   "Yale's football wrecks," *New York Times,* October 10, 1893.

4   Miller, John. J. *The Big Scrum: How Teddy Roosevelt Saved Football.* New York: Harper-Collins, 2011, p.149.

5   "The American Boy." *St. Nicholas Magazine,* May 1900.

6   Miller. *Op. Cit.*

7   "Football year's death harvest." *Chicago Tribune.,* November 26, 1905.

8   Zimmerman, Paul. *New Thinking Man's Guide to Pro Football.* New York: Harper Collins, 1984.

9   "OShea's back is broken." *Passaic Daily News,* October 14, 1929.

10 Ibid.

11 Bromberg, Lester. "Scholastic shortcuts." *New York Evening Post,* October 22, 1929.

12 Horowitz, Paul. "Hot football, warm sun, draw 200,000 fans." *Newark Evening News.* November 24, 1939.

13 Maloney, Walt. "Passes the dope along." *The Nutley Sun,* November 19, 1939.

14 McMahon, Art. "Sportsman's Corner." *The Herald-News,* October 9, 1937.

15 Del Greco, Al. "Gambling wide open while cops looking on at schoolboy classic." *Bergen Evening Record,* October 31, 1938.

16 Del Greco, Al.

17 Del Greco, Al. "Apologies to Englewood." *Bergen Evening Record.* October 25, 1937.

18 McMahon, Art. "Risky business." *The Herald-News.* October 26, 1937.

19 Hudak, Timothy L. with Pflug Jr., John R. *All the Way to No. 1.* Cleveland: Sports Heritage Publications, 2015, p.xiv.

CHAPTER SIX: THE BEGINNING

1   "Biscayne fadaway is the name of that thrilling play." *The Miami Metropolis.* November 21, 1911.

2   Bell, Jack. "Stinagrees trounce Hillsborough." *Miami Herald*, November 12, 1931.

3   "Coach Johnson silent as to grid break." *Tampa Morning Tribune*, November 13, 1931.

4   Bell, Jack. "A little meeting held over in Orlando." *Miami Herald*, November 24, 1931.

5   Godwin, Frank. "Miami High quits Big Ten after protest ruling." *Miami Daily News.* November 24, 1931.

6   Bell. Op. Cit.

6   Bell, Jack. "Freddy Major is leaving Miami High School." *Miami Herald*, December 7, 1931.

8   "Wright to remain Rock Hill coach." *The Greenville News.* June 26, 1932.

9   Godwin, Frank. "First Guesses." *Miami Daily News.* June 26, 1932.

10 "J.H. Yarborough favored as Miami High coach." *Miami Daily News*, July 8, 1932.

11 "Yarborough to coach Miami Hi." *The Greenville News*, July 16, 1932.

12 "Q and A with George McGugin." Commodore History Center, September 5, 2012.

13 Kolb, Joe. "Calling on Charley Bachman." *Fort Lauderdale Sunday News*, October 6, 1957

14 Bell, Walter. *Return to Glory Hole.* Bloomington, Indiana: Trafford Publishing, 2004.

15 "Garfield eleven trounces Leonia in crucial game." *Bergen Evening Record.* November 17, 1924.

16 "Purple and gold warriors battle state contenders in remarkable exhibition, winning loud praises." *Passaic Daily News.* November 4, 1924.

17 "Ridgefield Park eleven overlooks many chances and Garfield earns tie." *Bergen Evening Record*, November 3, 1924.

18 Del Greco, Al. "Samuel Dzikowski goes to his maker after sick bed fight." *Bergen Evening Record*, December 13, 1933.

19 Del Greco. Ibid.

20 "Sweet victory for kids—Chick DeVito." *Bergen Evening Record*, October 28, 1929.

21 Sutphen, James. "What hit Garfield? Wins two in a row without aid of mirrors. *Bergen Evening Record.* November 5, 1929.

22 "Speculation as to DeVito's 1930 successor runs rampant." *Bergen Evening Record*, November 11, 1929.

23 "Football secondary to studies, says Pete Tengi." *Bergen Evening Record*, November 15, 1929.

24 Del Greco, Al. "Garfield has the system." *Bergen Evening Record*, September 5, 1930.

25 Del Greco, Al. "A few predictions of scholastic games." *Bergen Evening Record*, September 26, 1930.

26 "Hundreds watch Dover High lose opening football game." *The Dover Advance*, September 29, 1930.

27 "Garfield provides upset by defeating Dover Champions." *Bergen Evening Record*, September 28, 1930.

28 Del Greco, Al. "At Random in Sportdom." *Bergen Evening Record*, November 28, 1930.

CHAPTER SEVEN: THE TEAMS

1 Kurland, Bob. "Marking golden anniversary." *The Record*, October 13, 1989.

2 Klein, Willie. "Football's silly—Babula "I want a baseball career." *Newark Star-Ledger,* November 7, 1939.

3 Ibid.

4 Ibid.

5 Bradenahl, Walter. Walter Bradenahl to Walter Young, June 8, 1938. From Walter Young estate.

6 Ibid.

7 Bradenahl, Walter. *Walter Bradenahl to Walter Young,* June 16, 1938. From Walter Young estate.

8 Kurland. Op. Cit.

9 Ibid.

10 Ibid.

11 "Christmas grid fans will watch Eldredge." *Miami Daily News*, December 17, 1939.

12 Holmes, Tommy. "Civil War revenge, not grid game, Georgia's mission here." *The Brooklyn Daily Eagle.* October 30, 1939.

13 Matlack, S.S., "Eldredge, seeking reelection as county purchasing agent has colorful, unique record." *Miami Daily News,* June 15, 1930.

14 "Christmas grid fans." Op. Cit.

15 Bell, Jack. "O'er the sports desk." *Miami Daily News,* May 15, 1939.

16 Kleinberg, Howard. "*The Stingaree Century.*" Miami: Howard Kleinberg, 2003, p.91.

17 Ibid.

18 Ibid.

CHAPTER EIGHT: THE SCOURGE

1   Bergener, John. "Boddy synonymous with Spartan championships." *Toledo Blade*, June 20, 1979.

2   Whipple, Plummer. "Waite gridders look good in scrimmage; Mac receives glowing reports on Miami." *Toledo Blade*, December 21, 1932.

3   Buckley, Frank. "'Beat Miami' slogan of Waite grid players." *The Toledo News-Bee*, December 26, 1932.

4   Morrison R. Waite High School, Round the Dial 1933 Yearbook, (Toledo, O. Graduating Class of 1933, 1933)

5   VanDyke, Ed. "Clint Williams can't go with his mates but he's dead game." *Elmira Star-Gazette*, December 10, 1935.

6   Ibid.

7   "'Proud of team all year,' says Hirst at dinner." *Elmira Star-Gazette*, December 12, 1935.

8   VanDyke, Ed. "Elmira footballers shake riding 'kinks' in practice session." *Elmira Star-Gazette*, December 21, 1935.

9   "Elmira High School football team in Miami for Christmas grid game." *Jamestown Evening Journal (Associated Press)*, December 24, 1935.

10 "EHS eleven is feted at banquet, speakers praise achievements." *Elmira Star-Gazette*, January 13, 1936.

11 "Negro back at Oak Park out of game." *Miami Daily News*, December 2, 1937.

12 Ibid.

13 "Score action of Oak Park grid coach." *The Chicago Defender*, December 11, 1937.

14 "Insulting loyalty." *The Chicago Defender*, December 18, 1937.

15 Stevens, Warren. "The scoreboard." *Oak Leaves*, December 9, 1937.

16 West, Stan, Sinko Peggy Tuck, Lipo, Frank. Suburban Promised Land. Oak Park, Il.: Soweto Press and Historical Society of Oak Park and River Forest, 2009, p.54.

17 "Letters from readers." *Oak Leaves*, December 23, 1937.

18 Smith, Kevin M., "50 years ago, the WPIAL football title belonged to McKeesport." *Pittsburgh Post-Gazette*, November 17, 1988.

19 "Colored star benched for bowl game." *Baltimore Afro-American*, December 23, 1939.

20 Ibid.

21 Carter, Robert L. *A Matter of Law*, New York: The New Press, 2005, p15.

22 "The Forbidden City." *The Chicago Defender*, October 2, 1926.

23 Reid, Ira DeAugustine. *The Negro Immigrant*, New York: Columbia University Press, 1939, p.189..

24 Bellamy, Jeanne. "Negro slum area rents increased." *Miami Tribune*, October 19, 1937.

25 George, Paul S. "Colored Town: Miami's Black Community, 1896-1930." *The Florida Historical Quarterly*, April, 1978.

26 Dunn, Marvin, *Black Miami in the Twentieth Century*. Gainesville: University of Florida Press, 1997, p.138.

27 "Quigg reappointed as Miami's top policeman." *Miami Tribune*, May 14, 1937.

28 "Police trail Willie just to see him run." *The Miami Herald*, November 12, 1937.

29 Willis Murray, interviewed by Jose Araujo and Venezia Reynoso, 2007, *Miami Oral Histories Collection*, Florida International University.

30 Wood, Jane, "Quigg's blistering career just healthy pace to him." *Miami Daily News*, January 17, 1954.

31 "Klan circus to open nine-day stand." *Miami Metropolis*, February 26, 1927.

32 "Klan official plans probe of charges." *Oakland Tribune (United Press)*, November 17, 1937.

33 "Miami night life loses 'hot pots.'" *New York Times*, November 22, 1937.

34 "Klan rides again." *The Miami Herald*, June 12, 1939.

35 Morris, Allen. "New Klan era seen in Miami." *The Miami Herald*, November 11, 1939.

36 Clay, Everett. "Harvey Comfort and unknown Delray darkie lead race for 1939 Cracked Coconut Award." *The Miami Herald*, January 6, 1940.

37 Bell, Jack. "Sports desk." *Miami Daily News*, October 2, 1939.

38 Dunn. Op. Cit.

39 Murray. Op. Cit.

40 Poston, Ted. "Miami shows the way to Negro America; Reaps great benefit from ballot use." *The Pittsburgh Courier*, June 22, 1940.

41 Poston, Ted. "Sam Solomon faced death; earned undying fame." *The Pittsburgh Courier*, January 2, 1940.

42 Ibid.

43 "Militancy in Miami." *The Pittsburgh Courier*, May 13, 1939.

44 "Miami blacks defy Ku Klux Klan. *The Chicago Defender*, May 13, 1939.

CHAPTER NINE: THE 1937 STINGAREES

1 Underwood, John. "The House that Earnie built." *Sports Illustrated*. January 3, 1972.

2 Ibid.

3 Ibid.

4 Bell, Jack. "O'er the sports desk." *Miami Daily News*, December 1, 1936.

5 Lewis, John. *Radio Master*. Minneapolis: Langdon Street Press, 2010, p.280.

6 Godwin, Frank. "We want peace and quiet if we have to fight for it." *Miami Daily News*, November 27, 1934.

7   Underwood. Op. Cit.

8   Ibid.

9   Harakas, Margo. "OB halftime something to shout about." *News/Sun-Sentinel.* January 2, 1984.

10 Bell, Jack. "O'er the sports desk." *Miami Daily News,* October 4, 1936.

11 "Stadium vote due tomorrow." *Miami Daily News,* October 6, 1936.

12 Casey, Robert J. *The Cannoneers Have Heavy Ears: A Diary of the Front Lines.* New York: J.H. Sears, 1927.

13 Bell, Jack. "O'er the sports desk." *Miami Daily News,* September 24, 1937.

14 "Miami gridmen begin practice." *Miami Daily News,* August 31, 1937

15 "Stingarees." *Miami Daily News,* September 12, 1937.

16 Bell, Jack. "O'er the sports desk. *Miami Daily News,* September 28, 1937.

17 Bell, Jack. "O'er the sports desk. *Miami Daily News,* May 18, 1938

18 Bell, Jack. "O'er the sports desk. *Miami Daily News,* December 27, 1936.

19 Bell, Jack. "O'er the sports desk. *Miami Daily News,* September 29, 1937.

20 Bell, Jack. "O'er the sports desk. *Miami Daily News,* October 6, 1937.

21 Barnhill, Les. "Schemer shows way for Miami team." *The Miami Herald,* Octiber 2, 1937.

22 Barnhill, Les. "Schemer and Stingarees whip Savannah." *The Miami Herald,* October 10, 1937.

23 Bell, Jack. "Stingarees win, 19 to 7." *Miami Daily News,* October 16, 1937.

24 Barnhill. Op. Cit

25 Bell. Op. Cit.

26 Bell, Jack. "Stingarees stave off late rally." *Miami Daily News,* October 23, 1937.

27 Bryant, Paul with Underwood, John. *Bear: My Hard Life & Good Times As Alabama's Head Coach.* New York: Little, Brown, 1975

28 Smith, Loran. *Wally's Boys.* Atlanta: Longstreet Press, 2005.

29 "Kentuckians whip Miami High." *Miami Tribune,* October 30, 1937.

30 Bell, Jack. "O're the sports desk." *Miami Daily News,* November 3, 1937.

31 "Eldredge runs as Stingarees fear Macon." *Miami Daily News,* November 10, 1937.

32 Ibid.

33 Kleinberg, Howard. "Parnell, Yarborough cut up old touches." *Miami Daily News,* November 27, 1957

34 Bell Jack. "Well matched prep elevens ready to step." *Miami Daily News,* November 24, 1937.

35 "Stingarees due to lose, says Edison." *Miami Daily News,* November 17, 1937.

36 "Yarborough predicts victory for Miami High." *Miami Tribune,* November 21, 1937.

37 Hughes, Bob. "Parnell thinks Red Raiders will shatter jinx theory." *The Miami Herald,* November 25, 1937.

38 Barnhill, Les. "Fair bunch of mugs says Stingaree coach." *The Miami Herald,* November 26, 1937.

39 Cavendish, Henry. "Stadium crowd breaks state mark for prep school games." *The Miami Herald,* November 26, 1937.

40 Cormack, Herbert. "Miami Hi wallops Cardinals." *Miami Tribune,* November 26, 1937.

41 Bell, Jack. "O'er the sports desk." *Miami Daily News,* November 30, 1937.

42 Barnhill. Op. Cit.

43 Ibid.

44 "Charity tilt may attract large crowd." *Miami Daily News,* November 30, 1937.

45 Bell, Jack. "O'er the sports desk." *Miami Daily News,* December 1, 1937.

46 "Butler runs many miles for visitors." *Miami Daily News,* December 3, 1937.

CHAPTER TEN: THE 1937 BOILERMAKERS

1 Lundquist, Carl. "Coach of week honor is given John Dagrosa." *The News-Herald (United Press),* October 10, 1945.

2 Carew, Wally. *A Farewell to Glory, The Rise and Fall of an Epic Football Rivalry—Boston College vs. Holy Cross,* New York: Ambassador Books, 2003, p.81.

3 Lovas, Joe. "DaGrossa assists Argauer in drilling Garfield Candidates." *The Herald-News,* September 14, 1937.

4 "Garfield loses practice clash." *The Herald-News,* September 20, 1937.

5 "Garfield eleven worries Argauer." *Bergen Evening Record,* September 21, 1937.

6 McMahon, Art. "Sportsman's Corner." *The Herald-News,* September 25, 1937.

7 Del Greco, Al. "At Random in sportdom." *Bergen Evening Record,* September 25, 1937.

8 Gotteher, Barry. *The Giants of New York.* New York: Putnam, 1963.

9 "Al Blozis, star athlete, killed in action." *The Jersey Journal,* April 9, 1945.

10 Del Greco, Al. "Argauer won't have to act." *Bergen Evening Record,* September 28, 1937.

11 Lovas, Joe. "Boilermakers show many other weaknesses as Dickinson wins." *The Herald-News,* September 27, 1937.

12 "Garfield shows improved form but loses second game in row." *The Herald-News,* October 4, 1937.

13 Del Greco, Al. "Garfield, Rutherford are lost." *Bergen Evening Record,* October 12, 1937.

14 Del Greco, Al. "At Random in sportdom." *Bergen Evening Record,* October 15, 1937

15 Hampson, Gene F. "Thru . . . Sportsland." *Plainfield Courier-News,* December 9, 1937.

16 Horowitz, Paul. "Columbia High's record best among Essex schools." *Newark Evening News,* October 20, 1937.

17 "Montclair and Orange only Bengal rivals to taste defeat." *The Independent Press,* October 22, 1937.

18 "Garfield aims for upset at Bloomfield." *The Herald-News,* October 30, 1937.

19 McMahon, Art. "Sportsman's Corner." *The Herald-News,* October 28, 1937.

20 McMahon, Art. "Tomorrow's outlook." *The Herald-News,* October 29, 1937.

21 Del Greco, Al. "At Random in sportdom." *Bergen Evening Record,* October 29, 1937.

22 "Bloomfield unimpressive in victory over Argauer's charges." *The Independent Press,* November 5, 1937.

23 Hill, Ed. "Garfield hands game to Asbury Park thru poor quarterbacking." *Asbury Park Press,* November 8, 1937.

24 Del Greco, A. "The Hackensacks to better Leonia, Garfield to win." *Bergen Evening Record,* November 5, 1937.

25 Falzer, G.A. "New Brunswick no match for Bengals." *Newark Sunday Call,* December 12, 1937.

26 Bowen, Bus. "Zebras defeated 54-0 in contest for state title." *The Sunday Times,* December 12,1937.

27 Horowitz, Paul. "Foley terms 1937 eleven Bloomfield's mightiest." *Newark Evening News,* December 13, 1937.

CHAPTER ELEVEN: THE SYSTEM

1   "Walter Edwin Short, Jersey sports figure." *Trenton Times,* December 8, 1978.

2   Merrill, Wendell. "Garfield must attend big meeting." *Passaic Daily News,* December 1, 1924.

3   Merrill, Wendell. "Merrill's sports talk." *Passaic Daily News,* December 2, 1924.

4   Del Greco, Al. "Higher mathematics gives Bloomfield tie with unbeaten Passaic." *Bergen Evening Record,* December 2, 1936.

5   bid.

6   Ibid.

7   Horowitz, Paul. "Comedy of errors marks selection." *Newark Evening News,* December 2, 1936.

8   McMahon, Art. "Passaic should quit state group." *The Herald-News,* December 3, 1936.

9   "Attention of state association angers followers of schools." *The Herald-News,* December 2, 1936.

10 "Mrs. Colliton's devotion to swimming and acting will help her in movies." *Trenton Times,* September 7, 1915.

11 "Mrs. Colliton on stand in divorce." *Trenton Times,* May 8, 1918.

12 "Colliton divorce suit thrown out." *Trenton Times,* May 9, 1918.

13 Short, Walter E. "Colliton system highlight of school sports campaign." *Asbury Park Press,* December 29, 1937.

CHAPTER TWELVE: THE 1939 BOILERMAKERS

1   Zanjani, Sally. Goldfield. *The Last Gold Rush on the Western Frontier,* Athens, O.: Swallow Press, 1992.

2   Ibid.

3   Kiley, Charles Jr. "About this town in sports." *The Jersey Journal,* October 23, 1937.

4   Ibid.

5   "Bloomfield's Builder." *Sports Illustrated,* October 31, 1960.

6   Wilcox, Dick. "Argauer's eleven in shape for invasion of Bloomfield's lair." *The Herald-News,* September 21, 1934.

7   Del Greco, Al. "Garfield-Bloomfield feature games." *Bergen Evening Record,* September 22, 1934.

8   Hill, Ed. "Coaches' annual cries of 'wolf' result in dire happenings." *Asbury Park Press,* September 25, 1934.

9   Horowitz, Paul. "East Side likely to meet stronger Bloomfield team." *Newark Evening News,* September 24, 1934.

10 "Matty Malkiewicz scores only touchdown after blocked kick." *The Herald-News,* September 24, 1934.

11 "Garfield aerials crush Bloomfield." *Bergen Evening Record,* September 23, 1934.

12 Arlen, Dennis J. "Bloomfield High shows state championship form." *The Independent Press,* October 18, 1934.

13 Rhodes, Arthur. "Why Coach Foley opposes spring football games." *The Bloomfield Mail,* December 21, 1934.

14 "Argauer rates 1938 combine one of the best Comet grid elevens." *The Herald-News,* September 20, 1938.

15 McMahon, Art. "The sportsman's corner." *The Herald-News,* September 25, 1932.

16 McMahon, Art. "The sportsman's corner." *The Herald-News.* September 21, 1938.

17 Del Greco, Al. "At random in sportdom." *Bergen Evening Record,* September 23, 1938.

18 "Powerful Garfield eleven sinks Hilltop in opener." *The Jersey Journal,* September 26, 1938.

19 "Garfield shows power beating Dickinson." *The Herald-News,* September 26, 1938.

20 "Comet choice to whip Camptowners at School Stadium game Saturday." *The Herald-News,* September 28, 1938.

21 "Pickett smiles as Camptowners plough through Garfield line." *The Herald-News,* October 3, 1938.

22 McMahon, Art. "Letters." *The Herald-News,* October 7, 1939.

23 McMahon, Art. "Week-end deductions." *The Herald-News,* October 3, 1939.

24 McMahon, Art. "Words." *The Herald-News,* October 4, 1939.

25 "Passaic refuses to join Comet stampede." *The Herald-News,* October 4, 1938.

26 McMahon, Art. "Tomorrow's outlook." *The Herald-News,* October 7, 1939.

27 "Expect 15,000 fans at scholastic tilts." *The Herald-News,* October 8, 1938.

28 Del Greco, Al. "Just a prediction that swellheadiditis will stiffen Garfield." October 11, 1938.

29 Ibid.

30 Fagan, Frank J. "Foley's 1938 team suffers by losses." *Newark Star-Eagle,* October 5, 1938.

31 "Free-for-all enlivens football game." *Passaic Daily News,* November 9, 1925.

32 McMahon, Art. "Tomorrow's outlook." *The Herald-News*, October 14, 1938.

33 Lovas, Joe. "Outplayed, Boilermakers triumph on long runs by Sekanics, Ciesla." *The Herald-News*, October 17, 1938.

34 McMahon, Art. "Garfield outplayed." *The Herald-News*, October 17, 1939.

35 "Rival coaches unexcited over night ball but fans turn out." *The Herald-News*, October 17, 1939.

36 Fagan, Frank J. "Bloomfield's defeat did not surprise." *Newark Star-Eagle*, October 17, 1938.

37 "Boilermakers favored to win but cockiness may spoil clean slate." *The Herald-News*, October 19, 1938.

38 McMahon, Art. "Tomorrow's outlook." *The Herald-News*, October 21, 1938.

39 Horowitz, Paul. "Garfield holds bag of tricks." *Newark Evening News*, October 26, 1938.

40 "Boilermakers' hopes of a state title rest on tomorrow's game." *The Herald-News*, October 28, 1938.

41 Ibid.

42 "Garfield shows improvement in Seton Hall drill." *The Herald-News*, October 26, 1938.

43 Lovas, Joe. "Bloomfield, the ex-powerhouse, plays Garfield Saturday and hopes." *The Herald-News,* October 26, 1938.

44 Fagan, Frank J. "Bengals have plan to stop Babula, Garfield star." *Newark Star-Eagle,* October 28,1938.

45 McMahon, Art. "The sportsman's corner." *The Herald-News,* October 11, 1938..

46 Lovas, Op. Cit.

47 Klein, William. "Babula, Ciesla big heroes of Boilermakers." *The Star-Ledger,* October 30, 1938.

48 Falzer, G.A. "Garfield bumps Bloomfield, 19-0, in title march." *Newark Sunday Call.* October 30, 1938.

49 Lovas, Joe. "Rout of Bloomfield moves Garfield to top in state." *The Herald-News*, October 31, 1938.

50 "Garfield hits peak, pointed to state title." *Bergen Evening Record*, October 31, 1938.

51 Fagan, Frank J. "Pick Boilermakers after Bengal rout." *Newark Star-Eagle,* October 31, 1938.

52 Hall, John J. "From where we sit." *Elizabeth Daily Journal,* October 26, 1938.

53 "No fear of big heads at Garfield, says Argauer." *The Herald-News*, November 1, 1938.

54 Zusi, Chris. "Tie with Paterson eleven blasts Jefferson's state championship hopes." *Elizabeth Daily Journal,* November 7, 1938.

55 Molnar, George. "Sports Echoes." *Woodbridge Leader Journal*, November 10, 1938.

56 Pinter, Gene. "Out on a limb." *The Daily Home News*, November 2, 1938.

57 Whiting, Bob. "Top ranking team in state in action at Baeurle Field." *Paterson Morning Call*, November 11, 1938.

58 Molnar, George. "Sports Echoes." *Woodbridge Leader Journal*, November 23, 1938.

59 Kernan, Kevin. "Babe's hideaway—Post finds old Bambino haunt well-preserved." *New York Post*, May 29, 2005.

60 "Honors showered on high school's football players." *Garfield Guardian*, December, 1939.

61 "Garfield fans call Argauer 'Miracle Man.'" *Newark Sunday Call*, November 27, 1938.

62 Ibid.

63 Fagan, Frank J. "Star-Eagle names all group choices." *Newark Star-Eagle*, December 3, 1939.

CHAPTER THIRTEEN: THE 1939 STINGAREES

1   Bell, Jack. "My! How big Ye Stingarees are this year." *Miami Daily News,* September 18, 1938.

2   Ibid.

3   Voltz, Luther. "Colonel eats peanuts and dreams of Miami victories." *Miami Daily News,* August 14, 1938.

4   Evans, Luther. "Miami High looks for big year." *The Miami Herald,* September 23, 1938.

5   Harris, Harold. "Expect record crowd to see Trojan-Miami game Friday." *The Knoxville News-Sentinel*, September 25, 1938.

6   "Fans give Miami High rousing trip sendoff." *The Miami Herald,* September 29, 1938.

7   Advertisement, *The Knoxville News-Sentinel*, September 29, 1938.

8   Sweet, Fletcher, "Jesse Yarborough's Miami High eleven opens season against Trojans in Knoxville." *The Miami Herald,* September 30, 1938.

9   Harris, Harold. "Breaks help Trojans to stay undefeated." *The Knoxville News-Sentinel*, October 1, 1938.

10 "Miami gets yardage but Knoxville wins." *The Miami News*, October 1, 1938.

11 "Lee gridmen entrain for Miami today." *Florida Times-Union*, October 8, 1938.

12 "Lee and Miami High to meet in Orange Bowl game today." *Florida Times-Union*, October 9, 1938.

13 Ibid.

14 "Miami coaches move to cure fumble mania." *The Miami News*, October 11, 1938.

15 Bell, Jack. "Jack Bell's Sports Desk.." *The Miami News*, October 12, 1938.

16 Evans, Luther. "Miami High tramples Central, 25 to 7." *The Miami Herald*, October 16, 1938.

17 Voltz, Luther. "Stingarees trounce Nashville Central, score 25 to 7." *Miami Daily News*. October 16, 1938.

18 Clay, Everett. "Eldredge leads Miami to 14-0 win." *The Miami Herald*, October 22, 1938.

19 "Stingarees, Beach, Edison score wins." *Miami Daily News*, October 22, 1938.

20 Clay. Op. Cit.

21 "Stingarees." Op.Cit.

22 "Stingaress drill until dark." *The Miami Herald*, October 26, 1938.

23 "Miami swamps junior high Bulldogs in 40 to 0 rout." *Fort Myers News-Press*, October 27, 1938.

24 Clark, Lem. "Lanier to meet Miami High tonight." *The Macon Telegraph*, November 11, 1938.

25 Latimer, Carter "Scoop." "Case of inexcusable negligence." *The Greenville News*, October 20, 1936.

26 Evans, Luther. "Miami High, confident after one-sided victory, will meet Edison Wednesday." *The Miami Herald*, November 20, 1938.

27 "Just a few notes gathered around town." *Miami Daily News*, August 28, 1938.

28 Clay, Everett. "Sports." *The Miami Herald*, November 25, 1938.

29 Ward, Ted. "Her're more notes on Edison's players." *The Miami Herald*, November 24, 1938.

30 Bell, Jack. "Huge crowd sees Bigart in star role." *Miami Daily News*, November 24, 1938.

31 Clay. Op. Cit.

32 Clay, Everett. "Miami Edison and Miami High and Xmas game." *The Miami Herald*, November 29, 1938.

33 Clay, Everett. "More about Christmas football game." *The Miami Herald*, December 6, 1938.

34 "Boys to play for city title next Monday." *Miami Daily News*, December 17, 1938.

35 Voltz, Luther. "Miami linemen subdue rivals for city title." *Miami Daily News*, December 20, 1938.

36 Ibid.

37 "McKeesport High reaches Miami for grid battle." *Pittsburgh Post-Gazette,* December 23, 1938.

38 Bell, Jack. "Stingarees score late to beat McKeesport." *Miami Daily News,* December 27, 1938.

39 Ibid.

CHAPTER FOURTEEN: THE CAUSE

1 "Pennsylvania will rigidly enforce its quarantine." *The Brooklyn Daily Eagle,* August 5, 1916.

2 "Miami youths to be isolated at their homes." *The Pam Beach Post,* July 31, 1939.

3 Hawkins, Leonard C. and Lomask, Milton. *The Man in the Iron Lung,* New York: Doubleday, 1956, p.15.

4 Ibid, p.133.

5 "17 Miami boy campers face 14-day isolation in homes." *Miami Daily News,* July 31, 1939.

6 "Miami alarms stirred when boys return." *Fort Myers News-Press,* July 31, 1939.

7 "Three local youths at stricken mountain camp; parents watch paralysis epidemic anxiously." *The Daily Democrat,* July 30, 1939.

8 "17 boy campers back in their Miami homes." *The Miami Herald,* July 31, 1939.

9 "Delray Beach family is placed under strict quarantine." *The Palm Beach Post,* August 1, 1939.

10 "Girl dies here, 4 more towns close schools." *Bergen Evening Record,* September 7, 1935.

11 "5 new paralysis cases reported, county total 37." *Bergen Evening Record,* September 9, 1935.

12 "East Rutherford boards hold emergency sessions." *The Herald-News,* September 6, 1935.

13 "Rutherford schools close as precautionary measure." *The Herald-News,* September 6, 1935.

14 "Four infantile cases added to county's total." *Bergen Evening Record,* September 18, 1935.

15 "Continuance of school advocated at Garfield." *The Herald-News,* September 7, 1935.

16 McMahon, Art. "Outside the law, but." *The Herald-News,* September 8, 1935.

17 "Rutherford '11' may not play with Garfield." *The Herald-News,* September 17, 1935.

18 McMahon, Art. "Tomorrow's outlook." *The Herald-News,* September 27, 1935.

19 "Garfield boy dies at Pines." *Bergen Evening Record,* September 26, 1935.

20 "Scare defers Rutherford-Garfield game." *The Herald-News,* September 28, 1935.

21 "Paralysis halts football game." *Bergen Evening Record,* September 28, 1935.

22 "The march of sports against infantile paralysis." Garfield-Miami Game Program, December 25, 1939.

23 Granger, Merrill. W. "The curbstone coach." *McKeesport Daily News,* November 20, 1944.

24 Ibid.

25 "Polio victim is 'fairly good.'" *Council Bluffs Nonpareil,* October 22, 1939.

26 "Greeley boy placed in iron lung." *Greeley Daily Tribune,* September 12, 1939.

27 "Bill Stevens says girls better looking." *Greeley Daily Tribune,* May 11, 1940.

28 "Jane Macy of Weld County Library staff and William Stevens are wed." *Greeley Daily Tribune,* April 8, 1950.

29 "Graduation day brings degree to 'Boiler Kid.'" *The Pittsburgh Press,* June 4, 1941.

30 Greene, June. "Boy completes year in 'lung.'" *The Pittsburgh Press,* September 20, 1940.

31 "Youth cheers for Bucs from his bed in iron lung." *The Pittsburgh Press,* April 16, 1940.

32 "Pittsburgh 'Boiler Kid', ardent Pirate fan, dies." *The Pittsburgh Press,* September 29, 1941.

33 "In 'lung' two years, Gibsonia boy dies." *Pittsburgh Post-Gazette,* September 29, 1941.

34 "Mother hangs self 18 hours after son dies in iron lung." *The Philadelphia Inquirer,* March 28, 1940.

35 "Camden, Brooklawn and Gloucester schools to open despite new deaths." *The Philadelphia Inquirer,* September 24, 1939.

36 "51 days in iron lung." *New York Times,* January 5, 1940.

37 "Double funeral tomorrow for polio victim and his mother." *Atlantic City Press,* March 28, 1940.

38 "Young Yon loses fight for life after 136 days in iron lung." *Atlantic City Press,* March 27, 1940.

39 "Mother hangs self." Op. Cit.

40 "Hundreds pay tribute to Yons in rites." *Atlantic City Press,* March 30, 1940.

Chapter Fifteen: The 1939 Stings

1 "Yarborough to Florida?" *The Palm Beach Post,* February 8, 1939.

2 Clay, Everett. "Around our town." *The Miami Herald,* March 22, 1939.

3 "Crabtree stays here." *Miami Daily News,* May 8, 1939.

4 Bell, Jack. "Sports desk." *Miami Daily News,* August 11, 1939.

5 "Yarborough family welcomes new tackle." *Miami Daily News,* September 8, 1939.

6 "Miami, Edison to be weaker than in 1938." *Miami Daily News,* August 27, 1939.

7 "Scrimmages carded at five camps." *The Miami Herald,* September 10, 1939.

8   Evans, Luther. Typhoons open season with 13-12 victory over aroused Stingarees." *The Miami Herald*, September 29, 1939.

9   "Stingarees are determined to avenge defeat." *Florida Times-Union*, October 6, 1939.

10   "Ye Stingarees need reserves for Knoxville." *Miami Daily News*, October 11, 1939.

11   "Stingarees prepare for Knoxville test." *The Miami Herald*, October 10, 1939.

12   McNeil, Glenn. "Poor tackling is blamed as Trojans get fourth licking." *The Knoxville News-Sentinel*, October 7, 1939.

13   Evans, Luther. "Stingarees out to snap Trojan jinx." *The Miami Herald*, October 13, 1939.

14   Bell, Jack. "Sports desk." *Miami Daily News*, October 13, 1939.

15   Bell, Jack. "Knoxville trimmed in 32-0 style." *Miami Daily News*, October 14, 1939.

16   Ibid.

17   "Weary Trojans start work for St. Xavier." *The Knoxville News-Sentinel*, October 16, 1939.

18   Bell. Op. Cit.

19   Evans, Luther. "Unbeaten Stingarees play Savannah tonight." *The Miami Herald*, October 21, 1939.

20   "Stingarees prepare for Savannah game." *The Miami Herald*, October 17, 1939.

21   "Injury bugaboo hits Miami High's eleven." *The Miami Herald*, October 24, 1939.

22   "And here's another great sports event that first sees the light of day in Miami." *Miami Daily News*, November 2, 1939.

23   "U-M's No. 1 grid fan faces assault charge." *Miami Daily News*, July 8, 1957.

24   "Charity clash billed here." *The Miami Herald*, November 2, 1939.

25   "Christmas football game to aid paralysis fund." *Miami Daily News*, November 1, 1939.

26   Bell, Jack. "Sports desk." *Miami Daily News*, November 3, 1939.

27   Anderson, Buck. "Dunham and Berman duel for All-GIAA laurels Friday." *The Macon Telegraph*, November 1, 1939.

28   "Stingarees display excellent blocking." *The Miami Herald*, November 7, 1939.

29   "Lanier eleven arrives today." *The Miami Herald*, November 10, 1939.

30   Voltz, Luther. "Poets suffer 19-0 defeat at stadium." *Miami Daily News*, November 12, 1939.

31   Evans, Luther. "Stingarees nearing record for victories." *The Miami Herald*, November 12, 1939.

32   "Tigers are humbled by Miami High 27-0." *Daily Clarion-Ledger*, November 18, 1939.

33   Evans, Luther, "Eldredge offensive standout." *The Miami Herald*, November 18, 1939.

34   Voltz, Luther. "Davey goes 99 yards." *Miami Daily News*, November 18, 1939.

35   "Bengals back in Jackson." *Daily Clarion-Ledger*, November 21, 1939.

36   "Few will observe Thanksgiving today." *The Palm Beach Post*, November 23, 1939.

37 Bell, Jack. "Sports desk." *Miami Daily News,* November 20, 1939

38 "Coaches quit bear stories to fabricate crazy tales about teams' new tactics." *Miami Daily News,* November 29, 1939.

39 Ibid.

40 Bell, Jack. "Sports desk." *Miami Daily News,* November 30, 1939.

41 Voltz, Luther. "Edison-Miami game notes." *Miami Daily News,* December 1, 1939

42 Clay, Everett. "Miami High's Eldredge defeats Edison, 13 to 0." *The Miami Herald,* December 1, 1939.

43 Ibid.

44 Bell, Jack. "Stingaree speed demon thrills crowd of 15,000." *Miami Daily News,* December 1, 1939.

45 Kelly, Whitey. "Edison-Miami game notes." *Miami Daily News,* December 1, 1939.

46 Voltz. Op. Cit.

47 Clay. Op. Cit.

48 Rollins, Larry. "Li'l David Eldredge has entire South voting for him." *Miami Daily News,* December 6, 1939.

49 "Boys High of Atlanta arrives today." *The Miami Herald,* December 6, 1939.

50 White, Roy. "Eldredge leads Miami to 26-to-0 victory over Boys High." *The Atlanta Constitution,* December 8, 1939.

51 Bell, Jack. "And so the Stingarees are Southern champions." *Miami Daily News,* December 8, 1939.

52 "L'il David Eldredge thinks it over and decides algebra isn't much fun." *Miami Daily News,* December 19, 1939.

53 Evans, Luther. "Miami annexes mythical Dixie grid crown." *The Miami Herald,* December 8, 1939.

CHAPTER SIXTEEN: THE 1939 BOILERMAKERS

1 Horowitz, Paul. "Coaches sing blues." *Newark Evening News,* September 2, 1939.

2 "Garfield High out to hold Jersey's football title." *The Newark Sunday Call,* September 17, 1939.

3 "Boilermaker power expected to carry team to easy opening win." *The Herald-News,* September 29, 1939.

4 Del Greco, Al. "Garfield still hot." *Bergen Evening Record,* October 3, 1939.

5 Ibid.

6 "Babula flashes in Garfield win." *Bergen Evening Record,* October 2, 1939.

7 Falzer, G.A. "Late Garfield rally nips Irvington, 14-12." *The Newark Sunday Call,* October 8, 1939.

8   Ibid.

9   Ibid.

10 Lovas, Joe. "Babula, Orlovsky star in victory." *The Herald-News,* October 9, 1939.

11 Falzer. Op. Cit.

12 McMahon, Art. "Passaic test for Garfield." *The Herald-News,* October 9, 1939.

13 "Passaic and Garfield in secret drills; Fadil lost to Indians." *The Herald-News,* October 10, 1939.

14 "Garfield given slight edge over Passaic." *The Herald-News,* October 11, 1939

15 Ibid.

16 Ibid.

17 "Passaic a threat." *Bergen Evening Record,* October 11, 1939.

18 "Garfield football fans driven back over river." *The Herald-News,* October 13, 1939.

19 Del Greco, Al. "Benny's the difference." *Bergen Evening Record,* October 15, 1939.

20 McMahon, Art. "Babula the difference." *The Herald-News,* October 15, 1939.

21 Del Greco, Al. "ER outraged as Garfield Board kicks contract around." October 17, 1939.

22 McMahon, Art. "Sportsman's Corner." *The Herald-News,* October 17, 1939.

23 "East Rutherford no breather for Garfield." *Bergen Evening Record,* October 21, 1939.

24 Del Greco, Al. "At random in sportdom." *Bergen Evening Record,* October 20, 1939.

25 McMahon, Art. "Tomorrow's outlook." *The Herald-News,* October 20, 1939.

26 McMahon, Art. "Weekend roundup." *The Herald-News,* October 23, 1939.

27 Fagan, Frank J. "Foley's magic wand is waving again; won-all field reduced." *Newark Star-Eagle,* October 30, 1939.

28 Kamm, Herb. "Garfield eleven may hit snag before it gets to the seashore." *Asbury Park Press,* October 31, 1939.

29 McMahon, Art. "The army threatens Garfield." *The Herald-News,* October 31, 1939.

30 "Boilermakers favored to capture important tilt at Foley Field." *The Herald-News,* November 3, 1939.

31 "Proud to march behind tiny boy." *The Herald-News,* November 13, 1939.

32 Dorfman, Sid. "Garfield rips Bengals." *The Star-Ledger,* November 5, 1939.

33 Miller, Lou. "Babula sparks powerful Garfield team." *New York World-Telegram.* November 6, 1939.

34 "A Day with Ben Babula, Garfield's all state quarterback." *The Newark Sunday Call,* November 5, 1939.

35 Fagan, Frank J. "Process of elimination among Essex County contenders continues tomorrow in game at Ashland Stadium." *Newark Star-Eagle.* November 6, 1939.

36 Lovas, Joe. "Boilermaker power turns back Bloomfield, 18-0, before 19,000." *The Herald-News,* November 4, 1939.

37 Burcky, Claire. "Honest Abe Shotwell, 159 pounds, is one of Pitt's greatest centers." *The Pittsburgh Press,* November 14, 1934.

38 Fagan, Frank J. "Shotwell likely to remain as coach of team." *Newark Star-Eagle,* November 24, 1939.

39 Falzer, G.A. "unbeaten teams to clash." *The Newark Sunday Call,* November 5, 1939.

40 Maloney, Walt. "Passes the dope along." *The Nutley Sun,* October 27, 1939.

41 Maloney, Walt. "Passes the dope along." *The Nutley Sun,* November 10, 1939.

42 Edmonston, John. "The sports record." *East Orange Record,* November 3, 1939.

43 McMahon, Art. "Two more bite the dust." *The Herald-News,* November 8, 1939.

44 Ibid.

45 Kamm, Herb. "Irons' dropkicks solve extra point problem for Asbury Park." *Asbury Park Press,* November 6, 1939.

46 McMahon, Art. "Tough sledding for Garfield." *The Herald-News,* November 6, 1939.

47 Kamm, Herb. "Elimination of kickoff won't remove dangers from gridiron." *Asbury Park Press,* November 7, 1939.

48 McMahon, Art. "Sportsman's corner." November 13, 1939.

49 Kamm, Herb. "Blue Bishops can find much for consolation in loss to Garfield." *Asbury Park Press,* November 13, 1939.

50 Ibid.

51 McMahon. Op. Cit.

52 Covella, Jerry. "Remembering Dallolio: VHS legend." *Vineland Times Journal,* February 14, 1983.

53 Sardella, Carlo. "Sports Chatter." *Vineland Evening Times,* November 14, 1939.

54 Horowitz, Paul. "Vineland puts feelers out for post-season game with Garfield." *Newark Evening News,* November 14, 1939.

55 "Post-season clash for Garfield hinges on Colliton grid ratings." *The Herald-News,* November 17, 1939.

56 Ibid.

57 "Garfield to purchase home football field." *Asbury Park Press,* November 13, 1939.

58 "Garfield game on Saturday five days from Central tilt." *Paterson Morning Call,* November 15, 1939.

59 Lovas, Joe. "Boilermakers in spectacular 48-6 Eastside rout for 19th win in row." *The Herald-News,* November 20, 1939.

60 "Garfield seeks invitation to 'Starlet Bowl'" *Paterson Morning Call,* November 20, 1939.

61 McMahon, Art. "Sportsman's Corner." *The Herald News,* November 21, 1939.

62   Sardella, Carlo. "Sports chatter." *Vineland Evening Times,* November 24, 1939.

63   Sardella, Carlo. "Sports chatter." *Vineland Evening Times,* November 25, 1939.

64   "Hoping for Miami bid." *The Herald-News,* November 24, 1939.

65   McMahon, Art. "Clifton always the bridesmaid." *The Herald-News,* November 26, 1939.

66   "Believe Garfield will refuse VHS bid for game." *Vineland Evening Times,* November 27, 1939.

67   Ibid.

68   Sardella, Carlo. "Sports chatter." *Vineland Evening Times,* November 27, 1939.

69   "Advance publicity causes state body to change mind." *Vineland Evening Journal,* December 1, 1939.

70   Marenghi, Anthony. "Why not Nutley?" *Newark Star-Ledger,* November 25, 1939.

71   McMahon, Art. "Passaic would like Garfield again." *The Herald-News,* November 24, 1939.

72   Del Greco, Al. "Park's champions sneer and jeer at another champ." *Bergen Evening Record,* November 30, 1939.

73   Ibid.

74   "VHS eleven may get bid to play in Starlet Bowl." *Vineland Evening Times,* December 4, 1939.

75   Sardella, *Carlo.* "Sports Chatter." *Vineland Evening Times,* December 4, 1939.

76   "State ass'n in trouble again." *The Jersey Journal,* December 5, 1939.

77   Horowitz, Paul. "Nutley win not enough." *Newark Evening News,* December 4, 1939.

78   "Garfield state champion team honored at testimonial dinner." *The Quill,* December 15, 1939.

Chapter Seventeen: The Choice

1   "Starlet Bowl grid game booked for Miami." *The Miami Herald,* November 17, 1939.

2   Considine, Bob. "Sports seek million for paralysis fund." *New York Daily Mirror,* November 18, 1939.

3   "Florida grid game for paralysis fund." *New York Daily Mirror,* November 17, 1939.

4   Miller, Lou. "Miami trip for Erasmus?" *The New York World-Telegram,* November 18, 1939.

4   Murphy, James J. "Erasmus-Miami grid classic looms." *Brooklyn Eagle,* November 17, 1939.

6   Bell, Jack. "Paralysis fund game approved for Miami." *Miami Daily News,* November 17, 1939.

7   Waldman, Leo. "Unbeaten Boys High football team snaps Erasmus winning streak at 12 games." *New York Herald-Tribune,* November 19, 1939.

8   Miller, Lou. "Seward leads in race for Miami game." *New York World Telegram,* November 22, 1939.

9   Murphy, James J. "Boys High in running for Miami game. *Brooklyn Eagle,* November 21, 1939.

10   Riss, John. "Erasmus may yet win Xmas trip to Miami." *Brooklyn Daily Eagle,* November 22, 1939.

11   Miller, Lou. "Educators may waive restrictions in the cause of charity." *New York World-Telegram,* November 18, 1939.

12   Daly, Fritz. "From scratch, Corcoran builds Boys Town football without setback in five seasons." *Omaha Evening World-Journal,* November 14, 1939.

13   "Boys Town '11' cops 35th in row." *The Binghamton Press,* November 24, 1939.

14   Blume, Carl. "Boys Town trims Cadets, 20 to 12. *The Los Angeles Times,* November 27, 1938.

15   Hopper, Hedda. "Hedda Hopper's Hollywood." *The Los Angeles Times,* December 2, 1938.

16   Taylor, Craig E. "Collegians remain undefeated in 38 successive games." *The Baltimore Sun,* November 19, 1939.

17   Lee, Michael. "Lawrence High's unbeaten and untied Golden Tornado has best claim to represent north in the Orange Bowl." *Long Island Daily Press.* November 22, 1939.

18   "Unbeaten Poughkeepsie eleven clips Middletown." *Middletown Times-Herald,* October 16, 1939.

19   North, Jack. "Dishing out Iowa's best crop of prep grid players." *Des Moines Sunday Register,* December 3, 1939.

20   Zadick, Bill. "Jitter, fumbles, 'Galloping' Frickey beat Bisons, 33 to 7." *Great Falls Tribune,* November 24, 1939.

21   "Broncs challenge any high school team in nation." *The Missoulian,* November 24, 1939.

22   "Powell praises Casper Mustangs." *Casper Star-Tribune,* December 5, 1939.

23   Ross, John. "Boys High strengthens for Miami Christmas game." *Brooklyn Eagle,* November 26, 1939.

24   Waldman, Leo. "Unbeaten Boys High hands Lincoln its first setback.." *New York Herald-Tribune,* November 26, 1939.

25   Considine, Bob. "All Metropolitan Schoolboy Team for Miami game solves a problem." *New York Daily Mirror,* December 11, 1939.

26   Gross, Milton. "Students are helping crippled youngsters." *New York Post,* December 4, 1939.

27   Weintraub, Seymour. Seward Park High School, *The Almanac* (New York, January 1940).

28   Ibid.

29 Murphy, James J. "Miami bowl bid finds pupil battling master." *Brooklyn Eagle,* November 30, 1939.

30 Waldman, Leo. "George Ross resigns as coach of Thomas Jefferson eleven. *New York Herald Tribune*, November 30, 1939.

31 Williams, Joe. "Come on, Mr. Mayor; Give The Seward Kids a Break." *New York World-Telegram*, December 1, 1939.

32 Ibid.

33 "Governor would send Billings to 'Bowl' game." *The Independent Record*, November 29, 1939.

34 "Mustang selection for Health Bowl is urged by governor." *Casper Star-Tribune*, December 3, 1939.

35 Del Greco, Al. "Objections." *Bergen Evening Record*, December 13, 1939.

36 Del Greco, Al. "At random in sportdom." *Bergen Evening Record*, December 3, 1939.

37 Rosell, Ed. "Breaks of the game." *Poughkeepsie Star-Enterprise*, December 4, 1939.

38 Cloney, Will. "With the schoolboys." *Boston Herald*, December 5, 1939.

39 Dalton, Ernest. "Brockton High may still have a chance to play Miami High." *Boston Globe*, December 6, 1939.

40 Ross, John. "Seward Park mourns loss of Miami trip." *Boston Eagle*, December 6, 1939.

41 Wood, Jimmy. "Sportopics." *Boston Eagle*, December 8, 1939.

42 "Seward Park sees new hope for trip." *New York Times*, December 7, 1939.

43 Lewin, Leonard, "Seward bowl bid okayed by mayor." *New York Daily Mirror*, December 7, 1939.

44 Ibid.

45 "Seward unlikely to make trip to Miami despite Mayor's help." *New York Journal-American*, December 7, 1939.

46 "Seward trip still in doubt." *New York World-Telegram*, December 7, 1939.

47 Murphy, James J. "LaGuardia's appeal saves football plum." *Brooklyn Eagle*, December 8, 1939.

48 Ibid.

49 Brumby, Bob. "Justice needs tempering." *New York Daily News*, December 10, 1939.

50 Minnoch, Jack. "Dressing room chatter." *Troy Record*, December 16, 1939.

51 "Not for high school boys." *The Saratogian*, December 19, 1939.

52 McMahon, Art. "Brockton, Mass., new 2nd choice for Miami coach." *The Herald-News*, December 9, 1939.

53 Fitzgerald, Tom. "Brockton's grid curtain down; Miami plays New York eleven." *Boston Globe*, December 12, 1939.

54 Considine. Op. Cit.

55 Lovas, Joe. "Miami coach had final say." *The Herald-News*, December 12, 1939.

56 Ross, John, "Brain trust maps routine for Met All Star gridders." *Brooklyn Eagle*, December 12, 1939.

57 Turkin, Hy. "Met All Stars trip hits more red tape." *New York Daily News*, December 13, 1939.

58 Daniel. "Official objection kills trip for school gridders." *New York World-Telegram*, December 13, 1939.

59 Del Greco, Al. "Moon over Miami—Garfield High boys look forward to it." *Bergen Evening Record*, December 14, 1939.

60 Ross, John. "Trail of red tape detours All Stars from Miami Game." *Brooklyn Eagle*, December 13, 1939.

61 "Garfield to play in Health Bowl." *The Herald-News*, December 13, 1939.

62 "Players jubilant over trip to Florida for Christmas night tilt." *The Herald-News*, December 14, 1939.

63 Lewin, Leonard. "Garfield accepts Miami game bid." *New York Daily Mirror*, December 13, 1939.

64 "Sports chatter." *Fitchburg Sentinel*, December 14, 1939.

65 Mann, Bob. "Stay East of Hudson seems good advice for Flushing High." *Long Island City Star-Journal*, October 17, 1939.

66 "Flushing escaped injuries in Bloomfield rout." *Long Island City Star-Journal*, October 17, 1939.

CHAPTER EIGHTEEN: THE TRIP

1 Goldberg, Hy. "Sports in the news." *Newark Evening News*, December 15, 1939.

2 Del Greco, Al. "Moon over Miami—Garfield High boys look forward to it." *Bergen Evening Record*, December 14, 1939.

3 "Kendricks hurt on golf course." *The Miami Herald*, December 11, 1939.

4 Wright, Frank. "Nutley players are supremely confident on eve of battle." *Florida Times-Union*, December 15, 1939.

5 Maloney, Walt. "Passes the dope along." *The Nutley Sun*, December 8, 1939.

6 Maloney, Walt. "Passes the dope along." *The Nutley Sun*, December 15, 1939.

7 "Coach George Stanford confident Maroon will defeat Sewanee High." *The Herald-News*, December 15, 1939.

8 Bozworth, Charley. "Nutley scores 14-0 victory over Live Oak." *Gainesville Sun*, December 16, 1939.

9 Maloney, Walt. "Passes the dope along." *The Nutley Sun*, December 22, 1939.

10 Del Greco, Al. "At Random in Sportdom." *Bergen Evening Record*, December 15, 1939.

11 Johnson, Art. "Tabaka, Grembowicz watch Garfield teammates drill." *Bergen Evening Record,* December 16, 1939.

12 McMahon, Art. "Garfield, Babula star attractions to Miami folks." *The Herald-News,* December 21, 1939.

13 Kamm, Herb. "Jersey football mild compared to setup in other parts." *Asbury Park Press.* August 8, 1941.

14 National Sports Council Press Release, Release date unknown, published in *Bradford Evening Star,* December 2, 1939.

15 Considine, Bob. "On the line." *New York Mirror,* December 15, 1939.

16 Ibid.

17 National Sports Council Press Release, Release date unknown, published in *Santa Ana Register,* December 21, 1939.

18 Ibid.

19 "Blondes rival grid aces in Health Bowl." *The Montana Standard (Associated Press),* December 16, 1939.

20 National Sports Council Press Release, Release date unknown, published in *Carlisle Sentinel,* December 19, 1939.

21 "Garfield team off for Miami." *Asbury Park Press,* December 19, 1939.

22 "Mayor, officials, high school band drive parade." *Carteret Press,* December 21, 1939.

23 "Babula & Co. off to Miami for big game." *Bergen Evening Record,* December 19, 1939.

24 "Garfield football team arrives to play Miami." *Miami Daily News,* December 20, 1939.

25 "Garfield given warm welcome." *Asbury Park Press,* December 21, 1939.

26 McMahon, Art. Op. Cit.

27 Gumucio, Ron X. "Boilermakers' field wagon found." *The Shopper,* October 15, 1999.

28 Horowitz, Paul. "Heat saps Garfield pep." *Newark Evening News,* December 22, 1939.

29 Clay, Everett. "Tabaka may not play at Miami." *The Star Ledger,* December 21, 1939.

30 Horowitz, Paul. "Argauer wary of overconfidence." *Newark Evening News,* December 21, 1939.

31 "Garfield gridders arrive; stage brisk drill." *The Miami Herald,* December 21, 1939.

32 Clay. Op. Cit.

33 Bell, Jack. "Sports Desk." *Miami Daily News,* December 20, 1939.

34 Kurland, Bob. "Marking golden anniversary Garfield's heroes reunited." *The Record,* October 13, 1989.

25 Ibid.

36 Horowitz. "Heat saps." Op. Cit.

37 McMahon, Art. "Florida heat slows Garfield team down." *The Herald-News,* December 22, 1939.

38 Ibid.

39 Bell, Jack. "Sports desk." *Miami Daily News,* December 27, 1939.

40 McMahon, Art. "Sportsman's Corner." *The Herald-News,* December 1, 1939.

41 Bell, Jack. "Sports desk." *Miami Daily News,* December 24, 1939.

42 Horowitz, Paul. "Garfield eleven shines under lights." *Newark Evening News,* December 23, 1939.

43 McMahon, Art. "Babula's passing makes 'em sit up." *The Herald-News,* December 23, 1939.

44 "Jersey champions have few backers." *Bergen Evening Record,* December 23, 1939.

45 Horowitz. Ibid.

46 "Arauca skipper hopes for fog as he tells of flight from speedy British craft." *Fort Lauderdale Daily News,* December 20, 1939.

47 Ibid.

48 "Pass in review." *Fort Lauderdale Daily News,* December 26, 1939.

49 Lopp, John D. "Broward County's ten best newspaper stories for 1939 listed for readers." *Fort Lauderdale Daily News,* December 30, 1939.

50 Bell, Jack. "Sports Desk." *Miami Daily News,* December 24, 1939.

51 McMahon, Art. Some Rockne in Argauer." *The Herald-News,* January 4, 1940.

52 Johnston, Bob. "The Sportsman." *The Bergen Sunday Star,* December 24, 1939.

CHAPTER NINETEEN: THE GAME

1 Bell, Jack. "Sports desk." *Miami Daily News,* December 25, 1939.

2 Ibid.

3 Clay, Everett. "National title claim goes to winner." *The Star-Ledger,* December 25, 1939.

4 Voltz, Luther. "Miami High plays big Garfield team for national high school grid championship." *Miami Daily News,* December 25, 1939.

5 "Miami celebrates Yuletide under warming rays of sun." *Miami Daily News,* December 25, 1939.

6 "Miami enjoys greatest Yule." *The Miami Herald,* December 25, 1939.

7 Morris, Allen. "Yule spirit rules Miami." *The Miami Herald,* December 25, 1939.

8 Clay, Everett. "Garfield beats Miami, 16 to 13." *The Star-Ledger,* December 26, 1939.

9 "The Health Bowl." *The Independent Press,* January 4, 1940.

10 McMahon, Art. Game program.

11 McMahon, Art. "Garfield beats Miami on field goal by Babula." *The Herald-News,* December 26, 1939.

12 Melching, Dale. "Sports sputters." *Miami High Times,* January 11, 1940.

13 "Garfield team sings over radio." *The Herald-News,* December 26, 1939.

14 Bell, Jack. "Sports desk." *Miami Daily News,* December 26, 1939.

15 "2,300 in Garfield school for 'broadcast.'" *The Herald-News,* December 26, 1939.

16 Kurland, Bob. "Marking golden anniversary Garfield's heroes reunited." *The Record,* October 13, 1989.

17 Whritenour, Hardy. "Babula and Eldredge stage great show in Miami grid battle." *Paterson Evening News,* December 26, 1939.

18 Ibid.

19 Ibid.

20 McMahon. Op Cit.

21 Clay. Op Cit.

22 McMahon. Op Cit.

23 Horowitz, Paul. "Grembowicz is Garfield's game-saver." *Newark Evening News,* December 26, 1939.

24 Strauss, Emanuel. "Garfield beats Miami High in health Bowl football game." *New York Times,* December 26, 1939.

25 "David and giant Babula do battle under moon." *Miami High Times,* January 11, 1940.

26 Voltz, Luther. "Garfield High edges Stingarees, 16 to 13, in nerve-chilling Paralysis Fund game." *Miami Daily News,* December 26, 1939.

27 Bell. Op.Cit.

CHAPTER TWENTY: THE AFTERMATH

1   McMahon, Art. "Sportsman's Corner." *The Herald-News,* January 4, 1940.

2   Ebben, Jimmie. "Sports in the News." *Newark Evening News,* January 2, 1940.

3   McMahon, Art. "Bruised Garfield players relax in Florida sunshine." *The Herald-News,* December 27, 1939.

4   "Fans greet Garfield team." *The Jersey Journal,* January 4, 1940.

5   "Garfield gets wild reception." *The Star-Ledger,* January 4, 1940.

6   McMahon. Op. Cit.

7   Forbes, Harry. "Garfield heroes welcomed home." *New York Daily News,* January 4, 1939.

8   "Garfield." Op. Cit.

9   Forbes. Op. Cit.

10 "Crowd of 20,000 turn out for ceremonies at City Field—speeches all but unheard in tumult." *The Herald-News,* January 4, 1939.

11 Ibid.

12 "E.J. Schulz is new No. 1 fan as club president." *The Independent Press,* January 26, 1940.

13 Supko, Michael. "Garfield takes over World's Fair for day; city 'deserted village.'" *The Herald News,* June 6, 1940.

14 Bell, Jack, "Sports desk." *Miami Daily News,* May 23, 1940.

15 Bell, Jack. "Sports desk." *Miami Daily News,* January 4, 1940.

16 Horowitz, Paul. "Drive for new Garfield field planned as 15,000 greet team." *Newark Evening News,* January 4, 1940.

17 Kamm, Herb. "Argauer turns up with post-mortems on Miami game." *Asbury Park Press,* December 7, 1940.

18 Sandler, Gil. "City's legendary streak." *The Baltimore Sun,* November 22, 1994.

19 Del Greco, Al. "Garfield's Sekanics will make fans forget Benny Babula." *Bergen Evening Record,* August 29, 1940.

20 McMahon, Art. "Sportsman's corner." *The Herald-News,* June 2, 1939.

Chapter Twenty-One: The War

1 Trimble, Jack C. "Former cheer leader of Garfield High School on 34 flying missions." *Garfield Guardian,* January 26, 1945.

2 "Sergeant Simko awarded air medal for aerial flights." *Garfield Guardian,* September 15, 1944.

3 "Mayor in Army still the mayor." *Asbury Park Press,* October 1, 1942.

4 Butler, Guy. "Davey Eldredge and Johnny Bosch." *Miami Daily News,* September 15, 1941.

5 Bradberry, Johnny. "Flashy soph 'furriners' run best at Tech." *The Atlanta Constitution,* September 19, 1941.

6 "Obituary, Paul Adolph Louis." *The Miami Herald,* May 27, 2008.

7 Spach, Jules, *Every Road Leads Home.* Chapel Hill, N.C.: Professional Press, 1996, p.118.

8 Bell, Jack. "Town crier." *The Miami Herald,* October 26, 1943.

9 "Medal awarded to parents of late Stanley Saganiec." *Garfield Guardian,* April 27, 1945.

10 "Sergeant Maciag reported killed on German front." *Garfield Guardian,* May 18, 1945.

11 "Valentine Maciag at German front." *Garfield Guardian,* January 26, 1945.

12 "Report of Aircraft Accident." War Department, U.S. Army Air Forces, March 9, 1944.

13 Simonaro, Joe. "Garfield mourns Grembowitz." *Garfield Guardian,* March 10, 1944.

Chapter Twenty-Two: Epilogue

1 Underwood, John. "Parnell enjoys bumps, dousing." *Miami Daily News,* November 28, 1952.

2 May, Patrick. "Harvey James, was coach at Edison, Norland." *The Miami Herald,* September 9, 1988.

3 Smallwood, Jack. "Harveygiechyjames is Kelly's Cinderella story." *The Miami Herald,* November 4, 1976.

4 "Coinmen you know." *The Billboard,* November 26, 1949.

5 "Cinderella weds sailor this week." *The Philadelphia Inquirer,* November 16, 1941.

6 "Shreveport sailor tells how New York's Cinderella girl won his heart." *The Shreveport Times,* November 15, 1941.

7 "Josie and sailor Bill marry to cap storybook romance." *Trenton Evening Times (Associated Press),* November 21, 1941.

8 "1932-57 men of achievement." *Sports Illustrated,* December 23, 1957.

9 Lovas, Joe. "Sportsman's corner." *The Herald-News,* September 28, 1948.

10 Lio, Augie. "Garfield fans happy Art Argauer is back." *The Herald-News,* September 23, 1958.

11 Glicken, Lloyde S. "Top coach Argauer dies at 85." *The Star-Ledger,* February 6, 1986.

12 "Irons cool, Jesse plans MHS return." *Miami Daily News,* January 28, 1946.

13 "Official: Jesse back at Miami Hi." *Miami Daily News,* February 16, 1949.

14 "'Should have stuck to football': Jess." *Orlando Evening Star (Associaated Press),* September 13, 1972.

15 Arnold, John. "Jess Yarborough, ex-Commissioner, legislator, and always the 'coach.'" *The Miami Herald,* April 12, 1980.

16 "Obituaries." *The Record,* June 17, 2003.

17 McMullan, John. "Davey vindicates himself in Hurricanes' 20-12 triumph." *Miami Daily News,* October 12, 1946.

18 McLemore, Morris. "And the party goes on . . ." *Miami Daily News,* May 9, 1962

INDEX

Photographic references are denoted in italics

ABOUT THE TYPEFACE

Minion Designed by Robert Slimbach, and released by Abobe Systems in 1990, Minion is
based on classic, Renaissance-style type and intended for body text and long-form works.
It is slightly condensed, with large apertures that improve readability. The term "minion"
comes from the traditional classification and naming of typeface sizes; minion is a size
in between brevier (the type size traditionally used to print breviaries) and nonpareil (so
named because of its great or unparalleled beauty) points of type.

Copperplate Designed in 1903 by Frederic W. Goudy (renowned for his Goudy Old Style),
Copperplate is evocative of engraving, as suggested by its name. While it appears Gothic
(sans-serif), it does possess subtle serifs. A solid, all-caps typeface, it is especially well-
suited for headlines and titles.